early, high, and late Scholasticism. McSorley regards such a thorough statement of the question as indispensible if one is to answer the important ecumenical-theological question: is Luther's central reformation protest one that must irrevocably divide Protestant and Catholic Christianity? The answer of this book is: No!

THE AUTHOR

Harry J. McSorley, C.S.P., is a Roman Catholic Priest, scholar, and Professor of Ecumenical Theology and Ecclesiology at St. Paul's College, Washington, D.C. A graduate of Bucknell University, he studied at the Universities of Munich, Heidelberg, and Tübingen, under such scholars as Karl Rahner, Michael Schmaus, Edmund Schlink, Hans Küng, and the Bornkamms.

In 1966 he received the degree of Doctor of Theology *summa cum laude* from the University of Munich. The present volume is the result of his five years of doctoral study.

LUTHER: RIGHT OR WRONG? has been published in German under the title *Luthurs Lehre vom unfreien Willen,* Volume I of the new ecumenical theology series: *Beiträge zur ökumenischen Theologie.* In addition, Father McSorley has written numerous articles on this subject for ecumenical journals.

Luther:
Right or Wrong?

An Ecumenical-Theological Study of Luther's Major Work, The Bondage of the Will

by

Harry J. McSorley, C.S.P.

NEWMAN PRESS

New York, N.Y.   Glen Rock, N.J.
Toronto   Amsterdam   London

and

AUGSBURG PUBLISHING HOUSE
Minneapolis, Minnesota

This edition, co-published by Newman Press and Augsburg Publishing House, was originally published under the title *Luthers Lehre vom unfreien Willen nach seiner Hauptschrift De servo arbitrio im Lichte der biblischen und Kirchlichen Tradition* in: *Beiträge zur ökumenischen Theologie*, Band II, hrsg. H. Fries (Max Hueber Verlag: Munich, 1967).

Library of Congress
Catalog Card Number: 68-59159

Published by Newman Press
Editorial Office: 304 W. 58th St., N.Y., N.Y. 10019
Business Office: Glen Rock, New Jersey 07452
and
Augsburg Publishing House
Minneapolis, Minnesota

Printed and bound in the United States of America
by Wickersham Printing Co., Lancaster, Pennsylvania

Acknowledgments

Grateful acknowledgment is hereby made for permission to quote from the following published works:

To Doubleday & Company, Inc. for permission to quote from *The Idea of Freedom* by Mortimer J. Adler. Copyright © 1959 by Institute for Philosophical Research, and from *The Jerusalem Bible*, English ed. Alexander Jones. Copyright © 1966 by Darton, Longman & Todd, Ltd. and Doubleday & Company, Inc.

To Beacon Press for permission to quote from *The Reformation of the Sixteenth Century* by R. Bainton, fifth printing, 1960.

To Desclee Company, Inc. for permission to quote from *Augustine: Philosopher of Freedom* by Mary T. Clark, published 1958.

To Charles Scribners & Sons, Inc. for permission to quote from *Theology of the New Testament*, vol. 1 by R. Bultmann, published 1951.

iv

To Sheed & Ward, Inc. for permission to quote from "Reformation, Preaching, and *Ex Opere Operato*" by H. Oberman, published in *Christianity Divided,* edited by Callahan, Oberman and O'Hanlon, © Sheed & Ward, Inc. 1961.

To Verlag Friedrich Pustet for permission to quote from *Der Römerbrief,* vol. 1 by Otto Kuss, published 1957.

To Les Éditions du Cerf for permission to quote from *Les Épitres de Saint Paul aux Galates et aux Romains* by S. Lyonnet, published 1959.

To Holt, Rinehart and Winston, Inc. for permission to quote from *Forerunners of the Reformation,* edited by Heiko A. Oberman. Translation by Paul L. Nyhus. Copyright © 1966.

To The Belknap Press of Harvard University Press for permission to quote from *The Harvest of Medieval Theology* by Heiko Oberman, published 1963.

To James Clarke & Co., Ltd. for permission to quote from *On the Bondage of the Will,* translated by Packer & Johnston, published 1957.

To Abingdon Press for permission to quote from *The Riddle of Roman Catholicism* by J. Pelikan, published 1959.

To Concordia Publishing House for permission to quote from *Luther's Works,* vol. 26, edited by J. Pelikan, published 1963.

To Henry Regnery Co. for permission to quote from *A Guide to the Thought of St. Augustine,* by E. Portalié, translated by R. Bastian, published 1960.

To Herder & Herder, Inc. for permission to quote from *Theological Dictionary* by K. Rahner and H. Vorgrimler, published 1965.

To Patmos Verlag for permission to quote from *Paulus Lehrer der Väter* by K. Schelkle, published 1959.

To Helicon Press, Inc. for permission to quote from *Problems of Authority* by J. Todd, published 1962.

To Frederick Ungar Publishing Co., Inc. for permission to quote from *Erasmus: A Study of His Life, Ideals and Place in History* by P. Smith, new printing 1962.

To Vandenhoeck & Ruprecht for permission to quote from *Das Freiheitsverständis bei Thomas von Aquin und Martin Luther* by H. Vorster, published 1964.

To The Newman Press for permission to quote from *Eucharistic Sacrifice and the Reformation* by F. Clark, published 1960.

To The Clarendon Press for permission to quote from *Grace and Reason: A Study in the Theology of Luther* by B. A. Gerrish, published 1962.

To The Westminster Press for permission to quote from *Theology of the Old Testament*, vol. II by Walther Eichrodt, tr. by A. J. Baker. Published in the U.S.A. by The Westminster Press, 1961. Copyright © 1961 SCM Press Ltd.; and from *Luther: Lectures on Romans,* edited by Wilhelm Pauck. LCC, Vol. XV. The Westminster Press. Copyright © 1961, W. L. Jenkins.

To Fortress Press for permission to quote from *The Coming Christ and the Coming Church* by E. Schlink, published 1968; and from *Luther's Works,* vol. 31, edited by H. J. Grimm, published by Muhlenberg Press, 1957.

To Harper & Row, Publishers, Inc. for permission to quote from *Old Testament Theology,* 2 vols. by G. von Rad, published 1962 and 1965; from "The Tridentine Decree on Justification in the Light of the Later Medieval Theology" by H. Oberman, published in *Journal for Theology and the Church,* vol. 3, 1967 by Harper Torchbooks; and from *The Epistle of Paul to the Romans* by C. H. Dodd, Second Impression, published by Fontana Books, 1960.

Abbreviations

AE	*Luther's Works: American Edition,* ed. J. Pelikan and H. Lehmann. Philadelphia-St. Louis, 1955ff.
Conc. Trid.	*Concilium Tridentinum.* Diariorum, Actorum, Epistularum, Tractatuum nova Collectio, ed. Societas Goerresiana . . . Freiburg, 1901ff.
Copleston	F. Copleston, *A History of Philosophy,* Image Books Edition. 6 vols.+ New York, 1962ff.
Denifle	H. Denifle. *Luther und Luthertum.*
DLA	Erasmus of Rotterdam. *De libero arbitrio diatribe sive collatio* (1524).
DS	Denzinger-Schönmetzer. *Enchiridion Symbolorum. . . ,* 33rd ed. Barcelona-Freiburg-Rome, 1965.
DSA	M. Luther. *De servo arbitrio* (1525).
DTC	*Dictionnaire de théologie catholique,* ed. A. Vacant and E. Mangenot; continued by É. Amann. Paris, 1930ff.
Hyp.	Erasmus of Rotterdam. *Hyperaspistes:* I & II (1526/27).
Jedin	H. Jedin. *A History of the Council of Trent.* 2 vols.
JB	*The Jerusalem Bible.* New York, 1966. (Biblical citations are ordinarily taken from this version.)
KuD	*Kerygma und Dogma.* Göttingen, 1955ff.
Lortz	J. Lortz. *Die Reformation in Deutschland.* 4th ed. 2 Bde. Freiburg-Basel-Wien, 1962.
LThK	*Lexicon für Theologie und Kirche,* hrsg. v. J. Höfer u. K. Rahner. 2nd ed. 10 vols. Freiburg, 1957-66.
LuJ	*Luther-Jahrbuch.*
MA	*Münchener Luther-Ausgabe.* Ergänzungsreihe. Bd. I: *Dass der freie Wille nicht sei.* München, 1954. Reprinted, 1962.
P & J	J. I. Packer and O. R. Johnston. *M. Luther: On the der freie Wille nicht sei.* München, 1954. Reprinted, 1962.
PG	*Patrologia Graeca,* ed. J. P. Migne. Paris, 1857-66.
PL	*Patrologia Latina,* ed. J. P. Migne. Paris, 1878-90.
RGG	*Die Religion in Geschichte und Gegenwart.* 3rd rev. ed. Tübingen, 1957-1962.
RJ	*Enchiridion Patristicum. . . ,* ed. M. J. Rouët de Journel. 18th ed. Freiburg, 1953.

vii

Seeberg   R. Seeberg. *Lehrbuch der Dogmengeschichte.*

Tappert   *The Book of Concord,* tr. and ed. T. Tappert. St. Louis, 1959.

TDNT   *Theological Dictionary of the New Testament,* ed. G. Kittel and G. Friedrich, tr. G. W. Bromiley. 3 vols. + Grand Rapids-London, 1964ff.

Theol. Inv.   K. Rahner, *Theological Investigations,* tr. C. Ernst and K. Kruger. 4 vols. Baltimore, 1961-1966.

ThStKr   *Theologische Studien und Kritiken.* (Hamburg) Gotha, 1828ff.

ThW   *Theologisches Wörterbuch zum Neuen Testament,* hrsg. G. Kittel, fortges. v. G. Friedrich. Stuttgart, 1933ff.

WA   *D. M. Luthers Werke. Kritische Gesamtausgabe* 1883ff.

WABR   *D. M. Luthers Werke. Kritische Gesamtausgabe: Briefwechsel.* 1930ff.

WATR   *D. M. Luthers Werke. Kritische Gesamtausgabe: Tischreden.* 1912ff.

Walter   *Desiderius Erasmus: De libero arbitrio diatribe sive collatio,* hrsg. v. J. von Walter. 2. Druck. Leipzig, 1935.

Foreword

In 1959 the Paulist Fathers offered me the opportunity to go to Europe to do scholarly research into Protestant theology and ecumenical questions. The *Decree on Ecumenism* of the Second Vatican Council which officially committed the Roman Catholic Church to ecumenism was at that time not yet in sight, and I believe I was the first Catholic priest from this country who went abroad precisely for ecumenical studies.

This book is one of the results of that research program, which extended from September, 1960 to March, 1966. During that time I encountered many persons—Protestant and Catholic—who helped in countless ways to shape the perspective and content of this book. To the following persons above all I wish to record my indebtedness:

To Professor Albert Brandenburg, of the Johann-Adam-Möhler-Institut in Paderborn, for introducing me to methods of Luther research and for alerting me to the central significance of Luther's *The Bondage of the Will*. To Professors Eduard Stakemeier and Peter Bläser, M.S.C., also of the Möhler-Institut, for their competent and willing assistance during my periods of research in Paderborn.

To Professor Michael Schmaus of the University of Munich, who supervised the writing of the German manuscript which was eventually accepted by the theological faculty of Munich as a doctoral dissertation and which provided the basis for the present book. For his scholarly example, but above all for his truly fatherly concern for me during my time in Munich, I shall be forever grateful.

To Professor Heinrich Fries, Director of the Ecumenical Institute of the University of Munich, for accepting the German manuscript as the first volume in the new ecumenical series of which he is the editor. Professor Fries' Preface to the German version has been included in the present revised edition.

I further wish to express my gratitude for the warm reception and scholarly assistance I received from the members of the Protestant theological faculties of Heidelberg and Tübingen during the semesters I spent at those universities. Especially to be thanked is Professor Edmund Schlink of Heidelberg who read the manuscript and delighted me one morning during the final session of Vatican II when he told me in one of the coffee bars in St. Peter's that my study had passed his critical muster with flying colors. To Professors Heinrich Bornkamm, Hans von Campenhausen, Peter Brunner and Albrecht Peters—all of Heidelberg—I am also indebted for many insights. From quite a different perspective, yet with the same cordiality, Professor Ernst Käsemann of Tübingen placed me greatly in his debt. Other Protestant scholars whose counsel helped me greatly include Professor Gerhard Ebeling, Professor Hermann Diem, Dr. Hans Vorster and Professor Gordon Rupp of Cambridge, who read the manuscript in both English and German.

To Father Karl Rahner, S.J. and Professor Otto Kuss, my two most highly esteemed teachers, I am profoundly grateful. Neither is a Luther scholar, yet each offered me, respectively, countless systematic and biblical insights that helped facilitate my dialogue with Luther.

To another great teacher and guide, Father Ben Hunt, C.S.P., Professor of Philosophy and Dean of St. Paul's College in Washington, I am thankful for his constant wise counsel and for his responses to the several philosophical questions that I posed to him from across the Atlantic.

To the dean of Roman Catholic Luther scholarship, Professor Joseph Lortz, and to the distinguished Lutheran theologian, Professor Krister Skydsgaard of Copenhagen, I am grateful for encouraging me to accept the challenge of *The Bondage of the Will* while at the same time warning me about the shoals surrounding it.

Thanks also to Professor Hans Küng of Tübingen who made some valuable suggestions toward improving my manuscript.

To the Augustinians of the Assumption who staff the *Bibliothèque Augustinienne* in Paris for their expert guidance during the summer I spent there researching my chapter on St. Augustine.

Mention should also be made of my indebtedness to those Catholic friends and colleagues in Germany whose zest for Luther research, ecumenism or theology in general helped form the exciting atmosphere in which I worked: Richard Heinzmann, Otto Pesch, O.P., Wim Boelens, S.J., Albert van Paasen, O.F.M.Cap. Reinhard Kösters, Johannes Brosseder and the members of "The American Theological Society of Munich."

A word of sincere thanks is also in order for the patience, under difficult circumstances, of Mrs. Marti Lydick in typing the manuscript.

My final expression of thanks is to the Paulist Fathers for the opportunity they gave me to do the research that lies behind this book. It was an opportunity that provided me with maximum freedom, with no limitations of time or place being imposed. In characteristic Paulist fashion, I was simply asked to go and learn all I could and then to come back when I was ready.

The present book is based upon the German study, as we have indicated, but has been revised to make it more readable by those who are not professional theologians. The American version also differs from the German in that the more recent literature has been incorporated as far as possible. Reflection on Edward Schillebeeckx's short essay, "The Tridentine Decree on Justification: A New View," *Concilium*, vol. 5 (Paulist Press: New York, 1965) has led me to do further research into the *Acta* of the Council of Trent. This resulted in modification of the excursus in Chapter 6: "The Axiom: 'God does not deny grace to one who does what is in him' and Merit—Neo-Semipelagianism?"

The author regrets that neither G. Rost's monograph, *Der Prädestinationsgedanke in der Theologie M. Luthers* (Berlin, 1966) nor G. Hennig's *Cajetan und Luther: Ein historischer Beitrag zur Begegnung von Thomismus und Reformation* (Stuttgart, 1966) caught his attention in time to give them the evaluation they deserve. Hennig's study has particular relevance for our excursus in Chapter 6: "Did Luther Know Thomas Aquinas?" Hennig has studied Luther's contact with Thomism in the person of Cardinal Cajetan, O.P. during their confrontation at Augsburg in 1518. Valuable as this study is, we do not regard its findings as a contradiction of our thesis that Luther lacked adequate knowledge of the theology of Thomas Aquinas.

There are far too many differences between Cajetan and Thomas for one to assume that knowing Cajetan's thought is the same as knowing Thomas'. On this point see A. Maurer, *Medieval Philosophy*, 3rd printing (New York, 1950), p. 350. Precisely on the question of the certitude of salvation, a question on which Hennig focuses, Thomas is far more compatible to Luther than is Cajetan. Hennig's effort (pp. 167-171) to refute the study of Stephen Pfürtner, *Luther and Thomas on Salvation*, in which the fundamental harmony between Thomas and Luther is elaborated, seems to us quite unsuccessful. Here and throughout his book Hennig assumes that every form of divine-human cooperation is foreign to Luther's thought. Hennig would have seen the incorrectness of such an assumption had he taken into account the monograph of Martin Seils, *Der Gedanke vom Zusammenwirken Gottes und des Menschen in Luthers Theologie* (Gütersloh, 1952).

A third volume that reached me too late for consideration is *Pelagius: Inquiries and Reappraisals* (New York: Seabury Press, 1968) by Robert F. Evans.

October 31, 1968

Harry J. McSorley
St. Paul's College
Washington, D.C.

**TO
MY MOTHER AND FATHER
WHO INTRODUCED ME
TO
THE LUTHERAN-CATHOLIC DIALOGUE**

Contents

xiii

PART TWO
ERASMUS: DE LIBERO ARBITRIO

PART THREE
LUTHER: DE SERVO ARBITRIO

Preface

The word "ecumenical" is on everyone's lips today. No theologian, no theology, indeed, no statement, attitude or action within the Church wishes to expose itself to the suspicion or the charge of not being ecumenical. The movement toward ecumenism is not new within the Catholic Church. Through Pope John XXIII and the Second Vatican Council, however, it has received a powerful new impetus and animation. With the promulgation of the Constitutions on the Church and Revelation, as well as the Decree on Ecumenism, ecumenism has become a structural principle and life element of the Church and, above all, of theology. In the post-conciliar age the ecumenical spirit must not be allowed to diminish. It must actualize itself concretely in a genuine and convincing practice of ecumenism.

The Decree on Ecumenism speaks expressly about theology. It states that theology must be taught with due regard for the ecumenical point of view so that it "may correspond as exactly as possible with the facts." This ecumenical theology is distinguished both from polemics as well as from a mutually deceptive glossing over of differences. Neither of these positions permits a true encounter. The duty of being true to one's self is linked with the task of presenting Catholic belief more profoundly and precisely in such a way and in such a language that our separated brethren can also really understand it. The openness that is called for by the Decree expresses itself in an ecumenical dialogue in which Catholic theologians "search together with the separated brethren into the divine mysteries," an enterprise which "calls for love for the truth, charity and humility." In this connection mention is also made of the fundamental idea of the "hierarchy of truths" within Catholic doctrine, a hierarchy based upon the varying relationship of these truths "to the foundation of the Christian faith." A merely additive or "all-on-the-same-level" understanding of Catholic belief is thus rejected. Such a conception, because it simply counts and does not evaluate the various doctrines, likewise prevents a genuine dialogue from taking place. Only a theology which is sensitive to the hierarchy of truths and which seeks a sense of proportion and dimension can prepare the way for the kind of "fraternal ri-

1

valry" which "will incite all to a deeper realization and a clearer expression of the unfathomable riches of Christ."

The foregoing is a statement of what ecumenical theology, according to a Catholic understanding of it, wants to be and can be. This understanding of ecumenical theology has by no means always been so clear. It only became clear as a result of a sustained process of differentiation. The concept of ecumenical theology presented in the Decree on Ecumenism is itself the fruit of such a development and would not have been possible without methodological, historical and theoretical reflection.

Ecumenical theology is—when seen from these viewpoints—not one division of theology alongside other divisions; thus not another instance of the specialization which has become unavoidable even in theology. It is rather the result of theological differentiation and reflection on the aspects and dimensions of theology. This means concretely:

Ecumenical theology is set in motion by the problem of separated Christianity and of a possible unity in faith. The factual situation, the separation of Christianity, is not simply accepted as something given, perhaps even as an unchangeable given or as some necessity that is theologically welcomed. On the contrary, ecumenical theology regards this factual situation as a scandal and as a challenge. Further, ecumenical theology recognizes the unity of Christians in faith not as an unrealistic Utopia, but as a task and it permits itself to be engaged by this task. It is clear that no area of theology can exclude itself from this impulse. On the other hand, it is just as clear that every area of theology is not challenged by this task to the same degree.

Ecumenical theology is not the same as comparative symbolics (*Konfessionskunde*), which describes the differences and similarities of the confessions and which limits itself to the very important task of information and orientation. Ecumenical theology is also different from the once widespread controversial theology (*Kontroverstheologie*), which makes the opposition between the confessions the object of its reflections, searches for the roots of the disagreements and tries to furnish justification for them. Ecumenical theology would understand itself and its task incorrectly, however, if it overlooked the results of comparative symbolics and controversial theology. It simply does not wish to be satisfied with these results. For these areas of research alone would not lead us to a movement, to a new phase in the history of the Church and of Christianity, to an ecumenism, but, at best, to a coexistence and heightening of isolation. For this reason, ecumenical theology tries to see not only the separating factors in the other confessions but also that which unites them and discovers in the process that that which is common is proportionately greater than that which separates. The differences are then seen and evaluated on the horizon of the elements which are held in common. In this way a new possibility of encounter and openness is created.

Such a theology oriented around the things which are held in common questions itself as to the theological motives for the division of Christianity. It asks whether in the faith and the life of the Catholic Church something which was the occasion of separation and which sought a new and more intensive realization outside the Catholic Church was given too little attention and entered too little into the existential life of the Church. It asks whether and how the Christian concerns and realizations which are alive in the other confessions can also be represented and accepted within the Catholic Church in order that they might again find their home, in all their integrity. An ecumenical theology, as a theology of theological causes, must further ask: Against what is the "No" of the other confessions directed? Is it directed against a contemporary expression of a truth of the faith or against this truth itself? Do the differences consist in diverse formulations or in the doctrine itself? Can the same thing be said with diverse formulations, different things with the same formulations? To what extent is a multiplicity of expressions, a theological pluralism possible in the unity of the faith?

Ecumenical theology is, further, a theology of understanding: it not only strives to understand the others but is also intent upon so expressing its own faith and its own understanding of the faith that the others are also able to understand it with their theological presuppositions and their vocabulary on the basis of their context. In so doing, it becomes clear that it is ultimately a matter of understanding the other in order to articulate more deeply and more adequately the truth of the Word of God which binds us all.

Ecumenical theology is a theology of origins and of sources. It wishes to gather its statements from the testimony of the Bible which is recognized by all confessions as the foundation and norm, and to present them in the light of the Bible. It has the courage to put up with the tension between the biblical times and our own and to allow itself constantly to receive new life from the biblical origins. At the same time, the theological enterprise is always to be undertaken in a spirit of co-operation and participation. As Möhler has said, we are not to develop a foolish theological rivalry but a competition based on faith and love, the purpose of which is a deeper understanding of the truth and of the Word of God. The theologians of other Christian confessions are thus seen not only in their opposition to one's own doctrine, as if this were their main value, but they are also regarded as "colleagues in search of truth."

Ecumenical theology is, finally, a theology of the whole. As such, it is not satisfied with developing partial aspects of the whole. It wishes, on the contrary, to present everything that is Christian in an all-embracing perspective. It wishes to articulate the undisguised fullness and to assign everything that is truly Christian its rightful place. It is not only interested in rejecting error but in retaining the truth which is to be found even in an error. Its own thought and language is deepened, expanded and renewed by the creative encounter with the others and by the return to the sources. This is neither minimalism nor indifferentism, but a maximalism of the inner dimensions which comes from truly ecumenical and catholic thinking. It should not be forgotten that, looking at the original meaning of the words, ecumenical and catholic mean the same thing.

If it is true, as we have suggested, that ecumenical theology is not a special discipline but a dimension and a structure of theology in general, and that it consequently ought to be present in all theological themes and disciplines, it is nonetheless necessary that there be particular models which, in a special way, illustrate the ecumenical as a dimension and as a structure. These models should exemplify and clarify the manner in which the ecumenical can manifest itself within theology. This is the meaning and the justification of institutes for ecumenical theology; it is also the meaning and the task of the contributions to ecumenical theology that begin with this volume.

The study of Luther's work, *De servo arbitrio,* by Father McSorley, a member of the Paulist Fathers, fulfills the conditions of an ecumenical theology in an exemplary manner.

The investigation deals with a central theme of Luther's theology, a theme found in that work which the Reformer himself designated as the most important of his writings. The special value of McSorley's study consists in the fact that the theme in question—it is the central theme of justification with all of its theological implications and consequences—is not only portrayed within the framework of Luther's theology, but is also developed in the light of the biblical and ecclesial traditions. The author achieves his objective by drawing upon a comprehensive knowledge of the sources and of the literature and by his impressive presentation of the material in his treatment of Paul and Augustine, the early Councils, Thomas, the late Scholastics and the direct confrontation of Luther with Erasmus. In this kind of presentation, the decisive elements of an ecumenical theology are unfolded: the search for causes, the consideration of the total problem, the common origins, the sources, and the use of theological research as a cooperative venture in the discovery of truth. From this methodology flow also the decisive theological criteria. In this way the thematic of *De servo arbitrio* is developed in its meaning for Christian theology in general.

The author deals with his theme on a broad theological horizon with remarkable scholarly energy, with a feel for problems, relationships and differences. He has the capacity to make a clear and well-founded judgment, the courage to criticize and to enter into a many-sided scientific confrontation with the historical and systematic research, and last, but not least, he has the ability for ecumenical *engagement*. This ability is not concealed by the strictly scientific character of the study, but is revealed in its full theological potential. The relationship between ecclesiology and the doctrine of justification which McSorley points out will significantly enrich the theological encounter between the confessions and the dialogue of the Churches.

I am happy that the *Contributions to Ecumenical Theology* [1] can be opened with the work of an American theologian who became interested in this theme in Germany and completed it there during five years of intensive research.

Munich, April 1967 HEINRICH FRIES

---

[1] Ed.—The German version of Father McSorley's book was the first volume in the new series edited by Professor Fries: *Beiträge zur ökumenischen Theologie.*

Introduction

One of the paradoxes of contemporary ecumenical discussions between Catholics and Protestants is that many of the theological issues which are today regarded as separating factors were not at all the issues that led Martin Luther to precipitate the separation in the sixteenth century. Much time is spent today, for example, discussing Mariology. Yet, for Luther, Mary was always "Gottes Mutter," and belief in her immaculate conception, her perpetual virginity and possibly even her assumption posed no problem for him.[1] Similarly, questions such as the relationship of Scripture and Tradition, the ministry, papal infallibility and the nature of the sacraments, which figure so prominently in ecumenical conversations today,[2] were *not* regarded by Luther as his supreme concern.[3]

---

[1] Cf. H. Hennig, "Die Lehre von der Mutter Gottes in den evangelischen Bekenntnisschriften und bei den lutherischen Vätern," *Una Sancta*, XVI (March, 1961), 55-80, esp. 77ff.; H. Schütte, *Um die Wiedervereinigung im Glauben*, 3rd ed. (Essen, 1960), pp. 146-149; W. Tappolet, ed. in collaboration with A. Ebneter, *Das Marienlob der Reformatoren* (Tübingen, 1962); A. Brandenburg, introduction to Luther's *Das Magnifikat* (Freiburg, 1964), pp. 16ff.; T. Harjunpaa, "A Lutheran View of Mariology," *America* (Oct. 21, 1967), 436-441. H. Graef, *Mary: A History of Doctrine and Devotion*, vol. II (New York, 1965) is inadequate in her treatment of Luther's view of Mary. Cf. Brandenburg, *Maria in der evangelischen Theologie der Gegenwart* (Paderborn, 1965), p. 83.

[2] W. Kampe lists seven topics which he thinks are the most important ecumenical questions today: "Die zweite Periode des II. Vatikanischen Konzils und ihre ökumenischen Aspekte," *Ökumenische Rundschau*, XIII (April, 1964), 157. He does not even mention the problems of grace, free will and justification! It is commonly accepted today that the ultimate issue separating Protestants and Catholics is an ecclesiological one. Thus, Heinrich Bornkamm thinks that Joseph Lortz and other Catholic scholars are perfectly correct in saying that the decisive difference was, and still is, the question of the infallibility of the Church's teaching office. Cf. Bornkamm, *The Heart of Reformation Faith* (New York, 1965), pp. 90 and 92. For the same view see Hubert Jedin, "Der Abschluss des Trienter Konzils 1562-63. Ein Rückblick nach vier Jahrhunderten," in: *Katholisches Leben und Kämpfen im Zeitalter der Glaubensspaltung*, No. 21 (Münster/Westf., 1963), p. 76. Too little attention has been paid, in our judgment, to the relation between Luther's ecclesiology and his doctrine of justification. Was it an explicit re-thinking of the nature of the Church that led to Luther's break with the medieval Church? Or was his ecclesiology conditioned by his doctrine of justification by grace alone? The latter

7

What *was* the central issue of Luther's protest? With unmistakable clarity Luther himself answers this question in the closing paragraph of *De servo arbitrio* (1525),[4] his powerful reply to the long-awaited attack made by Desiderius Erasmus in *De libero arbitrio* (1524). Fully confident that he has refuted Erasmus, Luther offers him a singular word of consolation: "Moreover, I give you hearty praise and commendation on this further account—that you alone, in contrast with all others, have attacked the real thing, that is, the essential issue [*res ipsa;*

seems to us to have been the case. Luther's rejection of the papacy and the hierarchical Church of his day is not based on any direct ecclesiological argument, but on the conviction that this hierarchical, papal Church was teaching a Pelagian doctrine of grace and justification. The dependence of Luther's ecclesiology on his doctrine of justification is seen clearly in his Commentary on Galatians of 1535. In Chapter 3 we find the remarkable sentence: "I am willing to kiss your feet, pope, and to acknowledge you as the supreme pontiff, if you adore my Christ and grant that we have the forgiveness of sins and eternal life through his death and resurrection and not through the observance of your traditions" WA 40, 357; AE 26, p. 224; cf. p. 99.

3 Albert Brandenburg has helpfully distinguished those differences which immediately catch the eye, such as Mariology, the papacy, ecclesiology, the sacraments, etc., which he calls the visible symptoms and foreground phenomena of Christian division, as opposed to those principles in the background which are not readily evident, but which are the real theological bases of the separation. See Brandenburg, "Hinweise zur Methodik der Arbeit an der Luthertheologie," *Begegnung der Christen: Festschrift für Otto Karrer*, eds. M. Roesele and Oscar Cullmann (Frankfurt-Stuttgart, 1959), p. 497. At this point it may be well to emphasize against a still widespread popular interpretation of the Reformation, that Luther was not primarily motivated by the abuses in late-medieval Catholicism, but by what he considered to be the false teaching of the Church. Cf. WATR, 1, Nr. 624; 880; 4, Nr. 4338. Among those who make this point abundantly clear is Roland Bainton in *The Reformation of the Sixteenth Century,* 5th ed. (Boston: Beacon, 1960): "Not the abuses of medieval Catholicism, but Catholicism itself as an abuse of the Gospel was the object of his onslaught. Luther congratulated Erasmus for perceiving what others had missed, that the quarrel centered on the view of man and God" (p. 24). Cf. Joseph Lortz, *Die Reformation in Deutschland,* 4th ed. (Freiburg-Basel, Wien 1962), I, 390.

4 WA 18, 600-787. The title of this work has been translated in various ways. Luther himself once translated Augustine's phrase "servum arbitrium," with the words "eyn gefangenen willen" WA 7, 446, 19. In English there is no uniform translation. The most frequently encountered is "The Bondage of the Will" (Packer and Johnston, Ernst Winter, also M. Bertram and R. Fischer in their translations of H. Bornkamm and F. Lau respectively). Packer and Johnston note that the literal rendering is "on the enslaved will." This translation is adopted by the English translator of H. Grisar, E. M. Lamond. We have chosen to speak of "the unfree will" not only for the sake of consistency, but also because this translation brings out the sharpness of Luther's opposition to Erasmus' book "On the Free Will." We think, however, that "the imprisoned will" or "the bondage of the will" corresponds more to Luther's intention and to his own German translation: "eyn gefangenen Willen." In German literature one frequently finds DSA referred to as "Vom unfreien Willen."

summa causae]. You have not wearied me with those extraneous issues about the papacy, purgatory, indulgences and such like—trifles, rather than issues—in respect of which almost all to date have sought my blood (though without success); you, and you alone, have seen the hinge on which all turns [*cardo rerum*], and aimed for the vital spot. For that I heartily thank you. . . ." [5]

Not the doctrines of the papacy, purgatory or indulgences, but the doctrine of the freedom of the will was the real issue—the *res ipsa* of Luther's reformation protest! This was not merely an isolated, passing statement. Already in 1520, in the *Assertio omnium articulorum M. Lutheri per bullam Leonis X. novissimam damnatorum,* Luther singled out the thirty-sixth article—the one in which he defends the thesis that the free will, after Adam's fall, is a name devoid of content (*res de solo titulo; eyn eytteler name*)—as the real issue of his reformation. Again he speaks of the other questions about the papacy, councils and indulgences as "trifles" (*nugae*) but explicitly insists that this article is the most important point of his doctrine. [6]

Did Luther change his mind after 1525 about the importance of his doctrine of the unfree will? It seems very unlikely that he did. Twelve years after he wrote *De servo arbitrio,* Luther could still write to Wolfgang Capito (July 9, 1537), in reference to the forthcoming publication of his collected works: "I consider none of my books to be worthwhile, except perhaps *De servo arbitrio* and the *Catechism.*" [7]

The great systematic theologian of early Lutheranism, Philip Melanchthon, saw clearly—even before Luther wrote *De servo arbitrio*—that Erasmus had attacked the very center of Luther's thought. In his

---

[5] P & J, p. 319. WA 18, 786, 26-31.

[6] WA 7, 148, 14-17. K. Zickendraht is one of the few authors to make the important observation "that Luther designates this article (36) as the center of his belief—a belief which was to lead to the rejection of the papal Church": *Der Streit zwischen Erasmus und Luther uber die Willensfreiheit* (Leipzig, 1909), p. 8. A. Sirrala, "Freedom and Authority in Erasmus and Luther," *Dialog* 7 (1966), 108-113 is seriously mistaken when he suggests that the "real issue" of *The Bondage of the Will* is not the bondage of the will but "the question of the character of divine authority in man's life."

[7] WABR 8, 99-100, No. 3162. Concerning the Catechism, Schwiebert, *Luther and His Times* (St. Louis: Concordia, 1950), p. 641, informs us that Luther himself never distinguishes between the Large (Der deutsche Katechismus) and the Small (the Enchiridion) Catechisms. Both were simply "the Catechism." For a possible exception see WATR 4, 434, 11. In the light of Luther's statements of 1520 and 1525, this remark to Capito loses none of its force even though Luther in the *Table-talk* often spoke highly of other doctrinal and biblical works, such as his Lectures on the Epistle to the Galatians and his Exposition of Chapters 14-16 of St. John's Gospel. Cf. WATR 5, 204, 28; 323, 26.

letter to Erasmus of September 30, 1524, written immediately after *De libero arbitrio* appeared, Melanchthon pointed out that all of Luther's theological views were essentially related to the question of free will.[8]

The supreme importance of *De servo arbitrio* has not escaped the attention of modern researchers. Preserved Smith in an older study [9] and Jean Boisset more recently [10] both regard *De servo arbitrio* as incontestably one of the most important works of the sixteenth century. And although Luther's essay *On the Freedom of a Christian Man* (1520) may have been "the most widely read of Luther's writings," [11] many Lutherans would agree with the Norwegian Luther scholar, Bishop Normann, that *De servo arbitrio* was "the finest and most powerful *Soli Deo Gloria* to be sung in the whole period of the Reformation." [12]

In the lengthy historical and theological introduction to their English translation of *De servo arbitrio,* Packer and Johnston call Luther's reply to Erasmus "the greatest piece of theological writing that ever came from Luther's pen." [13] Other authors express themselves more moderately by claiming that *De servo arbitrio* is at least Luther's greatest piece of systematic-theological writing.[14]

Anyone even slightly acquainted with the theology of Luther or with Lutheran theology may be surprised to find that Luther calls the doctrine of the unfree will the "res ipsa" and the "summa causae" of his

---

[8] *Corpus Reformatorum,* ed. Bretschneider et Bindseil (Halis Saxoniae, 1834ff), I, 674ff. Melanchthon himself later rejected Luther on precisely this vital point.

[9] *Erasmus: A Study of His Life, Ideals, and Place in History* (New York, 1923; new printing 1962), p. 354.

[10] *Érasme et Luther: Libre ou serf-arbitre?* (Paris, 1962), p. 28.

[11] Karl A. Meissinger, *Luther: Die deutsche Tragödie,* (München, 1953), p. 161. DSA was also an enormous publication success, with eight Latin and two German editions appearing within one year! Cf. A. Freitag, *Einleitung zu Luthers De servo arbitrio,* WA 18, 597-98.

[12] *Viljefrihet og forutbestemmelse i den lutherske reformasjon inntil 1525* (Oslo, 1933); cited by G. Rupp, *The Righteousness of God: Luther Studies* (London, 1953), p. 283.

[13] J. I. Packer and O. R. Johnston, "Historical and Theological Introduction" to *The Bondage of the Will* (London: J. Clarke, 1957), p. 40. Cf. Chr. Ernst Luthardt, *Die Lehre vom freien Willen in seinem Verhältnis zur Gnade* (Leipzig, 1863), p. 123. The Russian philosopher Nicholas Berdyaev, in *The Destiny of Man* (New York: Harper Torch, 1960), p. 19, n. 1, has called DSA "the most remarkable of Luther's works." Berdyaev's own understanding of freedom bears an interesting resemblance to Luther's. Cf. F. Copleston, S. J. *Contemporary Philosophy,* 4th printing (Westminster, Md.: Newman, 1963), p. 118.

[14] Martin Doerne, "Gottes Ehre am gebundenen Willen," *LuJ,* XXII (1938), 45; Lortz, I, p. 150; Rupp, p. 88; Robert Frick, "Erläuterungen" to Luther's work *Wider den Löwener Theologen Latomus* (München, 1961), p. 141: G. Ritter, *Luther: His Life and Work,* trans. John Riches (London, 1963), p. 177; P & J, p. 45.

teaching. Is not the doctrine of justification by faith alone the heart of Luther's reformation thinking, the *articulus stantis et cadentis ecclesiae?*[15] Actually there is no real inconsistency in asserting that the doctrine of the unfree will is just as important and central for Luther as his teaching on justification. For if the doctrine of justification is the article on which the Church stands and falls, then the doctrine of the unfree will is the *foundation* of the article on which the Church stands and falls, or the article on which Luther's doctrine of justification stands or falls.[16] Almost a century ago Plitt pointed out that everything that is peculiar to Luther's teaching on justification depends on his doctrine of the unfree will.[17] Preserved Smith has called Luther's teaching on the unfree will "the reverse side" of his doctrine on justification.[18]

No one has seen more clearly the centrality and radical importance of the doctrine of the unfree will for Luther's thinking than the careful scholar, Hans Joachim Iwand, when he wrote: ". . . evangelical theology stands and falls with this doctrine of the unfree will." [19] Luther himself says that St. Paul's teaching on justification and grace in the Epistle to the Romans is nothing more than an assault on the doctrine of free will ("disputationem adversus liberum arbitrium pro gratia Dei").[20] It is therefore no exaggeration when Erikstein says of *De servo arbitrio:* "For Luther the very heart of Christianity is at issue in this book." [21] Nothing less than "the inmost center of the Reformation" is at stake.[22]

---

[15] Cf. Friedrich Loofs, "Der articulus stantis et cadentis ecclesiae," *ThStKr,* (1917), 323-420.

[16] When Edmund Schlink, *The Coming Christ and the Coming Church* (Philadelphia, 1968), p. 165, writes: "The justification of the sinner can . . . not be taught without the distinction of Law and Gospel," one must also add that it is equally impossible to teach Luther's doctrine of justification without his doctrine of the unfree will, for this is an essential component of Luther's understanding of Law.

[17] G. L. Plitt, *Luthers Streit mit Erasmus über den freien Willen in den Jahren 1524-1525.* Studien der evangelisch-protestantischen Geistlichen des Grossherzogthums Baden, 2 (1876), p. 206.

[18] P. Smith, p. 339: ". . . this dogma lay at the very heart of the Protestant system, being, in fact, no more than the reverse side of the famous doctrine of justification by faith only. Where everything is performed by the grace of God there is nothing left for the human will."

[19] Iwand, "Theologische Einführung" to MA, p. 253. Cf. Schwiebert, p. 688, who says, with reference to J. MacKinnon, *Luther and the Reformation,* Vol. III (London, 1929), pp. 241f: "Luther's whole doctrinal system would crumble" if the thesis of *De servo arbitrio* were invalid.

[20] WA 18, 757, 10f; 762, 29-33.

[21] Einar Erikstein, *Luthers Praedestinationslehre geschichtlich dargestellt bis einschliesslich* "De servo arbitrio," unpublished diss. (Göttingen, 1957), p. 159.

[22] Iwand, MA, p. 312. Cf. Denis de Rougemont, Introduction to his translation of DSA, *Traité du serf arbitre* (Paris, 1936). He speaks of "l'importance centrale du traité que nous publions: je le vois au centre du débat occidental par excellence,

In making *De servo arbitrio* the object of an ecumenical-theological investigation, it is clear from what has already been said that one is not dealing with a single, isolated question, the favorable resolution of which would lead to only a partial agreement between the Lutheran Reformation and the Catholic Church.[23] What is involved here is the hinge on which Luther's entire theology turns (the "cardo rerum").[24] Luther's doctrine of the unfree will is essential to his justification teaching and, as we shall see, to his concept of faith. To affirm the one is to affirm the other. And to reject the doctrine of the unfree will in whole or in part is to alter not only Luther's teaching on justification, but his entire theological structure.[25]

In 1958, one of the leading Catholic experts on Luther's theology, Albert Brandenburg, expressed regret over the relative lack of Catholic contributions to scientific and critical research in the theology of Luther in comparison to numerous and valuable studies by Catholics in the field of Reformation history.[26] Since then there has been a remarkable upsurge of Catholic Luther research.[27] Among Protestants there is a comparable new interest in Thomas Aquinas. According to Thomas Bonhoeffer, Aquinas should be ranked as one of the "Fathers of Protestant theology." Bonhoeffer goes so far as to call Thomas the "doctor communis" of both Protestant and Catholic theology.[28]

---

mais au centre, aussi, de la Réforme, et de l'effort dogmatique de Luther" (p. 17). Doerne, p. 52 calls DSA "ein klassiches Dokument des eigensten Themas der Reformation." And according to Walter, p. vii, DSA presents "das zentrale Problem der Frömmigkeit und Theologie Luthers." In his judgment "der ganze Kampf mit Rom tritt fur den Reformator hinter jener einen Frage zurück."

[23] That is how Ansgar Ahlbrecht evaluates the otherwise fine study by Stephanus Pfürtner, *Luther und Thomas im Gespräch: Unser Heil zwischen Gewissheit und Gefährdung* (Heidelberg, 1961). See "Neue katholische Versuche zur Würdigung der theologischen Anliegen Luthers," *Una Sancta*, XVIII (July 1963), 178f. Cf. Pfürtner, *Luther and Aquinas on Salvation* (New York, 1965).

[24] WA 18, 786, 30.

[25] This is a general rule of theology. As Karl Rahner points out, to the extent that a theological question sets the whole of theology in motion, to that extent it can be presumed that the question has been properly stated and treated in its appropriate dimension. *Über die Schriftinspiration*, 2nd ed. (Freiburg, 1958), p. 42. Cf. the English translation by C. H. Henkey: *Inspiration in the Bible* (Edinburgh-London, 1961), p. 34.

[26] "Um Luthers Theologie heute," *Rheinischer Merkur* (Oct. 28, 1958). Cited by Thomas Sartory: "Martin Luther in katholischer Sicht," *Una Sancta*, XVI (March, 1961), 46f.

[27] See O. H. Pesch, "Twenty Years of Catholic Luther Research," *Lutheran World*, XIII (1966), 3-16.

[28] Bonhoeffer, *Die Gotteslehre des Thomas von Aquin als Sprachproblem* (Tübingen, 1962), p. 3. Hans Vorster, like Bonhoeffer a protégé of Gerhard Ebeling, has published his doctoral dissertation under the title *Das Freiheitsverständnis bei Thomas von Aquin und Martin Luther* (Göttingen, 1964). This work is far

The present study is an effort to contribute to the growing dialogue between the Father of the Reformation and the teaching of the Catholic Church. More specifically, this investigation is an attempt to fill the need for the new Catholic study of *De servo arbitrio* called for by Brandenburg when he wrote: "It is urgently necessary that Protestant and Catholic theologians engage in a common exchange of views on this most puzzling and most profound work of Luther, namely, *De servo arbitrio*." [29]

Instead of presenting an extensive survey of the relevant literature in this introduction,[30] we shall limit ourselves here to describing three broad categories of the interpretations that have been made of this complex book:

1. Authors who consider only that part of *De servo arbitrio* which treats the biblical doctrine of bondage to sin and who emphasize that Luther allows for free will in the things that are "beneath" us, the natural things,[31] but who do not take seriously Luther's teaching that, as a result of God's infallible foreknowledge, all things happen by absolute necessity.[32] Also included in this group are those who think that, for Luther, faith involves a free decision on the part of man, or who think that Luther means "freely" when he uses the words "voluntarie" or "sponte." [33]

2. Authors who try to read into *De servo arbitrio* certain modern philosophical-theological categories.[34]

3. Authors who see that the affirmation of universal necessity in *De*

superior in its understanding of and openness for St. Thomas and Scholasticism than, for example, W. Link's *Das Ringen Luthers um die Freiheit der Theologie von der Philosophie,* 2nd ed. (Münich, 1955). Pesch gives a brief critical appraisal of Vorster's book in: "Thomas von Aquin im Lichte evangelischer Fragen," *Catholica,* XX (1966), 72-76. Writing independently from Vorster, but treating the same problem, Pesch has provided a brief Catholic counterpart to Vorster's investigation: "Freiheitsbegriff und Freiheitslehre bei Thomas von Aquin und Luther," *Catholica,* XVII (1963), 197-244.

29 Brandenburg, "Vom Geheimnis der Geschichte nach Luther," *Catholica,* XV (1961), 155. An indication of the increasing new interest in DSA can be seen in the fact that this central work of Luther has in recent years been made the theme of theological seminars at the Universities of Heidelberg, (P. Brunner), Zurich (G. Ebeling), and Hamburg (H. Thielecke), and also at the Gregorian University in Rome (J. Witte, S. J.). The results of the first three seminars were fortunately accessible to us.

30 For a survey of the more important studies of the controversy between Erasmus and Luther, see the beginning of chapter 10.

31 WA 18, 672ff; 752, 7ff.

32 WA 18, 614, 27-616, 12; 747, 22ff. Cf. WA 7, 146, 6ff.

33 This group includes, among others, Pinomaa, G. Ebeling, J. Boisset, H. Bornkamm, D. Löfgren, E. Erikstein.

34 For example, F. Gogarten and J. Boisset. H. J. Iwand rightly says of such

servo arbitrio has deterministic overtones which exclude any activity of free will and deprive faith of its decision-character. This group can be subdivided into: (a) those who reject this aspect of Luther's teaching in *De servo arbitrio;* [35] (b) those who seem to accept this teaching in all its radicality; [36] and (c) those who try to distinguish what they consider to be Luther's sometimes misleading statements and expressions from his sound, biblical intention.[37]

The ecumenical problem posed by *De servo arbitrio* may be stated as follows: Is Luther's doctrine of the unfree will—his "summa causae"— a doctrine that truly, that is, in the dimension of its deepest intention, separates Catholics and Christians of the Reformation tradition? [38] We do not think so. In our statement of the problem, emphasis has been placed on Luther's intention, and this important aspect of the Reformer's book shall continually be stressed throughout our analysis of *De servo arbitrio.* To search for the intention and the basic concern behind the wording of a doctrinal statement is an essential characteristic of ecumenical theology.[39] We wish to discover not merely what Luther *said,* but also what he *intended.*[40] This is, after all, the difference be-

---

interpretations of DSA: Wir werden "einen grundlegenden Unterschied zwischen ihnen und der Schrift [Luthers] selbst feststellen können": MA, p. 255.

[35] A. Ritschl, Th. Harnack, F. Kattenbusch, K. Zickendraht, K. Holl, M. Doerne, K. Meissinger, Y. Alanen, W. Pannenberg, et al.

[36] H. Lammers, H. J. Iwand, Packer and Johnston, et al. These authors often fail to face the problem of the at least apparent contradiction between Luther's affirmation of free will in the "naturalia" on the one hand and his doctrine of absolute necessity on the other. Cf. notes 32 and 33 above.

[37] C. E. Luthardt, H. Bandt, E. Schlink, for example.—Our own interpretation of DSA approximates this view.

[38] The term "Lutheran Christianity" has deliberately been avoided here, so as not to give the impression that Luther was the only one of the Reformation Fathers to hold to the doctrine of the unfree will. Since it would distract us from our purpose to present here detailed evidence for the existence of this doctrine in the writings of the other Reformers, we are content simply to express agreement with Packer and Johnston, p. 58, who write: "Historically, it is a simple matter of fact that Martin Luther and John Calvin, and for that matter, Ulrich Zwingli, Martin Bucer, and all the leading Protestant theologians of the first epoch of the Reformation, stood on precisely the same ground here."

[39] As George Tavard puts it, we must try to seek "correspondence of thought beneath the divergences of language": *Protestantism,* trans. Rachel Attwater (London, 1959), p. 31. See also the paper read at the Fourth World Conference for Faith and Order (Montreal, 1963) by Albert C. Outler: "From Disputation to Dialogue," published in *The Ecumenical Review,* XVI, No. 1 (1963), 14-23.

[40] This distinction assumes great importance in the interpretation of Luther's writings. For as H. Bandt says in his masterly study of Luther's doctrine of the hidden God (*Deus absconditus*): One must remember "dass bei ihm das 'Gemeinte', der Intentionssinn seiner Sätze vielfach mit deren nacktem, logisch-grammatischem Wortsinn nicht eindeutig zusammenfällt. Ja, er hat sich manchmal so paradox zugespitzter Formulierungen bedient, . . . dass Wortsinn und Intentionssinn bei ihm gelegentlich geradezu in Widerspruch geraten. Es ist darum in Luthers

tween merely learning someone's doctrinal formulations and entering into dialogue with him. When there is true dialogue, men find themselves repeatedly asking the question: What did you *mean* by that?

The substance of divinely revealed truth and its formulation are not the same. This distinction, made by Pope John XXIII in his opening address at the first session of the Second Vatican Council, has been embodied in the council's *Decree on Ecumenism* as an official principle of Catholic ecumenical theology.[41] What practical significance does this principle have for ecumenical theology? It means at least that it is possible to have a unity of faith and dogmatic truth *without* a uniformity of dogmatic formulations.[42] Just as in the liturgy, where Catholic unity

---

Schrifttum . . . zu prüfen, ob er . . . tatsächlich das sagen will, was er auf den ersten Blick zu sagen scheint." *Luthers Lehre vom verborgenen Gott: Eine Untersuchung zu dem offenbarungsgeschichtlichen Ansatz seiner Theologie* (Berlin, 1958), p. 20.

The search for Luther's intention is not a search for something "hidden" that is not subject to the scrutiny of scientific historiography. On the contrary, in seeking Luther's basic intention we are indicating our dissatisfaction with the often oversimplified versions of his thought that reflect only a few of his more radical statements. Such oversimplifications of the complex thought of Augustine, Aquinas and Luther can be found by the score in many standard works of church history and the history of Christian thought. We seek to discover Luther's genuine intention by doing more—not less—intensive historical research, by studying the larger context of a number of his writings and refusing to be content with an inadequate historical view based on only a few of his works.

[41] *The Teachings of the Second Vatican Council* (Westminster, Md.: Newman, 1966), pp. 7 and 190f. Cf. *A.A.S.* 54 (1962), p. 792: *Decretum de Oecumenismo*, chapt. II, n. 6.—Speaking in the name of the Observer-Delegates at a reception given by Cardinal Bea on Oct. 15, 1962, Prof. Edmund Schlink pointed to the importance of this distinction and added: "I am convinced that separated Christianity has more common substance than is apparent when one looks for the first time at widely varying doctrinal formulations." Reported in *Herder Korrespondenz*, 17 (Nov., 1962), p. 92, (Trans. ours).

[42] In the Scripture itself one finds a diversity of expressions and formulations of the same divine truth. Cf., for example, the New Testament teaching about the Church, baptism, faith and works and, above all, the person and the work of Christ himself. From the history of the development of Christian doctrine one may cite the example of St. Augustine and other Church Fathers who often said that Christ is present in the eucharist "secundum praesentiam spiritualem," so that the eucharist is the "figuram" of the body and blood of Christ. Such expressions, which fell into disuse during later centuries of doctrinal development, were in no way intended to oppose belief in the "real presence," as is evident when one makes a study of the totality of the eucharistic doctrine of the Fathers in question. Abundant illustrations can be found in the Reformation period, as ecumenical studies are continually discovering. When Luther, for example, says that we are justified by faith alone, he is not disagreeing with the Catholic doctrine that good works done out of faith and love are necessary for salvation, for he himself teaches: "Die Werke sind nötig zum Heil, aber sie wirken nicht das Heil. . . ," WA 39/I, 96, 6ff. Cited by Paul Althaus, "Sola Fide nunquam sola: Glaube und Werke in ihrer Bedeutung für das Heil bei Martin Luther," *Una Sancta*, XVI (Dec., 1961), 235. And when Luther speaks of man's nature as being totally

of worship does not mean uniformity of rite or language, so also Catholic unity of belief does not absolutely demand uniformity of doctrinal formulations.[43] On the other hand, this principle can also mean that unity of doctrinal formulations does not necessarily guarantee unity in the substance of belief.[44] Certainly there must be a regulation of doctrinal formulations in the Church, precisely because a dogmatic statement has an ecclesial character which calls for common faith and a common profession, especially when the Church confronts a common contemporary spiritual situation.[45] Nevertheless, the very important

---

corrupt, one must not immediately conclude that he places himself outside the Catholic tradition. For in his *Commentary on Galatians* (1535), to cite just one example, Luther admits that the natural qualities of man—including will, reason and free choice!—remain sound and incorrupt even after the Fall; WA 40/1, 293. Tavard, p. 33f., has pointed out another example: the Catholic doctrine of the *ex opere operato* efficacy of the sacraments is explicitly rejected in the *Augsburg Confession* and in the *Apology of the Augsburg Confession,* yet the essence of the doctrine is taught by Luther himself in another confessional book, *The Large Catechism.*

[43] Very important for the method used in this dissertation and for the entire problem of the tension between what is meant and what is said in a dogmatic statement are the two essays: E. Schlink, "The Structure of Dogmatic Statements as an Ecumenical Problem," in: *The Coming Christist. . . .,* pp. 16-95 and K. Rahner, "What Is a Dogmatic Statement?", *Theol. Inv.* V, pp. 42-66.

[44] For example, Pelagius and Luther both teach justification "sola fide," but they mean something totally different despite their use of identical formulae. For a listing of the numerous places in which Pelagius speaks of "sola fides," see A. Souter, *Pelagius' Expositions of Thirteen Epistles of St. Paul,* Vol. I (Cambridge, 1922), p. 70. A classic example of our point is the identity of some of the formulations used by Baius and St. Augustine. The Baian propositions were condemned by Pius V because of the heretical intention that lay behind them; not because these formulations could never have and have never had a Catholic sense. Pius V says this expressly when he admits: ". . . nonnulae aliquo pacto sustineri possent" (DS 1980). That the Church herself has not always used the same terms in the same way to express the unchanging substance of Christian revelation is likewise conceded by Pius XII in *Humani Generis* (DS 3883). One could cite as another example the oath which candidates for ordination must take in most of the Lutheran Landeskirchen in Germany to uphold in their teaching the Scripture and the Lutheran Confessional Statements (RGG, 4, 1674). Quite clearly a candidate for the ministry who has accepted the principles of Bultmann's exegesis, when professing his belief in Jesus Christ and in his resurrection, will mean something radically different from that which a student of Edmund Schlink understands by the same creedal formulation. In fact, Barth, Buri, Schlink, Bultmann, K. Rahner and Cardinal Ruffini can all profess belief in the same *formula* "one, holy, catholic and apostolic Church," but what they mean by this formula varies considerably. The case of Rahner and Ruffini differs from that of the others just mentioned in that the Catholic Church does not see *their* difference of understanding of the formula as sufficient to destroy that unity in the profession of faith which binds them to one another and to the other Christians in full communion with the Catholic Church.

[45] Rahner, *Theol. Inv.,* V, pp. 53ff. A doctrinal formula may also be true, but not legitimate, insofar as the formulation invites misinterpretations. Such a regu-

and very complex question remains: How much diversity of dogmatic formulation is compatible with the full Christian unity willed by Christ? It is impossible for us, in this study, to pursue further this question which might well be called the most important single ecumenical question today.[46]

Although our investigation must continually seek to discover the intention and the concern behind Luther's doctrinal formulations about the unfree will,[47] the formulations themselves must be taken seriously, for it was because of them that Luther was condemned as a teacher of error by Leo X in the Bull *Exsurge Domine* (DS 1451-1492).[48]

lation of theological language would not, however, be irreformable, as R. Kösters points out, *op. cit.*, p. 77, footnote 62. Cardinal Ottaviani, the former Secretary of the Congregation of the Doctrine of the Faith, indicated very clearly his concept of the function of his Congregation as a regulator of theological language when he said: It is not necessary to hear the author of a censured book. For it is "not what he thought but what he wrote that we judge; the possible harm to souls is caused by that which has been printed, not from that which the author in question may have intended to say": *Katholische Nachrichten Agentur Konzilssonderdienst*, No. 89 (Dec. 4, 1963), p. 9. The first part of this sentence seems to be a confirmation of K. Rahner's view that "ecclesiastical statements of dogma also contain implicitly a determined terminology about which one cannot pose the question of truth but at the most the questions of aptness" (*Theol. Inv.* V, p. 55). Thus it is possible, says Rahner, to be "a person who really believes in Christ even where, judging merely from the objective meaning of an objectified statement, there seems only non-belief" (*Theol. Inv.* V, pp. 47f).—There is nothing especially modern about the distinction between verbal expression and actual intention. Aristotle seems to have used it when he says of Heraclitus: "What a man says is not necessarily the same as that which he thinks" (*Metaph.*, III, 1005b, 5f).— Although the Congregation of the Doctrine of Faith is not necessarily concerned with the thought and the intention of an author, the ecumenical theologian is. The ecumenist sees that there is a vast difference between an author who denies the Catholic faith in its substance as well as its formulation, and an author who truly believes in the Catholic faith, but whose expression of that faith is judged to be inadequate or misleading.

[46] In his opening speech at the Second Session of the Vatican Council Pope Paul VI referred to this problem when he spoke of the "possibiles varietates in unitate." Cf. *L'Osservatore Romano*, No. 226 (Sept. 30-Oct. 1, 1963), 2 and *Herder Korrespondenz*, XVIII (Nov., 1963), 81.

[47] L. Grane, in his fine recent study on Gabriel Biel and Luther's reaction against him, has criticized the work of J. Lortz and Ludger Meier on the grounds that neither author takes Luther's reformation intention seriously: *Contra Gabrielem: Luthers Auseinandersetzung mit Gabriel Biel in der Disputatio Contra Scholasticam Theologiam 1517* (Gyldendal, 1962), p. 28, footnote 57. Grane has not, however, considered Lortz's latest contribution to Luther research: "Luthers Römerbriefvorlesung. Grundanliegen," *Trierer Theologische Zeitschrift*, LXXI (1962), 129-153; 216-247. Concerning Grane's criticism, see O. Pesch, "Catholic Luther Research," Lutheran World, XIII (1966), 307f. Humbertclaude's careful and still valuable study, *Erasme et Luther: Leur polémique sur le libre arbitre* (Fribourg, 1909), is somewhat marred by its tendency to interpret Luther more according to the letter than the intention.

[48] Cf. the statement of Cardinal Ottaviani in footnote 45. Vorster does a great

To discover Luther's intention in *De servo arbitrio,* one must view this work in an historical perspective. A purely systematic statement of his doctrine, abstracted from the Reformation situation, is inadequate if we are to understand his book as a classic and all-important Reformation document and not simply as an interesting aspect of Luther's theology.[49]

This means first of all that an examination of Erasmus' *De libero arbitrio* and its background is in order.[50] Important for our ecumenical viewpoint are the questions: Did Erasmus present a true picture of the traditional Catholic understanding of free will? Did the Catholic theologians themselves, at the time of the Reformation, have a clear and unified understanding of free will, its relation to grace, etc.? [51]

Of all the characters of the Reformation period, Erasmus is second only to Luther in complexity. Abundant testimony to this effect can be found in the widely varying, often contradictory, judgments that later historians and theologians have made about him. It is our conviction that a correct understanding of Erasmus' position on free will—and therefore a correct understanding of the immediate front against which Luther was fighting—is impossible unless one reads his answer to Luther "in the much reviled but little read" [52] *Hyperaspistes diatribae*

---

service in searching out the common motives of Aquinas and Luther in their respective teaching on free will, but at times he passes over differences in expression that reflect differences in meaning.

[49] Heinrich Bornkamm has rightly objected to much of the research done on Luther's theology for its tendency to use "eine rein systematische und abstrakte Methode, die oft ohne jede Rücksicht auf Entwicklungsstufen und historische Situationen in Leben Luthers arbeitet": "Probleme der Lutherbiographie," in *Lutherforschung Heute:* Referate und Berichte des 1. Internationalen Lutherforschungskongresses, ed. V. Vajta (Berlin, 1958), p. 16. G. Ebeling, in his article "Luther: II. Theologie," RGG, 4, 496, likewise emphasizes the need for a historical approach to the presentation and interpretation of Luther's theology as opposed to a purely systematic approach.

[50] Neither M. Doerne, "Gottes Ehre am gebundenen Willen. Evangelische Grundlagen und theologische Spitzensätze in De servo arbitrio," *LuJ* (1938), 45-92, nor Vorster think it important to study DSA in relation to Erasmus' book and to the general situation of the Reformation controversy. Doerne's study suffers from this methodological defect more than Vorster's, since Vorster, as was noted in footnote 49, consistently seeks to find the motives behind Luther's sometimes exaggerated statements.

[51] This question has reference to Lortz's contention that "die theologische Unklarheit innerhalb der katholischen Theologie war eine der besonders wichtigen Voraussetzungen für die Entstehung einer kirchlichen Revolution. Sie ist einer der Schlüssel, die das Rätsel des gewaltigen Abfalls einigermassen lösen": Lortz I, p. 137; cf. pp. 138, 205-207 and "Reformation," *LThK,* 8, 1071-1072. This thesis has been attacked—in our judgment, unsuccessfully—in an important work by Heiko Oberman, *The Harvest of Medieval Theology,* (Cambridge, Mass., 1963), p. 186.

[52] Walter, p. XII.

adversus servum arbitrium M. Lutheri.[53] The fact that numerous authors have maintained that Erasmus says nothing new or nothing important in the *Hyperaspistes* indicates only that they have not taken the great amount of time required to read this often tedious, but sometimes very revealing, and almost "criminally neglected book of Erasmus." [54]

Any discussion of the problem of free—or unfree—will is rendered complex not only by the nature of the subject matter, but also by the terminological difficulties peculiar to this question. One need only consult the encyclopedic study of twenty-five centuries of man's reflections on the nature of freedom written by Mortimer Adler in conjunction with the Institute for Philosophical Research in San Francisco [55] to see the extraordinary variety of conceptions and definitions of freedom developed by philosophers and theologians of the West. The Reformation doctrine of the unfree will has heightened the terminological problem.

As is well known, Luther extolled the freedom of the Christian man in 1520, and yet he opposed Erasmus' defense of free will in 1525. To help clarify some of the terminological confusion and obscurity surrounding *De servo arbitrio*—and *De libero arbitrio*—and to bring into sharper focus precisely the "free will" which Luther rejected, we have decided to present the "status quaestionis," a statement of the development of the relevant issues and concepts that had formed the traditional Catholic pre-Reformation teaching on free will.

Starting with a general clarification of concepts and from an examination of the relevant biblical material, we shall proceed to sketch the development of the Catholic tradition of free will through Augustine up to the late Scholastic period in which Luther was formed. The transition from Luther's belief in free will to his affirmation of unfree will shall also be traced in his early writings.[56] Only then are we in a position to answer the question: Was the theological formation which Luther re-

---

53 Liber I (Basel, 1526); Liber II (Basel, 1527).

54 J. von Walter, "Die neueste Beurteilung des Erasmus," *Jahres-Bericht der Schlesischen Gesellschaft für vaterländische Cultur: Abteilung der Evangelischen Theologie*, 89 (1911/12), I, 5d., p. 16. The *Hyperaspistes* is longer than both DLA and DSA combined.

55 M. J. Adler, for the Institute for Philosophical Research, *The Idea of Freedom: A Dialectical Examination of the Conceptions of Freedom*, 2 vols. (Garden City, New York, 1958-1961).

56 By considering the genesis of Luther's teaching on the unfree will, one avoids the error of over-concentration that arises from isolating a single work of Luther's from its historical setting. One of the most commonly encountered misinterpretations of DSA resulting from such over-concentration is that described long ago by J. Lütkens, in his still valuable *Luthers Praedestinationslehre im Zusammenhang mit seiner Lehre vom freien Willen* (Dorpat, 1858). Lütkens criticizes those who assert that Luther's intense ardor in the controversy with Erasmus "ihn dazu

ceived concerning the role of free will in man's salvation in conformity
with the Catholic tradition? The answer to this question is all-important.
For we know that Luther rejected what he had learned about the free
will from such late Scholastic authors as Gabriel Biel. Was the teaching
about free will that Luther rejected the common teaching of the Catholic
Church, or was it a theological opinion of certain Catholic theologians
that had never been endorsed by the teaching authority of the Church? [57]

Finally, we shall analyze Luther's teaching in *De servo arbitrio* in
detail. This teaching will be compared to his views in his later works, as
well as to the teaching of the Lutheran confessional statements and to
the views of modern Protestant theologians. We shall see that Luther's
argument for the unfree will rests on two pillars, distinctly different in
structure. In fact, one can speak of two distinct concepts of unfree will
in *De servo arbitrio*.

One concept involves what E. Schlink calls the "structure of description," [58] in which the relationship between God's foreknowledge and

---

verleitet habe, äusserlich angewöhnte Sätze unüberlegt zu gebrauchen." If one is
aware of the development of Luther's doctrine of the unfree will, however, says
Lütkens, "so wird man von der Schrift de servo arbitrio durchaus nicht mehr in
der Weise überrascht, dass man zu so gefährlichen Erklärungs—und Entschuldi-
gungsversuchen Zuflucht nehmen könnte": p. 9.

On the other hand, by thoroughly studying one of Luther's central writings, such
as DSA, one avoids the opposite danger of over-extension that appears, for example, in some of the Swedish Luther research. Characteristic of this method is
the study of a particular problem or aspect of Luther's theology as it presents itself throughout Luther's entire corpus: 85 thick Weimar volumes or parts of volumes, not counting the WA *Bibel!* It seldom happens that such studies, especially
when made by young Luther researchers, are not guilty of important oversights.

Our method is an attempt to find a *via media* between the method described by
D. Löfgren, *Die Theologie der Schöpfung bei Luther* (Göttingen, 1960), p. 7
(over-extension), and that set forth by M. Doerne, p. 46-47 (over-concentration).
We agree with Brandenburg that: "Das einzelne Werk Luthers ist in seiner Ges-
amtgesalt zu erfassen . . . In sorgfältigen Einzelvergleichen müsste festgestellt
werden, wo das Neue bei Luther ist, was Theologen der Vorwelt und Umwelt, die
Luther benutzte, zum selben Thema gesagt haben." Cf. his "Hinweise zur Methodik . . . der Luthertheologie," p. 498.

[57] One will note that Heinrich Denifle, O.P., raised similar questions three generations ago in his unfortunately polemical work, *Luther und Luthertum in der
ersten Entwicklung* (Mainz, 1904). While we agree that Denifle's interpretation of
Luther requires much correction, it would be regrettable if one were to overlook
his permanent contributions to the investigation of Luther's relation to the theology
of late Scholasticism. Even Denifle's strongest critics must admit that the mere fact
that he has said something is no proof that the opposite is true. It suffices to
point out here that not only Denifle, but also such unpolemical authors as Lortz,
Küng, Bouyer, Moeller and Philips, (cf. C. Moeller and G. Philips, *The Theology
of Grace and the Ecumenical Movement*, trans. R. A. Wilson [London, 1961],
p. 21) accept the view that Luther was struggling against un-Catholic elements
in the Catholic Church.

[58] Schlink, *The Coming Christ. . . ,* pp. 174ff.

man's will is made an object of reflection, as so many philosophers and theologians before and after Luther have done. In this concept of unfree will Luther argues that God's infallible foreknowledge imposes an absolute necessity on all things. Even though it is possible to defend Luther against the charge of determinism and to show, by a painstaking exegesis, that his necessitarian argument for the unfree will need not be understood as a denial of man's natural free will, it is nonetheless never completely clear that Luther's emphasis on the necessity of all human actions does not rob faith of its character of personal, free decision.

Luther's necessitarian argument is based on speculative theological reasoning. Luther, very uncharacteristically, makes no effort to give biblical support for this argument. The necessitarian concept of unfree will has, moreover, never been accepted by the Church—before or after Luther—as a legitimate expression of the biblical doctrine of fallen man's bondage to sin and death. Most significantly, even though Luther's necessitarian concept of unfree will can be interpreted in a non-deterministic sense, and therefore in a sense compatible with Trent, the fact that Luther excludes man's free cooperation in saving faith makes his teaching on this point unacceptable not only to Trent, but also to the Lutheran confessional statements, as well as to the overwhelming majority of modern Protestant theologians, Lutherans included.

On the other hand, Luther's second main argument against the doctrine of free will taught by certain Catholic theologians of the fifteenth century involves a solidly biblical concept. It stands independently of the other basic argument, and has a different structure, that of personal encounter.[59] Further, this argument expresses well Luther's primary reformation concern, namely, to defend the biblical truth that the sinner can in no way break through the bonds of guilt and condemnation by any effort of his own.[60] This deeply biblical understanding of "servum arbitrium," we hope to show, is not only Johannine and Pauline, but also Augustinian, Thomistic, Lutheran and Tridentine. It is both Evangelical *and* Catholic.

---

[59] *Ibid.*, pp. 172ff.
[60] *Ibid.*, p. 175.

PART ONE

THE STATE
OF
THE QUESTION

1

Preliminary Clarification of Concepts

In ordinary language as well as in the language of philosophers and theologians, the word "freedom" and its adjective "free" are given a variety of meanings.[1] Quite clearly there are "senses of the word 'freedom' so diverse that it is obvious that they refer to things which are not the same."[2] In one sense a man is said to be free who is able to will or not will something, who can't decide for or against a course of action, or to choose between alternatives. This type of freedom has been called freedom of the will, free will, psychological freedom,[3] freedom of judgment,[4] freedom of choice,[5] and freedom of decision.[6] The Adler study

---

[1] The study by the Institute for Philosophical Research, directed by Adler, devotes the greater part of Book II (over 500 pages) to a clarification and classification of the various concepts of freedom. In a related study of Western philosophers, Vernon J. Burke, *Will in Western Thought: An Historic-Critical Survey,* (New York, 1964), finds no less than eight distinctive views on the nature of the will.

[2] Adler, p. 83.

[3] See E. Schott, "Willensfreiheit," RGG, 6, 1772. Schott calls freedom of the will "metaphysische Freiheit" when it is seen "auf dem Hintergrund eines Intentionalen Weltbildes."

[4] G. Siewerth, "Freiheit: I. Philosophisch," *LThK* 4, 325-328.

[5] K. Rahner, *Theological Investigations,* vol. II, (Baltimore-London, 1963), pp. 90 and 246; cf. *Schriften,* II, p. 259ff; also *Schriften* IV, pp. 215f. On the distinction between choice (Wahl) and decision (Entscheidung) see K. E. Løgstrup, "Wahl," RGG, 6, 1507 and W. Keller, *Psychologie und Philosophie des Wollens* (1954), p. 236. Cf. H. Küng, *Rechtfertigung: Die Lehre Karl Barths und eine katholische Besinnung* (Einsiedeln, 1957), pp. 181ff.; cf. trans. by T. Collins, E. Tolk and D. Granskou, *Justification* (New York-Toronto, 1964), pp. 181-185; O. Pesch, "Freiheitsbegriff. . . ," *Catholica,* XVII (1963), p. 201ff. Küng, trans., p. 183ff. favors substituting "the capacity to choose" (Wahlvermögen) for "freedom." He proposes to restrict "freedom" and *libertas* to that which the Bible calls freedom from sin and the freedom of the children of God. According to Küng, only when the *Wahlvermögen* is used in a *good* way should it be called "free."

[6] M. Schmaus, *Katholische Dogmatik,* II/1, 6th ed. (München, 1962), pp. 400f;

25

uses the word "natural" to designate this widely recognized type of free-dom.[7] It is natural because all men possess it, regardless of the circum-stances in which they live, regardless of whether they are good or bad men. In other words, "whoever is a man, and simply in virtue of being a man, is always and actually in possession of an ability to determine for himself what he wishes to do or become." [8]

A second type of freedom that has been distinguished by philosophers and theologians [9] is that which Adler calls "circumstantial freedom." This is a freedom that "consists in an individual's ability to realize his desires or to act as he wishes. . . ." [10]

Here the operative word is "to realize." It often happens that a man possessing the first freedom described, natural freedom, is unable to carry into action that which he wills because of such freedom-impeding circumstances as coercive force, fear through duress, disabling condi-

---

K. Rahner, *Schriften,* II. p. 259: "Entscheidungsfreiheit;" *Theol. Inv.,* II, p. 246. K. A. Meissinger, *Erasmus von Rotterdam,* 2nd ed. (Berlin, 1948), p. 289 suggests "freie Entscheidung" instead of free will as the best translation of *liberum arbitrium.* Adler, p. 400, says that "free judgment" is the literal English translation of *liberum arbitrium.* According to V. J. Bourke, pp. 67f., *liberum arbitrium* should be translated "free choice"; "free will," he maintains, would be *libera voluntas.* Literal translation is not too helpful here, for one could hold that "free choice" transates *"libera electio"* and "free judgment" corresponds to *"liberum judicium."* In keeping with widespread practice and for the sake of consistency we shall translates *"libera electio"* and "free judgment" corresponds to *"liberum judicium."* is unable to convey adequately the meaning of *liberum arbitrium.*

[7] In selecting terms to categorize the different ways in which men conceive of freedom, Adler seeks words that express what is common to the thinking of different authors, and yet which are, as far as possible, theologically and philo-sophically neutral. By this he means that a term "must succeed in catching some-thing common to the freedom being thought about by a group of authors without prejudicing what any of them thinks about it. It must unite them in spite of their diversity. . . ," p. 107. Cf. pp. 55f., 111, 400-403. On p. 403 he explains that "natural freedom" is preferable to "free will" or "free choice" because it is less ambiguous and because some authors affirm a natural freedom involving choice but refuse to speak of "free will." Others speak of free will, but mean the will's freedom from sin, injustice or domination by the passions. This is clearly not a natural freedom which all men possess.

[8] *Ibid.,* p. 154. Among the authors affirming this natural freedom Adler lists Luther, along with Aristotle, Cicero, Augustine, Anselm, Aquinas, Scotus, Suarez, Descartes, Kant, Hegel, W. James, Bergson, Dewey, Maritain, Tillich, et al., p. 148. Adler, pp. 219ff. points out the interesting fact that some philosophers such as Hobbes, Hume, M. Schlick and A. J. Ayer, hold that man can choose, but that his choices are necessitated. Man's choices are not exempt from necessity, but only from coercion or compulsion.

[9] Adler emphasizes the objective, impartial character of his study. He does not assert that the types of freedom he describes actually exist; he simply asserts that there are groups of authors who have upheld the existence of these different kinds of freedom: pp. 107f.

[10] *Ibid.,* pp. 110f.

tions or lack of true alternatives.[11] Conversely, there are favorable circumstances which "permit the individual to execute the movements that carry out or enact his wishes." [12] Thus the man in prison lacks circumstantial freedom, or what Hobbes calls "corporal liberty," [13] even though he retains his natural freedom of the will. Likewise the sick man and the poor man who are not able to travel abroad lack freedom in this second sense, but always possess their natural freedom. Some authors designate this kind of freedom as freedom of operation,[14] the operational area of freedom,[15] or even freedom of choice.[16] Adler maintains that such "freedoms" as "economic freedom," "political freedom," "civil liberty," "individual freedom," "the freedom of man in society," "freedom in relation to the state," and "external freedom" are all varieties of circumstantial freedom. Circumstantial freedom, he says, is the kind of freedom that authors have in mind when they speak of "freedom from coercion or restraint," "freedom from restrictions," "freedom of action," or "freedom under law." [17]

A third way in which freedom may be said to be possessed by men is called by Adler "acquired freedom," a freedom which is not natural to man, but "to which all men should aspire and to which only some men attain." [18] It is the freedom to live as one ought,[19] the freedom to do the morally good.[20] Unlike natural and circumstantial freedom, this

---

[11] For a further explanation and illustration of these four types of circumstances see Adler, pp. 113-133.

[12] *Ibid.*, p. 115.

[13] *Ibid.*, p. 117. Thomas Aquinas also uses "servitus corporalis" in this sense. (Cf. *In Ioann.*, 8, 34, n. 1204.)

[14] E. Schott, *op. cit.*, RGG, 6, 1722; G. Siewerth, *op. cit.*, LThK, 4, 326.

[15] K. Rahner, *Theol. Inv.*, II, p. 248ff.; *Schriften* II, p. 263ff.: "der Raum der Freiheit."

[16] Max Müller and Alois Halder, in *Herders Kleines Philosphisches Wörterbuch*, 3rd ed. (Freiburg, 1961), p. 57 designate freedom of action as freedom of choice (Wahl-freiheit), and call the simple freedom to choose (which we have named natural freedom) freedom of the will (Willensfreiheit).

[17] Adler, *op cit.*, p. 127. Authors who uphold the idea of circumstantial freedom, according to Adler, include Aristotle, Aquinas, Spinoza, Hobbes, Locke, Hume, Rousseau, Kant, Hegel, J. S. Mill, Freud, Russell, Schlick, Ayer, Dewey and Maritain. Cf. p. 110.

[18] *Ibid.*, p. 134. Anticipating a possible misunderstanding, Adler explains that *acquired freedom* does not necessarily mean a freedom attained by man's unaided efforts, nor does this term imply an active "getting" instead of a passive "receiving." He is keenly aware of the theological controversies on this point.

[19] *Ibid.*, pp. 143ff.; 167ff.

[20] E. Schott, *op. cit.*, RGG, 6, 1723 calls this freedom "ethische Freiheit" or "sittliche Freiheit." What Pesch, "Freiheitsbegriff. . . ," following Oeing-Hanhoff and H. Krings, calls "Wesensfreiheit" is a type of acquired freedom. Schmaus, II/1 pp. 401f. includes both circumstantial and acquired freedom under "Wesensfreiheit." Rahner, *Theol. Inv.*, II, pp. 93ff. calls it "the freedom of freedom" and

type of freedom can only be possessed by men who are "good," "right-eous," "virtuous," "holy," "sound," or "healthy." [21] This kind of free-dom can be enjoyed even by the prisoner and the slave, as the one-time slave Epictetus believed when he said that the virtuous man is the only truly free man, while the bad man is never free.[22] It is also the type of freedom intended by the biblical authors when they wrote of the truth which "shall make you free" (Jn. 8: 32) or of ". . . the freedom wherewith Christ has made us free" (Gal. 5: 1).[23]

Before considering the biblical concept of freedom in greater detail, it will perhaps be helpful to pause and to note what has and has not been accomplished by this preliminary clarification of the concepts of free-dom based on the massive study by Adler and his collaborators of the Institute for Philosophical Research.

1. The three types of freedom just described are the result of an objective impartial, comprehensive study (Adler calls this a dialectical study) of the ideas which more than one hundred leading Western thinkers have held about freedom.

2. These three dimensions of freedom represent a non-philosophical, non-historical classification in which no effort has been made to evaluate or to investigate philosophically or theologically the subject matter in-cluded under each of the three categories, for example, the role of will and intellect in natural freedom; and the relationship of God's fore-knowledge to free choice.

3. Each of the three categories of freedom is broad and is subject to almost as many nuances and qualifications as there are authors. Never-theless, the three neutrally formulated terms do identify three distinct types of freedom found in the voluminous literature on freedom, even if the authors concerned do not actually use these precise terms.

4. Besides the terms "natural," "circumstantial" and "acquired," "no fourth term, coordinate with these three, is needed to identify the ways in which authors conceived freedom as being possessed by man." [24]

5. Finally, "all three of these terms are needed to identify the distinct subjects which are treated in the literature on freedom. So far as the identification can be accomplished by reference to mode of possession,

---

identifies it with "the gift of salvation," p. 98. In *Schriften,* VI, pp. 235ff. he calls it "liberated freedom" (*befreite Freiheit*).

[21] Adler, p. 153.

[22] *Ibid.,* pp. 83ff.

[23] In Küng's Barth-oriented terminology (cf. footnote 5), the natural freedom of a sinner (*Wahlvermögen*) would not be called *liberum arbitrium,* but *servum arbitrium.* He shows, however, how his explanation is readily distinguished from similar propositions condemned by the Church. Cf. Küng, pp. 184f.

[24] Adler, *op. cit.,* p. 108.

no more than these three terms is needed, and no less than these three will suffice." [25]

This preliminary clarification of concepts is indispensable for our investigation of *De servo arbitrio*. We shall see that a lack of conceptual clarity and an inadequate definition of terms by both Erasmus and Luther caused such confusion in their debate that a true meeting of minds rarely took place. Ecumenical discussion in general, and our investigation in particular, can profit considerably by keeping in mind Adler's observation: "Much that is called 'controversy' is that in name only. . . . That controversy requires men to accept in commonly understood terms the very questions to which they give opposed answers is a truism often forgotten. The claim to disagreement must always be examined. When contestants are not answering the same question, no amount of discussion can lead to a common truth." [26]

---

[25] *Ibid.* Points (4) and (5) are categorical assertions; they are, however, ably supported by vast research and keen dialectical analysis.
[26] *Ibid.*

2

The Biblical Understanding of Freedom and Bondage

The Bible recognizes all three types of freedom that have just been described. However it limits the use of the words "freedom" and "free" to social or political freedom (circumstantial freedom) [1] and to the Christian freedom from law, sin, death and slavery to corruption that constitutes the "freedom of the sons of God" (acquired freedom).

1. *Natural freedom,* freedom of choice or free will is "presupposed on every page of the Scriptures," even though Scripture never dignifies it with the name "freedom." [2] Characteristic of biblical anthropology is the flesh-spirit structure (*bâśar-rûaḥ; sarx-pneuma*), which is quite distinct from the body-soul dualism of Plato, Plotinus, and Descartes and the hylomorphic anthropology of Aristotle and Thomas Aquinas.[3] And instead of an intellect-will psychology, we find in the Bible that the heart (*lēb-kardia*) is not only the central organ of the body and the seat of physical life, but also the source and seat of man's thoughts, understand-

---

[1] This is the only kind of freedom formally mentioned in the Old Testament. Cf. Peter Bläser, "Freiheit. II: Im Verständnis der Schrift," LThK, 4, 328; W. Rudolph, "Das Menschenbild des Alten Testamentes," in: *Dienst unter dem Wort. Festschrift H. Schreiner* (Gütersloh, 1953), pp. 241ff.: cited by Küng, *Justification,* pp. 181f. K. Niederwimmer, *Der Begriff der Freiheit im Neuen Testament* (Berlin, 1966) offers the most thorough recent study of the biblical theology of freedom, even though his brief reference to the attitude of Augustine and Luther on human freedom is unreliable. *Ibid.,* p. 86f.

[2] Küng, p. 182.—Freedom of decision ("Entscheidungsfreiheit") or formal freedom "wird vom NT überall vorausgesetzt, sie ist im jeden Satz impliziert, . . . dem NT selbstverstandlich". Cf. Niederwimmer, p. 89.

[3] C. Tresmontant, *A Study of Hebrew Thought* (New York, 1960), pp. 87-99; A. Hulsbosch, "Biblisches und scholastisches Denken," *Trierer theologische Zeitschrift,* 70 (1961), pp. 135ff.; O. Kuss, *Der Römerbrief,* vol. 2 (Regensburg, 1959), pp. 506-595; C. Spicq, *Dieu et l'homme selon le Nouveau Testament,* Lectio Divina, 29 (Paris, 1961), pp. 111ff.

ing, decisions and volition.[4] The will as a power or faculty of volition is as unknown to the biblical writers as it was to the vast majority of ancient Greek thinkers.[5]

Quite obviously, in the framework of such an anthropology, one cannot expect to find a doctrine of natural freedom expressed in terms of free will or *liberum arbitrium,* terminology that arose only in post-biblical times. The reality itself, however—natural freedom—is found in the scriptural view of man, even though explicit language is lacking. This is evident, first of all, from the fact that the same Hebrew and Greek words that the biblical authors used to describe God's free actions (even though these are, significantly never called "free"), are applied also to human choice and action.[6] Thus, the words for God's eminently free act of election [7] are predicated also of man's choices and decisions.

For example, in the case of *eudokeō,* this verb indicates God's choice of good pleasure,[8] as well as man's preference and choice.[9] The verb

---

[4] Tresmontant, pp. 119ff.; Spicq, pp. 26-33; F. Baumgärtel, "*kardia,* :A.: *leb,* in the OT," TDNT 3, 606f.; J. Behm, "*kardia:* D. *kardia* in the New Testament," *ibid.,* 611f.; F. H. von Meyenfeldt, *Het Hart (Leb, Lebab) In Het Oude Testament* (Leiden, 1950). One must not think of the heart as the exclusive source of thought, volition, etc.; cf. Spicq, p. 140. In the LXX the *pneuma* is sometimes made the seat of all spiritual functions. Cf. W. Bieder, "*pneuma:* C. Geist im Judentum," ThW 6, 368, 4f. There is no perfect anthropological synthesis in the Bible; cf. G. von Rad, *Old Testament Theology,* vol. 1 (New York, 1962), pp. 151f. and Spicq, pp. 141ff.

[5] In the New Testament *thelēma* means primarily that which is willed, the content of the willing. Only with Athanasius and Augustine, and above all during the Monothelitic controversy, do we encounter "will" as a power or source of willing. Cf. G. Schrenk, "*thelēma,*" TDNT 3, 62, and J. N. Sevenster, "Die Anthropologie des Neuen Testaments," in: Bleeker, *Anthropologie religieuse* (Leiden, 1955), pp. 166f. Schrenk exaggerates, however, when he says that in the Monothelitic controversy *thelēma always* meant the "organ" of the will. Against this view, see I. Solano, *Tractatus de Verbo Incarnato,* in: *Sacrae Theologiae Summa,* vol. III, 3rd ed. B.A.C. 62 (Madrid, 1956), p. 173, footnote 2. The ancient Greeks, including Plato and Aristotle, had little awareness of what the later Judaeo-Christian tradition called "will." Cf. F. Copleston, *A History of Philosophy,* 1/2 (New York, 1962), p. 81; Vernon J. Bourke, Foreword to: *Augustine, Philosopher of Freedom,* by M. T. Clark, (New York-Tournai, 1958) and Bourke, *Will in Western Thought,* pp. 29-33.

[6] M. Burrows, *An Outline of Biblical Theology* (Philadelphia, 1946), p. 231.

[7] See G. Schrenk, "*eudokeō,*" TDNT 2, 739f., who lists *thelein, hairetizein, eklegesthai, prosdechesthai,* and *eudokein* as terms for election. In the Old Testament *bahar* is the fixed dogmatic term for election. Cf. G. von Rad, *Theologie des Alten Testaments,* I, pp. 191f.; tr. I, p. 178, and G. Quell, "*eklegomai:* B. Die Erwählung im AT," ThW 4, 148-156. It is, however, by no means the only term used to signify election; cf. Peter Altmann, *Erwählungstheologie und Universalismus im Alten Testament* (Berlin, 1964).

[8] LXX: Ps. 49 (39), 14; Mt. 3: 17; 17: 5; Gal. 1: 15.

[9] LXX: Jgs. 17: 11; 20: 13; I Thess. 3: 1; Rom. 15: 26f.

haireomai [10] denotes not only man's preferential decision between two possibilities,[11] but also God's election of the Christian community.[12] Similarly *eklegomai* [13] is used to indicate not only the choosing of the good part by Mary and the choosing of the first places by the dinner guests, but also the choosing of the twelve by Jesus and the election of men by God.[14] In the Old Testament, when the Psalmist says he has chosen the precepts of the Lord, he employs the same verb *bahar* that is used to denote the election of Israel by Yahweh.[15] The inference to be drawn from this set of facts is obvious: If the Bible expresses human choice and election by the same words used to designate God's eminently free action of election, one has at least a philological argument that man himself acts freely, that he is able to will or not will, choose or not choose that which he in fact wills or chooses.

Possibly the most direct scriptural testimony to natural freedom is found in I Cor. 7: 37, which speaks of: *hos . . . mē echōn anagkēn, exousian de exei peri tou idiou thelēmatos.* Here necessity or constraint (*anagkēn*) is seen to be the direct opposite of "free will," as Nestle translates the phrase, *exousian . . . thelēmatos.*[16] These words seem to convey exactly the same meaning as the structurally similar word later used by the Greek Fathers of the Church to denote natural freedom or free will, *autexousion.*[17] The argument of G. Schrenk, that this passage *must* be translated: "to have control over one's own sexual drives," is not convincing.[18]

In the deuterocanonical literature Sir. 15: 14ff. is the *locus classicus* for natural freedom: the ability to choose freely between two alternatives.[19] Sirach probably refers to the role of choice in salvation. In Jer.

---

[10] Cf. H. Schlier, *"haireomai,"* TDNT 1, 180.
[11] Phil. 1: 22; Heb. 11: 25.
[12] II Thess. 2: 13, Heb. 11: 25 and similar texts cannot be used as examples of natural freedom without begging the important question as to fallen man's natural ability to choose good instead of sin. In any case, this text is evidence that *acquired* freedom—freedom to do good—involves decision or election by man. This point will be discussed more fully later.
[13] Cf. G. Quell, *"eklegomai,"* ThW 4, 147-173 and G. Schrenk, ThW 4, 173-181.
[14] Lk. 10: 42; 14: 7; Jn. 6: 70; Mk. 13: 20; Acts 13: 17, 15: 7; I Cor. 1: 27f.; Eph. 1: 4.
[15] Dt. 7: 6f., 10: 15, 14: 2; Ps. 119 (118), 173.
[16] E. Nestle, *Novum Testamentum Graece et Germanice,* 17th ed. (Stuttgart, 1960), p. 438.
[17] Cf. Justin, RJ 142; Gregory of Nyssa, RJ 1035; John Chrysostom, RJ 1219. The treatise of Methodius on free will bears the title: *Peri tou autexousiou:* PG 18, 239.
[18] G. Schrenk, *"thelēma,"* ThW 3, 60, 42ff.; cf. TDNT 3, 60.
[19] The Jerusalem Bible introduces vv. 11-20 with the title: "Man is free." It calls v. 14 "a classic text for the doctrine of the free will": p. 1055. Sir. 31:10b has also been cited by many exegetes as biblical testimony to free will. But

21: 8ff, however, it is perfectly clear that it is a case of natural freedom of choice between physical life or death.

Jewish and Christian exegetes have traditionally found indirect biblical evidence for the existence of natural freedom in (1) the numerous commands, threats, callings, prohibitions, invitations and exhortations as well as in (2) the constant biblical assumption that man is responsible for his actions and that sin is to be attributed to man, not God.

Concerning (1), if a man is commanded, exhorted, or invited to do something, the assumption is that he can at least will to do so; otherwise the command or invitation would be in vain. This does not discount the possibility that commands may be made simply to taunt someone and to show a person that he is, in some respect or other, powerless. This is always, however, an exceptional use of commands. Commands, invitations, etc. further presuppose that one can refuse to obey the command or to accept the invitation; otherwise the command or invitation would be unnecessary. Obedience or acceptance would be inevitable.

In the parable of the wedding feast, for example, the clear assumption is that all those who have been invited can accept the invitation or they can refuse it. Some in fact did refuse it, and the basis for the refusal is not ascribed to any intervention on the part of the king who issued the invitation, but simply to the will of those who refused: *kai ouk ēthelon elthein* (Mt. 22: 3).[20] One of the most remarkable texts, from the standpoint of our investigation, is Dt. 30: 19, where Moses, speaking in the name of the Lord, exhorts the Israelites to *choose* (again the verb is *bahar;* LXX: *eklexai*) life (and good) instead of death (and evil). Here we have much more than an exhortation presupposing free choice; choice itself is exhorted.

Practically all exegetes of past and present agree that the law, with its commands and prohibitions, naively presupposes the natural freedom of the will to obey or disobey.[21] Luther, however, as we shall see, rejected the argument that the existence of the law is a proof for the existence of

---

since this text is concerned primarily with freedom to do good, we shall recall what was said in footnote 12 and reserve this passage for treatment in our consideration of acquired freedom. Albert Gelin, *The Key Concepts of the Old Testament,* tr. by George Lamb (New York, 1963), p. 86, calls Sir. 15: 14ff. "a hymn to the freedom of [the] will."

[20] Some authors regard any kind of language or verbal address as an argument for natural freedom. Cf. E. Schott, "Willensfreiheit," RGG, 6, 1720f. R. Bultmann, *History and Eschatology* (New York, 1962), p. 152, states: "Preaching is address, and as address it demands answer, *decision.*"

[21] M. Burrows, p. 227, expresses the view of most exegetes when he writes: "In law, prophecy, the wisdom literature and the historical and poetical writings, the necessity of choice and man's responsibility for his choices are asserted or implied constantly." W. Eichrodt, *Theology of the Old Testament,* vol. II,

free will. Diametrically opposed to Luther's view of law is that of Pelagius, who so absolutized the natural freedom of the will presupposed by the law that he ignored or minimized the scriptural teaching on the necessity of God's assistance for all human actions. Without at this point entering into a discussion of these historical problems, it is sufficient to note here that the Bible nowhere seeks to solve the problem of the relationship between grace or God's action and man's free will.

In the Bible one simply finds the assumed fact of man's freedom to will or not will compliance with the law naively juxtaposed to the doctrine of man's helplessness without God. Scripture sometimes speaks as if man does all and sometimes as if God does all. The later theological concern for a systematic and speculative analysis of the relationship between the "two wills"—God's and man's—was not a concern of the biblical authors. For them a juxtaposition of the two was sufficient. Fuchs expresses the opinion of most exegetes when he says: "It is a mistake simply to transfer to the theology of the New Testament the problematic of the will which came to light in the history of freedom." [22] We can fully agree, therefore, with Gotthard Nygren, who writes: "Just as the formal problem of the freedom of the will very seldom becomes the object of a special discussion in the Bible, so also the question of the cooperation of grace and man's will hardly ever presents a perceptible problem. This does not mean, however, that the question concerning the understanding of this relationship is not a problem for *us*." [23]

What Nygren says above about grace and man's will is true also of the relation between God's foreknowledge, providence and predestination and the freedom of man's will. The Bible teaches that there is a divine foreknowledge,[24] providence [25] and predestination,[26] but does

---

p. 179: "The whole ethical exhortation of the prophets is based on the conviction that decision is placed in the hands of men. But the law, too, setting before Man the choice of life or death, rests on this presupposition." Cf. J. Schmid, "Notwendigkeit: II. Die heilsgeschichtliche Notwendigkeit in der Schrift," LThK, 7, 1056ff. See also Niederwimmer, pp. 90-102.

[22] E. Fuchs, "Freiheit I. Im NT," RGG, 2, 1103.

[23] G. Nygren, *Das Prädestinationsproblem in der Theologie Augustins* (Göttingen, 1956), p. 104. According to Nygren, the problem clearly emerges only in the apocryphal and rabbinic literature. He refers us on this point to the studies of W. Lütgert, "Das Problem der Willensfreiheit in der vorchristlichen Synagoge," *Beiträge zur Forderung christlicher Theologie*, 10 (1906) and R. Meyer, *Hellenistisches in der rabbinischen Anthropologie* (Stuttgart, 1937), pp. 69ff.

[24] Cf. R. Bultmann, *"proginōskō, prognōsis,"* TDNT, 1, 715f.

[25] Cf. R. Bultmann, *Primitive Christianity in its Contemporary Setting* (N.Y., 1959), pp. 25-34; J. Behm, *"pronoeō, pronoia,"* ThW 4, 1007-1011; W. Eichrodt, "Vorsehungsglaube und Theodizee im Alten Testament," in: *Festschrift Otto*

not attempt to explain how these truths can be reconciled with man's free will. Certainly the Bible nowhere invokes these truths to deny that man has free will or to teach that man acts out of necessity, that is, out of some determination not willed by man which makes it impossible for him to be, to will or to do other than he *actually* is, wills or does. This Aristotelian and Stoic understanding of *anagkaios* is never connected with the doctrine of predestination taught in the Bible.[27] Neither is the prophetic compulsion that motivated the prophets to be interpreted as a necessity which deprived the prophets of their free choice and power of decision.[28] Even in the "theologically thought-out concept of predestination" of Paul,[29] where the gift-character of faith is stressed, man's free decision is by no means excluded.[30] Still less does the fact of

Proksch (Leipzig, 1937), pp 45-70; Eduard Stakemeier, *Über Schicksal und Vorsehung* (Lucerne, 1949), pp. 156ff. The effort of later Christian theologians to relate God's providence and man's free will found expression in the doctrine of the *concursus divinus;* cf. E. Schott, *op. cit.,* RGG, 6, 1724.

[26] Cf. K. L. Schmidt, *"proorizō,"* ThW 5, 457, 11ff.; Burrows, p. 231; E. Dinkler, "Prädestinationslehre bei Paulus," in: *Festschrift für G. Dehn* (Neukirchen, 1957), pp. 81-102 and his article, "Prädestination im NT," RGG, 5, 481-483; H.-M. Dion, "La Prédestination chez saint Paul," *Rech. de Science Religieuse,* 53 (1965), 5-43. Commenting on Rom. 9:15-16, S. Lyonnet, *Les Épitres de Saint Paul aux Galates et aux Romains,* 2nd ed. (Paris, 1959), p. 108, note b) says: "Le texte cité ne parle que de la miséricorde divine; sans elle, volonté et efforts de l'homme sont vains; mais Paul ne dit pas que, la miséricorde une fois supposée, ces efforts soient inutiles; ailleurs il dit expressément qu'ils sont nécessaires" (v.g. ch. 6 et ch. 12 et s.). In view of our effort to show that the biblical doctrine of predestination does not exclude free will, it is almost amusing to find J. Köberle, saying: "A religion such as the Jewish, which so emphatically stresses freedom of the will, could not arrive at a genuine doctrine of predestination.": *Sünde und Gnade im religiösen Leben des Volkes Israel bis auf Christum* (München, 1905), p. 662, n. 1: (Trans. ours).

[27] Aristotle, *Metaphysics V,* 1015 a, 20ff., esp. lines 34f. in the Loeb Classical Library edition. Cf. Bultmann, *Primitive Christianity,* p. 27. Most exegetes will subscribe to the statement of W. Fairweather, "Development of Doctrine in the Apocryphal Period," *A Dictionary of the Bible,* ed. J. Hastings, 6th printing (Edinburgh, 1927). Extra volume, p. 293: "The Old Testament clearly affirms, on the one hand, the doctrine of Divine providence and foreordination and, on the other, the freedom of the human will." Fairweather, *ibid.,* believes that Sirach is actually fighting against a group of predestinarians who were denying free will in the name of predestination. Cf. Stakemeier, pp. 128-136; Schmid, LThK, 7, 1056ff.

[28] G. von Rad, *Old Testament Theology,* vol. II (New York, 1965), pp. 70-79. W. Grundmann's comments on the meaning of *anagkē* in I Cor. 9: 16 in his article *"anagkazō"* TDNT 1, 346f. require completion by von Rad's emphasis on the freedom that remains even under the "divine constraint."

[29] Dinkler, RGG, 5, 481.

[30] Burrows, p. 230 points out that, even though Paul teaches predestination, "he still insists on man's responsibility and often seems to assume freedom of choice." R. Bultmann is well known for the emphasis he places on free decision, both apart from faith ("relative freedom") and in the event of faith itself. Cf.

reprobation militate against natural freedom. It presupposes such freedom because, as Rom. 10: 16f. shows, reprobation is the result of man's own guilt inasmuch as he refuses to obey the Gospel.[31]

This last thought suggests further indirect biblical support for the existence of natural freedom: the fact of sin and man's responsibility for it.[32] How does one account for sin except by the free will of man? Surely the God who has revealed himself as holy, sinless and righteous cannot be the origin of, or bear the responsibility for man's unholiness, sin and unrighteousness.[33] To say that Satan is the source of sin is also

---

History and Eschatology, pp. 44ff. and 150ff.; *Glauben und Verstehen*, vol. II (Tübingen, 1958), p. 161; *Theology of the New Testament*, vol. I (New York, 1951), pp. 329f. See also Bläser, LThK, 4, 330 and the statement of Lyonnet cited in footnote 26.

[31] Dinkler, RGG, 5, 482.

[32] Sin is a polyvalent concept in the Bible, especially in the early books of the Old Testament. For the great variety of terms used to signify sin in the LXX and in the Hebrew Od Testament, see G. Quell, "*hamartanō* . . . A. Sin in the OT," TDNT 1, 267-271 and von Rad, *OT Theology*, vol. I, pp. 262-268. The concept of sin that is widely accepted today namely, an act or attitude of deliberate refusal to obey God's will, is much more precise and restrictive than the Old Testament concept, which includes faults that arise even through ignorance. The concept of legal sin and holiness is discarded in the New Testament. On the other hand, the Old Testament is aware of the distinction between merely legal or ritualistic—and at times involuntary—"sin" and "guilt," and ethical-religious or theological sin that is a willful rebellion against God, a hatred of God (Ex. 20: 5; Dt. 5: 9; Num. 15: 30). This difference, precisely with respect to the voluntary or involuntary character of sin, is expressed in the LXX by the terms *hekousios, hekōn* and *akousios, akōn* (Lev. 4: 2, 22, 27; Num. 15: 25; Ex. 21: 13, Job 36: 19. In the NT see Heb. 10: 26). Cf. E. Hauch, "*hekōn*. . . ," TDNT 2, 469f. On the distinction between legal and theological sin, see also G. Quell, TDNT 1, 271-280; P. Heinisch, *Theology of the OT*, pp. 254-258; A. Gelin, pp. 80-86; Th. C. Vriezen, "Sünde und Schuld: Im A. T.," RGG, 6, 478ff.; B. Vawter, "Missing the Mark," in: *The Way*, 2 (1962), pp. 19-27. The latter is summarized in "Scriptural Meaning of 'sin'," *Theology Digest*, 10 (1962), pp. 223-226. We are concerned here, of course, only with sin in its ethical-theological sense.

[33] See Ps. 71(70): 22; 77(76): 14; 78(77): 41; Is. 1: 4; 6: 3 on God's holiness; Ps. 5: 5; Jos. 1: 13; I Jn. 3: 9 on his sinlessness and Dt. 32: 4; Ps. 92(91): 15; Rom. 3: 5; 9: 14 on his righteousness. Eichrodt, vol. II, pp. 179f. shows that many of the Old Testament texts which seem to attribute sin or hardening of the heart to God are capable of being interpreted so that man's will is the real cause of the sin. Cf. Grundmann, "*agathos*," "TDNT 1, 13-16 and "*kakos*," TDNT 3, 476-480. God does, however, cause what certain later theologians will call physical evil, Job 2: 10; 12: 14-25; Is. 45: 7. The Vulgate translation of Osee 13: 9 has been used by many of the older exegetes to show that the reason for man's damnation lies in man's sinful will, not God's. Cf. Thomas Aquinas, *Super Epist. ad Romanos Lect.*, cap. IX, lect. 2, n. 763 (Taurini-Romae: Marietti, 1953), p. 139 and the *Solid Declaration of the Formula of Concord*, art. XI, nn. 7 and 62, in: *The Book of Concord: The Confessions of the Evangelical Lutheran Church*, tr. T. B. Tappert, 2nd printing (St. Louis, 1959), pp. 617 and 626. The corrected text, however, results in a complete change of mean-

an unsatisfactory answer, for how does one account for *his* sin and fall except by his free will? According to Mt. 23: 37 God's will as revealed in Jesus Christ is directly opposed by man's will. Here we have the very essence of sin: opposition to the will of God arising from man's will.

It is important to note that the biblical authors make no attempt to speculate or to reflect on this question of the origin of sin.[34] There can be, however, no doubt that the clear tendency of Scripture—in contrast to Babylonian, Zoroastrian or Marcionitic theodicy—is to attribute sin ultimately to man, not to God or to a dualistic evil principle.[35] Both Gen. 3 and Rom. 5 describe Adam's fall as being essentially an act of disobedience, that is, a freely willed rebellion or decision against God.[36] Did man lose this natural freedom as a result of Adam's fall? As we

---

ing. Cf. the Vulgate: "Perditio tua ex te, Israel, tantum in me auxilium tuum," and the translation of the Jerusalem Bible: "I mean to destroy you, Israel; who can come to your help?"

Secondly, as in the case of the respective workings of God's grace and man's will, the biblical authors are often content naively to juxtapose statements attributing the cause of evil to God, man and Satan. It remained for theologians of a much later era, equipped with sharper conceptual tools and animated by greater speculative interest, to distinguish the sinful action as being or action (the act viewed ontologically) and as sinful. If these later theologians were prepared to say that God is the cause of the act of sin, but not of the sin itself (see, for example, Thomas Aquinas, *S. Theol.* I-II, q. 79, a. 2), it is not at all surprising that the Old Testament "theologians" attribute the cause of sin to God *in some imprecise sense*. Cf. Schnackenburg, "Prädestination: I. Aussagen der Schrift," LThK 8, 661.

Thirdly, and most importantly, the entire context of the Bible excludes the possibility that God formally causes or wills sin: sin and Satan are invariably presented as God's enemies. God's gracious purpose and will to save is frustrated by sin. God hates sin and punishes sinners for their sins. None of these facts is compatible with a theory that would make God's will the cause of disobedience to his own will.

[34] Except, of course, for the harmartiology in Gen. 3-11. See G. von Rad, I, p. 154; K. Stendahl, "Sünde und Schuld IV. Im NT," RGG, 6, 484; A. Gelin, p. 86. According to Eichrodt, vol. II, p. 406, the two essential affirmations of the Old Testament concerning evil are that "evil does not come from God, and it is subject to God's power."

[35] See Th. C. Vriezen, RGG, 6, 481. Conscious and voluntary evil thoughts (*hoi dialogismoi hoi kakoi*) are said to arise from the heart of man: Mk. 7: 21ff.; Mt. 15: 19. In the O.T. cf. Ps. 28 (27): 3; Jer. 7: 24; 9: 13. Cf. W. Grundmann, *"kakos,"* TDNT 3, 479f. and the literature mentioned above in footnote 4.

[36] Grundmann, TDNT 1, 309: "Sin thus derived from the freedom of man." Bultmann stresses the fact that sin is disobedience and self-will. See, for example, *Primitive Christianity*, pp. 51ff. But if the obedience of faith involves a free decision, as Bultmann, *Glauben und Verstehen,* vol. 1, (Tübingen, 1958), p. 34; *Theology of the NT,* p. 329; and G. Kittel, *"hypakoē,"* TDNT 1, 224, note, the same must also be true of the *parakoē* of Adam's sin (Rom. 5: 19). Unbelief is also called disobedience in Jn. 3: 36 and Acts 14: 1. Cf. Bultmann, *"apeitheō,"* ThW 6, 10,12-11,19.

shall see shortly, Adam and his descendants did lose their freedom from sin and death as well as their freedom to do the good that is pleasing to God, as a result of the original disobedience. In our terminology, this is the loss of acquired freedom but not of natural freedom. The sins which men commit after Adam's fall never lose their decision-character.[37] Men are still responsible for their sins. And when we speak of decision and responsibility we are speaking about man's natural freedom of choice. Man's responsibility for sin, based on the control he has over his actions, is never questioned.[38] Except perhaps for the Qumran community which had deterministic inclinations, the Jews always recognized the natural freedom of the will.[39] Sin was not seen as something unavoidable.[40]

One must never forget this fact, even in the face of the strong biblical emphasis on fallen man's inclination to sin. To say that man has a tendency to sin is not the same as saying that he sins out of an irresistable or unavoidable necessity.[41] Not even the sin of Judas is regarded as

---

[37] It is the disobedience of the Kings, for example, the sinful, free human decision against Yahweh's revelation which the Deuteronomist sees as the reason for Israel's rejection. Von Rad says: ". . . it was in the kings' hearts [the German, I, p. 351 adds: 'and nowhere else'] that the decision whether Israel was to be saved or rejected had to be taken": I, 339. Eichrodt, vol. II, p. 410, writing on the late Jewish concept of sin, says: "Man of his own free decision turns to sin; each man in turn becomes his own Adam." Sir. 31: 10b is a classical example of the free, non-necessitated character of sin. In underscoring the free element in "actual" sin, we must not forget the teaching of both Old and New Testaments, that man does not simply commit sin but finds himself in a sinful condition from the very outset. Cf. Eichrodt, vol. II, pp. 406-413 and Kuss, *Der Römerbrief*, I (Regensburg, 1957), pp. 243f.

[38] Burrows, p. 227, says: "For most of the Bible the emphasis is on responsibility, which implies freedom of choice." Eichrodt, vol. II, pp. 382f. finds that sin in its moral-juristic sense always involves a "conscious and responsible act." He sees as essential to sin "the conflicting directions of two wills, the divine and the human."

[39] Bläser, LThK, 4, 329. C. H. Dodd, *The Epistle of Paul to the Romans,* 2nd impression (London-Glasgow, 1960), p. 170, maintains that the Hebrew mind tended to determinism. Against this view see Heinisch, *Theology of the OT* (Collegeville, 1955), p. 72, and Eichrodt, vol. II, p. 179. On p. 244 Eichrodt says: "Israel's history is from the very beginning controlled by the decisions of the tribal patriarchs. . . . This does not indeed do away with the importance of personal decision for the individual citizen. History is not fixed by a collective determinism, but leaves room for obedient or disobedient attitudes on the part of men to the divine decree." It is also significant that the Pharisees, despite their affirmation of divine providence against the Sadducees, always presupposed man's free will in their doctrine of providence. Cf. E. L. Dietrich, "Sadduzäer," RGG, 5, 1278; *idem,* "Pharisäer," RGG, 5, 327; K. Schubert, "Pharisäer," LThK, 8, 439; Burrows, p. 229.

[40] E. Lohse, "Sünde und Schuld: III. Im Judentum," RGG, 6, 482.

[41] Cf. A. M. Dubarle, *The Biblical Doctrine of Original Sin* (New York, 1964),

the result of an unavoidable pre-determination.[42] And although Satan is at work in Judas (Lk. 22: 3; Jn. 13: 2, 27), Satan cannot carry out his work unless Judas is willing.[43] The reason for this is that Satan is always subject to the power of God,[44] and that God permits no one to be tempted beyond his strength (I Cor. 10: 13).[45]

Do our previous exegetical findings that man's free decision is the ultimate origin of formal moral evil require correction in the light of the phenomenon, mentioned often in Scripture, of the hardening of man's heart by God? In an important monograph on this problem, F. Hesse [46] analyzes the texts concerning (1) hardening of Pharaoh described in the Pentateuch sources, together with Paul's use of Ex. 9: 16 in Rom. 9: 17-18; [47] (2) the hardening of Israel, both as a people and as individuals; [48] (3) the hardening of hearts by God in the prophetic literature.[49] In the case of Pharaoh, Hesse maintains that, since Yahweh was not Pharaoh's God, "one cannot speak of the hardening of Pharaoh as a

---

pp. 16-21; J. Gnilka, *Die Verstockung Israels* (München, 1961), p. 273. Cf. P. Schoonenberg, *Man and Sin* (Notre Dame, 1965), pp. 16-20.

[42] Schnackenburg, LThK, 8, 662.

[43] Jas. 4: 7; I Pet. 5: 9. Cf. W. Foerster, *"diabolos:* D. The NT View of Satan," TDNT 2, 79. Likewise in the OT and in late, pre-NT Judaism, Satan is never presented as having irresistible power over men. Cf. Heinisch, p. 144 and Foerster, *ibid.,* "C. The Later Jewish View of Satan," TDNT 2, 75-79. In Acts 5: 3f. we find a typical biblical attribution of the same action to two agents. Satan is said to have filled the heart of Ananias with temptations and yet Ananias is asked by Peter why he conceived the evil in his heart. The interrogative form of v. 3 also indicates that Ananias had some control over Satan's work in him.

[44] Foerster, TDNT, 2, 80 and *"exousia,"* TDNT 2, 567f.

[45] Cf. J. Jeremais, *"anthrōpinos,"* TDNT 1, 366f. and H. Seesemann, *"peira,"* TDNT 6, 28, 44f. Surprisingly, Schlier, in his monograph, *Principalities and Powers in the New Testament* (Freiburg-Edinburgh-London, 1961), does not treat these important problems of Satanology.

[46] *Das Verstockungsproblem im Alten Testament* (Berlin, 1955). Despite the overall excellence of this work, it is necessary to keep in mind the criticism of von Rad, II, pp. 151-155, namely, that Hesse regards the idea of the hardening of the heart as the result of an effort to solve an intellectual difficulty. Whoever tries to understand the biblical notion of hardening of the heart "as the way out from a theological dilemma," says von Rad, "has, from the point of view of hermeneutics, assumed a standpoint from outside the text itself" (p. 153). Without doubting that the hardening of the heart is a punishment for sin, von Rad rejects as too simple the view that it is exclusively such. The hardening of the heart must also be understood with reference to saving history. Is. 6: 9f.; 8: 17 and 30: 8ff. present the phenomenon of hardening not merely as punishment, "as the end, the final stage of a process which operates . . . according to fixed laws," but place it "emphatically at the beginning of a movement in the saving history" (pp. 154f.).

[47] Hesse, pp. 18-34.

[48] *Ibid.,* pp. 35ff.

[49] *Ibid.,* pp. 55-62.

sin in the deepest sense of the word." [50] Neither does Pharaoh's hardening refer to his eternal damnation, but to his welfare in this world.[51]

But Paul's view of Pharaoh's hardening is different, says Hesse. When Paul speaks of Pharaoh and of his anti-type, Moses, in Rom. 9: 17 "it is not a question of temporal demonstrations of grace and power, but of eternal acceptance or reprobation. In so equating hardening and reprobation, however, the Exodus text is over-interpreted." [52] Against Hesse's view, "that Pharaoh is for [Paul] the type of man who is destined to eternal corruption," [53] Lyonnet maintains that neither the Old Testament nor Paul teaches the damnation of Pharaoh, nor even that he is guilty of "formal" sin.[54] In both places, says Lyonnet, Pharaoh is seen as an instrument freely used by God for the realization of his plan of salvation.[55] The emphasis is on God's liberty in calling a certain people to salvation, not on the helplessness of individuals caught in some plan of predestination and destruction.

Concerning the hardening of *Israel* as a people and as individuals, however, it *is* a question of eternal damnation, contends Hesse. Here there is a willful hardening of the Israelites against the Yahweh revelation. For the prophets, the continuation of this voluntary hardening of the heart can lead to nothing else than reprobation. The same applies to such individuals as the sons of Heli whom Yahweh hardened (I Sam. 2: 25b). "That which cannot be said of Pharaoh, Sichem or the Chanaanites" says Hesse, "applies to them: the hardened are condemned." [56]

How do we explain this hardening of man's heart? First of all, it is essential to notice that Scripture ascribes the hardening of man's heart to

---

[50] *Ibid.*, p. 31.

[51] *Ibid.*, pp. 31ff.

[52] *Ibid.*, p. 33.

[53] *Ibid.*, p. 34. Hesse admits that this idea is present in Paul "nur dem Sinne nach," but that Luther in DSA asserts it explicitly.

[54] Lyonnet, p. 108, footnote c): "Mais il ne s'agit ni dans l'A.T. ni chez Paul de la damnation du Pharaon, ni même de son péché formel. Quelle que soit sa culpabilité personnell, connue de Dieu seul, son indocilité entre dans le plan divin ordonné par des voies mysterieuses au salut de tous (cf. 11, 32)." According to Dion, "La Prédestination chez Saint Paul," in: *Recherches de Science Religieuse,* 53 (1965), 6, modern exegetes are in almost complete agreement that Rom. 9 says nothing about damnation of individuals.

[55] Lyonnet seems thus to agree with von Rad's emphasis on the salvation-history significance of the hardening of the heart. See footnote 46 above. Schnackenburg, LThK, 8, 661 similarly holds that the hardening of the heart is concerned "nicht zuerst um persönliche Prädestination oder Reprobation, sondern um Entscheidungen für die Heilsgeschichte." That freedom of choice and moral responsibility are not eliminated by God's omnipotence, says Schnackenburg, is shown in such texts as: Dt. 11: 26ff.; 30: 15-20; Jos. 8: 34; 24: 15; Jer. 21: 8.

[56] Hesse, p. 37.

man as well as to God. Pharaoh is said to harden his own heart [57] and God is said to harden him.[58] What has been said previously about the attribution of evil to God [59] applies here also. The Israelites did not have such refined distinctions as direct and indirect, primary and instrumental causality. They did not consider an action insofar as it exists and insofar as it is sinful. Yet they were keenly aware of two things: that God is at work in all human events and actions, and that man is responsible for his actions, that he alone, not God, bears the guilt of sin. Thus the Israelite authors express God's omnipotence by saying that God hardens the hearts of men. Man's moral responsibility is recognized, on the other hand, when man is said to harden his own heart.

In his source analysis of the Pentateuch, Hesse finds that the Priestly tradition, in contrast to the Yahwist and Elohist traditions, saw the problem most sharply. The Priestly tradition knew that God's omnipotence could not be denied. Yet if it simply made Yahweh the cause of the hardening of the heart, "this could border on blasphemy." [60] "In the face of this predicament," says Hesse, "there was only one possibility: one had to place both ideas next to one another and simply endure the great tension they caused." Modern theology has not been able to improve upon this "solution," asserts Hesse.[61]

The prophetic tradition is equally unable to find any solution to the problem except that of juxtaposition. Even the prophets, who see Yahweh at work in the hardening of men, notes Hesse, take pains to assert the sinner's responsibility. Although they cannot give clear reasons for it, they simply assert that man remains responsible and will be called to give an account of his deeds. "The tension between God's causality and the freedom of man's will is insoluble." [62] Hesse's conclusion is identical with that reached by Eichrodt: "The basic postulate of ethical freedom is stated with the same force alongside of the religious conviction of the omnipotence of God, with no attempt being made to reach a harmonic synthesis of the two truths." [63]

This "solution"—it is really not a solution, but simply a statement of the biblical revelation concerning the mysterious relationship that exists

---

[57] Ex. 7: 13, 22; 8: 15, 28; 9: 7, 34; 13: 15; I Sam. 6: 6; cf. Ps. 95 (94): 8; Heb. 3: 7f., 15; 4: 7; Prov. 28: 14; Zach. 7: 11ff.

[58] Ex. 7: 3; 9: 12; 10: 20, 27; 11: 10; 14: 4, 8; cf. Dt. 2: 30; Is. 63: 17.

[59] Cf. footnote 33 above.

[60] Hesse, p. 47.

[61] *Ibid.*, p. 48.

[62] *Ibid.*, p. 72.

[63] Eichrodt, vol. II, p. 179. Cf. J. Gnilka and L. Scheffczyk, "Verstocktheit," LThK, 10, 740-743.

between God's action and man's—of the problem of the hardening of the heart by God is fully acceptable to Catholic theology. For it gives full recognition to both "poles"—every illustration here fails—of the unique relationship existing between the creator and the human creature made in the creator's likeness. It recognizes fully that God is omnipotent, that he is unceasingly at work in every created action and event, even in the act of creaturely freedom.[64] It also recognizes fully that man is free in that sense which we are calling natural freedom, and that man, not God, is alone guilty of sin.

Christian theologians have never had much difficulty in saying that man is not God and that man's being and God's being are radically distinct. But that man's *actions* are, in a distinct but mysterious way, not God's actions, has not been easy for some theologians to uphold.[65] This has been especially true when theologians have addressed themselves to the problem of sin. Whenever theologians have failed to affirm clearly the natural freedom of man's will, they have never been able adequately to explain why man, not God, is the only formal cause of sin. And if this is not made clear then the absolute holiness, sinlessness and righteousness of God proclaimed by the Bible are brought into question or at least are not affirmed with the clarity of the Bible. If, however, a theologian unhesitatingly and clearly affirms the righteousness, sinlessness and active omnipotence of God, but denies the natural freedom of man's will,[66] he cannot explain how man alone is responsible for sin. To say that man is not free and yet to say that he alone is responsible for sin is to make a demand on our reason—and our faith—which the Bible does not make.

Our treatment of the biblical difficulties that seem to militate against the natural freedom of the will may be summarized in the following general principle: the only kind of solution that does justice to all the biblical statements concerning the relationship between God and man in such events as predestination, sin, the hardening of the heart—and salvation itself—is one in which we let God be God—and man be man.

2. *Circumstantial freedom,* unlike natural freedom, is expressly designated by the name "freedom" in the Bible. Whenever the Bible mentions freedom, captivity and liberation in the sense of political or bodily freedom (or imprisonment), or of slavery as opposed to the social

---

[64] Eichrodt, vol. II, p. 178: God "is himself also at work within these acts of personal freedom."

[65] Later theologians point out, as we have already noted, that in one sense man's actions *are* God's actions, that is, insofar as they are being.

[66] This can be taken as a preliminary statement of one aspect of Luther's doctrine of the unfree will.

status of a freeman, then we are dealing with that which we have called circumstantial freedom or its absence.[67] The Bible shares this political and social concept of freedom with the contemporary Greek and Hellenistic world.[68] It requires no proof to see that a man's natural freedom of willing or not willing neither depends on nor results from his circumstantial freedom. Even when a man is in captivity or in the service of another as a slave,[69] that is, when he has lost his political or civil liberty, his natural freedom to will or not will remains.

Important as the question of circumstantial freedom is in itself especially today in such areas as political and civil liberties, freedom of religion and of the press—it has little relevance for the matter we are investigating. What the Scripture has to say about:

3. *Acquired freedom,* on the other hand, is of supreme importance for our study. For here we are concerned with the specifically biblical concept of freedom—Christian freedom. A man can have his natural freedom of the will; he may be politically free enjoying all the "freedoms" of a democratic society; he may even enjoy that acquired freedom of self-mastery over his own passions characteristic of the Hellenistic ethic,[70] but unless he "knows the truth" revealed by Jesus Christ (Jn. 8: 32), unless he is freed from sin by Jesus Christ (Jn. 8: 34, 36),

---

[67] Under the old covenant, slaves were freed after seven years: Ex. 21: 2; Dt. 15: 12; Jer. 34: 9, 14, 15, 17. Israel was freed from the bondage in Egypt by Yahweh: Ex 14; 20: 2; Dt. 5: 6. Isaiah proclaims liberty to the captive Israelites in Babylon: Is. 61: 1.

[68] Cf. G. Bornkamm, *Das urchristliche Verständnis von der Freiheit* (Heidelberg, 1961), pp. 7-10; H. Schilier, "*eleutheros:* A. and B.," TDNT 2, 487-496; *idem,* "The Law of Perfect Freedom," in: *Man Before God* (New York, 1966), pp. 52ff.; H. Rengstorf, "*doulos. . . .*" TDNT 2. 261-265; 270-273.

[69] A slave can be forced into slavery against his will or, in certain circumstances—when he has a benevolent master, for example—he freely wills to serve his master. In any case, he experiences a limitation of his independence. Cf. Rengstorf, *ibid.,* 266.

[70] We do not pretend here to offer a full statement on Christian freedom. Our main interest is to show that this freedom does not exclude natural freedom and that the absence of this freedom, slavery to sin, death and the law, likewise does not mean that man no longer has natural freedom. Since it is man's bondage to sin that is Luther's chief concern in DSA, we shall limit our attention to the relation between natural freedom and fallen man's slavery to sin. For the difference between the Stoic and the specifically Christian concept of freedom from sin, law and death, cf. H. Jonas, *Augustin und das paulinische Freiheitsproblem* (Göttingen, 1930), pp. 8-15; R. Bultmann, *Primitive Christianity in its Contemporary Setting,* pp. 185ff.; H. Schlier, TDNT 2, 493-502 and "The Law of Perfect Freedom," pp. 54-67; G. Bornkamm, "Die christliche Freiheit," in: *Das Ende des Gesetzes,* 3rd ed. (Munich, 1961), pp. 136f. and *Das urchristliche Verständnis von der Freiheit,* pp. 10-13. For an excellent statement of the meaning of Christian liberty, especially in respect to freedom from the law, see: S. Lyonnet, "Saint Paul: Liberty and Law," in: *The Bridge, A Year-*

then he does not have the "freedom of the children of God" (Rom. 8: 21) and he is still bound to "the law of sin and death" (Rom. 8: 2). On the other hand, even one who is a slave, in a condition of servitude to a human master (one who lacks circumstantial freedom) can be a freedman in Christ: "For a slave who has been called in the Lord, is a freedman of the Lord; just as a freeman who has been called is a slave of Christ" (I Cor. 7: 22).[71]

One of the most important differences between Christian freedom and the acquired freedom of the Greek philosophers is that Christian freedom is "acquired" by receiving it as a gift from God through Jesus Christ. It is a being-freed, a liberation.[72] The freedom of the Stoic ethicians, on the other hand, is acquired by active efforts to achieve full dominion over oneself.[73]

Christian freedom is found in those who live according to the law of the Spirit (Rom. 8: 2; II Cor. 3: 17). But the gift of the freedom-inspiring Spirit comes to the believer in baptism.[74] Thus it is through faith and baptism that we die to sin and are thereby freed from sin (Rom. 6: 2.6).[75]

Having fully recognized the essential gift-character of the acquired freedom which we find in the New Testament, the important questions arise: Is the unjustified man, the man who is a slave to sin, completely passive in receiving the gift of Christian freedom? Is a decision of his free will required for the acquisition of Christian freedom or is his will so enslaved as a result of Adam's fall and his own sins that he makes no free decision at all in his liberation from sin by Christ? Since, as we have

---

book of *Judaeo-Christian Studies*, vol. 4 (New York, 1961), pp. 229-251. A summary of the article can be found in *Theology Digest*, XI (1963), 12-18.

[71] On the basis of this text and Rom. 6: 16-22, Christian liberty can paradoxically be called Christian servitude. Aquinas, *Ad Rom.* 6: 22, n. 513 says: "Haec autem vera est libertas, et optima servitus." Paul indicates in Rom. 6: 19a, however, that this possibly shocking metaphor is not meant to be taken literally; cf. Kuss, *Römerbrief*, II, pp. 386 and 390. Nevertheless the frequent New Testament use of the concepts *doulos Christou (theou, kuriou)*: (Rom 1: 1; Phil. 1: 1; Tit. 1: 1; Gal. 1: 10; Eph. 6: 6; II Tim. 2: 24; Jas. 1: 1; I Pet. 2: 16) and the milder *diakonos Christou* (Jn. 12: 26; II Cor. 11: 23; Col. 1: 7; I Thess. 3: 2) shows how conscious the early Christians were that they *belonged* to Christ and to God and that they were "purchased" by Jesus Christ (Gal. 3: 13; 4: 5; I Cor. 6: 20, 7: 23). Cf. Kuss, *ibid.*, I, p. 3; Rengstorf, TDNT 2, 273-277; F. Büchsel, *"agorazō,"* TDNT 1, 125f.; H. Beyer, *"diakonas,"* TDNT 2, 88f.

[72] Rom. 6: 18, 22; Gal. 5: 1 (4: 31). Cf. G. Bornkamm, *Das urchristliche Verständnis von der Freiheit,* p. 11 and "Die christliche Freiheit," p. 137.

[73] *Ibid.* Cf. Schlier, "The Law of Perfect Freedom," p. 65.

[74] Schlier, *ibid.*, p. 61f.; Bultmann, *Theology of the N.T.* I, pp. 138f. and 333.

[75] Cf. Kuss, *Römerbrief* I, p. 248.

seen, the liberation from sin takes place through faith in Christ, and through baptism into Christ, the basic question really is: Does the faith in Christ which frees us from sin involve a free decision on the part of man? To this we must answer with all Catholic theologians and with the great majority of Protestant exegetes in the affirmative.

In one of his excursuses to Rom. 3: 24, "Der Glaube," [76] O. Kuss clearly affirms the character of free decision of the faith that sets us free: "The man who examines the gospel of faith must make a decision: for he can really say either yes or no. Faith is therefore—from man's standpoint—a *decision* for an acceptance of the Gospel which will affect his whole life; it is essentially *obedience,* just as unbelief is essentially disobedience. . . . [Faith involves] a real decision by man and to this extent faith is ultimately also an 'achievement,' even though it is, of course, not a 'work' in the sense in which Paul speaks of 'works' of the law. . . . Man is justified by pure grace (Rom. 3: 24). But even the conviction that—from God's standpoint—the entire event of salvation is in all of its phases God's work (Rom. 8: 28ff.) cannot prevent the Apostle from ascribing a role to the free decision of man's will in his belief or unbelief. In the last analysis it is this alone which enables us to explain Paul's missionary activity." [77]

The same view of faith as God's gift and man's decision is held by Bultmann: "Faith can . . . be said to 'come' and 'to be revealed' (Gal. 3: 23, 25). This, of course, does not take from the concrete 'faith' of the individual that decision-character which belongs to its very nature as 'obedience'. . . . Since the believer experiences the possibility of the faith—decision as grace, it is only as a gift of grace that he can understand his decision—his own decision! . . . [A] faith brought about by God outside of man's decision would obviously not be genuine obedience. Faith is God-wrought to the extent that prevenient grace first made the human decision possible, with the result that he who has made the decision can only understand it as God's gift; but that does not take its decision-character away from it." [78]

---

76 *Ibid.,* pp. 131-154.

77 *Ibid.,* p. 138; (Trans. ours).

78 *Theology of the NT,* I, pp. 329f. The last sentence is an unusually concise and accurate expression of the biblical theology of the relation between grace and free will in the act of faith. This statement accords fully with the doctrine of the Catholic Church. For other statements of Bultmann on the free character of faith see G. Hasenhüttel, *Der Glaubensvollzug* (Essen, 1963), pp. 156-164. The Johannine concept of faith also involves free decision: Cf. Bultmann, "*pisteuō,*" ThW 6, 227, 34ff.; *Theology of the NT,* II, p. 21ff.; H. Braun, "Glaube III. Im NT," RGG, 2, 1596. According to a list compiled by H. Schütte, *Um die Wiedervereinigung im Glauben,* 3rd ed. (Essen, 1960), pp. 80ff., other

It is noteworthy that both Kuss and Bultmann see obedience as the basis of the moment of free decision in the act of faith. According to Kuss, Paul understands faith as "essentially" obedience;[79] according to Bultmann it is "primarily" obedience.[80] The slavery spoken of in Rom. 6: 16ff. is actually defined in terms of obedience: we are slaves or servants [81] of whomever we obey, slaves either of sin or of justice. But obedience: (*hypakoē*) as used in the New Testament is a free act,[82] an act of religious decision.[83] In fact, obedience is the word used to describe the eminently free, saving work of Jesus himself (Rom. 5:19; Heb. 5: 8, etc.). Further, when Paul uses the expression "yield" or "offer" yourselves (*paristanein*) in Rom. 6: 13. 16. 19, it is even more evident that "an element of will and decision" is involved.[84] As Kuss comments on Rom. 6: 16: "The Apostle is clearly convinced that man is capable of surrendering himself to either one of these powers, i.e., to the power of sin or to God." [85]

Besides these Pauline texts there are, as was noted above, other texts indicating that man's salutary acts—whether they be the initial act of liberating faith [86] or the acts of loving service to God and neighbor,[87]

Protestant exegetes who hold that faith involves a free decision by man include: K. L. Schmidt, E. Stauffer, Fr. Büchsel, H. D. Wendland, G. Kittel and H. Strathmann. This list could be lengthened considerably. Cf. Eichrodt, vol. II, pp. 469ff.

[79] Kuss, *Römerbrief* II, p. 138.

[80] Bultmann, *Theology of the NT* I, pp. 314f.

[81] Dodd, *The Epistle of Paul to the Romans*, p. 116 notes that "slave" is a more proper translation of *doulos* than "servant." Paul deliberately used "this human analogy, to bring the truth home to your weak nature" (Dodd's translation of Rom. 6: 19; pp. 115 and 117). The milder idea of "servant" is conveyed by *diakonos*.

[82] Bultmann, I, p. 316. It is interesting that Dodd, who defines the Pauline view of faith in almost completely passive terms—"the negation of all activity," "the moment of passivity"—overlooks the role of obedience, and therefore of free decision, in the response of faith; cf. Dodd, *The Epistle of Paul to the Romans*, p. 43.

[83] G. Kittel, *"hypakoē,"* TDNT 1, 224f.

[84] Kuss, *Römerbrief* II, p. 392.

[85] *Ibid.*, p. 386.

[86] Jos. 24: 15. 22. 24; Heb. 11: 24ff. Concerning the Josue texts, Schrenk, *"eklegomai,"* ThW 4, 153, 24-27, grants that: "Es scheint, dass man schärfer kaum sagen kann, als hier durch Anwendung des Begriffs der Wahl geschieht, dass Israels Bekenntnis zu seinem Bundesgott . . . ein verstandesmässig, wohl begründeter Willensakt war." But Schrenk is suspicious of this "fast ganz isolierte Aussage über eine Wahl Jahwes durch das Volk" (p. 154, 2), and therefore examines it carefully. Referring to M. Noth's literary analysis of Jos. 24, "Das System der zwölf Stämme Israels," (1930), pp. 133ff., which recommends the elimination of v. 22, Schrenk suggests that v. 22 is meant sarcastically (p. 154, 5-28). In any case, he says, the idea of "choosing" Yahweh is so rare "dass sich diese starke Formulierung im Kanon nur ganz unbedeutend oder gar nicht ausgewirkt hat" (p. 155, 18-21). To this we wish only to observe that,

which characterize the life of the free Christian man—involve free decision or choice on the part of man. It is important to recognize that the free decision that is involved in these salutary acts is no longer simply "natural freedom" of the will. Man—or man's will—truly makes a free decision, but this is not a "natural" decision, since it is not possible for men to make such a decision of faith simply in view of the fact that they are men. This free decision is itself a free gift of God. It is grace, not nature. Nevertheless, there is something which the graced decision of faith has in common with natural freedom: both involve a free decision by man.

The important questions now arise: What does the Bible mean when it speaks of slavery to sin? Does it mean that man no longer has free will, *liberum arbitrium,* or what we have called "natural freedom"? Does it mean that every action he performs is sinful, that he can do no good whatever?

First of all one might say that man's slavery to sin is also an obedience (Rom. 6: 16), and therefore on the basis of what has already been said, man willingly and freely "yields" himself to sin and the consequent slavery to sin. The question is not so simply answered, however, since man is also said to be constituted a sinner through the disobedience of Adam. He simply discovers that he is already a sinner.[88] To express this reality, Paul personifies sin and speaks of it as an active power which dominates, enslaves,[89] dwells in and imprisons (Rom. 7: 23) the sinner.[90] In short, man lives in the "power of darkness" (Col. 1: 13) and the "power of Satan" (Acts 26: 18; II Tim 2: 26). Being born into slavery and imprisonment to sin, man *cannot* alter his condition unless he is "bought with a price" (I Cor. 6: 20; 7: 23) or freed from this slavery by a liberator, a Redeemer, whose own life is the price of redemption.[91]

Here we have the essence of the biblical doctrine of human bondage to sin. Man is bound and enslaved to sin and he cannot free himself

---

although this "starke Formulierung" is "eine fast ganz isolierte Aussage," it nevertheless is in full harmony with both the intention and the formulation of the other biblical statements we have presented which indicate the element of free decision in man's religious activity. The formulation might be isolated, but the meaning is not.

[87] Ps: 118; 173 (LXX); Sir. 31: 10b; Phil. 1. 22ff. Schrenk, ThW 4, 174, 61ff. See footnotes 12 and 19 above.

[88] See Kuss, *Römerbrief* I, pp. 238ff.; 243f.; 272ff.; Dubarle, pp. 142-200.

[89] Kuss, p. 244.

[90] Just as Paul applies the metaphor of slavery both to sin and justice, so he uses the "prisoner" image not only to signify captivity to sin, but also to Christ: Rom. 7: 6, 23; II Cor. 10: 5; Eph. 4: 8. Cf. Kittel, *"aichmalōtos,"* TDNT 1, 196; *"desmos,"* TDNT 2, 43.

[91] Mt. 20: 28; Jn. 8: 36; Gal. 5: 1 (4: 31); Tit. 2: 14; I Pet. 1: 18f.

from this slavery. He is *not free* to leave this prison or to set aside his condition as a slave. This liberation takes place through faith in Jesus Christ and in no other way.

For our purpose, the important thing to note is that man's slavery to sin is analogous to the type of "unfreedom" we have considered under the heading: circumstantial freedom. It is an inability to act in a certain way—to act as one ought. This is a lack of acquired freedom. It is *not* a loss or lack of the first type of freedom we have considered, natural freedom. The biblical doctrine of bondage to sin has nothing to do with a doctrine of an "unfree will" if we take "unfree will" to mean that man no longer is able to choose or make a free decision, or that whatever he does is done by absolute necessity, and that he never has the possibility of doing other than what he actually does. If, however, we understand by "unfree will" man's total helplessness to break free by his own efforts from the slavery to sin in which he finds himself, then man indeed, in this sense, has an "unfree will."

In either case, however, the term "unfree or enslaved will" is not a biblical term. Scripture is not interested in describing man's *will* as unfree or enslaved. It teaches simply but unmistakably that sinful *man* is a slave to his sin: he cannot escape from it and he even yields himself up to it obediently. The scriptural doctrine is the bondage of man, not the bondage of the will.[92] Just as one does not say of a man in prison who has thereby lost his circumstantial freedom that he no longer has free will (this would be to confuse the natural freedom and the circumstantial freedom which we have taken pains to distinguish), so also would it be misleading and confusing to say of a man who is a slave to sin and

---

[92] C. Lindhagen, *The Servant Motif in the O.T.* (Uppsala, 1950), in a minute and lengthy biblical-philological analysis of the concept "ebed," never finds this concept identified with unfree or enslaved *will*. The nearest the Scripture comes to speaking about the bondage of man's *will* is in the highly controverted passage, Rom. 7: 15-21, where, according to most modern exegetes, it is a question of the *homo sub lege* before Christ and apart from Christ. (See below footnote 109). Even here it is not a question of the *will* being unfree, but of the incapacity to do the genuine good that one wills. Scripture knows of an unfree man, but not an unfree will. More precisely, it is a question here not so much of incapacity, but of a *de facto* non-execution of the good willed. Cf. Kuss, II, p. 454. Concerning the man described in Rom. 7: 15, Thomas Aquinas writes: ". . . qui facit quod non vult non habet liberam actionem, sed potest habere liberam voluntatem": *De Malo,* q. 6, a. un., ad 22. When Eichrodt, vol. II, pp. 389-392 attributes to the prophets a doctrine of *servum arbitrium* which leaves man with no free will, he is not denying that man, according to the OT, has an innate power of free decision. He has elsewhere clearly recognized that such a power of free decision is essential to Old Testament anthropology. Cf. above nn. 21, 33, 37, 39. As Eichrodt, vol II, pp. 468ff. points out, the prophets held that man lacks freedom to convert or redeem himself. Man's "free and conscious yes" is nevertheless essential to conversion.

who has not yet been freed by Jesus Christ, that he does not have free will or that he has an enslaved will.[93] The desire to avoid this confusion has undoubtedly been one of the main reasons why the Church, as we shall see, has never seen fit to describe man's helpless condition as a slave to sin and to the power of Satan as one involving an unfree or an enslaved *will*.

Finally, what does Scripture say about the actions of men while they are enslaved to sin? Can man do anything good while he is in the power of Satan? Does he sin necessarily in all his actions? These questions, of great importance in the history of Christian theology, have a particular relevance for the aspect of Luther's theology which we are investigating. They are ambiguous questions. One cannot answer them with a simple affirmative or negative. One must make distinctions.

As we have already seen, Scripture describes not only man's sinful actions, but also his sinful condition or sinful state of existence.[94] The man not yet liberated by the saving power of Christ's death, which becomes our death to sin in baptism,[95] is not simply a man who commits sins. He is a man who lives in the sphere of sin,[96] in the domain of Satan.[97] He is a dead man because of his sins [98] and is only resurrected from this death and brought back to life by a gracious and loving God (Eph. 2: 4f.). Here we have an example of the kind of distinction that must be made to answer the questions we have just posed. A man enjoying physical, biological life is said to be dead because of his sins. The death of sin is the most real and most destructive kind of death, for it is eternal death, death in the full sense of the word.[99] No matter how much a sinner may exercise his physical life he is still not alive in the full sense. He does not "live to God" (Gal. 2: 19). But if he is baptized, then he dies to sin and rises with Christ to a life hidden with Christ in God.[100] This is life in the full sense of the word, for it is eternal life.

---

[93] Bultmann contributes to such confusion when he speaks of the *will* being in bondage to evil: *Primitive Christianity*, p. 181. This terminology is dependent on Bultmann's exegesis of Rom. 7: 15-18 (cf. *Theology of the NT*, pp. 223f.), which is rightly criticized by Kuss, II, pp. 468ff. Similarly, K. Barth, *Church Dogmatics*, tr. G. W. Bromiley, IV/2 (Edinburgh, 1958), p. 485, says that Jn. 8: 34 contains "the whole doctrine of the bondage of the will." The German reads: "die Lehre vom unfreien Willen." Despite their use of these misleading formulations, neither Bultmann nor Barth deny that man retains his power of free decision.

[94] Grundmann, TDNT 1, 309.

[95] Kuss, I, p. 248.

[96] *Ibid.*

[97] Foerster, TDNT 2, 261.

[98] Rom. 6: 16; Eph. 2: 1, 5; Col. 2: 13; cf. Rom. 11: 15.

[99] Kuss, I, p. 251.

[100] Rom. 6: 2-7; Col. 3: 1-3; Gal. 2: 19. Cf. Kuss, I, pp. 254f.

Does the Bible offer any similar distinctions that will help us answer the question: Can a man do anything good as long as he is still dead in his sins? In the face of abundant and constant biblical teaching from Old and New Testaments that fallen man before his liberation through faith is totally sinful and unjust,[101] it would seem to be a contradiction to say that he is capable of doing anything good. The contradiction is only apparent. It is resolved as soon as one applies the distinction made by Paul, the first Christian theologian,[102] between the justice of God (of faith) and the justice of men (of works of the law).[103]

On the basis of this Pauline distinction we can say that a man who is a slave to sin can do something which is *in a certain sense* good and righteous. As far as the justice of the law is concerned, a Jew could lead an irreproachable life.[104] There are even some heathens who fulfill the main precepts of the Mosaic law.[105] Nevertheless this "relative," personally acquired justice is not true justice which alone pleases God.[106] The only true justice is the justice of God, that justice which God graciously gives man through faith. The justice and goodness that are one's own, which come through keeping the precepts of the Mosaic law or of the law written in the heart, cannot be justice or goodness in the full sense. In fact, in comparison with the justice "which is from faith in Christ, the justice from God based on faith," all of this human, legal

---

[101] Gen. 6: 5; 8: 21 (cf. Kuss, I, p. 243 for other OT texts); Mt. 7: 17f.; (Lk. 6: 43); Rom. 1: 18; 2: 8; 3: 5, 7, 9-12; 5: 8, 19; 7: 14, 18; I Cor. 6: 1, 9; Eph. 2: 3. It would be incorrect, however, to understand Rom. 14: 25 in this sense, as Luther did. Calvin did not follow Luther here. His interpretation is much closer to that of Thomas Aquinas. Cf. Lyonnet, *Les Épîtres de Saint Paul*, pp. 126, footnote e) and 129, footnote e) and Dodd, p. 222, says that Rom. 14: 23 "has been disastrously misunderstood. It was once taken to mean that unless a man held the Christian creed, he was incapable of doing right in the sight of God; the virtues of the heathen were nothing but 'brilliant vices.' This monstrous doctrine (which is in clear contradiction to ii. 14-15) is quite foreign to this passage." Dodd, like Aquinas, Calvin and many others, takes it to mean: all that is against one's conscience is sin.

[102] Schrenk, "*dikaiosynē*," TDNT 2, 202, notes that Paul's "whole theology is rooted in this radical clarification of the question of the law." According to the comment of the Jerusalem Bible to Phil. 3: 9, the differences between the two types of justice "form the entire subject of Paul's letters to the Christians of Galatia and Rome."

[103] Cf. Rom. 3: 22; 10: 3-6; Phil. 3: 6, 9; Tit. 3: 5.

[104] Phil. 3: 6; Tit. 3: 5. Cf. Schrenk, TDNT 2, 189f. Thomas Aquinas, *Ad Philip.*, 3, 6, n. 112 calls this exterior—as opposed to interior—justice and notes that Paul says "sine querela" and not "sine peccato." Thus Paul does not contradict what he said in Eph. 2: 3; "quia veram iustitiam fidei, quae fecit hominem purem, tunc non habuit, sed solum legis." Cf. P. Bläser, "Gesetzesgerechtigkeit," LThK, 4, 829.

[105] Rom. 2: 14, 15. Cf. Kuss, I, p. 75 and Dodd, *Romans*, p. 62.

[106] Rom. 8: 8; Heb. 11: 6. Cf. Schrenk, TDNT 2, 202.

justice is to be regarded as worthless.[107] It cannot be pleasing to God for it is the justice of a man who is still not subjected to God in the obedience of faith.[108]

We have seen that those enslaved to sin can perform actions that are in a certain sense good. The justice that a man acquires through his own efforts may win him glory in the eyes of men—but not in the eyes of God (Rom. 4: 2). These "good" actions are worthless as far as true justice and true liberty are concerned. This is why Scripture hardly ever refers to them as good or just [109] but almost always emphasizes the total sinfulness of man before his true justification and liberation through Jesus Christ.[110]

It would be perfectly in accordance with the spirit of the New Testament which understands neither "good," "sin," "life," nor "justice" univocally, to call even the works of human justice sins,[111] as long as we realize that there is an *ethical* difference between an unbeliever who is to some extent faithful to the law written in his heart and an unbeliever, who deliberately flaunts even this norm of human justice.[112] Thus, it is perfectly legitimate from a biblical-theological point of view to

---

107 Phil. 3: 7f. Cf. the very careful exegesis of these verses by A. Stumpff, "zēmia," TDNT 2, 890f. The verb of this same root, zēmioomai, occurs only once in the Synoptics: Mt. 16: 26, par. We see here also a radical comparison of the values. If we were to transfer this Synoptic usage to Phil. 3: 7f., it would read: what does it profit a man if he should possess perfect justice of the law and not have the justice of faith?

108 Rom. 4: 2; 8: 8. Thomas Aquinas, *Ad Rom.* VIII, 8, n. 624: "Unde illi qui ei non subiciuntur, non possunt ei placere, quamdiu tales sunt."

109 Cf. Schrenk, "dikaios," TDNT 2, 189f.; Grundmann, "agathos," TDNT 1, 16f.; Kuss, II, 454f. and 468. On the problem of the "good" mentioned in Rom. 7: 18-22 see Kuss, II, 482f. and Dodd, p. 62.: In concrete cases Paul "allows that in some measure at least the good pagan . . . can do the right thing. We note this as against the doctrines of 'total depravity,' and the complete impotence of the human will which have been attributed to Paul." Dodd seems to be more balanced than Bultmann, *Primitive Christianity*, p. 143, who interprets Paul as saying: ". . . man is radically incapable of doing what he wants to do. His will is corrupted from the outset. . . ." As Gaudel says, DTC 12, 313f.: Paul "ne nie pas le *vouloir*, mais le *pouvoir* de l'homme déchu."

110 Cf. footnote 101.

111 We must remember that, strictly speaking, no one is good except God alone (Mt. 19: 17 par); cf. Grundmann, "agathos," TDNT 1, 16.

112 The "ethical" view of sin may be contrasted with the "theological" view which dominates the NT. Cf. Grundmann, "hamartanō," TDNT 1, 315 and "agathos," TDNT 1, 16; Schrenk, "dikaios," TDNT 2, 189f. The Bible understands neither "good" "sin" nor "righteous" univocally. On the basis of this qualification and in light of the total biblical perspective we have considered, it seems clear that one could legitimately sustain some theses otherwise censured (in varying degrees) by the Catholic Church, for example, the first half of DS 1925, DS 1935 and similar theses concerning the condition of the unbeliever. Accordingly, the thesis "omnia opera infidelium sunt peccata" could be sustained

speak of the "good" pagan or the "good" Jew as sinners, and even to say that their "good" acts are sinful if they are done apart from the obedience of faith in Christ, which alone makes man and man's actions pleasing to God. From the point of view of ethics or moral philosophy on the other hand, it would clearly be false to say that the virtues of a good pagan are the same as the vices of a bad pagan, or that the Old Testament Jew who faithfully tried to keep the law of Moses is no different from a Jew who totally disregarded the law.

Does the spiritually enslaved man sin necessarily in all his actions? We have just seen that there is a legitimate biblical sense in which we can say that all the actions of an unbeliever are sins. As long as the unbeliever remains in his condition of spiritual slavery, therefore, he cannot avoid sin.[113] This does not mean, however, that he sins by absolute necessity or that he no longer has free will.[114] Scripture, as we have already seen, knows no such doctrine of necessity. To say that a man cannot do something does not imply that he no longer has natural freedom. It implies that he lacks freedom of action (circumstantial freedom) or freedom to do as he ought (acquired freedom). Even though the sinner is a captive of sin and Satan, he still retains like any other prisoner or slave the ability to make free decisions.[115] But since his captivity is a spiritual one involving his *obedience* to sin, the ability to make free decisions does not extend, by the very nature of his captivity, to the freedom to decide to obey "obedience unto justice," to use the inexact parallel of Rom. 6: 16b. His will is powerless to will true justice

---

if we understood "opera" to mean works unaided by grace, and took "peccata" to mean acts which have no value before God (Rom. 4: 2; 8: 7) and which are not pleasing to God (Rom. 8: 8; Heb. 11: 6). Pius V himself admitted that some of the censured theses "aliquo pacto sustineri possent" (DS 1980). Although A. Hartmann, for example, "Gut," LThK 4, 1285, maintains that the supernatural good is the only true and absolute good, his lack of attention to the biblical texts we have considered prevents him from expressing more sharply the miserable situation of the man who performs "nur natürliche gute Akte." We leave aside here the whole question of the "anonymous Christian." We wish simply to register our recognition that, through the hidden action of Christ, there can be true, saving faith not only in Jews but also in those who do not accept the biblical revelation.

[113] Thomas Aquinas, *In Ioann.*, 8, 34, n. 1204: "Quae quidem servitus peccati gravissima est, quia vitari non potest: nam quocumque homo vadat, peccatum intra se habet, licet actus et delectatio eius transeat. . . ."

[114] See footnote 27f. above.

[115] Thus even the slave to sin is capable of deciding for or against works of human justice, for or against an ethical virtue or good deed. In neither case, however, according to the NT, is he any closer to liberation from sin or any better disposed for justification, for this liberation and the bestowal of *true* justice is a pure gift of God, not the result of any ethical excellence or purely human moral righteousness (Eph. 2: 8; Phil. 2: 12f.; Jn. 6: 66; 8: 36).

and liberty. (It enjoys natural freedom but not acquired freedom.) Otherwise he would be free to change his servile condition by his own efforts. But in the light of the New Testament this is impossible, since the free decision that is "obedience unto justice," and therefore liberation from sin, is a gift of God, the gift of faith.

Other questions pertaining to grace and free will naturally arise at this point. These we shall leave for our next section when we consider them in their historical setting in the controversy between Augustine and the Pelagians.

By way of summary, our biblical-theological investigation has led us to the following conclusions:

1. The Bible recognizes three types of freedom, which we have named natural, circumstantial and acquired freedom. Although Scripture applies the name freedom only to the last two types of freedom, there is no question that the reality we have called natural freedom is also recognized and presupposed throughout the Bible.

2. The view that God's foreknowledge or predestination imposes absolute necessity on human actions has no basis in Scripture.

3. The Bible recognizes a corporal, social and political slavery or imprisonment (absence of circumstantial freedom) and a spiritual or theological slavery to sin, Satan, to the law and to death (absence of acquired freedom—to do and be as one ought in the light of Christian revelation).

4. Slavery to sin does not mean that man has lost the power of free choice and decision (natural freedom), but that man cannot free himself from his enslaved condition. Slavery to sin means, therefore, that the enslaved man is not free to be or to become what he ought to be: a slave to God and to the justice of God by the obedience of faith which alone makes him truly free (acquired freedom in the Christian sense). To say that a man cannot do something is not to say that he no longer has natural freedom, but that he lacks freedom of action (circumstantial freedom) or freedom to do as he ought (acquired freedom).

5. Captivity to Satan likewise does not mean that Satan deprives man of his natural freedom, but of the acquired freedom to live as he ought, as a servant of God. Man finds himself in the power of Satan and under the law of sin from birth without his willing it. Yet man's own sins are to be distinguished from his sinful condition of estrangement from God. Man *is* responsible for the sins resulting from his obedience to Satan's will. He allows Satan to dominate him. He does freely will his sins. Unless we say this, it is impossible to account for man's responsibility for his sins and the judgment God will pass on him.

6. The legally righteous acts (the so-called naturally good works) of the man still enslaved to sin are not pleasing to God and are worthless in comparison with the true justice and goodness which are made possible only by faith in Christ.

7. The slave to sin is truly liberated, therefore, only by faith in Christ and through the power of the Holy Spirit, who comes to him in baptism.

8. Scripture speaks neither of "liberum arbitrium" nor "servum arbitrium". "Liberum arbitrium," in the sense in which we have defined it (natural freedom), is presupposed by the Bible. "Servum arbitrium" can only be accepted as a legitimate expression of the biblical doctrine of man's enslavement to sin if we take it to mean that the sinner, apart from grace and faith in Christ, can in no way free himself from his miserable condition. To understand by it any kind of necessitarianism that excludes natural freedom is seriously to misunderstand the biblical anthropology as well as the biblical doctrines of faith and justification.

3

Freedom of the Will
in the Pre-Augustinian Fathers

There can be no doubt whatever that the Greek and Latin Fathers of the Church from the very beginning held to the natural freedom of man's will both before and after the fall of Adam. Indeed, the concept—as well as the actual expression—"free will" (*autexousion; liberum arbitrium*) was so emphasized and so firmly and constantly defended,[1] that some have questioned whether the early Fathers, especially the Apostolic Fathers and the Apologists, were really faithful to the New Testament teaching on redemption through the sacrificial death of Christ and justification by grace and faith.[2]

To avoid the one-sided assessment that the early Fathers were mere moralists, however, one must remember several things:

1. The concepts of grace and historic redemption through Christ were never fully absent.

2. In the period of oral tradition (Cullman, von Campenhausen) prior to 150 A.D. when the Church still had not made any effort toward shaping a biblical canon—and long after 150 A.D.—the Pauline and Johannine corpus was not in the hands of each ecclesiastical writer. Quite understandably, then, we cannot expect to find specific theses of Pauline theology, for example, in the works of these early writers.[3]

---

[1] K. Rahner, "Freiheit. IV. Freiheit in der Tradition," LThK, 4, 332. On the use of the Stoic word and concept *autexousion* in the patristic interpretation of Paul see K. H. Schelkle, *Paulus: Lehrer der Väter,* 2nd ed. (Düsseldorf, 1959), pp. 439f.

[2] Cf. R. Seeberg, *Lehrbuch der Dogmengeschichte,* Bd. I, 3rd ed. (Basel-Stuttgart-Leipzig, 1960), pp. 177ff. (the apostolic Fathers); 351f. (the Apologists); 484ff. (Clement of Alexandria); 543 (Origen); Fr. Loofs, *Leitfaden zum Studium der Dogmengeschichte,* 1st and 2nd part, 6th ed. (Tübingen, 1959), p. 93; O. Cullmann, *The Early Church* (London, 1956), p. 96; T. F. Torrance (a student of Cullmann), *The Doctrine of Grace in the Apostolic Fathers* (Edinburgh-London, 1948).

[3] Seeberg, I, p. 180: "Wer nur das gesetzliche Element in das Auge fasst, dem

3. Neither Greek nor Latin Fathers ever denied the necessity of grace for justification and for works pleasing to God.[4]

4. The early Fathers were not primarily fighting against Jewish-Christian legalism and justification by works, as was Paul in Romans and Galatians. Their main efforts were directed against the more fundamental errors concerning God, creation and sin that were being propagated by the contemporary pagan mystery religions of the Stoic philosophers and, above all, of the Gnostics. These groups agreed that man is inexorably controlled by fate. Deliverance from this fate and from an evil for which man was not responsible was preached by Gnosticism and the mystery religions.[5] Other related movements, such as that of the Marcionites and the later Manichees, sought to identify evil with material substance. The Christian Fathers could not accept the basic assumptions of these pagan movements: the dualistic or polytheistic concept of God and the denial that man is responsible for his sins. Seen from this perspective the patristic concern to defend man's natural freedom is more understandable. We can similarly appreciate the tendency of the early Fathers to concentrate more on personal, actual sin—insisting always on its origin in man's free will—and less on what we now call original sin.

5. There is a "moralism," more precisely a parenesis, throughout the New Testament, including the Pauline writings. The charge of "moralism" has, of course, also been made of such New Testament books as the Epistle of James. This charge has validity only if one presupposes such a "canon within the canon" as a onesided Paulinism, or an overemphasized doctrine of justification.[6]

6. The Fathers of the Church had to deal with many problems that the Scriptures neither answered nor even formulated. Just as, for example, the developing Christological and Trinitarian theology prior to the great Councils of Nicaea, Ephesus and Chalcedon fell into considerable "material heresy," so also was the emerging patristic theology of

---

kann sich das Christentum in der ersten Hälfte des 2. Jahrhunderts fast wie eine Abart des Judaismus darstellen, wer tiefer blickt, nimmt die Kräfte des erlösenden Geistes der Gnade wahr." Cullmann, p. 96, likewise admits that "the Church Fathers who wrote after 150—Irenaeus and Tertullian—. . . understood infinitely better the essence of the Gospel" than the authors of the first half of the century.

[4] M. Schmaus, *Katholische Dogmatik*, III/2, 5th ed. (München, 1956), p. 269; J. Van der Meersch, "Grâce: III. Nécessité," in: DTC 6, 1574.

[5] Bultmann, *Primitive Christianity*, pp. 153f.; Gaudel, "Péché Originel: II. La Tradition ecclésiastique avant la controverse pélagienne. Les Pères grecs," DTC, 12, 323.

[6] Schelkle, p. 440, invoking M. Werner for support, urges Protestant scholars to make sure that they measure the Paulinism of the Church Fathers according to Paul himself in his entirety, and not according to Luther and Calvin's understanding of Paul.

predestination, original sin, grace and free will not without its errors and shortcomings.

Unmistakable throughout the pre-Augustinian period of doctrinal development, however, is the patristic affirmation of the divine foreknowledge, providence and a predestination (however one understood its relation to the foreseen merits of man),[7] the necessity of grace for all salutary acts [8] and the natural freedom of man's will, even after the Fall.[9]

In contrast to the Old and New Testament belief in God's providential care, the late Greek (Stoic and Pythagorean) concept of providence was a doctrine of destiny, fatalism or necessitarianism that left no place for the free will of man.[10] The Christian Fathers, reacting against these originally Oriental ideas which found wide acceptance in the politically turbulent Graeco-Roman world, and which led to star worship and astrology,[11] taught a doctrine of providence and predestination that respected man's natural freedom. A fatalism that took away man's re-

---

[7] A. *Foreknowledge:* Cf. RJ 116, 166, 177, 202, 371, 397, 521 (English translations of the RJ entries can be found in *The Teachings of the Church Fathers,* ed. J. R. Willis, New York, 1966; see the Table of Reference on pp. 524-530 of the TCF). B. *Prédestination:* Cf. H. D. Simonin, "Prédestination: II . . . d'après les Pères grecs," DTC, 12, 2815-2832; J. Saint-Martin, "Prédestination: III . . . d'après les Pères latins, particulièrement d'après Saint Augustin," DTC, 12, 2832-2896; A. Auer, "Prädestination: II. Geschichtlich," LThK, 8, 662-665; Schelkle, pp. 17ff.; 308-312; 336-353; 380-384; 436-440. C. *Providence:* H.-D. Simonin, "Providence: II. . . . selon les Pères grecs." DTC, 12, 941-960; A. Rascol, "Providence: III . . . selon les Pères latins," DTC 12, 961-984; RJ 202, 422, 1014, 1134, 1377; H. Beck, *Vorsehung und Vorherbestimmung in der theologischen Literatur der Byzantiner* (Rome, 1937).

[8] J. Van der Meersch, DTC 6, 1574; Schmaus, III/2, pp. 269-272; J. Auer, "Gnade: III. Zur Geschichte der Gnadenlehre," LThK, 4, 984-988; Schelkle, p. 219; RJ 114, 220, 251, 253, 348, 808, 963, 1003, 1153, 1165, 1177, 1204, 1219, 1302.

[9] See F. Wörter, *Die christliche Lehre über das Verhältnis von Gnade und Freiheit von den apostolischen Zeiten bis zu Augustinus,* 2 parts (Freiburg, 1855/60); D'Alès, "Liberté, Libre Arbitre," *Dict. apol.* 2, 1852f. Cf. Schelke, pp. 18f.; 66-69; 72-75; 106f.; 218ff.; 337ff.; 347-350; 380-383; 436-440; RJ 123, 142, 156, 184, 244, 355, 446, 466 etc. God's predestination and foreknowledge do not take away man's free will: RJ 116, 1059, 1175, 1272. Free will remains even after the sin of Adam: RJ 244, 349, 398, 1022, 1406. No actual sin is possible without the consent of free will: RJ 123, 244, 335, 1151. Grace does not take away free will: RJ 244, 446, 704, 1034, 1151.

[10] See A. Chollet, "Destin," DTC 4, 632-634; J. Bouché, "Fatalisme," DTC 5, 2095-2098; G. Bardy, *La Conversion au Christianisme* (Paris, 1949), pp. 134-145. F. Copleston, *A History of Philosophy* I/2, pp. 140f.; R. Bultmann, *Primitive Christianity,* pp. 27; 136-140; D. Amand, *Fatalisme et liberté dans l'antiquité grecque* (Louvain, 1945). Some of the late Stoics (Seneca, Epictetus) broke through the traditional Stoic determinism—at least in the practical doctrine—and emphasized the role of the will in virtue and sin. Cf. Copleston, I/2, pp. 174-177. The same is true of the Gnostics. Cf. Dupont, pp. 266-377, esp. 282-327.

[11] Bultmann, *Primitive Christianity,* pp. 146-155.

sponsibility for sin was abhorrent to them, but equally repugnant was Cicero's argument against fatalism. The great Roman eclectic was too much of a humanist and moralist to deny free will. Yet he saw that the Stoic idea of providence was incompatible with free will. Cicero unfortunately identified the divine foreknowledge with the Stoic view of providence and held in his *De Fato* that, if God foreknows all future things, then there is no such thing as free will. Therefore, said the Roman moralist, since free will must be upheld, one must deny God's foreknowledge.[12] We shall see later that Luther used basically the same type of argumentation. Convinced, however, as a Christian, of the divine foreknowledge, he thought it necessary to deny free will! The Christian Fathers rejected this type of either-or argumentation. They insisted always that both truths were to be upheld. Augustine, for example, confronted Cicero's argument directly [13] and showed that the divine foreknowledge and man's free will are not alternatives.

If one were to summarize the motives for the insistence upon free will by the early Fathers, one could say that they were theological and not anthropological motives. The early Church had to struggle against pagan dualism to uphold monotheism and the holiness of the one God. To the Fathers this meant that sin could not be attributed to any personal principle of evil co-existing with the good God, or to the material creation of a creator-God as opposed to the redeemer-God.[14] It meant further that man could not have been created naturally evil by the good God and that the good God was in no way responsible for sin. Sin had to originate from some change in man for which man himself was responsible, a change that he freely willed.[15]

---

[12] Cf. Chollet, DTC 4, 634; Adler, I, p. 443; Garrigou-Lagrange, "Providence: IV . . . selon la Théologie," DTC 13, 988.

[13] Augustine deals with Cicero's argument in *De civ. Dei* I, 5, 9.

[14] Cf. A. von Harnack, *Marcion*, 2nd ed. (Leipzig, 1924), pp. 94-143; J. D. N. Kelly, *Early Christian Doctrines*, 2nd ed. (New York, 1960), pp. 348-357.

[15] Justin, *Apol.* I, 6: defends the one God in whom there is no evil; *Dial.* 88, 4: every man is responsible for his own sin; Tatian, *Adv. Graec. Orat.* 11 (PG 6, 829); Irenaeus, *Adv. Haer.* IV, 11, 2 (PG 7, 1002; RJ 229): against the view of Valentinus that some men are good by nature and do not require good works; cf. *ibid.* I, 1, 11-12; III, 40, 2; Gaudel, DTC 12, 323; Tertullian, *Adv. Marc.*, II, 5: opposes Marcion's view that the Creator-God can't be good because he permits sin, by insisting that sin arises from man's "arbitrii libertas"; cf. RJ 324, 335. Hippolytus, *Phil.* 10, 33 (RJ 398): God neither made nor does evil; Clement of Alexandria: cf. Gaudel, DTC 12, 329f.; Origen, *De princ.* I, Praef. 5 (PG 11, 118; RJ 446): testifies to the firm tradition of the Church ("definitum in ecclesiastica praedicatione") that man always retains free will and is never necessitated to good or evil. He so emphasizes free will that predestination is limited to a foreknowledge of man's merits. Cf. Seeberg, I, pp. 538ff.; H.-D. Simonin, DTC 12, 2822-2828. In the writings of the Fathers of the fourth century the conviction that sin is caused by a misuse of free will

Likewise, when the Fathers argued that free will was necessary for merit or demerit, they were not seeking to extol the power of man to merit his salvation. They were simply taking seriously the scriptural teaching that God judges all men according to their works, and from this theological standpoint—from the revealed truth of the coming judgment of God—they insisted against their pagan contemporaries, Marcion above all, that the God who judges is the good God and that man had to have free will if a judgment of God is to be at all meaningful and just.[16] One misunderstands the patristic teaching on free will, then, if one interprets it as mere moralism or as an assertion of autonomous humanism. It was much more an assertion of the justice and the holiness of the one God, the recognition of the original goodness of his creation and a confession of the biblical faith in the coming judgment of our works by God.

The doctrine of man's bondage or enslavement to sin is never absent in the pre-Augustinian Fathers.[17] However, it was only in the struggle of Augustine against the Pelagians that the doctrine of fallen man's total powerlessness to do anything truly good without grace—the doctrine of *servum arbitrium*—fully emerged.

---

is so widespread that we need not make individual citations. One can find an excellent summary of the patristic defense of free will against the teaching of the pagans and heretics in Schelkle, pp. 248-252.

[16] Cf. J. Rivière, "Mérite: II. . . . dans la tradition patristique," DTC 10, 612-661; J. Loosen, "Gericht: IV. Tradition," LThK 4, 732f.; E. Kähler, "Prädestination: III. Dogmengeschichtlich," RGG 5, 484: Schelkle, pp. 70-76.

[17] For example: Clement of Alexandria: cf. Gaudel, DTC 12, 330f.; John Chrysostom: *ibid.*, 352.

4

Free Will and Unfree Will
in Augustine

To speak of Augustine's doctrine of the will as a doctrine of the unfree or enslaved will is one-sided and misleading. For Augustine's doctrine was a doctrine of grace *and* free will.[1] He did use the term "servum arbitrium" once, in the midst of a controversy with his Pelagian opponent, Julian of Eclanum, and it was this phrase which Luther appropriated as the title of his reply to Erasmus.[2] But what

---

[1] The literature on this central aspect of Augustine's theology is enormous. Cf. the treatment of Augustine's doctrine of grace, free will and predestination in the older, but perennially useful study by E. Portalié, "Augustin (Saint)," DTC, 1, 2375-2408; tr. R. J. Bastian, *A Guide to the Thought of St. Augustine* (Chicago, 1960). Portalié's great work is unfortunately marred, as Jacquin, van Crombrugghe and others have pointed out, by his determination to find the roots of the Molinist doctrine of predestination in Augustine. See esp. DTC, 1, 2401f.; tr. pp. 219-223. Valuable also is the chapter on Christian liberty in É. Gilson, *Introduction à l'Étude de Saint Augustin,* 3rd ed. (Paris, 1949), pp. 185-216. A comprehensive view of the newer literature can be obtained by consulting the specialized bibliographies offered by A. Michel, "Augustin," DTC: Tables Générales, 2, 307; M. Schmaus III/2, pp. 450ff.; V. Capanaga, in: *Obras de San Agustin,* Vol I: *Introduccion General Y Primeros Escritos,* BAC 10, 3rd ed. (Madrid, 1957), pp. 306f.; 322-326; Capanaga, in: *Obras de Saint Agustin,* Vol. VI: *Tratados Sobre La Gracia,* BAC 50, 2nd ed. (Madrid, 1956), pp. 116f. (In this latter volume Capanaga offers a fine introduction to Augustine's writings on grace: pp. 3-115); *Repertoire Bibliographique de Saint Augustin,* ed. T. van Bavel (Den Haag, 1963), pp. 513-519; 714-719. Among the important recent monographs dealing with Augustine's teaching about free will are: G. Nygren, *Das Prädestinationsproblem in der Theologie Augustins* (Lund, 1956); M. T. Clark, *Augustine: Philosopher of Freedom* (New York-Tournai-Rome-Paris, 1958). J. Chéné, *La Théologie de Saint Augustin: Grâce et Prédestination* (LePuy-Lyon, 1961). Each of these works offers an extensive bibliography. See also chapts. 29-33 of Peter Brown's superb biography, *Augustine of Hippo* (Berkeley and Los Angeles, 1967).

[2] Augustine, *Contra Iulianum,* II, 8, 23 (PL 44, 689): "Sed vos festinatis et praesumptionem vestram festinando praecipiatis. Hic enim vultis hominem perfici atque utinam dei dono, et non libero, vel potius servo proprie voluntatis

did Augustine mean by "servum arbitrium"? Did he mean that "servum arbitrium" is opposed to the "liberum arbitrium" which we call natural freedom? Because of the importance that Augustine's phrase, *servum arbitrium,* had for Luther, and also because of Augustine's singular role in the development of the doctrine of grace and free will, it is necessary that we look at the teaching of this great Father more closely than we have done in the case of the earlier Fathers.

Although Augustine at times uses ambiguous terminology,[3] there is never any ambiguity about the fact that he always held to the natural freedom of the will even in fallen man. Equally clear, on the other hand, is the fact that, especially in his controversy with the Pelagians, Augustine emphasized the radical impotence of man's will apart from divine grace even to *will* to do something truly good. This is the only sense in which Augustine uses the phrase, "servum arbitrium." In our terminology, then, Augustine upholds the existence of natural freedom in man even after the Fall. As a consequence of Adam's sin, however, the human race has lost its true liberty, the liberty of acting or living rightly or justly, as one ought. Man thus has lost his acquired freedom, but never his natural freedom. His *liberum arbitrium* is, as a result of the Fall, a "liberum arbitrium captivatum";[4] but it is still a *liberum arbitrium* in the sense of natural freedom. It is a *liberum arbitrium* in captivity, however, since it does not have the liberty to live a life of true goodness. This liberty unto justice can only be acquired from God, who liberates and aids the captive *liberum arbitrium.*[5]

That Augustine's doctrine of *servum arbitrium* has nothing whatever to do with universal determinism, fatalism or necessitarianism can most easily be established by considering the fact that Augustine, throughout his Christian life, unceasingly defended the natural freedom of the will against the Manichaean doctrine of dualism, according to which one God was not the creator of all things and evil was attributed to material nature rather than to the fallible free will of man. Not only in his early work, *De libero arbitrio* (begun in 388, completed in 395), and in other books written directly against the Manichaean ideas, but also in his later anti-Pelagian writings, Augustine maintained unyielding opposition to

---

arbitrio." Cf. WA 18, 665. Luther had already cited this sentence from Augustine in the *Disputatio* of 1516: WA I, 148.

[3] In reply to the charge of a Pelagian opponent, Augustine admitted that his words could be misleading. Nevertheless he insisted that there was no contradiction between his earlier and later writings: *Contra Iul.* V, 5, 19 (PL 44, 795); 9, 37 (PL 44, 806). Cf. Clark, pp. 90f.

[4] *Contra duas epist. Pelag.,* III, 8, 24 (420 A.D.): "Et liberum arbitrium captivatum nonnisi ad peccatum valet. . . ."

[5] *Ibid.,* ". . . ad iustitiam vero, nisi divinitus liberatum adiutumque, non valet."

the Manichaean view that evil was natural and not the work of free will.[6]

1. De libero arbitrio (388–395)

In writing *De libero arbitrio* St. Augustine quite understandably did not emphasize the necessity of grace for liberating man from the captivity of sin and for helping him to live a life of true goodness. But it would be wrong to say that this work was simply an early philosophical discourse. It is true that Augustine shows himself primarily as a Christian philosopher in *De libero arbitrio,* but he unmistakably indicates even in this work, as we shall shortly note, that he is fully aware that the problem of free will can be treated not only in itself, but also from the perspective of the Christian theologian who considers the free will of man in the light of the Fall.

Augustine was to take up the theological consideration of free will in all its complexity against the Pelagians. But when he wrote *De libero arbitrio* the Pelagian heresy had not yet achieved its maturity, and Augustine's defense of free will is not too different from the similar defenses made by his contemporaries, John Chrysostom and the early Jerome.[7] Later, of course, against a completely different type of opposition—Pelagianism—Augustine had to point out the powerlessness of the free will of fallen man to do or to will true goodness.

But even when he emphatically and unceasingly proclaims the necessity of the "grace of God" or the "grace of the faithful" against the Pelagian identification of grace with the "grace attributed to nature" or

---

[6] *Op. cit.* III, 9, 25; IV, 3, 3; 6, 12; 12, 33.

[7] Neither Luther nor Erasmus seems to be aware that Jerome opposed Pelagianism late in his career. They both erroneously see an opposition between Jerome and Augustine on this point. An important factor contributing to this misunderstanding was undoubtedly that one of the central *loci* of Pelagius' thought, the *Expositiones in Epistolas Pauli libri XIV,* in an expurgated version, was for a long time attributed to Jerome. Erasmus went so far as to publish this Pelagian work under Jerome's name in 1516! Cf. R. Hedde and É. Amann, "Pélagianisme," DTC 12, 679f.; J. Forget, "Jérome (Saint)," DTC 8, 924. Jerome, who died in 419, eleven years before Augustine, would possibly have rivaled Augustine as a *doctor gratiae* had he lived longer. In several of his letters Jerome, weak from sickness, expressed admiration for the zeal with which Augustine was attacking the Pelagians (*Epist.* 141-2). In one of the last letters he wrote (*Epist.* 143) Jerome sorrowfully regretted that his illness prevented him from replying further to the "enemies of the faith." Cf. J. Forget, DTC 8, 906f. It is likely that the *De libero arbitrio libri quatuor* of Pelagius was a response to the attacks made by Jerome in his *Dialogus adversus Pelagianos* (415). Cf. Hedde and Amann, DTC, 12, 681. To place an opposition between John Chrysostom and Augustine on the question of the necessity of grace—as did Luther and Erasmus—is even more anachronistic than it is with Jerome, for Chrysostom died in 407, long before the onset of the Pelagian controversy.

the "natural gifts of God," [8] which made man's intellect and free will—and the revelation of the Law—the most important graces or "dona" which man receives from God, even then Augustine never withdrew the basic teaching that he developed in *De libero arbitrio:*

(1) God, whose justice it would be sacrilegious to deny, is not the author of moral evil.[9]

(2) The first cause of evil is not nature, but the free will of man.[10]

(3) Even though it is impossible for man to sin without free will, it would be wrong to regard free will as an undesirable gift. For God did not give man free will for the purpose of sinning, but in order that he might be able to do good and live justly. Without free will man cannot live justly.[11]

(4) If man lacked free will it would be unjust either to punish him or to reward him.[12]

(5) Free will is a gift of God and is, as such, good. But it is not the highest kind of good, for it can be put to bad use. Virtue is the highest kind of good, since it can by definition never be badly used.[13]

(6) The turning of the will from God to creatures, which constitutes sin,[14] does not happen naturally or by natural necessity—a stone falls by natural necessity—but voluntarily, by one's own will.[15] The difference between the voluntary and the naturally necessary is that the will is able to prevent its tendency to turn away from God in favor of creatures.[16]

---

[8] Augustine, *De praed. sanct.* (428/9), 5, 10.

[9] *De lib. arb.,* I, 1, 1.

[10] *Ibid.,* I, 16, 35; III, 16, 45; 17, 48-49.

[11] *Ibid.,* II, 1, 1 and 3. Cf. *ibid.,* II, 19, 48 and 50.

[12] *Ibid.,* II, 1, 3. Cf. *ibid.,* I, 14, 30. In *De vera relig.* (389-391), 14, 27, Augustine uses the fact of sin's existence as a proof of free will. Augustine reaffirmed this view in *Retract.* I, 13, 5.

[13] *Ibid.,* II, 18, 48—19, 50. Cf. *Retract.,* I, 9.

[14] *Ibid.,* II, 20, 54.

[15] *Ibid.,* III, 1, 2: ". . . nulla re fieri mentem servam libidinis, nisi propria voluntate:. . . ." Even in this early work Augustine uses the "servus" concept. See also *ibid.,* I, 12, 24; II, 13, 37. In the latter text Augustine speaks of the Christian liberty that results from subjection to the truth. Cf. III, 10, 30 and 18, 51, which show that Augustine, even in *De lib. arb.,* is able to consider man not only in himself, in his essential structure, but also from the point of view of the history of salvation. Against the view of Loofs and Seeberg, he is therefore not to be considered simply as a Christian philosopher in this early period. Cf. Clark, pp. 56f.; Nygren, pp. 41, footnote 66.

[16] *Ibid.,* III, 1, 2. Highly important for our later comparison of Luther's doctrine of *servum arbitrium* with that of Augustine is the fact that, for Augustine, the voluntary is the same as the naturally free. We find Augustine using interchangeably the expressions: "voluntas," "arbitrium voluntatis," "liberum arbitrium," and "liberum voluntatis arbitrium" to designate natural freedom. The voluntary and the "compulsion" and "coercion" of *natural* necessity exclude one another. This

(7) Every "nature" is from God as is every good thing. Sin is not something positive; it is a defect rather than a created nature. This defect or absence of good is not the work of God. It is a voluntary defect and it is in the power of our will to cause it.[17]

(8) If an action cannot be avoided there can be no sin; sin can only be committed when the sinful act can be avoided or resisted.[18]

(9) God's foreknowledge of our sins does not mean that he is the author of sin. Whatever he causes, he foreknows, but it does not follow that whatever he foreknows, he causes.[19]

(10) Fallen man does not have the free will to choose a truly just way of living.[20]

(11) One can speak of sin not only in its proper sense, as when a sin is committed with knowledge and free will, but also in an improper or broader sense, namely, of sins that result from ignorance and weakness.

---

necessity is not the same as extrinsic force, for natural necessity involves a "proper movement," such as the *proprius motus* of natural necessity which causes a stone to fall. Thus, if we do anything by natural necessity we do it unwillingly (*invitus*). Augustine, however, doesn't regard every kind of necessity as being incompatible with the voluntary. Like many of the Scholastics he holds that the will is moved by a necessity of end to will happiness—even though he does not use the term. See *De nat. et gr.*, 46, 54—47, 55. Cf. *De civ. Dei*, V, 10, 1. Bourke, p. 82, overlooks these texts which show that Augustine recognizes that the will has some necessary activities. Augustine also says that if God foresees the future blessedness of someone, nothing else can happen than that which he foresees: *De lib. arb.* III, 3, 7. Yet he does not consider this a necessity that deprives the will of its freedom: *ibid.*, 8. Here is a foreshadowing of the later Scholastic distinction between *necessitas absoluta* (*consequentis*) and *necessitas conditionalis* (*suppositionis; consequentiae*). Seeberg, *Dogmengeschichte*, II, p. 419, footnote 1 is incorrect in seeing here a distinction between a "durch Gottes Vorherwissen gesetzten metaphysischen Notwendigkeit einer Handlung" and a "psychologischen Willentlichkeit." That will (*voluntas*) is for Augustine always a naturally free *voluntas* can be ascertained from the following texts: "Quid enim tam in voluntate, quam ipsa voluntas sita est?": *De lib. arb.*, I, 12, 26. "Quapropter nihil tam in nostra potestate, quam ipsa voluntas est": *ibid.*, III, 3, 7. Cf. *Retract*, I, 22. "Voluntas igitur nostra nec voluntas esset, nisi esset in nostra potestate. Porro, qui est in potestate, libera est nobis. Non enim est nobis liberum, quod in potestate non habemus, aut potest non esse quod habemus": *ibid.*, III, 3, 8. Here Augustine does not say that the will would not be will unless it acts spontaneously or willingly, "sponte et libenter," but that the will would not be will unless it is *free*, that is, in our power. In *De duab. an. contra Manich.* (391/2), 11, 15 he says explicitly: "Quamquam si liberum non sit, non est voluntas." Augustine reaffirms his earlier teaching in the *Retractationes*: I, 13 (PL), 5; 15, 2 and 4.

[17] *De lib. arb.*, II, 20, 54. Cf. *De div. quaest. LXXXIII*, 6: evil is a privation —"speciei privatio." Cf. Copleston, *A History of Philosophy*, II/1 (New York, 1962), pp. 99f.

[18] *De lib. arb.*, III, 18, 50. Cf. Nygren, p. 38. In *De nat. et gr.*, 67, 80f. Augustine repeats what he teaches here, emphasizing, however, that sin can only be resisted by the grace of God.

[19] *De lib. arb.*, III, 2, 4—3, 8; 4, 11. II, 3, 8. Cf. *De civ. Dei*, V, 10, 1 and 2.
[20] *De lib. arb.*, III, 18, 51-52.

These are called "sins" because they are the result of original sin, which was caused by free will.[21]

EXCURSUS: *The Different Meanings of "Sin," "Good" and "Virtue" in Augustine and the Problem of the "Good Works" of Unbelievers.*

It is difficult to overestimate the importance of the different meanings which Augustine attaches to the word "sin." No more than Scripture itself, as we have already seen, does Augustine use the terms "sin," "good" and "just" univocally. But failure to realize that Augustine speaks of sin sometimes in a proper, strict sense and sometimes in an improper, broad or analogous sense (as indicated in Thesis 11 above which we have extracted from *De libero arbitrio*) has resulted in serious misrepresentations or misunderstandings of Augustine's thought. Failure to make the distinctions which Augustine made undoubtedly occasioned much of the controversy that arose when the Reformers, Baius and the Jansenists appealed to Augustine to support this concept of the doctrine of the total sinfulness of the unjustified man. It seems clear that the condemnations of certain theses by the Church concerning the sinfulness of fallen man were reactions to statements in which "sin" is used univocally, without any distinctions (DS 1486, 1557, 1925, 1927f., 1935, 2308, 2311). Cf. Ch. 2, footnote 112. It is therefore incorrect to say, as Pelikan does, that the condemnation of the Jansenists by the Church was also a condemnation of Augustine: *The Riddle of Roman Catholicism* (New York-Nashville: Abingdon, 1959), p. 69. Pelikan makes this assertion even though he admits that the Jansenists distorted Augustine's doctrine. The same lack of attention to Augustine's distinctions concerning sin has led to innumerable errors on the part of historians who content themselves with such inaccurate generalizations as: Augustine "has only evil to say of free will when unattended by grace; it is capable only of doing wrong": G. Leff, *Bradwardine and the Pelagians* (Cambridge: University Press, 1957), p. 74.

In later writings Augustine speaks of another way in which sin can be understood in a strict or in a broad sense. On the one hand, he teaches in *Contra Faust. Manich.* (400 A.D.) 22, 27: "Sin is any deed, word or thought contrary to the eternal law. But the eternal law is the divine order or will of God commanding the preservation of the natural order and forbidding its disturbance."

Here we have a traditional Catholic definition of sin. Yet, on the other hand, should a "good" pagan (*impius; alienus a fide*) conform to the natural order of things by practicing such virtues as mercy, modesty, chastity and sobriety without the help of grace as Julian suggests (*Contra Iul.* [421] 4, 3, 16), this still would not be "true virtue unless he be just. And it is unthinkable that he be truly just unless he lives by faith." (*Ibid.*, 17). Here Augustine takes his stand on the biblical distinction between true justice—the justice of faith which avails before

---

[21] *Ibid.*, III, 19, 54.

God—and the justice of works, which has value only before men. The "impii" may have a certain kind of human justice and human virtue, but this cannot be *true* virtue or *true* justice; otherwise Christ would have died in vain (*ibid.*): "Christ has died in vain if men without the faith of Christ arrive by any other means at true faith, true virtue, true justice or true wisdom."

Augustine cites Gal. 2, 21 as his biblical proof: "If the law can justify us, there is no point in the death of Christ." His theological argument is this: the "virtutes impiorum" are not true virtues because they are not referred to God as their end (*finis*). "Thus neither the continence nor the modesty of the ungodly is true virtue" (*ibid.*). Augustine thus admits that unbelievers can practice continency, temperance and other virtues of the natural law, (even "caritas humana": *Serm.* 349, 1, 1), but he denies that they are true virtues. They are in no sense true virtues because they are without value for attaining true happiness (*Contra Iul.* 4, 3, 19): "If human virtues are of no avail (*nihil prosunt*) for achieving true happiness, they can in no way be true virtues." (Cf. *De gr. et lib. arb.* 18, 37; *De spiritu et litt.* 27, 48). They may seem to be true and beautiful virtues, but they are not. In *De civ. Dei* (413-426) 19, 25 Augustine says of these "virtutes impiorum": "they are vices rather than virtues." This is the nearest Augustine comes to saying: "all virtues of pagans are splendid vices," a phrase he never actually used, despite assertions to that effect made from the time of Leibniz, through Seeberg and Harnack, to the present day. (See for example, J. Dillenberger—C. Welch, *Protestant Christianity* [New York: Scribner's, 1958], p. 29; cf. Denifle's examination of the "splendid vices" question in *Luther und Luthertum* [2nd ed., Mainz, 1906], pp. 857-860.)

In *Contra Iul.* 4, 3, 21 Augustine presents what might be called an analysis of a moral act when he says that Julian fails to see that the virtues of pagans are not true virtues because he considers only the "officium" of the act, but not the "finis." "The *officium* is that which is to be done; the end (*finis*) is that for which it is to be done." The "officium" is that which later theologians will call the object of the act, "the natural inner ethical quality" (Schmaus III/2, p. 284). If a man does something good, therefore, but does not do it to serve God, it is a sin even though it may appear to be good if we simply consider the "officium": "Whatever good a man does that is not done because true wisdom dictates that it ought to be done is a sin by the very fact that the end is not good—even though the act may seem good as officium."

Here Augustine frankly calls even the good actions of the unjustified —objectively good, that is—sins. Augustine further analyzes the moral act when he says, *ibid.*, 31 that the act of an unbeliever can be *per se ipsum* good, but it is "used" badly—and sinfully—when done without faith in Christ: "In itself an act of natural compassion is good. But he who uses this good work in an unbelieving way uses it badly. And he who does this good act unbelievingly does it in an evil way. But whoever does something in an evil way sins." The virtues of the ungodly are, "in God's eyes, sterile . . . and hence are not good" (*ibid.*, 33). Cf. *Enarr. in Ps.* 37, 2, 4; *In Io. evang. tract.* 45, 2.

It is quite clear from the texts cited that for Augustine not only "sin," but also "justice," "virtue" and "good" are used diversely. For Augustine, an infidel can indeed be spoken of as doing good works, living justly and being virtuous. But apart from the faith in Christ that works through charity the infidel never does truly good works nor does he possess true justice or virtue, for nothing that he does has value before God, nothing has value for attaining true, eternal happiness.

If the analogous character of Augustine's terminology is overlooked, he is bound to be misinterpreted. To say simply and without qualification, therefore, that, for Augustine, all actions of unbelievers are sins, is to falsify Augustine's thought by over-simplification and by univocal interpretation of his analogous language. For Augustine, unbelievers can perform acts which are good in their "officium," such as prudence and temperance. Such acts can never be called bad from the point of view of the "officium." In this respect they clearly differ from acts of imprudence and intemperance.

Luther, already in 1516, tends to overlook the distinctions which Augustine makes concerning the good acts and virtues of infidels. In the *Disputatio de viribus et voluntate hominis sine gratia,* which contains numerous citations from Augustine, Luther writes in reference to Mt. 7, 18: "In many places St. Augustine teaches that man apart from grace is an evil tree. Whatever he does, therefore, in *whatever manner* he may use his reason, elicit, command or do an act, he always sins when he lacks faith working through love" (Concl. II, Corr. 2: WA 1, 148). The first of these sentences is a correct statement of Augustine's thought but the second is not, for the words which we have emphasized suggest an absoluteness and a univocity in Augustine's doctrine that is not to be found in his writings. On the contrary, as we have seen, Augustine admits that there is a "modus" by which we can speak of "good acts" of infidels or "virtues of [unbelieving] men"—even though there is no "modus" in which these can be *truly* good acts or *true* virtues: "nullo modo verae possunt esse virtutes" (*Contra Iul.* 4, 3, 19).

It is not always clear from the *immediate* context that Augustine uses his terms diversely. Thus, one could misinterpret Augustine's intention if he were to isolate from the context of the entire Augustinian corpus such a text as: "Nor does free will avail for anything except sin should the way of truth be hidden" (*De spir. et litt.* 3, 5). When Luther refers to this text in his *Assertio omnium articulorum* (1521), WA 7, 145, he implies that Augustine speaks of sin univocally. However, he neglects to introduce Augustine's qualification that the free will of unbelievers can be the cause of some good works (*aliqua bona opera*)—even though these are without profit for salvation (cf. *De spir. et litt,* 27, 48). It seems very likely that the condemnations by Leo X and by Trent concerning the capacity of the free will of fallen man (DS 1476 and 1557) were occasioned by authors who used the concept "sin" univocally and without qualification.

In Luther's favor, however, and in the interest of ecumenical understanding, it must be noted that he was perfectly aware of an analogous concept of "justice" and "good" and therefore of "injustice" and of "sin." He fully recognized the New Testament distinction between the righteousness before God and before men.

But during the heat of the Reformation controversy, when access to all of Luther's works was not possible and when the spirit of today's ecumenical dialogue was virtually non-existent, we see certain of Luther's theses being isolated from their total context and condemned by the Church authorities as erroneous and heretical. It would be easy to demonstrate that the condemned theses do not always represent a balanced statement of Luther's doctrine in its full context. With Luther as with Augustine we must seek out the meaning not simply from the immediate context, but from the context of the entire corpus. Fortunately, Luther's name is never attached to any of the propositions anathematized in the canons of the Council of Trent. Even should certain of Luther's propositions have been explicitly censured at Trent, one would still have to keep in mind the nature of a dogmatic pronouncement, as we have indicated in the Introduction, and ask: Was the teaching office of the Church declaring that the person condemned really had lost or abandoned the Catholic faith? Or was it performing the function, necessary to maintaining Church unity, of regulating theological language—in this case, affirming that "sin" and "good" can have several meanings?

What value have the "virtutes impiorum" if they are not true virtues? Augustine concedes that they are better—or are less evil—than vices or actions which are bad in themselves (*per se ipsas*) because the "good" pagans will be more tolerably punished in hell than the bad ones (cf. *Contra Iul.* 4, 3, 25 and *De spir. et litt.* 28, 48). This view was adopted by Luther in the *Disputatio de viribus et voluntate hominis sine gratia* of 1516 (Concl. I, Corr. III: WA I, 126f). An important monograph on this entire question has been written by J. Wang Tch'ang-Tche, *Saint Augustin et les vertus des Paiens* (Paris, 1938) showing that Augustine never states flatly that non-Christians are lost. His position is rather: *If* they are saved they are saved by the grace of Christ.

A still broader concept of sin is revealed by Augustine in *De perf. iust.* (415), 6, 15, when he states that an act is sinful when either due love is absent or when there is less love than there ought to be. G. de Broglie, *De fine ultimo humanae vitae* (Paris, 1948), pp. 35f. points out that Augustine's broad concept of sin never prevailed in the Catholic Church. By the time of Thomas Aquinas, as we shall see, while there is a fundamental agreement with Augustine as to the fruitlessness of the ethically good acts of sinners, these acts are no longer called sins—but neither are they called truly virtuous in the strict sense.

Finally, an awareness of Augustine's diverse use of the word "sin" is essential for understanding his doctrine on the concupiscence that remains after baptism. In *De nupt. et concup.* (419/420) I, 23, 25; *Contra Iul.* (421) 2, 3, 5 and elsewhere, Augustine teaches that concupiscence in a baptized person is sin only according to a manner of speaking (*modo quodam loquendi peccatum vocatur*) because concupiscence is a result of original sin and can be the occasion of actual sins. In his *Lectures on Romans* (1515/1516), WA 56, 352f., Luther accepted this distinction, but later abandoned it. Augustine's view is explicitly rejected in Luther's book against Latomus (1521), WA 8, 108, 24-109, 10.

The following points conclude the basic theses developed in *De libero arbitrio:*

(12) True liberty is the liberty of the blessed and of those who keep the eternal law. This is not to be confused with the liberty of those who think they are free merely because they have no human master, and the liberty which is desired by those who wish to be set free from human masters.[22]

(13) One is never guilty of sin unless he is obliged to do or avoid something. But there can be no obligation unless we have free will and fully sufficient power of acting.[23] Although there is no responsibility and guilt for sins (in the improper sense) involuntarily committed through ignorance or because of the weakness of will resulting from Adam's sin,[24] one is personally guilty of sin in the proper sense when he neglects to seek from God the truth of which he is ignorant and when he despises him who wishes to heal the weakness of the will. For God is the victor over the error and concupiscence of men and he is present everywhere, calling back those who have abandoned him, and hearing and answering their prayers for help.[25]

Of the thirteen theses which we have extracted from *De libero arbitrio,* the first twelve represent a permanent part of Augustine's thought. One could show that he held to them throughout the Pelagian controversy until his death. To speak of a total retreat by the later Augustine from the positions taken in *De libero arbitrio,* or to suppose that in *De libero arbitrio* we meet only Augustine the philosopher as opposed to a later Augustine the theologian is to betray a superficial understanding of either the early or the later Augustine—or perhaps of both.[26]

Concerning thesis (13), however, Augustine does make an important change. Thesis (13) assumes that the initiative to accept God's offer of

[22] *De lib. arb.,* I, 15, 32: "Deinde libertas, quae quidem nulla vera est, nisi beatorum, et legi aeternae adhaerentium: sed eam nunc libertatem commemoro, qua se liberos putant qui dominos non habent, et quam desiderant ii qui a dominis hominibus manumitti volunt." Here it is perfectly clear that Augustine recognizes the distinction between that which we have called circumstantial freedom and acquired freedom. Thus we find in *De lib. arb.* all three types of freedom.

[23] III, 16, 45.

[24] See thesis (11) above.

[25] *De lib. arb.,* III, 19, 53.

[26] In the *Retractationes* (426/7), we find no "retraction" of *De lib. arb.* On the contrary, one finds explanations of many points of the early work in the light of the later controversies as well as reaffirmations of the theses of *De lib. arb.* Cf. *Retract.* I, 9; *Epist.* 143 (412).

salvation still belongs to fallen man. G. Nygren correctly states the early Augustine's concept of free will as follows: "The idea of free will, this cornerstone of Augustine's religious and ethical thought—without which his concept of justice, reward and punishment loses its meaning—is nevertheless, in view of the fact of original sin and after the loss of man's original freedom, completely oriented toward grace: the rationality of his entire outlook now depends on the freedom of the will to accept or reject grace." [27]

2. De diversis quaestionibus VII ad Simplicianum (396/7)

It is no exaggeration to say that the early Augustine, prior to his elevation to the episcopate in 393, held the same error that he himself was later to combat—the error of Semipelagianism, which attributed the beginning of salvation (initium salutis [fidei]) to man's free will.[28] The Semipelagians in fact cited Augustine's early works to support their view that, although grace is necessary for every truly good act, the beginning of the good act (and therefore of faith and salvation) depends solely on man's free will. In his answer in De praedestinatione sanctorum (428/9) Augustine simply and humbly admitted that he now understood the doctrine of grace, faith and works better and had to correct his early

---

[27] P. 41. Nygren correctly sees that, already in this early work, the original freedom of Adam and the free will of fallen man are not the same.

[28] Cf. Portalié, DTC, 1, 2378; tr., p. 181: ". . . before his episcopacy he had not yet understood how the first good disposition of the will, faith for example, must come from God; he attributes this beginning of salvation exclusively to freedom of choice. This could really be an opening for Semipelagianism, but not Pelagianism, as the Jansenists supposed. This single error was the inspiration of various expressions which he himself corrected later." Cf. De dono persev., 21, 55. For an introduction into the issues of the Pelagian and Semipelagian controversies, see R. Hedde and É. Amann, "Pélagianisme," DTC, 12, 675-715; É. Amann "Semi-Pélagiens," DTC, 14, 1796-1850; H. Rondet, Gratia Christi, pp. 112-121; G. de Plinval, Pélage (Lausanne, 1943); J. N. D. Kelly, Early Christian Doctrines, pp. 357-361; 370ff. An ample bibliography on Pelagius and Pelagianism can be found in J. Ferguson, Pelagius (Cambridge, 1956), pp. 188-192. Ferguson's book itself is actually a defense of Pelagius against Augustine, whose theology is seriously misrepresented. Ferguson merits praise for examining Pelagius' writings in detail, thereby overthrowing many loose and erroneous impressions of Pelagius' actual thought. Had he done the same for Augustine's writings and had he not been content with vague and erroneous clichés about Augustine's doctrine (such as: Augustine's "theory of predestination . . . left no room for human freedom," p. 175; "Jerome does not hold the extreme predestinarian views of Augustine. He is rather a synergist, holding that God's grace and man's free will come together in the work of salvation. . . ," p. 80—as if Augustine never wrote De gratia et libero arbitrio!), perhaps his study as a whole would have great merit. The positive Christian ethical values which Pelagius stressed are given due recognition by P. Brown, "Pelagius and his Supporters: Aims and Environment," Journal of Theological Studies, 19/1 (1968), pp. 93-114.

works, especially his *Expositio quarumdam propositionum ex Epistola ad Romanos* (394).[29] He says that his opponents should not only read his books, but they should also keep in step with the progress and development of his thought.[30] Then, in the very important sentence which follows, Augustine states precisely where he made the change from his earlier works: it was in the first of two books that he wrote to Simplicianus, the successor of Ambrose to the See of Milan: *De diversis quaestionibus VII ad Simplicianum* (396-397).[31]

It is difficult to overemphasize the importance of this work which Augustine, in his very latest period, regarded as a "solution of the problem" of faith and works "according to the truth of the divine Scriptures." Portalié says that this book—more precisely, Book I, Quaest. 2—constitutes the key to the Augustinian system, and agrees with Loofs that *Quaest. II ad Simplicianum* contains all the elements of the doctrine of grace which Augustine was later to defend against the Pelagians and Semipelagians.[32]

For our problem, it is important to notice the following changes in *De div. quaest.* arising from Augustine's new understanding of Rom. 9: 10-29:

1. The basis or motive of God's predestination is no longer understood to be election, that is, *temporal* election to glory based upon the just man's cooperation with grace.[33] Instead the election itself is based upon God's eternal decree of predestination.[34]

2. Contrary to the implication of thesis (13) of *De libero arbitrio*—see above—and to the general teaching of Augustine in his earlier writings, according to which man's response to God's offer of grace in prayer and faith was something dependent solely on man's free will,

---

[29] Cf. *Retract.*, I, 23, 3-4; *De praed. sanct.* (428/9), 3, 7; *De dono persev.* (428/9), 21, 52. V. Bourke, *The Essential Augustine* (New York, 1964), p. 77, overlooks these texts when he asserts flatly: "Augustine was never a Pelagian."

[30] *De praed sanct.*, 4, 8.

[31] *Ibid.*: "Nam si curassent, invenissent istam quaestionem secundum veritatem divinarum Scripturarum solutam in primo libro duorum, quos ad beatae memoriae Simplicianum scripsi episcopum mediolanensis Ecclesiae. . . ." Augustine then cites what he had already written about this work in his *Retractationes*, II, 1, 1.

[32] Portalié, DTC, 1, 2379; tr., pp. 182f. Cf. the helpful introduction, bibliography, and supplementary notes to *De div. quaest.* by V. Capanaga, *Obras de San Augustin*, vol. IX, pp. 3-58; 170-183. Portalié's call for a special study of *De div. quaest.* has been answered by T. Salgueiro, *La doctrine de Saint Augustine sur la grâce d'après le tráité à Simplicien* (Porto, Portugal, 1925). Cf. G. Nygren's faithful exposition of the work, pp. 41-48.

[33] *De div. quaest.*, I, 2, 6. Augustine distinguishes an eternal election corresponding to predestination and a temporal election based on the merits of the justified man. Cf. V. Capanaga, vol. IX, pp. 174f. and Salgueiro, pp. 44ff.; 151f.

[34] *De div. quaest.*, I, 2, 6.

Augustine now teaches that it is God who, in his mercy, inspires the very response of faith in the helpless sinner.[35] What was previously unclear for Augustine, if it was not in fact rejected, is now an essential part of his teaching on grace: the very good will by which we respond to grace is the work of God in us.[36]

3. God's action on the will is more precisely described when Augustine takes up the text: "Igitur non volentis neque currentis, sed miserentis est Dei" (Rom. 9:16).[37] Besides "inspiring" faith in the unbeliever, God *gives* us a good will.[38] Without his mercy and calling we simply do not will what is good.[39] God's calling is so productive of a good will that everyone who is called follows the call.[40] God is so able to move [41] the will that Augustine doesn't see how one can say that man's will can frustrate God's merciful calling.[42]

4. The hardening of Pharaoh (Rom. 9: 17f.; Ex. 9: 16) is interpreted as God's not willing to be merciful to him.[43] This hardening involves no injustice by God, whose justice is of a hidden nature not penetrable by man.[44] What is clear is that, because of Adam's fall, all men form a "massa peccati" and deserve the punishment imposed by divine justice. Therefore, there can be no injustice if God chooses to exact this punishment by hardening the heart or if he chooses to pardon the sin.[45] The hardening of the heart is in no way to be understood as if

---

[35] *Ibid.*, I, 2, 9: "miseretur inspirando fidem."

[36] *Ibid.*, I, 2, 12: Paul "ostendit etiam ipsam bonam voluntatem in nobis operante Deo fieri." This expresses Augustine's new awareness of Phil. 2: 13. In I, 2, 9 Augustine uses another biblical text which will appear again and again in the anti-Pelagian writings: I Cor. 4: 7: "What do you have that was not given to you?"

[37] See (2) in text above. Cf. *De div. quaest.*, I, 2, 21.

[38] *Ibid.*, I, 2, 12: "Nam si quaeramus utrum Dei donum sit voluntas bona, mirum si negare quisquam audeat."

[39] *Ibid.*

[40] *Ibid.*, I, 2, 13: ". . . vocatio ista ita est effectrix bonae voluntatis, ut omnis eam vocatus sequatur. . . ." Here we have the notion of God's infallibly efficacious movement of the will.

[41] Augustine speaks in this work of the will being "moved" (*ibid.*, I, 2, 12, 14, 21) and "excited" by God (*ibid.*, I, 2, 21).

[42] *Ibid.*, I, 2, 12: ". . . nescio quomodo dicatur, frustra Deum misereri, nisi nos velimus. Si enim Deus misereatur, etiam volumus; ad eamdem quippe misericordiam pertinet ut velimus." I, 2, 13: ". . . quoniam non potest effectus misericordiae Dei esse in hominis potestate, ut frustra ille misereatur, si homo nolit; quia si vellet etiam ipsorum misereri, posset ita vocare, quomodo illis aptum esset, ut et moverentur et intelligerentur et sequerentur." The phrase "quomodo illis aptum esset" seems to indicate Augustine's concern to retain free will as well as God's infallibly efficacious activity. Cf. Portalié, DTC, 1, 2385; tr. p. 192.

[43] *Ibid.*, I, 2, 15: ". . . obduratio Dei sit nolle misereri."

[44] *Ibid.*, I, 2, 16: ". . . aequitate occultissima et ab humanis sensibus remotissima iudicat." But cf. footnote 68 below.

[45] *Ibid.*: "Sunt igitur omnes homines . . . una quaedam massa peccati, suppli-

God forces anyone to sin. It means that he does not have mercy on them, not that he impels them to sin.[46]

5. Man's free will can do many things, but when it is sold to sin (Rom. 7: 14) what value does it have? Who can live justly and do good things unless he is justified by faith? Who can believe unless he is called?[47]

The following remarks of G. Nygren at the end of his fine exposition of *Lib. I Quaest. II ad Simplicianum* are worth citing in their entirety: "It is somewhat difficult to see how Augustine can still speak of man's merit and guilt when his thoughts about the operation of grace are so completely determined by the doctrine of predestination. We have reached that point in Augustine's theological development where predestination becomes a burning problem. The impression cannot be avoided that here there is a clear paradox. This paradoxical character is henceforth inseparably connected with Augustine's theology.

"Nevertheless the fact remains that Augustine operated in the same conceptual framework for the next thirty years without showing visible concern about this paradox. Nowhere do we find him deviating from the truth once he had found it. For the rest of his life he remains faithful to his solution of the problem in *Ad Simplicianum*. Even though the doctrine of predestination received increasing emphasis in his work because of external reasons, this did not signify anything basically new.

"A glance at Augustine's late work *On Grace and Free Will* will confirm this. . . ."[48]

Concerning this testimony of a careful scholar that Augustine never abandoned the affirmations of God's grace and man's free will that he made in 397 A.D., we wish to comment first of all on Nygren's remark that "it is not easy to see how Augustine can still speak of man's merit and guilt when his thoughts about grace are so dominated by the doctrine of predestination." From the very fact that Christianity is the revelation of divine, transcendent truth—truth that is conceptual as well as inter-personal—we must expect that it is not easy to understand such things as the relation between predestination and divine grace on the one hand, and created freedom on the other. The problem of the relation

---

cium debens divinae summaeque iustitiae, quod sive exigatur, sive donetur nulla est iniquitas."

[46] *Ibid.*: ". . . quia non eorum miseretur, non quia impellit ut peccent."

[47] *Ibid.*, I, 2, 21: "Liberum voluntatis arbitrium plurimum valet; imo vero est quidem, sed in venumdatis sub peccato, quid valet?" Here again we have a free will which is not free to do anything truly good, which lacks acquired freedom. This goodness and the acquired freedom which it presupposes come to man only by a *donum Spiritus Sancti*.

[48] Nygren, pp. 47f. Tr. ours.

between predestination and man's guilt and merits is really only an aspect of this more basic problem.

The concept of created freedom itself—even in its natural structure, apart from the problem of its interaction with grace—brings us face to face with the mysterious relationship between creation and its creator. Both exist, both are real, but in essentially different ways: the creator is the Infinite Being and Ground of Being, and all creation is finite being, totally dependent on the creator in every instant of its existence. How is it that creation genuinely exists, that it totally depends on the creator, and yet is not identified with the Being of the creator? This is also not easy to see! Neither is it any easier to see how God, who creates and conserves in existence all finite being and action, can create some beings who are not moved solely by natural necessity or animal spontaneity, but who so resemble the creator that they are not only able to make free choices in relatively unimportant matters, but are also given the opportunity and the command to make the ultimate fundamental decision for or against the creator himself: the decision of saving faith or of sinful unbelief.

Augustine was the first of a long line of Christian thinkers who have tried to throw some light on this mystery encountered both in the realm of nature and of grace. None of the so-called systems that have tried to throw light on this mystery have been able to penetrate it, to solve it, or to make it "easy to see how." This is true simply because we are confronted with a mystery rooted in the incomprehensibility and unsearchability of God himself (Rom. 11: 33). As K. Rahner puts it: ". . . In our case we must realize that the incomprehensible coexistence of God's absolute sovereignty with man's genuine freedom is only the most extreme instance of the incomprehensible coexistence of God's absolute being with the genuine being of creatures: the incomprehensibility *must* be permanent if God is to be God." [49] Rahner's suggestion: "Utterances of God concerning himself and man . . . that seem to contradict each other are best left side by side as an expression of the plenitude of reality which man can never master," [50] corresponds with the dialectical method which Schmaus proposes in his approach to this problem.[51]

There is, as our scriptural analysis has shown, an unembarrassed juxtaposition of statements in the Bible pertaining to predestination and

---

[49] K. Rahner-H. Vorgrimler, *Theological Dictionary* (New York, 1965), p. 197. Cf. Rahner, "Prädestination, III. Systematisch," LThK, 8, 669f.

[50] *Theol. Dictionary*, p. 197.

[51] Cf. Schmaus, I, p. 600; II/1, pp. 177f.; III/2, p. 355. This method is based on the view that all of reality has a dialectical structure. Cf. R. Guardini, *Der Gegensatz*, 2nd ed. (Würzburg, 1955).

grace on the one hand, and free will and human responsibility on the other. Although the biblical authors did not interest themselves in a speculative harmonization of these apparently irreconcilable truths, later Christian thinkers, for a variety of reasons—the necessity of clarification in the midst of controversy; the defense of the traditional doctrine against heretics; the attempt to develop a Christian theological synthesis for its own sake, etc.—found it necessary or worthwhile to attempt to do so. The hallmark of orthodoxy in these efforts was the upholding of *both* truths of the dialectical polarity, however one sought to relate the apparently opposed truths to one another. The dissolution of the dialectic by a denial of either man's free will or God's predestination and efficacious grace has always been rejected by the Church. Each of the different systems of grace permitted to coexist in the Church are "Catholic" because they uphold both man's free will and the truth that God's grace excites us to action by moving the will itself.[52] Each of the different systems throws some light on one or another aspect of the mystery, but the mystery remains: the two truths still remain in a dialectical juxtaposition, just as they do in the Scriptures.

Despite our admiration of Nygren's generally very faithful presentation of Augustine's thought on free will, we cannot agree with several of his contentions. Nygren holds that the predestination *problem*—as opposed to the Pauline predestination *doctrine*—first arose in the theology of Augustine (p. 294). Having raised the problem, says Nygren, Augustine became involved in internal contradictions as a result of his "theoretical-causal oriented conceptual framework" (p. 137). This conceptual framework, he maintains, involves a transformation of the biblical doctrine of predestination (p. 294) under the influence of Augustine's "religious-philosophical starting point" (*ibid.*) and is "completely different" from the "personal orientation of Paul's conceptual framework" (p. 137). If one applies causal thinking to the Pauline statements concerning grace and predestination, Nygren insists that an either-or situation results: "*either* everything is caused by the predestining omnipotence of God, thus making it impossible for us to speak of a self-sufficient (*selbständig*) human activity, *or* there is a self-sufficient human factor at work, thus depriving the concepts 'omnipotence' and 'predestination' of their absolute character, which leads unavoidably to synergism" (p. 127).

---

[52] Pope Paul V (1607) made it clear at the conclusion of the famous *Disputationes de auxiliis divinae gratiae* between the Jesuits and Dominicans, that both parties of the dispute upheld not only free will, but also the truth that "Deum, gratiae suae efficacia, nos ad agendum excitare, et facere de nolentibus volentes, et flectere et immutare hominum voluntates; discrepent autem explicandi modo. . . ." Citation from S. González, *Sacrae Theologiae Summa*, III (Madrid: BAC 62, 1956), p. 665, footnote 297.

We offer the following critical observations concerning Nygren's views:

1. Church Fathers prior to Augustine did concern themselves with the *problem* of predestination, that is, with the defense of the various elements of the biblical revelation: divine foreknowledge, election, predestination, grace and justice on the one hand, and man's free will on the other. (Cf. Schelkle, *Paulus*, pp. 336-353 and 436-440; Simonin, DTC 12, 2816-2832; J. Auer, "Prädestination II. Geschichtlich," LThK 8, 662ff., and our own presentation of the doctrine of the pre-Augustinian Fathers above.)

2. Paul himself cannot be said to have been unaware of the problem. True, Paul was concerned primarily with teaching the *doctrine* of predestination as an integral part of the Gospel of salvation, not with clarifying or seeking to resolve the *problem* of predestination. However, one aspect of the predestination problem is the upholding of the justice of God electing some and not others. Paul shows in Rom. 9, 14ff. that he is aware of this difficulty, but he does not give a direct answer to it (Dodd, *Romans*, p. 169). He "simply asserts [God's] justice without solving the difficulty," says Schelkle (*Paulus*, p. 340). But the early Fathers found it necessary to clarify this aspect of the predestination problem (Schelkle, *ibid.*; Simonin, DTC 12, 2816).

3. Nygren stresses Paul's "personally oriented conceptual framework" to such an extent that he overlooks the framework presupposed by the Pauline statements concerning God's all-embracing activity in both the realm of grace and of nature. Such texts as Phil. 2: 13; I Cor. 12:6; Acts 17: 24-28 and Col. 1: 15-17 speak of the universal creative and conserving work of God, an operation which extends even to our very will acts (Phil. 2: 13). The word "causality" does not appear in these texts, but in the light of them it would surely be one-sided to say: "Everything that is said in the Epistles is concerned with proclamation and response," with statements that have meaning only within the sphere of personal existence (pp. 127f.). It is significant that, in his reflections on predestination in his chapter on the Pauline background (pp. 125-138). Nygren cites neither I Cor. 12: 6 nor Phil. 2: 13. Augustine, on the contrary, in his anti-Pelagian writings, where his doctrine on the relationship between grace, predestination and free will is most fully developed, appeals constantly not to "theoretical-causal" arguments to support the doctrine that God governs even the wills of men, but to such biblical texts as Phil. 2: 13; Jn. 15: 5; Prov. 8: 35 (LXX) and Ezech. 36: 26f. Further, Augustine draws his radical doctrine that the good will itself is dependent on God from such a "personally oriented" text as I Cor. 4: 7: "What do you have that you have not received?" That personalist thinking does not exclude, but is complementary to, causal thinking, is brought out by L. Smits in his review of Nygren's book: *Revue d'Histoire Ecclésiastique*, 55 (1960) 954-959; cf. Seeberg, II, p. 421.

4. Just as Nygren constructs a false either-or between personal and causal thinking, so too he sets up an unreal opposition between a causal view of predestination and the free will of man. In the first place, Augustine tries to defend a concept "of a self-sufficient human activity" (p.

127) or "a self-sufficient free will" neither in Adam (p. 81) nor in fallen man (p. 82). Augustine would also be surprised to learn that: "The concept of merit presupposes by its very definition the self-sufficient function of the will" (*ibid.*). This is precisely the Pelagian understanding of merit against which Augustine fought! (Cf. *Contra duas. ep. Pelag.*, IV, 6, 12 and 13.) Having assumed such an un-Augustinian definition of merit, Nygren then finds it difficult to reconcile the self-sufficient function of the will that is presupposed by *his* definition of merit with Augustine's supposed teaching that man is not able to reject the gifts of God which are the foundations of merit. This difficulty also is created, not by Augustine, but by Nygren, when he translates Augustine's words from *De corr. et gr.*, 14, 43: "nullum hominum resistit arbitrium. . . ." with the words: no human will "*is able* to resist. . . ." —Later in Nygren's book (p. 269) we find a clarification: the "self-sufficiency of man's will," which Augustine supposedly teaches, is only a "relative" self-sufficiency, which "is not to be understood as a total independence, as self-sufficiency in an absolute sense." Even this must be qualified, however, for Nygren's concept of merit compels him to say (p. 289): "Although man is regarded as *relatively* self-sufficient from an ontological standpoint in relation to the creator, as a *causa secunda* in relation to the *causa prima,* the ethical-religious perspective of merit forces the idea of an *absolute* self-sufficiency to the fore." Nygren brings forward no texts from Augustine which teach such an absolute self-sufficiency. His interpretation of Augustine on this point clearly is the result of his own tendentious definition of merit, a definition that is not to be found in Augustine's writings, and one which Augustine would surely reject. For Augustine, the human will is unquestionably not God's will any more than man's being is God's being. They are distinct ontologically and ethically, but never—neither ontologically nor ethically —does the Catholic Augustine conceive of a created being or good action as being absolutely self-sufficient in relation to God, the source of all good and of all good use of the will. (*Retract.* I, 9, 6: "Quia omnia bona, sicut dictum est et magna, et media, et minima ex Deo sunt; sequitur ut ex Deo sit etiam bonus usus liberae voluntatis, quae virtus est, et in magnis numeratur bonis.") Man is absolutely self-sufficient only to "do" nothing, the nothing of the *causa deficiens* that is essential to sin (*De civ. Dei,* XII, 7 and 8).

Finally, because Nygren uses the concept of causality in a univocal sense, he feels that one is forced into an unacceptable either-or situation of predestination if understood causally. If we imagine that God's causality is essentially the same as human causality or any created causality, then Nygren is correct in saying that it is impossible to speak any longer of human activity. For if a man, through the power of his human causality, really, and in the strict sense, does *all* the work on a given project, then it follows that there is no other human activity working on the same project. But God inspires the variety of workings in us—"all in everyone" (I Cor. 12: 6), and yet there *is* human activity and working. He works in us both our willing and our working (Phil. 2: 13) and yet it is *we* who will and work. This is clearly a type of working, a causality that transcends all the causality and working of our experience. Augustine expresses God's transcendent movement, government or working of our wills in many ways. He says, for example: Deus "magis habet in potestate voluntates hominum quam ipsi suas," *De. corr. et gr.* 14, 45. On the transcendence of the divine action and the subordination of human activity according to Augustine see J. Saint-Martin, DTC 12, 2844f.

Undoubtedly the most explicit statement of Augustine's recognition of the biblical dialectic between the power of God's grace and the free acceptance of that grace by man—a free acceptance which is itself the work of grace, as we have already seen in the *De div. quaest.* (cf. above footnote 35f.)—is found in his late work, *De gratia et libero arbitrio* (426/7). Since this important work was written late in Augustine's career, thirty years after the books to Simplicianum and at least fifteen years after he had begun his long literary activity against Pelagianism, we should first note any significant developments during that period before we turn to *De gratia et libero arbitrio*.

3. *De peccatorum meritis et remissione et de baptismo parvulorum (412)*

With his work, *De peccatorum meritis et remissione et de baptismo parvulorum,* Augustine began his campaign against Pelagianism.[53] After combatting the errors of the Pelagians concerning original sin and the baptism of infants in Book I, Augustine corrects in Book II the false view which the Pelagians had of free will. The Pelagians, he says, attribute so much to man's free will that they deny that man needs divine help in order to keep from sinning. All he needs to have is free will.[54] As a consequence, says Augustine, we would not have to pray "lead us not into temptation," which is clearly contrary to the Christian religion.[55]

Against this view, Augustine lays down the following theses: (1) We do not need God's help in order to sin. (2) But we cannot act justly or fulfill completely the commandment of justice unless we are aided by God.[56] Here for the first time we find Augustine contending with a heresy concerning man's free will: too much is attributed to it, while the necessity of God's assistance is ignored. How does Augustine combat this error? Does he deny the existence of man's free will? Does he oppose the "tantum" by a "nihil"? On the contrary, although Augustine

---

[53] *Retract.,* II, 36: ". . . contra donatistas vehementer exercebamus et contra pelagianos iam exerceri coeperamus."

[54] *De pecc. mer. et rem.,* II, 2, 2.

[55] *Ibid.*

[56] *Ibid.,* II, 5, 5.

insists that it is impossible for the unaided will to do anything truly good, he explicitly states that (3) he does not want to defend grace in such a way that he seems to deny free will, nor does he want to assert free will in such a way that he would appear proud and ungrateful for the grace of God.[57] Then, invoking a biblical text that is of decisive importance for his doctrine of grace, a text which appears again and again in his anti-Pelagian writings, Augustine adds: unless we maintain that God gives us not only the (natural) *free* will by which we are able to perform naturally good acts, but also the *good* will which is able to perform truly good acts, how can we explain the words of Scripture: "What do you have that was not given to you?" (I Cor. 4: 7).[58]

4. *De spiritu et littera* (*412*)

The same dialectic of grace and free will is also retained by Augustine in his great anti-Pelagian work of the same year, *De spiritu et littera*, written to the same Marcellinus who received *De pecc. mer. et rem.* This work assumes special importance for us, since Luther informs us in the preface to volume I of the Wittenberg edition of his *Opera Latina* (1545) that he was pleased to find in *De spiritu et littera* a confirmation of his interpretation of "iustitia Dei" as the "justice by which we are justified." [59]

In this work Augustine first states his fundamental thesis on grace in a negative manner as follows:

1. Whoever thinks that he can attain justice or can make progress in tending toward justice without the help of God, through the power of the human will itself, is to be opposed most sharply and vigorously.[60] Immediately Augustine answers the subtle objection of the Pelagians who say, in effect: We don't deny that the aid of God is needed to achieve justice. In fact, we admit that God aids us not only by giving us free will

---

[57] *Ibid.*, II, 18, 28: ". . . ne sic defendamus gratiam, ut liberum arbitrium auferre videamur; rursus, ne liberum sic asseramus arbitrium, ut superba impietate ingrati Dei gratiae iudicemur."

[58] *Ibid.*, II, 18, 30. Cf. above footnote 36. Note that naturally good acts are those which can be used badly, that is, as we have seen in our excursus on ". . . the Good Works of Unbelievers," they can be good according to their "officium," but be bad because of a bad or inadequate "finis."

[59] WA 54, 186, 16. Luther does not say that he found *all* of his doctrine in this work of Augustine. On the contrary, he says Augustine still speaks "imperfecte" on this matter, and is unclear on the question "de imputatione."

[60] *De spir. et litt.*, 2, 4: "Sed illis acerrime ac vehementissime resistendum est, qui putant sine adiutorio Dei per se ipsam vim voluntatis humanae vel iustitiam posse perficere, vel ad eam tenendo proficere. . . ." *De spiritu et littera* had an important influence on Luther's *Lectures on Romans* (1515/16). So highly did Luther regard this book that he himself published it in 1518.

by which we can merit eternal life, but also by revealing to us the law, so that we know what we should avoid and what we should seek.[61]

2. Against this view, which limits the concept of grace to the natural gift of free will and the revealed gift of knowledge of the law, Augustine insists that there must be a divine assistance above and beyond free will and the revealed doctrine of how man ought to live. This grace is nothing less than the Holy Spirit himself, who inspires man to turn to the creator and to seek true blessedness,[62] and through whom God pours charity into the hearts of those whom he has foreseen, predestined, called and justified.[63]

3. Free will can do nothing but sin if it does not know the path of truth. But even when the right course of action is made known, there is no right living unless this way of truth is loved. For this purpose the charity of God is poured forth into our hearts—not by the free will which originates within us, but by the Holy Spirit who has been given to us.[64]

4. When Paul says, "The letter kills, but the spirit gives life" (2 Cor. 3: 6), he does not mean that a general prohibition as "Thou shalt not covet" is to be taken figuratively, or that it is evil. On the contrary, this command is most clear and most salutary: whoever fulfills it will have no sin whatever. In this sense the law is good and praiseworthy. But when the Holy Spirit does not help by inspiring good desires in us in place of evil ones, that is, by pouring forth charity into our hearts, then

---

[61] *De spir. et litt.*, 2, 4: "Sed aiunt, ideo ista sine ope divina non fieri, quia et hominem Deus creavit cum libero voluntatis arbitrio, et dando praecepta ipse docet quemadmodum homini sit vivendum. . . ." Cf. *De gest. Pel.* (417), 10, 22; *De gr. Chr. et de pecc. orig.* (418), I, 2, 2-3, 3. Ferguson, pp. 113f., seems unaware that Pelagius uses the term "grace" equivocally. Cf. Souter, I, pp. 69f.

[62] *De spir. et litt.*, 3, 5: "Nos autem dicimus humanam voluntatem sic divinitus adiuvari ad faciendam iustitiam, ut praeter quod creatus est homo cum libero arbitrio voluntatis, praeterque doctrinam qua ei praecipitur quemadmodum vivere debeat, accipiat Spiritum Sanctum, quo fiat in animo eius delectatio dilectioque summi illius atque incommutabilis boni quod Deus est. . . ."

[63] *Ibid.*, 3, 5 and 5, 7.

[64] *Ibid.*, 3, 5: "Nam neque liberum arbitrium quidquam nisi ad peccandum valet, si lateat veritatis via; et cum id quod agendum et quo nitendum est coeperit non latere, nisi etiam delectet et ametur, non agitur, non suscipitur, non bene vivitur. Ut autem diligatur, charitas Dei diffunditur in cordibus nostris, non per arbitrium liberum quod surgit ex nobis, sed per Spiritum Sanctum qui datus est nobis." As we have already seen in the excursus, it would be false to take this passage to mean that Augustine denies any possibility of naturally good acts when the charity of God is absent from our hearts. Later in the same work Augustine explicitly tells us that such acts are possible—and are even to be expected—in unbelievers, and are to some extent praiseworthy, even though they are not works of true justice. *Ibid.*, 27, 47. 48; 28, 48.

the law, good in itself, increases evil desires in us by its prohibitions.[65] For this reason we say that the letter of the law, which teaches us not to sin, kills unless the vivifying Spirit is present. The purpose of the law may be stated more positively by saying that the law has been given that grace might be sought for; and grace has been given that the law might be fulfilled.[66]

The necessity of the Holy Spirit and charity for all right action in no way excludes the necessity of the action of the free will. For Augustine there is no either-or in this matter, but a dialectic between grace (or the Spirit) *and* free will. Thus Augustine can say:

5. Without free will there can be neither good nor bad living.[67]

6. We shall be judged according as we have used our free will for good or for evil.[68]

7. Grace does not make free will void, but establishes it.[69]

8. There is no reason for boasting about free will before we are liberated from sin, nor even after we are liberated. Before liberation we were slaves of sin. After liberation, why should we act as if the liberation took place by our own efforts and why should we glory as if we have not *received* the liberation from God? [70]

9. Rom. 3: 20-24 means that we are not justified by the law nor by our own will, but freely by his grace. But this does not mean that we are justified *without* our free will.[71]

---

[65] *Ibid.*, 3, 6.

[66] *Ibid.*, 6, 8: ". . . legis littera quae docet non esse peccandum, si spiritus vivificans desit, occidit." *Ibid.*, 19, 34: "Lex ergo data est, ut gratia quaereretur; gratia data est, ut lex impleretur." Augustine speaks more fully of the pedagogical function of the law in *De perf. iust.* (415) 5, 11. On this point see the study of J. Plagnieux, "Le Chrétien en face de la loi d'après le De Spiritu et Littera de saint Augustin," in: *Theologie in Geschichte und Gegenwart: Michael Schmaus zum 60. Geburtstag* (München, 1957), pp. 725-754. In *Contra duas epist. Pelag.* (420), III, 7, 20—III, 8, 23 Augustine's doctrine of the law and the difference between the "iustitia legis" (*hominis; non vera*) and "iustitia fidei" (*Dei; vera*) is presented more fully.

[67] *Ibid.*, 5, 7: ". . . homini Deus dedit liberum arbitrium, sine quo nec male nec bene vivitur."

[68] *Ibid.*, 33, 58: "Vult autem Deus omnes homines salvos fieri, et in agnitionem veritatis venire: non sic tamen, ut eis adimat liberum arbitrium, quo vel bene vel male utentes iustissime iudicentur."

[69] *Ibid.*, 30, 52: "Liberum ergo arbitrium evacuamus per gratiam? Absit; sed magis liberum arbitrium statuimus. Sicut enim lex per fidem, sic liberum arbitrium per gratiam non evacuatur, sed statuitur. Neque enim lex impletur nisi libero arbitrio . . . ita liberum arbitrium non evacuatur per gratiam, sed statuitur, quia gratia sanat voluntatem, qua iustitia libere diligatur."

[70] *Ibid.* Again the distinction is made between free will and freedom. It is possible to have the former without the latter.

[71] *Ibid.*, 9, 15. Here Augustine speaks simply of *voluntas,* not of *liberum arbi-*

10. The same is true of faith. Even though the very will to believe is given by God to man, the consent to, or dissent from, God's call to faith is an act of one's own will.[72]

In *De civitate Dei* (413-426), as we have already noted,[73] Augustine insists upon the dialectic of the divine prescience and of man's free will against the either-or thinking of Cicero.[74]

5. *De natura et gratia* (*415*)

In *De natura et gratia,* Augustine again defends the necessity of grace against the Pelagian exaltation of man's natural powers. He does not argue that these powers have been totally destroyed by original sin, but that they are weakened and infirm:

---

trium. But our view that these terms are used interchangeably by Augustine is supported by *ibid.,* 30, 52 where, in substantially the same context, Augustine uses the term *liberum arbitrium.*

[72] *Ibid.,* 34, 60: ". . . profecto et ipsum velle credere Deus operatur in homine, et in omnibus misericordia eius praevenit nos; consentire autem vocationi Dei, vel ab ea dissentire, sicut dixi, propriae voluntatis est." *Ibid.,* 35, 63, Augustine emphasizes that faith is both the work of God and the work of man. In Lk. 17: 6, Jesus speaks of *your* faith, says Augustine: "Certe, *vobis,* dixit; non: 'Mihi aut Patri'. . . ." And yet, adds Augustine, the most important thing to remember, the truth that prevents us from glorying in ourselves, is that man has this faith only because God gives it to him and "works" it in him: "et tamen hoc nullo modo facit homo, nisi illo donante et operante." *Ibid.,* 34, 60, he shows again that I Cor. 4: 7 applies even to our consent to faith, since *what* we have and *what* we receive in faith comes from God.

[73] Cf. p. 67, footnote 19 above; Ch. 3, footnote 13.

[74] *De civ. Dei,* V, 10, 2: "Quocirca nullo modo cogimur, aut retenta praescientia Dei tollere voluntatis arbitrium, aut retendo voluntatis arbitrio Deum (quod nefas est) negare praescium futurorum; sed utrumque amplectimur, utrumque fideliter et veraciter confitemur." As Christians, says Augustine, we profess God's foreknowledge as a part of our faith; as philosophers, we profess free will as a condition of responsible living. No man sins unless he chooses to sin, and even this choice is foreseen by God. Like the later Scholastics, Augustine answers the classic objection against either God's foreknowledge or man's free will by distinguishing two types of necessity: one which does not take away free will and which is actually involved in the free choice itself, and the other which excludes free will. Unlike the Scholastics, he does not call them *necessitas absoluta* (*consequentis*) and *conditionalis* (*consequentiae*)—but his meaning is the same. When Boethius (480-524/5) takes up the argument of Cicero, *De consolatione philosophiae,* V, prosa 6: PL 63, 861, he makes basically the same distinction of the "duae necessitates": "Duae sunt etenim necessitates; simplex una, veluti quod necesse est omnes esse mortales; altera conditionis, ut si aliquem ambulare necesse est. Quod enim quisque novit, id esse aliter ac notum est, nequit. Sed haec conditio minime secum illam simplicem [necessitatem] secum trahit. Hanc enim necessitatem non propria facit natura, sed conditionis adiectio. . . . (S)i quid Providentia praesens videt, id esse necesse est, tametsi nullam naturae habeat necessitatem. Atqui Deus ea futura, quae ex arbitrii libertate proveniunt, praesentia contuetur. Haec igitur, ad intuitum relata divinum, necessaria fiunt per condi-

1. The nature of man after Adam's fall requires a doctor, because it is not healthy.[75] As he explains in the *Retractationes,* he sought to defend grace not *against* nature, but as the liberator of nature.[76]

2. Thus, even though he recalls the biblical texts which teach that salvation is impossible without God's merciful grace, Augustine assures his readers that he is not taking away man's free will when he preaches grace. He simply wishes to destroy any pride that would arise from the erroneous belief that the power of one's own will is sufficient for achieving justice.[77]

3. The law is exceedingly good if it is used legitimately. For we firmly believe that the good and just God cannot command the impossible. We learn from the commandments, then, what we are to do in easy matters and what we should ask for in difficult matters.[78]

Augustine refuses to admit to Pelagius that ecclesiastical writers do not support his views. We shall cite what Augustine says of Jerome in order to show that Augustine did not find the opposition between himself and Jerome that later writers have claimed to find. Pelagius had cited Jerome's words from his book against Jovinian: "God created us with free will. We are drawn neither to virtue nor vice by necessity, for where necessity is present there can be no reward." [79] Augustine says this is undeniable: "Who believes that human nature was created in any other way? But in acting rightly there is no bond of necessity, because the freedom of charity is present." [80] What is implied in these statements is made explicit in the next chapter: as a result of the fall from the original state of creation, from the vices of nature—not from nature as such—there is a certain necessity of sinning. Man should therefore pray, as does the Psalmist, to be delivered from this necessity. Through the aid of grace the evil necessity will be removed and full liberty restored.[81]

---

tionem divinae notionis: per se vero considerata, ab absoluta naturae suae libertate non desinunt."

[75] *De nat. et gr.,* 3, 3: ". . . natura . . . hominis . . . iam medico indiget, quia sana non est." Augustine speaks more strongly (*ibid.,* 43, 50) when, in the language of Lk. 10: 30-34, he says fallen man is like a "semivivum" whom the robbers have left by the wayside. Human nature is said to be "vitiata": *ibid.,* 64, 76.

[76] *Retract.,* II, 42: "Liberum ergo quo huic respondi defendens gratiam, non contra naturam, sed per quam natura liberatur et regitur."

[77] *De nat. et gr.,* 32, 36: "Non enim, cum ista commemoramus, arbitrium voluntatis tollimus, sed Dei gratiam praedicamus."

[78] *Ibid.,* 69, 83. Cf. *ibid.,* 43, 50; "non igitur Deus impossibilia iubet; sed iubendo admonet, et facere quod possis, et petere quod non possis."

[79] *Contra Iovinianum,* 2, 3.

[80] *De nat. et gr.,* 65, 78.

[81] *Ibid.,* 66, 79.

Here we have a fine illustration of the distinction Augustine makes between freedom (*libertas*) and free will (*liberum arbitrium*).[82] At the same time, it is a good illustration of how confusing Augustine's teaching about free will must have been to some of his readers. Is Augustine saying that free will is something that is given to man at creation, but that it was lost as a result of the fall? Does he mean that free will is restored again only when charity is poured forth into our hearts? All that we have seen in Augustine up until now, including statements found in this very book, incline us to say "no" to both of these questions. True, he doesn't say free will is restored by grace, but that "full liberty" is restored.[83] Yet this language, not found in the writings of his contemporaries, did in fact raise doubts in the minds of his Catholic followers as to whether Augustine really held to the existence of free will after the fall.

6. *De gestis Pelagii* (417) and *De gratia Christi* (418)

There seems to be no ambiguity about Augustine's *thought* at this time, for in the *De gestis Pelagii,* he clearly endorses the condemnation by the Synod of Diospolis (415) of the proposition: "There is no free will if the help of God is necessary; for everyone finds in his own will the power to do or not do something." [84]

Nevertheless, Augustine shows his awareness of the difficulty of retaining the dialectic of grace and free will when he writes in *De gratia Christi et de peccato originali* (418):

Because in this question concerning free will and the grace of God it is so difficult to make the correct distinctions, with the result that, when free will is defended the grace of God seems to be denied, and when God's grace is affirmed free will is thought to be eliminated—because of this difficulty, Pelagius is able to hide himself in the shadows of this

---

[82] According to Clark, p. 45, footnote 1, Augustine uses "free choice" (*liberum arbitrium*) to indicate the free will found in all men and "freedom" or "liberty" (*libertas*) as a synonym for the good will "which is the fruit of the grace of God and the effort of man." This is basically the view of Gilson, pp. 212ff. Gilson's rules for interpreting the Augustinian texts concerning liberty are most helpful, yet one must agree with Küng, tr., p. 182 when he says: "It is possible that Gilson has exaggerated the contrast between *liberum arbitrium* and *libertas* and that his interpretation does not correspond with all the texts. . . . But it probably has to be conceded that we can find such a fundamental distinction in Augustine."

[83] Gilson would say, and we agree with him, that Augustine is to be understood here as saying that man's liberty for doing good is lost by original sin— but not his free will. There is a "certain necessity of sinning" not because the will is necessitated by an internal necessity, but because man is incapable of "recte faciendi" apart from the grace of God which liberates him from his bondage to sin. This would be "plena libertas."

[84] *De gest. Pel.,* 35, 65.

obscure matter in such a way that he can claim to agree with the things
we have quoted from Saint Ambrose. . . .[85]

7. *Contra duas Epistolas Pelagianorum* (420)

A further and lengthier clarification of Augustine's doctrine of freedom, free will and grace is found in Book I of the *Contra duas epistolas
Pelagianorum,* where Augustine answers the charge of Julian of Eclanum [86] that the Catholic teaching on free will was the same as that
of the Manichees:

> By defending free will, however, they [the Pelagians] make the mistake
> of confiding more in it for achieving justice than in the help of the Lord.
> But who among us would say that free will was lost to the human race
> because of the sin of the first man? Freedom, certainly, was lost to the
> human race by sin—the freedom that existed in paradise, of having
> perfect justice with immortality. For this reason human nature needs
> divine grace, for as the Lord has said: "If the Son has freed you, then
> you shall be truly free" (Jn. 8: 36), free that is, to live rightly and
> justly. For free will still is sufficiently present in sinners that through it
> they might sin, especially all those who sin with delight and love of sin.
> . . . Thus they are not free from justice except through free will, but they
> become free from sin only by the grace of the Savior (Rom. 6: 20-22).
> He says that they are free from justice, not freed. But he doesn't say
> they are free from sin, lest they attribute this to themselves, but he most
> carefully chose to say "freed" from sin, referring to the statement of the
> Lord: "If the Son has freed you, then you shall be truly free." Since the
> sons of men, therefore, do not live rightly unless they are made sons of
> God, why is it that they wish to attribute the power of living uprightly to
> free will if this power is only given through the grace of God through
> Jesus Christ our Lord? [87]

Immediately following this argument, Augustine attacks the Pelagian
view that the grace of justification is merited by the free will, unaided by
grace. He calls this a destruction of grace and, basing his argument on
Phil. 1: 28f., Eph. 6: 23 and Jn. 6: 44, 64ff., he concludes that faith
itself, through which one is drawn to the Father and made a son of God,

---

[85] *De gr. Christi et pecc. orig.,* I, 47, 52. Instead of considering the condemnation of the Pelagians by the Council of Carthage (418) at this point, we shall
examine them together with other early magisterial pronouncements in the next
chapter.

[86] Julian was one of eighteen Italian bishops who refused to subscribe to the
excommunication of Pelagius and Caelestius by Pope Zosimus subsequent to the
Council of Carthage. Although some of the bishops eventually submitted, Julian
became the chief representative of Pelagianism. Cf. Ferguson, pp. 111ff.; F.
Refoulé, "Julien d'Éclane, théologien et philosophe," *Recherches de science religieuse,* 52 (1964), pp. 42-84 and 233-247; P. Brown, *Augustine,* pp. 381-397.

[87] *Contra duas epist. pelag.,* I, 2, 5. Cf. II, 5, 9.

is a gift. This gift, he says, must be from God. It cannot come from man's free will "because [the free will] is not free for good which the Liberator has not yet set free." "No one therefore can have a just will unless he has received—without any preceding merits—true, that is, gratuitous grace from above." [88]

It is not our purpose to present here a full exposition of the Augustinian doctrine of merit. For this, one can consult J. Rivière, "Mérite," DTC, 10, 642-651. We simply wish to correct a widely held misconception about Augustine's teaching on merit and to make a specific criticism of G. Nygren's critique of Augustine on this point. It is well-known that Augustine vigorously opposed the Pelagian doctrine of merits preceding grace. The passage we have just cited from Book I of the Contra duas. epist. Pelag. is an example of this opposition as is Augustine's approval of the condemnation of the following proposition by the Synod of Diospolis: "Quod Dei gratia secundum merita nostra detur; et propterea ipsa gratia in hominis sit posita voluntate, sive dignus fiat, sive indignus" (De gest. Pel. 35, 65. Cf. ibid., 18, 42).

Authors such as Packer and Johnston, however, op. cit., p. 49, who think that "the Augustinian position . . . denies all merit," betray an inadequate understanding of Augustine. G. Nygren, op. cit., p. 66 correctly describes Augustine's thought on merit when he writes: "The biblical witness thus shows that God's grace is not given according to our merits. It is true that we begin to gain merit once grace has been given. However, we merit only because of grace. . . . For this reason a man who begins to merit should not attribute this to himself, but to God." Nygren rejects the Augustinian position, however, claiming that it involves a causal view of the action of grace on free will that is foreign to the Pauline doctrine of reward. Such causal thinking, says Nygren, if drawn to its logical conclusion, would lead to the denial of free will. This would amount to a contradiction in Augustine's work which the great Church Father did not perceive. "Grace, as Augustine presents it here," contends Nygren (p. 71), "seems to completely exclude any concept of the free will as an independent (selbständig) causal factor, thereby taking away the foundation of any doctrine of merit."

Nygren's criticism is unjustified, we believe, because Augustine nowhere in his writings seeks to defend a concept of the free will as an "independent causal factor." It is not clear which Augustinian concept is supposed to correspond with "selbständig," the adjective which Nygren repeatedly uses to describe Augustine's idea of the will (Cf. pp. 73, 81, 82, 85). In the light of what we have urged above concerning the dialectic between creator and creature, grace and nature (free will), one can never speak of a "selbständige" creature or of a "selbständige" free will in relation to the creator, to his divine concursus or to his grace.

And the same is true of the relation between grace, free will and merit. The free will can never merit in any "selbständig" way. Nygren's view that "the concept of merit presupposes as a principle that the

[88] Ibid., I, 3, 6f.

human will be regarded as an independent causal factor" (p. 73) finds no counterpart in the thought of Augustine. According to Augustine, the Holy Spirit "breathes where he wills, not following merits, but causing the merits themselves": *De pecc. orig.* II, 24, 28. Neither Augustine nor any later writer in the Church has claimed to have "solved" the problem of the mysterious relationship between God's unceasing action on the will and man's freedom, and between God's action through grace and the free action of man which is involved in merit. Augustine and the later theologians of the Church have sought to describe these actions more completely and to defend the reality of *both* of them against various writers who have erroneously sought to destroy the dialectical tension. But it would be wrong to criticize Augustine for creating the problem. The elements of this problem are already present in the Scriptures, even though the problem was not the object of theological reflection by the biblical authors.

It would be equally wrong to criticize Augustine for failing to "solve" an insoluble problem, insoluble because it involves a mystery whose inner truth and rationale are withheld from us as long as we walk by faith and not by sight. The mystery consists precisely in our inability to understand the transcendent activity (causality) of God. This activity is infinitely powerful, all-embracing and all-penetrating. It infinitely surpasses any other created activity or causality of which we have knowledge. It is a dynamism which is able to work in us both our willing and our working, according to God's good pleasure, and yet, it is able to work this in us so that we do it freely!

EXCURSUS: *The Meaning of "Servum Arbitrium" in Augustine*

As Augustine's thought developed in his controversy with the Pelagians, we see him emphasizing more and more the lack of true freedom in sinners. The more the Pelagians extolled the power of the free will in the practice of asceticism and Christian morality, the more Augustine insisted that man was not truly free, that he had lost his true freedom as a result of original sin and was actually a slave of sin. Man could only be made truly free, Augustine argued, by the grace of God which comes to man totally gratuitously, not as the result of any merits of the free will preceding grace.

Apparently unable to grasp the fact that Augustine was talking about a different kind of freedom than free will, the Pelagians accused Augustine of denying free will. Augustine explicitly denied this charge many times and tried to clarify his meaning in such passages as we have cited above from *Contra duas epist. Pel.* (cf. above footnote 87): "But who among us would say that free will was lost to the human race because of the sin of the first man?" And in the same work, he expresses his thought in a paradoxical but clear manner when he speaks of the free will being captive: "Et liberum arbitrium captivatum nonnisi ad peccatum valet: ad iustitiam vero, nisi divinitos liberatum adiutumque, non valet": (III, 8, 24). Here it is perfectly clear that Augustine conceives of at least two types of freedom: free will (natural freedom) and liberated free will (acquired freedom). The captive free will is able only to sin. (Here we must not forget what we have noted in the excursus on naturally good acts of unbelievers. Because Baius ignored the total Augustinian context, the Church judged it necessary to condemn his use of Augustine's words [DS 1927], since he used them in an un-Augustinian sense.) The captive free will, (*liberum arbitrium captivatum*), however, becomes the liberated free will (*liberum arbitrium liberatum*) only when it is divinely aided and liberated. It alone can do things which are truly just.

Despite his explicit denial that man lost his *liberum arbitrium* after Adam's fall, Augustine continued, in the heat of his struggle against the Pelagians, to use even more radical language than he had previously used to indicate the powerlessness of the *liberum arbitrium* to will that which is truly good and just. In his work *Contra Iulianum* of 421 we find him for the first, and as far as we have been able to determine, the only time saying that the *liberum arbitrium* is so powerless for willing that which is truly good that it is not simply a *liberum arbitrium captivatum,* as he had said in *Contra duas epist. Pelag.,* but a *servum arbitrium:* ". . . utinam dei dono, et non libero, vel potius servo proprie voluntatis arbitrio": (*Contra Iul.,* 2, 8, 23). (Cf. above footnote 2.) And in his *Enchiridion ad Laurentium, De fide, Spe et Charitate,* written in the same year, Augustine speaks even more radically when he says that *liberum arbitrium* itself is lost through sin! ". . . Nam libero arbitrio male utens homo, et se perdidit et ipsum; . . . cum libero peccaretur arbitrio, victore peccato amissum est liberum arbitrium": (*Ench.,* 30, 9).

Clearly it is very easy to misrepresent Augustine's meaning if one considers certain texts, such as the two we have just cited, in isolation from the Augustinian context. Concerning the citation from the *Enchiridion* we are fortunately able to clarify its meaning from the immediate context, which shows that Augustine really means that *libertas* (in the sense of the freedom, before the Fall, to live justly), not *liberum arbitrium* (in the sense of the power to choose), is lost through sin. Augustine cites II Peter 2:19b to show that a man is a slave of sin if he commits sin. Then he returns to his teaching of *Contra duas epist. Pelag.,* 1, 2, 5 (cf. above footnote 87) when he writes: ". . . qualis, quaeso, potest servi addicti esse libertas, nisi quando eum peccare delectat? Liberaliter enim servit, qui sui domini voluntatem libenter facit. Ac per hoc ad peccandum liber est, qui peccati servus est. Unde ad iuste faciendum liber non erit, nisi a peccato liberatus esse iustititiae coeperit servus" (*Ench.,* 30, 9). For the same interpretation see K. Heim, *Das Wesen der Gnade und ihre Verhältnis zu den natürlichen Funktionen des Menschen bei Alexander Halesius* (Leipzig, 1907), p. 8.

From the texts examined in this excursus, considered in the light of the whole Augustinian context that we have already studied, we may draw the following conclusions:

1. *Servum arbitrium,* for Augustine, in no way implies a loss of the natural freedom to choose between alternatives.

2. It means that a sinner cannot choose what is truly good or just.

3. The *servum arbitrium* has efficacy only for sinning, if we take sin here to mean any action not animated by faith, charity and the Holy Spirit. The *servum arbitrium* of the sinful man is capable of performing naturally good acts which, however, are totally without value for salvation and for achieving true freedom and justice. This we have shown in the excursus on the meaning of sin in St. Augustine.

4. *Servum arbitrium* cannot mean the exclusion of natural freedom (*liberum arbitrium*), since it signifies man's slavery to sin. Sin in the proper, personal sense, and slavery to sin are, for Augustine, unthinkable unless man sins freely or unless he freely and willingly serves sin (and Satan, the prince and author of sin): *De nup. et concup.*, I, 23, 26.

5. The meaning of Augustine's phrase, *"servum arbitrium"* is best expressed by his other phrase, *"liberum arbitrium captivatum."* Here the paradox of the enslavement to sin of the naturally free man finds full expression without, however, giving the mistaken impression that man's slavery to sin involves a loss of the natural freedom of the will.

We are therefore in complete agreement with R. Seeberg, *Lehrbuch der Dogmengeschichte,* II, pp. 512ff., when he writes:

"Even though the race descending from Adam has become sinful or a *massa perditionis,* even though a *misera necessitas peccandi* hangs over the human race, despite all of this one can still speak of a *liberum arbitrium* even in the sinner, not, however, in the sense of the Pelagian *possibilitas utriusque partis,* since a man cannot be both a good tree and a bad tree at the same time (*gr. Christi,* 18, 19). . . . The *libertas* of Paradise is lost: *habere plenam cum iustitia immortalitatem,* for this freedom (*liberi ad bene iusteque vivere*) is only made possible by the working of grace, which is precisely what the sinner lacks. There remains to him, however, the freedom to sin with his own will. . . .

"The necessity [of sinning] is . . . in no way to be understood as a physical or metaphysical determinism. On the contrary, Augustine explicitly recognizes that even the sinner has psychological freedom. . . . [The will] can choose even under the drives of concupiscence, it can occasionally overcome these drives, it can avoid grave sins as well as exercise the natural virtues of prudence, fortitude, etc. . . . In denying the freedom of the sinful will Augustine does not mean, as the Pelagians thought, that man's natural freedom is extinguished. . . . He means that the sinner is a captive of his own self-determination and cannot escape from it. . . ."

It is therefore incorrect when D. Löfgren, *Die Theologie der Schöpfung bei Luther,* p. 116, says of Augustine's position: Through the fall "Adam lost both his *liberum arbitrium* as well as the help of grace. . . . After the fall, therefore, Adam was forced to sin." Cf. Vorster, pp. 223f. Seeberg, II, p. 535, continues: "One thing is certain: Augustine taught that the will of the sinner before his conversion is indeed free to choose things which lay within the sphere of his natural thinking and willing, but that he is incapable or unfree to emerge from this sphere. To do this he must be liberated by grace."

A final word from Seeberg, II, p. 536: "If we look at man's life as a whole, then we can say that from the point of view of Augustine, man is always free in regard to his individual will acts, but these are conditioned by the total direction of his will. Thus the sinner is free, but the area in which his freedom operates is one dominated by evil. The justified man is free, but the area in which his freedom operates is one which is directed toward God. . . ."

If Augustine seems to speak of the irresistibility of grace (Seeberg, II, p. 534 and Loofs, p. 304 footnote 9 recognize that this expression is not found in Augustine), this is likewise not to be taken as a denial of free will. For, as Seeberg, II, p. 538f., puts it: ". . . even the divinely effected transition into this new life-condition (justice) takes place with free will in that the irresistible grace brings about the very turning of ourselves and our wills to God. . . . The good will is indeed caused or willed by God, but God wills it in such a way that the will itself wills. These are Augustine's thoughts. The insight that the good will exists only insofar as it is willed by God was just as self-evident to him . . . as the psychological fact that the will exists only in the form of free self-determination."

For further analysis of the controversial Augustinian phrases from *De Correptione et gratia* (426-7)—"humanas voluntates non posse resistere" (14, 45) and "divina gratia indeclinabiliter et insuperabiliter" (12, 38)—see Portalié, *DTC*, I, 2406; G. de Broglie, "Le 'De Correptione et Gratia'," *Augustinus Magister*, III, pp. 317-337; Clark, *op. cit.*, pp. 98-115.

8. *De gratia et libero arbitrio* (426/7)

Not only did Augustine have to correct Pelagian misunderstandings of his doctrine of *servum arbitrium* and *liberum arbitrium captivatum*, but he also had to explain his meaning to Catholics, who feared that his emphasis on grace excluded man's free will. We have already seen how easily Augustine's thought can be misunderstood not only because of his strong insistence on the powerlessness of the will of the sinner to do anything truly good, but also because of his lack of strict and consistent terminology. His book, *De gratia et libero arbitrio*, written in 426-427, only three years before his death, was Augustine's effort to set the record straight once and for all as to the meaning of his doctrine on the necessity of liberating grace and the powerlessness of fallen man's will.

De gratia et libero arbitrio is addressed to the abbot Valentinus and his monks of Hadrumetum in North Africa.[89] These monks, as Augustine notes in the first chapter, had been troubled by dissension on the question of the relation between grace and free will, undoubtedly as a result of reading the anti-Pelagian writings of Augustine. In the opening

---

[89] For the genesis of this work see Portalié, DTC, I, 2298f.; tr. p. 58 and Nygren, p. 49, footnote 101. Nygren discusses *De gr. et lib. arb.*, pp. 49-69.

lines of the book, Augustine states his purpose very clearly and gives us
an indication that an either-or solution of the question is erroneous:

Because of those who preach and defend man's free will to such an
extent that they dare to deny and seek to set aside the grace of God by
which we are called to him and liberated from our evil merits, and
through which we acquire the good merits that enable us to attain eternal life, we have already written many things as the Lord has seen fit to
allow us. But because there are some persons who defend grace to such
an extent that they deny man's free will or who think that, when grace is
defended, free will is denied, I have decided to write something to you,
brother Valentinus . . .[90]

In the introductory chapter Augustine admits to the monks that the
question about which they had consulted him is indeed obscure.[91] He
then offers a beautiful example of prayerful humility to all Christian
theologians when he tells the monks that they should thank God for
whatever understanding they already have about the question and
should pray to God that they might understand further.[92]
Augustine begins to unfold his doctrine with the unhesitating affirmation that God "has revealed to us through his holy Scriptures that there
is free will in man." [93] This can be seen first of all, he says, from the
divine precepts: How could they have any value for man unless he had
free will by which he could follow the precepts and thus attain the
promised rewards? [94] Further, man has to have free will if he is to be
alone responsible for his sins. Augustine cites Sir. 15: 11-18 [95]—as
theologians before and after him have done—to show that man, not
God is the author of sin, for God has left man "in the hands of his own
counsel." "See how clearly free will is taught here," exclaims Augustine.[96]
Augustine returns to the argument for free will based on God's law:
How does God command if there is no free will? [97] A command is

---

[90] *De gr. et lib. arb.* 1, 1: "Sed quoniam sunt quidam, qui sic gratiam Dei
defundunt, ut negent hominis liberum arbitrium; aut quando gratia defenditur,
negari existiment liberum arbitrium; hinc aliquid scribere ad vestram charitatem,
Valentine frater . . . curavi."

[91] *Ibid.:* "ne vos perturbet . . . huius quaestionis obscuritas. . . ."

[92] *Ibid.*

[93] *Ibid.*, 2, 2: "Revelavit autem nobis per Scripturas suas sanctas, esse in
homine liberum voluntatis arbitrium."

[94] *Ibid.:* ". . . ipsa divina praecepta homini non prodessent, nisi haberet liberum
voluntatis arbitrium, quo ea faciens ad promissa praemia perveniret."

[95] He also uses Jas. 1: 13ff and Prov. 19: 3 in support of this argument.

[96] *Ibid.*, 2, 3: "Ecce apertissime videmus expressum liberum humanae voluntatis
arbitrium."

[97] *Ibid.*, 2, 4: "Quommodo iubet, si non est liberum arbitrium?" The numerous

addressed to the will,[98] says Augustine. That is why the meaning of such prohibitions as: "Do not be overcome by evil . . ." (Rom. 12: 21) and "Be not without understanding as the horse and the mule . . ." (Ps. 31: 9) is really "Be unwilling to be overcome by evil . . ." and "Be unwilling to become as the horse and the mule. . . ."[99] "What do these texts show," asks Augustine, "except the free judgment of the human will?"[100]

The bishop of Hippo then lays down this general principle of interpretation: "Wherever the Scripture says: 'Don't do this and don't do that' and wherever the work of the will is required to do or not do something commanded by God, the free will is sufficiently demonstrated."[101] Thus not only the biblical imperatives are proof of free will for Augustine, but also the indicative and conditional statements which speak of the activity of the will.[102] Again we find Augustine using will and free will interchangeably.

After giving what he believes are abundant "divine testimonies" on behalf of free will, and having asserted that there are undoubtedly many more such testimonies in defense of free will, Augustine then proceeds to give a Catholic, anti-Pelagian balance to the biblical teaching on free will by citing the equally clear Scriptural doctrine of the necessity of God's grace for all good living and action.[103]

As a point of comparison between Augustine and Luther, it is most important to notice Augustine's biblical argument for free will. He maintains: (1) that the biblical imperatives (law) make no sense unless man has free will, (2) that sin cannot be attributed to man unless he has free will, and (3) that wherever Scripture speaks of the activity of the human will in carrying out the law, free will is by that very fact "sufficiently demonstrated."

In contrast to what we will notice in Luther, we do not find Augustine saying: to produce arguments for free will from certain biblical texts,

---

precepts of love that are found in the New Testament are given "vainly" to men if they do not have free will: *ibid.*, 18, 37.

[98] Again it is clear that Augustine identifies "voluntas" with "free will." Nygren, p. 52, rightly translates "voluntas" as "freier Wille."

[99] *De gr. et lib. arb.*, 2, 4. As other examples he cites: Prov. 1: 8; 3: 7, 11, 27, 29; 5: 2; Ps. 35: 4; Mt. 6: 19; 10: 28; I Cor. 15: 34; I Tim. 4: 14; Jas. 2: 1; 4: 11; I Jn. 2: 15.

[100] *Ibid.*: ". . . quod ostendunt, nisi liberum arbitrium voluntatis humanae?"

[101] *Ibid.*: "Nempe ubi dicitur: 'Noli hoc et noli illud' et ubi ad aliquid faciendum vel non faciendum in divinis monitis opus voluntatis exigitur, satis liberum demonstratur arbitrium."

[102] Cf. Mt. 16: 24; Lk. 2: 14; I Cor. 7: 56f; 9: 17; I Tim. 5: 11. *De gr. et lib. arb.*, 3, 5: "Et utique cui dicitur: *Noli vinci*, arbitrium voluntatis eius sine dubio convenitur. Velle enim et nolle propriae voluntatis est."

[103] *Ibid.*, 4, 6.

especially from the imperatives, is Pelagian, for such arguments prove too much, namely, that man's free will alone is capable of fulfilling the commandments. Never does Augustine argue that we must choose *either* the free will defended by Pelagius *or* the unfree will and grace. Instead, he agrees with Pelagius and his followers that the free will is taught by many passages of Scripture, but he disagrees absolutely with Pelagius that the free will is sufficient for truly good living. The grace of God must precede and accompany the good action of the free will.

Thus, Augustine partly agrees and partly disagrees with Pelagius, and he does this in the name of Scripture, which teaches neither free will without grace nor grace without free will, but grace *and* free will. Nowhere does the Bible offer a theological harmonization of the two realities, grace and free will; more or less it simply places side by side texts presupposing free will on the one hand and the necessity of grace on the other. Both sets of texts must be considered in any biblical-theological statement of the problem that is to be considered truly Catholic. Augustine's unyielding retention of both poles of the biblical dialectic is undoubtedly one of the main reasons why the Church has recognized him as her pre-eminent "doctor of grace."

Confident that he has proven from Scripture that man, in order to live and to act rightly, has a free will, Augustine turns his attention to the "haeresis pelagiana" when he says: "Let us also see what divine testimonies we have concerning the grace of God, without which we are unable to do anything good." Augustine selects an illustration of the necessity of grace that has personal meaning for the monks of Hadrumetum: monastic continence. It is impossible to follow this counsel of the Lord, says Augustine, without grace, for Jesus told his disciples that continence is a gift (Mt. 19: 11). At the same time, however, Paul speaks of continence as a matter of free will.[104] Thus, concludes Augustine, the acceptance of this word of the Lord is both a gift of God and a work of the free will.[105]

The same interplay of grace and free will is illustrated by the Scriptural teachings on conjugal chastity and chastity in general, says Augustine.[106] "The victory by which the sin (the context refers to a sin against chastity) is overcome is nothing else than the gift of God helping the free will in this struggle." [107]

---

[104] *Ibid.*, 4, 7: Augustine cites I Tim. 5: 22 and I Cor. 7: 37.

[105] *Ibid.*, "Itaque, ut hoc verbum, quod non ab omnibus capitur ab aliquibus capiatur, et Dei donum est, et liberum arbitrium."

[106] *Ibid.*, 4, 8.

[107] *Ibid.*: "Ergo et victoria qui peccatum vincitur, nihil est quam donum Dei, in isto certamine adiuvantis liberum arbitrium."

Again, the injunction of the Lord to watch and pray that we may not enter into temptation (Mt. 26: 41) is interpreted by Augustine as clear evidence of the need for grace.[108] On the other hand, the command to "watch" is an admonition to man's will. Similarly, the text: "My Son, do not scorn correction from Yahweh" (Prov. 3: 11b) is addressed to man's free will, says Augustine. But when the Lord says: I have prayed for you, Simon, that your faith may not fail" (Lk. 22: 32), this shows that man is aided by grace in order that his will will not be given a senseless command.[109] Two types of biblical texts are constantly cited by Augustine: those showing free will and those showing the need for helping grace. Augustine never asserts one of these sets of texts to the exclusion of the other. He admits and insists upon the powerlessness of the free will without grace to do anything truly good, but he never argues from this powerlessness of the unaided free will to its non-existence.

Commenting on Zac. 1: 3, "Return to me, and I will return to you," a text which has traditionally been cited by theologians to show that man is not merely passive in conversion and justification, Augustine agrees that the text does refer to the activity of man's will in conversion. But he warns against the error of the Pelagians who claim that this text means that man works his own conversion and thereby merits the grace through which God turns toward us.[110] The Pelagians, says Augustine, do not realize that our very conversion to God is itself a gift of God. Otherwise, he argues, we could never pray with the Psalmist: "Help us, God our savior," [111] and: "Will you not give us life again? . . . Bring us back, God our savior." [112] Nor could Jesus have said: "No one could come to me unless the Father allows him." [113]

One of Augustine's clearest statements on the dialectic of grace *and* free will is based on I Cor. 15: 10. The need for grace is obviously expressed by the words: "But by God's grace that is what I am." Paul shows the role of free will, says Augustine, when he immediately adds: "And the grace that he gave me has not been fruitless." Other texts teach free will in the same way, such as II Cor. 6: 1: "We beg you once again not to neglect the grace of God that you have received." "Why does he entreat them," asks Augustine, "if the reception of grace means

---

108 *Ibid.*, 4, 9.

109 *Ibid.*: "Homo ergo iuvatur, ne sine causa voluntati eius iubeatur." Cf. footnote 137 below.

110 *Ibid.*, 5, 10: "Talia ergo de Scripturis (Zach. 1: 3) colligunt . . . ut secundum meritum conversionis nostrae ad Deum, detur gratia eius, in qua ad nos et ipse convertitur."

111 Ps. 79: 8.

112 Ps. 84: 7, 5.

113 Jn. 6: 65.

that they lose their own will?" [114] But for Paul to avoid the impression, continues Augustine, that the will itself is able to do something good without God's grace, he adds, after I Cor. 15: 10, the phrase: "I, or rather the grace of God that is with me." Thus, Paul's apostolic labor is neither from the grace of God alone, nor from himself alone, but from the grace of God with him.[115] Augustine makes the immediate clarification that man's efficacious vocation to conversion is to be attributed to the grace calling him to conversion, since all of his "merits" were evil.[116]

Man begins to have good merits only *after* he has been given God's grace.[117] Even then, however, he merits through grace (*per illam*). If it is withdrawn, he falls down. Thus, even when he gains merits, he should not attribute them to himself.[118] The Pelagian concept of merit is erroneous, maintains Augustine, not because it teaches that man merits, but because it forgets that man's merits themselves are gifts of God. Citing I Cor. 4: 7—one of his favorite anti-Pelagian texts—along with other texts that speak of God's gifts to man,[119] Augustine concludes with an essential aspect of his—and any truly Catholic—doctrine of merit: "If therefore your good merits are gifts of God, then God does not crown your merits insofar as they are your merits, but insofar as they are his gifts." [120]

After showing, in opposition to the Pelagians, that faith itself is a gift of God and not the basis for the grace he gives us,[121] and after rejecting an antinomian interpretation of Rom. 3: 28: "As we see it, a man is justified by faith and not by something the law tells him to do," [122]

---

114 *De gr. et lib. arb.*, 5, 12.

115 *Ibid.*: ". . . id est, non solus, sed gratia Dei mecum; ac per hoc, nec gratia Dei sola nec ipse solus, sed gratia Dei cum illo."

116 *Ibid.*: "Ut autem de caelo vocaretur, et tam magna efficacissima vocatione converteretur, gratia Dei erat sola, quia merita eius erant magna, sed mala." II Tim. 1: 8f., and Tit. 3: 3-7 are cited as biblical evidence.

117 *Ibid.*, 6, 13: "Sed plane cum data fuerit incipiunt esse etiam merita nostra bona, per illam tamen."

118 *Ibid.*

119 Jas. 1: 17; Jn. 3: 27; Eph. 4: 8.

120 *De gr. et lib. arb.*, 6, 15: "Si ergo Dei dona sunt bona merita tua, non Deus coronat merita tua tanquam merita tua, sed tanquam dona sua." It is difficult to understand how, in the light of this statement, G. Nygren can say that Augustine presumes a "Selbständigkeit des freien Willens" in his doctrine of merit. W. Pannenberg similarly creates a false opposition between natural freedom of the will and the "Freiheit der Gottesgemeinschaft," by defining free will as a "radikale Selbstmächtigkeit": "Christlicher Glaube und menschliche Freiheit," in: KuD, 4 (1958), 270.

121 *Ibid.*, 7, 17.

122 *Ibid.*, 7, 18.

Augustine returns in Chapter 8 to the problem of grace and merit. How can Scripture teach us most clearly on the one hand that eternal life is rendered according to good works: God "will reward each one according to his behavior" (Mt. 16: 27), and on the other hand that eternal life comes through grace, if grace is not given according to works, but freely? [123] It is impossible to solve this question, answers Augustine, unless we realize that even our good works, according to which eternal life is granted, pertain to the grace of God, according to the words of Jesus: "Cut off from me you can do nothing" (Jn. 15: 5). What Paul means, therefore, in Rom. 11: 6, when he says "not by works," is: not by your works insofar as they arise from you, but insofar as God has fashioned, formed and created them in you.[124]

Augustine's doctrine of merit receives a further clarification when he tells us that eternal death is indeed in the strict sense rendered as a debt for sin: "The wage paid by sin is death" (Rom. 6: 23). Eternal life could also have been called a wage by Paul—"and rightly," says Augustine. Paul chose, however, to say: "The present given by God is eternal life" (Rom. 6: 23b), so that we might understand that God leads us to eternal life because of his mercy.[125] Augustine does not contradict his earlier statements that eternal life is merited, and that Paul could rightly call it a "wage." He seeks to clarify his meaning when he asks: "Isn't the crown spoken of by the Psalmist in Psalm 103 (102): 4 given because of good works?" Instead of flatly answering, "No," Augustine accepts the assumption of the question and adds: Because the good works themselves are worked in us by him of whom it has been said: "It is God, for his own loving purpose, who puts both the will and the action into you" (Phil. 2: 13), therefore the Psalmist says: He crowns "you with love and tenderness," because it is by his mercy that we do the good things for which the crown is given.[126]

Concerning Phil. 2: 13—a very important text for his concept of grace—Augustine insists that one must not think that free will is taken away because God is said to work in us both to will and to accomplish. If this were so, says Augustine, Paul could not have said in the previous verse: "Work for your salvation in fear and trembling." For when it is commanded that they so act, it is their free will that is commanded.[127]

---

[123] He cites Rom. 4: 4; 11: 5f.; 6: 23.

[124] *Ibid.*, 8, 20.

[125] *Ibid.*, 9, 21.

[126] *Ibid.*

[127] *Ibid.*: "Non enim quia dixit Deus est enim qui operatur in vobis et velle et operari, pro bona voluntate, ideo liberum arbitrium abstulisse putandus. Quod si ita esset, non superius dixisset: *Cum timore et tremore*. . . . Quando enim iubetur ut operentur, liberum eorum convenitur arbitrium. . . ."

Until now we have examined the text of *De gratia et libero arbitrio* in detail. Since our primary purpose is not to make a comprehensive study of Augustine's doctrine, but to study Augustine insofar as he is relevant for a historical-theological understanding of Luther's *De servo arbitrio*, we shall not mention those points of Augustine's anti-Pelagian doctrine that we have already examined; we shall mention only those points in the remaining chapters of *De gratia et libero arbitrio* that have special value for a comparison between Augustine and Luther.[128]

1. The Law: Paul in Rom. 3: 20 says through the law comes knowledge of sin. Augustine points out that Paul says "knowledge," not "destruction" (*consumptio*). This leads him to cite texts showing the fundamental goodness of the law. The knowledge of sin becomes a disaster and a "consumptio" only if grace does not aid man that he might avoid the sin which he knows.[129]

2. We always have free will, but it is not always good.[130] This well-known text is really not a proof that Augustine teaches free will, for he uses the phrase: "libera voluntas" in the sense of Rom. 6: 16-20: a man is either free from sin and a slave of justice or he is free from justice and a slave of sin. Freedom is clearly used here in a sense other than that of natural freedom of the will.[131] In the same chapter and paragraph Augustine speaks of *liberum arbitrium* in the sense of natural freedom, and cites a number of biblical texts,[132] "lest anyone think that men do nothing through their free will" when God sanctifies them by removing their hearts of stone.[133]

3. The paradox of God's commands and gifts. Augustine sees two types of biblical texts: one commanding man to do something, the other saying that God will give to man the very thing commanded.[134] "Why

---

[128] A more detailed treatment of these remaining chapters can be found in Nygren, pp. 61-69.

[129] *De gr. et lib. arb.*, 10, 22.

[130] *Ibid.*: "Semper est autem in nobis voluntas libera, sed non semper est bona. Aut enim a iustitia libera est, quando servit peccato, et tunc est mala; aut a peccato libera est, quando servit iustitiae, et tunc est bona."

[131] Ferguson, p. 171 is totally unjustified when he calls this passage "mere verbal juggling" which "confuses two separate and distinct meanings of the word 'free'." That there are at least two separate and distinct meanings of the word "free" is recognized by Scripture as well as by common experience. And whether Augustine confuses these meanings can only be determined by a full reading of *De gratia et libero arbitrio*, which Ferguson cites nowhere else in his book. Nygren also fails to distinguish clearly the two types of freedom in Augustine. That is the only way one can explain his statement on p. 82: "Der Mensch besitzt unter der Sünde zwar *potentiell* einen freien Willen, aber dieser ist zu allem Guten unfähig. . . ." (italics ours).

[132] Ps. 95: 8; Ez. 18: 31f.

[133] *De gr. et lib. arb.*, 15, 31.

[134] Cf. Ez. 18: 31a and Rom. 4: 5; Ez. 18: 31b and 36: 26.

does he command if he is going to give the same thing? Why does he give, if man is going to do it? The only explanation is that he gives what he commands when he aids men to do what he commands." [135]

4. God does not command the impossible.[136] Augustine's insistence on the necessity of grace for any good work or for the keeping of the commandments led to the Pelagian objection: God does not command the impossible; therefore man can by his own powers do what God has commanded. Augustine does not deny the Pelagian premise, but the conclusion. "Who is unaware," rejoins Augustine, "that God doesn't command things if he knows man cannot do them?" But the point is, he adds, God "commands some things which we are unable to do so that we may know what we ought to ask from him. For it is by faith that we, in our prayers, ask for that which the law commands." [137]

5. *Gratia operans* and *cooperans.* Augustine makes a famous distinction of two moments or types of grace, the *gratia operans,* through which the good will itself is given, and the *gratia cooperans,* through which God cooperates with our free will in the actual performance of the good act. It seems that Augustine arrived at this distinction through the fact of experience that one can want to fulfil a command of God, yet not be able. Such a person indeed has good will, says Augustine, but it is still a "small and weak" will; it can fulfil the commandment when it is "great and strong." [138] God "works" or "operates" the good will in us without us, i.e., without our assent (*gratia operans*). But when we will and do that which is good, he cooperates with us. In either case, unless he operates in order for us to will or cooperates when we will, we are

---

[135] *De gr. et lib. arb.,* 15, 31.

[136] Already in 415 Augustine taught this doctrine in a non-Pelagian sense. Cf. *De nat. et gr.,* 43, 50.

[137] *De gr. et lib. arb.,* 16, 32: "Magnum aliquid pelagiani se scire putant, quando dicunt: 'Non iuberet Deus, quod sciret non posse ab homine fieri.' Quis hoc nesciat? Sed ideo iubet aliqua quae non possumus, ut noverimus quid ab illo petere debeamus. Ipsa est enim fides, quae orando impetrat quod lex imperat." Cf. *ibid.,* 4, 9 and 14, 28.

[138] *Ibid.,* 17, 33: "Et quis istam etsi parvum dare coeperat charitatem, nisi ille qui praeparat voluntatem et cooperando perficit, quod operando incipit? Quoniam ipse ut velimus operatur incipiens, qui volentibus cooperatur perficiens."

[139] *Ibid.,* 17, 33: "Ut ergo velimus, sine nobis operatur; cum autem volumus, et sic volumus ut faciamus, nobiscum cooperatur; tamen sine illo vel operante ut velimus, vel cooperante cum volumus, ad bona pietatis opera nihil valemus." In the previous chapter (16, 32), Augustine made it abundantly clear that *we* indeed keep the commandments when we will to do so, but only because our will is prepared by the Lord (Prov. 8: 35). It is also certain that *we* will when we will, but it is God who causes us to will the good. Likewise, *we* act when we act, but it is God who enables us to act ("facit ut faciamus") by endowing the will with very effective powers.

able to do no good works of piety. Augustine cites Phil. 2: 13 and Rom.
8: 28 as support for *gratia operans* and *cooperans* respectively.

EXCURSUS: *Synergism and Semipelagianism*

When Ferguson, *Pelagius,* pp. 79f. claims to detect an opposition
between Jerome and Augustine on the grounds that Jerome "is a
synergist, holding that God's grace and man's free will come together in
the work of salvation," he provides us with a representative statement of
a frequently encountered confusion surrounding the word "synergism."
If synergism is taken to mean a view of the relationship between God's
grace and man's free will in which God and man are each *partial* causes
of man's salvation, then synergism is rightly to be rejected as a misunderstanding of God's sovereign working in us (his transcendental causality) of both the willing and the accomplishing of the salutary act
(Phil. 2: 13). But if synergism is understood simply as a co-working or
co-operation of God and man in the work of salvation (without suggesting that they work on the same or on an equal plane), if it is taken to
mean simply that man *does something essential* in the work of salvation,
or that grace and free will are both involved in justification and salvation, then this is not only not a Semipelagian viewpoint—as some suppose—but a viewpoint that is central to Augustine's doctrine of grace.
In the *De gratia et libero arbitrio,* especially where Augustine speaks of
the *gratia cooperans,* we find the fullest statement of Augustine's
"synergism."

A. Adam, "Die Herkunft des Lutherwortes vom menschlichen Willen
als Reittier Gottes," in: *Luther-Jahrbuch* (1962), p. 27 erroneously
brands as Semipelagian and un-Augustinian a doctrine of divine-human
cooperation held by Augustine himself. Even though he does not actually cite W. von Loewenich, "Zur Gnadenlehre bei Augustin und bei
Luther," in: *Von Augustin zu Luther* (Witten/Ruhr, 1959), Adam
seems to be referring to Loewenich's essay, p. 87, when he says that
Augustine conceives of the relationship between grace and free will as
an interaction ("Ineinander") while the Semipelagians understood it as
a juxtaposition ("Nebeneinander"). The pseudo-Augustinian *Hypognosticon,* of Semipelagian origin, is cited by Adam as an illustration of
the "semi-Pelagian juxtaposition": "And thus neither grace without free
will enables a man to have a blessed life nor free will without grace"
(*Hypo.,* III, 11, 20: PL 45, 1632). But this is hardly peculiar to the
Semipelagians. One can find many such texts in Augustine. See, for
example, *De gr. et lib. arb.* 5, 12, where, commenting on I Cor. 15: 10,
Augustine says: ". . . not alone, that is, but the grace of God with me;
and thus, neither the grace of God alone nor himself alone, but the grace
of God with him."

Von Loewenich, p. 87, cites a similar text from Augustine's *Enchiridion* (421) 32, 91, and says: ". . . it appears to be a situation involving
an addition of grace and will. I would rather suppose that we are dealing

here with an intentional paradox. Then this formula would not be so far removed from Luther's intention. The Catholic tradition however settled upon the addition idea (*Additionsschema*)."

We do not agree with von Loewenich. The Catholic tradition indeed retains the Augustinian paradox—we prefer to call it the Augustinian dialectic—by insisting on both grace *and* free will. The various explanations of the relation of these two realities by the Catholic schools cannot be adequately or fairly described as an "Additionsschema". One loses the Augustinian dialectic when one denies either grace or free will and teaches grace alone to the exclusion of free will *or* free will to the exclusion of divine grace. The dialectic can also be lost, as von Loewenich suggests, when one holds that grace is added to free will in the manner of a partial cause operating with another partial cause to produce a common effect. This is a naïve synergism, an "Additionsschema" that is foreign to Augustine and to the Catholic tradition.

Heinrich Barth admirably conveys the nature of the Augustinian dialect when he writes: "God's assistance is neither placed alongside of man's action nor before it in time. The entire action is the action of man. And the entire action of man is, on the other hand, the action of God. In the temporal order faith is the starting point and the source of the spiritual life. But because grace is what is really prior, one can regard it as the starting point of faith, a starting point and a source, to be sure, which is outside of the temporal event. 'Ut esses, ut sentires, ut audires, ut consentires, praevenit te misericordia eius. Praevenit te in omnibus. . . .' (*Sermo.* 176, 5). Even in this unique 'going before' (*Vorangehen*), one's 'own will' is not by-passed or set aside. . . . Proof of this is found in Augustine's countless references to the text: 'Praeparatur voluntas a Domino.' Thus both are true: that God prepares the vessels for honor and that they prepare themselves (*Op. imp.* I, 134)": *Die Freiheit der Entscheidung im Denken Augustins* (Basel, 1935), p. 137. Cf. G. Nygren, p. 41.

It is important to remember that one can find the roots of an acceptable doctrine of synergism in the Bible, which refers to men as *theou . . . synergoi*: I Cor. 3: 9. Augustine cites Rom. 8: 28 in this connection, as we have seen above in our presentation of his doctrine of *gratia cooperans*. Cf. G. Bertram, *ThW* 7, 872, 13-17; 873, 5-10.

Semipelagianism was therefore not simply a doctrine of synergism. Nor was it the attempt to reconcile "God's foreknowledge and foreordination . . . with man's freedom" in opposition to a supposed view of Augustine "that God predestined everything and that, as far as merit went, the human will was absolutely impotent to do aught but sin," as P. Smith suggests in *Erasmus* (New York: F. Ungar Co., 1923; reprinted 1962), p. 337. Nor was it the fact "that Augustine attributed the salvation of the redeemed solely to God's grace while these [the Semipelagians] believed that every man could decide what his destiny was to be," as we are told by Fr. Loofs, p. 352. Nor was Semipelagianism characterized by the view that one "must make the right use of the saving grace received through the sacraments" in order to "merit the gift of salvation": A. C. McGiffert, *Protestant Thought Before Kant* (New York: Harper Torchbooks, 1962), pp. 3f.

The essence of the Semipelagian doctrine which was attacked by Augustine and by Prosper of Aquitaine and later condemned by the Second Council of Orange (529) was, rather, the idea that it belongs to the natural power of the free will to initiate belief and salvation, to accept the gift of faith once it was offered by God. Augustine—and the Church—insisted against the Semipelagians that the only reason for the acceptance of the gift of faith by the will is that God's grace precedes the act of the will and prepares it for the acceptance of faith. As Augustine put it, the very desire for the help of grace is the beginning of grace: "Desiderare auxilium gratiae initium gratiae est," *De correp. et gr.* (426/7), 1, 2. Cf. *De dono persev.* (428/9), 17, 42; 21, 55.

An extensive exposition of Semipelagianism can be found in É. Amann, "Semi-Pélagiens," *DTC* 14, 1796-1850. Cf. K. Rahner, "Augustin und der Semipelagianismus," *Zeitschr. für katholische Theol.* 62 (1938), 71-196; J. Chéné. "Que signifiaient 'initium fidei' et 'affectus credulitatis' pour les semipélagiens?", *Recherches de science religieuse* 35 (1948), 566-588; J. Auer, "Initium fidei," *LThK,* 5, 67, 6f.; M. Seckler, *Instinkt und Glaubenswille* (Mainz, 1961), pp. 90ff.; M. Flick, "Semipelagianismus," *LThK,* 9, 650ff. See also the articles by P. Godet on two important Semipelagians: "Cassien, Jean," *DTC* 2, 1823-1829 and "Fauste de Riez," *DTC* 5, 2100-2105.

Seeberg, II, p. 573, does not do justice to the differences between Augustine's doctrine of grace and free will and that of the Semipelagians. On page 579 he more correctly places the difference in the fact that a Semipelagian such as Faustus has no concept of grace as an interior movement of the will. Even this is not precise, for, as P. Godet points out, *DTC* 5, 2103f., Faustus held against Pelagius that grace works interiorly, but he failed to see with Augustine that grace acts on the will and moves it to will good. See also Denifle's criticism of Dieckhoff, who claims that Thomas Aquinas was also a Semipelagian: *Luther und Luthertum* (Mainz, 1906), pp. 875-878. Loofs, p. 358, is incorrect when he says that the so-called "gratia irresistibilis" is the difference between Augustinianism and Semipelagianism. The same criticism of Loofs is made by Portalié, "Augustinisme," *DTC,* 1, 2527. The definition of Semipelagianism held by Loofs is the same as that of Jansenius. Cf. DS 2004.

6. The final point from *De gratia et libero arbitrio* which has relevance for a comparison between Augustine and Luther is Augustine's treatment of Pharaoh's hardening. In earlier writings Augustine explained the hardening of sinners by God simply by saying that God did not have mercy on them. One cannot explain this phenomenon, he maintains, by saying that God impels them to sin.[140] God blinds and hardens by deserting and by not helping the sinner. But this is always

---

[140] *De div. quaest. ad Simpl.* (396/7), I, 2, 16.

done justly, for those who are so punished have merited the punishment. If God aids and forgives the sinner, he does so mercifully; if he does not aid him, but hardens and blinds him, he does so justly. His judgment may be hidden to us, but it is never unjust. This is an absolutely unshakable truth.[141]

In *De gratia et libero arbitrio* Augustine stresses the positive working of God in hardening the hearts of men.[142] This is biblically more exact than his previous explanations. Nevertheless, the explanation of the hardening of the heart by God remains essentially that of his earlier writings: (i) Pharaoh's hardening is a punishment for his previous sins; [143] (ii) The hardening of the heart is not solely a work of God, for Pharaoh hardens his own heart by his free will; [144] (iii) Whether God hardens the sinner or has mercy on him, there is never any injustice with God. For God returns evil for evil because he is just and good for evil because he is good, and good for good because he is both good and just.

---

[141] *In Ioannis Evangelium Tractatus* (416/7), 53, 6: "Etiam hoc [excaecare and indurare] eorum voluntatem meruisse respondeo. Sic enim excaecat, sic obdurat Deus, deserendo et non adiuvando; quod occulto iudicio facere potest, iniquo non potest. Hoc omnino pietas religiosorum inconcussum debet inviolatumque servare. . . . Si ergo absit ut sit iniquitas apud Deum; sive quando adiuvat, misericorditer facit; sive quando non adiuvat, iuste facit. . . ."

[142] *De gr. et lib. arb.*, 21, 42: "Agit enim Omnipotens in cordibus hominum etiam motum voluntatis eorum, ut per eos agat quod per eos agere ipse voluerit, qui omnino iniuste aliquid velle non novit . . . (I)lle qui in caelo et in terra omnia quaecumque voluit fecit, etiam in cordibus hominum operatur." *Ibid.*, 21, 43: ". . . satis, quantum existimo, manifestatur, operari Deum in cordibus hominum ad inclinandas eorum voluntates quocumque voluerit, sive ad bona pro sua misericordia, sive ad mala pro meritis eorum. . . ." It is clear from the biblical examples cited in ch. 21, 42 that Augustine is not saying that God inclines the will to *sin*. He uses "mala," not "peccata," and means by this the temporal punishments that sinners justly merit by their sins, or the temporal evils which sinners can bring upon others when they are used as instruments of God's powers, as was the case with Pharaoh and Judas. Ch. 20, 41 is clearer than 21, 43: ". . . ita esse in Dei potestate, ut eas quo voluerit, quando voluerit, faciat inclinari, vel ad *beneficia* quibusdam praestanda, vel ad *poenas* quibusdam ingerendas, sicut ipse iudicat. . . ." In *De pecc. mer. et rem.*, II, 18, 30 Augustine made it perfectly clear that our good will is from God, but not our bad will.

[143] *De gr. et lib. arb.*, 20, 41: "Nam invenimus aliqua peccata etiam poenas esse aliorum peccatorum . . . sicut est induratio Pharaonis, cuius et causa dicitur ad ostendendam in illo virtutem Dei. . . ." *Ibid.*, 21, 43: "Ac per hoc quando legitis in litteris veritatis, a Dei seduci homines, aut obtundi vel obdurari corda eorum, nolite dubitare praecesisse mala merita eorum, ut iuste ista paterentur. . . ." *Ibid.*, 23, 45: "Quando ergo auditis . . . quod ait Apostolus: *Cuius vult miseretur, et quem* vult obdurat (Rom. 9: 18); in eo quem seduci permittit vel obdurari, mala eius merita credite." The understanding of hardening as a "permissio" is still retained by Augustine, despite the emphasis of a positive "inclinatio" that we pointed out in footnote 142 above.

[144] *De gr. et lib. arb.*, 23, 45: "Ac per hoc [Ex. 4—14 passim and Ex. 8: 32] et Deus induravit per iustum iudicium, et ipse Pharao per liberum arbitrium."

But he never returns evil for good because he is not unjust.[145] God's judgment is sometimes manifest and sometimes hidden, but it is always just.[146]

A final question remains. Did Augustine in his final writings—those written after *De gratia et libero arbitrio*—retract his earlier clear teaching that man possesses natural freedom of the will before and after the fall? *A priori* one might rule out such a possibility on the grounds that such an about-face would have so shaken Augustine's doctrine of grace, sin and law that he would have had to make a special, *ex professo* retraction affirming that personal sin *is* possible without free will and that the precepts of the law *do* make sense even if we lack free will to accept or reject them—positions, of course, which he had constantly rejected in his earlier works. In the *Retractationes* of 426/7 there is no indication of such a drastic departure from his earlier teaching. On the contrary, as we have seen in various references to the *Retractationes,* Augustine confirms his earlier teaching that man always enjoys natural freedom, even though he does correct some of his early opinions which did not conform to the truth that grace is necessary for the very beginning of conversion, faith and salvation.

9. *De praedestinatione sanctorum* and *De dono perseverantiae* (428/9)

Does Augustine's teaching on predestination and the gift of perseverance, which he developed at length in two of his very latest works, *De Praedestinatione sanctorum* and *De dono perseverantiae,* both written between 428 and 429, imply an abandonment of his early conviction that man always retains natural freedom of the will? Few authors maintain that Augustine actually denied man's natural freedom in these late writings.[147] Such a contention appears to be not only improbable on *a priori* grounds, as we have suggested above, but it is also irreconcilable with Augustine's clear teaching in the two works in question.

First of all, as we have already noted,[148] in *De praedestinatione*

---

145 *Ibid.*: "Reddet omnino Deus et mala pro malis, quoniam iustus est; et bona pro malis, quoniam bonus est; et bona pro bonis, quoniam bonus et iustus est; tantummodo mala pro bonis, non reddet, quoniam iniustus non est."

146 *Ibid.*, 21, 43: ". . . iudicio utique suo aliquando, aperto, aliquando occulto, semper tamen iusto." *Ibid.*, 20, 41: ". . . sicut ipse iudicat, occultissimo quidem iudicio, sed sine ulla dubitatione iustissimo."

147 Even Ferguson, p. 175 does not claim that Augustine directly denied natural freedom. He simply says: "As Augustine formulated his full theory of predestination he left no room for human freedom." This view is characteristic of a position, to be examined below, which holds that Augustine's assertion of man's free will is simply incompatible with his doctrine of predestination and grace, even though he himself does not realize it.

148 Cf. footnote 29ff. above.

sanctorum, Augustine, after pointing out corrections he had made of some of his earlier writings, expressly states that he had already arrived at a solution of the problem of faith and works and of grace and free will in *De diversis questionibus VII ad Simplicianum* (396/7).[149] In trying to solve this problem, Augustine says he worked to uphold free will (literally: on behalf of free will; "laboratum est pro libero arbitrio voluntatis humanae"), but the grace of God triumphed.[150] How the grace of God triumphed we have already seen in our examination of *De div. quaest.* It did not triumph by the denial of the existence of free will, but by the assertion that *good* will itself, the very beginning of faith and salvation, is to be attributed to grace.

Secondly, we find that Augustine even in *De praed. sanctorum* continues to assert the natural freedom of man's will, even after the fall. He teaches, for example, that one would contradict I Cor. 4: 7 if one should claim that faith is one's own and not something received from God. This claim is false, says Augustine, not because believing or not believing does not pertain to the free will, but because the will itself is prepared by the Lord, as Prov. 8: 35 (LXX) teaches.[151] That faith involves free choice on the part of man is further seen from a consideration of Jn. 15: 16: "You have not chosen me, but I have chosen you." Augustine points out that it is beyond doubt that the Apostles did indeed choose Christ when they believed in him. Therefore the only explanation for the words of the Lord transmitted in Jn. 15: 16 is: the Apostles did not choose Christ in order that he might choose them, but he chose them in order that they might choose him.[152]

Clear evidence that Augustine did not change his position on the existence of natural freedom even in fallen man is found in the very last of his works, the *Opus imperfectum contra Iulianum,* begun in 429 and terminated by his death in 430. Augustine says that the free will of Adam was given him by the creator, was vitiated by the deceiver and

---

149 *De praed. sanct.*, 3, 7—4, 8.

150 *Ibid.*, 4, 8: "In cuius quaestionis solutione laboratum est quidem pro libero arbitrio voluntatis humanae; sed vicit Dei gratia."

151 *Ibid.*, 5, 10: "Quid autem habes quod non accepisti? quisquis audet dicere: Habeo ex me fidem, non ergo accepi, profecto contradicit huic apertissimae veritati, non quia credere vel non credere non est in arbitrio voluntatis humanae, sed *in electis praeparatur voluntas a Domino.* Ideo ad ipsam quoque fidem, quae in voluntate est, pertinet: Quis enim te discernit? Quid autem habes. . . ?" We have already pointed out (footnote 16) that Augustine uses "arbitrium voluntatis" and "liberum arbitrium" interchangeably.

152 *De praed. sanct.*, 17, 34: "Et ipsi quidem procul dubio elegerunt eum, quando crediderunt in eum. Unde non ob aliud dicit: *Non vos me elegistis, sed ego vos elegi;* nisi quia non elegerunt eum ut eligeret eos, sed ut eligerent eum elegit eos. . . ."

was healed by the Savior.[153] The vitiation of free will does not, however, take away man's natural freedom, for Augustine speaks of the
"infirmity of the free will." Fallen man indeed always has free will, but
it is an infirm free will until it is healed by the grace of the Savior.
Man—or the will—is not free, however, in the sense of having acquired
freedom which, as Augustine says, is the freedom to do good.[154]

The question debated among Augustine scholars is not: Did the later
Augustine deny his earlier teaching on the existence of natural freedom
in fallen man? There is simply too much evidence that he did not. The
controversy has centered much more around the question: Granted that
Augustine had no intention of denying the natural freedom of man's
will, does his doctrine of all-powerful, efficacious grace and predestination in fact leave any room for natural, psychological or, as some call it,
metaphysical freedom of the will? Do Augustine's statements affirming
free will have "only a purely formal significance?"[155] Without entering

---

[153] *Op. imp. contra Iul.*, 3, 110: ". . . hoc est liberum arbitrium, tale omnino
accepit Adam: sed quod datum est a conditore, et a deceptore vitiatum, utique a
Salvatore sanandum est." "Natura vitiata" and "depravata" never mean for
Augustine that nature is so totally corrupt that it is not healed by grace. *Ibid.*, 1,
101 Augustine says of human nature: "verum etiam cum per vitium mala est,
capax est boni, quo bona sit." Cf. *Contra Iul. pelag.*, 4, 54 and *De gr. et lib. arb.*,
20, 41. As H. Barth, p. 28, explains: "Zwar nicht in der Natur als Natur, aber in
ihrem Fehler liegt die Sünde. . . ."

[154] *Op. imp. contra Iul.*, 3, 110: ". . . hinc convincimini . . . quod arbitrii liberi
infirmitatem ad agendum bonum nonnisi per Christi gratiam potest humana re-
parare natura." "Arbitrii liberi infirmitas" corresponds to the phrase "liberum
arbitrium captivatum," which we hold to be the least ambiguous explanation of
Augustine's doctrine of *servum arbitrium*. If we keep these phrases in mind we
shall not make the mistake of thinking that Augustine denies the natural freedom
of the will in such statements as *Op. imp. contra Iul.*, 6, 7, where he rebukes
Julian for denying that "liberum arbitrium vires suas perdidisse peccando. . . ."
One can interpret this statement in two ways: (1) by sinning, the free will lost
the "integrrimas vires" which it had in Paradise and was left with weakened
powers. Augustine makes this contrast himself in the same place, book 6, ch. 7;
(2) by sinning, the weakened will no longer has the power to do good. The
second possible explanation seems to be supported by Augustine's words, *ibid.*, 6,
14: "Ubi quod non vis, interim confiteris, scilicet libertatem voluntatis suo malo
usu perire potuisse, quia perficiendo malum minus idonea facta est ad perficiendum
bonum." Here the loss of the liberty of the will is said to be a lack—or lessening
—of its ability to do good. Free will itself, however, is "congenitum et omnino
inamissabile": *ibid.*, 6, 11.

[155] Nygren, pp. 97-102, offers a summary of the dispute and the names of the
disputants, mostly those favoring the view that Augustine's doctrine of the *gratia
efficacissima* cannot be harmonized with a genuine concept of free will. This view
is held not only by the majority of Protestant historians of theology, but also by
such Catholic scholars as O. Rottmanner, A. M. Jacquin, T. Salgueiro, H. Lange,
M. Cappuyns, B. Bartmann, K. Rahner and B. Altaner. The opposite view is
represented by J. Mausbach, H. Rondet, F. Cayré, E. Portalié, F. Diekamp, G. de
Broglie and M. Clark.

into this controversy directly, we wish simply to note two things: First, Augustine faithfully upholds the dialectic between grace (and predestination) and free will which he finds in Scripture. To surrender either of these realities—the ever-present and supernatural divine action or the free, human activity—would be, in his eyes, heretical. It would be a surrender to either the Pelagians or the Manichaeans. Secondly, is it really historically valid to seek in Augustine's writings an effort to harmonize this divine-human relationship? Was this Augustine's problem? To these questions the historian must answer in the negative. The attempt to develop "systems" which carefully express the relation between grace and free will was not even the task of high Scholasticism, but of post-Reformation Scholasticism in its encounter with the thought of the Reformers and of the Jansenists. Clark brings the issue into clear focus when she writes: "The Jansenist problematic was: How does one reconcile free choice, which seems to condition the responsibility of man, with the primacy of predestination and the order of grace? They do not seem to have asked themselves this question: Was Augustine offering the theory of such a reconciliation?" [156] Clark's question: ". . . is it correct for the Jansenists to interpret a fifth century text of Augustine in the light of concepts and problems bequeathed to them by scholasticism?",[157] may well be asked of the twentieth-century scholars who find in Augustine "extreme statements" and "exaggerations" instead of a well-thought out statement on the relation between grace and free will.

10. Summary

The results of our investigation of the meaning of *liberum arbitrium* and *servum arbitrium* in Augustine may be summarized in the following theses:

1. Among the types of freedom recognized by Augustine, the following are especially relevant for our investigation: (i) *liberum arbitrium,* which is the ability to choose, the freedom to act or not to act (natural freedom) and (ii) the freedom of those who have been liberated from the bondage of sin by the grace of God (acquired freedom).

2. God's foreknowledge does not exclude man's free will.

3. The fact of personal sin and the biblical commands and prohibitions are seen by Augustine as the chief biblical arguments for *liberum arbitrium.*

4. Although Adam, before the fall, was free also to will and to do that which is truly good, he and his decendants have lost this freedom as a result of original sin.

---

[156] Clark, p. 110.
[157] *Ibid.*

5. The loss of the Adamic freedom does not mean that *liberum arbitrium* has been lost, but that *liberum arbitrium* cannot will to do that which is truly good.

6. Even though Augustine describes this inability to do good and the bondage of sin as *servum arbitrium*—the phrase occurs only once in his writings—any supposition that Augustine intends to deny the existence of *liberum arbitrium* when he speaks of *servum arbitrium* is shown to be incorrect when one considers the other formulations he uses to describe the same reality: *liberum arbitrium captivatum* and *infirmitas arbitrii liberi*. These formulations convey less ambiguously than *servum arbitrium* the truth that fallen man indeed has free will (and can choose even ethically good acts), but that he is not free to do that which is truly good, that is, a good which has value for salvation, unless he is liberated by faith in Christ.

7. The initiative in man's liberation from sin and his movement toward justification, faith and salvation is always taken by God. His grace prepares the will of man for faith and justification, but never excludes the operation of free will.

8. Justification involves a *consensus* by man's will; belief (*credere*) involves an *electio* by the *arbitrium voluntatis humanae*.

9. Whereas the Scripture emphasizes that the unjustified *man* is a slave to sin and Satan, Augustine, in his fight against the Pelagian exaggeration of free will, says that the will itself is in captivity to sin.

10. Augustine means by *servum arbitrium* nothing more than that the free will of fallen man is a slave to sin and can be liberated from this condition of bondage only by the grace of God. His doctrine of *servum arbitrium* is, therefore, a doctrine of grace and free will.

5

Early Conciliar and Papal Teaching on Free Will and Unfree Will

No single theologian in the history of the Church has influenced the formulation of the Church's official doctrine on grace, free will and the bondage of the will as has Augustine. His tremendous theological output on these questions has been recognized by the Church as being so faithful to the teaching of divine revelation that Augustine has come to enjoy the title of the Church's "doctor gratiae." Beginning with the letter of Pope Coelestinus I to the bishops of Gaul (431) and continuing to the present day, various Roman pontiffs have praised the orthodoxy of Augustine's doctrine of grace and free will.[1] Augustine's authority as "doctor of grace" is not, however, unlimited.[2] In the central doctrines of faith concerning grace and free will, Augustine is indeed the Church's authentic witness against the Pelagians, Semipelagians and Manichaeans.[3] But in the more subtle questions concerning the mode of action of grace on the free will, the precise explanation of predestination, etc. the Church has left the field open to development by later theologians.[4] The so-called *Indiculus* or *Capitula Coelestini* already

---

[1] The text of this letter is found in PL 50, 528ff. Cf. DS 237 and the related footnote 2. A more extensive list of the papal statements recognizing Augustine's authority is found in Portalié, DTC, I, 2463-2466; tr., pp. 315-320.

[2] This has not been self-evident to some Catholic authors. The Roman Catholic Church therefore found it necessary formally to censure the view of the Jansenists that Augustine's authority is absolute: DS 2330. Cf. the warning by Pius XI in the encyclical "Ad salutem" that Augustine's authority is not to be set above the authority of the teaching Church. AAS 22 (1930) 204. An exposition and critique of this exaggerated Augustinianism can be found in Portalié, DTC, I, 2466-2469; tr., pp. 321-327.

[3] Portalié, DTC, I, 2469f.; tr., p. 327 therefore rightly criticizes the view of some Roman Catholic theologians who claimed to have found an unorthodox predestinarianism in Augustine which sacrifices man's free will to God's sovereign action.

[4] As Portalié says, DTC, I, 2470; tr., pp. 328f.: ". . . in the important questions

contains a "restriction" [5] on Augustine's authority in the "more profound and difficult" questions.[6] Augustine himself realized that his doctrine was not without its defects, and he himself said that he was not to be followed on all points.[7]

1. Conciliar Decisions during Augustine's Lifetime

It is not surprising, in view of this early approbation of Augustine, to find the main lines of his doctrine on grace and free will reflected in the various conciliar pronouncements of that age. Already during his lifetime Augustine exerted decisive influence on the teaching of the diocesan Synod at Jerusalem (July, 415) [8] and on the indictment of the doctrine of Caelestius drawn up at the provincial council held in Diospolis (the town called Lydda in Acts 9: 32) in December of the same year.[9] Pelagius was present at both of these meetings, but was not condemned. Through a series of equivocations and evasions he was able to agree at Jerusalem to the anathematizing of anyone who held that a man could advance in virtue without God's help.[10] At Diospolis, using the same tactics, he was able to disavow the following propositions attributed to him by the Council: (1) God's grace and aid are not given for individual actions, but consist simply of the gifts of free will, the law and revealed doctrine. (2) There is no free will if one needs the aid of God, for every man has the power in his own will to act or not to act.[11]

Augustine's doctrine unmistakably influenced the formulations of the

which constitute the faith of the Church in the matter of freedom of the will and grace, the doctor of Hippo is really and truly the authorized witness of tradition against the Pelagian and Semipelagian errors as St. Athanasius was against Arius and St. Cyril against Nestorius. . . . On the other hand, the more subtle explanations of secondary problems which concern the manner rather than the fact are left by the Church, for the moment at least, to the prudent study of theologians."

5 This is Portalié's expression: tr., p. 316.

6 DS 249: "Profundiores vero difficillioresque partes, incurrentium quaestionum, quas latius pertractarunt qui haereticis restiterunt . . . non necesse habemus adstruere."

7 Cf. De dono persev. (428/9), 21, 55 and Portalié, DTC, 1, 2469; tr., pp. 326f. Catholic theologians, with the sanction of the Church, have thus felt free to reject Augustine's rigid view on the fate of unbaptized infants and his vacillations in the interpretation of I Tim. 2: 4. (On the latter point cf. A. d'Alès, "Prédestination," DAC, 4, 213-216; J. Saint-Martin, "Prédestination. S. Augustin," DTC, 12, 2889-2892; Clark, pp. 98f.; M. J. Farrelly, Predestination, Grace and Free Will (Westminster, Md., 1963), pp. 96ff.

8 Cf. Portalié, DTC, 1, 2280; Hedde and Amann, DTC, 12, 690f.; Ferguson, pp. 82-85.

9 Portalié, DTC, 1, 2281; Hedde and Amann, 691-694; Ferguson, pp. 85-89; A. Hamman, "Pelagianismus," LThK, 8, 246f.

10 Ferguson, p. 84.

11 Hedde and Amann, DTC, 12, 691; Ferguson, pp. 88f. Cf. Augustine, De gest. pelag., 14, 30; 35, 65.

anti-Pelagian canons of the Council of Carthage held in May of 418, which was attended by practically all the bishops of Africa.[12] All of the canons are concerned either with original sin or with the necessity of grace, but only the fifth [13] speaks directly of free will. Canon 5 anathematizes anyone who says that the grace of justification is given to us simply to enable us to do more easily those things which we are commanded to do by means of our free will, as if we could fulfill the divine commands without grace, albeit with greater difficulty.[14] Approved by Pope Zosimus I,[15] this Augustine-inspired canon makes the Catholic position on grace and free will perfectly clear: the divine commands are addressed to man's free will, but they cannot be fulfilled unless the grace of God is given. This papally approved teaching of a provincial council is the first statement we have declaring so authoritatively that the Catholic doctrine is grace *and* free will, not grace *or* free will. This teaching has been reinforced by many stronger and still more authoritative pronouncements in later centuries and, despite the inevitable development of the doctrine, the basic dialectic of grace and free will has never been surrendered by the subsequent Catholic tradition.

Shortly after Augustine's death the Ecumenical Council of Ephesus (431) officially condemned the heresy against which Augustine had struggled so long. While canons 1 and 4 of this Council reject by name only the thought of Caelestius, the most outspoken of Pelagius' early colleagues,[16] it is evident from the historical information that we have concerning the Council that the doctrine of Pelagius himself was held to be equally heretical.[17] Unfortunately however, since the Council of Ephesus was preoccupied with Nestorianism, it did not bother to draw up a specific list of the Pelagian errors, but was content simply with making a general condemnation.

2. The "Indiculus de gratia Dei"

Quite specific, on the other hand, is the teaching of the so-called *Indiculus de gratia Dei* or *Capitula Coelestini*, long attributed to Pope

---

[12] Ferguson, p. 111.

[13] DS 227. In Quesnel's collection (PL 56, 486-490) it is canon 6. Cf. Amann, "Milève (Conciles de)," DTC, 10, 1754-1758; Hedde and Amann, DTC, 12, 698f.

[14] DS 227. Cf. DS 245.

[15] Portalié, DTC, 1, 2282; Hedde and Amann, DTC, 12, 700ff.; Amann, "Zosime (Saint)," DTC, 15, 3712-3715; Ferguson, pp. 112f.; Hamman, LThK, 8, 247. P. Fransen holds that the great authority of the canons of the Council of Carthage arises not so much from the fact of their approbation by Zosimus, but from the recognition given them by the Church universal. "The Authority of the Councils," in: *Problems of Authority*, ed. J. M. Todd (Baltimore, 1962), pp. 63f.

[16] DS 267f.

[17] Cf. Hedde and Amann, DTC, 12, 711ff.

Celestine I, but now regarded by most scholars as probably the work of Augustine's disciple, Prosper of Aquitaine.[18] Regardless of its authorship, this collection of anti-Pelagian theses faithfully presents the doctrine of Innocent I, Zosimus, the Council of Carthage and Augustine. And, as Portalié says: "The great authority of the *Capitula* is incontestable, either by reason of the pontifical and conciliar documents from which they are taken, or because of the approbation given the *Capitula* by subsequent pontiffs and the universal veneration they have received from the Church." [19]

Important for our purposes are the following points extracted from the *Indiculus:*

1. The preamble announces that the collection of theses that is to follow are pronouncements of the See of Peter and of the African councils approved by the bishops of the Roman See against the "enemies of the grace of God" and the "most noxious defenders of free will." [20]

2. Innocent I is cited in support of the proposition that "through the sin of Adam all men have lost their natural possibility and innocence and no one is able to arise from the depth of that fall by means of free will unless the grace of the merciful God should raise him up." [21] Here we have a good statement of the Augustinian concept of the bondage of the free will. The existence of *liberum arbitrium* is not denied. What is denied is the possibility of free will apart from grace to liberate man from the misery of this fallen condition.

3. Chapter 3: even when one has been renewed by the grace of baptism, he is not able to overcome the temptations of Satan and the concupiscence of the flesh unless he daily receives God's assistance to persevere in a good life.[22]

4. Chapter 4: No one uses his free will well except through Christ.[23] This chapter is related to Chapter 2, where we read: "No one is good by himself, unless He who alone is good gives him a participation of Himself." [24] In both theses "good" is taken in the sense of true, salutary good. The question of "natural" or ethical goodness, goodness *ex officio,* as Augustine calls it, is simply not considered here.

---

18 Portalié, "Célestin," DTC, 2, 2053; Amann, DTC, 14, 1830; K. Gross, "Coelestin I.," LThK, 2, 1254; J. Martin, "Prosper," LThK, 8, 812.

19 Portalié, DTC, 2, 2053. Cf. *idem.,* DTC, 1, 2464; tr., p. 318: "These *chapters* have always been regarded, at least since the sixth century, as a document officially expressing the faith of the Church."

20 DS 238.

21 DS 239.

22 DS 241.

23 DS 242.

24 DS 240.

5. Chapter 5: All efforts, all works and all merits of the saints are to be referred to the glory and praise of God, because no one can please God except by means of that which God himself has given.[25] Then an excerpt is given from a letter (no longer extant) of the African bishops to Pope Zosimus, in which the influence of Augustine is evident. The bishops refer to a letter of Zosimus which attacked "those who extol the freedom of the human will against the grace of God." [26] Citing Prov. 8: 35 (LXX) the bishops teach: "for anything good which the sons of God do, it is necessary that God touch their hearts by his fatherly inspirations." [27]

6. Chapter 6 treats even more specifically than the foregoing chapter the question of God's action on the free will: "God so acts in the hearts of men and in the free will itself that every holy thought, every pious resolution and every movement of good will is from God, because through him we can do good and without him we can do nothing." [28]

7. In Chapter 7 we find a reaffirmation and a repetition of the text of canons 3, 4 and 5 of the Council of Carthage of 418.[29]

8. In Chapter 8 the teachings of the first seven chapters are summarized by the author when he refers to "the inviolable decrees of the most blessed and Apostolic See, according to which our most holy fathers . . . have taught us that the beginning of good will, the increase of good works and the perseverance in them till the end are to be referred to the grace of Christ."

Then he develops an argument from the liturgy, applying the principle: the Church's prayer determines her rule of faith (legem credendi lex statuat supplicandi). The Church constantly prays, argues the author, that infidels be given faith, that idolators be freed from their unholy errors, that the veil may be removed from the hearts of the Jews so that the light of the truth may be manifest, that heretics may receive the spirit of renewed charity, that lapsed Catholics may be brought to the medicine of penance, and finally, that catechumens, after they have been led to the sacraments of regeneration, may have opened to them the court of heavenly mercy.[30] But the results of these prayers show that they are not made to the Lord in vain, since it pleases God to draw

---

[25] DS 243.
[26] Ibid.
[27] Ibid.
[28] DS 244.
[29] Cf. DS 245ff. and 225ff. See footnote 14 above.
[30] DS 246.—The liturgical reference is undoubtedly to the orationes of the Good Friday liturgy. This is the oldest known document containing the explicit wording "legem credendi lex statuat supplicandi." Cf. K. Federer, "Lex orandi-lex credendi," LThK, 6, 1001f.

many men away from all kinds of errors as we see in such texts as Col.
1: 13 and Rom. 9: 22f. This work of conversion is regarded as being so
much the work of God that thanksgiving and praise are continually
given to God for illuminating or correcting such persons.[31]

In the second paragraph of Chapter 9 the foregoing doctrines are
once again summarized: On the basis of these ecclesiastical definitions
and sacred documents we are convinced, by the aid of God, that (i) all
good inclinations and works and all efforts and all virtues by which we
are directed to God from the very beginning of faith have God as their
author; (ii) all of man's merits are preceded by the grace of him through
whom we begin to will and to do anything good; (iii) free will is
certainly not taken away by this help and assistance of God, but it is
liberated; (iv) God's goodness toward men is so great that he wills those
things to be our merits which are his own gifts and he wills to give
eternal rewards for those gifts he has given us; (v) he acts in us in such
a way that what he wills, we also will and do . . . in such a way that we
are co-operators with his grace.[32]

3. *The Condemnation of Predestinarianism in the Fifth Century*

Until now all the magisterial decisions we have considered have been
concerned largely with correcting Pelagian and Semipelagian errors. The
fifth century, however, witnessed not only a struggle between the followers of Augustine and such anti-Augustinian figures as Cassian, Vincent of Lerins and Faustus of Riez,[33] but there emerged also the first of
the Christian predestinationists, Lucidus. Little is known about Lucidus,
a priest of Gaul, other than his involvement in the predestinationist
heresy.[34] Among the "ultrapredestinationist" [35] views upheld by Lucidus, views which he retracted and condemned at the Council of Arles
(473 or 475), were the following: (i) after the fall of the first man free
will was totally extinct; (ii) Christ did not die for all men; (iii) those
who are lost, are lost by God's will. In his assertion of the true faith,
Lucidus affirmed (iv) that the liberty of the human will has been at-

---

[31] DS 246: In ch. 9 (DS 247) we find another liturgical argument to support
the truth that all salutary events are to be attributed to God: the universal practice of exorcising Satan prior to the acual baptism signifies that the victor takes
possession of the one previously held captive by Satan.

[32] DS 248.

[33] Cf. Portalié, "Augustinisme (Développement historique de l')," DTC, 1, 1519-
2522; Amann, DTC, 14, 1833-1837.

[34] É. Amann, "Lucidus," DTC, 9, 1020-1024; Portalié, DTC, 1, 2522ff.; Seeberg,
II, p. 580; J. Auer, "Prädestinatianismus," LThK, 8, 660; R. Garrigou-Lagrange,
Predestination, 5th ed. (St. Louis-London, 1953), pp. 17-23.

[35] The expression is Seeberg's, II, p. 580.

tenuated and infirmed, but has not been made extinct and (v) that he who is lost could have been saved.[36]

4. The Condemnation of Semipelagianism at the Second Council of Orange (529)

Parodoxically, the man who so vigorously opposed predestinationism and who was commissioned by the Council of Arles to draw up an indictment of the exaggerated Augustinianism of Lucidus, Bishop Faustus of Riez, was himself more of a Semipelagian than Cassian or Vincent of Lerins.[37] An ascetic, as were most of the Pelagians and Semipelagians, Faustus condemned the Pelagian doctrine of grace and original sin without reservation.[38] But in his opposition to the errors of the predestinarians, in his eagerness to defend the existence of free will, he fell into a kind of synergism that was quite foreign to the Augustinian concept of cooperation which accorded a clear sovereignty and primacy to the action of grace.[39]

Faustus was soon attacked by the devoted follower of Augustine, Fulgentius of Ruspe, in a work, *Contra Faustum Libri VII*, no longer extant.[40] While rejecting the teaching of Faustus that predestination is nothing more than God's foreknowledge and that the will takes the initiative while grace cooperates with it, Fulgentius firmly maintained that predestination and grace do not take away man's free will.[41] In 520 Pope Hormisdas, in a letter to the African bishop, Possessor, assured him that the writings of Faustus have no authority in the Church. Further, on the question of free will and grace, Hormisdas says that, although the teaching of the Roman Catholic Church can be ascertained in various books of Saint Augustine, especially those written to Hilary and to Prosper, it is, however, also to be found in the documents preserved in the archives of the Church. In any event, whoever examines diligently the words of the Apostle will clearly know what he ought to follow.[42]

Although in the Church of the fifth century "Semipelagianism as a

---

[36] DS 330-333; 339. Seeberg is incorrect when he suggests that it is un-Augustinian and Semipelagian to say "der menschliche Wille ist zwar verwundet durch die Sünde, aber eine gewisse Freiheit ist ihm doch geblieben": II, 573. We have already seen that Augustine himself speaks not just of "einer gewissen Freiheit" after the fall, but of *liberum arbitrium*, even though it is only a *liberum arbitrium captivatum* and *infirmatum*.

[37] See Loofs, p. 353; Seeberg, II, pp. 577f.; Godet, DTC, 5, 2103ff.

[38] Godet, *ibid.*

[39] *Ibid.*, 2104.

[40] Godet, DTC, 5, 2101; cf. Portalié, DTC, 1, 2521f.; Seeberg, II, pp. 584f.

[41] Godet, DTC, 5, 2524f.

[42] Portalié, DTC, 1, 2465; DS 366.

theory was not accepted in official circles," [43] the recurring anti-Augustinian doctrines in Gaul, especially those of Faustus, are proof that the teaching of the earlier African councils and of the Roman bishops had not yet become universally normative. This uncertain situation was finally clarified by the official and unequivocal condemnation of Semipelagianism at the Second Council of Orange (529), one of the most important provincial councils in Church history.[44] This synod is rightly termed "the so-called Second Council of Orange" [45] because its teaching—twenty-five canons, eight under the form of anathemizations,[46] seventeen in the form of positive theses,[47] followed by a profession of faith [48]—was not the result of deliberations by an assembly of bishops as is normally the case. Rather, Caesarius of Arles, seeking to put an end to the Semipelagian ideas still circulating in the south of Gaul, submitted to Pope Felix III (IV) a list of nineteen "chapters," based largely upon Augustine's works, which condemned Semipelagianism. The Pope selected eight of these, set them into their definitive form, and added sixteen theses extracted from a collection of Augustinian texts drawn up by Prosper of Aquitaine at Rome circa 450 (*392 sententiae ex Augustino delibutae*). These canons were sent back to Caesarius, who modified them slightly, added a seventeenth thesis himself (canon 10), summarized the doctrine in a profession of faith, and on the occasion of the consecration of a basilica in Orange, succeeded in having the entire declaration signed by fourteen bishops and eight laymen.[49] Aubert writes: "The council seems to have been less a deliberating assembly than a docile audience which was used to promulgate the traditional teaching on grace in the very area in which it had been attacked." [50]

Directly relevant to our study is the following teaching from the Synod of Orange: (1) It is Pelagian and contrary to Scripture to say that the "liberty of the soul" remains intact after Adam's sin.[51] From the scriptural texts cited in the canon [52] it is clear that the "liberty"

---

[43] Seeberg, II, p. 585.

[44] For a detailed account of the events leading up to this council see Portalié, DTC, 1, 2520ff.; 2524ff.; Fritz, "Orange (deuxième Concile d')," DTC, 11, 1087ff.; Amann, DTC, 14, 1837-1844; J. Aubert, *Le Problème de l'Acte de Foi*, 3rd ed. (Louvain, 1958); Fransen, "Orange, 3," LThK, 7, 1188f.

[45] Fransen, LThK, 7, 1188.

[46] DS 371-378.

[47] DS 379-395.

[48] DS 396f.

[49] Fritz, DTC, 11, 1089-1092; Seeberg, II, pp. 586f., footnote 4; Amann, DTC, 14, 1842ff.; Aubert, pp. 35f.; Fransen, LThK, 7, 1188f.

[50] P. 36.

[51] DS 371, can. 1: "animae libertate illaesa durante."

[52] Ezech. 18: 20; Rom. 6: 16; II Pet. 2: 19.

referred to here is not *liberum arbitrium* but freedom from sin. (2) To say that God waits for our will to cleanse us from sin and to deny that our very desire to be cleansed comes about through the infusion and operation of the Holy Spirit within us is to resist the Holy Spirit speaking through the Scriptures.[53] (3) ". . . [N]ot only the increase of faith but also its beginning and the very desire for faith, by which we believe in Him who justifies the ungodly" is a gift of grace and does not belong to us by nature.[54] (4) Anyone is heretical who asserts that he can, by the power of nature, conceive . . . any good thought which pertains to the salvation of eternal life, or that he can choose or consent to the salutary preaching of the Gospel without the illumination and inspiration of the Holy Spirit, who gives to all delight in consenting to and believing the truth.[55] (Here we have a firm statement on the necessity of grace for every salutary act. Further to be noted is the plain implication that faith or belief involves an *electio* and a *consensus,* something that we have already found in Augustine.) (5) The *liberum arbitrium* of Adam's descendants is wounded (*vitiatum; laesum*),[56] weakened (*infirmatum*) [57] and diminished (*inclinatum; attenuatum*),[58] but its existence is not denied. (6) God and man cooperate in good works. For as often as we do good, God acts in us and with us in order that we might act.[59] (7) A reward is due to good works if they are performed; but grace, to which we have no claim, precedes these works in order that they might be performed.[60] (8) Man of himself has nothing but sin and error.[61]

---

[53] DS 256, canon 4. Two of Augustine's favorite texts are cited: Prov. 8: 35: LXX and Phil. 2: 13. Cf. can. 6, DS 376.

[54] DS 375, can. 5. Tr. J. Leith, *Creeds of the Churches* (New York, 1963), p. 39. For a detailed explanation of these terms see J. Chéné, "Que signifiaient 'initium fidei' et 'affectus credultatis' pour les Semipélagiens?," *Recherches de science religieuse,* 35 (1948), 566-588; Aubert, p. 37 and M. Seckler, *Instinkt und Glaubenswille,* p. 91.

[55] DS 377, can. 7: "Si quis per naturae vigorem bonum aliquid, quod ad salutem pertinet vitae aeternae, cogitare, ut expedit, aut eligere, sive salutari, id est evangelicae praedicationi consentire posse confirmat, absque illuminatione et inspiratione Spiritus Sancti, qui dat omnibus suavitatem in consentiendo et credendo veritati haeretico fallitur spiritu. . . ." Cf. canon 20, DS 390.

[56] DS 379, can. 8.

[57] DS 383, canon 13. Leith, p. 41, is misleading when he translates "infirmatum" as "destroyed."

[58] DS 396.

[59] DS 379, can. 9: ". . . quoties enim bona agimus, Deus in nobis atque nobiscum, ut operemur, operatur."

[60] DS 392, can. 18: "Debetur merces bonis operibus, si fiant; sed gratia, quae non debetur, praecedit, ut fiant."

[61] DS 392, can. 22: "Nemo habet de suo nisi mendacium et peccatum." This is the 323rd thesis of Prosper's collection. It comes from Augustine *In Ioann. tract.,* 5, 1. Cf. Augustine, *Contra duas epist. pelag.,* III, 8, 24.—Concerning the simi-

Appended to the twenty-five canons is a profession of faith composed by Caesarius,[62] to which all the bishops (fourteen) and "distinguished men" subscribed. This confession has special importance, since it, and not the canons themselves, was the specific object of the magisterial approval granted by Pope Boniface II in his letter to Caesarius of January 25, 531 which, it should be mentioned, praised Augustine by name.[63] According to the profession of faith: (1) the *liberum arbitrium* of man has been so weakened through Adam's sin that no one can ever love God unless the grace of the divine mercy has preceded him.[64] (2) The faith of the saints of the Old and New Testaments was not bestowed through any good of nature originally given to Adam, but through the grace of God. This grace, even after the coming of the Lord, is not in the power of the *liberum arbitrium* of those desiring baptism, but is conferred by the goodness of Christ. (3) All baptized persons, if they wish to labor faithfully, can and ought, with the aid and cooperation of Christ, to do those things which pertain to salvation.[65] (4) If anyone wishes to believe that some are predestined to evil by God's power, he is anathema.[66] (5) In every good work it is not we who take the initiative and are afterward aided by God, but it is God himself who, prior to all merit on our part, inspires in us both faith and love for him.[67]

---

larity of this proposition to the censured propositions 25 and 27 of Baius (DS 1925 and 1927) see our excursus on the different meanings of "sin" in Augustine, as well as Fritz, DTC, 11, 1099 and Amann, DTC, 14, 1846ff. Fritz accepts the explanation of J. Ernst, *Die Werke und Tugenden der Ungläubigen nach S. Augustinus, nebst einem Anhang über den 22ten Canon des Arausicanum secundum* (Innsbruck, 1871), according to which works that are only naturally good are called sins by Augustine because they are worthless for salvation. A possible support for this view can be found in other canons of Orange II. When can. 7 (DS 377) speaks of "bonum aliquid, *quod* ad salutem pertinet," doesn't this imply that there is another kind of *bonum* which does not pertain to eternal life? Can. 17 (DS 387) attributes fortitude to pagans. Even though this is not the same as Christian fortitude, it must still be considered to be natural or pagan "virtue" which is *ethically* better than cowardice. Cf. Schmaus, III/2, p. 264. Finally, in the confirmation of the confession of faith attached to the canons, Pope Boniface II says: "nihil esse prorsus secundum Deum boni, quod sine Dei quis gratia aut velle, aut incipere aut perficere possit. . . ." (DS 399). Boniface is therefore saying that grace is needed to make an action *entirely* good, i.e., good before God. This would seem to imply the possibility of only partially good actions or actions good from a certain point of view or "secundum hominem."

[62] DS 396f.

[63] DS 398: ". . . confessionem vestram . . . auctoritate Sedis Apostolicae firmaremus." Caesarius sought papal confirmation because of continued Semipelagian resistance. Cf. Fritz, DTC, 11, 1102f.; Amann, DTC, 14, 1848f. Fransen, LThK, 7, 1189 maintains that it is only the summary of the profession of faith found in Boniface's letter which can be regarded as a strictly defined dogma of faith.

[64] DS 396.

[65] DS 397.

[66] *Ibid.*

[67] *Ibid.*

Catholic [68] and Protestant [69] scholars agree that, although Orange II does not represent a total endorsement of Augustine's anti-Pelagian teaching on sin, grace, free will and predestination, it nevertheless is an unmistakable, official acceptance by the Church of the decisive theses [70] that constitute "moderate" Augustinianism. The Church thereby received "a great heritage" and Orange II can therefore be considered as "a real step forward." [71]

Until the eighth century, the decrees of the Council of Orange enjoyed considerable authority, but from the tenth to the middle of the sixteenth century, as H. Bouillard has shown,[72] theologians seem to have been completely unaware of the existence of the Council of Orange and its

[68] Cf. Portalié, DTC, 1, 2526f.; Fritz, DTC, 11, 1102; Amann, DTC, 14, 1850; Fransen, LThK, 7, 1189; Schmaus, III/2, p. 373.

[69] Seeberg, II, 588-591. W. von Loewenich, "Zur Gnadenlehre bei Augustin und bei Luther," in: *Von Augustin zu Luther* (Witten/Ruhr, 1959), writes: Orange II "bewahrt die religiös entscheidenden Sätze von Augustins Gnadenlehre, es hat aber nicht alle Spitzensätze übernommen": p. 111. Loofs, pp. 356f. sees even Orange II as tending toward Semipelagianism! He reaches this conclusion, it seems, because of his tendency to identify almost any anti-Augustinian thesis with Semipelagianism. Such a view of Orange II is rightly rejected by von Loewenich: "Man hat dem Arausicanum einen schlecht verhüllten Semipelagianismus vorgeworfen. Dieses Urteil dürfte zu scharf sein.": *Ibid.* Loewenich reminds those who point out that Orange II does not accept the idea of double predestination and *gratia irresistibilis* (Seeberg, Loofs) that these doctrines are "tatsächlich bedenkliche Elemente in Augustins Gnadenlehre": *Ibid.* For our part, we do not think that it has been proven that Augustine actually held such ideas; they are certainly not explicitly taught by him. We can, however, agree with Amann's view, held by many Catholic Augustine scholars, that: "Ni la valeur universelle de la rédemption, ni la volonté salvifique du Père céleste n'avaient obtenu du Docteur de la grâce toute la considération que méritaient ces thèses capitales" DTC, 14, 1850.

[70] This is Portalié's expression: DTC, 1, 2527. It is adopted by Fritz, LThK, 11, 1102 and Fransen, LThK, 7, 1189. Cf. F. Cayré, "The Great Augustinism," *Theol. Digest*, 2 (1954), 169-173.

[71] Seeberg, II, p. 589. Fransen, "The Authority of the Councils," pp. 63f. evaluates the canons of the Council of Orange the same as he did those of Carthage (418): They "have a special dogmatic value, and this is in great part due to the fact that for centuries the Universal Church has recognized that these texts contain a singularly profound statement of her faith. . . . Few local councils have acquired such authority as these in the Universal Church and this as early as the beginning of the Middle Ages. This recognition given by the Universal Church is a sufficient guarantee that the teaching of these councils is of faith, even if we cannot use the technical term 'a formal definition of faith'."

[72] *Conversion et Grâce chez Thomas d'Aquin* (Paris, 1944), pp. 94f.; 97; 98-102; 114-121. Bouillard emphasizes that, although the decrees of Orange were lost during the Middle Ages, the doctrine they expressed was not. This doctrine—including the doctrine of the necessity of grace for the "initium fidei"—became known to Thomas Aquinas and other medieval theologians through the writings of St. Augustine. *Ibid.*, p. 121. So great was the authority of Augustine in the Middle Ages, says Bouillard, that "on admit comme vérité de foi ce qu'il connait comme tel": *ibid.*, pp. 114f. This is why Thomas could say in the *S. Th.*, I-II, q. 114, a. 5, ad 1, that it is a "veritas fidei" that the *initium fidei* is from God.

teachings. Only at the time of the Council of Trent were they recovered and reaffirmed. Since Trent they have been restored to their rightful place as important witnesses of the tradition of the ancient Church in Catholic treatises on grace.

5. *The Condemnation of Predestinarianism in the Ninth Century*

Semipelagianism disappeared almost completely after the Council of Orange, but not forever, as we shall see. The necessity of grace for the beginning of salvation had been forcefully and authoritatively asserted and the biblically-formed Augustinian dialectic of grace and free will had been preserved. The only other serious assault on this dialectic in the remaining centuries of the first millennium came from those who would destroy the dialectic by denying free will. These were not resurgent Manichaeans, whose brand of determinism was long since refuted by Augustine, but the Predestinarians of the ninth century,[73] led by the Benedictine monk, Gottschalk of Orbais.[74] This controversy, which still awaits a definitive study, is complicated not only by reason of its subject-matter and terminology, but also because of our still incomplete understanding of the actual opinions held by the various participants in the controversy.[75] Thus it is really not possible to say definitively whether Gottschalk really held the proposition that, after the fall, man's free will can only be used for evil, so that good can never be attributed to the cooperation of the human will, but to grace alone.[76] Further, some of the formulations of the provincial councils involved were so obscure and

---

As we shall see, while Augustine was for Thomas the highest authority next to Scripture itself on the doctrine of grace, Erasmus regarded Augustine as somewhat of an extremist.

[73] As early as c. 785, Pope Hadrian I judged it necessary to clarify the doctrine of predestination in his letter to the bishops of Spain (DS 596). Against the either-or thinking of those who, in the face of God's power say there in no need for human effort, and those who, considering man's power of free will see no need for prayer, Hadrian simply cites the teaching of Fulgentius, who has come to be called the "Augustinus Abbreviatus." God indeed prepares from all eternity works of mercy and justice, says Hadrian, but he does not prepare evil wills or evil works, only the just and eternal punishments that they deserve.

[74] On Gottschalk see the articles by Godet, DTC, 6, 1500ff. and K. Vielhaber, LThK, 4, 1144f.; *idem.*, RGG, 2, 1813. Cf. also Vielhaber, "Hinkmar v. Reims," LThK, 5, 374f.

[75] A good summary of the controversy can be found in B. Lavaud, "Prédestination. IV. La controverse sur la prédestination au IXe siècle," DTC, 12, 2901-2935. Shorter accounts are offered by Portalié, "Augustinisme," DTC. 1, 2527-2530; Seeberg, III, pp. 65-71; J. Auer, "Prädestination, II. Geschichtlich," LThK, 8, 665f.

[76] Lavaud, DTC, 12, 2930, thinks this is unlikely. Seeberg, III, p. 67, on the other hand, thinks that Gottschalk is guilty of "schroffen Determinismus."

ambiguous, that instead of clarifying things, they contributed to a prolongation of the controversy.[77] Added to this is the fact that the discussion was led away from the biblical and Augustinian theology of predestination by the introduction of the neo-Platonic philosophical categories of John Scotus Eriugena.[78]

In spite of this highly entangled state of the question, it is possible to find some agreement resulting from the ninth century predestination controversy, despite the lack of unanimity on the more obscure questions: (1) God wills all men without exception to be saved, even though all in fact are not saved.[79] (2) That certain persons are saved is a gift of him who saves; that some are lost is the fault of those who are lost.[80] These are not lost because they could not be good, but because they did not want to be good and have remained in the state of condemnation (*massa damnationis*) either by original or actual demerit.[81] (3) God's foreknowledge and predestination impose on man no necessity of doing evil in such a way that he could be nothing else than he is.[82] (4) There is a predestination of some to eternal life through mercy and grace.[83]

---

[77] The Council of Quierzy (853), for example, confuses in canon 2 (DS 622) *liberum arbitrium* and *libertas arbitrii,* natural and acquired freedom. See the criticism of this canon by Portalié, DTC, 1, 2528. Although the Council of Valence (855) partially corrected the Council of Quierzy, adds Portalié, "il n'est pas moins certain que les expressions de Valence sont encore plus malheureusees, plus obscures que celles de Kiersy. . . ." *Ibid.*

[78] Lavaud, DTC, 12, 2911ff. and L. Scheffczyk, "Johannes Skotus Eriugena," LThK, 5, 1082.

[79] DS 623.

[80] *Ibid.* Cf. the *Liber de tribus epistolis* which emanated from the Church of Lyon (c. 852): "Quod ergo non possunt salvari eorum est vitium non Dei. . . ." PL 121, 997.—Loofs, p. 375, is incorrect when he calls the possibility of resistance to grace which is presupposed in this book "Krypto-Semipelagianismus." Cf. footnote 69 above.

[81] DS 627. Augustine's concept of the "massa damnationis" is found in both the councils of Quierzy and Valence: DS 621 and 627.

[82] DS 626f. concerns God's foreknowledge; DS 628f. predestination. DS 628 expressly approves the teaching of Orange II on this point (DS 397). The kind of necessity that is excluded as a result of God's foreknowledge and predestination is that which prevents the wicked from being other than they are: "ut aliud esse non posset." This understanding of necessity is found in both canons: DS 627 and 629.

[83] DS 621 and 628. While the Council of Quierzy holds that there is "unam Dei praedestinationem tantummodo" (DS 621), Valence asserts that there is a "praedestinationem electorum ad vitam et praedestinationem impiorum ad mortem." Any opposition between single or double predestination here is purely verbal. The double predestination taught at Valence involves a predestination of the wicked to death that is essentially different from the predestination of the elect: "in electione tamen salvandorum misericordiam Dei praecedere meritum bonum: in damnatione autem periturorum meritum malum praecedere iustum Dei iudicium" (DS 628). Cf. E. Schlink, "Der theologische Syllogismus als

(5) God's foreknowledge of sin is the basis for reprobation, (i.e., predestination of the wicked to damnation).[84] (6) Free will is weakened (*infirmatum*) by the sin of Adam but is restored and healed by the grace of the Lord Jesus in his faithful.[85] "Where predestination is conceived as the destruction of man's responsibility and freedom in the work of salvation (theological determinism)," says K. Rahner, "there we have heretical Predestinationism." [86]

The ninth century predestination controversy, as Lavaud correctly notes,[87] was not merely an argument over words, even though there was a considerable amount of verbal confusion. On a much more fundamental level it was a struggle between two diverse mentalities which have always been present in the Church, at least since the time of Augustine. The one tendency, professing loyalty to Augustine and Paul, seeks to affirm before all else the absolute primacy of the divine will in predestining and preparing man for salvation. The other tendency, refusing to concede that it is any less faithful to Augustine or to St. Paul, insists on safeguarding, in the name of the holiness of God and his desire to save all men, the free will of man in salvation. Otherwise, this group argues, God alone will bear the responsibility—if he alone has free will—for sin and salvation alike, for damnation to hell and predestination to glory.

Indeed, "the episode of the ninth century contains in germ all the later debates. Two conceptions came into conflict. They remain even today, each expressing in its own manner something of the incomprehensible mystery." [88] These tendencies, if they are to be considered as belonging to the Catholic tradition, must be understood as emphases of different poles of the mystery, not as the exclusion of either pole by a denial either of God's sovereign will, upon which the very beginning of man's salvation depends, or of man's free cooperation with God's omni-

---

Problem der Prädestinationslehre," in: *Einsicht und Glaube, Festchr. für G. Söhngen* (Freiburg-Basel-Wien, 1962), p. 312. Defensible as it is to speak of a double predestination, the Church nevertheless ceased to use this concept.

[84] DS 621 and 628.

[85] DS 633. The Council of Valence expressed its intention to remain within the tradition of the teaching on grace and free will which had been formed by the Fathers, who based their teaching on the authority of Scripture, by the definitions of the Councils of Carthage and Orange and by the doctrine of the Roman pontiffs.

[86] K. Rahner, "Prädestination, III. Systematisch," LThK, 8, 669. Rahner cites in this connection DS 596, 621ff., 625ff. as well as the later doctrine of Trent: DS 1556 & 1567. Cf. *idem.*, "Freiheit, III kirchl. Lehramt," LThK, 4, 331; *Theol. Dictionary*, p. 373.

[87] DTC, 12, 2933.

[88] *Ibid.*

potent action. Such an exclusivist theology would destroy the dialectical tension of the mysterious relationship between the all-embracing activity of God and the free will of the creature. It would result in either Pelagianism (Semipelagianism) or Predestinarianism.

6. The Defense of Grace and Free Will in the Magisterial Decisions of the 11th and 12th Centuries

Two centuries later we find a very concise statement of the Catholic belief concerning predestination, grace and free will in the profession of faith composed by Pope Leo IX which was sent to Peter, Bishop of Antioch in 1053: [89] "I believe that God predestines only good things, but that he has foreseen both good things and bad. I believe and profess that the grace of God precedes (praevenire) and follows man, in such a way, however, that I do not deny that a rational creature has free will." [90]

The previous document indicates that the concept of free will was firmly and clearly upheld as the Church entered her second millennium. However, a Semipelagian tendency to exaggerate the power of the free will came to the surface in the writings of Peter Abelard (1079-1142). Along with a number of other errors, the following propositions attributed to Abelard were condemned by the Council of Sens (1140/1): "Christ did not become incarnate in order to liberate us from the yoke of the devil," [91] and: "Free will is sufficient of itself to do something good." [92] The condemnations of the Council of Sens were confirmed by Pope Innocent II.[93] The following year, under the influence of Peter the Venerable, Abelard retracted his errors at Cluny in a profession of faith shortly before his death.[94]

---

[89] DS 680-686.

[90] DS 685. Here the general formula "ita tamen" indicates the desire of the official teachers of the Church not to try to settle the "how" of the relationship between the efficacious grace of God and man's free will. The Church is interested above all in maintaining the dialectic which constitutes the mystery. The question of the "how" is committed to free discussion among the theologians. The Church has given authoritative endorsement to none of the proposed "solutions." On the other hand, she has always reacted unfavorably when one of the poles of the dialectic has been endangered. Cf. Rahner, LThK, 4, 332.

[91] DS 723. Portalié, "Abélard," DTC, 1, 47 says that Abelard completely denies the redemption in this thesis, holding that the Word was made flesh simply to provide us with a splendid example of love.

[92] DS 725. Portalié, ibid., notes that Abelard, like the Pelagians, does not deny the necessity of grace, but that he identifies grace with any gift from God, even the natural gift of free will. Cf. J. Rivière, "Mérite, (Analyse théologique: Abélard)," DTC, 10, 668-671.

[93] DS pp. 235f.

[94] Portalié, DTC, 1, 38.

7. The "lex orandi"

In this chapter we have been concerned until now, only with dogmatic statements of the Church of the early Middle Ages concerning free will and grace. But the belief of the Church is manifested not only in her doctrinal pronouncements. The dogmatic statement is, as Schlink rightly points out, "Only *one* in the midst of many other statements of faith. Faith answers God for his act of salvation also in prayer, worship, testimony, doctrine, etc. The dogmatic statement is also not the only statement in which the *consensus* of faith achieves formulation. Even statements of the liturgy, of catechesis, of the traditions of the fathers, of religious tracts, etc., signify in the life of the Church more than just the statements of the individual believers who formulated them, but they are effective as statements which form and define the Church community." [95]

When we look at the Church's liturgy—we confine ourselves here simply to the *Missale Romanum*—we find that her official prayer (*lex orandi*) is an expression of her authentic belief (*lex credendi*) [96] about grace and freedom. We have already seen that the *Indiculus* demonstrated the Catholic belief from the Good Friday liturgy (1) that the beginning of conversion and of good will as well as the perseverance in the Christian life is to be attributed to the grace of Christ.[97] The prayers from various Masses during the liturgical year also teach: (2) man's powerlessness and inability to do good apart from God's help,[98] (3) that grace works internally by illuminating our minds, exciting our hearts and wills and directing our actions,[99] and finally, (4) that it is

---

[95] *The Coming Christ*, p. 168.

[96] DS 246. Cf. footnote 30 above. Piepkorn, "Grace," in: *Encyclopedia of the Lutheran Church*, II, 952, notes that an anti-Pelagian thrust characterizes the collects of the Leonine, Gelasian and Gregorian sacramentaries.

[97] *Ibid*. Cf. also the oration from the Mass of the 16th Sunday after Pentecost, where we pray that God's grace may always precede and follow us (*praeveniat et sequatur*), the same language used by Leo IX (DS 685; cf. footnote 90 above).

[98] Cf. the *Orationes* from the following Masses: 2nd Sunday of Lent; 1st, 3rd and 18th Sunday after Pentecost; Feast of St. Martin (Nov. 11th). As a result of our powerlessness to do good without God, we can have no confidence in our own justice or actions: collects from the 2nd Common of a confessor and Sexagesima Sunday. Our confidence is solely in God: collect from Mass of the 5th Sunday after Epiphany.

[99] Cf. the collects from the Masses of the 2nd Sunday within the octave of Christmas; 5th Sunday after Epiphany; 2nd Sunday of Lent; 5th Sunday after Easter; 18th Sunday after Pentecost; Last Sunday after Pentecost. Also: the prayers over the people for Ember Wednesday and Friday in Lent and the 5th oration of Ember Saturday in Lent. In the Introit of the 21st Sunday after Pentecost, the Church instructs her faithful concerning the omnipotence of God's

God who converts and liberates us from bondage to sin and to Satan.[100] It is important to notice that the liturgical prayers of the Church have no interest whatever in defining or even asserting man's natural free will. The only freedom that is sought in the liturgical prayers is freedom from sin and from Satan.

---

will by citing Esther 13:9f. (Vulgate): ". . . non est qui possit resistere voluntati tuae. . . ." Cf. Schmaus, III/2, p. 255.

[100] Besides frequent use of such biblical texts as Ps. 17: 3 and 49 (cf. Introit from the Mass of Wednesday of Passion week) and the daily Lord's Prayer, where God is called upon as our Liberator, the theme of the Father or the Son as the Liberator is also found in the ordinary of the Mass in the embolism: "Libera nos quaesumus, Domine . . ." This prayer is simply an expansion of the final petition of the Lord's Prayer. Cf. Jungmann, *The Mass of the Roman Rite*, II, pp. 284f. According to Jungmann, II, p. 345, this prayer dates from the 8th century.

6

Free Will and Bondage to Sin
in Early Scholasticism
and Thomas Aquinas

I
t would carry us too far from our purpose to trace carefully the
development of the doctrine of grace and free will from the tenth
century teaching through early Scholasticism,[1] or even to compare
the teaching of Thomas Aquinas on this point with that of the other
masters of high Scholasticism. We shall therefore simply sketch briefly
the developments in the understanding of free will and bondage to sin
during the Scholastic period which deepen our comprehension of the
state of our question.

I. FROM ANSELM TO BONAVENTURE

In Anselm of Canterbury (1033/4-1109) [2] we meet an ardent disciple of Augustine who is, at the same time, the first of the Scholastics.[3]
In his *Dialogus de Libertate Arbitrii* Anselm seeks a definition of free
will (*libertas arbitrii*) that applies to God as well as to rational crea-

---

[1] We have already seen in our treatment of the 9th century predestination controversy the contribution to our question made by the pre-Scholastics. By way of
contrast, the 10th century was, as M. Grabmann, *Die Geschichte der katholischen
Theologie* (Darmstadt, 1961), p. 28, puts it, "a time of scientific decline." And,
although the 11th century saw a rise of interest in eucharistic theology in reaction
to the unorthodox speculations of Berengarius, the first half of that century, at
least, contributed little of importance to the question of grace and free will.

[2] See J. Verweyen, *Das Problem der Willensfreiheit in der Scholastik* (Heidel-
berg, 1908), pp. 44ff.; O. Lottin, *Psychologie et Morale aux XIIe et XIIIe siècles*,
T. 1, *Problèmes de Psychologie* (Louvain-Gembloux, 1942), pp. 12ff.; F. Bäum-
ker, *Die Lehre Anselms v. Canterbury über den Willen und seine Wahlfreiheit*
(Münster, 1912); Seeberg, III, pp. 161ff. and 218f.; J. Bainvel, "Anselme (Saint),"
DTC, 1, 1327-1350; F. S. Schmitt, "Anselm v. Canterbury," LThK, 1, 592ff.; *idem.*,
RGG, 1, 397f.; Adler, pp. 417f.

[3] Cf. Grabmann, pp. 29f. Schmitt, LThK, 1, 593, calls Anselm the "most important disciple" of Augustine. A comparison between the Augustinian and
Anselmian doctrine of freedom is found in Clark, ch. X.

tures, presupposing always, of course, that it will be found in different ways in creatures and creator. This leads Anselm, building upon Augustine, to exclude from the outset any definition of free will in terms of the power of sinning or not sinning, since such freedom could not be present in God, the blessed or in the fallen angels.[4] Free will is, rather, the *power* of preserving the rectitude of the will.[5] Adam had this power and it was natural to him.[6] It could therefore not be lost even when he fell into sin, that is, when he did not preserve the rectitude of will which God had given him.[7] But whether he has rectitude of will (justice) or not, he always has *libertas arbitrii* and it can, in this sense, always be called *liber*.[8]

Anselm distinguishes the power from the act of the power and asserts that there is no power that is sufficient to act by itself.[9] This distinction, rooted in Aristotle, together with its corollary: no created power can reduce itself to act, became the common property of the later Scholastics. It is important for our problem because, if it is always maintained, it implicitly provides us in advance with an answer to the question: Can a man do anything for salvation by his own powers? Anselm—and the majority of the Scholastics—would consider this possibility excluded by the very way in which they define "power." All of man's powers must be "actualized" ultimately and immediately either by God's general (com-

---

[4] Anselm, *De libertate arbitrii*, I, PL 158, 488: ". . . non pertinet ad diffinitionem libertatis arbitrii posse peccare. Denique nec libertas nec pars libertatis est potestas peccandi. . . ." Cf. Augustine, *De correptione et gratia*, 12, 32f.

[5] *De lib. arb.*, III, PL 158, 494: "Quapropter restat libertatem arbitrii datam esse rationali naturae ad servandam acceptam rectitudinem voluntatis." Cf. *ibid.*, X, PL 158, 502: "Semper itaque habet rationalis natura liberum arbitrium; quia semper habet potestatem servandi rectitudinem voluntatis. . . ." The same definition is found in Anselm's much later work, *De concordia praescientiae et praedestinationis nec non gratiae Dei cum libero arbitrio*, I, 6, PL 158, 517: "Haec enim est libertas, quam esse dixi potestatem servandi rectitudinem voluntatis propter ipsam rectitudinem."

[6] *De lib. arb.*, III, PL 158, 494; *De veritate, Prolog.*, PL 158, 467. In the latter passage Anselm explains that in *De lib. arb.* he discussed "naturalem tantum fortitudinem voluntatis ad servandam acceptam rectitudinem." In *De concordia . . .* he speaks of "liberum arbitrium naturale." In *ibid.*, III, 13, PL 158, 540 he uses the term: "naturalis libertas arbitrii."

[7] *De lib. arb.*, III, PL 158, 494: "Etiamsi absit rectitudo voluntatis, non tamen rationalis natura minus habet quod suum est."

[8] *Ibid.*, X, PL 158, 502: cf. footnote 5 above. *De concordia*, etc., I, 6, PL 158, 517: "Semper enim haec potestas libera est. . . . Hac ipsa libertate rationalis naturae, et arbitrium liberum et voluntas libera dicitur." In this way, even though Satan never has rectitude, he can be said still to have the *power* of preserving rectitude. This power is precisely his natural liberty: "servandi potestas sive libertas."

[9] *De lib. arb.*, III, PL 158, 495: "Nullam namque potestatem habemus, ut puto, quae sola sufficiat sibi ad actum."

mon) concursus or by his special concursus, which is grace.[10] On the other hand, even though the free will is a power which is not sufficient of itself to act, it is still a *real* power; we cannot say that we do not have it.[11] Anselm illustrates his point by noting that a tool cannot operate or act of itself; nevertheless we still *have* the tool, even if we do not have the things needed to operate it.[12]

Anselm's doctrine of man's bondage to sin can be expressed in the following paradoxical statements: Man's *libera voluntas,* which remains even after he abandons rectitude, is a slave to sin, since it is impossible for the *libera voluntas* to recover the lost rectitude by itself.[13] Even though man always possesses *naturalis libertas arbitrii,* his will is never

---

[10] Unless one keeps in mind the doctrine of God's immediate cooperation in man's acts, much confusion results—as it did during the Reformation controversies—when one asks the question: What can man do for salvation by his own natural powers? Cf. Luther's *Disputatio* of 1516, *Quaestio de viribus et voluntate hominis sine gratia,* WA 1, 145ff., which was a Reformation reaction to late Scholastic unclarity, if not error, on this point. Such confusion is seldom found among the great Scholastics, for whom God's creative *concursus* was a basic premise of all their thinking. To cite just one example, when William of Auxerre (d. 1231) writes of what the *liberum arbitrium* can do *per se, sine gratia,* he immediately adds "non tamen excluso Deo, sine quo nihil tale bonum est," *Summa Aur.,* II, tr. 11, pr. 4. 1. Thomas Aquinas in *II Sent.,* d. 28, qu. 1, a. 1 similarly qualifies his use of the phrase, the *per se* power of the will, by saying: "ut ly 'per se' non excludat divinam causalitatem, secundum quod ipse Deus in omnibus operatur ut universalia causa boni. . . ."—What Anselm expresses here rather primitively came to full flowering in the 13th century with the beginning of the development of the doctrine of the divine concursus. When one remembers with Thomas Aquinas, for example, *De potentia,* q. 3, a. 7 that: ". . . Deus est causa actionis cuiuslibet in quantum dat virtutem agendi, et in quantum conservat eam, et in quantum applicat actioni, et in quantum eius virtute omnis alia virtus agit," then one is unlikely to give a Pelagian, Semipelagian or falsely synergistic answer to the question: What can man do by his own powers? In fact, he would probably not even formulate such a misleading and ambiguous question. Cf. F. Mitzka, "Anfänge der Konkurslehre im 13. Jahrhundert," in: *Zeitschr. f. kath. Theologie,* 54 (1930), 161-179; V. Frins, "Concours divin," DTC, 3, 781-796; K. Rahner, "Mitwirkung Gottes," LThK, 7, 502f. Cf. further: A. Landgraf, "Die Erkenntnis der helfenden Gnade in der Frühscholastik," in *Zeitschrift für katholische Theologie,* 55 (1931), 177-238; 403-438; 562-591.

[11] *De lib arb.,* III, PL 158, 494.

[12] *De lib arb.,* III, PL 158, 494. Clark is therefore incorrect when she says, p. 171, that, for Anselm, "*libertas* . . . is an actuality only by the grace of God." She should have said: the rectitude of the will or the justice through which the will is *libera* is an actuality only by the grace of God. We have *libertas arbitrii,* however, even when we do not have rectitude of the will. On p. 169, Clark cites Anselm: "Potestatem autem servandi rectitudinem semper habet, et cum rectitudinem habet, et cum non habet; et ideo semper est liber." Her interpretation, however, seems to be exactly the opposite of Anselm's meaning when she says: "Man is potentially free always, but only actually free when grace enables man to love God for himself."

[13] *De lib. arb.,* X, PL 158, 502.

libera without justice.[14] These statements are paradoxical only because Anselm uses "freedom" in two different senses: the natural, permanent freedom of the will and the acquired freedom that we enjoy only when we have the justice or rectitude which is received (*accepta*) from God through grace.[15]

Concerning the relationship of grace to free will, Anselm is faithful to Augustine and the previous Catholic tradition when he says that whereas infants are saved by grace alone since they are completely inactive in their salvation, in mature persons grace always aids the natural free will of man which, without grace, can do nothing for salvation.[16] He likewise makes his own Augustine's teaching in *De gratia et libero arbitrio*[17] that neither grace alone nor free will alone effect the salvation of man, but both do it together,[18] even though the primacy belongs to grace, which precedes and follows the action of the free will.[19]

According to Anselm, neither the divine foreknowledge nor predestination of man's just acts deprive man of *liberum arbitrium* by causing these acts to happen of necessity. For man has no justice which he does not preserve by free will.[20] The power of necessity and the election of

---

14 *De concordia.* . . , III, 13, PL 158, 539: The will "per se redire nequit ad iustitiam, sine qua numquam libera est, quia naturalis libertas arbitrii sine illa otiosa est."

15 *De concordia.* . . , III, 13, PL 158, 524; III, 13, PL 158, 539. That Anselm uses "freedom" in at least two ways is unquestionable. But to say with Gilson, p. 213, that "La terminologie augustinienne s'est clarifiée et fixée chez saint Anselm" is to read into Anselm's works a terminological precision that simply is not there. Küng and Clark have followed Gilson here. Anselm does not simply substitute "à *liberum arbitrium* l'expression *libertas arbitrii*" (Gilson, *ibid.*). He continues to use the terms interchangeably as not only the texts but also the very titles of his works show: *De libertate arbitrii* and *De concordia praescientiae . . . Dei cum libero arbitrio*. In *De concordia*, II, 3. PL 158, 521 Anselm likewise uses *liberum arbitrium* and *libera voluntas* interchangeably. Gilson is also inaccurate when he suggests that Anselm's doctrine of freedom is: "L'homme a toujours un *arbitrium*, mais qui n'est pas toujours *liber*," p. 213. This judgment is based on a misreading of *De lib. arb.*, II, PL 158, 492 and III, PL 158, 194, where Anselm unmistakably teaches that man is *always* free in the sense that he always has the power of preserving rectitude.

16 *De concordia.* . . , III, 3, PL 158, 524: ". . . invenimus gratiam ad salvandum hominem cum libero arbitrio concordare, ita ut gratia sola hominem salvare nihil eius libero arbitrio agente—sicut fit in infantibus—et in intelligentibus ipsa semper adiuvet liberum arbitrium naturale, quod sine illa nihil valet ad salutem. . . ."

17 Cap. 5, 12: ". . . nec gratia Dei sola, nec ipse solus, sed gratia Dei cum illo."

18 *De concordia.* . . , III, 5, PL 158, 526: ". . . nec sola gratia nec solum liberum arbitrium salutem hominis operetur."

19 *Ibid.*, III, 4, PL 158, 525: "liberum arbitrium non nisi per gratiam praevenientem et subsequentem rectitudinem habet et servat."

20 *Ibid.*, II, 3, PL 158, 521: ". . . neque praescit Deus neque praedestinat quemquam iustum futurum ex necessitate. Non enim habet iustitiam, qui eam non

the will are mutually exclusive.[21] Anselm does distinguish however, a necessity which precedes an act and causes it, and a necessity which follows the act.[22] The latter would be compatible with *liberum arbitrium*.[23]

We are indebted to Bernard of Clairvaux (c. 1090-1153) [24] for the clarification that grace and free will are not related as partial causes—which would be a false synergism—but as total causes of the act of justification, each on its own proper plane.[25] Bernard maintains the Catholic-Augustinian tradition by insisting that man's natural freedom (*liberum arbitrium*) remains even after the fall. It is a wretched, but nonetheless integral free will.[26] This natural freedom of the will, possessed by the just and sinners alike,[27] enables us to will, but not to will what is good. It is grace alone that gives us good will.[28]

Bernard knows of other types of freedom besides the natural freedom which is always found in man. He speaks of freedom from necessity, freedom from sin and freedom from misery.[29] Freedom from necessity, without which our activities cannot be voluntary, is the same as natural

---

servat libera voluntate." Anselm repudiates the argument that man is not free if God foresees everything he does, by pointing out that this argument would also deny God's freedom. For God foresees everything that he himself will do and he is not necessitated by this foreknowledge. *De concordia*, I. Following Boethius he also points out that God's *praescientia* should properly be called *praesentium scientia*, "cui enim semper omnia sunt praesentia non habet futurorum praescientiam": *De casu diaboli*, cap. 21.

[21] *Ibid.*, I, 6, PL 158, 517: ". . . nec aliud facit vis necessitatis, ubi operatur electio sola voluntatis."

[22] *Ibid.*, II, 3, PL 158, 521: "quaedam . . . praedestinata non eveniunt ea necessitate quae praecedit rem et facit, sed ea quae rem sequitur."

[23] Here Anselm employs the distinction, already found in Augustine and Boethius, which will later come to be known as absolute and conditional necessity or *necessitas consequentis* and *necessitas consequentiae*.

[24] See. E. Vacanard, "Bernard (Saint)," DTC, 2, 746-785, esp. 776; B. Opfermann, "Bernard v. Clairvaux," LThK, 2, 239-242. For a brief comparison of the definitions of free will given by Augustine, Anselm and Bernard, see Auer, *Die Entwicklung der Gnadenlehre in der Hochscholastik*, vol. II (Freiburg, 1951), p. 126, footnote 38. Cf. also O. Lottin, La théorie du libre arbitre depuis S. Anselme jusqu'à Thomas d'Aquin," reprint from the *Revue Thomiste*, 1927-1929 (Louvain, 1929); idem., *Psychologie et Morale. . .*, vol. I, pp. 79f.

[25] *De gratia et libero arbitrio* (c. 1127), 14, 47, PL 182, 1026f.: Grace and free will act "mistim, non singillatim; simul, non vicissim. . . . Non partim gratia, partim liberum arbitrium, sed totum singula opere individuo peragunt. . . ." Cf. Auer, II, p. 191, footnote 62, who points out that, while the system of Thomas Aquinas admits only of a subordination of causes, in the later Franciscan thought there is a co-ordination of partial causes (*causae partiales*) especially in Scotus' doctrine of the will.

[26] *De gr. et lib. arb.*, 8, 24, PL 182, 1014: "miserum, tamen integrum."

[27] *Ibid.*, 4, 9, PL 182, 1006f.

[28] *Ibid.*, 6, 16, PL 182, 1010: ". . . liberum arbitrium nos facit volentes, gratia benevolos."

[29] *Ibid.*, 3, 6f., PL 182, 1005: "libertas a peccato, a miseria, a necessitate."

liberty for Bernard.[30] Although he holds that free will and necessity are mutually exclusive, Bernard, like Anselm,[31] recognizes a necessity which follows the free act and which, by definition, does not exclude freedom.[32]

It remained for Peter Lombard (c. 1095-1160) [33] to summarize the Augustinian tradition on free will as well as the more or less Augustinian teachings of his contemporaries, and to provide us with a clear terminology concerning the various types of freedom.[34] The contribution of Lombard, from our point of view, consists much more in his clarification of the state of the question than in his penetration of the problem of the relationship between grace and free will.

In Book II of the *Sentences,* distinction 25, we find the following teaching about free will and freedom relevant to our theme:

1. *Liberum arbitrium* pertains to future contingents,[35] that is, to those futures which, through free will, can take place or not take place.[36]

2. *Liberum arbitrium* cannot be defined as the ability to will good or evil; otherwise God couldn't be said to have *liberum arbitrium*.[37]

3. The *arbitrium* is called *liberum* because, without force or necessity, it can desire or choose what is decided by reason.[38]

---

[30] *Ibid.*

[31] Cf. footnote 22f. above.

[32] Bernard, *In Cant. Canticorum,* Sermo 81, PL 183, 1174 (after 1148). Cf. R. Mousnier, "Saint Bernard and Luther," *American Benedictine Review,* 14 (1963), 460. Addressing himself to the remarks of Luther recorded in the Table-Talk (WATR 1, 272, 4; 435, 32; 3, 295, 1; 5, 154, 6), to the effect that Bernard in his sermons excelled all other doctors, even Augustine, because he preached so beautifully about Christ, but that in his disputations, such as *De lib. arb.,* Jesus was nowhere to be found, Mousnier shows that even in the sermons Bernard upheld man's free will. Mousnier, pp. 458f., cites as an example *De diversis sermonibus,* 29, PL 183, 620.

[33] See J. de Ghellinck, "Pierre Lombard," DTC, 12, 1941-2019; Seeberg, III, pp. 247f.; Grabmann, pp. 40-43; I. Brady-A. Emmen, "Petrus Lombardus," LThK, 8, 367ff. Cf. also O. Lottin, "Les définitions du libre arbitre au XIIe siècle," in: *Revue Thomiste,* 10 (1927), 118-120; *idem., Psychologie et Morale,* I, pp. 28ff.; J. Schupp, *"Die Gnadenlehre des Petrus Lombardus"* (Freiburg, 1932).

[34] De Ghellinck, DTC, 12, 1995, says Robert of Melun, Lombard's contemporary, contributed far more to this problem than did Peter. This judgment has recently been confirmed in the study by U. Horst, *Die Trinitätslehre und Gotteslehre von Robert von Melun* (Mainz, 1964), pp. 267-273.

[35] This is the first time in our study we have encountered this word in relation to free will. It actually occurs earlier in Hugh of St. Victor, *De sacramentis,* PL 176, 256 B-C: "Liberum arbitrium spectat semper ad futuros eventus et solum qui in contingenti consistunt."

[36] *Libri IV Sententiarum,* Lib. II, d. 25, cap. 1.

[37] *Ibid.* He expressly wishes to follow Augustine here. Similarly Augustinian is his idea that the will which is unable to sin is more free than one which can.

[38] *Ibid.,* dist. 25, cap. 5: "liberum videtur dici arbitrium, quia sine coactione et necessitate valet appetere vel eligere quod ex ratione decreverit."

4. There are four states of free will: (i) before sin, when man had grace and nothing impeded him from doing good: man could do good without difficulty; (ii) after sin but before the repairing (of the will) by grace: man can sin and is not able not to sin; (iii) after the repairing by grace, but before the confirmation in grace: man is able to sin because of his liberty and weakness, but he is able not to sin because of his liberty and helping grace; (iv) after confirmation in grace: man is not able to sin.[39]

5. Besides the other penalties incurred by Adam's sin, man also suffered a corruption of free will. This does not mean that, after the fall, man no longer has *liberum arbitrium,* but that he has lost liberty of the will (*libertas arbitrii*). He has not however lost liberty of the will entirely but only liberty from misery and from sin.[40]

6. There are three kinds of liberty of the free will: freedom from necessity, from sin and from misery.[41]

7. *Liberum arbitrium* is free from necessity both before and after the fall. Where there is necessity, there is no liberty. This liberty is in everyone, whether he be good or evil.[42]

8. Freedom from sin is the freedom spoken of in II Cor. 3: 17 and John 8: 36. This freedom, described in Rom. 6: 18-20, frees us from the slavery of sin and makes us slaves of justice. It is this freedom that man has lost by sin.[43] Thus, when Augustine says that man, by using free will badly, has lost both it and himself,[44] he does not mean that freedom from necessity has been lost, but freedom from sin.[45]

---

[39] *Libri IV Sent.,* II, d. 25, cap. 7. According to de Ghellinck, DTC, 12, 1996 and Lottin, *Psychologie et Morale,* I, 30, the Lombard borrowed this division from the *Summa Sententiarum,* III, 9.

[40] *Ibid.,* d. 25, cap. 8, PL 192, 707f. Here, finally, is the sharp distinction between *liberum arbitrium* and *libertas arbitrii*—free will and freedom of the will. Corruption of the will for Lombard does *not* mean the absence or loss of it. He explicitly says it means wounding—not a privation ("vulneratus . . . non privatus")—otherwise it could not be "repaired." The gratuitous gifts are indeed "subtracta" but not the natural gifts ("naturalia"). These are "corrupta" in the sense in which he explains it. Since Seeberg, III, 247, does not make these clarifications, his readers are liable to be misled when he simply says "der Lombard eine Korruption . . . des freien Willens lehrt."

[41] *Libri IV Sent.,* II, d. 25, cap. 8. Cf. above footnote 29.

[42] *Ibid.* Peter seems to identify *necessitas* here with what later Scholastics will call *necessitas coactionis,* i.e. necessity imposed by an extrinsic force. For a survey of the thinking of the High Scholastics on the concept of external *coactio* and internal necessity cf. Auer, p. 131, footnote 62.

[43] *Libri IV Sent.,* II, d. 25, cap. 8.

[44] Augustine, *Enchiridion,* 30, 9. Cf. our excursus: The Meaning of *servum arbitrium* in Augustine.

[45] Peter Lombard, *Sent.* II, d. 25, cap. 8. This is a helpful terminological clarification that fully accords with Augustine's meaning.

9. The will of man is always free in some way, but it is not always good. Even though it is only good when it is liberated from sin, it is, however, free from necessity.[46]

10. Freedom from misery is the freedom from the slavery of corruption of which Paul speaks in Rom. 8: 21.[47] Before the fall, man had this freedom and he will have it even more fully in heaven. But since it is a punishment for sin, no one in this life is free from "miseria."[48]

11. (By way of summary): Free will is always free in very person; however, it is not free in the same way in good persons and bad. It is more free in good men, where it has been liberated, than in wicked men, where it has not been liberated.[49]

12. Unless the free will is liberated and aided by grace it cannot do good.[50]

13. Freedom from sin and from misery comes through grace. Freedom from necessity comes from nature.[51]

Bonaventure [52] (1217/18-1274) follows the tradition of Augustine, Anselm, Bernard and Peter Lombard, by teaching that the will is always free.[53] *Liberum arbitrium* belongs to the *esse* of man and can never be lost or diminished even by sin.[54] *Libertas a poena* and *culpa,* on the other hand, belong to man's *bene esse* and are lost by sin, permanently lost in those who are damned.[55] Similar distinctions had already been drawn, as we have seen, by Peter Lombard. Like Bernard [56] and

---

46 *Ibid.*

47 *Ibid.* Peter seems to refer here to the misery resulting from the loss of the gifts of physical and spiritual integrity.

48 *Ibid.*

49 *Ibid.* Here the Master of the Sentences employs the same terminology that we found in Augustine: "liberum arbitrium liberatum" as opposed to "liberum arbitrium non liberatum." This paradoxical terminology is really an admirable way of expressing the fact that freedom is used in two different senses: as natural freedom (free will or *liberum arbitrium*) and acquired freedom (liberation from sin through Jesus Christ the Liberator).

50 *Ibid.,* cap. 8 and 9. This Pauline-Augustinian doctrine is even more clearly expressed by Peter in *Sent.* II, d. 27, cap. 7, where he says it is: "gratia, qua excitatur liberum arbitrium et sanatur, atque adiuvatur voluntas hominis, ut sit bona." See Schupp, p. 258.

51 *Sent.* II, d. 25, cap. 9.

52 See E. Smeets, "Bonaventure (Saint)," DTC, 2, 962-986; Grabmann, pp. 66-69; 297f.; Seeberg, III, 353-359; O. Lottin, *Psychologie et Morale,* I, pp. 174-182; É. Gilson, *La Philosophie de saint Bonaventure,* 3rd ed. (Paris, 1953); E. W. Platzeck, "Bonaventura," LThK, 1, 582ff.; Bourke, pp. 62f.; 133f.

53 Seeberg, III, 357.—Bonaventure was consciously a "traditional" theologian: "Non enim intendo novas opiniones adversare, sed communes et approbatas retexere": *In IV Sent.,* II, praeloc.

54 *In Sent.* II, d. 25, p. 2, dub. 1 and resp. ad 1.

55 *Ibid.*

56 See footnote 25 above.

Thomas Aquinas,[57] Bonaventure has no place for a *partim-partim* synergism in his explanation of the act of justification.[58]

Important for our *status quaestionis* are Bonaventure's reflections on the relation between *liberum arbitrium* and necessity. With all the authors of his time—and like Luther in a later age—Bonaventure held that external force (*necessitas coactionis*) was incompatible with free will.[59] But Bonaventure distinguished another kind of necessity, *necessitas immutabilitatis,* which he said did not exclude free will. Bonaventure explains that the *arbitrium* is called *liberum* not because it is able to will the opposite of what it actually wills, but because it desires everything that it wills according to its own command. And therefore in the act of willing it moves itself and masters itself. Thus the *arbitrium* is called free even though it is immutably ordered to the thing willed.[60]

In the same place Bonaventure takes a position which is precisely the opposite of a stand later to be taken by Luther: Free and voluntary are the same thing; whatever is produced through the mediation of the will is produced freely.[61]

---

[57] *Summa Theol.,* I, q. 23, a. 5.

[58] *In Sent.,* I, d. 45, a. 2, q. 2 c: "nec una causa derogat alteri, sed totus effectus est a causa creata et totus a voluntate increata."

[59] *Ibid.,* II, d. 25, p. 1 art. un., q. 3, sed contra 1: "quod liberum arbitrium non possit cogi, hoc indicat ipsum nomen; si enim possit cogi, non esset liberum." Cf. Auer, II, p. 131, footnote 62.

[60] *In Sent.,* II, d. 25, p. 2, a. un., q. 2: ". . . duplex sit necessitas, coactionis et immutabilitatis. Necessitas coactionis repugnat libertati arbitrii, necessitas vero immutabilitatis non. Pro eo quod arbitrium dicitur liberum non quia sic velit hoc, ut possit velle eius oppositum, sed quia omne quod vult appetit ad sui ipsius imperium, quia sic vult aliquid, ut velit se velle illud et ideo in actu volendi se ipsum movet et sibi dominatur. Et pro tanto dicitur liberum quamvis immutabiliter ordinetur ad illud." Cf. *ibid.,* II, d. 7, p. 1, a. 2, q. 3 ad 1, where Bonaventure teaches that the "necessitas immutabilitatis ad bonum" which is present in those who are confirmed in good "nullo modo repugnat libero arbitrio." This distinction can be found in Bonaventure's teacher, Alexander of Hales. Cf. Grane, *Contra Gabrielem,* p. 220. Gabriel Biel, *In Sent.,* II, d. 25, q. un. D rejects the view that *necessitas immutabilitatis* is compatible with *liberum arbitrium.* Further, he misunderstands the passage from Bonaventure cited above and thinks the *Doctor seraphicus* teaches that *liberum arbitrium* doesn't mean the ability (*posse*) to will the opposite of that which it wills. *Ibid.,* C. Bonaventure simply says that *liberum arbitrium* does not derive its *name* from its ability to will opposites, but from its *imperium-dominium* character; he certainly does not deny that the *liberum arbitrium* chooses between opposites. Cf. Grane, p. 119. It must further be noted that Bonaventure is discussing the question: "Utrum confirmatio in bono, vel obstinatio in malo diminuat libertatis dominium?" He is not talking about the freedom of man's will *in via,* as Biel supposes. By "necessitas immutabilitatis ad bonum," therefore, Bonaventure means nothing more than what Thomas means when he says "immutabiliter in particulari bonum debitum appetunt beatorum mentes" (*De Ver.,* q. 24, a. 8c).

[61] *In Sent.,* II, d. 25, p. 2, a. un., q. 2: "Illo modo ergo idem est liberum et voluntarium. Et libere producitur quiquid producitur mediante voluntate."

II. THOMAS AQUINAS

Our central concern in this book is to develop an ecumenical-theological evaluation of Luther's doctrine of *servum arbitrium* as found in *De servo arbitrio*. The attempt to present here a full treatment of the doctrine of free will and bondage to sin of Thomas Aquinas would therefore divert us from our purpose. Fortunately there are enough competent studies of Thomas' teaching on free will [62] to make this task unnecessary here.[63]

---

[62] The same cannot be said concerning studies on Thomas' doctrine of man's bondage to sin and its opposite, the specifically Christian freedom of the children of God. One finds this doctrine primarily in expositions of Thomas' teaching on the necessity and gratuity of grace. See also R. Egenter, *Von der Freiheit der Kinder Gottes* (Freiburg, 1941); B. Lonergan, "St. Thomas' Thought on 'Gratia operans'," *Theological Studies,* 2 (1941), 289-324; 3 (1942), 69-88; 375-402; 532-578; H. Bouillard, *Conversion et Grâce chez Thomas d'Aquin* (Paris, 1944); R. Garrigou-Lagrange, *De Gratia* (Turin, 1946); H. Rondet, *Gratia Christi* (Paris, 1946); T. A. Deman, *Kommentar zu Summa Theologiae,* I-II, qq. 106-114, in: *Deutsche Thomas-Ausgabe,* vol. 14 (Heidelberg-Graz, 1955); Küng, p. 183f. Still needed is a study of Thomas' "konkret-heilsgeschichtliche"—as distinct from his "ontischmetaphysischen" (Schmaus, III/2, pp. 264ff.)—reasons for the necessity of grace. Cf. *S. Theol.,* I-II, q. 109, 9.

[63] A partial list of these studies includes: G. Feldner, *Die Lehre des heiligen Thomas von Aquin über die Willensfreiheit* (Graz, 1890); N. del Prado, *De gratia et libero arbitrio,* 3 vols. (Fribourg, 1907); M. Wittman, "Die Lehre von der Willensfreiheit bei Thomas von Aquin, historisch untersucht," *Philosophisches Jahrbuch,* 40 (1927), 170-188; 285-305; O. Lottin, "Le libre arbitre chez S. Thomas d'Aquin," *Revue Thomiste,* 12 (1929), 400-430; idem., *La théorie du libre arbitre depuis S. Anselme jusqu'á S. Thomas d'Aquin* (Louvain, 1929); idem, *Psychologie et Morale aux XIIᵉ et XIIIᵉ siècles,* vol. I (Louvain, 1942); J. Auer, *Die menschliche Willensfreiheit im Lehrsystem des Thomas von Aquin und des Johannes Duns Scotus* (München, 1938); idem., *Die Entwicklung der Gnadenlehre in der Hochscholastik,* 2 vols. (Freiburg/Br., 1942/51); J. Maritain, "The Thomist Idea of Freedom," Chapter V of: *Scholasticism and Politics* (New York, 1940); Image Book ed., (New York, 1960), pp. 117-138; idem., "Reflections on Necessity and Contingency," in: *Essays in Thomism,* ed. R. E. Brennan (New York: Sheed & Ward, 1942); idem., "The Free Existent and the Free Eternal Purposes," in: chapter IV of: *Existence and the Existent,* tr. L. Galantiere and G. B. Phelan (New York, 1948); Image ed. (1957), pp. 92-128; A. Rzadkiewicz, *The Philosophical Bases of Human Liberty according to St. Thomas Aquinas* (Washington, D.C., 1949); G. Siewerth, *Thomas von Aquin: Die menschliche Willensfreiheit* (Düsseldorf, 1954); L. Oeing-Hanhoff, "Zur thomistischen Freiheitslehre," *Scholastik,* 31 (1956), 161-181; G. P. Klubertanz, "The Root of Freedom in St. Thomas's Later Works," in: *Gregorianum,* 42 (1961), 701-721 (an extensive specialized bibliography is added to this article, pp. 722ff.); O. H. Pesch, "Philosophie und Theologie der Freiheit bei Thomas von Aquin in quaest. disp. 6 De Malo," *Münchener theolog. Zeitschrift,* 13 (1962), 1-25; V. Bourke, *Will in Western Thought* (New York, 1964), pp. 61-70. For comparisons of the Thomistic and the Bonaventurean views of free will see L. B. Gillon, "Thomas d'Aquin. V," DTC 15, 690-693 and C. M. O'Donnell, *The Psychology of St. Bonaventure and St. Thomas Aquinas* (Washington: Catholic Univ. Press, 1937).

Of special interest from the standpoint of ecumenical theology are several recent studies by Protestant and Catholic theologians bringing Thomas and Luther into dialogue on precisely the question of free will.[64]

How does one explain the new [65] appreciation of the common ground existing between the *doctor communis* of the Catholic Church and the Father of the Reformation? One factor, certainly, has to do with the very nature of ecumenical theology, which seeks to re-open supposedly closed questions of the Reformation and to question some long-unchallenged assumptions of both Catholics and Protestants.

EXCURSUS: *Did Luther Know Thomas Aquinas?*

We have just mentioned the increasing awareness of areas of agreement between Saint Thomas and Luther. It should be pointed out, however, that Luther himself was not aware of this common ground. In fact, he expressed practically nothing but contempt for Thomas, mainly on the grounds that Thomas had admitted Aristotle into theology and had become seduced by metaphysics. Cf. WA 7, 737, 14; 8, 127, 19; WATR 3, 564, 10. But one can ask, did Luther actually have a sufficient knowledge of Thomas to dismiss him so abruptly? Was his rejection of Thomas based on a firsthand reading of Thomas' works, or on an indirect knowledge derived from the citations of Thomas in the writings of the late Scholastic theologians? These questions, raised by Denifle long ago, must not be dismissed simply because they are Denifle's.

A strong case can be made to support the view that Luther did not

---

[64] See our Introduction, p. 12 and footnote 28. Hans Vorster, *Das Freiheitsverständnis bei Thomas von Aquin und Martin Luther* (Gottingen, 1965) devotes almost two hundred pages solely to Thomas' teaching. From the Catholic side see the essays by O. H. Pesch, "Freiheitsbegriff und Freiheitslehre bei Thomas von Aquin und Luther," in: *Catholica*, 17 (1963) and H. J. McSorley, "Luther und Thomas von Aquin über die Prädestination," in: *Oekumenica, Prof. E. Schlink zum 60. Geburtstag* (Heidelberg, 1963), pp. 17-20. It is no accident that both Vorster and Th. Bonhoeffer, the author of another fine study of Thomas Aquinas, are disciples of the Tübingen theologian, Gerhard Ebeling. Perhaps more than any Protestant Luther scholar, with the exception of H. Oberman, Ebeling sees the necessity of understanding Thomas and the late Scholastics for an accurate and historically sound interpretation of Luther.

[65] As is so often the case with supposedly new ideas, this new appreciation isn't entirely new or modern. Vorster has discovered a work by the 17th century theologian, J. C. Dorscheus, who defends the thesis that Luther is not really opposed to Thomas Aquinas, but rather to Bellarmine and Trent. Vorster himself contributes much to ecumenical theology by showing the basic common concerns of Thomas and Luther in the question of free will and grace. He has unfortunately accepted too uncritically the alleged opposition between Thomas and the teachings of Trent.

have an adequate knowledge of this greatest and most representative of Catholic theologians since Augustine. Without attempting to develop this thesis fully, we shall simply mention a few points which tend to support it. First of all, it is difficult to find in Luther's works a direct— or even an indirect—citation from Thomas. Luther is content to make generalizations concerning Thomas' Aristotelianism (WA 8, 127, 19; WATR 1, 118, 1), his lack of the Spirit (WA 7, 774, 15; 17/2, 27, 27), his failure to inspire trust in Christ (WATR 2, 193, 5), etc. In one place Luther seems patently unfamiliar with Thomas' writings when he refers to the *prima pars* of the *Summa Theologiae* as the "prima primae" (WATR 1, 118, 3).

Secondly, had Luther carefully studied Thomas' teaching on the evangelical law (*S. Theol.*, I-II, q. 106, aa. 1 and 2) and the necessity of grace (I-II, q. 109, aa. 1-10), as well as Thomas' doctrine on faith and works, grace, predestination and man's bondage to sin as set forth above all in his commentaries on the Pauline epistles, there is every reason to suspect that he would not only have accepted this doctrine, but would actually have cited it, along with the teaching of Paul and Augustine, against the errors he found in some of the late Scholastics concerning the unaided powers of man's fallen nature in respect to justification.

Although he dissociates himself from the polemical tone of Denifle's work, T. M. McDonough, *The Law and the Gospel in Luther* (Oxford, 1963), pp. 32f. finds Denifle's argument convincing that Luther had but a superficial understanding of Thomas. Cf. Denifle, *Luthertum*, I, pp. 522-590. Seeberg maintains that Luther studied Thomas during the early years of his theological formation, yet he believes that Luther's exaggerated criticisms of Thomas indicate the lack of a deep penetration of Thomas' thought. "At least Luther was incorrect" writes Seeberg, IV/1, p. 76, footnote 2, "when he claimed that Thomas was the representative of the Pelagian and deistic Scholasticism against which he was fighting." Other Protestant scholars who recognize Luther's lack of genuine acquaintance with Thomas' writings include Loofs, p. 690; K. A. Meissinger, *Der Katholische Luther* (München, 1952), p. 109; P. S. Watson, *Let God be God* (London, 1947), p. 29, footnote 27; B. A. Gerrish, *Grace and Reason* (Oxford, 1962), p. 21, footnote 3; Vorster, p. 18. F. Lau, on the other hand, *Luther* (London, 1963), pp. 44f., asserts that Luther did become familiar with Thomas, but he offers no proof for this view. L. Grane, *Contra Gabrielem* (Gyldendal, 1962), p. 314 follows the view upheld by R. Hermann, *Luthers These "Gerecht und Sünder Zugleich"* (Darmstadt, 1960[2]), pp. 32f., that Denifle's thesis is unimportant, since the difference between Thomism and Scotism—and, presumably, between Thomism and the late Scholastics —on the points criticized by Luther is "inconsiderable." On the very page where he rejects Denifle's position, however, Grane inadvertently substantiates Denifle's argument by citing WA 56, 349, 22ff., which offers us one of the clearest examples of the differences between Thomas' teaching and that of the theologians against whom Luther was reacting. Commenting on Rom. 7: 17, Luther says "our theologians," since they hold that sin is entirely destroyed through baptism or absolution, cannot understand how Paul can speak of "the sin that lives in me." They therefore say, continues Luther, that Paul's words apply not to himself, but to the carnal man. But when we look at Thomas' exegesis of Rom. 7: 17 we find that his position is exactly the opposite of the theologians whom Luther is criticizing and is almost identical with Luther's own understanding of the text! Commenting on the words "the sin that lives in me," Thomas writes: ". . . and thus it is clear that I am a slave of sin inasmuch as sin acts within me as a master. And this can quite rightly and easily be understood of the man who is constituted in grace. . . . But it cannot properly be understood of the man who is in sin. . . ." (*Super Epist. ad Rom. Lect.*, Cap. VII, lect. 3, nn. 569f).

It is true that Thomas understands "sin" here to mean the tendency to sin (*fomes peccati*) which gives rise to the stirring of concupiscence: *ibid.*, n. 570. But it would be incorrect to see an opposition between Thomas and Luther (at least the Luther of the *Lectures on Romans*) on this point. For Luther also teaches, following Augustine, that *concupiscentia* is called "sin" by Paul, but it is not sin "formally" but "causally and effectually": WA 56, 353. At this stage of his development Luther is in agreement not only with Augustine and Thomas but also with the doctrine which was later defined at Trent (DS 1515).

Apart from the methodology essential to ecumenical theology there is another factor, still insufficiently explored, accounting for the new interest in bringing Thomas and Luther into dialogue. Thomas Aquinas has been regarded for so long as a Christian Aristotelian [66] or as the theologian who "baptized Aristotle" that his Augustinianism [67] and Paulinism [68]

---

[66] The Aristotelianism of Thomas has often been misunderstood as an element which excludes or replaces certain aspects of the Gospel. Thus, K. A. Meissinger, p. 225: "In dem Aristoteles streckt nun einmal ein der Lehre des Evangeliums fremdes säkulär-rationalistiches Element. Das Evangelium war ja doch (I Cor. 1, 20ff.) 'den Griechen eine Torheit' gewesen . . . Thomas' Ehrgeiz war es ja gerade den Griechen keine Torheit zu sein." Had Meissinger consulted Thomas' commentary on I Cor. 1: 20ff. it is unlikely that he would have written what we have just cited. Cf. Thomas, *In I ad Cor.*, cap. 1, lect. 3, nn. 41-62.

A much more positive and sympathetic evaluation of Thomas' Aristotelianism is offered by Vorster, pp. 257f.: "Die Behauptung, Thomas habe alles Licht für das von ihm zu Sagende von einer unsachgemässen Lichtquelle bezogen und deshalb stünde bei ihm alles nur in dem Irrlicht, das diese Lichtquelle allein verbreiten könne, ist jedenfalls zu schablonhaft. Wenn nicht nur der Mensch, sondern auch sein Verstehen geschichtlich ist, und wenn Menschenwort nicht nur (in seiner Selbstherrlichkeit) Lüge ist, sondern (gnadenhaft) doch immer in seine Funktion zurückgerufen und zum Träger des Gotteswortes werden kann, dann lässt sich nicht apriorisch ausschliessen, dass dem Denken des Aristoteles in einer bestimmten geschichtlichen Stunde diese Tragfähigkeit nicht geschenkt werden könnte. Mann könnte, ja man müsste diese Tragfähigkeit sonst für die ins biblische Denken eingegangen Vorstellungen der vorderorientalischen Religionswelt ebenfalls bestreiten. . . ."

[67] Seeberg, III, p. 462 shows an exceptional awareness of Thomas' Augustinianism: Thomas "hat sich treuer als die Franziskaner Augustins Gnadenlehre angeschlossen. . . ." He adds, p. 484: "Auch Thomas folgt . . . augustinischen Gedanken, und er hat das *sola gratia* mit grösster Energie betont." When V.

have been overlooked—in some circles almost completely. Although the speculative and metaphysical aspects of Thomas' theology have been universally recognized, the biblical-historical elements have been almost as universally forgotten or ignored. And it is precisely these elements—salvation history, Paulinism, Augustinism—which were so pronounced and so decisive in Luther's Reformation theology. How many Protestant—or Catholic—theologians seek to balance or complement the systematic statements of the *Summa Theologiae,* for example, with the biblical formulations found in Thomas' extensive biblical commentaries? Many surprises await the theologian who compares, say, Luther's *Lectures on the Epistle to the Romans* with those of Thomas.[69]

Bourke, p. 133 says that "the Franciscans are usually closer to the thought of St. Augustine" than is Thomas, we should understand this in reference to Augustine's psychology, not his teaching on grace. Seeberg, III, p. 462, also recognizes that the Franciscans follow the Augustinian psychology more closely than does Thomas. More recently, J. Pelikan, *The Riddle of Roman Catholicism* (New York: Nashville, 1959), p. 148, has pointed out the Augustinian character of Thomas' writings: "Far from being a repudiation of Augustinianism, Thomism was Augustinianism purged of some of its concessions to Neoplatonic philosophy." Cf. Portalié, "Augustinisme," DTC, 1, 2531-2535 and B. Decker, "Augustinismus," LThK, 1, 1092ff. By the same token, Protestant scholars are recognizing more and more that Luther cannot be considered to be a completely faithful disciple of Augustine. Cf. A. Hamel, *Der junge Luther und Augustin* (Gütersloh, 1934/35); A. Nygren, *Augustin und Luther* (Berlin, 1958); G. Nygren, *op. cit.;* B. Gerrish, p. 126.

68 One should naturally not look for Thomas' Paulinism when Thomas is discussing such matters as the nature of the soul and its union with the body. In such questions the Philosopher, Aristotle, plays a decisive, but by no means exclusive, role. But when Thomas treats a truly Pauline theme, then Paul and Augustine are his masters. In his treatment of grace and justification, for example, in I-II, qq. 109-113, Thomas cites the Old Testament twenty-two times, the New Testament thirty-two times (of which 26 are citations from Paul), Augustine twenty times, other Church Fathers six times, and Aristotle only nine times.

69 J. Pelikan has won deserved praise for his study, *The Riddle of Roman Catholicism.* Especially remarkable is his essentially positive evaluation of "The Angelic Doctor," the title he gives to chapter X of his book. Pelikan's admiration for Thomism as an intellectual system even leads him to say that "there is no orthodox Christian tradition in the modern world that demands less of an intellectual surrender than Rome!" (p. 153). We believe, however, that Pelikan should see Thomas' biblical commentaries as more than just a preparation for "his great theological work," the *Summa Theologiae* (the "other great work" being the *Summa Contra Gentiles*): pp. 145 and 147. These commentaries, especially those on the Pauline epistles, ought to be considered in their own right as belonging to Thomas' great works. Thomas' great commentary on Romans, for example, was not written as a preparation for the *Summa Theol.* It was in fact written after the completion of the *prima pars* of the *S. Theol.,* and very probably during or after the writing of the *prima secundae.* Cf. P. A. Walz, "Thomas d'Aquin. Écrits," DTC, 15, 639f.; Bouillard, pp. 225-241.

Pelikan unfortunately gives new life to an old legend about Thomas that goes back to Luther himself. Whereas Luther could say: "Hic est Thomae ordo: Principio accipit sententias ex Paulo . . . postea concludit: Aristoteles autem sic dicit,

When we look at Thomas' entire teaching as found in his biblical as well as in his systematic works, we find all three of the types of freedom described in our first chapter. For this reason we cannot expect to find a single, all-inclusive definition of freedom in St. Thomas. Since circumstantial freedom or freedom of activity has little direct relevance for our problem, we shall limit ourselves to an investigation of Thomas' understanding of natural freedom and acquired freedom.[70] Thomas, of course, does not use the Adlerian terminology but his writings show unmistakably that he is aware of the distinct realities signified by these terms.

A. NATURAL FREEDOM

Thomas refers to natural freedom by various names: *liberum arbitrium*,[71] *libertas arbitrii*,[72] *libertas voluntatis*,[73] *libera voluntas*,[74] *libera electio*,[75] *vis electiva*,[76] *liberum iudicium*,[77] and *libertas naturalis quae*

---

et secundum Aristotelem interpretatur scripturam": WATR 1, 118, 1 (cf. WATR 5, 686, 15: 687, 31), Pelikan states, p. 156: "The Sermon on the Mount . . . at the hands of Thomism sounds like a combination of Aristotle's ethics and the rules of the monastic life. . . ." A brief survey of the contents of Thomas' *Super Evangelium S. Matthaei Lectura*, cap. V-VII, nn. 396-679 fails to produce any basis for the "ordo Thomae" alleged by Luther or for the Aristotelian legalism seen by Pelikan. In fact, the first twelve verses of Thomas' commentary on the Sermon on the Mount alone contain some 72 citations of the Old Testament, 43 citations of the New Testament, 10 references to Augustine and 12 to other Fathers—but only five references are made to Aristotle. *Ibid.*, nn. 396-449. In his commentary on the Lord's Prayer to which Pelikan makes reference, p. 254, footnote 17, there is no reference at all to Aristotle, only to Scripture and to the Fathers of the Church. *Ibid.*, nn. 583-602.

[70] Whenever Thomas speaks of the freeman as distinct from the slave—in a social or political sense—he is speaking of circumstantial freedom. In *De Malo*, q. 6, a. un., ad 22 this kind of freedom is called "libera actio" in distinction to natural freedom, which is there termed "libera voluntas." Elsewhere, *De Veritate*, q. 24, a. 1, ad 1, Thomas uses the terms "electio operum" and "executio operum" to distinguish circumstantial from natural freedom. Man always has the power of choosing but cannot always carry out what he chooses to do. This is why he is said to be "liber electionis" and not "liber suarum actionum."

That Thomas assigns various meanings to "libertas" is evident in *De Malo*, q. 6, a. un., ad 23, where—in the tradition of Lombard and Bonaventure—he distinguishes *libertas a coactione, libertas a culpa* and *libertas a miseria*. In *S. Theol.*, I, q. 83, a. 2, ad 3, Thomas refers to the same three "libertates" and calls the *libertas a coactione* "libertas naturalis." Cf. *De Ver.*, q. 24, a. 1, ad 7 for the same identification of *liberum arbitrium* as "naturaliter."

[71] This is the most frequently used term. Cf. *De Ver.*, q. 24; *S. Theol.*, I, q. 83.

[72] See *De Ver.*, q. 22, a. 6c; *S. Theol.*, I, q. 23, a. 6c; q. 62, a. 8, ad 3; q. 82, a. 1, ad 1; q. 83, a. 1, ad 5.

[73] *De Ver.*, q. 22, a. 6c; I, q. 59, a. 3, *sed contra*; q. 82, a. 1, ad 1.

[74] *De Malo*, q. 6, a. un., ad 22.

[75] The question of *De Malo*, q. 6, a. un. is not stated in terms of *liberum arbitrium* but of *libera electio*: "Et videtur quod non libere sed ex necessitate eligat." Cf. I-II, q. 13, a. 6.

est a coactione.[78] This freedom is natural because it belongs to all men [79] and, as we shall see later, is not lost even by Adam's fall.

By natural liberty Thomas means the power [80] of the will [81] to choose [82] between objects which are related as means to an end.[83] Thomas offers us a simple definition of *liberum arbitrium* when he speaks of it as the *vis electiva,*[84] that is, the power of electing those things which are related to the end.[85] The following can be taken as a descriptive definition of free will: having apprehended the end, and deliberating on the end and the means proportionate to it, the free person can either be moved toward the end or not moved toward it— according as he chooses.[86] Only when acts proceed from deliberative willing are they in the proper sense of the word human actions.[87] Although the actions of brute animals are considered by Thomistic psychology to be in some way voluntary,[88] they are in no way free, responsible actions, because animals lack the ability—in this case, the rationality—to deliberate concerning the end and the means to achieve the end.[89] Because man, in distinction to irrational creatures, performs

---

[76] I, q. 83, a. 4c.

[77] *S. Theol.,* I, q. 83, a. 1c: "homo . . . agit libero iudicio." In the body of the article and in the answer to the first objection of I, q. 83, a. 2 Thomas explains that *liberum iudicium* is really the act of the *liberum arbitrium,* which is a *potentia* and the principle of the act of *liberum iudicium.* Although *liberum arbitrium* is sometimes called *liberum iudicium* (cf. I, q. 83, a. 2, obj. 2 and *ibid.,* a. 3, obj. 2), according to common usage ("secundum communem usum") it signifies the principle of the act of freely judging. On the nature of this *iudicium* see *De Ver.,* q. 24, a. 1, ad 17.

[78] I, q. 83, a. 2, ad 3.

[79] *De Ver.,* q. 24, a. 15c: ". . . in nullo inveniuntur omnes homines convenire nisi in aliquo naturali. . . ." Cf. footnote 78.

[80] *Ibid.,* a. 2.

[81] *Ibid.,* aa. 3 and 4.

[82] *Ibid.,* a. 3c: "Proprium liberum arbitrium est electio." Cf. III, q. 18, a. 4c: "electio . . . est proprius actus liberi arbitrii"; I, q. 83, a. 4: "liberum arbitrium . . . nihil aliud est quam vis electiva."

[83] For Thomas, following Aristotle, it is axiomatic that *electio,* the proper act of *liberum arbitrium* is "eorum quae sunt ad finem," while the *voluntas,* whose simple act of appetition is *velle,* "est finis": *S. Theol.,* I-II q. 13, a. 3; a. 6c and ad 2. Cf. I, q. 82, a. 1, ad 3; q. 83, a. 4c; II-II, q. 24, a. 1, ad 3; SCG I, cap. 88, par. 4.

[84] Cf. footnote 81.

[85] Cf. I, q. 62, a. 8, ad 3.

[86] I-II, q. 6, a. 2c.

[87] I-II, q. 1c: "Illae ergo actiones proprie humanae dicuntur, quae ex voluntate deliberata procedunt."

[88] I-II, q. 6, a. 2c: "voluntarium imperfectum."

[89] *Ibid.* This corresponds to Thomas' basic conviction that man has free will by the very fact that he is rational. Cf. *De Ver.,* q. 24, aa. 1 and 2; I, q. 19, a. 3; q. 59, a. 3; q. 83, a. 1; I-II, q. 17, a. 1, ad 2; *De Malo,* q. 6, a. un.

actions which proceed from the deliberation of reason, he is said to be master of his actions.[90]

How does Thomas support his conviction that the will is free? He uses three kinds of argument: philosophical-psychological, ethical and biblical. The philosophical-psychological argument deduces free will from the fact of rationality, as was indicated in the previous paragraph.[91] Unless man has free will, so goes the ethical argument, counsels, exhortations, commands, prohibitions, rewards and punishments would be in vain.[92] If man acts of necessity and cannot avoid doing what he does, then the basis for merit and de-merit in human acts is taken away, and all principles of moral philosophy are overthrown.[93] Again, it is an ethical axiom that man is master of his acts,[94] but this would not be true if man did not have free election of his acts.[95] Finally, Thomas sees Sir. 15:14 as biblical evidence for the existence of free will in man.[96] To deny that man has free will or to affirm that man's will is moved by necessity to choose something is, for Thomas, an "heretical opinion" which is contrary to faith, for it implicitly denies that man's acts are meritorious or demeritorious.[97]

---

[90] Cf. I-II, q. 1, a. 1c and ad 3; q. 6, a. 2c and ad 2. I, q. 82, a. 1, ad 3: ". . . sumus domini nostrorum actuum secundum quod posssumus hoc vel illud eligere."

[91] Cf. footnote 88. I, q. 83, a. 1: "Et pro tanto necesse est quod homo sit liberi arbitrii, ex hoc ipso quod rationalis est."—We are fully aware that such early texts emphasize the "intellectualist" view of free will in comparison with the "voluntarist" emphasis in I-II and De Malo. Cf. Pesch, "Philosophie und Theologie der Freiheit. . . ," pp. 8-15.

[92] I, q. 83, a. 1c.

[93] De Malo, q. 6, a. un. Benignus, Nature, Knowledge and God (Milwaukee, 1947), p. 249, points out that Thomas' ethical argument is not a purely pragmatic one: we treat men as if they have free will (by our exhortations, commands, etc.); therefore they are free agents. This is not Thomas' argument. The explanation Thomas gives for the inanity of commands, etc., if man is not free is that man enters into a particular action not by natural instinct, but by a certain process of rational comparison, that is, by a free judgment which enables him to be inclined to diverse courses of action. Cf. De Ver., q. 24, a. 1, sed contra 5 and 6; SCG, III, cap. 73, 5. In De Ver., q. 2, a. 12c, where Thomas says that if there were no free will, it would be unnecessary to seek counsel, he sees counsel as a sign of free will.

[94] Cf. De potentia, q. 3, a. 7, ad 12; I, q. 82, a. 1, ad 3; I-II, q. 1, aa. 1 and 2c; q. 6, a. 2, ad 2; SCG, I, cap. 88.

[95] De Malo, q. 6, a. un., sed contra 3.

[96] He cites this text as an argument for free will in De Ver., q. 24, a. 1, sed contra 1; I, q. 83, a. 1, sed contra; De Malo, q. 6, a. un., sed contra 1. Cf. De potentia, q. 3, a. 7, ad 12; De Ver., q. 5, a. 5, ad 4; SCG, III, cap. 73, 6; 90, 8.—In III, q. 18, a. 4, sed contra. Is. 7: 15 is cited to show that Christ had liberum arbitrium. In the body of this article Thomas speaks of election as the "actus liberi arbitrii."

[97] De Ver., q. 24, a. 1c; De Malo, q. 6, a. un. c.

It is important to notice that Thomas does not teach that the will is free in every respect. Man's will acts freely only concerning things which are related to his ultimate end. The ultimate end itself—beatitude, perfect happiness, the perfect good—is in no way subject to man's free choice or free judgment.[98] The will tends naturally and of necessity toward beatitude; man cannot not-will it.[99] The desire for the ultimate end is not one of those acts of which we are the master.[100] Thomas clarifies the extent of the natural freedom of the will by distinguishing between freedom of exercise and freedom of determination or specification. No object, not even the most perfect, i.e., beatitude itself, can cause the will to act necessarily from the point of view of exercise. The reason for this is that man is always free not to think about beatitude, etc. and therefore he is able not to will it in act.[101] From the standpoint of the specification of the will-act, on the other hand, an object which is universally good, i.e., good in every respect, does necessitate the will. The will is not free in regard to it. It cannot will the opposite but tends toward the universal good of necessity once this perfectly good object has been proposed to it.[102] Other objects which are not perfectly good,

---

[98] *De Ver.*, q. 24, a. 1, ad 20; I, q. 19, a. 1 c; q. 82, a. 1c; q. 83, a. 1, ad 5; I-II, q. 13, a. 3: ". . . ultimus finis nullo modo sub electione cadit."

[99] *De Malo*, q. 6, a. un., c: ". . . homo ex necessitate appetit beatitudinem." Cf. I, q. 19, 3c; q. 82, a. 1; I-II, q. 5, a. 4, ad 2; q. 10, a. 2c. In I, q. 41, a. 2c Thomas points out that the will differs from nature in that nature "determinata est ad unum; sed voluntas non est determinata ad unum." But in the ad 3 of the same article Thomas says that even the will can be considered as nature, and under this aspect it wills certain things naturally and therefore necessarily. Cf. I-II, q. 5, a. 4, ad 2. Thomas' terminology is sharper in *S. Theol.*, III, 18, a. 3c, his final word on the will, where, following John Damascene and the Lombard, he neatly distinguishes *thelesis* or *voluntas ut natura* from *bulesis* or *voluntas ut ratio* He himself names the former *simplex voluntas* and the latter *consiliative voluntas* which, *ibid.*, a. 4, he identifies with *electio,* the proper act of *liberum arbitrium.* An interesting and a much more subtle distinction is made by Thomas when he says: in relation to the ultimate end we have *liberam voluntatem,* or *libertas voluntatis,* since the natural necessity of inclination (of the will to the ultimate end) does not exclude liberty, as Augustine says in *De civitate Dei,* 5, 10; however, we do not have *liberum iudicium* in regard to the ultimate end since the ultimate end does not fall within the scope of election. Cf. *De Ver.*, q. 24, a. 1, ad 20 and *S. Theol.*, I, q. 82, a. 1, ad 1.

[100] I, q. 82, a. 1, ad 3. Cf. footnote 90.

[101] Cf. I-II, q. 10, aa. 1 and 2; *De Malo,* q. 6, a. un.

[102] *Ibid.* Pesch, "Freiheitsbegriff . . . bei Thomas . . . und Luther," p. 201, emphasizes that the necessary ordination of the will to its transcendental object—good in its universality—is what makes the will's freedom of choice possible in the first place. By pointing out that, for Thomas, the will is "immer schon aktive Tendenz der Geistform," "immer schon ein Wollen," p. 209, Pesch implicitly but effectively corrects the misconception of H. Lammers, *Luthers Anschauung vom Willen* (Berlin, 1935) and others that Thomas has a static concept of the will. Pfürtner, pp. 61f. and Clark, p. 185, footnote 2 and 193, footnote 5 likewise stress this important point.

i.e., good from every conceivable aspect, do not necessitate the will. In relation to them, therefore, the will is said to enjoy freedom of specification.[103]

In the foregoing paragraph we have encountered Thomas' concept of necessity for the first time. Because of the important role this idea will play in our examination of Luther's doctrine on the unfree will, we must look at it here more closely. That the will necessarily wills beatitude and that this necessity neither excludes the liberty of the will nor prevents this natural willing from being voluntary is an idea that Thomas finds in Augustine.[104] For Thomas "necessity" has many meanings.[105] Necessity is generically defined as that which is unable not to be,[106] or that which is immutably determined to one.[107] The natural necessity by which the will tends toward beatitude is not incompatible with voluntariness or liberty of the will, but it does exclude free judgment taken in the proper sense, that is, as involving election.[108] Necessity of coercion,

---

[103] Cf. I-II, q. 10, a. 2; *De Malo*, q. 6, a. un.

[104] Cf. Thomas: *De Ver.*, q. 24, a. 1, ad 20; I, q. 82, a. 1, ad 1 and Augustine, *De civ. Dei*, 5, 10: PL 41, 152; *De Trinitate*, 13, 4: PL 42, 1018. Adler, p. 567 observes: "For Augustine and Aquinas man's freedom of choice is grounded in a 'natural necessity' a necessity born of the will's own nature as a rational appetite for which the infinite or perfect good is the only completely satisfying object." Cf. Maritain, *Scholasticism and Politics*, p. 120. Pesch also emphasizes the ordination of man's will to the ultimate end. We cannot agree with him, however, when he thinks that this "bondage" to the ultimate end involves basically the same reality as Luther's bondage of the will. Cf. Pesch, "Freiheitsbegriff. . . ," p. 219. Thomas and Luther both teach that the will is "immer schon ein Wollen, ein In-Tätigkeit-Sein." *Ibid.*, p. 220. For Luther the will is enslaved not because of *this* basic "bondage" but because God's foreknowledge imposes absolute necessity on all things and primarily because, according to the biblical revelation, sinful man is enslaved to sin and no effort of his "free will" can release him from this unrighteous condition.

[105] I, q. 82, a. 1c: "necessitas dicitur multipliciter." Cf. SCG, II, cap. 138, 2 and 3.

[106] *Ibid.*

[107] *De Ver.*, q. 22, a. 6c.

[108] I, q. 82, a. 1c: "Necessitas autem finis non repugnat voluntati . . . Similiter etiam nec necessitas naturalis repugnat voluntati." *Ibid.*, ad 1: "Necessitas autem naturalis non aufert libertatem voluntatis. . . ." Cf. *De Ver.*, q. 24, a. 1, ad 20: Habemus ergo respectu eius finis ultimi liberam voluntatem, cum necessitas naturalis inclinationis libertati non repugnet . . . non autem liberum iudicium, proprie loquendo, cum non cadat sub electione." Cf. *ibid.*, q. 23, a. 4 and footnote 99 above.—Here is another example of Thomas' manifold use of the word "free." What is willed by natural necessity or by natural instincts, I, q. 19, 10c, cannot be willed by *liberum arbitrium* or *liberum iudicium* since *electio* is not involved. But this does not mean that the will is not free: i.e. that we do not have *libertas voluntatis* when we will the ultimate end necessarily. As Pesch points out: essential to freedom is "nicht nur Selbstbestimmung und Selbstbewegung. . . , sondern darüber hinaus ein secundum rationem et secundum se operari, also ein Handeln in Richtung auf das Wesensgemässe, d. h. auf das Gute." "Freiheitsbegriff. . . ," p. 204, footnote 32. In the light of *S. Theol.*, I,

on the other hand, is incompatible with voluntariness and therefore of liberty.[109] An act of man that is done because of some violent force acting from outside him is for this reason called an involuntary act.[110]

(a) Free Will, Necessity and God's Knowledge

We encounter the concept of necessity, and its counterpart, contingency, not only in Thomas' teaching on creation, but also in his teaching on God, especially in the questions concerning the divine knowledge, will, providence and predestination. Interestingly, Thomas does not ask: Does God's *foreknowledge* impose necessity on things? He is so convinced that some events happen contingently—and not by absolute necessity—that he asks: Does God have knowledge of future contingents?[111] In his treatment of this question, Thomas answers an objection similar to the one raised by Cicero—to which Augustine offered a rebuttal—and similar also to an objection later used by Luther in *De servo arbitrio* (WA 18, 614f.):

. . . others have said that God has knowledge of all future things, but all things happen of necessity. Otherwise God's knowledge of them would be liable to error. But this cannot be, for according to this view *liberum arbitrium* would be lost and it would no longer be necessary to seek counsel; it would also be unjust to give punishments or rewards for merits if all things are done out of necessity.[112]

---

q. 82, a. 1c and *De Ver.*, q. 24, a. 1, ad 20 one can also say that the will is free when it operates *secundum inclinationem naturalem*. Thus Thomas can say that God and those who enjoy perfect beatitude in heaven are not only free, even though they cannot sin, but that they have a greater *libertas arbitrii* than those who are able to sin. The ability to sin, the *posse peccare*, is a defect of liberty and a sign of liberty, but is by no means essential to liberty: I, q. 62, a. 8, ad 3; II-II, q. 88, a. 4, ad 1; *De Ver.*, q. 22, a. 6; SCG, II, cap. 138; *De Malo*, q. 16, a. 5c. It is a "libertas perversa": *In Ioann.*, cap. 8 lect. 4, n. 1209. See the additional texts cited by Pesch, *ibid.*, p. 205, footnote 32, 2. Thomas is breaking no new ground here. He follows a position taken by Augustine and Anselm. After Thomas, this view was maintained by such theologians as Gregory of Rimini, Ockham and Gabriel Biel. Cf. Biel, II *Sent.*, dist. 44, q. un., art. 2.

[109] I, q. 82, a. 1c.

[110] I-II, q. 6, aa. 4 and 5. Violence can only be brought to bear on those acts which are commanded by the will and which are executed by some powers other than the will. The will itself cannot be moved to act by some violent force from outside, for by its very definition an act of the will is an inclination proceeding from an interior principle. Cf. I-II, q. 6, a. 4 and a. 5, ad 1.

[111] I, q. 14, a. 13; *De Ver.*, q. 2, a. 12.—On the development of the concept of contingency see RGG, 3, 1793f.; LThK 6, 507ff.; Vorster, pp. 400ff.; Gilson, *The Spirit of Mediaeval Philosophy* (New York, 1940) pp. 64-83.

[112] In his answer to this objection, Thomas uses the same argument that he uses in I, q. 19, a. 8 *sed contra*. Cf. I, q. 14, a. 13, obj. 2.

And therefore it must be said that while God knows all futures this does not prevent some things from happening contingently.[113]

To the objection: "It is necessary that everything that is known by God exists necessarily," [114] Thomas answers with a famous distinction:

The statement: Everything that is known by God is necessary, can be understood in two ways, either in reference to the proposition (*de dicto*) or to the thing itself (*de re*). If we understand it *de dicto*, then we take it in a composite sense and it is true in this sense: Whatever is known by God is necessary [the formulation in I, q. 14, a. 13, ad 3 is clearer: This *proposition:* What is known by God exists, is necessary] i.e., because it is impossible that God should know that something exists which does not exist. But if we take the statement to refer to the thing itself, then we understand it in a divided sense and it would be false, for then the meaning would be: Everything which is known by God exists necessarily.[115]

An argument against free will similar [116] to Luther's is also found in *De Ver.*, q. 24, a. 1, obj. 13:

Whatever God foreknows necessarily happens, since his foreknowledge cannot be deceived. But God foreknows every human act. Therefore these happen of necessity; and thus man does not act according to free will.[117]

Thomas answers this objection by employing the same distinction he used in *De Ver.*, q. 2, a. 12, ad 4. The only difference is that in *De Ver.*, q. 24, a. 1, ad 13, instead of speaking of necessity in the composite (*de dicto*) or divided (*de re*) sense, he uses the terms "necessary by absolute necessity, which is called necessity of the *thing* consequent" and "necessary by conditioned necessity, which is called necessity of consequence." Thus, says Thomas: "It cannot be concluded from God's foreknowledge that our acts are performed out of absolute necessity, which

---

[113] *De Ver.*, q. 2, a. 12c.

[114] *Ibid.*, obj. 3, 4 and 5.

[115] *Ibid.*, ad 4. This distinction is explained more fully in other places: *De Ver.*, q. 23, a. 4, ad 1; *Quodl.*, 11, q. 3, a. un., ad 1.; I, q. 14, a. 13c and ad 2 and 3; *De Malo*, q. 16, a. 7, ad 15.

[116] We emphasize that this argument is only *similar* to Luther's; we shall notice some important differences.

[117] *De Ver.*, q. 24, a. 1, obj. 13: ". . . quidquid Deus praescit, necesse est evenire, cum praescientia Dei falli non possit. Sed omnes actus humanos Deus praescit. Ergo de necessitate eveniunt; et ita homo non est liberi arbitrii ad agendum."

is called necessity of the thing consequent, but out of conditioned necessity, which is called necessity of consequence. . . ." [118]

EXCURSUS: *Contingency and Necessity in Thomas Aquinas*

The contingent, for Thomas, is that which is not necessary or that which is subject to free will: I, 14, 13 *sed contra*. It is "that which is able to be and not be": I, 86, 3c. The will is a contingent cause, for it does not have power limited to one outcome but rather has the ability to produce this effect or that: SCG III, 73, par. 2. In all discussions of contingency and necessity, one must be clear as to whether he is discussing logical contingency or necessity, or ontological contingency or necessity. Thomas does not use the terms, logical and ontological, in this connection, but there is no doubt that this language conforms to his thought and helps clarify it. If a proposition is logically necessary, the necessity spoken of refers to the truth or validity of the proposition, *not* to the nature or mode of the being or event. Only ontological contingency and necessity refer to the mode of existence of beings or events as they are in themselves. Thus, in the proposition: Whatever God wills happens of necessity, we say the proposition is true when we understand it to mean that the apodasis of this conditional sentence necessarily follows from the protasis. Nothing has been said about the nature or mode of the being—that is, of its ontological structure, be it necessary or contingent—or of the event which is willed by God. The following proposition offers perhaps a clearer illustration: If I see an old friend, then he necessarily is still alive (necessarily still exists). Again the proposition is true since the apodasis necessarily follows from the protasis. But again, nothing whatever has been said about my friend's ontological structure, even though it is said that he necessarily exists. The necessity spoken of here is logical, not ontological necessity. This is

---

118 *De Ver.*, q. 24, a. 1, ad 13: ". . . ex praescientia Dei non potest concludi quod actus nostri sint necessarii necessitate absoluta, quae dicitur necessitas consequentis; sed necessitate conditionata, quae dicitur necessitas consequentiae. . . ." The same distinction is also found in SCG, I, cap. 67, 10: "Praeterea, si unumquodque a Deo cognoscitur sicut praesentialiter visum, sic necessarium erit esse quod Deus cognoscit, sicut necessarium est Socratem sedere ex hoc quod sedere videtur. Hoc autem non necessarium est absolute, vel, ut a quibusdam dicitur, necessitate consequentis; sed sub conditione vel necessitate consequentiae. Haec enim conditionalis est necessaria: si videtur sedere, sedet. . . ." Luther's understanding of the distinction between *necessitas consequentis* and *necessitas consequentiae* is, like his concept of contingency, radically different from that of Thomas. Cf. WA 18, 617 and 720ff. For Thomas, conditional necessity is involved in everything that God wills and this does not take away free will (I, q. 23, a. 3, ad 3 and a. 6). God can will that some things occur freely. To deny this would be to limit his power to communicate his perfections—existence, life, intelligence *and* freedom—in an analogous way to creatures. This difference accounts to a great extent for the distinctly different answers Luther and Thomas give to the questions: Does man have *liberum arbitrium?* Does God's will impose necessity on all things?

what Thomas called *necessitas consequentiae:* the necessity by which the conclusion of a syllogism follows from its premises, or the necessity by which the apodasis of a conditional proposition follows from its protasis.

Illustrations from the created order are less ambiguous in showing the distinction between logical and ontological necessity because it is self-evident that our logically certain and necessary conclusions about things say nothing about their ontological makeup. Thus, when I ascertain that there is something seated on a chair, it is logically necessary that there be something on the chair as long as it is there. This logical necessity in no way implies that the thing on the chair is sitting there freely (contingently) or necessarily: the thing, considered in its own mode of being, can, in fact, be a man, who is free at any instant to get up, or it can be a dummy, which must of necessity remain there until some other force moves it (cf. *De Malo,* q. 16, a. 7, ad 15). When we draw up conditional propositions or syllogisms in which a logically necessary conclusion follows from one of God's attributes, especially his creative powers of knowledge and will, it is easy to confuse the two orders of mental and real being. The reason for this is, of course, that God's omnipotent will can create beings which exist or act necessarily. But as long as it is admitted that God's creative will is so transcendently powerful that it can will some things to exist or to happen in either a contingent or a necessary way, then we are faced with the possibility of beings and actions which exist or happen not by ontological or absolute necessity but by logical, conditional or suppositional necessity. Contingency is excluded only by absolute necessity, not by conditioned necessity (*S. Th.* I, q. 23, a. 3, ad 3) or the necessity which results from the immutability of the divine will (I, q. 23, a. 6, ad 3). Cf. I, q. 19, a. 7, ad 4 and *De Ver.* q. 23, a. 4c, where Thomas calls this *necessitas immutabilitatis.* As Thomas explains elsewhere: "The necessity of supposition in the cause . . . does not require an absolute necessity in the effect. But God wills something in the creature, not by absolute necessity, but only by a necessity of supposition. . . . From the divine will, therefore, an absolute necessity in created things cannot be inferred. But only this excludes contingency, for even the contingents open to opposites are made necessary by supposition: for example, that Socrates be moved, if he runs is necessary. . . . Hence it does not follow, if God wills something, that it will of necessity take place. But this conditional is true and necessary: If God wills something, it will be. But the consequent does not have to be necessary" (SCG, I, ch. 85, 5f.; tr. A. Pegis).

To avoid a misunderstanding of Thomas' teaching on contingency and liberty in relation to the divine knowledge, we must note a distinction that he makes in several places (cf. I, q. 14, a. 13 c; SCG, I, ch. 67), namely, that the contingent event can be considered in itself, according as it already exists in act—as present (*in seipso, secundum quod iam actu est . . . ut praesens*) or the contingent event can be considered as it is in its cause—as future (*ut est in sua causa . . . ut futuram*). Considered as present, the contingent event is not contingent to both sides, but is determined in one way (*determinatum ad unum*). For, according as it is in itself, the contingent as present and as existing in act is subject to the ontological principle of contradiction: it cannot be and not-be; it can only be, insofar as it is present in act. Considered as future, however, it can not-be, for it is not yet determined in one way: because a contingent cause is open to opposites. Thomas states this all very concisely when he writes in II-II, q. 171, a. 6, ad 2: Although future contingents, considered as they are in themselves, are *determinatum ad unum,* nevertheless, considered in their causes, they are not determined in such a way that they cannot happen otherwise (*non sunt determinata, quin possint aliter evenire*). To God's eternal knowledge all things that happen in time are present. Thus God knows all future contingents infallibly because they are always present to him, i.e., as *determinatum ad unum,* but—as Thomas emphasizes in both I, q. 14, a. 13 c and SCG, I, ch. 67—although God has from eternity an infallible knowledge of contingent singulars they do not cease to be contingent.

We shall see that the concept of contingency, which is of decisive importance in discussions concerning free will, seems to have an altogether different meaning for Luther than it does for Thomas (cf. WA 18, 616, 7-12).

Vorster gives a careful exposition of Thomas' teaching on contingency in *S. Th.,* I, q. 14, a. 13 but unfortunately, on the decisive point, he misinterprets Thomas. He fails to take seriously Thomas' view that a contingent cause—such as man's free will: SCG, III, ch. 73, 2—can be considered *as future,* and therefore as not yet *determinatum ad unum.* When the contingent event is considered as future it can not-be.

True, God's knowledge of all events is eternal and all things which occur in time are eternally present to him. But Vorster exaggerates one aspect of Thomas' teaching when he concludes that, for Thomas, the contingence of human actions, the "openness to both sides," is only an illusion ("der Schein der Kontingenz") because God knows all human events as present and therefore as determined *ad unum* (cf. pp. 354f.). Nowhere does Thomas say that man's acts only give the "illusion of contingency" or freedom. They are *really* contingent and *really* free. They are such as a result of God's all-powerful, creative will. As long as we can consider contingent actions as future they are *not yet* determined to one. They receive this determination from a free, contingent human decision.

In *De Ver.,* q. 5, a. 5, ad 1 Thomas teaches that acts of human election are not determined to one by God's providence as are the acts of beings without free will. Cf. *S. Th.,* I-II, q. 10, a. 4, and *De Potentia,* q. 3, a. 7, ad 13. Further, in *S. Th.,* I, q. 19, a. 8; q. 22, a. 4; q. 23, a. 6 and SCG, I, ch. 85. Thomas expressly denies that God's will, providence or predestination imposes absolute necessity on all things. Man *can* resist God's grace: *Quodl.* I, q. 4, a. 2, ad. 2. Some things really happen necessarily, that is "always in the same way" and some things really—not seemingly—happen contingently, that is "variably" (*S. Th.,* II-II, q. 95, a. 5), and they do so because God wills it that way. In I, q. 14, a. 13, ad 2 and 3 Thomas says that if God knows something, it will be—and it will be necessarily, that is, according as it is subject to God's knowledge of praesentiality, but it will *not* be necessary in itself, which is the only kind of necessity that would prevent it from being contingent (cf. Garrigou-Lagrange, *De Deo Uno* [Paris, 1937], pp. 353-360). Only absolute necessity excludes contingency from things (SCG, I, ch. 85, 5), not the necessity of the logical order (e.g., the *necessitas infallibilitatis* mentioned in I-II, q. 112, a. 3 does *not* make it absolutely impossible for man to say "no" to God, as Vorster suggests, pp. 320f.), resulting from the condition that God knows or wills something. Vorster stresses the fact that when God sees temporal events in his praesentiality, they are, as present, *determinatum ad unum,* but he overlooks the decisive point that "effects are foreseen by God, as they are freely produced by us": SCG, III, ch. 94, par. 15.

(b) *Free Will, Necessity and God's Will*

Luther's speculative-theological argument against free will in *De servo arbitrio* is based on the immutability of God's foreknowledge.[119] Thomas is, like Luther, completely convinced of the immutability of the divine will.[120] He is equally certain, however, that: (1) God does not will by absolute necessity whatever he wills.[121] (2) God has *liberum arbitrium* concerning the things other than his own goodness.[122] These he does not will by absolute necessity, but only by necessity of supposition.[123] (3) God's will is always fulfilled.[124] (4) God's will is not

---

[119] The "bolt of lightening" which overthrows *liberum arbitrium* is God's immutable, eternal and infallible will by which he foresees, proposes and does all things: WA 18, 615, 12-17 and 26-33; WA 18, 720ff.

[120] I, q. 19, a. 7: ". . . voluntas Dei est omnino immutabilis."

[121] I, q. 19, a. 3. Again Thomas distinguishes two kinds of necessity, *necessitas absoluta* and *ex suppositione*. Cf. *De Ver.*, q. 23, a. 4, ad 1; SCG, I, cap. 85, 5. It is thus absolutely necessary that man is an animal and that the whole is greater than any part, but it is not absolutely necessary that a man be sitting. Sitting can be necessary *ex suppositione,* that is, on the supposition that a man is sitting, it is necessary that he sit as long as he is sitting. According to a distinction Thomas makes in I-II, q. 10, a. 4, ad 3, we can say that it is not impossible for the man to stand, but as long as he is sitting it is impossible that he stand. *De Ver.*, q. 23, a. 4, ad 1 Thomas says that, from the fact that God willed or wills the salvation of someone, his salvation is not absolutely necessary, but it is necessary *ex suppositione*. This means that, granting that God has willed or wills the person's salvation, it is impossible that he did not will it or does not will it, since his will is immutable. This necessity, says Thomas, is called *necessitas immutabilitatis* by the theologians: I, q. 23, a. 6, ad 3. In I-II, q. 112, a. 3c Thomas speaks of *necessitas infallibilitatis.*—Luther also makes use of the term *necessitas immutabilitatis* (WA 18, 720, 32). However, since he uses it in the sense of *necessitas absoluta* when dealing with the problem of free will, he reaches a completely different conclusion than Thomas.

[122] I, q. 19, a. 10; SCG, I, cap. 80ff.; II, cap. 23.

[123] I, q. 19, a. 3 and a. 7, ad 4; SCG, I, cap. 83. *Necessitas ex suppositione* is the same as *necessitas conditionata* and *consequentiae*. Cf. footnote 118 above.

[124] I, q. 19, a. 6: "Cum igitur voluntas Dei sit universalis causa omnium rerum, impossibile est quod divina voluntas suum effectum non consequatur." —*Ibid.*, ad 1, Thomas introduces the celebrated distinction of John Damascene concerning God's antecedent and consequent will: whatever God wills *simpliciter*

mutable; however, his immutable will wills mutability in creatures.[125] (5) God's immutable will does not impose absolute necessity on all the things he wills. Since his will is most powerful, it not only follows that those things happen which God wills to happen, but that they happen in the way in which he wills them to happen, that is, either necessarily or contingently (or freely).[126]

Because of the importance of this "most celebrated article" (I, q. 19, a. 8) as Garrigou-Lagrange calls it, we shall examine it more closely. The first and third objections are similar. The first: It seems that the will of God imposes necessity on all things, because Augustine says in his *Enchiridion,* 103: PL 40, 280: "If God wills something, it is necessary that it happen." The third: This conditional proposition is true: If God wills something, it happens. But every true conditional proposition is necessary. Therefore everything that God wills is absolutely necessary. Both of these objections are easily answered by means of the distinction between absolute necessity (*nec. consequentis*) and conditional necessity (*nec. consequentiae*). Thus, in his answer to the first objection, Thomas says that Augustine's words are to be understood as meaning that the necessity in things willed by God is not absolute, but conditional. In the answer to the third objection Thomas repeats the point he made in the body of the article: those things which happen because of the divine will have such necessity as God wills them to have, namely, either absolute or conditional necessity. Thus not all things happen of absolute necessity.

The second objection maintains that, since the will of God cannot be impeded (Rom. 9:19), it follows that the will of God imposes necessity on things. Thomas gives his basic answer to this objection in the body of the article. (See footnote 126.) In his direct answer to the second objection he grants that nothing resists the divine will. From this, he says, it follows not only that those things happen which God wills to happen, but also that they happen contingently or necessarily, according as God wills them to happen.

On the basis of Thomas' teaching in this article, it is contradictory to hold that God's will is immutable, eternal and all-powerful, and at the same time to affirm that, precisely because God's will is so powerful, man's will cannot be free, since all things happen by absolute necessity. One who holds such a view is really denying that God's will is sufficiently powerful to communicate free will to creatures. Such a person must then explain satisfactorily how it is that God's creative power is so

---

or *consequenter* happens; but what he wills *secundum quid* or *antecedenter* may not always happen. Cf. *De Ver.,* q. 23, a. 2.

[125] I, q. 19, a. 7, ad 3. Benignus, p. 547 states it as follows: "God's will cannot change, but God can will change." Cf. Garrigou-Lagrange, p. 436.

[126] I, q. 19, a. 8c: ". . . divina voluntas quibusdam volitis necessitatem imponit, non autem omnibus. . . . Cum igitur voluntas divina sit efficacissima, non solum sequitur quod fiant ea quod Deus vult fieri; sed quod eo modo fiant, quo Deus ea fieri vult. Vult autem quaedam Deus fieri necessario, et quaedam contingenter. . . ." Cf. *De Ver.,* q. 23, a. 5; SCG, I, cap. 85; I-II, a. 10, ad 4.

great that God can communicate to creatures the dignity of being, life, intelligence, will and the divine life itself through Christian rebirth, but that the divine creative power is not great enough to enable God to communicate to creatures the perfection of free will. Once it is admitted that God *can* will to endow some creatures with free will, then it is self-contradictory to suppose that the divine foreknowledge excludes free will, for one would be saying: God can will infallibly and efficaciously that the conversion of a sinner take place freely, but this conversion cannot take place freely because the decree of the divine will is absolutely efficacious and the divine knowledge of this conversion is infallible.

The principle upon which Thomas' teaching in this article is based is the universal, supremely efficacious power of the divine will. This is clear from Thomas' reference in I, q. 19, a. 6 c (cf. above footnote 24) to God's will as the "universal cause of all things" and from his description of the divine will in article 8 of the same question as "most efficacious." It is precisely because of this all-powerful will, or what later Thomists would call God's transcendent causality, that Thomas can conclude that "not only do those things happen which God wills to happen but also that they happen in the way (*secundum modum fiendi vel essendi*) in which he wills them to happen" that is, necessarily or contingently. Whoever denies, therefore, in the name of the all-powerful, immutable will of God, that God can will certain things to happen freely or contingently, does so because he fails to attribute to the divine will such tremendous, transcendent power and efficaciousness as does St. Thomas.

The recognition that God's causality is unique and transcendent, infinitely and essentially different from all created causality of our experience, is a commonplace of Catholic theology. Cf. Garrigou-Lagrange, *God: His Existence and His Nature,* vol. III, 6th ed. (St. Louis, 1955), pp. 203ff. When authors such as G. Nygren (see chapter 4) and W. Pannenberg, "Christlicher Glaube und menschliche Freiheit," in: *Kerygma und Dogma* 4 (1958), 251-280 find difficulty with "causal categories" as a means of describing the creative omnipotence of God, it is because they think of God's transcendental causality in terms of the finite causality of creatures. Thus, it is only because Pannenberg conceives of causality univocally that he can write: "The power of expression of causal concepts is very limited when we are trying to understand God's activity (Wirken). . . ." p. 279. Only when one forgets or fails to see that God, the transcendent cause of all being and action, is the ultimate, transcendent cause even of man's free will acts, can one formulate, as does Pannenberg, p. 269, the following false alternative: "If man has free will in reference to the gospel of God's grace then it is man—not God—who makes the actual and ultimate saving decision."

In contrast to this viewpoint it would be helpful to consider the following statement of the thought of Thomas Aquinas which is offered by L. Bouyer, *The Spirit and Forms of Protestantism* (Westminster: Newman Press, 1961), p. 54: "For St. Thomas, God is the absolute master, not only of the faculty, but of its entire range of employment, and of its least acts. As such, he moves us, albeit freely, to assent to grace when we actually do so. This divine impulse it is which makes grace efficacious in us; it is not we who make it so." For a concise explanation of the meaning of analogous concepts, the reader is referred to K. Rahner-H. Vorgrimler, *Theological Dictionary*, pp. 17f.

(c) Free Will, Necessity and Divine Providence

In I, q. 22, a. 4 Thomas asks whether God's providence [127] imposes necessity on things.[128] His reply is that "divine providence imposes necessity on certain things, but not on all things as certain persons have believed." [129] "And therefore that takes place infallibly and necessarily which divine providence disposes to take place infallibly and necessarily. And that happens contingently which divine providence ordains to happen contingently." [130]

(d) Free Will, Necessity and Predestination

While God's providence applies to all creatures, his predestination has reference only to rational creatures. Thomas defines predestination as the leading or sending of rational creatures to that goal—eternal life—which exceeds the proportion and power of their created natures.[131] Following Augustine, he teaches that predestination most cer-

---

127 For Thomas' understanding of God's providence see *S. Theol.*, I, q. 22, aa. 1-3 and *De Ver.*, q. 5.

128 The same question is treated in *SCG*, III, cap. 72, 73 and 94 and in *De Malo*, q. 16, a. 7, ad 15. In *SCG*, III, cap. 94 we find an extensive discussion of the question in which Thomas comes to grips with Cicero and the classical dilemma formulated by him: God's providence or man's freedom.

129 I, q. 22, a. 4c.

130 *Ibid.*, ad 1. Cf. SCG, III, cap. 94: whatever God foresees happens in the way he foresees it. But God foresees that something would happen contingently. Therefore it follows infallibly that it will happen contingently and not necessarily.

131 *S. Theol.*, I, q. 23, a. 1: "Finis autem ad quem res creatae ordinantur a Deo, est duplex. Unus, qui excedit proportionem naturae creatae et facultatem; et hic finis est vita aeterna . . . quae est supra naturam cuiuslibet creaturae . . . Ad illum autem ad quod non potest aliquid virtute suae naturae pervenire, oportet quod ab alio transmittatur. . . . Unde, proprie loquendo, rationalis creatura, quae est capax vitae aeternae, perducitur in ipsam quasi a Deo transmissa . . . Unde ratio praedictae transmissionis creaturae rationalis in finem vitae aeternae, praedestinatio nominatur: nam destinare est mittere." At first glance it would seem that Thomas' flight into philology, with the resulting identification of *destinare* and *mittere*, *praedestinatio* and *transmissio creaturae rationalis*, etc., is an adulteration of the biblical concept of *proorizō*. The element of determination seems to be lost. When Thomas' doctrine of predestination is explored more carefully, however, this objection proves to be groundless. Predestination is seen to be not only a kind of sending, but also an *ordinatio* (I, q. 23, a. 3), *praeordinatio*, a *definitio* and a *praefinitio principalis* (I, q. 23, a. 7 and 8; III, q. 24, a. 1 and a. 4, ad 3), as well as a *directio* (III, q. 24, a. 1 and a. 2) and a *determinatio* (III, q. 24, a. 2, ad 1).—In his earlier treatise on predestination in *De Ver.*, q. 6, Thomas takes the word *destinatio*, from which he says predestination derives its name, to mean "directionem alicuius in finem." The later commentary on the Epistle to the Romans agrees more with the article in the *Summa*: cf.

tainly and infallibly achieves its effect.[132] It does not, however, cause its effect to take place out of necessity.[133]

Thomas develops his thesis in the following way: Predestination is a part of God's providence. But the order of providence is infallible even though it does not impose necessity on all things. Similarily, the order of predestination is certain even though *libertas arbitrii,* through which the effect of predestination contingently takes place, is not taken away. Thomas then asks the reader to consider what he had said previously concerning God's knowledge and will. Even though these are most certain and infallible, they do not take contingency away from things.[134] As Thomas says in the closing sentence of *Quodl.,* XI, q. 3, a. un., where he gives a lengthy reply to the question: Does predestination impose necessity?: ". . . because God knows and wills that someone will attain such a goal, predestination is certain. But because God wills that he be directed to such a goal according to free will, this certitude does not impose necessity on the one predestined."

A final aspect of this question needs to be mentioned: God predestines men to salvation solely because of his merciful goodness, by grace alone (*ex sola gratia*), and not because of any good merits, such as the good use of grace, which he foresees in the creature.[135]

(e) *Free Will, Necessity and Reprobation*

Thomas understands reprobation to mean that God permits some men to fail to reach eternal life.[136] Reprobation is more than the mere foreknowledge by God that some men will fail to reach their eternal goal. Just as predestination includes, over and above the divine foreknowledge concerning the elect, God's will to confer the graces needed

---

In Rom., cap. 1, lect. 3, n. 43. For further discussion of this question see the article by C. Williams, "Prädefinition und Prädetermination," LThK, 8, 659f., 672f. and Garrigou-Lagrange, *Predestination,* fifth printing (London-St. Louis, 1953), pp. 183-191.

[132] Augustine's definition of predestination found in *De dono perseverantiae,* 14, 35 is cited by Thomas in the *sed contra* of I, q. 23, a. 6 as a gloss on Rom. 8: 29f.: "praedestinatio sanctorum, nihil aliud: praescientia scilicet et praeparatio beneficiorum Dei, quibus certissime liberantur, quicumque liberantur."

[133] I, 23, 6c: "praedestinatio certissime et infallibiliter consequitur suum effectum: nec tamen imponit necessitatem, ut scilicet effectus eius ex necessitate proveniat."

[134] *Ibid.* Cf. SCG, III, cap. 173.

[135] I, q. 23, a. 5c and ad 1; *In Rom.,* cap. 1, lect. 3, n. 48; cap. 8, lect. 6, n. 703; cap. 9, lect. 2, nn. 757-764; lect. 3, nn. 771f. Cf. Garrigou-Lagrange, *Predestination,* pp. 194-205. *In Rom.,* cap. 1, lect. 3, n. 48 Thomas says not even Christ was predestined "propter merita praecedentis, sed ex sola gratia . . . ita et nos ex sola gratia, non ex meritis, praedestinamur ut simus filii adoptiva."

[136] I, q. 23, a. 3: ". . . pertinet etiam ad divinam providentiam, ut permittat aliquos ab isto fine deficere. Et hoc dicitur reprobare."

to attain eternal life, so also reprobation includes God's will to permit some men to commit sin and to impose the penalty of damnation because of this sin.

Despite the similarity between predestination and reprobation it would be incorrect to hold with Pannenberg and others that, in a causal concept of predestination, one is forced to assume a "structural parallel of election and reprobation" which would correspond to a "double predestination." [137] Thomas Aquinas teaches indeed, as we have seen, that God's all-powerful causality is operative not only in his providential ordering of all creation but also in that special area of providence known as predestination. However, he explicitly denies that there is a parallel in the causality involved in reprobation and predestination.[138]

Later theologians have thus come to distinguish between positive and negative reprobation.[139] Negative reprobation means that God permits some creatures to sin. The reprobated creatures themselves, however, are alone the responsible cause of the sin by virtue of their free wills. For Thomas, as for Augustine, the most unsearchable aspect of the mystery of reprobation is not that God does not elect and predestine all men to eternal life, but that God elects *this* person and reprobates *that* one.[140] There can be no question of injustice on God's part, however, for, in relation to God, *no* creature has a *right* to exist, to be conserved in goodness or to be predestined to eternal life. This is purely a matter of God's freedom and grace and has nothing whatever to do with his justice.[141]

---

[137] Pannenberg, "Der Einfluss der Anfechtungserfahrung auf den Prädestinationsbegriff Luthers," in KuD, 3 (1957), 130.

[138] I, q. 23, a. 3, ad 2: ". . . aliter se habet reprobatio in causando, quam praedestinatio. Nam praedestinatio est causa et eius quod expectatur in futura vita a praedestinatis, scilicet gloriae; et eius quod percipitur in praesenti, scilicet gratiae. Reprobatio vero non est causa eius quod est in praesenti, scilicet culpae; sed est causa derelictionis a Deo. Est tamen causa eius quod redditur in futuro, scilicet poenae aeternae." Cf. *In Rom.*, cap. 9, lect. 2, n. 764.

[139] See Garrigou-Lagrange, *Predestination*, pp. 206-212.

[140] I, q. 23, a. 5, ad 3: "Sed quare hoc elegit in gloriam, et illos reprobavit, non habet rationem nisi divinam voluntatem." Cf. *In Ioann.*, cap. 6, lect. 5, n. 938.

[141] I, q. 23, a. 5, ad 3: "Neque tamen propter hoc est iniquitas apud Deum, si inequalia non inequalibus praeparat. Hoc enim esset contra iustitiae rationem, si praedestinationis effectus ex debito redderetur, et non daretur ex gratia. In his enim quae ex gratia dantur, potest aliquis pro libito suo dare cui vult, plus vel minus, dummodo nulli substrahat debitum, absque praeiudicio iustitiae." Cf. *In Rom.*, cap. 9, lect. 3, nn. 766-773. This concept of God's graciousness corresponds with Thomas' ontological insight that creation itself and the conservation of the creature in existence and in natural goodness is so absolutely dependent on God that the creature would cease to exist or would cease to have any goodness whatever except for God's conserving action. Cf. I-II, q. 109, a. 2, ad 2. Here Thomas' thought approaches most closely the teaching of canon

Positive reprobation, according to the principles of Thomas, is the actual damnation imposed as punishment for the sin freely committed. God is indeed the cause of the punishment of eternal damnation,[142] but he is in no way the cause of the sin for which the punishment is justly imposed.[143]

Negative reprobation requires no foreknowledge whatever by God of the sinful demerits of the creature. Positive reprobation, on the other hand, presupposes that God foresees the demerits of the creature, since it would clearly be unjust for God to decree a punishment where there is no guilt.[144]

(f) The Created Free Will: Totally Dependent on God for Existence and Operation

To conceive of man's free will as a "radical self-dynamism" or as "faith in man's self-dynamism" [145] is to place oneself in complete op-

---

22 of the Second Council of Orange when he says that man "in se considerata est nihil." Cf. In Rom., cap. 3, lect. 2, n. 277: "ex se quilibet est peccator." Also, In Ioann., cap. 15, lect. 1, n. 1993.

Vorster, pp. 193-199 has extensively criticized the Thomistic concept of reprobation. He proposes no alternative concept, however, which would be faithful to Rom. 8: 29f., 1 Tim. 2: 3f. and to the biblical truths that predestination and election are absolutely gratuitous, that man alone is responsible for sin against God and that God's will of not predestining some is not determined by his foreknowledge of man's sins. Vorster unfortunately limits his examination of Thomas' doctrine of reprobation to the brief statement of it found in I, q. 23, a. 3 and thus misses the extensive biblical-theological development of this theme found in Thomas' commentary on Romans.

[142] I, q. 23, a. 3, ad 2: God "est tamen causa eius quod redditur in futuro, scilicet poenae aeternae."

[143] Ibid.: "Sed culpa provenit ex libero arbitrio eius qui reprobatur et a gratia deseritur." Cf. I-II, q. 79, a. 1; De Malo, q. 3, a. 1; In Rom., cap. 9, lect. 3, n. 764. For one of the finest contemporary expositions of the Thomistic understanding of the relation of God and human freedom to moral good and moral evil, see J. Maritain, Existence and the Existent (New York, 1957), pp. 94-112, esp. footnote 9 on pp. 101-106. On the divine permission of sin see M. Pontifex, Providence and Freedom (London, 1960), pp. 78f. and Maritain, God and the Permission of Evil (Milwaukee, 1966).

[144] Cf. Garrigou-Lagrange, p. 206.

[145] Pannenberg, "Christlicher Glaube und menschliche Freiheit," in: KuD, 4 (1958), 268ff. A similar view is put forward by G. Ebeling, Luther: Einführung in sein Denken (Tübingen, 1964), p. 257, who maintains that through the Scholastic teaching that man has free will "ist . . . der Mensch im Prinzip als Gott gegenüber selbständig in Ansatz gebracht. . . ."—It is curious that Pannenberg in his 1958 article rejects the doctrine of free choice (Wahlfreiheit) on the ground that it is "Glaube an die Selbstmächtigkeit des Menschen," while in his earlier article, KuD, 3, (1957), 109-139, he asserts that Augustine, Thomas, Peter Lombard and other Scholastics are guilty of determinism, a charge made long ago by Loofs, p. 438 and Seeberg, III, 402-405. This juxtaposition of mutually exclusive criticisms results from Pannenberg's failure to conceive of causality in any other way than as univocal.

position to Thomas' concept of the divine creative will, *concursus*,[146] providence and predestination. It is true that, for Thomas, "liberum arbitrium est causa sui motus" and that man truly moves himself to action by his free will.[147] But it would be grossly misleading to stop one's investigation at this point and simply conclude that Thomas teaches that man possesses a radical self-dynamism, independent of God's power. Man has dominion over his actions because he directs himself freely. This free self-direction has been entrusted to him by God. However, just as the lawful authority which God has entrusted to men does not imply absolute authority over the men they govern, so also man's dominion over his actions in no way implies that man is absolutely autonomous or has absolute dominion over himself.

The free will is the cause of its own motion, but it is not the *first* cause.[148] The fact that man moves himself voluntarily, that is, by

---

In the one article, Pannenberg thinks that the affirmation of *liberum arbitrium* as a genuine power of human self-determination implies human self-sufficiency and autonomous independence from God (Pelagianism). In the other essay he interprets the doctrine that God is the ultimate cause of all being and operation as the negation of true created causality and created freedom. The Thomistic conception, on the other hand, maintains that God's causality is transcendent, i.e. it is a causality infinitely more powerful than any created causality of our experience. His power is so great that he is able to be the ultimate and the primary cause even of man's free acts. Cf. *De Malo*, q. 6, a. un., ad 4. The only necessity involved in man's free choice, from the standpoint of God's causality, is a conditional necessity of infallibility or immutability.

After correctly stating that God is the total cause ("Totalursache") of our salvation, *KuD* 3 (1957), 114, Pannenberg mistakenly concludes that God is the *sole cause* involved in salvation. *Ibid.* When he says this, he is no longer dealing with the doctrine of Thomas or even of Bernard for, as we have seen, it was Bernard who pointed out that God and man are not partial causes of the salvation event, but that each are total causes in their own proper plane of operation. Cf. Ch. 5, footnote 25. When Pannenberg supposes that it is the Thomistic view that God is the "sole cause of salvation," he overlooks the whole concept of secondary causality that is absolutely essential to Thomas' theology. Cf. *De Ver.*, q. 6, a. 3c where *liberum arbitrium* is called "causa proxima salutis"; also *ibid.*, a. 2 and I, q. 23, a. 5c, where Thomas teaches that one and the same effect proceeds from the primary and the secondary cause, from grace and free will.

[146] Cf. V. Frins, "Concours divin," DTC, 3, 785ff. We need not discuss here the controversy concerning Thomas' teaching on the nature of this *concursus*. The perennial controversy flared up again as a result of the writings of J. Stufler during the early 1930's. For a summary of the literature for and against Stufler's interpretation of Thomas, see I. F. Sagues, *Sacrae Theologiae Summa*, II (Madrid, 1955), p. 751, footnote 6. Cf. Pesch, "Philosophie und Theologie der Freiheit," pp. 21ff.

[147] I, q. 83, a. 1, ad 3. Cf. I, q. 105, a. 4, ad 3.

[148] I, q. 83, a. 1, ad 3: ". . . liberum arbitrium est causa sui motus: quia homo per liberum arbitrium seipsum movet ad agendum. Non tamen hoc est de necessitate libertatis, quod sit prima causa sui id quod liberum est. . . ."

means of an intrinsic principle, doesn't exclude the possibility that this intrinsic principle, the will, can be moved from without by an extrinsic principle.[149] This extrinsic principle is God alone, who is the cause of the very movements of the will.[150] If God causes the very movement of the free will, why isn't he the cause of the sin that arises from free will? It would take us too far afield to discuss this problem. For Thomas' answer to it, see *De Malo*, a. 3, as well as the presentation by Maritain mentioned above.[151]

In discussing the dependence of created freedom on uncreated creativity, we once again encounter the paradox or the dialectic that we have previously noted. This paradox cannot be dissolved without destroying reality itself. For to affirm the existence and the activity of the creator and not to recognize fully the creature and his freedom, or to affirm created freedom and fail to see the total dependence of this finite freedom on the creator is to deny the real order of things. As we have insisted in an earlier chapter, it is not sufficient to say: Let God be God. If one is to do justice to reality as it is grasped by man's mind in philosophical reflection and as it is given to man's mind and heart in the biblical revelation, one must say: Let God be God and man be man. Augustine had to struggle mightily to defend God's sovereignty and Godness against the Pelagians, but he never did it by denying man's free will. This would have been an assault on man's man-ness. Thomas Aquinas, although he theologized in historical circumstances quite different from those surrounding Augustine, was no less faithful than Augustine in letting God be God and man be man.

B. ACQUIRED FREEDOM

The natural freedom of the will belongs to all men and is not lost even by Adam's fall from grace.[152] In I, q. 83, a. 2, obj. 3, Augustine's authority is used to support the contention that *liberum arbitrium* is taken away by sin: "By misusing free will, man destroys both it and himself" (Augustine, *Ench.*, 30, 9). In his reply to this objection

---

[149] I, q. 105, a. 4, ad 2 and 3; *De Malo*, q. 6, a. un., ad 20.

[150] I-II, q. 9, a. 6. Cf. SCG, III, cap. 88, 89 and 91; *De Malo*, q. 6, ad 1 and 4. *Ibid.*, ad 4 Thomas writes: "voluntas . . . ipsa enim est quae operatur, sed mota a Deo." Cf. *In Rom.*, cap. 9. lect. 3, n. 778. The Protestant church historian, Heiko A. Oberman, presently at the University of Tübingen, gives a faithful presentation of Thomas' doctrine on this point in his book: *Archbishop Thomas Bradwardine* (Utrecht, 1958), p. 87. From the Catholic side see Garrigou-Lagrange, *God: His Existence and His Nature*, vol. II, Ch. 4.

[151] Cf. footnote 143 above.

[152] Cf. footnote 78 and 79 above.

Thomas offers a correct interpretation of Augustine's doctrine when he writes: "By sinning man is said to have lost his *liberum arbitrium* not in the sense of natural freedom from coercion but in the sense of freedom from guilt and from misery." [153]

For Thomas, as for Augustine, man always has natural liberty or freedom. This is not, however, "true" freedom, since man can have "natural" freedom and still not enjoy freedom from sin [154] and from the unhappiness which results from sin. Thomas follows the usage of Romans and the fourth gospel by calling fallen man a slave of sin, but unlike Augustine he does not call the *liberum arbitrium* of fallen man a *servum arbitrium,* or even a captivated free will. But he is no less radical than Augustine when he refers to the free will or to the circumstantial freedom of fallen man as "perverse freedom," [155] "not true, but apparent freedom" [156] (referring to the abuse of free will: sin), and "vain," "temporal" or "carnal" freedom [157] (in reference to the civil or political freedom of the free man as distinct from the slave). On the other hand, corporal slavery—servitude to another man—is not true slavery.[158] True or spiritual slavery is the slavery to sin and to Satan.[159] Similarly, true or spiritual liberty is freedom from sin [160] and slavery to justice and to God.[161]

(a) *Slavery to Sin*

When man sins he becomes a slave of sin. But what does Thomas understand by the biblical doctrine of man's slavery to sin? As we have

---

[153] I, q. 83, a. 2, ad 3.: ". . . homo peccando liberum arbitrium dicitur perdidisse, non quantum ad libertatem naturalem, quae est a coactione; sed quantum ad libertatem, quae est a culpa et a miseria." The identical reply is found in *De Malo,* q. 6, a. un., ad 23. Cf. *De Ver.,* q. 24, a. 1, ad 7; *De Malo,* q. 16, a. 5c; *In Rom.,* cap. 6, lect. 4, n. 508. See the excursus above: The Meaning of "servum arbitrium" in Augustine.

[154] *In Ioann.,* cap. 8, lect. 4, n. 1199, Thomas speaks of freedom from error, from the slavery of sin and from corruption. I-II, q. 109, a. 8, ad 3, fallen man is called "servus peccati."

[155] *Ibid.,* cap. 8, lect. 4, n. 1209.

[156] *In Rom.,* cap. 6, lect. 4, n. 508.

[157] *In Ioann.,* cap. 8, lect. 4, n. 1209.

[158] *Ibid.,* n. 1203; II-II, q. 104, a. 6, ad 1.

[159] *In Ioann.,* cap. 8, lect. 4, n. 1208; III, q. 48, a. 4c and ad 2. H. Rückert, *Die Rechtfertigungslehre auf dem Tridentinischen Konzil* (Bonn, 1925), p. 167, is quite mistaken when he says that Thomas has no doctrine of the slavery of the will to sin and to Satan.

[160] II-II, q. 183, a. 4c; *In Rom.,* cap. 6, lect. 4, nn. 507-513; *In Ioann.,* cap. 8, lect. 4, n. 1209.

[161] III, q. 48, a. 4, ad 2; *In Rom.,* cap. 6, lect. 4, n. 513: "Haec autem vera est libertas, et optima servitus."

already stressed, slavery to sin does not mean the loss of man's natural free will. The domestic or political slave and the slave to sin both indeed have free will,[162] and the man in bodily slavery is perhaps even able to free himself from his slavery by fleeing. But this is precisely what the spiritual slave to sin is unable to do.

Herein lies the utter misery of his slavery: (1) Wherever he goes, he has sin within him and thus he cannot flee from his slavery.[163] (2) The sinner is truly a slave because a slave does not act according to his own principles of activity, that is, according to his own free will, but according to the will of another. The free man, on the other hand, acts of himself and is not acted upon or driven by another.[164] (3) The slave to sin is subject to the devil.[165] (4) He is inclined always toward further sins.[166] (5) He has no natural power to free himself from the sin to which he has subjected himself.[167] (6) By his own natural powers,

---

[162] *De Ver.*, q. 24, a. 1, ad 7: ". . . servitus peccati non dicit coactionem. . . . Et ideo semper in homine remanet libertas a coactione, per quam naturaliter est liberi arbitrii." Cf. *In Rom.*, cap. 6, lect. 4, n. 508.

[163] *In Ioann.*, cap. 8, lect. 4, n. 1204: "Quae quidem servitus gravissima est, quia vitari non potest: nam quocumque homo vadat, peccatum intra se habet, licet actus et delectatio eius transeat. . . . Servitus autem corporalis, saltem fugiendo, evadi potest."

[164] *Ibid. In Rom.*, cap. 7, lect. 3, n. 569: ". . . servus peccati . . . ipse non agit sed agitur a peccato. Ille enim qui est liber, ipse per seipsum agit et non ab alio agitur." Cf. I, q. 96, a. 4c; *In II Cor.*, cap. 3, lect. 3, n. 112; *In Gal.*, cap. 5, lect. 3, n. 302. This kind of slavery—just as its opposite, slavery to God—involves free consent and obedience on man's part: *In Rom.*, cap. 6, lect. 4, n. 509: "Servitutem quidem peccati qua trahitur ad consentiendum peccato, contra iudicium rationis." *Ibid.*, n. 513: "Similiter . . . sicut in statu peccati est aliquis servus peccati cui obedit, ita in statu iustitiae est aliquis servus Dei voluntarie obediens. . . ." Cf. *ibid.*, cap. 6, lect. 2, n. 481; cap. 7, lect. 4, n. 588. Unlike the slave to sin, however, who is "movetur quasi ab altero," the slave to justice and to God is so led by the Holy Spirit that there is a perfect conformity and harmony between what the just man wills and what God wills because the Holy Spirit causes the very movements of the free will of the just man when he makes us lovers of God. See *In Rom.*, cap. 8, lect. 3, n. 635; SCG, IV, cap. 22. Cf. footnote 188 below.

[165] III, q. 48, aa. 2 and 5.

[166] *De Ver.*, q. 24, a. 1, ad 7: ". . . servitus peccati dicit . . . inclinationem, in quantum peccatum praecedens aliquo modo inducit ad sequentia." *In Rom.*, cap. 6, lect 4, n. 508: "Semper ergo homo, quantum ad arbitrium rationis, remanet liber a coactione, non tamen est liber ab inclinatione. . . . Quandoque . . . arbitrium inclinatur ad malum per habitum peccati: et tunc habet servitutem peccati et libertatem iustitiae." Cf. *De Malo*, q. 2, a. 12, ad 5: "pronitas ad malum"; *ibid.*, q. 3, a. 1, ad 9: "impellens ad malum"; II-II, q. 183, a. 4c.

[167] I-II, q. 109, a. 7c: ". . . homo nullo modo potest resurgere a peccato per seipsum sine auxilio gratiae." *In Rom.*, cap. 7, lect. 4, n. 592: "Non enim homo propriis viribus potest liberari a corporis corruptione, nec etiam animae . . . sed solum per gratiam Christi. . . ." Cf. *De Ver.*, q. 24, a. 1, ad 7; SCG, III, cap. 157; II-II, q. 137, a. 4, ad 3. Cf. Auer, II, pp. 49-58.

without the aid of grace, the slave to sin is unable: (a) to avoid sin,[168] (b) to fulfill all the precepts of the natural law,[169] (c) to love God above all things even with a natural love [170] or (d) to do anything that is perfectly good.[171] (7) The slave to sin, by his own natural powers, without the help of grace, can in no way dispose or prepare himself for liberation from sin (justification).[172]

It is highly important for our later analysis of Luther to notice Thomas' logic at this point. Keenly aware as he is of the impotency of the slave to sin not only in regard to salvation, but also in regard to the natural law, Thomas never draws the conclusion that the slave to sin no longer has natural free will. For him, the existence of the free will and the powers of the free will are two different matters.[172a] The fact that Luther does not draw this distinction sharply, as we shall see, is one of the reasons for his denial of man's *liberum arbitrium*.

We should also note Thomas' logic concerning the commands and prohibitions of the law in relation to free will. While it is true that the Church in a later century rejected the teaching of Baius that the proposition: "God does not command man to do the impossible," is Pelagian,[172b] there is nevertheless a true sense in which one can say that God commands many things that are impossible, namely, if we consider

---

[168] *In Hebr.*, cap 10, lect 3, n. 516; I-II, q. 63, a. 2, ad 2; q. 109, a. 8. *Ibid.*, ad 1 Thomas explains that the slave to sin can avoid some mortal sins without grace. This view does not differ from Augustine's, who admitted that the sinner could perform "aliqua bona opera, sine quibus difficillime vita cuiuslibet pessimi hominis invenitur": *De spir. et litt.*, c. 28, 48.

[169] I-II, q. 109, aa. 2 and 4.

[170] *Ibid.*, a. 3.

[171] II-II, q. 23, a. 7c and ad 1.

[172] I-II, q. 109, a. 6; SCG, III, cap. 149. In these texts Thomas invokes Jer. 31: 18; Lam. 5: 21; Jn. 6: 44; 15: 5; Rom. 9: 16 and Tit. 3: 5 to support his conclusion that "homo non potest se praeparare ad lumen gratiae suscipiendum nisi per auxilium gratuitum Dei interius moventis" (I-II, q. 109, a. 6c). This refutes the error of the Pelagians, says Thomas, who held that the beginning of our justification is from ourselves and only its completion is from God: SCG, III, cap. 149. Thomas interprets Zach. 1: 3: "Convertimini ad me, et ego convertar ad vos" to mean that "conversio hominis ad Deum fit quidem per liberum arbitrium." But on the basis of Jer. 31: 18: "Converte me, et convertar. . . ." and Lam. 5: 21: "Converte nos, Domine, ad te, et convertemur." Thomas concludes that "liberum arbitrium ad Deum converti non potest nisi Deo ipsum ad se convertente" (I-II, q. 109, ad 1). This understanding of Zach. 1: 3 is remarkably similar to that of Augustine in *De gr. et lib. arb.*, 5, 10. See above p. 97.

[172a] Cf. *De Ver.*, q. 24, a. 1, ad. 2: "homo dicitur esse liberi arbitrii secundum quod potest agere hoc vel illus, non secundum quod potest sic vel sic agere. . . ."

[172b] DS 1954; cf. 1536f., 1568, 2619.

man's natural powers alone, without the aid of grace.[172c] Augustine himself recognizes this distinction when he writes: "God does not command the impossible. By commanding, he both admonishes you to do what you can and to pray for what you cannot." [172d] Thus both Augustine and Thomas recognize that God commands some things which are impossible for man *without the aid of grace.* They are not, however, "altogether impossible." The necessity of grace, therefore, does not mean that the free will is excluded, nor does the fact that free will is involved in man's response to the commandments imply that the will is sufficient without grace. There was much speaking beside the point in the controversy between Erasmus and Luther because this distinction was not made.

EXCURSUS: *The Different Meanings of "Justice," "Virtue," and "Good" in Thomas Aquinas*

Like Augustine, Thomas admits that sinners can perform ethically good actions, that is, actions which are generically good (*ex suo genere;* II-II, q. 23, a. 7c and ad 1; *De Malo,* q. 2, a. 5, ad 7). Cf. the Excursus: The Different Meanings of "Sin", "Good" and "Virtue" in Saint Augustine. . . . Whereas Augustine at times calls the human virtues of sinners or unbelievers vices or sins, Thomas employs less radical terminology, calling them true, but imperfect, virtues (II-II, q. 23, a. 7c). An act performed by one in mortal sin can have a certain natural goodness. But it is "not perfectly good" (*ibid.,* ad 1). Cf. *In Rom.,* cap. 14, lect. 3, n. 1141. Moreover, such acts are totally worthless for eternal salvation: *In I Cor.,* cap. 13, lect. 1, nn. 766-70. They have value before men, but not before God.

It is further to be emphasized that, since man after the fall lives in a state of corrupt nature which implies a proneness and an impulsion to sin (*De Malo,* q. 3, a. 1, ad 9), even man's naturally good acts require the help of divine grace—*gratia sanans.* Cf. *ibid.,* I-II, q. 109, aa. 3 and 4. Even though Thomas concedes in I-II, q. 109, a. 2c (cf. *De Ver.* q. 24, a. 14c) that man even in the state of corrupt nature can, by the power of his nature, perform such "good" actions as building homes and planting vines, he still is able elsewhere to say flatly that without grace man cannot do good (*non potest bonum operari*) and without it he cannot avoid sin: *In I Cor.,* cap. 12, lect. 1, nn. 718f. Cf. *Quodl.* I, q. 4, ad 2. With this teaching, and with his assertion, reminiscent of canon 22 of Orange II (DS 392), that "of himself any man is a sinner" (*In Rom.,* cap. 3, lect. 2, n. 277), Thomas shows his fundamental agreement with the Pauline-Augustinian outlook.

172c See *Summa Theol.,* II-II, q. 2, a. 5, ad 1; I-II, q. 109, a. 4, ad 2; a. 8, ad 2.
172d *De nat. et gr.,* c. 43, 50.

For Thomas, as for Paul and Augustine, there is more than one kind of justice and goodness. *Iustitia acquisita* (justification by the works of the law) is caused or acquired by the works of man, but *vera iustitia* (justification by faith) is infused in us by God through his grace. This is the only justice that makes us just before God: I-II, q. 100, a. 12c. In Thomas' *Lectures on Romans,* cap. 4, lect. 1, n. 325, acquired justice is called "human justice," in distinction to the "justice which has glory in God's eyes (*apud Deum*) . . . which excedes human capability." Cf. *In Gal.,* cap. 3, lect. 4, n. 141, where the justice of works is called justice before men (*apud homines*). That human justice is totally worthless as far as salvation is concerned can be gathered from Thomas' statement that: "no one is just in himself of himself, but of himself any man is a sinner; his justice is from God alone" (*ex solo Deo; In Rom.,* cap. 3, lect. 2, n. 277). True saving justice comes to us only by faith in Christ (*solum ex fide Christi; In Gal.,* cap. 2, lect. 4, n. 94).

Gerrish, p. 130 seems to overlook the fact that Thomas firmly upholds the biblical distinction between the two justices. This explains his statement that: "The 'Catholic' mind appears unwilling to think of anything rendering a man morally acceptable to God other than actual moral attainment." This is a modified and somewhat milder version of the criticism of Thomas made by P. S. Watson, *Let God be God,* 5th ed. (London: The Epworth Press, 1960), pp. 52-59. For Thomas Aquinas, the *doctor communis* of Catholic theology, there is only *one* thing that makes a man acceptable to God and that is the grace of God! "God only gives grace to those who are worthy, not however in the sense that they were worthy to begin with, but because he made them worthy through grace": I-II, q. 114, a. 5, ad 2. See *De Ver.,* q. 27, a. 1 c; *II Sent.,* d. 27, q. 1, a. 4, ad 4; SCG, III, cap. 150; I-II, q. 113, a. 2, and all of Thomas' commentaries on those texts of the Pauline epistles which proclaim that we are justified by faith in Christ and not by the works of the law.

Gerrish's (p. 130) criticism of Garrigou-Lagrange for saying that God does not love sinners as he loves his friends and children is based more on a difference of language than of theology. "Sinners" can be considered from one point of view as those who persist in their hardness of heart even until death—and beyond. These rightly deserve God's wrath. They are the ones whom God does not hear (Jn. 9: 31). They are the proud whom God resists (Jas. 4: 6; I Pet. 5: 5; Prov. 3: 34). "Sinners" may also mean those who, as a result of God's merciful love and predestination, will be brought to repentence and to eternal life. Cf. Thomas, *In Ioann.,* cap. 9, lect. 3, n. 1347. From still another point of view, one can say with Thomas that God loves sinners insofar as they exist and insofar as they retain any of the good gifts he has given them, but not insofar as they are opposed to him by sin or by unbelief (cf. I, a. 20, a. 2c and ad 4; II-II, q. 25, a. 6). Finally, we should consider that for Thomas, as well as for the Bible, God's love is *merciful* love. Thomas can never say that God loves sin or the sinner insofar as he is a sinner, but he does say that God loves the sinner and has mercy on him and that the motive of this mercy is precisely the *malum* or the *defectus* of the sinner (cf. II-II, q. 30, aa. 1, 2, 4; I, q. 21, a. 2).

EXCURSUS: *The Axiom: "God does not deny grace to one who does what is in him" and Merit: Neo-Semipelagianism?*

The distinction between natural and supernatural goodness is found constantly in Thomas' theology: "The good proportionate to nature is the good of acquired virtue" and "the good transcending nature is the good of infused virtue" (I-II, q. 109, a. 2c). There is no question that Thomas had a greater interest than Augustine in speculating on the ability of man, both in the state of integral and of corrupt nature, to perform good acts proportionate to his nature. Cf. I-II, q. 109, aa. 2ff. This is to be explained primarily by the different theological-historical situation in which Thomas found himself. Unlike Augustine, he was not engaged in a life-or-death struggle to defend the necessity of divine grace against the clever and appealing arguments of Pelagianism. His concern was much more with the problems of faith and reason and of the relation between philosophy and theology which were posed by Arabian Aristotelianism. Thomas indeed rejected some of Augustine's philosophical views in favor of the newly emerging Aristotelian insights. Cf. Gillon, DTC, 15, 586-693; M. Chossat, "Dieu (sa Nature selon les Scolastiques)," DTC, 4, 1174-1202. It never entered his mind, however, to abandon what he regarded as the authoritative Augustinian teaching on the necessity of grace and on the depravity of fallen human nature without grace.

Even though Thomas had no knowledge of the text of the decrees of the Second Council of Orange, his reading of Augustine led him to regard it as "truth of faith" that the "beginning of salvation" comes from God (I-II, q. 114, a. 5, ad 1). Cf. Bouillard, pp. 114-121; Seckler, pp. 90ff. The contrary view, as we have seen, was precisely the error of the Semipelagians. Thomas, of course, did not use the 16th century term, "Semipelagianism," to designate this error; he simply attributed it to "the Pelagians": cf. SCG, II, cap. 149 and 152; I, q. 23, a. 5c; II-II, q. 6, a. 1c; *In Rom.*, cap. 7, lect. 3, n. 579; *In II Cor.*, cap. 3, lect. 1, n. 86; *In Philip.*, cap. 1, lect. 1, n. 12.

Among the other errors Thomas attributed to the Pelagians are the following: (1) that man can fulfill all the precepts of God's law without grace or charity: *Quodl.* I, q. 4, a. 2; I-II, q. 109, a. 4, *sed contra; De Malo,* q. 2, a. 5, ad 7; *In I Cor.*, cap. 12, lect. 1, n. 714; (2) that man can avoid sin without grace: SCG, III, cap. 16; *De Ver.*, q. 24, a. 12c; (3) that the grace of God is given to men according to merit: *De Malo,* q. 8, a. 4, arg. 2; *In Rom.*, cap. 9, lect. 3, n. 771; (4) that man can merit grace solely by the natural power of free will: SCG, III, cap. 147; *De Ver.*, q. 16, a. 1, ad 12; (5) that man only needs divine assistance in order to know what he ought to do: *Quodl.* I, q. 4, a. 2; (6) that man can attain eternal life by free will without grace: *ibid.; De Ver.*, q. 24, a. 12, arg. 2; (7) that there is no original sin: SCG, IV, cap. 50 and 52; (8) that man can rise from sin by his own free will: SCG, III, cap. 157.

Despite the clear evidence that we have just seen of Thomas' anti-

(Semi)pelagianism, there is still a suspicion in some quarters that by his affirmation of the axiom "facienti quod in se est, Deus non denegat gratiam" (God does not deny grace to one who does what is in him), Thomas slipped into a subtle form of Pelagianism. A recent expression of this attitude is found in R. Schwarz, *Fides, Spes und Caritas beim jungen Luther* (Berlin, 1962), p. 373: According to Luther man "can in no way necessitate grace by his disposition. But this is what is affirmed in the generally accepted Scholastic thesis that grace is infallibly infused when man does what he can to prepare for it. Not only the Franciscans upheld this axiom, so did Thomas."

The first thing to be noted here is that *facienti quod in se est,* etc., is indeed a "generally accepted Scholastic thesis," but this thesis has been interpreted quite diversely by the Scholastics. Secondly, as far as much of high Scholasticism is concerned, Schwarz's statement of the axiom is incomplete, for it omits the important condition that God does not deny grace to the one who does what is in him *under the influence of grace.* In regard to Schwarz's assertion, therefore, the crucial question is: What does "his disposition" mean?

Since the early Scholastics had little or no knowledge of the Semipelagian controversy, it is not altogether surprising that some of them, such as Abelard (cf. above ch. 5, p. 125), "approached Semipelagianism in their explanation of the preparation for justification": M. Flick, "Semipelagianismus," LThK, 9, 652. Cf. A. Landgraf, *Dogmengeschichte der Frühscholastik,* Bd. I/1 (Regensburg, 1952), pp. 241-264; Dhont, pp. 277f.

Even Alexander of Hales shows a complete lack of awareness of Semipelagianism. As proof of this we need only consider the question he raises in the *Glossa in II Sent.* (Quaracchi 1952), d. 28, n. 5, p. 268: "In justificatione hominis quaeratur utrum homo prius moveatur in Deum, an actus Dei in hominem primo." (In justification does man first move toward God or does God first turn toward man?) He reaches no conclusive answer, but simply quotes Origen, Isadore and Augustine. The citation he offers from Augustine is from the *Confessions,* not from any of the great anti-(Semi)pelagian treatises where Augustine deals with this question *ex professo.*

The high Scholastics, however understood the "doing what is in one" as an activity "which is made possible by a free gift of grace, a 'gratia actualis entitative supernaturalis' ": J. Trütsch, "Facienti quod in se est," LThK, 3, 1336f. Cf. J. Van der Meersch, "Grâce," DTC, 6, 1603; L. Capéran, *Le problème du salut des infidèles* (Toulouse, 1934), II, pp. 49-57; S. González, "De Gratia," in: *Sacrae Theologiae Summa,* III, BAC 62 (Madrid, 1956), pp. 556ff. As Denifle, p. 557 says: "To do what one is able to do in the formula: *facienti quod in se est,* is understood to mean: to do what one is able to do when aroused and moved by grace."

Thomas' understanding of the axiom is seen clearly in the following texts: I-II, q. 109, a. 6, *sed contra:* "A man cannot prepare himself for grace without the help of grace." Cf. *ibid.,* corpus and ad 2; I-II, q. 112, aa. 2 and 3; *In Rom.,* cap. 10, lect. 3, n. 849: "That some do what is in them, that is, by turning themselves to God, is made possible by God moving their hearts to good." *In Hebr.,* cap. 12, lect. 3, nn. 688f:

"Although grace is not given because of merits—otherwise grace would not be grace—it is nevertheless necessary that man do what he is able to do. But God, by his most generous will, gives grace to everyone who prepares himself. [Rev. 3: 30 and I Tim. 2: 4 are cited.] And therefore the grace of God is lacking to no one. . . .

"On the contrary. For if grace is not given on the basis of works but only on the basis that someone does not present an obstacle to it, the possession of grace would depend on free will alone and not on God's election, which is the error of Pelagius.

"I respond by saying that the very fact that a person does not present an obstacle is itself the result of grace. Thus if someone should present an obstacle to grace and if his heart should then be moved to take away the obstacle this is because of the gift of God's grace calling him by his mercy."

Against the view of several older (Cajetan, D. Soto) and newer (Scheeben, Denifle, Rivière, Lange, Flick, L. Ott. Trütsch) Catholic theologians, Del Prado, pp. 91ff.; Portalié, DTC, 1, 2535 and, more recently, Bouillard, pp. 3–9 deny that the younger Thomas in his *Commentary on the Sentences* has a Semipelagian understanding of the axiom in question. Cf. Seeberg, III, pp. 460f.; Rivière, DTC, 8, 2120; Pesch, *Die Theologie der Rechtfertigung bei M. Luther und Thomas von Aquin* (Mainz, 1967), pp. 659-669.

For a time it was thought, even in Catholic circles (Scheeben), that Scotus tended toward Semipelagianism in his explanation of man's preparation for justification. But studies such as those of P. Minges, *Die Gnadenlehre des Duns Scotus* (Münster, 1906), especially pp. 56-102, have shown that Scotus is at worst guilty only of unclear terminology, especially concerning the meaning of the "common (general) influence of God." Although Scotus teaches that the "dispositions to grace have the character of congruous merits," *In II Sent.,* d. 7, q. 2, he nevertheless seems to regard even these dispositions as being the fruit of grace (contrary to Auer, "Rechtfertigung," LThK, 8, 1040), since he elsewhere affirms that one approaches the Pelagian error who says that a purely natural act is meritorious. *Ordinatio* I, d. 17, pars i, n. 160. Cf. P. Raymond, "Duns Scot," DTC, 4, 1899-1904; J. Rivière, "Justification," DTC, 8, 2128 and "Mérite," DTC, 10, 704f.; Bouillard, pp. 115f.; Dohnt, pp. 300f. Seeberg, III, p. 482, has rejected the claim of Loofs and Heim that the Franciscans of the high Scholastic period were "Neosemipelagians." For the rejection of a similar charge against the high Scholastics by Harnack and Dieckhoff, see Auer, II, p. 86; Denifle, pp. 875ff.; and Seckler, pp. 87ff.

Seeberg points out that, although the Franciscans of the high Scholastic era stressed the *facere quod in se est,* they also presupposed the *gratia gratis data:* III, p. 448, footnote 1 and p. 461. We agree with Oberman, *The Harvest,* p. 147, footnote 3, however, that an investigation of the concept "gratia gratis data" in the high Scholastics is still necessary.

According to Trütsch, LThK, 3, 1336, the Nominalists (Ockham, Biel) understood the *facere quod in se est* in a different way, namely, as an "activity undertaken without internal grace and thus stemming from merely natural powers." Trütsch adds: "Only according to this interpretation did Luther know of the axiom and he justifiably attacked it." We shall examine this development in more detail in the next chapter.

The Scholastics were in general agreement that only the actions of a man constituted in grace could be meritorious in the strict or full sense (*de condigno*). Cf. H. Quilliet, "Congruo (De), Condigno (De)," DTC, 3, 1138-1152; Rivière, DTC, 10, 689-693; Auer, II, p. 73. Although it is customary to distinguish merit in the full sense from congruous merit (*meritum de congruo*) by designating the former as "true" or "perfect" merit, it must be pointed out, in order to avoid misunderstanding, that even *meritum de condigno,* for Thomas at least, is not a matter of strict justice. Justice in the strict sense exists only between equals. "It is clear that between God and man there is the greatest inequality: for they are infinitely different and all of man's good is from God" (I-II, q. 114, a. 1c). Thus, continues Thomas, between God and man one can speak only of a "certain kind of justice" and of a merit "secundum quid," that is, of a merit *essentially* different from, though in some way the same as, the justice and merit that are found among men.

What makes the merit of man before God essentially different from all simply human merit involving strict justice is that merit before God presupposes an ordinance of God that he will reward a particular work. The work itself, apart from this ordinance, has no claim in justice on God. This divine ordinance constitutes, according to Thomas, the *principle* factor in merit (*ibid.,* a. 4c). Cf. Auer, II, pp. 64ff. Scotus, with his doctrine of the divine acceptance, seems to us to be saying the same thing. See W. Dettloff, *Die Lehre von der acceptatio divina bei Johannes Duns Scotus* (Werl, 1954), pp. 84ff. Important to recognize is that Scotus, with his concept of divine acceptation, and Thomas, with his doctrine of the divine ordination, both wish to reject the notion that meritorious acts are meritorious because of some inner value they possess apart from God's ordinance. See Dettloff, pp. 106ff.; 112ff.; 123ff. Oberman, *Forerunners of the Reformation* (New York, 1966), p. 130, misses this point.

Thomas insists that God is never a debtor to us in the strict sense. He is rather in debt to himself insofar as he has pledged himself to fulfill his promise or ordinance. Cf. I-II, q. 114, a. 1, ad 3. Clearly then, "merit" is, for Thomas, an analogous concept. Failure to keep this in mind is the source of most of the criticisms against the Thomistic—and the Catholic —concept of merit. Gerrish, for example, p. 133, following Watson, pp. 53f., regards Thomas'—and the Catholic Church's—doctrine that man can merit a heavenly reward as "legalistic without being Pelagian, or even semi-Pelagian," because Thomas understands man's merit before God simply as "a *quid pro quo,* a price paid for work done." Gerrish cites I-II, q. 114, a. 1 for this definition of merit, but because he does not take the entire article into account, he unfortunately misses the main point, namely, that, for Thomas, man's merit before God is essentially different from man's merit before men, as we have seen above.

Some of the misunderstanding about the Catholic concept of merit is occasioned by Catholic authors who fail to make perfectly clear that even *meritum de condigno* involves justice only *secundum quid,* that is, only in a certain analogous sense, and therefore that it is merit only in a *secundum quid* sense (I-II, q. 114, a. 1c). A reader is therefore very likely to misunderstand Thomas' notion of *meritum de condigno* when he reads in McDonough, p. 157, footnote 1, that this refers to merit "according to a strict rule of justice. . . ." Much more faithful to Thomas' meaning—and wording—is the editor's note in the Marietti edition of the *Summa Theologiae* to I-II, q. 114, a. 1 (p. 591). There the reader is told:

"Note the difference between *meritum de condigno* and that which is said to be merit in strict justice. Even though both bespeak some right to a reward, they do so in different ways. Merit in strict justice implies an absolute equality without any grace given to the person who merits. But merit *de condigno* involves an equality which arises from grace which has been given to the one meriting."

Catholic authors likewise customarily refer to *meritum de condigno* as merit in the true or proper sense. But even this designation is misleading. To indicate the completely (*simpliciter*) different character of merit before God and before men, one should speak of the former as merit in a proper but analogous sense. Cf. Schmaus, III/2, p. 411.

It is to Gerrish's credit, p. 133, that he recognizes with R. Prenter, *Spiritus Creator* (München, 1954), the Augustinian character of the Scholastic doctrine of merit. "This Scholastic idea of merit," writes Prenter, p. 36, "is so far removed from Pelagianism that one would have to say that it is the genuine expression of the Augustinian doctrine of grace." In the face of this statement, it seems odd that Grane, p. 315, footnote 13, can refer to this same page of Prenter's study to support his view that Thomas' doctrine of merit represented "the triumph of Aristotelian ethics in the doctrine of grace."

When one studies carefully what Thomas Aquinas (and Augustine) understand by merit, one encounters a paradoxical problem. The difficulty is not that this doctrine of merit over-emphasized the power of free will, as Schwarz, pp. 373f. maintains, nor that it is "legalistic" (Gerrish, Watson), but that Thomas "so understood merits *de condigno* . . . to be the products of grace that it is hard to maintain their meritorious character": Seeberg, III, p. 481. Unlike anything that one man merits in strict justice from another man, man's merits before God are themselves gifts of God. *In Rom.*, cap. 9, lect. 3, n. 771: ". . . even man's good merits are themselves from God and are the effect of predestination." Cf. Augustine, *De gr. et lib. arb.*, 6, 15: "If therefore, your good merits are gifts of God, God does not crown your merits as your merits but as his gifts" (cf. DS 248, 1548). For the finest available presentation of the evangelical character of Thomas' doctrine of merit see O. Pesch, *Die Theologie der Rechtfertigung,* pp. 771-789.

As O. Karrer, "Der Galaterbrief," in *Liturgisch-bibl. Monatsschrift,* 9

(1949), p. 32, has said: "When Catholic doctrine paraphrases by the expression 'merit' the objective salvific meaning of the moral-religious efforts of the sons of God, it must be granted that this expression, as a transference of human relationships to our relationship with God, is only used in an analogous sense. This means that it conveys only imperfectly, in a manner just as dissimilar as it is similar, the reality described in the Bible as 'heavenly reward'. . . . Naturally it is perfectly correct when Protestants emphasize—and this is what is manifestly intended in their 'attack on the doctrine of merit'—that one cannot boast of his works before God since these are ultimately gifts of God. Nor can one base his trust on these works since the entire constancy of our trust is based on God. . . . There is in reality no difference of opinion whatever in this matter between Catholic and Protestant theologians and educators. Here as elsewhere we have carried on controversies with straw men! Any difference of opinion is limited to the question: Is the word 'merit' which the Scholastics took from Augustine a particularly fortunate expression for designating what we mean? Concerning the issue itself, however, as to how the believer assesses his openness for grace and his works which are motivated by grace, there is no difference of opinion in the theological literature and in any of the relatively good Christian devotional literature."

From the Evangelical side we find a confirmation of Karrer's basic point in K. A. Meissinger's, *Erasmus von Rotterdam* 2nd ed., (Berlin 1948), p. 323: "The main attitude of the old system of faith was to retain as much of the doctrine of Augustine, the most important Father of Church, as was compatible with daily pastoral needs and with a cautious interpretation of the Scripture. This was to be done, however, in such a way as to exclude clearly the heretical pride and activism of the Pelagians. That the grace of God was ultimately decisive was just as indisputable here as it was with Luther." More recently H. A. Oberman, "Reformation, Preaching and *Ex Opere Operato,*" in: *Christianity Divided* (London-New York: Sheed and Ward, 1962), p. 228, has written: "If asked to state in just one phrase the most fundamental rediscovery of the Reformation, one should not simply answer: the authority of the Scriptures, or the sole efficacy of grace. . . . (T)hroughout the Middle Ages, in Augustinian and Dominican circles, the sole efficacy of grace was clearly stated."

If *meritum de condigno,* as we have seen, expresses "just as dissimilarly as similarly" that which is called "merit" in human relationships, how much more this is true of *meritum de congruo!* And, as Karrer suggests, if it is doubtful whether "merit" is a particularly fortunate designation for what is meant in theology, one can surely ask whether what is meant by *de congruo* merit—a "merit" that has nothing to do with God's justice but only his mercy (Schmaus, III/2, p. 441)—should be called merit in any sense at all. On the origin of the concept, *meritum de congruo,* see Auer, II, p. 78 and Rivière, DTC, 10, 693f.

When Thomas speaks of *meritum de congruo* in the *Summa,* it is important to notice that, in contrast to *In II Sent.,* d. 28, q. 1, a. 4, he does not speak of it in connection with the preparation for the grace of justification. Cf. I-II, q. 12, aa. 2 and 3; q. 114, aa. 3 and 5. Grane, p.

298, footnote 39 points out that Kawerau, in an explanatory note to the Weimar edition of Luther's *First Lectures on the Psalms* (Scholion to Ps. 115: 1), mistakenly interprets the *praeparatio* spoken of in I-II, q. 112, a. 3, as a *meritum de congruo*. Ficker, in his note to WA 56, 503, and Link, *Das Ringen Luthers*, p. 176, have repeated this error. For Thomas, there is no preparation for justification except that which is worked in man by God: I-II, q. 112, a. 2, ad 3; q. 113, a. 7c. Cf. Bouillard, p. 94. Further, this preparation is not understood by Thomas as merit in any sense. Following Augustine, he says in *De Ver.*, q. 29, a. 6c: ". . . before grace there are no merits except demerits. Before grace man is ungodly and the merits of the ungodly deserve punishment, not grace." Nor can anyone merit the first grace: I-II, q. 114, a. 5c. It is only when one is "constituted in grace" that he can merit the first grace *for another de congruo:* ibid., a. 6.

Thomas' doctrine on the preparation for justification which excludes all merit—*de congruo* or *de condigno*—of justification and of the first grace, is in perfect conformity with the later Tridentine teaching that "nothing that precedes justification, neither faith nor works, merits the grace of justification" (*Sess.* 6, cap. 8: DS 1532) and that those who are called to justification "are called by no merits of their own" (*Sess.* 6, cap. 5: DS 1525).

Not so easy to reconcile with the wording of this decree, however, is the view of "the entire medieval Franciscan School" (V. Heynck, *Franziskanische Studien,* 33 [1951], 57) that the preparation or disposition for justification, made possible by prevenient grace, is also a *de congruo merit* of justification. Cf. Jedin, II, p. 179. Rivière, DTC, 10, 751 gives evidence from the conciliar debates to show that the majority of the Fathers, led by the Superior General of the Franciscan Conventual order, intended only to exclude the conferral of justification as a result of merits *de condigno,* or "merits in the proper sense (*proprie*), to which grace is owed." Rivière exaggerates somewhat, however, when he concludes, *ibid.,* 754, that the council "clearly endorsed the idea" of *de congruo* merit, even though it avoided the technical term. Cf. E. Stakemeier, *Glaube und Rechtfertigung* (Freiburg, 1937), p. 120. More precise is the view of F. Hünermann, *Wesen und Notwendigkeit der aktuellen Gnade nach dem Konzil von Trient* (Paderborn, 1926), pp. 77-85, that Trent neither teaches nor excludes the theory that, *with the aid of actual grace,* one can merit justification *de congruo* (cf. Schmaus, III/2, p. 425). This is similar to the interpretation of Andreas de Vega, the influential Franciscan theologian at Trent. Cf. H. Oberman, "The Tridentine Decree on Justification in the Light of Late Medieval Theology" *Journal for Theology and the Church,* 3 (1967), p. 54.

In this study Oberman goes beyond Vega and, similar to Rivière and Stakemeier, maintains that it was "the decision of the Tridentine fathers to safeguard the merit *de congruo* as a merit based on God's justice" (*ibid.*). Oberman reaches this conclusion not only by analyzing the Council debate itself, as did Rivière, but also by a historical analysis of the term "promereri" which was used in the final form of the decree (*Sess.* 6, cap. 8: DS 1532). This term, Oberman shows, was deliberately used instead of "mereri" to convey the idea that only merit "in the full sense," i.e. *de condigno,* was excluded, as distinct from merit in a less than full sense, i.e., *meritum de congruo.*

With Schillebeeckx, "The Tridentine Decree on Justification: A New View," *Concilium* 5 (1965), p. 177, we agree that Trent did not decide in *favor* of the Scotist *meritum de congruo.* Trent's intention was rather not to exclude or "destroy" the doctrine of *de congruo* merit of justification. Cf. *Conc. Trid.* V, 695, 2; 737, 28; 764, footnote 3. We likewise welcome Schillebeeckx's important reminder (p. 178) that Trent's teaching on justification, while not incorrect, is incomplete and must be supplemented by earlier as well as later Church teaching.

We disagree with Schillebeeckx, however, when he says Trent "leaves open the *possibility* that man can prepare himself for grace in some way . . . by his own strength and without grace": pp. 177f. The reason for our disagreement will become clear in our criticism of Oberman's view that: ". . . the fashionable presentation of the Tridentine decree on justification as the *via media* between the extreme of Pelagian nominalism and Lutheran Augustinianism stands corrected" (*Journal for Theology and the Church,* p. 54; the German version, p. 282, reads: "requires correction"). In other words, Trent, because it accepted the idea of a merit of justification *de congruo,* did not exclude "Pelagian nominalism" or, as Oberman puts it on page 39, "nominalistic Pelagianism." And when he says, *ibid.,* that "the nominalistic doctrine of justification has substantially contributed to the final formulation of the decree," the implication is clear that it was the justification doctrine of "nominalistic Pelagianism" that influenced Trent. Cf. *idem.,* "Duns Scotus, Nominalism and the Council of Trent," in: *John Duns Scotus: 1265-1965* (Washington, 1965), pp. 311-344.

The following considerations prevent us from accepting Oberman's interpretation of Trent. The mere fact that Trent may have allowed a *de congruo* merit of justification does not prove the influence of "nominalistic Pelagianism" or "Pelagian nominalism." According to Jedin, II, p. 180, it was only Nominalism which "found no defenders at Trent." Moreover, older Franciscans such as Bonaventure, who cannot be considered Nominalist or Pelagian, admitted the possibility of a *de congruo* merit before justification.

At the Council of Trent itself the greatest defender of Augustinianism, Cardinal Seripando, was among those who voted not to exclude *meritum de congruo* prior to justification! Cf. *Conc. Trid.,* V, p. 737; Rivière, DTC, 10, 751. That Seripando's view of *de congruo* merit presupposes the merciful grace of God is clear from his statement on justification of July, 1546: *Conc. Trid.* XII, 616—619; 629, 41ff.—630, 18; cf. XII, 681 and H. Jedin, *Girolamo Seripando,* vol. I (Würzburg, 1937), pp. 371ff.

The Scotist, Antonio Pinarolo, O. F. M. Conv., likewise defended the possibility of *de congruo* merit of justification at Trent, but insisted that the works involved in this merit must always be performed "by a divine instinct, prompting and motion." Pinarolo held that "no works produced by natural power alone, that is, without some grace antecedent to the natural will, . . . either merit justification or dispose so that justifying grace is fittingly given" (*nec disponunt ut congruenter donentur gratia gratificans*): *Conc. Trid.,* V, 274ff. Cf. Rivière, DTC, 10, 736. The same is true for the Franciscan bishop of the Canary Islands, Antonio de la Cruz, who categorically denied the possibility of merit—even in the *de congruo* sense—without the help of grace. Cf. Jedin, II, p. 186.

Not even Bonaventura Costacciarius, the General of the Conventual Franciscans, can be cited as a representative of Pelagian nominalism at Trent. It is true, as Oberman points out on pp. 48ff., that this theologian, like Seripando, argued for merit *de congruo* of justification. But it is also true that, with all the fathers of Trent, he believed that man's disposition and preparation for justification are possible only when man is aroused and aided by divine grace. This is clear from the vote of approval he gave to Chapter 6 of the reformed decree on justification which deals with the "mode of preparation" and which insists that we are disposed for justification by the action of grace: *Conc. Trid.,* V, 698, 20. Cf. V, 369. This interpretation of *de congruo* merit by the General of the Fransican Conventuals, is, as we shall observe, essentially different from that of Gabriel Biel on this important point.

In contrast to such issues as the certitude of grace, there was actually no controversy at Trent about the belief that the beginning of justification takes place by the prevenient grace of God through Jesus Christ (cf. *Conc. Trid.* XII, 681, 5-38), regardless of whether one held that the preparation initiated by grace could be considered merit *de congruo.*

Even Andreas de Vega, the influential Franciscan council-theologian whom Oberman rightly lists as one of the chief advocates of *de congruo* merit of justification, held that man's preparation for justification is preceded by the special action of God. In his draft on justification of July 1546, Vega stated: "Although God first awakens and enlightens man apart from man's initiative (*sine homine*), man nevertheless prepares and changes himself and inclines and opens his heart, but by God preparing, changing and inclining him" (*Conc. Trid.,* XII, 639, 45ff). This clear affirmation of the gracious prevenient and internal action of God is evidence that Vega stands firmly in the Catholic tradition.

While we should not forget Vega's affirmation of the divine initiative in justification, we must acknowledge a subtle point raised by Oberman, "The Tridentine Decree," p. 53, which illustrates that Trent's doctrine of justification is in some respect incomplete. Trent did not *explicitly* rule out what Vega and certain post-Tridentine theologians regarded as the ability of fallen man to *dispose* himself for justification to some extent by his unaided natural powers.

To be sure, Vega does not say that this natural disposition constitutes merit *de congruo.* Such a merit would surely be the kind of preparation that requires prevenient grace as Vega affirmed in the passage cited above.

Francisco Suarez (d. 1619), the leader of Spanish Scholasticism after Trent, regards Vega's view as seriously erroneous. Contrary to some of his theological contemporaries, however, Suarez does not call Vega's position heretical.

In his treatise *De Gratia,* Lib. VIII, cap. 7, 2 (*Opera Omnia,* vol. IX, [Paris, 1858]), Suarez teaches that any "act disposing [the sinner] to justifying grace (*ad habitualem gratiam*) must be supernatural." As opponents of this view he lists Gabriel Biel, Vega and several others who teach that a *remote* disposition to sanctifying grace can be achieved naturally, without grace (*ibid.,* cap. 7, 8). Some, adds Suarez, even say that a *proximate* disposition is similarly possible. Suarez insists, however, that it is a matter of faith (*de fide*) that those acts which can be proximate dispositions to justification and forgiveness of sin cannot take place without grace. This has been defined with sufficient clarity at Trent, he says, as well as "in earlier councils and by the fathers; what is more, it has been sufficiently stated in Scripture." "There is thus no doubt or controversy among modern theologians on this point," he adds.

The older theologians cannot be excused from material error on this point, says Suarez. But they should not be called formal heretics because they have not spoken obstinately against the Church's doctrine. They erroneously thought that the ancient doctrine about the necessity of grace for acting rightly as one ought applied only to acts which were strictly meritorious (*de condigno*), or else referred to any kind of grace, or to gratuitous acceptation, etc. (*ibid*). Cf. Chapter 7, footnote 95.

The same criticism ought also to be made concerning their assertion about the remote disposition, says Suarez, referring to his earlier evaluation of Semipelagianism. The definitions against that heresy, he maintains, implicitly exclude the view that man is able by a merely natural act to dispose himself *even remotely* for the reception of justifying grace.

For this reason, says Suarez, several important theologians (whom he does not mention) flatly condemn this opinion as heresy. Suarez tells us that he has refrained from doing likewise for two reasons: (1) because he does not find an explicit universal definition condemning that opinion in terms of "disposition," but only in terms of "merit," "impetration" or equivalent words, and someone could say that "remote disposition" is a broader term not touched by the condemnations; (2) because he sees theologians using that language without scruple, and not only Scotus, Biel and Durandus, but even Richard Middleton, Cajetan, Medina and Domingo Soto.

Even though Medina (d. 1580), for example, teaches that a purely natural good work cannot be a disposition to grace, he adds a "remarkable example," says Suarez, when he says that such a work is "like the dryness in wood." Suarez notes that the dryness of wood is an important disposition for burning the wood. Medina clarifies the point by noting that a naturally good work, "though it can be called a certain remote disposition (*quaedam dispositio remota*) for grace, cannot be called merit *de congruo*" (*ibid.* Lib VIII, cap. 7, 9).

Domingo Soto, says Suarez (*ibid.*), recognizes an "improper and very remote [natural] disposition" which is neither sufficient nor necessary for justification. But Soto explains: because it does not arise from the special action of the Holy Spirit it cannot be regarded as a disposition in the proper sense.

Suarez (*ibid.*) then comes to the opinion of Andreas de Vega, which he describes as "more unfavorable" (*durius*). He cites the same sentence from Vega's work *De iustificatione* as Oberman does in "The Tridentine Decree," p. 53, fn. 115, to the effect that even natural acts can be remote dispositions and therefore dispositive causes of justification.

For the foregoing reasons Suarez repeats that he has always refrained from judging the thesis in question as heretical, "even though I hold it to be entirely true and certain that no disposition toward grace, even a remote one, is possible without the aid of special grace. For a disposition in the strict sense is a true cause and a positive reason for the conferral of grace. But the councils sufficiently exclude every such cause or reason when they say that we do not anticipate (*praevenire*) God but he anticipates us. . . . Such talk [about the possibility of a remote natural disposition for justification] should be completely avoided because it is a bad way to speak (*male sonat*); even more, when taken in the strict sense (*in sensu proprio*) it is incompatible with the doctrine of the fathers and of the Councils" (*op. cit.*, Lib. VIII, cap. 7, 9).

Suarez's caveat has been observed by nearly all Catholic theologians since his time. Thus, the representative tract on grace by S. González, in: *Sacrae Theologiae Summa,* Vol. III (Madrid, 1956), pp. 544f. teaches that it is a definition of divine and Catholic faith "that fallen man by his natural powers alone can merit the first grace neither *de condigno* nor *de congruo.*" Concerning Vega's notion that man could remotely dispose himself for justification by the powers of his fallen nature. González points out that, since Suarez, it has commonly been held that no positive natural disposition for grace, "not even the most remote," may be taught by Catholic theologians (*ibid., p.* 552).

The decisive question, then, in our examination of Oberman's thesis, is not: Did Trent leave the door open for a *de congruo* merit of justification?, but: Was the *de congruo* merit of justification which was defended at Trent by the Augustinian, Seripando, and by many Franciscans a merit which is made possible through the power of God's prevenient grace, or by man's unaided natural powers? In other words, does the beginning (*exordium:* DS 1525) of justification come from man's natural fallen powers "doing what is in them" without the aid of grace— which is a Semipelagian concept of *de congruo* merit of justification—or does the beginning of justification come "through the prevenient grace of Jesus Christ"—which is the Tridentine teaching (DS 1525f., 1553) as well as that of Orange II (DS 375ff.)?

Granting that Trent left open the possibility of *de congruo* merit of justification, this does not prove the influence of "nominalistic Pelagianism," especially when we interpret *de congruo* merit in the light of Chapters 5 and 6 of the Decree on Justification and keep in mind the influence at Trent of the re-discovered canons of the Second Council of Orange.

In full agreement with Orange II, Chapter 5 of Trent's justification decree (DS 1525) teaches against Pelagianism and Semipelagianism that the ". . . beginning of justification in adults must be understood as arising from the prevenient grace of God through Jesus Christ. That is, it comes about through God's call, a call which is based on no merits on man's part. The purpose of this call is that those who have been turned away from sin by God may be disposed by his grace, which arouses and aids them, . . . to turn to their own justification. . . . Without the grace of God the sinner cannot move himself to justice in God's eyes by his own free will."

Two things should be noted about Chapter 5: (1) The beginning of justification lies solely with God through the grace of Christ, not partly with God and partly with man as Oberman suggests: "The Tridentine Decree," p. 35. (2) The prevenient grace that is spoken of here and elsewhere at Trent is not to be equated with the "divine acceptation" of Scotus or of the "divine ordinance" of Thomas Aquinas. As at Orange II, this grace is conceived to be the *interior* action of God through Christ and in the Spirit "awakening," "aiding," "enlightening" and "inspiring" (DS 374-377; 397; 1525f; 1553f.). (This is not to deny, of course, that Thomas and Scotus recognized that grace also involves an interior movement of man by God.) Both of these reasons support our view, to be developed in the next chapter, that, contrary to Oberman, *ibid.*, p. 36, Trent's doctrine of justification does imply a correction of the view of Gabriel Biel on the *de congruo* merit of justification.

The thesis that "nominalistic Pelagianism" had an influence on Trent is highly questionable, to say the least. On the other hand, the dominant influence of the doctrine of Augustine and Orange II is indisputable. According to Jedin, II, p. 142, footnote 1, the Tridentine fathers had the anti-Semipelagian decrees of Orange II in their hands. The canons of that council were even appended to the second schema on justification of September 23, 1546 (*ibid.*, p. 241) and were cited frequently during the deliberations, often to emphasize the debility of the will of the sinner. See, for example, *Conc. Trid.*, V, p. 450, 42f. Further, the discussions on the various schemata on justification show that the chief authorities cited, apart from Scripture and the Fathers of the Church, were Thomas Aquinas (approximately 50 times) and Augustine (almost three times as often as Thomas). Of the leading Nominalists, on the other hand, Biel was cited twice and Ockham not at all.

Granting with Oberman and Rivière that Trent's decree on justification did not exclude a *de congruo* merit of justification, we have emphasized that this merit is impossible without prevenient, interior grace. But, in the light of what we have already seen, how are we to understand such a "merit?"

In an intervention at Trent on behalf of the thesis that the preparation —under grace—of the sinner for justification is the same as a *de congruo* merit of justification, the General of the Franciscan Conventuals stated: ". . . all theologians except Gregory of Rimini hold to these improper, relative (*secundum quid*), interpretative merits, that is, merits *de congruo,* as distinct from proper, true, gratuitous and *de condigno* merits" (*Conc. Trid.* V, 480).

Thus merit *de congruo,* as understood by one of its foremost defenders at Trent, is an improper, "non-true" merit. Should it, then, really be called "merit?" As we have seen above, for Thomas Aquinas any merit in relation to God is already a relative merit (*secundum quid*) in comparison to merit in the strict sense between men. Hence, to call merit *de congruo* a relative merit (*secundum quid*) is misleading. If the "meritorious character" of merit *de condigno* "is difficult to maintain" (Seeberg), how much more this is true of merit *de congruo!* In fact, merit *de congruo* is not even analogous to merit *de condigno,* for it lacks the same character (the *proprium*) as merit *de condigno*. It should therefore be recognized for what it is: an *equivocal* use of the concept "merit." Theological language becomes almost ludicrous when certain authors (e.g., those mentioned in the Marietti edition of the *Summa Theologiae*, I-II, p. 597, footnote 1) distinguish two kinds of improper or *de congruo* merit: a "proper and strict" type, and the other, a "broad and improper" type. In the latter case we thus have an improper kind of *de congruo* merit which, applied to Thomas' definitions of merit, would mean relative merit (any merit before God is *secundum quid*) in a relative or improper sense!

(b) *Christian Freedom and Free Will*

As we have seen, Thomas Aquinas continues the tradition of Scripture, of Augustine and of the ancient Church in recognizing that man can enjoy freedom in one or another respect (natural freedom of the will; civil or corporal freedom, of which the Jews boasted in Jn. 8:33) and yet, in a profound, spiritual sense, he can be enslaved to sin. Fallen man, by his own natural efforts, is totally unable to free himself from his enslaved condition. He is only freed by passing from sin to grace.[173] This transition from slavery to freedom takes place through the "charity which is poured forth in our hearts by the Holy Spirit." [174] It is the grace of Christ—and his grace alone—which frees us from slavery to sin.[175] It is Jesus Christ, the eternal Son of God, who is our Liberator.[176] It is only through faith in him and his truth, not through any Old Testament sacrifices or ceremonies, that we can be liberated.[177] It is thus perfectly evident that Christian freedom is a gift of Christ the Liberator, not a freedom which we naturally possess or attain by any natural efforts of our own.

What is this Christian freedom, the freedom of the sons of God? In its negative aspect, Christian freedom is the liberty or law of the Spirit, by

---

[173] II-II, q. 184, a. 4, ad 2: ". . . cum aliquis transit de peccato ad gratiam, transit de servitute ad libertatem."

[174] *Ibid.*, q. 183, a. 4, ad 1: ". . . libertas a peccato fit per charitatem, quae diffunditur in cordibus nostris per Spiritum Sanctum, ut dicitur Rom. 5. Et inde est quod dicitur II ad Cor. 3: Ubi Spiritus Domini, ibi libertas."

[175] *In Rom.*, cap. 7, lect. 4, n. 592: "Non enim homo propriis viribus potest liberari a corporis corruptione, nec etiam animae . . . sed solum per gratiam Christi, secundum illud Jo. 8, 36. . . ." Cf. *ibid.*, cap. 9, lect. 4, n. 792; SCG, III, cap. 157.

[176] *In Ioann.*, cap. 8, lect. 4, n. 1207: "nos autem . . . per ipsum (Filium) a peccato liberamur." *Ibid.*, n. 1208: "Liberationis autem potestatem habet Filius. . . : per eum liberamur non a barbaris, sed a diabolo." Cf. *In Gal.*, cap. 4, lect. 9, n. 275; cap. 2, lect. 1, n. 62; III, q. 35, a. 8, ad 1; q. 46; a. 1, ad 3; aa. 2 and 3.

[177] *In Ioann.*, cap. 8, lect. 4, nn. 1199 and 1210. III, q. 35, a. 8, ad 1: "Christus venerat nos in statum libertatis reducere de statu servitutis."

which we are freed *from* sin,[178] death,[179] error,[180] and the law.[181]
Freedom from the law does not mean that we are no longer obliged to
keep the moral law or that we may sin, for this would simply make us
slaves to sin once more.[182] Freedom from the law means (a) that
Christians are not bound to keep the ceremonial law of the Old Testament [183] and (b) that, even though the Christian is still obliged to fulfill
the moral law, and in this sense, like Christ (Gal. 4: 4), he is still under
the law, he is, however, not under it in the sense that he fulfills the law
out of compulsion, shame or fear of punishment. An observance to the
law out of fear of punishment would be the slavish observance of the
law of those who "have the will to do evil." [184] *In II Cor.,* cap. 3, lect. 3,
n. 112, Thomas writes: "He who avoids evil not because it is evil but
because the Lord forbids it is not free. But he who avoids evil because it
is evil is free."

Looking at Christian freedom in its positive sense—not just as freedom *from* something, but as freedom *for* something—Thomas teaches
that grace frees men to fulfill the law.[185] The old law is replaced by a
new one, the evangelical law of perfect liberty, the law of the Spirit,

---

[178] *In Rom.,* cap. 8, lect. 1, nn. 601-605; 609. N. 605 reads: ". . . liberavit
me. . . . Et hoc a lege peccati, id est, a lege fomitis quae inclinat ad peccatum.
Vel a lege peccati, id est, a consensu et operatione peccati, quod hominem tenet
per modum legis." *Ibid.,* cap. 13, lect. 1, n. 1017. In his earlier commentary on
John, Thomas showed a more eschatological view of man's freedom from the
inclination to sin: "Vera et spiritualis, quae est libertas gratiae . . . quae est im-
perfecta, quia caro concupiscit adversus spiritum, ut non ea quae volumus faciamus, Gal. 5, 17. (Libertas) gloriae, et perfecta atque plena, quae erit in patria:
Rom. 8, 21 . . . et hoc erit, quia nihil erit ibi inclinans ad malum, nihil
opprimens, quia ibi erit libertas a culpa et a poena." But cf. *In Rom.,* cap. 8,
lect. 4, n. 666, where Thomas distinguishes the "libertas iustitiae, quae est a
servitute peccati" and the "libertas gloriae, quae est a servitute miseriae."

[179] *In Rom.,* cap. 7, lect. 4, n. 593: "Haec autem liberat a corpore mortis
huius dupliciter. Uno modo ut corruptio corporis menti non dominetur, trahens
eam ad peccandum; alio modo ut corruptio corporis totaliter tollatur. Quantum
ergo ad primum . . . iam iustus liberatus est . . . quantum ad secundum . . .
ut scilicet in corpore meo non sit corruptio peccati, aut mortis; quod erit in
resurrectione." Cf. *ibid.,* cap. 8, lect. 2, nn. 628ff.

[180] *In Ioann.,* cap. 8, lect. 4, n. 1199.

[181] *In Gal.,* cap. 5, lect. 1, n. 277.

[182] *In Rom.,* cap. 6, lect. 3, n. 501; *In Gal.,* 5, lect. 5, n. 318.

[183] *In Rom.,* cap. 6, lect. 3, n. 497; *In Gal.,* cap. 5, lect. 1, n. 277; cf. *ibid.,*
lect. 5, n. 318.

[184] *In Gal., ibid.:* "Et sic iusti sunt sub lege obligante tantum, non cogente,
sub qua sunt solum iniusti." Cf. *In Gal.,* cap. 4, lect. 2, n. 208; *In Rom.,* cap. 6,
lect. 3, n. 497. If those who are free from the law commit sin, this is an
"abusus libertatis": *In Gal.,* cap. 5, lect. 3, n. 300.

[185] *In Rom.,* cap. 6, lect. 3, n. 497f.: ". . . per gratiam . . . homo servet
legem, non quasi sub lege existens, sed sicut liber. . . . Hanc autem gratiam
facientem homines libere legem implere, non conferebant legalis sacramenta, sed
conferunt eam sacramenta Christi. . . ."

which not only teaches us what is to be done, but also helps us to fulfill it.[186] It is the Holy Spirit himself, dwelling in us, who inclines us to right action[187] so that we freely [188] and lovingly [189] serve God. "This is true liberty and the noblest servitude." [190]

A final point in our investigation of Thomas' doctrine of freedom concerns the relation of Christian freedom to the natural freedom of the will. First of all, it is clear from what we have seen that, for Thomas, Christian freedom is a gift dependent solely on God's mercy and grace, totally beyond the powers of fallen man without grace. It is equally clear, however, that man's natural free will—healed and aided by grace —is involved in the transition "from sin to grace . . . from slavery to liberty" which we call justification.[191] Further, Christian freedom is the freedom of a Christian *man,* that is, of a human person endowed with free will. Thomas is therefore convinced that man's free will is active even when he is acted upon or led by the Holy Spirit, who causes the very motion of the free will within man.[192]

---

[186] I-II, q. 106, a. 1, ad 2. The new law principally consists in the "gratia Spiritus Sancti, quae datur per fidem Christi": *ibid., corpus art.* Evidencing a pneumatology no less radical than that of Luther or Calvin, Thomas, following Augustine, teaches in the remarkable second article of I-II, q. 106, that the law of the Gospel justifies only if we consider this law as the very grace of the Holy Spirit. The new law considered as documents of faith and as precepts ordering man's actions does not justify: "Unde etiam littera Evangelii occideret, nisi adesset interius gratia fidei sanans."

[187] *In Rom.,* cap. 8, lect. 1, nn. 602f.; *ibid.,* lect. 3, n. 635.

[188] *Ibid.;* ". . . homo spiritualis non quasi ex motu propriae voluntatis principaliter sed ex instinctu Spiritus Sancti inclinatur ad aliquid agendum. . . . (I)psum motum voluntatis et liberi arbitrii Spiritus Sanctus in eis causat, secundum illud Phil. 2, 13." Cf. *In Rom.,* cap. 6, lect. 4, n. 513: ". . . in statu iustitiae est servus Dei voluntarie obediens."

[189] *In Gal.,* cap. 5, lect. 5, n. 318: ". . . iusti non sunt sub lege, quia motus et instinctus Spiritus Sancti, qui est in eis, est proprius eorum instinctus, nam charitas inclinat ad illud idem quod lex praecipit." Cf. *In II Cor.,* cap. 3, lect. 3, n. 112; I-II, q. 108, a. 1, ad 2. SCG, IV, 22: "Spiritus autem Sanctus sic nos ad agendum inclinat ut nos voluntarie agere faciat, inquantum nos amatores Dei constituit. Filii igitur Dei libere a Spiritu Sancto aguntur ex amore, non serviliter ex timore."

[190] *In Rom.,* cap. 6, lect. 4, n. 513.

[191] Cf. II-II, q. 184, a. 4, ad 2 and I-II, q. 113, a. 1c. *Ibid.,* a. 3c: ". . . in eo qui habet usum liberi arbitrii, non fit motio a Deo ad iustitiam absque motu liberi arbitrii; sed ita infundit donum gratiae iustificantis, quod etiam simul cum hoc movet liberum arbitrium ad donum gratiae acceptandum. . . ."

[192] *In Rom.,* cap. 8, lect. 3, n. 635. After saying that man is inclined to action by the instinct of the Holy Spirit, he adds: "Non tamen per hoc excluditur quin, viri spirituales per voluntatem et liberum arbitrium operentur, quia ipsum motum voluntatis et liberi arbitrii Spiritus Sanctus in eis causat, secundum illud Phil, 2, 13: Deus est qui operatur in nobis velle et perficere." Failing to distinguish adequately Thomas' concept of *necessitas absoluta* and *conditionata,* Vorster, pp. 265f., thinks that when Thomas speaks of the *neces-*

For Thomas and the Scholastics in general, it is a commonplace that free will must be involved in Christian living if our judgment by God with its subsequent rewards and punishments is to make any sense. This judgment presupposes a man who "could have sinned but did not sin" (Sir. 31: 10). Thus, it is always possible for the Christian man to abuse his Christian freedom by a misuse of free will, that is, by sinning. Only on such a supposition can imperatives such as Gal. 5: 1 have any meaning. Finally, man's free will remains steadfast in the life of Christian freedom only through God's gift of perseverance, a gift which the Christian man cannot merit since it depends solely on God's graciousness.[193]

---

sitas infallibilitatis (I-II, q. 112, a. 3) which results from God's intention to move man's heart, he excludes the possibility of man's saying "no." But man, in Thomas' view, always has free will under grace. There is therefore no *necessitas absoluta* imposed on him; man *can* resist God's motion: *Quodl.*, I, q. 4, a. 2, ad 2. However, on the condition that God intends to move man's heart, there is a logical necessity or a *necessitas infallibilitatis* present, enabling us to say that God infallibly moves man's will freely! Once again we are confronted with the transcendent, all-powerful operation or *energeia*, of God which operates in a manner that exceeds human categories. This is a power that is even able to "work"—a biblical term with more of a physical connotation than the metaphysical concept "cause" which is so repugnant to G. Nygren, Pannenberg, *et. al.*—man's free will actions.

193 I-II, q. 114, aa. 9 and 10.

7

Free Will, Unfree Will and
Neo-Semipelagianism in
Late Scholasticism

We turn now to a consideration of the final phase of our statement of the question, a phase which is absolutely indispensable for a theologically and historically correct evaluation of Luther's central concern.

I. PRELIMINARY OBSERVATIONS ON LATE SCHOLASTICISM

Before tracing the developments in this period which are most decisive for the state of our question, some preliminary remarks are in order. First of all, generalizations about this complex theological era, which encompasses roughly the two centuries between the deaths of Duns Scotus (d. 1308) and Gabriel Biel (d. 1495), are almost always erroneous. As. F. Clark, in a very useful and comprehensive survey of the present state of research on late medieval Scholasticism, has pointed out: "If one conclusion emerges from all these studies, it is that sweeping generalizations in this matter can only mislead." [1]

So varied are the currents and the viewpoints expressed even among the members of the same "school," that it is a sure indication that one has failed to consult the sources when one attaches to such a diversified period as late Scholasticism such general labels as "Semipelagian," or when one states, for example, that since the high Middle Ages, the concept of freedom developed in the direction of autonomy. [2] There is no such thing as *the* concept of freedom in late Scholasticism! One

---

[1] *Eucharistic Sacrifice and the Reformation* (London, 1960), p. 300.

[2] Vorster, p. 95. A similar generalization is made by Freitag, WA 18, 596. The tendency to pass imprecise universal judgments on such diverse intellectual movements as Scholasticism and to identify the teachings of some theologians of that age with the teaching of "the Scholastics" can already be found in Luther. Cf. Denifle, p. 536.

cannot even say that the Nominalists had a common concept of freedom. For, as Ehrle [3] and Feckes [4] have pointed out long ago, there are
highly diverse currents of thought even within Nominalism, currents
which H. Oberman [5] has named the right-wing (led by Gregory of
Rimini, d. 1358), the left-wing (Robert Holcot, d. 1349; Adam Woodham, d. 1358), the Ockham (d. 1349)-Biel School and the syncretist
"schools." In the face of this diversity there is much merit in the proposal of N. Häring and C. Prantl, which Clark endorses, to abandon the
very elusive category, "Nominalist theology," in favor of the broader
term, "modern way" (via moderna), which was used by the anti-Realist
schoolmen themselves.[6] It is therefore important to bear in mind that
the followers of Ockham or the Ockham-Biel School, important as they
were, still were only one group among the "moderns." Similar diversity
within the so-called Scotist School has been brought to light by W. Dettloff in his study, Die Entwicklung der Akzeptations-und Verdienstlehre
von Duns Scotus bis Luther.[7]

Important as this highly diverse Nominalist current was, it is quite
erroneous to suppose that Nominalism dominated late Scholastic theology. With numerous references to the intensive research in the field of
late Scholasticism during the past forty years, Clark [8] lists the following
schools or movements which flourished alongside late Scholastic Nominalism: (1) the revitalized Thomist school,[9] (2) the flourishing school

---

[3] Der Sentenzenkommentar Peters von Candia: Ein Beitrag zur Scheidung der
Schulen in der Scholastik des vierzehnten Jahrhunderts (Münster, 1925), pp.
106-251.

[4] Die Rechtfertigungslehre des Gabriel Biel und ihre Stellung innerhalb der
nominalistischen Schule (Münster, 1925), pp. 100-138.

[5] The Harvest, p. 4.

[6] Clark, p. 304.

[7] (Münster, 1964).

[8] Clark, pp. 301ff. Cf. Grabmann, Die Geschichte der katholischen Theologie,
pp. 95-132.

[9] In addition to the studies cited by Clark, p. 301, footnote 7, see also
Grabmann: "Das Weiterleben und Weiterwirken des moraltheologischen Schrifttums des hl. Thomas von Aquin im Mittelalter," in: Aus Theologie und Philosophie, Festschrift f. F. Tillmann (Düsseldorf, 1950), p. 81. Y. Congar, "Thomas
d'Aquin," DTC 15, 417 points out that the canonization of Thomas in 1325 in-
creased his authority considerably. G. Ritter, Via Antiqua und Via Moderna
auf den deutschen Universitäten des XV. Jahrunderts (Heidelberg, 1922), p.
142 adds that already in the 15th century Thomas enjoyed "almost canonical
recognition." Copleston, A History of Philosophy, III/2, pp. 153ff. speaks of the
"remarkable revival" of non-Nominalistic Scholasticism in the 15th and 16th
centuries. Although Mandonnet, DTC, 6, 905 and 14, 1711 is not quite so
convinced as Grabmann of the extent of the Thomistic revival in the 15th century, he nevertheless concedes that there was "une vitalité doctrinale notable"
of Thomism in that century. Cf. H. de Jongh, L'ancienne faculté de théologie de
Louvain au premier siècle de son existence (Louvain, 1911), pp. 286, 306f.

of orthodox Scotism, (3) the Augustinian tradition, (4) a revived Albertism, (5) medieval Mysticism, with its varied emphases and (6) an influential group of individual theologians who were not committed to any one school, such as John Gerson (d. 1429), Nicholas of Cusa (d. 1465) and Denis the Carthusian (d. 1471).

When one reflects on what has just been said about the diversity of late Scholasticism and the consequent danger of generalization, it is easy to see the improbability, if not the folly, of the thesis that late Scholasticism, or even Nominalism, was one uninterrupted movement of decadence in comparison to the balanced synthesis achieved by the high Scholastics.[10] Equally untenable, however, is the view put forth recently by Oberman that late medieval Nominalism was the "harvest" of medieval theology, a term Oberman intentionally uses to oppose the traditional view that late Scholastic theology represented a "decline." [11] According to Oberman, "late medieval nominalism should be viewed as a basically catholic movement." [12]

How does Oberman arrive at this conclusion, which replaces the old generalization that Nominalism is basically an uncatholic decline with the new generalization that it is basically Catholic? First of all, although Oberman recognizes the existence of several schools within Nominalism, as we have noted above, he seems to forget about the anti-Pelagian school of right-wing Nominalism when he concludes that "nominalism has not been able to avoid a Pelagian position." [13] Secondly, after determining correctly that the Nominalist doctrine of justification of the Ockham-Biel school is "at least semi-Pelagian," [14] Oberman asserts that

---

[10] Oberman, *The Harvest*, pp. 423 and 325 is only partly correct when he associates Denifle with the thesis of the "disintegration of late medieval thought." That there was *some* disintegration, *some* decay in late medieval theology, Oberman himself admits when he concludes that the doctrine of justification of Durandus, Ockham, d'Ailly, Biel and Usingen was "at least semi-Pelagian" (p. 426). Similarly, Denifle never claims that late Scholasticism was a time of *total* decline. He says on p. 536: "Luther [not Biel, as Oberman maintains, *The Harvest*, pp. 141 and 178; cf. p. 208, footnote 59] war . . . nur ein theologischer Halbwisser und unglücklicherweise war jene Hälfte, die er kannte, gerade jene, die ungesund war. . . ." According to Denifle, then, not all of late Scholasticism, but about half of it, was unsound and un-Catholic. When Denifle says on p. 587 that the theology which Luther knew was only the decline of Scholasticism, it is clear from the context that he believes there was a sound current of thought which originated within Scholasticism in the 13th century and continued through the 14th, 15th and 16th centuries.

[11] *The Harvest*, pp. 5 and 423.

[12] *Ibid.*, p. 428.

[13] *Ibid.*, p. 427.

[14] *Ibid.*, p. 426. In his more recent study, *Forerunners of the Reformation*, pp. 125-131, Oberman does not make this assertion when speaking of Ockham, Holcot and Biel. He simply says that "it is a matter of debate" whether they

this doctrine, "important as it is, should not be identified with its theological system as such" and that "a second and . . . even more important part of the nominalistic system is its doctrine of Tradition and its understanding of the authority of the Church." [15] Oberman concludes: "On this vital point, and on derivative doctrinal issues such as Mariology, late medieval nominalism can be regarded as the forerunner of the Tridentine formulation of the relation of Scripture and Tradition and is therefore in agreement with beliefs basic and characteristic for what has come to be known as Roman Catholicism. When catholicity is understood in this sense, we are altogether willing to defend the thesis that late medieval nominalism should be viewed as a basically catholic movement." [16]

By suggesting that the Semipelagian Ockham-Biel school belongs to a movement that is "basically catholic," Oberman seems to us to be unduly extending and thereby distorting the meaning of "catholic" and "catholicity." In our view, his evidence enables him to draw only these conclusions: (1) On the doctrine of the relation of Scripture and Tradition, and concerning derivative doctrinal issues such as Mariology, late medieval nominalism should be viewed as a basically catholic movement.[17] (2) On the other hand, at least one school of late medieval nominalism, the Ockham-Biel current, "held a doctrine of justification which cannot according to any interpretation of the word be termed fully 'catholic,' " [18] a doctrine which is "at least semi-Pelagian." [19]

When Oberman's conclusions are formulated in this more careful

---

yielded "to the influx of Pelagian ideas": pp. 130f. In saying "that all medieval theologians attempted to be as faithful as possible to St. Augustine's teaching" (p. 127) on justification, Oberman does not venture to suggest how well these theologians succeeded. Nor does he, in stressing the anti-Pelagianism of all the medieval schoolmen, take sufficiently into account the fact that a theologian could be an Augustinian anti-Pelagian and still be an un-Augustinian and un-Catholic Neo-Semipelagian. For this reason, Oberman's reminder (p. 131) that Augustine had not been forgotten by the late Scholastics is misleading. The same criticism applies to his statement: "The Reformation period is not marked . . . by the sudden discovery of the radical anti-Pelagianism of Augustinian theology" (*ibid.*). Augustine was so radically anti-Pelagian that he denounced the merely anti-Pelagian doctrine of grace held by those who were later to be called Semipelagians.

[15] *Ibid.*, p. 428.

[16] *Ibid.*

[17] We do not wish to discuss here the merit of this thesis; we merely set it forth as a correct statement of one of Oberman's conclusions.

[18] *The Harvest*, p. 426.

[19] *Ibid.* We are in complete agreement with this conclusion. In his lengthy review of Oberman's book, F. Clark, "A New Appraisal of Late-Medieval Theology," *Gregorianum*, vol. XLVI (1965), 741-751 rejects Oberman's finding— which is also our own—that Biel fell into substantially the same error as that of the Semipelagians. See our reply to Clark, "Was Gabriel Biel a Semipelagian?"

manner, they do not seem to be too far from the main thesis of Denifle. Although Denifle did not treat at any length the question of Mariology and that of Scripture and Tradition, he did admit the existence of a truly Catholic current, perhaps not in Nominalism,[20] but at least in other schools of late medieval theology. Concerning the other conclusion, that the Ockham-Biel school had a Semipelagian understanding of justification, Oberman is in full agreement with Denifle.

Having made these necessary distinctions, we are now in a position to see quite readily the fallacy and the truth that are contained in K. Meissinger's assertion: At Trent, the "modern way" (*via moderna*), whose chief spokesmen were Ockham and Biel, was in no way condemned; therefore no Catholic theologian is forbidden to adopt this theological position.[21] Insofar as the "modern way" was Semipelagian, it was most certainly condemned by Trent. This was not a direct condemnation, for the Tridentine fathers were not interested in uncovering the errors of the schoolmen. It was indirect, in the sense that Trent did intend to reaffirm the doctrine of justification found in the Scripture in the light of the Catholic, anti-Semipelagian tradition shaped by Augustine and canonized by the Second Council of Orange. On the other hand, in *most*

---

in: *Festschrift f. Michael Schmaus zum. 70. Geburstag* (Paderborn, 1967), vol. II, pp. 1109-1120.

[20] Later studies showing the diversity of "schools" within the Nominalist school have corrected Denifle on this point.

[21] *Der katholische Luther* (München, 1952), p. 106. Cf. F. Lau, *Luther*, (London, 1963), p. 44, who also emphasizes that Nominalism has to this day not been condemned. Grane, p. 29, noting that Ockhamism "als philosophisches und theologisches System" has never been condemned by the Church, agrees with Meissinger that one can be a Roman Catholic and an Ockhamist at the same time. Aside from the fact that Pope John XXII on June 22, 1330 wrote that Ockham was a heresiarch who publically taught various heresies and who had written books full of errors and heresies, and apart from the fact that Ockham's anti-papal writings were placed on the Index by Pope Paul IV in 1564 (Amann, DTC, 11, 868, 903), it is true that Ockham's "system" has never been formally condemned by the Church. Luther, however, was under the impression that Ockham "centum annos pro haeretico damnatus fuit" WATR, 4, 679, 3. The Church censures erroneous *doctrines*, not "systems." Although some of the propositions of the Semipelagians, for example, were condemned, one cannot speak of a condemnation of their theological system as such. There were too many orthodox points in their teaching to warrant a total condemnation. Not even Luther's "system" has been condemned by the Roman Church! In many, indeed in most points of doctrine, Ockham was perfectly orthodox. While Catholic theologians and Church historians of today may express amazement that Ockham's more glaring errors were never formally condemned by the 14th century Church, there is general agreement today that some of Ockham's teachings were heretical, as Pope John XXII himself recognized. And even though there seems to be an Ockham-Rennaisance underway today (cf. Rupp, p. 88, footnote 6 and Clark, *Eucharistic Sacrifice*, pp. 308f.) which has happily beeen able to correct some of the prejudiced caricatures of Ockham's doctrine, no one since Trent and its renewed

questions of theology, the "modern" theologians were unquestionably Catholic. This applies even to those *moderni* who had fallen into error concerning the role of grace and free will in justification. To this extent Meissinger is fully correct when he says that no Catholic theologian is forbidden to adopt this theological position.

Clark calls attention to the recent scholars who have "protested against what they consider the unjustified denigration of Ockhamism in the past and the prejudice which must at all costs make that school the scapegoat for the Reformation tragedy." [22] Dettloff has recently offered a very careful and nuanced assessment of Ockham in which he criticizes Ockham's concept of God as "extraordinarily pallid." [23] According to Dettloff, Ockham as a theologian "is not especially original." [24] He is a logician who "neglects, however, to use logic and dialectics as a genuine *service* to theology. One is thus forced to ask the question whether Ockham was really concerned more with theology and the penetration and illumination of its truths or with the exercise of the arts of logic and dialectics." [25] Despite this sharp criticism, Dettloff cannot accept without reservations E. Iserloh's [26] almost totally negative judgment of Ockham.[27] Dettloff agrees that Ockham contributed to the negative development of the Scotist system. He points out, however, that Ockham was not the first to truncate and distort "the great Scotist concept of the "divine acceptance." If one studies the period before Ockham, maintains Dettloff, one finds theologians who had an even more superficial understanding of charity and a much more extreme concept of God's arbitrariness than did Ockham.[28]

One of the special merits of Dettloff's study is that he points out the unacceptable features in the thought of Ockham and other late Scholastics not from any "Thomistic prejudice," [29] but from the standpoint of the doctrine of Scotus, with whom, says Dettloff, "the great Franciscan School of theology really came to an end." [30]

---

awareness of the teaching of the Second Council of Orange has attempted to defend Ockham's teaching on the preparation for justification as a tenable Catholic position any more than they have sought to revive his anti-papal doctrine.

[22] *Eucharistic Sacrifice*, p. 308.

[23] *Die Entwicklung*, p. 284.

[24] *Ibid.*, p. 286.

[25] *Ibid.*

[26] *Gnade und Eucharistie in der philosophischen Theologie des Wilhelm von Ockham* (Wiesbaden, 1956).

[27] *Die Entwicklung*, p. 288.

[28] *Ibid.*, pp. 289f.

[29] Denifle has often been accused of this. Cf. Meissinger, *Der katholische Luther*, pp. 104ff.; Grane, p. 21, footnote 8. For a similar criticism of Feckes, see Oberman, *The Harvest*, p. 126.

[30] *Die Entwicklung*, p. 365.

Concerning the influence of late Scholastic Nominalism on Luther, opinions of scholars are extremely varied and often conflicting. However, the distinction made by Grisar between a positive and negative influence of Nominalism on Luther's formation still retains its validity and usefulness.[31]

To determine the positive influence of Nominalism on Luther, that is, those elements in Nominalism which aided Luther to create his theological system, is much more difficult than to discern the negative influences, those elements *against which* Luther reacted. Grane,[32] followed by Vorster,[33] maintains categorically that the Nominalist theology of Ockhamism exercised no creative influence whatever on Luther's theological development. Rupp [34] concedes "that Luther owed much to the stern discipline of logical, critical enquiry which he learned in the schools," but he refuses to accept the thesis held by Iserloh [35] and Bouyer,[36] that Luther was so influenced and shackled by the Ockhamist-Nominalist theology that he was unable to arrive at a fully Catholic reformation theology. Gerrish,[37] on the other hand, is more generous in his determination of Luther's positive debt to Ockhamism.

At least one of the alleged positive Nominalist influences on Luther has been discredited by recent scholarship, namely, the view that there is a positive connection between Ockhamist speculations about the divine acceptance by the absolute power of God and Luther's doctrine of non-imputation of sin.[38]

Far more readily discernible, in our judgment, is the negative influ-

---

[31] *Luther,* vol. I (London, 1913), pp. 133-164. Cf. Grane, pp. 21f.

[32] Grane, p. 377. On pp. 20-42 Grane surveys the studies that have been made concerning Luther's relation to Ockhamism.

[33] Pp. 30f., footnote 59. Vorster seems to overlook the fact that Grane does not intend to treat completely the theme "Luther and Ockhamism," but only wishes to describe the problem from the *specific* point of view of his study. Cf. Grane, p. 377. Against the earlier view of C. Stange, *Theologische Aufsätze,* No. 8 (Leipzig, 1905), who similarly admitted no positive relation between Luther and the school of Ockham, see W. von Loewenich, *Luthers Theologia Crucis,* 4th ed. (München, 1954), p. 79.

[34] Pp. 88ff. Cf. Rupp, *Protestant Catholicity* (London, 1960), pp. 41ff.

[35] P. 132.

[36] *The Spirit and Forms of Protestantism* (Westminster, Md., 1956), p. 160ff. Grane, p. 40, footnote 22 likewise criticizes Bouyer for seeing too strong a positive influence of Ockhamism on Luther.

[37] Pp. 43-56.

[38] This view had been held by Denifle, pp. 591-605; Grisar, I, pp. 123-132; Feckes and Bouyer, p. 162. Cf. McDonough, p. 162. Against this position see the arguments of Vignaux, "Sur Luther et Ockham," in: *Franziskanische Studien,* 32 (1950), 21-30; Weijenborg, "La charité dans la première théologie de Luther," in: *Revue d'histoire ecclésiastique,* 45 (1950), 617-660; Rupp, *The Righteousness,* pp. 90f.; Grane, p. 373. Vignaux stresses that Luther in 1517 *rejected* the doctrine, held by Ockham, Biel and others that God could, *de potentia absoluta,* accept a

ence of Nominalism on Luther. This is the doctrine of the Ockham-Biel school that fallen man, by his natural powers of reason and free will, without the aid of any divine help other than God's general concursus,[39] can prepare or dispose himself for justification. According to this teaching a sinner, by doing that which he is capable of doing (*facere quod in se est*) by his own natural, fallen powers, without any special preparation of the will or illumination of the mind by the Holy Spirit, can merit the grace of justification by a *meritum de congruo*. It is our conviction that this doctrine propounded by Ockham, Biel and other—but by no means all—Nominalists, represents a new variation of the old Semipelagian heresy which was combatted long before by Augustine and which was condemned by the Second Council of Orange. The emergence of this Neo-Semipelagianism [40] constituted the greatest single negative influence on Luther's Reformation theology. This teaching was, in Luther's eyes, that element in the Catholic Church of his time which was most contrary to the Gospel. It was the element against which he uttered his most powerful Reformation protest—and he was right in doing so! That this doctrine was publicly taught by influential theologians reveals what was probably the greatest of the many abuses in late medieval Catholicism: the lack of vigilance by the Church's teaching authority concerning the sound preaching and teaching of a central truth of the Gospel, namely, the doctrine that we are "justified freely by grace." [41]

---

man who lacked the grace of justification. Cf. thesis 57 of the *Disputatio contra scholasticam theologiam: WA* I, 227.

[39] For many Scholastics this is called the *influentia* or *concursus Dei generalis*. Ockham sometimes calls it simply the *auxilium divinum*. Vignaux, erroneously thinking that the latter term means actual grace for Ockham, believes that it is therefore unjust to accuse Ockham of Pelagianism. He thereby also shows his insensitivity to the distinction between Pelagianism and Semipelagianism. Cf. footnote 14 above and 50 below. Cf. also Vignaux, *Justification et Prédestination au XIVe siècle* (Paris, 1934), p. 139 and Oberman, *The Harvest*, pp. 209ff.

[40] We do not use this term in the manner of Loofs, *et. al.,* who has claimed that this heresy had permeated all of Scholasticism. Loofs erroneously identifies Semipelagianism with the doctrine that man can resist grace. We likewise dissociate ourselves from A. Jörgensen's view that any doctrine is Semipelagian which holds that there is a preparation for justification. This view overlooks the decisive question: Does God's grace prepare man, or does man prepare himself without the grace of the Holy Spirit? To answer the first part of the question affirmatively is Augustinian and Tridentine; an affirmative answer to the second part of the question is Semipelagian. Cf. Jörgensen, "Was Verstand man in der Reformationszeit. . . ," p. 80. See also the Excursus on Synergism and Semipelagianism in chapter 4.

[41] Rom. 3: 24. Thomas Bradwardine, who, as we shall see, was one of the most forceful opponents of Neo-Semipelagianism, did not hesitate to rebuke the papacy for its lack of vigilance in the face of the new error. Oberman, *Forerunners of the Reformation*, p. 22, says of Bradwardine: "Notwithstanding his belief that 'our one and only doctor Jesus Christ' safeguards and protects the

This laxity in the exercise of the Church's teaching mission caused far greater harm to the Church than any of the personal immoralities in the lives of the shepherds to whom Christ entrusted his flock. For, as we have emphasized earlier,[42] it was primarily against the *doctrine* that was being taught in the Church of his time [43] and not against personal and institutional abuses that Luther launched his Reformation. More specifically, it was against the erroneous exaggeration of the powers of fallen man's free will by certain influential theologians in the late medieval Church that Luther rightly protested. This protest was later to find its most radical expression in Luther's doctrine of the unfree will.

II. NEO-SEMIPELAGIANISM IN LATE SCHOLASTICISM

In our investigation of Neo-Semipelagianism in late Scholasticism we should recall first of all the difference that we have noted between Pelagianism and Semipelagianism in Chapters 4 and 5. The Semipelagians whom Augustine combatted believed that grace was necessary for salvation as well as for every truly good act.[44] But they held that the *beginning* of faith and salvation is the work of man's free will. Augustine's answer, and the answer of the Council of Carthage, the *Indiculus* and the Second Council of Orange was, of course, that the very good will by which we respond to God's grace is itself the work of Christ's grace in us,[45] that only through Christ is free will used rightly [46] and that the grace of God through Jesus Christ not only reveals to us the knowledge of the commandments and shows us what we are to seek, but that it also enables us to love and to do that which we know ought to be done.[47] Further, man's will must be prepared by God through the inspiration and operation of the Holy Spirit if it is even to will to be cleansed from sin.[48] To say that one is able by his natural power without the illumination and inspiration of the Holy Spirit even to think a good thought that has relevance to salvation is heresy.[49]

In the light of this Catholic tradition which we have traced from the Scripture through Augustine and the early Church decisions to Thomas

---

ship of Peter so that 'the teaching authority of all Christian doctrine resides with the Roman Church,' he feels forced to ask whether Peter has fallen asleep since he, Bradwardine, seems almost completely isolated in his struggle against the Neo-Pelagians."

[42] Introduction, footnote 3.

[43] This is not always the same as the official teaching of the Church.

[44] Cf. chapter 4, p. 73.

[45] DS 374.

[46] DS 242.

[47] DS 226, 245, 376.

[48] DS 374f.

[49] DS 377.

Aquinas, it is impossible to defend such theologians as Ockham and Biel against the charge of Semipelagianism simply by pointing to their belief that grace is necessary for salvation and merit. The Semipelagians said that also. The decisive question in determining whether a Neo-Semipelagianism has emerged in Ockham and Biel is not: Must God necessarily confer eternal life on those who perform good acts,[50] but: according to God's revelation, is it the Holy Spirit of God acting within man, or man himself who takes the initiative in the man's justification? Does God offer his grace to man and wait for the sinner to accept this grace freely, or does his grace precede and prepare the free will itself, making it possible for the will to accept the grace? Can fallen man begin to dispose himself positively for justification without the prevenient operation and inspiration of the Holy Spirit?

It is difficult to find a single Scholastic who, like Ockham and Biel, does not condemn Pelagius for one reason or another. The same cannot be so easily said concerning Semipelagianism, that subtle development of Pelagianism which attributes the beginning of salvation to man's fallen free will instead of to God's interior grace which precedes and converts the will and enables it to assent to grace.

---

[50] Vignaux, DTC, 11, 773f. and Dettloff, *Die Entwicklung,* p. 268 both exonerate Ockham from the charge of Pelagianism on the basis of what he says in I *Sent.,* d. 17, q. 1, L, M: "Ego autem pono, quod nulla forma, nec naturalis nec supernaturalis, potest deum sic necessitare . . . et ita ista opinio maxime recedit ab errore Pelagii, quae ponit deum sic posse necessitari et non gratuitam et liberalem dei acceptationem esse necessarium cuique": Göttingen, *Handschr. Theol.,* 118, fol. 129 va. Cited by Dettloff, pp. 267f., footnote 43. Biel shows exactly the same understanding of the Pelagian error: I *Sent.,* d. 17, q. 1, (E-F). Cf. Jörgensen, "Was verstand man in der Reformationszeit unter Pelagianismus?" *Theol. Studen u. Kritiken,* 82 (1909), 65ff. It need hardly be pointed out how inadequate this statement of Pelagius' position is: the concepts of *necessitas* and *acceptatio* are totally foreign to the thought of Pelagius. And as far as the doctrine of the *meritum vitae aeternae* by a person in the state of grace is concerned, we agree fully with Dettloff's judgment: "Die Ansicht des Wilhelm von Ockham weist sich *hier* nicht so sehr als ein Pelagianismus, sondern eher als dessen überspitztes Gegenteil aus: hatten der Pelagianismus, das menschliche Tun und Verhalten überbewertet, so wird es von Wilhelm von Ockham nahezu völlig unberücksichtigt gelassen": p. 268. We have underlined "hier" because Dettloff's investigation is limited to the question of *meritum vitae aeternae* in relation to the *acceptatio divina;* it does not include the problem of merit in preparation for justification. On *this* question Ockham's position is completely different. It can no longer be seen as anti-Pelagian; on the contrary, it represents a new form of Semipelagianism. Auer's observation is most interesting: "Es ist bemerkenswert, dass Thomas und seine Schule, die ein Verdienst der ersten Gnade durch würdige menschliche Vorbereitung entschieden ablehnte, für die Vermehrung der Gnade ein Würdigkeitsverdienst annahm, während die Franziskanerschule, die der menschlichen Vorbereitung auf die Gnade hohen Wert zuschrieb und darum für die erste Gnade ein interpretatives Verdienst annahm, für die Vermehrung der Gnade kein volles Verdienst wollte gelten lassen": *Gnadenlehre,* vol. II, p. 100.

A. ANTI-PELAGIAN PROTESTS IN LATE SCHOLASTICISM

1. *Thomas Bradwardine (d. 1349)*

In the preface of his book, *De causa Dei contra Pelagium et de virtute causarum*, completed just three years before he was named archbishop of Canterbury in 1348, Thomas Bradwardine declares that the book was written as a protest against the Pelagian views that he had heard during the time of his philosophy studies at Oxford.[51] Even before he began his theological studies Bradwardine, according to his own testimony, had a divine illumination which showed him the true meaning of Rom. 9: 16, namely, that everything pertaining to salvation depends on the merciful grace of God.[52] At once he saw the error of those philosophers who taught: (a) "That man cannot properly merit grace of himself, but he can prepare himself duly and then God will give him grace freely" (*De causa Dei*, I, 37); (b) "God always precedes by knocking and inciting us to grace . . . and man follows by opening and consenting, and he does this by his own powers" (*ibid.*, I, 38); (c) "Men fittingly (*de congruo*) merit the grace of God by their powers; but they do not merit grace strictly (*de condigno*)" (*ibid.*, I, 39).[53]

The last thesis, in Bradwardine's eyes, summarized all the other errors. Who these heretical teachers were, Bradwardine does not say. It is very likely, however, that one of them was William of Ockham, who was teaching at Oxford during the time of Bradwardine's studies.[54]

Concerning the propositions just cited, two things are to be noted: (1) Bradwardine was quite correct in judging that they were opposed to the traditional teaching of the Church. Although the first of the propositions could possibly be reconciled with the teaching of Orange II, the same cannot be said of the second and third propositions. The second proposition implies that God offers his grace to the sinner and then awaits the response of man's free decision to accept the grace. This is opposed to the teaching of Orange that the very willing that our sins be washed away is worked in us by the infusion and operation of the Holy Spirit (DS 374). The third proposition asserts or at least implies that fallen man is *naturally* able (*ex solis propriis viribus*), that is, without the gift of grace, without the inspiration of the Holy Spirit who corrects our will,

---

[51] De causa Dei, I, 31: ". . . fere omnes communiter aestimant solius liberi arbitrii viribus se posse declinare a malo, facere bonum, servare mandata. . . ." Cf. G. Leff, *Bradwardine and the Pelagians* (Cambridge, 1957), p. 14.

[52] P. Glorieux, "Thomas Bradwardine," DTC, 15, 770.

[53] Citations from Rivière, DTC, 10, 697f.

[54] Cf. É. Amann, "Occam. Vie," DTC, 11, 866. Robert Holcot was also a probable opponent. Cf. H. Oberman, *Forerunners of the Reformation*, pp. 134-37.

to initiate the event that results in justifying faith and grace. No mention is made of the need for God's grace to initiate the very desire of faith (*affectum credulitatis*), or the need for the gift of grace or for the inspiration of the Holy Spirit to correct the fallen will. This proposition is therefore just as incompatible with the teaching of Orange II as is the previous one (DS 375). (2) Both of these propositions, Semipelagian in character, were taught by William of Ockham and later by Gabriel Biel.[55]

We shall not go into the question here of how successful Bradwardine was in refuting his opponents. We do agree at least with the observation made by G. Leff: "Each side [of the controversy between Bradwardine and his opponents] was struggling to redefine the relation between the divine and the created; neither was willing, or able, to return to the balance achieved by St. Thomas Aquinas in the thirteenth century." [56]

A word about Bradwardine's concept of necessity is important for clarifying the state of our question. Portalié [57] lists Bradwardine, John of Mirecourt (his theses were condemned at Paris in 1347) and John Wyclif (d. 1384 or 1387) [58] among the proponents of predestinarianism and theological determinism in the late Middle Ages. Contrary to this widely held view, Glorieux [59] and Oberman [60] have given convincing evidence showing that Bradwardine does not teach a "fatalistic predeterminism" [61] or a determinism that excludes free will. Although he held to an "antecedent natural necessity," Bradwardine, *De causa dei,* III, c. 12, rejected as heretical the thesis that "everything that happens happens by absolute necessity." [62] The apparent contradiction is resolved by Oberman, who says that "necessitas" is used by Bradwardine in a different sense than in the earlier Scholastic tradition. Bradwardine does not use necessity in the traditional way, namely, in opposition to

---

[55] Others representing this position—all of them "moderni" and representatives of the Nominalist school—are Durandus of St. Pourcain (d. 1334), Robert Holcot (d. 1349) and Adam Woodham (d. 1358). Cf. Rivière, DTC, 10, 705f.; Feckes, *Die Rechtfertigungslehre,* pp. 124-127; Bouillard, p. 116; Oberman, *The Harvest,* pp. 168-178, 246f.; *idem,* " 'Facienti quod in se est Deus non denegat gratiam': Robert Holcot, O.P., and the Beginnings of Luther's Theology," *Harvard Theological Review,* 55 (1962) 317-342; *idem, Forerunners of the Reformation,* pp. 131-137; 142-150.

[56] P. 12.

[57] DTC, 1, 2535-2542; cf. Copleston, III/1, pp. 136f.

[58] Cf. the condemnation by the Council of Constance (1418) of Wyclif's thesis: "Omnia de necessitate absoluta eveniunt" (DS 1177).

[59] DTC, 15, 768-772.

[60] *Archbishop Thomas Bradwardine* (Utrecht, 1958).

[61] Portalié, DTC, 1, 2537.

[62] Glorieux, DTC, 15, 772.

liberty; he opposes it instead to contingency. The latter term, Oberman shows, takes on a new meaning for Bradwardine.

Contingency, as used by Bradwardine, conveys not only the idea of the non-necessary, which was the earlier Scholastic emphasis, but also the idea that events happen by chance, fate or fortune, apart from God's providential direction. Bradwardine rejects contingency as understood in this second sense. When he insists that all things happen of necessity, he means simply that God causes and directs them. That he does not, however, reject *all* contingency is expressly stated when he opposes those who say "that everything happens by a totally absolute necessity." Such an opinion, he says "takes away all liberty of the will—liberty of contradiction—and all contingency to alternatives." [63]

In contrast to Leff, Oberman finds it impossible to connect Bradwardine with any of the characteristic Reformation ideas. We wish to point out one area, however, where there is at least a real doctrinal similarity, if not an historical connection between Bradwardine and Luther. In *De servo arbitrio* Luther shows an understanding of contingency which is almost identical to the type of contingency rejected by Bradwardine: "A deed cannot be called contingent unless we do it contingently and, as it were, by chance. . . ." [64] In contrast to Luther, however, Bradwardine recognizes another type of contingency which is the basis of man's free will.

Perhaps the newer studies on Bradwardine, which render obsolete such one-sided interpretations as those of Portalié,[65] can shed some new light on the supposed determinism for which Bradwardine's countryman, Wyclif, was condemned.[66] It is quite possible that Wyclif intended nothing more by his doctrine of universal necessity than did Bradwardine, whose writings were undoubtedly known to Wyclif.[67] It seems most unlikely, for example, that a man who holds to a strict universal determinism could say that God's prevenient grace awakens and necessitates us to merit without detriment to free will (*salva libertate arbitrii*).[68]

---

[63] Oberman, *Bradwardine*, pp. 70-75.—It seems to us that Bradwardine's "antecedent necessity" is the same as the traditional "necessitas consequentiae!" Cf. ch. 6, nn. 108 and 118.

[64] WA 18, 616, 9-12.

[65] Cf. footnote 56 above.

[66] Cf. footnote 58 above.

[67] Cf. J. Cristiani, "Wyclif," DTC, 15, 3586; Loofs, pp. 530f.; Seeberg, III, pp. 778f.; M. Schmidt, RGG, 6, 863 and 1850.

[68] *De dominio divino*, pp. 226f. Cited from Seeberg, III, p. 779. Cf. the totally unfounded statement of H. Daniel-Rops, *The Protestant Reformation*, vol. I (New York, 1963), p. 215: "Wyclif declared that no free will existed. . . ."

2. *Gregory of Rimini* (*d. 1358*)

Another important historical witness to the emergence of a new type of Semipelagianism [69] is Gregory of Rimini, O.E.S.A., who was Superior General of the Augustinian order when he died. In his Commentary on the Second Book of the Sentences, which appeared in Paris in 1344,[70] Gregory, who combined great devotion to Augustine with certain Nominalist theses,[71] says that "it is the opinion of very many moderns that man, by his natural powers alone, with the general concurrence of God, can perform a morally good act in the present state of fallen nature, as for example, to love God above all things, to be sorry for and to detest one's sins, etc." [72]

These modern men, says Gregory, hold that by such naturally good acts a sinner can merit the first grace *de congruo*. This possibility he rejects categorically, saying: "No one can merit the first grace—neither *de condigno* nor *de congruo*—contrary to an opinion of the moderns." [73] While showing all due respect to the *moderni* who hold this opinion, Gregory maintains that they "depart from the doctrine of the saints and from the definitions of the Church and favor the condemned error of Pelagius. . . ." [74]

One should note that Gregory does not attribute this opinion to all the "moderns," but to "many" and he says nothing whatever about the older Scholastics (*antiqui*). It is therefore incorrect to conclude from Gregory's words that this new Pelagian tendency dominated the theology of his day.[75] Feckes and Müller do not even grant that it was the dominant position among the Nominalist *moderni*.[76] According to Müller this

---

[69] We shall shortly take note of the difference between this Neo-Semipelagianism and the earlier form.

[70] Cf. D. Trapp, "Gregor v. Rimini," LThK, 4, 1193; M. Schüler, *Prädestination, Sünde und Freiheit bei Gregor von Rimini* (Stuttgart, 1934); Bouillard, pp. 117f.

[71] After a careful examination of the evidence, Oberman, *The Harvest*, pp. 196-205, gives an affirmative answer to the debated question: Was Gregory truly a Nominalist?

[72] II *Sent.*, d. 26, 27, 28, q. 1, a. 1, fol. 92 G: ". . . plurium modernorum est opinio, quod homo per sola sua naturalia cum communi influentia Dei, et in statu praesenti et naturae lapsae actum bonum moraliter . . . potest elicere, ut ergo diligere Deum super omnia, dolere et detestari peccatum commissum . . . et sic de aliis. . . ." Citation from Grane, p. 208.

[73] This is the same conclusion Thomas reached in I-II, q. 114, aa. 5 and 7. Denifle, pp. 567f. shows that Gregory cited Thomas to support his views on the preparation for justification. Cf. Loofs, p. 509.

[74] II *Sent.*, d. 26-28, q. 1, a. 1, fol. 93 A. Citation from Oberman, *The Harvest*, p. 197, footnote 23.

[75] Grane, p. 208.

[76] Cf. Feckes, "Die Stellung der nominalistischen Schule zur aktuellen Gnade,"

doctrine represents "only one current of the Nominalist doctrine of grace." [77]

Gregory is strongly anti-Pelagian but, like Augustine, he always affirms the existence of *liberum arbitrium* even in the sinner, however powerless the will is without God's grace to do anything truly good: "God neither wills that we sin nor causes us to sin, but . . . permits free will" to sin. [78]

In his doctrine on the motive for predestination and reprobation Gregory stands squarely in the common Augustinian-Thomistic tradition which holds "there is no basis (*ratio*) in the creature," that is, that the ultimate basis of election and of reprobation is to be found solely in the absolutely free will of God. [79] Oberman has misinterpreted the position of John Eck (d. 1543) when he says that Eck "was the first to isolate Gregory of Rimini as someone who stood against the common Scholastic tradition." [80] It is true, as Oberman notes, that Eck lists Alexander of Hales, Bonaventure, Ockham, Thomas of Strasbourg, Henry of Ghent, Petrus Aureolus, Gabriel Biel, Silvester de Prierio, *et al.* as holding "that there is some basis in the creature for both predestination and reprobation." [81] But this is *not* the common opinion, as Eck explicitly says: "The first opinion, common and solemn, is that there is no basis in the creature for either predestination or reprobation; the difference rests solely in the divine will."

Among the "many doctors" following this opinion Eck lists: Peter Lombard, who deduces it from St. Augustine, St. Thomas, Albert the Great . . . Giles of Rome, Peter of Tarantasia, John Gerson, Gregory of Rimini, Peter D'Ailly, Marsilius of Inghen, Capreolus, Wimpina and Richard Middleton. [82]

3. *Other Voices*

Other Nominalists who hold, in opposition to the Ockhamist wing of Nominalism, that there is no *meritum de congruo* of justification by

---

Römische Quartalschrift, 32 (1924), 165; O. Müller, *Die Rechtfertigungslehre nominalistischer Reformationsgegner* . . . (Breslau, 1940), p. 53, footnote 166.

[77] *Ibid.*, p. 52.

[78] I *Sent.*, d. 46 and 47, q. 1, a. 1, fol. 153 A. Citation from Loofs, pp. 509ff., footnote 3. Cf. Seeberg, III, pp. 774f.

[79] Cf. Seeberg, III, p. 775.

[80] *The Harvest*, p. 144.

[81] *Ibid.*

[82] *Chrysopassus praedestinationis* (Augsburg, 1514), Centuria I, Art. 2, XCI: "opinio . . . communis et solemnis . . . non sit aliqua ratio ex parte creaturae, nec praedestinationis, nec reprobationis: sed tota illa diversitas sit ex sola voluntate divina." It is noteworthy that on the doctrine of predestination the Ockham-Biel school is aligned with the Semipelagians inasmuch as both held to a pre-

man's natural efforts include Heinrich Totting of Oyta (d. 1397),[83] Heinrich Heinbuche of Hessen (d. 1397), Marsilius of Inghen (d. 1396) [84] and John Mairo (d. 1550).[85] None of these authors seems to have attacked the opposite position as heretical, as did Bradwardine and Gregory. While the last three authors we have listed are not as pessimistic as Gregory and Heinrich of Oyta concerning the ability of fallen man to perform morally good acts apart from grace, it must be remembered that Gregory's "pessimism" is no greater than Augustine's. And although Gregory rejects the view of Thomas Aquinas that all of man's works in the state of sin are not necessarily sinful, we do not need to see a *real* opposition here, but a verbal one, hinging on the definition of "sin." Cf. the excursus: The Different Meanings of "Sin," "Good" and "Virtue" in Augustine in Chapter 4.

O. Müller [86] adds Luther's Augustinian teacher Usingen, and the Franciscan controversialist, Kaspar Schatzgeyer, to the list of Nominalist anti-Semipelagians. Müller sees an influence of Thomas Aquinas on Usingen in the doctrine of merit similar to that of Thomas' influence on Marsilius of Inghen and Heinrich of Oyta, this despite the fact that Usingen at times spoke sharply "against everything Thomistic." [87] Ritter has shown that such a "selective Thomism" is not improbable. It is one of Ritter's main theses that the philosophy and the theology of Ockham are to be strictly distinguished. Many who followed Ockham's "modern" philosophy did not depend on him for their theological insights.[88] Müller concludes his study by saying: Neither in Usingen, nor in Schatzgeyer do we find "Pelagian sentiments. On the contrary, both strongly emphasize the need for grace. . . . If there is any charge against these theologians that is unjustified, it is the charge of Pelagianism or Semipelagianism." [89]

Oberman insists, however, that Usingen is a true disciple of Biel with

---

destination *post praevisa merita*. Cf. Eck, *ibid*. See also Oberman, *The Harvest*, p. 211. According to K. Rahner, "Augustin und der Semipelagianismus," the main error of the Semipelagians is to be found in their concept of predestination.

[83] His "Nominalism" has also been questioned. Cf. Oberman, *The Harvest*, pp. 204f., footnote 50; Feckes, *Die Rechtfertigungslehre*, p. 115, footnote 84.

[84] Marsilius stands much closer to the theology of the high Scholastics than does Ockham. Cf. Ritter, *Marsilius von Inghen und die okkamistische Schule in Deutschland* (Heidelberg, 1921), p. 177.

[85] Cf. Feckes, *Die Rechtfertigungslehre des Gabriel Biel*, pp. 127-133; *idem.*, "Die Stellung der nominalistischen Schule. . . ," pp. 157-165; Rivière, DTC, 10, 706; O. Müller, pp. 52f.

[86] *Die Rechtfertigungslehre nominalistischer Reformationsgegner* (Breslau, 1940).

[87] *Ibid.*, p. 51.

[88] Ritter, *Via antiqua*, p. 132. Cf. footnote 84 above and Denifle, p. 551.

[89] *Die Rechtfertigungslehre*, p. 165. In the light of what we have seen in chapter

a clearly Pelagian doctrine of justification.[90] The chief text supporting Oberman's view is found in Usingen's *Libellus . . . contra Lutheranos*. After recognizing that God's "spiritual help" precedes the sinner and "aids him to dispose himself for . . . grace," Usingen uses the image of Rev. 3: 30 and pictures God standing at the door of man's heart and knocking with his spiritual help, while man opens the door "through penance." [91] Here there is no suggestion that the free acceptance of grace by the will is itself made possible by God's grace, as the Second Council of Orange teaches.

B. Neo-Semipelagianism in William of Ockham and Gabriel Biel

Historians of theology have found in the English Franciscan, William of Ockham and in the German Professor at the University of Tübingen, Gabriel Biel, virtually the same doctrine on the preparation for justification.[92] For this reason we have decided to limit our detailed examination of the rise of Neo-Semipelagianism in late Scholasticism to the writings of Biel, the most influential theologian in Germany on the eve of the Reformation and a man whose writings Luther had certainly studied at first hand.[93]

We have already discussed in an excursus the Scholastic axiom, "God does not deny grace to one who does what is in him." This axiom, we saw, was an expression of the general Scholastic doctrine that a sinner who is aided by God's grace moving him interiorly can prepare himself for justification by cooperating with that grace. Many Scholastics such as Bonaventure and Scotus and their disciples speak of this grace-facilitated preparation as a *de congruo* merit of justification. Most Thomists refer to it simply as a non-meritorious preparation for the grace of justification. With Gabriel Biel, following Ockham, we encounter an

---

4 it hardly seems adequate to say that simply because a person "betont die Gnade überaus stark" he is therefore not a Semipelagian.

90 *The Harvest,* pp. 178-181.

91 *Ibid.,* p. 180, footnote 106.

92 Cf. Loofs, pp. 506-509; Seeberg, III, pp. 765-769; Oberman, *The Harvest,* pp. 169-178; 209ff.; 424. Biel's essential Ockhamism is seen in his declared intention that his *Collectorium sive Epithoma in IV Libros Sententiarium* is an effort "dogmata et scripta venerabilis inceptoris Guilelmi Occam Angli indagatoris acerrimi circa IV Sententiarum libros abbreviare." Cf. Grabmann, p. 115; C. Ruch, "Biel, Gabriel," DTC, 2, 816.

93 H. Bornkamm, "Probleme der Lutherbiographie," in: *Lutherforschung Heute* (Berlin, 1958), p. 18 calls Biel's *Collectorium* "das Grundbuch von Luthers scholastischer Erziehung." Of Biel's *Lectura super canonem missae* Luther remarked: "Legite tantum Gabrielem supra canonem missae, qui optimus liber est papistarum, noch wie schendlich ding is drin. Es war für zeiten mein bestes Buch": WATR 3, 192, 24; 564, 5.

interpretation of *facienti quod in se est* . . . which must be regarded as a new form of Semipelagianism. For, according to this interpretation, it is fallen man's free will that takes the first step toward justification, a free will that is unaided by any special inspiration of the Holy Spirit (Augustine; II Orange) or by a "gratuitous assistance of God moving the soul from within or inspiring a good resolution" (Thomas, I-II, q. 109, a. 6).

The following is a typical statement of Biel's position on the disposition or preparation of the sinner for justification: "By his own natural powers man can do something morally right and dispose himself for grace, avoid sins and fulfill commandments." [94] By means of a common Scholastic distinction, Biel shows how his position differs from that of the Pelagians.[95] But he also shows that he is completely unaware of the Semipelagian error.

We can best see the Neo-Semipelagian character of Biel's teaching on the preparation for justification by considering two representative texts, one from the *Collectorium,* the other from his *Lectures* or *Exposition of the Canon of the Mass.* These texts make it perfectly clear what Biel means by fallen man's "doing what is in him."

By removing the obstacle and by a good movement toward God elicited by the power of free will, the soul can merit the first grace *de congruo.* The proof for this is as follows: God accepts the act of a person who does what is in his power as a basis for the bestowal of the first grace, not because of any obligation in justice, but because of his generosity. Now when the soul removes the obstacle by ceasing from the act of sin, by ceasing to consent to it and by eliciting a good movement toward God as its principle and end, it does what is in its power. Therefore God, because of his liberality, accepts this act of the removal of the

---

94 II *Sent.,* d. 28, q. un., art. 3 and dub. 2 (M): ". . . homo ex suis naturalibus posset moraliter bene agere et ad gratiam se disponere, peccata cavere et praecepta implere." Citation from Grane, p. 205, footnote 3. Grane, p. 206 notes that Gregory of Rimini is Biel's adversary in dub. 2. Cf. Biel, I *Sent.,* d. 17, a. 1, dub 3.

95 Biel, in common with most Scholastics (cf. Auer, *Gnadenlehre,* vol. II, pp. 40-49) distinguishes the fulfillment of the divine precepts "quoad actus substantiam" and "quoad intentionem praecipientis, que est consecutio salutis nostrae," II *Sent.,* d. 28 (K). Man is capable of the former *ex suis naturalibus,* but not the latter. In II *Sent.,* d. 27, q. un., art. 3, dub. 2 (R) Biel makes the usual distinction and says that the "determinatio ecclesiae" condemns the view that "homo potest implere praeceptum quantum ad . . . intentionem praecipientis." This "determinatio ecclesiae" to which Biel refers is canon 5 of the Council of Carthage (417/8), DS 227, which Biel relates as follows: "Qui dixerit, quod sine gratia possumus mandata Dei implere per liberum arbitrium anathema sit." Biel adds: "Contrarium enim fuit haeresis pelagiana . . ." That Biel is so careful to indicate his conformity to the "determinatio ecclesiae" seems to be a clear indication that he would have accepted the teachings of Orange II had he known of their existence. His Neo-Semipelagianism cannot therefore be considered to be a formal error, which implies that the teaching of the Church is knowingly defied.

obstacle and of the good movement toward himself and infuses grace into the soul.[96]

Biblical proof for this position, adds Biel, is found in Zach. 1: 3, Jas. 4: 8 and Rev. 3: 20. To turn to God—to draw near to God—to open the door to him is to do what is in one's power.[97] Then, invoking an interpretation of Rom. 5: 1 by Augustine,[98] Biel writes:

God receives those who have recourse to him. Otherwise he would be unjust. But this is impossible. Therefore it is impossible that God does not receive those who have recourse to him. But the person who does what is in his power has recourse to God. Therefore it is necessary that God should receive him. . . . By eliciting through the free will a good movement toward God a man does what is in his power. Of himself he cannot do anything more, supposing always the general influence of God without which man can do nothing whatever. . . . When therefore a man acts by his free will, having recourse to him whom he recognizes as his first principle and seeking from him the light of the knowledge of faith and of good he does that which is in his power. Generally speaking, any man is capable of this.[99]

Similar ideas are found in the *Exposition of the Canon of the Mass:*

Second proposition: A work which is generally or even morally good which is elicited by the will merits nothing . . . *de condigno* if grace does

---

[96] II *Sent.*, d. 27, a. 1, art. 2, concl. 4 (K); Latin text cited by Oberman, *The Harvest*, p. 172, footnote 80.

[97] *Ibid.*; Latin text in Oberman, p. 173, footnote 85. The same biblical texts are invoked in IV *Sent.*, d. 14, a. 2, a. 1, n. 2.

[98] *Ibid.*; Latin text in Oberman, pp. 174f., footnote 88. Was Biel aware that it was precisely Augustine's early (394) commentary on Romans which contained the same error on the *initium fidei* that Augustine later rejected and combatted when it emerged in the Semipelagians? Cf. chapter 4, pp. 73f.; Augustine, *Retractiones*, I, 23; *De praed. sanct.*, cap. 3 and 4. Actually this Glossa comes most likely from Rabanus Maurus (d. 856), *Enarr. in Ep. B. Pauli, Lib. II: Comment. in Rom.*, c. 3, v. 21. Highly interesting is the fact that Thomas uses this same argument—even the wording is almost identical—as an objection to his own position in I-II, q. 112, a. 3. In the response to the first objection of this article Thomas answers: "dicendum quod glossa illa loquitur de illo qui confugit ad Deum per actum meritorium liberi arbitrii iam per gratiam informati: quem si non reciperet, esset contra iustitiam, quam ipse statuit. Vel si referatur ad motum liberi arbitrii ante gratiam, loquitur secundum quod ipsum confugium hominis ad Deum est per motionem divinam: quam iustum est non deficere." According to neither interpretation does Thomas admit that man, *ex suis naturalibus,* can "ad Deum confugere!"

[99] II *Sent.*, d. 27, q. 1, art. 2, concl. 4 (K); Latin text cited by Oberman, *The Harvest*, pp. 174f., footnote 88f. Cf. Biel, IV *Sent.*, d. 16, q. 2, dub. 4 (K): ". . . peccator disponens se ad gratiam faciendo quod in se est meretur gratiam primam qua iustificatur de congruo."

not animate it. This is clear because the work lacks . . . worthiness on the part of the one who performs it. . . . Third proposition: A morally good work performed apart from grace merits a spiritual or temporal good *de congruo*. This is clear because nothing that is good goes unrewarded by the most generous rewarder. . . . The Lord gives grace to the sinner who does what is in his power, which he would not give unless the sinner did what was in his power. Zach. 1: 6,: Be converted. . . . Jas. 4: 8,: Draw near to God. . . . Perhaps you will ask, what does it mean to do what is in one's power? Alexander answers this question in Pars III, q. 69, art. 3.[100]

Then Biel cites the teaching of the *Summa Theologica* attributed to Alexander of Hales (=*Summa Halensis*) that any man, by natural reason, can know that there is a God and that we are to seek good things from God. If the man turns to this principle by his will and seeks from it the "light of the knowledge of good and evil, he does what is in him." By these lights of nature or faith (in the case of a believer who has fallen into mortal sin), continues Biel, the sinner ". . . recognizes the wickedness of sin. And resolving to arise from sin, he seeks the divine assistance by which he may be cleansed from sin. To one who does this, God gives his grace necessarily, not by a necessity of coercion but of immutability. . . . And these propositions agree with the teaching of Alexander . . . St. Thomas, . . . St. Bonaventure, . . . Scotus and others." [100a]

We can summarize Biel's teaching on the preparation for justification in the following way:

1. Fallen man is said to do what is in himself when he ceases to consent to sin, *and*, on the basis of his natural knowledge of God's existence, moves toward God or seeks refuge in him. This good movement toward God is the work of the fallen man's free will unaided by special grace.

2. When a fallen man thus does what is in himself, he merits the grace of forgiveness and justification *de congruo*.

3. God does not give his grace unless the sinner does what is in himself.

4. We know that this is God's plan of salvation because he has revealed it to us in such passages as Zach. 1: 3; Jas. 4: 8 and Rev. 3: 20.

5. The sinner merits the first grace *de congruo* and not *de condigno* since there is no debt in justice; there can be no such debt because the

---

[100] *Gabrielis Biel Canonis Misse Expositio*, ed. H. Oberman-W. Courtenay, Part II (Wiesbaden, 1965), Lectio LIX, O-P, pp. 442f.

[100a] *Ibid.*, P and R, pp. 441ff. Cf. *Summa Halensis*, III, Inq. 1, tr. q. 5, m. 3, solutio and ad 6.

sinner lacks the necessary dignity.[101] It is purely because of God's liberality that man is permitted to merit the first grace.

6. Because God in his liberality has so decreed to reward the efforts of the sinner with grace when the sinner does what he can and because God's decrees are immutable, it is proper to say that the grace which the sinner merits *de congruo* is conferred necessarily, by a necessity of immutability.[102]

7. Although it is through the natural power of man's free will that grace is merited *de congruo,* the "general influence of God" is always presupposed.

The first thing that strikes us about this teaching is that there is no mention or suggestion that any special grace, illumination by the Holy Spirit or preparation of the will by God is necessary to the sinner for his *de congruo* merit of justifying grace. The only *gratia* or *auxilium divinum* Biel mentions is the *gratia prima,* the grace by which we are cleansed from sin.[103] In the order of salvation generously willed by

---

[101] This "dignitas" consists in the fact that the one meriting is a friend of God: "in operantem quod sit amicus." The sinner is an "inimicus": "Ex quo sequitur quod peccator nihil meretur de condigno apud deum": *Exposition,* Lectio 59 N.

[102] Feckes, *Die Rechtfertigungslehre,* p. 43 is mistaken when he thinks that this type of necessity means that God is forced. Cf. Thomas I, q. 23, a. 6, ad 3 and I-II, q. 112, a. 3c. Thomas has no difficulty in admitting that a man can obtain grace from God by a *necessitas infallibilitatis*—if God wills that a man whose heart he moves should receive grace. Thomas differs from Biel in that he does *not* believe that God *has* intended or ordered that grace should be conferred *facienti quod in se est* without a special grace. In II *Sent.,* d. 27, q. un. art. 3, dub 4 (O) Biel refers to it as necessity "immutabilitatis et ex suppositione." The supposition is that God has so ordained that the sinner who *facit quod in se est,* without any special grace, will merit the first grace *de congruo.* In contrast to Thomas, Augustine and Orange II, Biel is convinced that this supposition is the true revealed order of things: "Illa ergo ordinatione stante et suppositione non potest non dare gratiam facienti quod in se est . . .": *ibid.* This distinction did not originate in late Scholasticism. Cf. *Summa Halensis,* III, Inq. 1, tr. 1, q. 5, m. 3, sol. For Bonaventure, see above chapter 6, footnote 59f. Cf. Vorster, pp. 86f., footnote 70.

[103] At times Biel does say that *gratia gratis data* is present in the meriting of the first *grace de congruo.* However, Oberman, *The Harvest,* pp. 135-139, in a very helpful analysis of Biel's use of the term "gratia," has shown clearly that "when the term 'gratia gratis data' is used, it is thoroughly naturalized and barely distinguishable from man's natural endowments." *Ibid.,* p. 138. Biel even applies the name "gratia" to the *concursus (influentia) Dei generalis* which is necessary for the action of any creature. Since the time of the (Semi-) Pelagians it is safe to say that no Christian thinkers have naturalized or minimized the concept of *gratia auxilians, operans,* or *gratia gratis data* as have Ockham and Biel. As Seeberg, III, p. 766 rightly observes: It "ist auffallend, dass Ockham wie Biel von einer Wirkung des *auxilium gratiae* . . . nichts wissen oder es ersetzen durch die *generalis influentia* oder den allgemeinen göttlichen Konkurs." It is perfectly legitimate to speak of the created order of nature as a "gratia" or "donum," as Augustine himself admitted in his Epistle to Pope Innocent I (416 A.D.) con-

God, says Biel, nothing more is necessary for the sinner to begin his journey toward God than the proper use of his own fallen intellect and his own fallen will. As we have already noted, it is Biel's position that "man can . . . dispose himself for grace by his own natural powers." [104] Thus, for Biel, it is fallen man's *facere*—not God's grace acting on man by illuminating his mind and preparing his will—which not only can, but must take the initiative in man's salvation.

Is this understanding of *facienti quod in se est* Semipelagian? If we apply to Biel's teaching the criterion laid down by Schmaus, an affirmative answer to this question is inescapable: "When in Scholastic theology the statement is made that God does not deny his grace to those who do what they are able to do, this is not a Pelagian distortion of revelation. Such would only be the case if the statement means that God gives—or must give—his grace to the man who does that which he is able to do by his natural powers."[105]

---

cerning the teaching of Pelagius, as long as we keep in mind that: ". . . alia est [gratia] tamen qua praedestinati vocamur, iustificamur, glorificamur": PL 33: 767. Cf. Schmaus, III/2, pp. 5f.; J. Auer, I, pp. 337-354. In contrast to Ockham and Biel the following late Scholastics insist that a disposition for, or a *meritum de congruo* of the first grace is impossible for fallen man by his natural powers without actual grace, i.e., without an "auxilium Dei speciale," "praeventio Dei specialis . . . ultra et praeter influxum communem," "motio specialis," "influentia specialis," "gratia gratis data" in the sense of "spiritus sancti aliquam specialem motionem factam per se immediate," etc.: Giles of Rome (d. 1316), Gregory of Rimini, Heinrich Heinbuche of Hessen, Marsilius of Inghen, Peter de Palude, Heinrich of Oyta, *et al.* Cf. Seeberg, III, pp. 733, 733f.; Loofs, p. 509, footnote 3; Denifle, pp. 551-557; Feckes, *Die Rechtfertigungslehre,* pp. 127-133.

[104] Cf. footnote 94 above.

[105] Schmaus, III/2, p. 292. Cf. Rahner-Vorgrimler, *Theological Dictionary* (New York, 1965), p. 431. Because he does not define Semipelagianism as clearly as Schmaus and Rahner, Rivière, DTC, 10, 705f., followed by McDonough, pp. 160f., mistakenly thinks that Biel's teaching is compatible with the doctrine of the Church. Paquier, "Luther," DTC, 9, 1187, although he speaks of "les nominalistes" without the necessary distinctions, shows far more discernment than Rivière when he concludes: "Ils en arrivaient à un véritable semi-pélagianisme." The Scotist John Maior (c. 1469-1550), in his *Commentary on the Sentences* which appeared only a few years after Biel's *Collectorium,* rejected an opinion which approximated that of Biel because it seemed to him to contradict the teaching both of Scripture and of the saints (*scripturam sanctam et sanctos*): II *Sent.,* d. 28, q. 2, concl. 1-4. Cf. Feckes, *Die Rechtfertigungslehre,* p. 133. Grane has given us an invaluable analysis of many central texts of Biel. However, when he insists on pp. 218-221 that it is incorrect to characterize Biel's doctrine as Semipelagian because Biel can say in all truth "that no one emphasizes the necessity of grace as much as he," Grane shows a poor understanding of the nature of Semipelagianism. Cf. footnote 50 above. This is all the more evident when he adds: "Hieran ändert auch sein Lehre über *facere quod in se est* nicht das geringste": *Ibid.* Grane fails to see that it is precisely in his doctrine of *facere quod in se est* that Biel is Semipelagian! When Clark, *Eucharistic Sacrifice,* p. 311 speaks of Biel's "well-attested orthodoxy," it must be noted that on the

The same conclusion is reached from a slightly different perspective. In common with Biel, many later theologians admit that the unjustified man is capable of a "negative" disposition toward justification without the aid of grace. By this they mean that the sinner ceases to perform new, deliberate acts of sin, that is "does not place an obstacle." [106] But in the light of the Second Council of Orange and Trent—or, for the pre-Tridentine Scholastics, in the light of the later writings of Augustine—none of these theologians will allow a *positive* disposition as Biel does when he says that fallen man can elicit a good movement toward God by the power of free will. González, therefore, lists Alexander of Hales, Durandus, Ockham and Biel among the Scholastic theologians who hold, in common with the Pelagians and Semipelagians, that man can positively dispose himself for grace "solely by natural powers." [107]

Contrary to Oberman,[107a] we maintain that Biel's teaching on the preparation for justification is incompatible with that of Trent. Nowhere in Biel can one find a doctrine of the preparation for justification in which: (a) the beginning (*exordium*) of justification is from God's prevenient grace inspiring and awakening him; (b) man is called by God without reference to any of his merits; (c) the sinner is disposed for justification by grace which arouses and aids him (*gratia excitans* and *adjuvans*), and not by his own natural powers; and in which (d) the sinner cannot move himself to justice before God by his own free will without the grace of God. But this is precisely the doctrine of Trent.[107b] We agree with Oberman in *The Harvest of Medieval Theology* when

---

following page he recognizes that "at some points indeed, chiefly concerning the theology of grace, there were real defects in the theories of Biel. . . ." On p. 303 Clark affirms that Biel, along with other Nominalists, "veered toward semi-Pelagianism." Cf. footnote 19 above.

[106] This is how Eck explains the "removere obicem" in *Chrysopassus*, IV, 3. He refers to the "doctores in dist. xxvii. secundi" for this interpretation. Paradoxically he adds: "Et ibi notabiliter dominus praepositus Gabriel!" Eck differs from Biel, however, in that he does not add to the "removere obicem" Biel's "ac bono motu in Deum . . ." or "et eliciendo bonum motum in deum." It is precisely this insistence on man's natural ability to dispose himself positively for grace that constitutes Biel's error.

[107] *Sacrae Theol. Summa*, III, pp. 550-558. González, p. 544 is inconsistent when he fails to mention Biel among the adversaries of the thesis: Homo lapsus, solis naturae viribus non potest gratiam mereri [neither *de condigno*, nor *de congruo*]. There can be no question, in the light of what we have seen, that Biel's teaching is irreconcilable with this thesis which González, p. 545, says is "de fide divina et catholica definita."

[107a] "The Tridentine Decree on Justification. . . ," pp. 36 and 49. Cf. the excursus in the previous chapter: "The Axiom: God does not deny grace . . ." and our essay: "Was Gabriel Biel a Semipelagian" in: *Wahrheit und Verkündigung*, (Paderborn, 1967), pp. 1109-1120.

[107b] DS 1525.

he says that Biel's doctrine of justification is essentially Pelagian,[107c] but disagree with him when he maintains in "The Tridentine Decree on Justification," [107d] that this doctrine does not have to be corrected in the light of Trent's teaching on justification.

This is a new form of Semipelagianism only to the extent that the Semipelagians did not use the Aristotelian category "disposition." The Semipelagians spoke instead of man's free will taking the initiative, or of the efficacy of God's grace being dependent on man's free acceptance— to the exclusion of an antecedent *gratia operans* which prepares the will of the sinner and enables it to will good. The terminology is different but the meaning—and the error—are the same in both Biel and the Semipelagians.

Another striking thing about the passages we have examined is that the biblical evidence which Biel offers for his doctrine of merit *de congruo* of the first grace by fallen man's natural powers is basically the same as that which the (Semi-) Pelagians used to support their teachings! We have noted that Scripture offers no harmonious doctrine of grace and free will. It simply presents us with texts which teach now the one, now the other truth. But with Biel and the (Semi-) Pelagians, one pole of the biblical dialectic is exaggerated, namely, the biblical imperatives or conditionals which imply man's freedom and the need for his activity.[108]

Against the one-sidedness of the (Semi-)Pelagian biblical argument which rightly upheld the existence of free will but wrongly exaggerated its powers without grace, the Church tradition from Augustine to Aquinas did not deny that the imperatives and conditionals proved the existence of free will. On the contrary, this tradition pointed to the two types of biblical statements: the one indicating free will, the other the need for God's preparing grace in order that the free will be a truly good will.[109] Thus, whereas Biel, like the Semipelagians, invokes Zach. 1: 3, "Return to me. . . ," etc. to support the view that the sinner takes the first step on the path to justification,[110] Thomas Aquinas admits that the sinner's free will is indeed involved in his conversion, as Zach. 1: 3 implies, but he cites Jer. 31: 18 and Lam. 5: 21 to show that the free will cannot turn to God unless God turns man's will to himself! [111]

107c P. 177.

107d P. 36.

108 E.g.: Zach. 1: 3; Jer. 29: 13; Ps. 22: 27; Jas. 4: 8; Rev. 3: 20.

109 Cf. Augustine, *De gr. et lib. arb.*, 2, 4-5, 12; Ch. Four, pp. 95ff.

110 *Expositio*, Lectio 59, Q.

111 I-II, q. 109, a. 6c, obj. 1 and ad 1. Cf. SCG, III, 149; I-II, q. 112, a. 3. Other biblical texts frequently cited by Augustine and Thomas to show that God

A further point where Biel's views coincide with those of Augustine's opponents is his emphasis on the primacy of knowledge in the "beginning of justification." [112] For Biel it is not the Holy Spirit or prevenient grace which illumines the mind and moves the will, but knowledge itself, which is the "root and foundation of all virtues. . . ." [113] According to Biel, the main reason for the lack of true religion among the Christian people is lack of knowledge; conversely, the principle cause of true religion is knowledge about God.[114] How reminiscent this is of the Pelagians who limited the concept of grace to the natural gift of free will and to the revealed knowledge of God's law. Against this error, as we have seen, Augustine wrote his great work, *De spiritu et littera,* in which he showed that knowledge of God's law is worthless unless we have the Spirit of God within us who inspires us to turn to God and who enables us to fulfill the law.[115]

At times, as one can see from the texts we have cited, Biel says that natural knowledge about God is sufficient for the unbeliever to begin the process of his conversion. For this reason Luther, in 1519, endorsed the judgment of Gregory of Rimini and said that the "moderns" were worse than the Pelagians (*Pelagianis deteriores*). The Pelagians, says Luther, at least affirmed that man was aided by God's *revealed* law. The *moderni,* on the other hand, hold that the "natural dictates of right reason" represent a knowledge of God's law sufficient for the beginning of an unbeliever's conversion.[116] Luther is incorrect when he isolates Gregory of Rimini's position from that of all other Scholastics and when he identifies the Scotists and Thomists in general with the teaching of the

---

takes the initiative in saving us include: Prov. 8: 35 (LXX); Pss. 79: 8; 84: 5 and 7; Jn. 6: 65.

[112] Cf. Oberman, *The Harvest,* pp. 164f.

[113] *Sermones de festivitatibus Christi* (Hagenau, 1510), 39 C; citation from Oberman, *The Harvest,* p. 165, footnote 61.

[114] Oberman, *ibid.*

[115] The Pelagian identification of grace with revelation of the law was likewise condemned by the Council of Carthage: DS 226; cf. DS 245.

[116] *Resolutiones Lutherianae super propositionibus suis Lipsiae disputatis:* WA 2, 394, 31-395, 6: "Certum est enim Modernos (quos vocant) cum Scotistis et Thomistis in hac re (id est libero arbitrio et gratia) consentire, excepto uno Gregorio Arimense, quem omnes damnant, qui et ipse eos Pelagianis deteriores esse et recte et efficaciter convincit. Is enim solus inter scholasticos contra omnes scholasticos recentiores cum Carolostadio, id est Augustino et apostolo Paulo, consentit. Nam Pelagiani, etsi sine gratia opus bonum fieri posse asseruerint, non tamen sine gratia coelum obtineri dixerunt. Idem certe dicunt scholastici, dum sine gratia opus bonum, sed non meritorium fieri docent. Deinde super Pelagianos addunt, hominem habere dictamen naturale rectae rationis, cui se possit naturaliter conformare voluntas, ubi Pelagiani hominem adiuvari per legem Dei dixerunt." Cf. WA 5, 485.

moderni: that by following the natural dictate of reason alone man could merit the first grace.[117] The Reformer is likewise in error in implying that "the Scholastics" taught that "heaven is attained without grace." Not even Ockham or Biel held such a crass doctrine.[118]

According to Jörgensen, Luther "did not correctly assess the historic Pelagianism," for the Pelagians—the same as Biel—taught that *every* man had the possibility of at least starting on the journey to salvation by means of natural reason and free will.[119] The revealed law was, for the Pelagians, only an aid that made it easier to achieve salvation. Jörgensen correctly shows that Biel, in contrast to Pelagius and Caelestius, insists on the necessity of grace for salvation.[120] In common with the Semipelagians, however, Biel holds that the disposition required for the reception of justifying grace belongs to fallen man's powers unaided by the grace of the Holy Spirit.[121] This is why Jörgensen concludes —and we agree with him—that one can only call the Ockhamists Semipelagians.[122]

It is interesting to note that Biel believes that his propositions are in accord with the thought of Thomas Aquinas, Alexander of Hales, and other High Scholastics. On the basis of what we have seen in the previous chapter, Biel is clearly in error when he thinks that Thomas agrees with him. Thomas knows of no *meritum de congruo* of the grace by which the sinner is cleansed of sin.[123] Further, fully foreign to Biel's thought is the conviction of Thomas that there can be no preparation for justification which does not presuppose "some gratuitous assistance of God moving the soul from within or inspiring a good resolution." [124]

Not to be overlooked as a point of difference from Thomas and as a

---

[117] Denifle's (II, pp. 565-568) criticism of Luther on this point is still valid despite the recent attempt of Oberman, *The Harvest,* pp. 143ff. to discredit it.

[118] Cf. footnote 50 above.

[119] P. 72.

[120] *Ibid.*

[121] By clearly distinguishing Pelagianism and Semipelagianism, as Jörgensen has done, we are able to see the fallacy in Grane's statement (p. 218): "Historisch gesehen wäre es jedoch sicher nicht richtig, Biels Lehre als Pelagianismus oder Semipelagianismus zu bezeichnen. Er kann mit vollem Recht behaupten, dass niemand die Notwendigkeit der Gnade so sehr betont hat, wie er." The Semipelagians could say the very same thing to the Pelagians! Cf. footnote 105.

[122] P. 72.

[123] Lacking foundation is Grane's assertion that Biel's doctrine of *facere quod in se est* in no way excludes him from basic agreement with Thomas Aquinas (p. 219).

[124] I-II, q. 109, a. 6. That Biel has seriously misunderstood what Thomas, I-II, q. 109, aa. 1-9, means by "auxilium gratiae" is, in Grane's opinion, "generally recognized" (pp. 151f.). Cf. Denifle, pp. 543ff., 573ff.; Scheel, *Martin Luther,* vol. II (Tübingen, 1917), pp. 163ff.; Feckes, *Die Rechtfertigungslehre,* p. 29; Seeberg, IV/1, pp. 76f., footnote 2; Oberman, *The Harvest,* pp. 140-143.

point of contact with the Pelagian concept of an autonomous free will is Biel's understanding of "liberty of contingency." This liberty excludes not only necessity of coercion but also necessity of immutability.[125]

A very important conclusion can be drawn from this statement. We have already seen Biel's view that when God confers grace to one who does what is in him, he does so not out of any freedom of contingency, but out of a necessity of immutability and of supposition.[126] The sinner, on the other hand, must enjoy freedom of contingency if he is to merit. Thus, if the sinner is to merit grace *de congruo,* it is impossible that he be moved infallibly or immutably by God's grace or even by God's general influence. This conclusion contradicts a basic principle of the Augustinian, Thomistic *and Lutheran* doctrine of grace and predestination.

For Thomas, as we have seen, God moves man's will by a necessity of infallibility (immutability, supposition, condition), without destroying its contingency.[127] Thus, the human will can, absolutely speaking, avoid doing what it is about to do. The will does not do what it does by absolute necessity, but only by conditional necessity, i.e., by a necessity of infallibility, of immutability, etc. According to Thomas, only absolute necessity is incompatible with freedom of contingency. In contrast, because he does not distinguish clearly between absolute and conditional necessity, and also because of his peculiar understanding of necessity of immutability, Biel is led to assert that God's omnipotence does not extend to moving man's will by a necessity of immutability and of infallibility—a conclusion which is utterly foreign to Augustine, Thomas and Luther!

Whether Biel is justified in claiming that his merit *de congruo*—"doing what is in one" doctrine agrees with the thought of the *Summa*

---

[125] Biel, II *Sent.,* d. 25, q. un. (D): ". . . opponitur necessitate, non tantum coactionis, sed etiam immutabilitatis. Haec dicitur libertas contingentiae. Sic accipitur quando est principium meriti vel demeriti. Nam per haec, quae vitare non possumus, nec meremur nec demeremur." It seems that Biel here understands *necessitas immutabilitatis* as *necessitas absoluta,* since he opposes it to *contingentia.* According to Thomas, however, God can move the free will of man *ex necessitate infallibilitatis* without depriving the will of its freedom (I-II, q. 112, a. 3). He also says that God moves the will "immutabiliter propter efficaciam virtitutis moventis; sed propter naturam voluntatis motae . . . non inducitur necessitas, sed manet libertas" (*De Malo,* q. 6, a. un., ad 3). If we wish to call this most efficacious movement of the will by God *necessitas immutabilitatis,* this can never be understood in the sense of *necessitas absoluta,* since the necessity in question does not exclude liberty. On Gabriel Biel's misunderstanding of the Bonaventurean view of *liberum arbitrium* and of the *necessitas immutabilitatis,* cf. chapter 6, footnote 60.

[126] Cf. footnote 102 above.

[127] Cf. chapter 6, footnote 122, 124 and 126. Cf. footnote 125 above.

Halensis is not clear. Holl [128] and Heim [129] see Alexander as the theologian who broke from the Augustinian balance of Peter Lombard and who introduced Neo-Semipelagianism into Scholastic theology. It would take us too far afield to attempt to solve this problem of historical theology. We wish only to note that the thought of the *Summa Halensis* is much more complex than Biel's citations seem to imply. It is true, as we have already noted, that the author of the *Summa Halensis,* like Durandus, Ockham and Biel, seems to be totally unaware of the Semipelagian heresy. [130] Further, in explaining the necessity of man's disposing himself to grace, the *Summa Halensis* uses basically the same type of scriptural arguments as Biel and the Semipelagians. [131] The analogies by which the author of the *Summa Halensis* illustrates the meaning of the "doing what is in one's power" principle betray a possible false synergism. [132]

On the other hand, there are considerable differences between the actual teaching of the *Summa Halensis* and the impression we gain of it from Biel's citations. In the first place, the author never calls man's disposition for justification a merit *de congruo;* it is only an "interpretative merit" which, according to Alexander, is not a true merit. [133] Secondly, whereas Biel says that the unbeliever's natural act of love of God is the final and sufficient disposition for the reception of grace, [134] the *Summa Halensis* holds that the ultimate disposition is not a natural

---

[128] *Gesammelte Aufsätze,* I, p. 116.

[129] *Das Wirken der Gnade . . . bei Alexander Halesius* (Leipzig, 1907). Whereas Holl judges the basic mistake to be Alexander's doctrine of *meritum de congruo,* Heim says the Neo-Semipelagianism of the Scholastics begins with the introduction of Aristotle's concept of *dispositio* into theology by Alexander and also with the mutation of the doctrine of predestination of Augustine and of Peter Lombard into a Semipelagian doctrine which reduces predestination to God's foreknowledge of man's *bonus usus gratiae.* H. Doms, *Die Gnadenlehre des seligen Albertus Magnus* (Breslau, 1929) has sharply attacked Heim's view.

[130] Cf. our excursus: The Axiom: "God does not deny grace. . . ."

[131] Cf. III, Inq. 1, tr. 1, q. 5, m. 2, cap. 1, art. 1, where Zach. 1: 3 is invoked without any mention of the other biblical texts which attribute our conversion to God.

[132] Cf. *Summa Halensis,* III, Inq. 1, tr. 1, q. 5, m. 4, sol. 1 and 2. In sol. 2 we find this example, already used by Anselm: ". . . si quis porrigeret eleemosynam duobus pauperibus, et extenderet manum, alter non, ille qui manum extenderet reciperet donum, alter non; et ipse Deus semper porrigit omnibus suam gratiam, non tamen omnes extendunt manum, id est voluntatem, ut recipient eam."

[133] Ill, Inq. 1, tr. 1, q. 5, m. 2, cap. 1, art. 1, sol: ". . . duplex est meritum, scil. meritum interpretativum et meritum congrui vel condigni. Meritum interpretativum appelatur quando non est aliqua condignitas in recipiente, et tamen ei exhibet Deus donum suum ex sua liberalitate acsi ille per opera sua meruisset, et tamen in veritate non meruit." Cf. Auer, III, pp. 78ff.

[134] Biel, II, *Sent.,* d. 28, t. 2, p. 4; cf. Paquier, DTC, 11, 1187; Rivière, DTC, 10, 706; Feckes, *Die Rechtfertigungslehre,* p. 41.

work of the unbeliever, but is the grace of justification itself.[135] Thirdly, although Biel borrows from the *Summa Halensis* the idea that the unbeliever can turn to God by his natural right reason and free will,[136] he overlooks other statements of the *Summa* which do not readily lend themselves to a Semipelagian interpretation.[137] Grane has pointed out that Biel, in his presentation of the doctrine of other theologians such as Bernard, Anselm, Peter Lombard and Augustine, likewise omits factors "which play an important role in the doctrine of the will of these authorities." [138]

Without pretending to offer a complete evaluation of the thought of the *Summa Halensis* on the relation of grace and free will in the preparation for justification, we simply wish to emphasize that, although this author makes many statements in his *Summa* which reassure us of his

---

[135] I, Inq. 1, tr. 2, q. 3, tit. 3, m. 2, cap. 6, sol: ". . . gratiae vero gratis data sive dona gratis data sunt sicut dispositiones quae animam ad hoc disponunt, sicut est prophetia, scientia et huiusmodi, nec tamen anima adhuc est templum dei; sed ultimo sequitur dispositio, quae est necessitas ad quam necessario sequitur quod anima sit templum in quo habitat Deus; et haec dispositio est gratia gratum faciens quae perficit templum." Because this important affirmation is not found in Book III of the *Summa Halensis,* but only in Book I, the teaching on the preparation for grace in Book III can easily be misunderstood.

[136] Cf. footnote 100.

[137] For example: III, Inq. 1, tr. 1, q. 5, m. 3, ad 5: ". . . nullus potest sufficienter se disponere ad gratiam nisi Deus ipsum disponat . . ."; III, Inq. 1, cap. 2, q. 1, sol.: ". . . juxta auctoritates Sanctorum, quod liberi arbitrii conatus ad bonum otiosi sunt, si a gratia non adiuvatur, nulli si a gratia non excitantur . . . et ideo liberum arbitrium non proficit in bonum, declinando malum et faciendo bonum, nisi virtute gratiae, et ita sine gratia non potest operari bonum et relinquere malum." Cf. III, Inq. 1, tr. 1, a. 1, ad. 4. In contrast to Biel's teaching that "Rectitudo . . . naturalis voluntatis, eius scilicet libertas, non corrumpitur per peccatum" (II *Sent.,* d. 30, q. 2, ad dub. 4; citation from Denifle, p. 535), Alexander holds that the *rectitudo voluntatis* "non potest esse . . . sine gratia": III, Inq. 1, tr. 1, q. 1, and 3. Similarly, Alexander recognizes that grace moves the *liberum arbitrium,* an insight that is lacking in Biel: III, Inq. 1, tr. 1, q. 6, cap. 3 and 4.

[138] P. 136. Thus, whereas Bernard, *De gr. et lib. arb.,* 4, 9 (ML 182, 1007) writes: "Manet ergo libertas voluntatis, ubi etiam fit captivitas mentis, tam plena quidem in malis, quam in bonis, sed in bonis ordinatior. . . ," Biel's citation in II *Sent.,* d. 25, q. un. art. 2, concl. 4 (H) reads: ". . . dicit beatus Bernardus. . . : Manet libertas arbitrii tam plena in bonis quam in malis. . . ." He thus ignores the biblical doctrine of bondage! Cf. Grane, p. 143. In II *Sent.,* d. 25, q. un. (F), when Biel cites the Augustinian definition of free will found in Peter Lombard's *Sentences,* II, d. 24, c. 3, he records it correctly. But in his commentary on it, he discusses only the contingent nature of *liberum arbitrium,* ignoring completely the Lombard's statement that the will chooses good "gratia assistente vel malum ea desistente. . . ." We agree with Grane, p. 136 that this indicates that Biel is primarily interested in a philosophical concept of freedom and has little concern for the Christian, theological concept. As a commentator on the *Sentences* he is, of course, aware of the different types of freedom outlined by Peter Lombard. Cf. Grane, pp. 78f., 123f., 144-147.

orthodoxy, the passage cited by Biel [139] would appear to be Semi-pelagian if taken from its larger context. It is precisely this that Biel has done. We believe that the *Summa Halensis* has all the elements of the Catholic tradition on grace and free will, but that these elements are poorly synthesized in comparison with the teaching of Thomas Aquinas and later theologians. For this reason the statement of H. Bouillard concerning Scotus can be applied equally to the author of the *Summa Halensis:* "Even if the context gives an acceptable meaning to the vari-ous affirmations, it is likely that [the author] would have expressed himself differently if he had known of the Second Council of Orange. He would at least have taken the precaution of explaining how he did not contradict it." [140]

Bouillard [141] has uncovered probably the most important explanation for the emergence of Neo-Semipelagianism in late Scholasticism: universal ignorance in the medieval Church of the existence of the Second Council of Orange and of its condemnation of the Semipelagian errors.[142] This lack of awareness of Orange II by no means resulted in a universal Neo-Semipelagianism, however, since theologians always had the Holy Scriptures as their primary font. Further, those theologians who knew of Augustine's great anti-Pelagian writings were protected from the temptation of Semipelagianism. Bouillard has argued well on behalf of the thesis that it was not Thomas Aquinas' discovery of the Second Council of Orange, but his discovery of the late works of Augustine that caused such a marked difference of expression, if not of doctrine, be-tween Thomas' early (Sentences Commentary) and later (SCG; S. Theol.) statements on the necessity of grace in the preparation for justification. Theologians of the Augustinian order, such as Gregory of Rimini, and other theologians who had a good knowledge of Augustine, such as Bradwardine, learned of the Semipelagian errors through the later writings of Augustine.[143] But where these late works of Augustine

---

[139] Cf. footnote 100.

[140] Cf. pp. 115f.

[141] *Conversion et grâce*. . . .

[142] Another factor which has not yet been explored is a possible over-emphasis on free will in reaction to the condemnations at Oxford and Paris (1277, 1284, 1286) of an alleged determinism in Aristotelian-Thomistic Scholasticism.

[143] The Augustinian orientation of the Franciscan school, from whose ranks came the most vigorous protests against the emerging Aristotelianism, is well known. Cf. Dettloff, "Franziskanerschule," LThK, 4, 285-288. That not all of these Franciscans were opposed to Aristotle has also been pointed out in studies such as those of Heim on the *Summa Halensis* and of F. van Steenberghen, *Siger de Brabant d'après ses œuvres inédites* (Louvain, 1942). The latter author has rejected the view that the opposition to Thomas represented a truly Augus-tinian school. We wish simply to emphasize here that, even though Thomas' opponents such as John Peckham, O. F. M. and Robert Kilwardby, O. P. undoubt-

are either unknown or unincorporated into a theological system, we find an understanding of the "beginning of salvation" that is at best ambiguous; the *Summa Halensis,* for example, and at worst Neo-Semipelagian, in such theologians as Durandus, Ockham and Biel.

It is our conviction that the Neo-Semipelagian tendencies of Ockham and Biel were the principle negative influences of late Scholastic theology on Luther.[144] We believe further that Lortz's judgment: "The system of Ockhamism is fundamentally un-Catholic," applies at least to the doctrine of Ockham and Biel that man takes the initiative in the preparation for justification.[145]

The question remains: Did the Ockham-Biel view represent the common or the majority teaching of Catholic theologians on the eve of the Reformation, as Luther believed? [146] More studies of the positions of the theologians of the late 15th and early 16th centuries are needed before this question can be decisively answered. These studies would have to examine the views of the theologians not only in Germany,[147] but also in Paris, Louvain, England, Spain and Italy. Our own view inclines toward that of Müller, for whom Biel's doctrine on the preparation for justification represents "only one direction of the

---

edly sought to retain Augustinian insights which were opposed to Aristotelianism, this anti-Aristotelian Augustinianism was *not* characterized by its devotion to—or knowledge of—Augustine's doctrine on grace, justification and predestination. Cf. D. A. Callus, "Robert Kilwardby," LThK, 8, 1340; T. Barth, "Johannes Peckham," LThK, 5, 1069f. The struggle against Aristotelian Thomism was primarily a struggle of philosophical—not theological—Augustinianism against Aristotelianism. Cf. B. Decker, "Augustinismus in der Theologie und Philosophie des MA," LThK, 1, 1092ff.; Gillon, DTC, 15, 654-693; Glorieux, "Tempier (Etienne)," DTC, 15, 99-107; Callus, *The Condemnation of St. Thomas at Oxford,* 2nd ed. (Oxford, 1955). In fact, due to his "discovery" of Augustine's later writings (cf. Bouillard, p. 109), Thomas was far more clearly Augustinian than any of his contemporaries on the doctrines of predestination, grace and the preparation for justification.

[144] This Neo-Semipelagianism also had its influence on the late medieval popular piety. Cf. Lortz, I, pp. 99-108, 197; Auer, "Rechtfertigung," LThK, 8, 1041, Lortz, I, p. 124 maintains, "dass *praktisch* das Verhalten eines grossen, vielleicht sogar des grösseren Teiles der Katholiken so war, *als ob* man mit eigenen Werken den Himmel verdienen könnte." To be sure, a truly exemplary popular piety existed alongside this nonauthentic devotionalism, as Lortz points out: I, pp. 111-118.

[145] *Die Reformation,* I, p. 173. We cannot, however, agree with Lortz, I, p. 176, that Biel corrected Ockham—at least insofar as Ockham's doctrine of the disposition for justification is concerned. Oberman also finds Lortz's judgment here unacceptable. Cf. *The Harvest,* pp. 424 and 425, footnote 169.

[146] Cf. footnote 117 above and Chapter 8, footnote 5 below.

[147] Ritter's investigation, *Via antiqua und Via Moderna auf den deutschen Universitäten des XV. Jahrhunderts,* offers us a methodological model for the needed studies on the doctrine of the preparation for justification in the German, French, English, Italian and Spanish theologians on the eve of the Reformation.

Nominalist doctrine of grace; there was also another orthodox direction.
. . . ." [148] We agree with Müller that Denifle, Grisar, Hermelink, Scheel,
et al., are incorrect in their assertion that Biel's doctrine was *the* Nominalist doctrine of grace at the turn of the 16th century.[149]

One must keep in mind that, just as it would be erroneous to try to
determine the common pre-Reformation Catholic doctrine by simply
studying the German theologians without considering the Spaniards,
Italians, etc., so it would also be wrong to forget that the teaching of the
majority of the *Nominalist* theologians is not the same as the teaching of
the majority of the late *Scholastic* theologians, whose different schools
we noted at the beginning of this chapter. Thus, even though Denifle and
Müller, for example, are at odds on the question of the dominant doctrine within *Nominalism,* Denifle never denies that the majority of the
late Scholastics had a Catholic understanding of *facienti quod in se
est*.[150] As far as Germany is concerned, however, Denifle affirms that
"a great precentage of the theologians in Germany" knew no other theology than that which Luther knew, namely, the Ockhamist theology.[151]

Contrary to the view of Denifle,[152] Grane,[153] Seeberg,[154] and Loofs,[155]
Vignaux,[156] and Tavard [157] hold that Nominalism and Ockham's influence dominated the universities of the 14th and 15th centuries. We
do not think Vignaux and Tavard have demonstrated this thesis. Much
more study is required before this debate can be settled.

---

[148] Pp. 52f. To say that Biel's view was not the majority view is not to reject
Jedin's judgment that he was "one of the most highly esteemed German theologians at the end of the 15th century": *Trent,* I, p. 143.

[149] P. 54, footnote 165.

[150] Pp. 564f.: "Nun sind es aber bedeutend mehr Scholastiker als die eben
genannten (Nominalisten), die ihnen entgegen mit der Kirche lehrten, die Vorbereitung zur heiligmachenden Gnade . . . nähme nicht von uns aus, sondern nur
von der Gnade Christi ihren Anfang." Cf. Holl, *Ges. Aüfsatze,* I, p. 172, proposes
that Denifle's words—"ein grosser Teil der Doktoren in Deutschland" should be
changed to: "die weit überwiegende Mehrzahl der Doktoren." Denifle's position
finds confirmation in Grane, pp. 14, 16, footnote 3; 89 and 208. Grane, p. 208,
says it would be incorrect to assert that the Ockham-Biel position was the dominant attitude of that time.

[151] P. 588, footnote 2.

[152] Cf. footnote 150.

[153] *Ibid.*

[154] III, pp. 750-755. Seeberg holds that there was a restoration of Thomism
and Scotism, coupled with a lessening influence of the *moderni* in the second half
of the 15th century.

[155] Pp. 505f. Loofs reaches the same conclusion as Seeberg when he says that
Nominalism was "only an episode" in Catholic theology. Cf. Mandonnet, "Frères
Prêcheurs (La théologie dans l'ordre des)," DTC, 6, 905-911.

[156] DTC, 11, 889.

[157] *Protestantism* (London, 1959), p. 20. Tavard goes farther than Vignaux in
asserting that Gabriel Biel's view were the most widely held. Cf. Holl, I, p. 116.

In any case, even if it were to be shown that Biel's Neo-Semipelagian doctrine was the common opinion of theologians at the turn of the 16th century, it still could not be shown that such a view was in conformity with or was supported by the authoritative doctrinal pronouncements of the Church. These pronouncements, as we have seen, affirm unmistakably that the beginning of faith and salvation is to be attributed to the grace of Christ and to the Holy Spirit of Christ working within us. This doctrine is not only irreconcilable with the Semipelagianism of the 5th and 6th centuries, but also with the Neo-Semipelagianism that emerged in the 14th and 15th centuries in the Ockham-Biel school of late Scholastic Nominalism.

8

Luther's Early Reaction: From *Liberum Arbitrium* to *Servum Arbitrium*

H aving traced the concept of freedom, both natural and acquired, from the Bible through Augustine and the Church's doctrinal decisions to Thomas Aquinas and Gabriel Biel, our statement of the question is complete. Instead of turning directly to Erasmus' *De libero arbitrio,* however, the work which provoked Luther's lengthy exposition of his doctrine on the unfree will, we should first look briefly at the development of this doctrine in Luther's works prior to his controversy with Erasmus.

We have noted that in the Catholic tradition there has been a constant defense of God's grace and of man's free will. Sometimes the one, sometimes the other was in danger of being minimized. When Ockham and Biel minimized the need for grace in the preparation for justification and when they exaggerated the role of fallen man's free will in salvation, no new Augustine arose within the Church to refute these unbiblical errors and to induce the bishops of the Church, including the bishop of Rome, to denounce such teaching. Instead, there arose a man who became convinced not only that virtually all of the theologians in the papal Church were Pelagians,[1] but also that the pope himself did not believe that God justifies sinners solely by grace through Christ.[2] And when Pope Leo X in 1520 condemned Luther's thesis: "Free will after sin is an empty word and when it does what is in itself it sins mortally," Martin Luther became more convinced than ever that the pope was the Antichrist. Unlike Augustine, who affirmed against the Pelagians the

[1] Cf. chapter 7, footnote 116.
[2] *Lectures on Galatians* (1535): WA 40/1, 181, 11.

Catholic doctrine of grace and free will, Luther proclaimed against the
Neo-Semipelagianism of his day a doctrine of *servum arbitrium*. Luther
did not always teach such a doctrine. What follows is a sketch of his
evolution from a doctrine of *liberum arbitrium* to one of *servum
arbitrium*.[3]

I THE NEO-SEMIPELAGIAN UNDERSTANDING OF FREE WILL IN LUTHER, THE COMMENTATOR ON THE SENTENCES AND EXPOSITOR OF THE PSALMS

A. LUTHER's *Marginal Notes* IN THE *Sentences* OF PETER LOMBARD (1509-1510)

When Luther made his marginal notes in the copy of Lombard's
Sentences that was in the Augustinian monastery in Erfurt, he was
undeniably a theologian who showed the influence of the Ockham-Biel
school.[4] Yet even at this early date there were other influences on his

---

[3] For general surveys of this development see J. Lütkens, *Luthers Prädestinationslehre im Zusammenhang mit seiner Lehre vom freien Willen* (Dorpat, 1858),
pp. 11-51; C. E. Luthardt, *Die Lehre vom freien Willen* . . . (Leipzig, 1863), pp.
87-122; F. Kattenbusch, *Luthers Lehre vom unfreien Willen* . . . *nach ihren
Entstehungsgründen untersucht* (Göttingen, 1875), pp. 38-77; K. Zickendraht, *Der
Streit zwischen Eramus und Luther über die Willensfreiheit* (Leipzig, 1909), pp.
186f. Kattenbusch's book presents a fine survey except for the unavoidable omis-
sion of Luther's development in the *Lectures on Romans*. The comparison of
Luther's early doctrine of freedom, unfreedom and slavery with that of "the
Scholastics" which is made by R. Schwarz, pp. 191-208 is very unreliable.
Schwarz does not make the needed distinctions between "libere" "libertas" and
other related concepts. He furthermore frequently misleads his readers by speaking
of the highly diversified opinions of Scholastic theologians under the one term
"the Scholastics."

[4] That Luther may have been sarcastic when he said "Sum enim Occanicae
factionis" (WA 6, 600, 11) and when he called Ockham "magister meus" (WATR
2, 516, 6) has been upheld by Holl, *Ges. Aufsätze,* I, p. 49, footnote 2 and
Grisar, I, p. 104, but firmly denied by Grane. If Holl means by this that Luther
did not remain an unchanged Ockhamist, then he is correct. As Gerrish says,
p. 45, Denifle's blunt assertion that Luther remained an Ockhamist (p. 591) contains both truth and error. Kattenbusch's remark, "Deus absconditus," in: *Festgabe
für J. Kaftan* . . . (Tübingen, 1920), pp. 209f., that Luther "ist Occamist
besonderer Ordnung geworden" is probably the best expression of the relationship.
No one can dispute Grane's statement, pp. 265 and 377, based on the studies of
Scheel, *Luther,* II, 397-480 and Vignaux, *Luther commentateur des Sentences*
(Paris, 1935), that Luther "als Ockhamist begann," and that he was an Ockhamist
when he made his marginal notes in the copy of Lombard's *Sentences* that was
in the Erfurt monastery. This Ockhamism was not simply philosophical. While
it is well established that the Faculty of Arts at Erfurt, where Luther studied
his philosophy (1501-1505), was officially committed to the *via moderna* of
Ockhamism, it is no less certain that Luther, in his preparation for the priesthood,
had imbibed the Ockhamist theology through Biel's *Lectura super canonem missae.*
Biel also influenced him after his ordination (1507) through his principal pro-

thought, mainly biblical and Augustinian, which enabled him to criticize both Ockhamist theology and Aristotelian philosophy.[5] In these early marginal notations we find Luther not only holding to the natural freedom of the will, and to the concept of *meritum de congruo,* in true Ockhamistic fashion,[6] but also asserting that even the man who is a slave of sin naturally wills the good insofar as he has a will, but not insofar as it is vitiated.[7]

In the preceding chapter we noted that Biel was not as clear on the distinction between absolute and conditional necessity as were most Scholastics. We saw also that Biel broke with Thomas Aquinas when he

fessor of theology, Johann Nathin, who had studied under Biel in Tübingen. Cf. Weijenborg, p. 620. L. Saint-Blancat, "La Théologie de Luther et un nouveau Plagiat de Pierre D'Ailly," in: *Positions Luthériennes,* 4 (1956), 61-77, argues on faulty *a priori* grounds against an influence of Ockham and Biel on Luther in favor of an influence by Gregory of Rimini. This view has been rightly criticized by Oberman, *The Harvest,* pp. 199ff. and Grane, pp. 19f.

[5] Cf. Rupp, *The Righteousness,* pp. 92ff. A. Zumkeller, in: *Augustinus Magister* (Paris, 1954), pp. 269-271 reaffirms his earlier rejection of A. V. Müller's thesis that there was a pre-Lutheran theology in the Augustinian school of the late Middle Ages. Zumkeller maintains that the Augustinian thought of Gregory of Rimini and Hugolin of Orvieto brought Luther at a very early date under the *indirect* influence of Augustine. This is a revival of the view held long ago by C. Stange, "Über Luthers Beziehung zur Theologie seines Ordens," in: *Neue kirchliche Zeitschr.* (1900), 574ff. Concerning the direct contact of Luther, the *Sentences* commentator, with the writings of Augustine, see A. Hamel, *Der junge Luther und Augustin,* I (Gütersloh, 1934), pp. 5-25. Cf. B. Lohse, "Die Bedeutung Augustins fur den jungen Luther," in *KuD,* 11 (1965), 116-135. Zumkeller, p. 271, thinks that despite the research of Scheel and Boehmer, the Ockham-Biel character of Nathin's theology has not yet been truly established. This seems to be an over-cautious reservation. It overlooks the distinctly Ockhamist theses that are to be found in the early Luther. We have indicated earlier our view that Luther's knowledge of Thomas Aquinas was very poor. It is of interest to note, however, that the text of the *Sentences* which Luther used during his bachelor year at Erfurt was accompanied by a Thomistic commentary, that of Henry of Gorcum, professor at Cologne from 1419-1431. Cf. Saint-Blancat, pp. 66. Grane, p. 16, footnote 31 makes the important point that the *theological* faculty of Erfurt was not dominated by Ockhamists; there were also Thomists and Scotists there. Further, the chair of the Franciscans was never occupied by Ockhamists— only by Scotists. This contradicts the view of F. Lau, "Luthers Eintritt ins Erfurter Augustinerkloster," in: *Luther,* 27 (1956), 52. At the University of Wittenberg the situation was similar. In 1505 there were four Thomists and four Scotists on the theological faculty—but no Ockhamists. Cf. E. Schwiebert, *Luther and His Times* (St. Louis, 1950), p. 294; W. Friedensberg, *Urkundebuch der Universität Wittenberg,* 2 vols. (Magdeburg, 1926/7). On the influence of Bernard of Clairvaux and John Gerson on the young Luther, see H. Strohl, *Luther jusqu'en 1520,* 2nd ed. (Paris, 1960), pp. 65-69.

[6] WA 9, 31f. Cf. Grane, pp. 265f. In WA 9, 7, 2. 27 Luther shows a fundamentally Catholic understanding of merit: "Quicquid habes meriti, praeventrix gratia donat: Nil deus in nobis praeter sua dona coronat."

[7] WA 9, 79, 10-35.

insisted that the will could not be free unless it were free from the necessity of immutability. He thus apparently identified necessity of immutability with what Thomas calls absolute necessity, the necessity which takes away free will. We find in Luther a similar lack of clarity concerning the concept of necessity. Luther notes in the margin of the *Sentences,* Lib. II, d. 26, c. 3, that from one point of view it is *impossible* for the blessed in heaven to choose good, but that they do not choose the good *necessarily,* although they are necessarily "in slavery to justice." The same is true for the damned in relation to evil. Both the blessed and the damned are in slavery, but in neither group is liberty diminished.[8] Luther recognizes that from another point of view one can say that the blessed choose the good necessarily. His hesitation indicates that he has an undifferentiated concept of necessity. Like Biel, he does not distinguish between absolute and conditional necessity as do Thomas Aquinas and other Scholastics.

In another marginal note Luther writes: "On the contrary, grace does not necessitate; it inclines."[9] Thomas Aquinas can agree with Luther that grace inclines the will but does not force the will or impose a necessity on it that would exclude freedom.[10] Yet, from the point of view of the infallible efficacy of grace and from the certitude of God's predestination, Thomas could say that grace necessitates the free will by necessity of infallibility or immutability.[11] If a theologian holds that grace inclines, but does not necessitate the will, but does not distinguish clearly absolute and conditional necessity, once he becomes aware, with Augustine and Thomas, of the most certain working of grace, he is liable to teach that grace *necessitates* the will. In other words, if he does not distinguish absolute and conditional necessity, he is liable to go from one extreme position to the other because he uses the concept necessity only in its absolute sense. We shall return to Luther's concept of necessity as we trace the development of his doctrine of *servum arbitrium.*

That Luther is not purely an Ockhamist at this early date is suggested by his readiness to criticize the "human reasons" of any "teacher in the Church" in the light of the supreme authority of the Bible.[12] Further indication of a certain degree of independence from the Ockhamist

---

8 WA 9, 71, 5-72. Cf. Rupp, *The Righteousness,* p. 99. Denifle, p. 507, takes this *glossa* as evidence that the early Luther held to a free choice by man in the work of salvation. He also cites WA 4, 295, 34, from the *First Lectures on the Psalms.*

9 WA 9, 62, 28.

10 I, q. 62, a. 3, ad 2.

11 I-II, q. 112, a. 3c.

12 WA 9, 45, 4; 46, 16.

school is found in Luther's handling of Lombard's doctrine of charity and the Holy Spirit.[13] He agrees with Lombard and Ockham that God himself is grace and that this uncreated grace is the sole basis of our redemption. He disagrees with Ockham's teaching, however, that, beyond the uncreated grace, there is still a created grace which can be considered to be a "habit" in the soul. The only *habitus* Luther recognizes is that of the Holy Spirit himself.[14] Keeping in mind Vignaux's warning that we should not look for too much self-sufficient thinking in Luther, the commentator of the *Sentences*,[15] we can agree fully with Grane, who says that it is clear that Luther "as early as 1509-1510 is preparing to rid himself of the Ockhamist thought pattern." [16]

B. *Dictata super Psalterium* (AUGUST, 1513—EASTER OR OCTOBER, 1515)

Several positions characteristic of Ockham and Biel are still evident in Luther's first *Lectures on the Psalms*.[17] The most important of these positions for our purpose is one which was not seen too clearly in the marginal notes on the *Sentences:* the Neo-Semipelagianism which the young Luther inherited from Biel and Ockham! Not only did Luther in the *Dictata* repeatedly affirm [18]—and extol [19]—the natural freedom of

---

[13] WA 9, 43, 2-8.

[14] Cf. Vignaux, *Luther Commentateur*, pp. 91ff.; Rupp, *The Righteousness*, p. 94; Grane, pp. 32ff.

[15] Cf. Lortz, I, p. 171.

[16] P. 377. This is the same conclusion reached by Scheel, *Luther*, II, p. 467: "Neben und unter occamistischen Formeln pulsiert ein Beben, das ernster ist als die occamistische Moralphilosophie . . . Den Dienst . . . haben der Lombarde und der durch ihn wirkende Afrikaner ihm geleistet, dass sie ihm trotz seiner occamistichen Schulerziehung, an der er noch nicht irre geworden war, ermöglichten . . . die Annäherung an eine Theologie zu erleichtern, die nicht nur das Elend, sondern auch die Gewalt der Sünde sich nicht durch Betrachtungen über die grundsätzliche Natur des Willens verschleiern liess."

[17] We must necessarily limit ourselves to a consideration of only one point of the "dogmatic" side of these lectures. For a penetrating study of the "existential" aspects, see Brandenburg, *Gericht und Evangelium* (Paderborn, 1960).

[18] Man's free choice is involved even in the work of salvation. Cf. *In Glossa* to Ps. 119: 109: "Anima mea in manibus meis semper: . . . Anima mea est in potestate mea et in libertate arbitrii possum eam perdere vel salvare eligendo vel reprobando legem tuam, q.d. licet ego sim liber ad utrumque, tamen 'legem tuam non sum oblitus.' Et hec glosa melior est. . . ." WA 4, 295, 19-35. Grane, pp. 299f. remarks: "Nach erneuter Überlegung hat also Luther gemeint, dass dieser Vers für libertas arbitrii spricht. . . . Es besteht kein Zweifel darüber, dass Luther hier an die ockhamistische Lehre vom Willen anknüpft." Cf. Kattenbusch, *Luthers Lehre vom unfreien Willen*, pp. 39ff.; Denifle, pp. 507f. On the inamissability of natural freedom see WA 9, 112, 34-38 (marginal notes to Anselm's *Opuscula:* 1513). That man is free "obicem ponere" and "gratiae resistere" is taught in Luther's *Sermo de propria sapientia et voluntate* of Dec. 26, 1514: WA 1, 32. In

the will, but he also passed on to his students the Ockham-Biel Neo-Semipelagian version of *meritum de congruo* and *facienti quod in se est.*
The following passage, Luther's Scholion to Ps. 113: 1, deserves to be cited in its entirety. It not only shows us the basic similarity between Luther's thought of early 1515 and the Neo-Semipelagian thought of Biel [20] on the decisive question of merit and the preparation for justification,[21] but it also provides us with a point of comparison by which we can measure Luther's radical rejection of this same position in his marginal notes to Gabriel Biel's main works and in his *Lectures on the Epistle to the Romans* written only a short time afterward:

The coming of Christ in the flesh was the result of the sheer mercy of God who promised him to us. This gift was not given in view of any merits of human nature nor was it refused because of any human demerits. Nevertheless there had to be a preparation and a disposition in order to receive him, and this actually happened throughout the Old Testament in Christ's ancestral lineage. That God promised his son was due to his mercy, but that he actually gave him was the result of his truth and faithfulness (*veritas et fidelitas*), as is said in the closing verse of the Book of Micah: "You will show truth to Jacob and mercy to Abraham, as you promised to our fathers from of old" (Vg.). He does not say "as we have deserved," but "as you promised." Hence, the fact that God makes himself our debtor stems from his merciful promise, not from the worth of the merits of human nature. All he requires of us is that we prepare ourselves so that we might be capable of his gift. . . . In the same way Christ comes to us spiritually through grace and comes in the future through glory, not because of our merits but because of the sheer promise of the merciful God. He promised the spiritual coming in the following way: "Ask and you shall receive; seek and you shall find; knock and it shall be opened to you. For everyone who seeks, finds, etc." Hence, the theologians rightly say (*recte dicunt Doctores*) that God infallibly gives grace to the man who does what he is able to do, and even though he cannot prepare himself for grace *de condigno,* since

---

Thesis 33 of the *Disputatio contra scholasticam theologiam* (1517), WA 1, 225, Luther rejects this view.

[19] WA 3, 331, 17ff. Cf. Grane, pp. 282, footnote 48; 289.

[20] Cf. Biel, II *Sent.*, d. 22, q. 2, art. 3, dub. 1; d. 27, q. un., dub. 4 (P); IV *Sent.*, d. 9, q. 2, art. 1; *Lect. super canone misse*, lect. 59 (P). These ideas are *not* the ideas of Thomas Aquinas. As Grane, p. 298, footnote 39 correctly notes: "Es ist geradezu peinlich, dass Kawerau hier auf Thomas von Aquin, *Summa Theologica* I-II, q. 112, art. 3 verweist, als ob Thomas dies lehrt. Leider hat Ficker diesen Hinweis übernommen, WA 56, 503, Anmerkung. Ebenso Link, *Das Ringen Luthers* . . . S. 176."

[21] Grane, p. 300, footnote 43 says that this section of the *Lectures on the Psalms* had to be written no later than the first half of 1515, before the marginal notes on Biel, for in the marginal notes "the opposition to Biel and his doctrine of the preparation for grace is formulated as sharply as possible."

this is disproportionate to him, he can, however, prepare himself for grace *de congruo* because of this promise of God and the agreement God has mercifully made.[22]

Does Luther here, in contrast to Biel, hold that the sinner's preparing himself is a work of God's grace? In the passage just cited, there is no mention of the need for grace preparing the will. However, in the Scholion to Ps. 118: 11 Luther writes: "He correctly seeks first the help of grace . . . For our resolution is nothing unless the grace of God disposes it." [23] There thus appears to be an unclarity similar to that which we have seen in Alexander, Bonaventure and Scotus. It is certain, as we have already noted concerning Luther's marginal notes to Peter Lombard, that Luther is wrestling with himself and with the theology which he has been taught. We feel however that Grane has not proven his assertion that, despite the retention of terminology, Luther has broken through the disposition-framework of Biel. "It is absolutely clear," asserts Grane, "that the insight which Luther attained in his first *Lectures on the Psalms* represents a complete break with Ockhamism." [24] Bandt comes closer to the truth, we believe, when he says that Luther's continued use of *facere quod in se est* and *meritum de congruo* in the *Lectures on the Psalms* simply shows that he was not yet able to see all the consequences that flowed from his present repudiation of the outlook he once held. "Fundamentally, however, the new insight is already there: God himself and he *alone* it is who moves man to repentance and to a humble acknowledgment of the divine judgment." [25]

---

[22] WA 4, 261, 25-262, 4; cf. WA 4, 312, 40; 329; 344.

[23] WA 4, 309.

[24] Pp. 299-302. Grane, pp. 305f. also speaks too absolutely about Luther's concept of grace that is found in the *Dictata*. Besides the concept of grace as *misericordia Dei* Luther also knows of the *gratia auxilians* and *disponens*. In WA 31/1, 473, 18f. and WA 56, 220, for example, Luther speaks also of *gratia infusa*. Grane, pp. 191f., and 204, says that Luther's biblical concept of *voluntas* and *obedientia* in the *Dictata,* in which the *spontanea, liberalis, hilaris* character of the will is emphasized, was seen by Luther as being "in ausgesprochenem Gegensatz zu dem philosophisch-theologischen Begriff der Scholastik." Grane, pp. 193-196 notes that such a voluntary, spontaneous and joyous obedience as is described in WA 3, 17, 1ff.; 30, 9ff.; 286, 17ff.; 336, 34f.; 467, 21ff., is also familiar to such medieval theologians as Bernard and Gerson. But he overlooks the fact that such a concept of obedience can also be found in the *doctor communis.* Cf. Thomas, I-II, q. 100, a. 9, ad 3: "quicumque cum tristitia operatur, non volens operatur" and Luther, WA 3, 26, 6ff.: "semiplena et languida voluntas non est voluntas." See also Thomas, *In Rom.,* cap. 8, n. 639; *In II Cor.,* cap. 9, n. 332.

[25] *Luthers Lehre vom verborgenen Gott* (Berlin, 1958), p. 62. He cites WA 3, 594, 10; 4, 38, 20 and 38; 115, 21; 461, 26. Cf. E. Vogelsang, *Die Anfänge von Luthers Christologie nach der ersten Psalmenvorlesung* (Berlin, 1929), pp. 122f.

It is not just the old terminology, as Grane suggests, but also some of the old ideas that still remain. Link [26] has also tried to interpret the text we have cited at length in a non-Bielian way, but Normann's view that Luther, even in the *Dictata,* retains a "residue of Pelagian Catholicism" seems to us more tenable.[27]

II. LUTHER'S BREAK WITH NEO-SEMIPELAGIANISM IN THE MARGINAL NOTES TO GABRIEL BIEL'S *COLLECTORIUM,* THE *LECTURES ON THE EPISTLE TO THE ROMANS* AND THE *DISPUTATIONES*

A. *Marginal Notes to Gabriel Biel: Collectorium in quattuor libros sententiarum* and *Sacri canonis missae expositio* (1515)

Here we find an unmistakable break with Biel's teaching and with his own earlier position on the power of fallen man's will. In a marginal note to Biel's statement: "The human will of the pilgrim is able to love God above all things by its natural powers," [28] Luther writes:

Consequently the will is neither sick nor does it require the grace of God. All of this is based on the proud principle of free will—as if free will could, by its own power, choose to follow opoosite paths when it is prone solely to evil. Even if it should overcome this proneness, it at least does so unwillingly and unlovingly.[29]

Again, alongside the sentence in Biel's printed text: "How astonishing it is that the will can conform itself to an erroneous dictate [of conscience] and not to a correct one," [30] we find Luther's sarcastic comment: "Rather, it is astonishing that you say this and agree so much with Pelagius. As if nature were not prone to evil." [31] Luther, in rejecting

---

26 *Das Ringen Luthers.* . . , p. 198.

27 *Viljefrihet og forutsbestemmelse.* . . , p. 98. Cf. E. Erikstein, *Luthers Prädestinationslehre geschichtlich dargestellt.* . . , p. 204. Whether the humility-theology that emerges in the *Dictata* is a pre-Reformation residue connected with the doctrine of man's preparation for justification, or whether it is nothing else than the Reformation doctrine of justification itself is a question that is still disputed. For the present state of the discussion see Grane, pp. 295f.; 321 and Brandenburg, *Gericht und Evangelium,* pp. 59-69.

28 Biel, III *Sent.,* d. 27, q. un., art. 3, dub. 2 (O).

29 From the text of H. Degering, in: *Festgabe der Kommission zur Herausgabe der Werke M. Luthers* (1933), pp. 14f.; corrected by L. Grane, p. 359, by a comparison with the original edition of the *Collectorium* containing Luther's notes: "Et per consequens non est infirma nec eget gratia dei. Omnia ista ex stulto fundamento procedunt liberi arbitrii, quasi liberum arbitrium possit ex se ipso in utrumque oppositorum, cum solum ad malum sit pronum. Aut si contra pronitatem se erigit, manet saltem invita: ut per hoc nec amativa."

30 III *Sent.,* d. 27, q. un., art. 3, prop. 1 (Q).

31 Cf. Degering, p. 15; Grane, p. 362.

Biel's teaching, returns to the Catholic tradition of Paul, Augustine, Orange II, Bernard and Thomas Aquinas [32] according to which fallen man's nature is corrupted, enslaved and prone to evil until it is healed and liberated by grace. In reminding Biel of the evilness of fallen man, of the proneness of his will to evil, Luther's doctrinal concerns are completely Catholic. When he bypasses the question of the possibility of the fallen will to will naturally good acts, and simply asserts that the *liberum arbitrium* is prone "only to evil," [33] Luther neither follows nor attacks the concept of natural goodness taught by Thomas Aquinas. He is only returning to the fully traditional language of Augustine and Orange II.[34]

B. *Lectures on the Epistle to the Romans* (EASTER OR NOVEMBER, 1515 TO SEPTEMBER, 1516)

By the end of 1515 Luther's theological breakthrough—or breakaway (primarily from Neo-Semipelagian Ockhamism)—was in full progress. Was it in this year that he had his critical "tower experience"? Without going into this perennially debated question,[35] and without disputing Ebeling's remark that the *Lectures on Romans* contain "hardly anything

---

[32] Cf. chapter 6, footnote 166; Thomas, I-II, q. 109, a. 3, speaking of the love of God "super omnia," says: ". . . in statu naturae corruptae homo ab hoc deficit secundum appetitum voluntatis rationalis, quae propter corruptionem naturae sequitur bonum privatum, nisi sanetur per gratiam Dei."

[33] One cannot say that Luther's concept of "natura viciata" is Manichaean, as many Catholic apologists of the Counter-Reformation have unjustly asserted: John Fisher, Erasmus, Albert Pighius, among others. Cf. Jörgensen, pp. 79-82. R.-C. Gerest, "Du Serf-arbitre à la liberté du chrétien," in: *Lumière et Vie*, 12 (1963), 90f. has recently implied that Luther denies the natural integrity of fallen man. Any charge that Luther is a Manichaean must consider three things: (1) not only Luther, but also Thomas Aquinas and Augustine speak of a "natura corrupta;" (2) in his *Lectures on Galatians* of 1535 Luther explicitly says that the natural qualities ("naturalia") of fallen man are sound and incorrupt ("integra"); it is the "spiritualia" that are corrupt: WA 40/1, 293; WA 18, 753, 6-15; (3) in Theses 8 and 9 of the *Disputatio contra scholasticam theologiam* Luther clearly distanced himself from the Manichaean understanding of *natura viciata*.

[34] Cf. the excursus: The Different Meanings of "Sin," "Good" and "Virtue" in Augustine.

[35] When speaking of the "tower experience" it is necessary to remember, as Bornkamm, "Luther: I," RGG, 4, 482f. points out, that Luther's new insight "nicht ein einmaliges Durchbruchserlebnis darstellt." Ebeling, "Luther:II," RGG, 4, 498, reminds us that Luther's basic Reformation discovery is the fruit of a theological transition along a broad front and that his breakthrough was neither the absolute beginning nor the end of the transition which turned Luther into a Reformer. The most complete survey of the discussion concerning the date of Luther's Reformation turning-point has been made by O. Pesch, "Zur Frage nach Luthers reformatorischer Wende," in: *Catholica*, 20 (1966), 216-246; 264-280. A short summary in English can be found in McDonough, pp. 17ff.

. . . that one does not already meet incipiently in the *First Lectures on the Psalms,*" [36] we simply call attention to the fact that these lectures demonstrate how rapidly Luther's thought was now developing. A number of points from this course of lectures are relevant to our investigation.

1. Whereas in the *Marginal Notes* to Biel Luther only hints at Biel's Pelagianism, in the *Lectures on Romans* he energetically denounces as Pelagian Biel's doctrine of "doing what is in one," and a phrase reminiscent of Bradwardine, maintains that nearly the whole Church has fallen into this error:

For although there are now none that profess Pelagianism and call themselves Pelagians, there are very many who in fact and in what they believe are Pelagians even if they are not aware of it. For example, there are those who think that unless one attributes the freedom of decision (*libertas arbitrii*), before grace, "the power to do what is in him," one sins, in case he sins, because God forces him to sin so that he, therefore, sins necessarily. Even though it is altogether impious to think so, they are so sure of themselves and so bold as to reckon that if they form a good intention, they will infallibly obtain God's infused grace. Thereupon they go about with the feeling of great security and, of course, they are certain that the good works they do are acceptable to God. They do not feel that they need to implore grace, because they are no longer fearful or anxious. They are also free from any fear that by being of this mind they are perhaps in the wrong, but they are certain that they are right in what they are doing (Is., Ch. 44). Why? Because they do not understand that God lets the ungodly sin even when they do good works. Certainly, they are then not forced to commit a sin, but they are doing only what they want to do according to their good intention. . . . Hence they that really do good works . . . know that man cannot do anything from himself. Hence, it is utterly absurd and it means strongly to support the

---

[36] RGG, 4, 501. Grane, pp. 331ff. is again guilty of incautious generalizing when he says that Luther in the *Lectures on Romans* has "totally" broken with the Scholastics. If any Scholastic terms remain, asserts Grane, they have a "completely new meaning." He says this, for example, of Luther's use of the term "opera praeparatoria," but he does not try to prove that this term has a completely new meaning. He further completely overlooks what Luther says about it in WA 56, 202. Grane seems to be too influenced by the assertions of E. Ellwein in the Munich edition of the *Römerbriefvorlesung* (1957), p. 486, footnote 18 and p. 488, footnote 22. Cf. Rupp, pp. 184f. Grane tries to demonstrate his thesis by pointing to Luther's apparent lack of certainty in speaking of "ignorantia invincibilis" in WA 56, 198f. When Luther says that the invincible ignorance of pagans is an excusing cause, and yet a few lines later asserts that ignorance of the law is no excuse, this apparent discrepancy is not to be explained by saying that Luther gives an entirely new meaning to a traditional concept, but by noting that Luther uses "ignorance" in two different senses: First, as ignorance of the *positive* law of circumcision, and second, as ignorance of the innate *natural* law. Ignorance of the first can be excused and tolerated but not ignorance of the second.

Pelagian error to hold the view that is expressed in the well-known statement: "God infallibly infuses grace in one who does what is in him" if the phrase "to do what is in him" is to be understood to mean "to do or to be able to do anything." Hence, it is not to be wondered at that almost the whole church is undermined, namely, by the trust one puts into that which this one sentence expresses.[37]

Luther's concern here is clearly Catholic. Like Augustine, he is struggling against those who so exalt the free will that the necessity of the grace of God is ignored. His theological language is also unobjectionable. For, even though he says that the *impii* sin even in their good works, it is clear from this very phrase that he is not rejecting the concept of natural goodness in unbelievers, but is simply employing an Augustinian concept of sin which is broader than that which was common in non-Augustinian Scholasticism. This is an effective way for Luther, as it was for Augustine, to emphasize that no naturally good acts or virtues—however glorious they may appear in the eyes of men—have any value whatever *coram Deo,* that is, for salvation. He doesn't deny the existence of naturally good works or of human righteousness; he only denies that these can save us.[38] Like Augustine, Luther here distinguishes between the good works and intentions of sinners (*opera bona impiorum; intentio bona*) and works which are *truly* good (*vere bona*).

The vigor of Luther's denunciation of the Neo-Semipelagianism that he had learned recalls the paradox pointed out by Lortz: "Luther's campaign against justification by works is a campaign against his *own,* innermost pre-Reformation conceptions." [39]

2. For the first time we see Luther explicitly speaking of *servum arbitrium:*

The power of free decision insofar as it is not under the sway of grace has no ability whatsoever to realize righteousness, but it is necessarily in

---

[37] WA 56, 502f.; cf. *ibid.,* 274f. Tr. W. Pauck, *Luther: Lectures on Romans* (Philadelphia, 1961), pp. 390f. Cf. Biel, *Expositio,* lect., 59 (P): "Haec facienti deus gratiam suam tribuit necessario."

[38] On the "sinfulness of all good works" see P. Althaus, *Paulus und Luther über den Menschen,* 3rd ed. (Gütersloh, 1958), pp. 122-127. On the necessity of works for salvation see Althaus, "Sola fide nunquam sola. . . ," in: *Una Sancta,* 16 (1961), 227-235.

[39] I, 176. To Bellucci, "Faith and Justification in the Early Works of Luther," *Unitas,* vol. XVII, n. 2 (1965), 120, Luther does not appear "so grossly ignorant of Catholic doctrine or infected by Pelagianism." He suggests that Luther's dissatisfaction was not with any "Pelagian" (we prefer to say Neo-Semipelagian) concept of justification but with "the true Catholic doctrine of Justification." At least insofar as the question of the *initium iustificationis* is concerned we must disagree sharply with Bellucci on the basis of texts which we have examined in this and the preceding chapter.

sins. Hence, Blessed Augustine is right, when, in his book against Julian, he calls it "the enslaved, rather than free, will." But when it has received grace, the power of decision really becomes free, at all events in respect to salvation. To be sure, it is always free according to its nature, but only with respect to that which is in its power and is inferior to it but not with respect to that which is superior to it, since it is held captive in sins and then cannot choose the good according to God.[40]

We find this passage to be wholly in conformity with Augustine's concept of *servum arbitrium* and with the Catholic tradition.[41] Several points are to be noted:

(a) Luther's recent discovery of Augustine's anti-Pelagian writings in the eighth volume of the Amorbach edition of 1506 played a great role in his attacks on late Scholastic theology and in the development of his own thought in the *Lectures on the Epistle to the Romans.*[42]

(b) The passage from Augustine's *Contra Iulianum* which he cites here as a patristic basis for his *servum arbitrium* doctrine is used in the same way in the *Disputatio* of 1516,[43] the *Heidelberg Disputation* of 1518,[44] in his work *Contra malignum Ioh. Eccii iudicium* of 1519 and in *De servo arbitrio.*[45]

(c) The main concern of Luther in this passage is to emphasize that the sinner is a captive to his sins, that is, he is not able to choose what is truly good, *bonum secundum Deum.*[46]

(d) It is by grace that we are made free in the proper sense, that is, for salvation. This is basically the understanding of freedom in John 8: 32, 36.

(e) There is no hint here of any determinism which excludes man's natural freedom: man is said to be always free according to the things of this earth (*se inferiora*), but not concerning the things of heaven (*se supra*).[47]

---

[40] WA 56, 385.

[41] Cf. the excursus: The Meaning of "servum arbitrium" in Augustine.

[42] Cf. A. Hamel, II (Gütersloh, 1935), pp. 130ff.; Rupp, *The Righteousness,* p. 160; Grane, pp. 378f. For reasons that we have given in our excursus: Synergism and Semipelagianism, we maintain that it is incorrect for Hamel, I, p. 132, to say that Augustine retained a vestige of Semipelagianism by accepting human merits, regardless of the improper sense in which he understood them.

[43] WA 1, 148.

[44] WA 1, 360.

[45] WA 18, 665, 10f.

[46] The implication is clear that the captive to sin can do something that is "bonum secundum hominem."

[47] Ebeling's formulation in RGG, 4, 501: "Der Wille des sündigen Menschen ist notwendig unfrei," is therefore misleading. Denifle, p. 510 likewise needs to be corrected when he says, in reference to this text: "According to Luther . . . the freedom of the will is completely destroyed by sin."

(f) The meaning of "it is necessarily in sins" (*necessario est in peccatis*) is clarified a few lines later when Luther writes: ". . . nobody is a sinner by coercion and against his will . . . for such are unavoidably (*necessario*) in sin by the immutability of necessity but not of coercion." [48] A sinner sins willingly and, we may assume, freely. But since he is unable to escape his sinful captive condition by himself, he can be said to be in his sins by a necessity of immutability. From the context it is clear that necessity of immutability, for Luther, does not exclude free will, since "liberum quidem semper est naturaliter" (it is always naturally free).

3. Despite his clear affirmation: "it is always naturally free," Luther, in his commentary on the same verse of Romans,[49] makes statements about necessity and contingency which indicate a departure from the Scholastic understanding of these concepts. As a result, a basic unclarity or confusion is introduced into his thought on predestination, necessity and free will, a confusion that we have not found in the biblical, Augustinian, Thomistic and Catholic doctrine of slavery to sin or *servum arbitrium* which is always a doctrine of grace *and* free will. This confusion eventually leads Luther to say in *De servo arbitrio* that, from the fact of God's foreknowledge, "free will is knocked flat and utterly shattered." [50]

The first indication we have that Luther's concept of necessity and contingency is inadequate is when, failing to distinguish kinds of necessity, he reaches the conclusion: the elect are not saved contingently but necessarily.[51] Here we have an either-or conclusion—and it is based on the either-or premise: *either* salvation is based on God's decree *or* on man's will and works. Unless it is based on God's decree, salvation would be contingent and uncertain.[52] By failing to use the Scholastic

---

[48] WA 56, 386.

[49] Rom. 8: 28; WA 56, 381ff.

[50] WA 18, 615, 12-15. It would take us too far from our course to trace this concept in all of the Scholastic "schools." A special study is still needed to see if there were antecedents to Luther's critique of the two types of necessity commonly distinguished by the Scholastics. The only special study of this question is the one written in Swedish by H. Olsson, "Det dubbla necessitas-begreppet i skolastiken och Luthers kritik darav," in: *Till Gustav Aulen* (Lund-Stockholm, 1939), pp. 279-310. Cf. Vorster, pp. 284-316. On the distinction itself see chapter 4 above, footnote 74; chapter 6, footnote 22, 60 and 118. See also Scotus, I *Sent.*, d. 39, q. 5, n. 35; Biel, III *Sent.*, d. 20, 2. un., art. 1 (B).

[51] WA 56, 381.

[52] *Ibid.*: "Quia si propositum Dei non esset et in nostro arbitrio et nostris operibus staret salus, contingenter staret . . . (N)on meritis nostris, sed electione mera et immutabili voluntate sua . . . salvet." We have already seen that either-or thinking in this question is foreign not only to the Scholastics but also to

distinction between absolute and conditional necessity Luther is unable
to say with the schoolmen that God moves some things necessarily and
some contingently, and that even those things which happen contingently are known infallibly by God and from the point of view of God's
knowledge and will they are said to happen by necessity of infallibility
or immutability. Such necessity is a conditional or suppositional necessity, which does not exclude free will. Luther has not only departed from
the generally held Scholastic concept of necessity, but he has also lost
the less precise but no less clearly differentiated understanding of necessity with which Augustine responded to Cicero's argument: *either* God's
foreknowledge *or* man's free will.[53] Luther was aware of the distinction
between the two types of necessity, but he refused to use it because he
did not see how it helped clarify the doctrine of predestination.[54]

After affirming several times that the elect are saved necessarily because of God's immutable will and love (*voluntas immutabilis; dilectio
immutabilis; inflexibilis et firma suae praedestinationis voluntas*), and
that only through the knowledge of the immutability of God's predestining will can man's despair be overcome,[55] Luther asks: "Now where is

---

Augustine and to Scripture. Cf. Augustine, *De gr. et lib. arb.*, 5, 12: ". . . id est,
non solus, sed gratia Dei mecum; ac per hoc nec gratia Dei sola nec ipse solus,
sed gratia Dei cum illo." We should remember, however, that for Augustine and
for Thomas the basis of predestination and election lies solely in God's gracious
and merciful will. Man's *personal salvation* is another matter, since God predestines that man be saved by grace moving and working with man's free will.
Luther does not keep clear in this text the distinction between predestination and
the effect of predestination—salvation; the former is *ex sola voluntate Dei*, the
latter is *ex gratia et libero arbitrio*.

[53] *De civitate Dei*, 5, 10; cf. cap. 4, footnote 74. Rupp, *The Righteousness*,
p. 186, gives the impression that Luther is only rejecting a distinction of "medieval thinkers."

[54] Vorster, pp. 285-288, says that here and in DSA, WA 18, 616, 1-617, 22;
722, 1-29, Luther does not deny the validity of the distinction. Although Luther
doesn't see how it has any revelance for the doctrine of predestination, he does
accept it as a means of showing that God's being is necessary, whereas created
being is contingent, and that God's action imposes on man not a *necessitas coactionis* but *immutabilitatis*. Vorster neglects to point out, however, that these were
not the reasons for which the Scholastics, following a long tradition reaching back
over Boethius and Augustine into Aristotle, distinguished the two necessities.
Their main purpose in using it was to show that there was a kind of necessity
which did not exclude free will.

[55] WA 56, 382. Luther's characteristic search for certitude of salvation is the
underlying motive in these reflections. Holl, I, p. 112 writes: "Erwählungsgewissheit hat er (beim gewöhnlichen Christen) nie für erreichbar gehalten und trotz-
dem 'Heilsgewissheit' gelehrt." H. Bandt, *Luthers Lehre vom verborgenen Gott*,
p. 161, seems to say that Luther already in the *Lectures on Romans*: WA 56,
382, 24, held to the possibility of certitude of election. Cf. Pannenberg, "Der
Einfluss der Anfechtungserfahrung auf den Prädestinationsbegriff Luthers," in:

our justice? Where are our good works? Where are freedom of the will and the contingency of things?" [56] Of importance here is not only the fact that Luther seems to see an opposition between God's certain, predestining will and man's works and free will, but also between the immutability of God's will and the contingency of things (*contingentia rerum*).[57]

Why does Luther think that the immutability of God's will excludes the "contingency of things?" Thomas held that God's will was indeed immutable, but he also upheld the contingency of some things.[58] He asserted just as strongly as Luther that whatever God wills and knows happens infallibly and most certainly.[59] And even though he will admit that man achieves the grace intended for him by God with a necessity of infallibility,[60] he still insists that this infallibility and certainty—and this kind of conditional necessity—do not take away the contingence of man's will.[61] This paradoxical conclusion is the result of Thomas' insistence on the dialectic of God's infallible, immutable and most efficacious will and man's free will. If we consider only the free will—the proximate cause—says Thomas, then man's salvation is not certain; but if we look at the first cause, predestination itself, then salvation is certain.[62] This kind of thinking is indeed more subtle and more paradoxical than Luther's, but it does far greater justice to the divine-human dialectic than does Luther's either/or: *either* salvation is necessary and certain *or* it is contingent; if salvation is necessary then there is no room for contingency or free will.

We have re-stated Thomas' position to emphasize that Thomas, no less than Luther, held to the immutability of God's will and to the infallibility and certitude of predestination. It seems highly unlikely, therefore, that Luther, in the passage we are now considering is attacking the predestination doctrine of Thomas. More probably, it seems, Luther has failed to understand the nature of the Scholastic distinction between necessity of the thing consequent and necessity of consequence.

KuD (1957), 120-124. Schlink, "Der theologische Syllogismus als Problem der Prädestinationslehre," pp. 314f. maintains: "Es ist völlig deutlich, dass in den neutestamentlichen Texten die Erwählungsgewissheit der Glaubenden bezeugt ist."

[56] WA 56, 382, 17.

[57] *Ibid.*

[58] I, q. 19, a. 8c and ad 3; cf. I, q. 23, a. 6, ad 3; *De Ver.*, q. 23, a. 4, ad 1 and above, chapter 6, footnote 121.

[59] I, q. 23, a. 6c.

[60] I-II, q. 112, a. 3c.

[61] I, q. 23, a. 6c.

[62] *De Ver.*, q. 6, a. 3c. A difference of emphasis and terminology is seen *In Rom.*, cap. 9, lect. 3, n. 775. Cf. below footnote 79.

Evidence for this view is found in the passage immediately following the one we have just cited:

Our theologians, to be sure, subtle as they are, imagine they have accomplished something, though I do not know what it could be, when they adduce in this context their notion of the "contingent." They say that the elect are necessarily saved, namely, by the necessity of the consequence but not by consequent necessity. This is nothing but empty talk, especially in view of the fact that they want to understand or at least give occasion to understand the concept of "consequent contingency" to mean that salvation can or cannot come by our decision. Thus I, too, once understood the matter.

This concept of "the contingency of the consequent" is irrelevant to the theme under discussion. Moreover, it is meaningless to ask whether this "consequent" is contingent, as if (and this is implied in the question) it could be necessary, inasmuch as only God is necessary in this sense. Therefore, it is a ridiculous addition if one says: The elect are necessarily saved by the necessity of the consequence, but not by consequent necessity, i.e., the consequent is not God, or: because it is not God, therefore salvation is by the necessity of consequence. What else does "to be contingent" mean than "to be a creature" and not God? They twist the understanding by turning the necessity of an occurrence into the necessity of the essence of a thing. This equivocation is here out of place. For no one raises the question or doubts whether a created thing is contingent in its being, i.e., whether it is mutable or whether it is God and thus immutable. But the question is about the necessity of the sequel or whether what God has predestined will necessarily happen, and they concede that it will. And yet they make this superfluous addition, after they have said all that can be said. For if you know that something will definitely happen by the necessity of the consequence, what does it matter if you know further whether, at this particular place, it is contingent or not? . . . They who raise this question are asking therefore whether a contingency can hinder the necessity of a chain of events, and they make the presupposition that they know the contingency, and you teach by a *petitio principii* that there are contingent things and that they do not hinder the necessary occurrence of a sequence of events. Your answer is correct, but what you teach is superfluous and irrelevant.

Simple people put the question at least in this way: Does the contingency of an event constitute an impediment of the certain predestination of God? The answer must be: With God there simply is no contingency, but only with us, because not even a leaf of a tree falls to the ground without the will of the Father.[63]

The following conclusions may be drawn from this passage:

---

[63] WA 56, 382, 21-383, 19. Tr. W. Pauck, pp. 248ff. Cf. Rupp, *The Righteousness*, pp. 186f.

(a) Luther thinks the distinction of the two necessities is a matter of "empty words" because it can give the impression that we are saved or not depending on how we use our free will. Thus, his either-or thinking about the relationship of God's and man's will in salvation is the cause, not the result of, his refusal to make use of the distinction in the question of predestination.

(b) Luther correctly sees that "contingency of the thing consequent" implies the activity of free will,[64] but he introduces a serious note of confusion when he identifies contingency with what Aristotle, Augustine and Thomas would have called chance or fortune.[65] When Luther says "nothing is absolutely contingent in God's eyes but only in our own" (*nulla est contingentia apud Deum simpliciter, sed tantum coram nobis*) he says of contingency precisely what Augustine and Thomas say of chance or fortune! [66] And when Luther says that not a leaf falls to the ground apart from the will of the Father, all Christians who believe in God's providence would agree; but they would not agree that this is an argument against the contingency or freedom of man's will. Both Augustine and Thomas admit that the contingent will is subject to providence and they even admit that a *certain* kind of necessity is compatible with the free will. Luther, then, is combatting a concept of free will which we do not find in Augustine or Aquinas, a free will which is removed from God's providential direction. He seems to be rather combatting a *contingentia* such as Thomas Bradwardine opposed, one which is identified with a chance that is outside the order of God's providence.[67] Impor-

---

64 Cf. Thomas Aquinas, I, q. 14, a. 13 *sed contra*.

65 Cf. Augustine, *De civ. Dei*, 5, 1 and Thomas Aquinas, I, q. 116, a. 1c and ad 2. In DSA, WA 18, 616, 7-12, Luther maintains that something happens *contingenter* which proceeds from a contingent and mutable will, "qualis in Deo non est." Again, we find no distinction as to whether God's will is absolutely immutable, in which case it could will nothing freely, or whether it is immutable *ex suppositione*. Cf. Thomas, I, q. 19, aa. 3 and 7. M. Schüler, "Luthers Gottesbegriff nach seiner Schrift De servo arbitrio," in: *Zeitschr. f. Kirchengesch.*, 55 (1936), 548 cites WA 18, 632 and 717ff., to show that Luther attributes to God the highest contingency in the sense that God's will is absolutely free. On the other hand, Luther holds in WA 18, 616, 7-12, that a contingent act (*opus*) can only be considered to be one that happens to us by chance ("velut casus") or without reflexion. Thomas, I, q. 23, a. 4, however, does not hesitate to say that some effects or things happen contingently because God has prepared contingent causes for them. Cf. chapter 10, nn. 130f.

66 Cf. WA 7, 146, 30-147, 2. When the Munich Edition of the *Römerbrief-vorlesung* and of DSA translate "contingenter" or "contingentia" as "des Zufalls freies Spiel" (MA-DSA, p. 24) or as "zufällig" (MA-DSA, p. 25; MA-Römerbr., pp. 290f.), this is certainly an incorrect translation of the high Scholastic meaning of *contingentia*, but it seems to convey what Luther understands by the term.

67 Cf. chapter 7, p. 195.

tant to notice here is that these comments are not written by Luther the existentialist, but by Luther the Scholastic.[68] These statements concerning *necessitas* and *contingentia* are not formulated according to the "structure of personal encounter," but according to the "structure of description." [69]

(c) Both here and in the corresponding passage of *De servo arbitrio* [70] Luther seeks to dismiss the distinction of the two necessities by a *reductio ad absurdum*. He tells us that the only result of this distinction is that it shows us that we are not God. For when we say that some things do not happen by *necessitas consequentis,* he asks, what else are we saying than that the thing consequent is a creature and not God? [71] Through this effort at a *reductio ad absurdum* Luther shows us that his understanding of the meaning of *necessitas consequentis* is not the same as that of Boethius, Thomas Aquinas, Scotus and other Scholastics.

Boethius,[72] although using the term *necessitas simplex* or *naturae*—as opposed to *necessitas conditionis*—instead of *necessitas consequentis* or *absoluta,* gives as an example of *necessitas simplex* the fact that all men are mortal.

Thomas says: "Something is said to be absolutely necessary because of a necessary relationship which the terms of a proposition have to each other. For example, man is an animal; every whole is greater than

---

[68] It is not true that Luther's personal vision as a believer "does not allow itself to be smoothly harmonized with the previous objectivizing manner of thinking of theology," as A. Peters, says, *Glaube und Werk* (Berlin-Hamburg, 1962), pp. 258f. On the contrary, Luther's "objectivizing" statements, at least in the passage we are considering, do not permit themselves to be harmonized with the previous "objectivizing" statements of Thomas Aquinas, *et al*. With Pesch, "Ein katholisches Anliegen an evangelische Darstellungen der Theologie Luthers," in: *Catholica,* 16 (1962), 310, we agree with Peters that every attempt to present Luther's thought in a purely objective, systematic way does violence "from the very outset to Luther's actual style of theologizing." But as Pesch, p. 312, has rightly pointed out, Luther is not an existential theologian always and in every sentence! To illustrate this he cites a central passage from DSA, WA 18, 615, 12-15, which is very similar to our text. Pesch writes: although the existential meaning of such a passage is quite clear, "dennoch handelt es sich um eine 'objektivierende' Aussage über das Verhältnis des Menschen in seinem Tun zu Gott in seinem Tun, eine Aussage, die sich zwar nicht dem sachlich Gemeinten, wohl aber ihrer 'objectiven' Struktur nach in jede katholisch-scholastische Denkstruktur einfügen liesse": *ibid.,* p. 313.

[69] Cf. Schlink, *The Coming Christ,* pp. 172-75.

[70] WA 18, 616, 13-617, 20. Whereas in the *Lectures on Romans* Luther calls the distinction "vacua verba" and "impertinens," in *DSA* he calls it "nihil," "illusio" and "ludibrium."

[71] As Luther says in WA 18, 617, 6-9: "Quid autem istis ludibriis verborum efficunt? Id scilicet, facta res non est necessaria, id est, non habet essentiam necessariam, hoc est aliud nihil dicere quam: res facta non est Deus ipse."

[72] Cf. above chapter 4, footnote 74.

its part, and the like." [73] For Thomas, absolute necessity, or *necessitas consequentis,* is the necessity in the thing itself which excludes contingent action or alternative mode of being. It does not imply that the creature *exists* by absolute necessity as does God. This is abundantly clear, for example, in the "third way" of the *Summa Theologiae,* I, q. 2, a. 3.

There is an ambiguity of language here which Luther unfortunately failed to overcome. The meaning of *absoluta* in the distinction we are discussing is that we consider the thing itself *absoluta,* that is *to the exclusion of* all conditions and suppositions which are not by definition inherent in the nature of the creature. The very fact that we are speaking of *creatures* shows that the concept of *necessitas consequentis* or *absoluta* in no way implies that the creature has any existence or operation *absoluta*—apart from—God's creative power. There is no suggestion whatever in this distinction that man is "absolutely free" or enjoys absolute existence in the sense of independence from God. Thus it is a serious misunderstanding of this Scholastic distinction to suppose, with Luther, that it results only in showing that a creature is not God. The effect of the distinction was to enable the Scholastics clearly to affirm man's free will, while at the same time affirming the infallible working of God's creating and saving activity. Because Luther rejects the distinction he is not only unable to say that salvation involves a free decision by man, but he also makes us wonder if he is really consistent in holding that man has free will in mundane affairs.

It should be noted that the distinction is not a *proof* of the existence of free will or the fact that some things happen necessarily and some contingently. It presupposes the arguments for the free will based on Scripture and reason and simply seeks to respond to a difficulty arising from a belief in God's infallibly certain knowledge of all human events and in the most efficacious power of his will which providentially directs all things. It deals with the difficulty by pointing out, as Augustine and Boethius did long before the Scholastics, that the certain knowledge that we—or God—have of some event in no way implies that the event is produced by necessity of nature (*absoluta, consequentis*) *or* by the contingent causality of man's free will. The *mode* of the action must be determined in other ways.

Neither does the distinction explain the mystery of the relation between divine and human activity. Rather, it enables us to state the mystery correctly and to retain it by affirming both God's transcendent, unfailing working and man's free will.

[73] *De Ver.,* q. 23, a. 4, ad 1.

The explanation of the "two necessities" given by Huter, a representative of Lutheran orthodoxy, which is related to us by Ellwein,[74] agrees, as Ellwein says, with the old Scholastic understanding of these concepts—but it has little resemblance to Luther's explanation of the terms in either the *Lectures on Romans* or in *De servo arbitrio*. It is therefore surprising when we find attributed to Luther a fairly accurate explanation of the distinction in Anton Lauterbach's collection of Luther's *Table Talk* (1538).[75]

(d) Luther's personal note: "Thus I, too, once understood the matter," reveals his belief that he had lived in error when he formerly held "that salvation can . . . come by our decision." Luther had been trained in the Neo-Semipelagian theology which exaggerated the role of free will in salvation. Instead of reacting against this doctrine with the traditional Catholic doctrine of grace *and* free will, Luther already gives indication that he will seek a more radical method of destroying this error: by denying altogether the role of free will in salvation.

4. That Luther has not actually taken the radical step just mentioned can be seen from his comments on Rom. 9, 16:

We must not understand this to mean: The only thing that matters is God's mercy and therefore it is not necessary for anyone to will and to run, but we must take it to say: A man owes his ability to will and to run, not to his own power, but to the mercy of God who gave him this power to will and to run. Without it, man could neither will nor run.[76] Now it does not follow from this text that a man's running and willing amount to nothing, but what follows from it is that they do not come from his own strength.[77]

Here Luther might still be considered to be in the tradition of Augustine[78] and Thomas Aquinas[79] for whom free will by itself is powerless regarding salvation. Nevertheless, when it is empowered by God's grace, it does take part in the work salvation. It should be noted, however,

---

[74] Commentary to the Munich Edition of the *Römerbriefvorlesung*, p. 503, footnote 55.

[75] Cf. Clemen, vol. 8, p. 198; Nr. 3915.

[76] WA 56, 398, 9-14.

[77] P. 399.

[78] Cf. *De div. quaest, ad Simpl.*, 1, 2, 12; *Enchir.*, 32; *De gr. et lib. arb.*, 7, 16. These texts had a considerable influence on Luther's *Marginal Notes to the Sentences*, Lib. II, d. 26, c. 2: WA 9, 70f.

[79] Cf. *In Rom.*, cap. 9, lect. 3, n. 775: ". . . ipsa salus hominis, non est, volentis neque currentis, id est non debetur aliqui per aliquam eius voluntatem. . . , sed est miserentis Dei, id est, procedit ex sola Dei misericordia." This interpretation is directly in line with Augustine's exegesis. Cf. esp. *ibid.*, n. 777 and Augustine, *De div. quaest. ad Simpl.*, 1, 2, 12.

that Luther does not speak here of *liberum arbitrium*, but of *voluntas*. For Augustine these terms are used interchangeably. This is not the case with Luther as we shall see. Luther never denied that man has a will, but that he has a *free* will.

5. Although Luther has very little to say about *liberum arbitrium* in his *Lectures on Romans*, he develops the concept of *voluntas* that we already met in the *First Lectures on the Psalms* [80] by emphasizing that sin paralyzes the human will in such a way that, even though man does outwardly what the law commands, there is no cheerful and spontaneous quality to this fulfillment. Thus the unjustified man fulfills whatever parts of the law he can, wholly from a servile fear or out of love of reward, but not out of a cheerful, free love of God.[81]

6. The idea of freedom which Luther developed at length in his brief work, *On the Freedom of a Christian* (1520) [82] is already contained germinally in the *Lectures on Romans,* above all in his commentary on Rom. 13: 1.[83] Neither here nor in the book of 1520 which we just mentioned does Luther speak of natural freedom or free will, but only of what we are calling circumstantial and acquired freedom.

Luther rightly observes that Paul uses the expressions "slavery" and freedom" in various ways: (i) to describe those who are freemen or slaves according to civil law (I Cor. 7: 21); (ii) in a metaphorical sense, to indicate the man who loses his freedom by getting involved in temporal affairs. Such people are to a certain extent imprisoned when they get so concerned with business affairs that they cannot direct their attention to God. According to Luther this is the meaning of the phrase "slaves of men" in I Cor. 7: 23; (iii) in Gal. 5: 13 we find a description of the noblest slavery of all: "By love serve one another." This servitude is really the greatest freedom because it needs nothing and takes nothing but is generous and outgoing. (iv) Finally, there is a slavery to the law and its burdens, a condition in which a man believes that the external works of the law are necessary for salvation. This is the worst kind of slavery of all. Everyone is a slave in this way who wishes to be saved in any other way than through faith in Christ. With anxious concern they try to satisfy the law with their many works. According to Luther such slavery was widespread in his day! [84]

---

[80] Cf. footnote 24 above.
[81] Cf. WA 56, 205, 22 and 36; 235, 6; 264, 31; 336, 14; 496. See Rupp, *The Righteousness,* p. 164.
[82] WA 7, 20-38. Cf. also the *First Lectures on the Psalms: WA 4, 227, 19; 256, 18f.
[83] WA 56, 480ff.
[84] *Ibid.*

7. The final significant point which we encounter is Luther's view of man's passive role in justification. Luther in the *Lectures on Romans* tells us that we must always hold ourselves passive toward the first grace just as a woman does when she conceives.[85] On the basis of this illustration alone it would be premature to claim that this is the concept of passivity which was later condemned by Trent.[86] At Trent both Andreas de Vega and the Superior General of the Franciscan Conventuals were among those who affirmed a "merely passive" moment in justification.[87] What Luther says in the next sentence makes his illustration no less acceptable: ". . . when grace comes and the soul is about to be impregnated with the Spirit, there must be neither prayer nor any action on our part but only a keeping still." Is not Luther saying here substantially what Augustine, Thomas Aquinas and other Scholastics say about *gratia operans*? Augustine, for example, referring to *gratia operans*, says: "In order that we might will, it operates without us." [88] And Thomas, in his explanation of this kind of grace, writes: "the will is related to it as that which is moved, with God as the mover." [89] That this is what Luther meant when he wrote: There is no "action on our part but only a keeping still" can be seen in his explanation which follows: "For God first gives operating grace; he lets it be used and he lets it co-operate until he is ready to infuse another one; and when it is infused, he again lets it become a co-operating grace. . . ." [90] This is surely not a doctrine of purely passive justification which excludes all human activity! [91]

---

85 WA 56, 379: "Ad primam gratiam sicut et ad gloriam semper nos habemus passive sicut mulier ad conceptum."

86 DS 1554.

87 *Conc. Trid.* V, 369: "Homo ad gratiam praevenientem habetur passive mere, ad gratiam gratum facientem habet se active. . . ." Cf. Vega, *Conc. Trid.* V, 275: "secundum est infundere, quod est Dei, et nos operamur passive. . . ," and footnote 90 below. See also Jedin, II, p. 180.

88 *De gr. et lib. arb.*, 17, 33: "Ut ergo velimus sine nobis operatur."

89 I-II, q. 111, a. 2: "voluntas se habet ut mota, Deus autem ut movens."

90 WA 56, 379: "Quia gratiam dat primo operantem, qua sinit uti et cooperari, usque dum aliam incipit infundere, qua infusa iterum sinit eam esse cooperantem, que tamen in primo sui infusione fuit operans et prima. . . ."

91 Rupp, *The Righteousness*, p. 185, speaking of Luther's concept of *gratia cooperans* in the *Lectures on Romans*, thinks that Luther "has given the older term a new setting." In our view Rupp exaggerates the passive aspect of man in Luther's doctrine of grace by failing to take into account Luther's recognition of man's activity, his "uti et cooperari." The same criticism can be made of J. Paquier, "Luther," DTC, 9, 1266 and 1272. As an example of Luther's "doctrine of passive justification," McDonough, p. 47, footnote 2, cites a text from the *Lectures on Romans*, WA 56, 392, 33-393, 1ff. This passage refers not to Luther's doctrine of justification but to his doctrine of the knowledge of God. Another text cited by McDonough, *ibid.*, is WA 56, 275, 22ff. (375, 22ff. was

C. The Disputation Theses for Bartholomäus Bernhardi:
Quaestio de viribus et voluntate hominis sine gratia disputata
(September, 1516)

A new sharpness and directness are seen in the attack which the young reformer makes against the theology of Gabriel Biel—and the "Gabrielists" [92]—in the theses for the *disputatio* of 1516. These theses were drawn up by Luther's pupil, Bernard of Feldkirch (Schwabia), but with the help and approval of Luther, who was able to refer to the teaching contained in the theses as "my position." [93]

Basing the theses exclusively on Scripture and Augustine, whom he calls the "defender of grace," [94] Luther teaches:

1. Apart from the grace of God man can never keep the commandments or prepare himself for grace either *de congruo* or *de condigno,* but necessarily remains under sin.[95]

This thesis is in conflict with the Ockham-Biel theology, but is fully in conformity—at least in substance, if not in formulation—with the teaching of Augustine, Orange II and Thomas Aquinas.[96]

2. God only punishes the person who deserves it (*debitam*), but he shows mercy only to the person who is undeserving (*indebitam*).[97]

In *De servo arbitrio* Luther departs from this Augustinian [98] thesis and holds that God can damn even the undeserving (*immeritos*).[99]

3. The will of man without grace is not free; it is a slave; [100] but it is not so unwillingly.[101]

It is perfectly clear from Luther's explanation of this thesis that what

---

obviously intended). Luther speaks indeed of our "purely passive" relation to God. However, the question remains: What did Luther *mean* by "semper nos habemus passive?" McDonough does not pay sufficient attention to Luther's own explanation of what he means by man's passive role in WA 56, 379. On Luther's concept of "active-passivity" see W. Joest, *Gesetz und Freiheit* (Göttingen, 1961), pp. 114ff.; 218f.

[92] WABR 1, 65, 18.

[93] *Ibid.*

[94] Augustine in his day called Paul "gratiae defensor": *De spiritu et littera,* 24, 40.

[95] WA 1, 147, conclusio secunda.

[96] This thesis is also compatible with the doctrine of Trent. Even though Trent insists that man be disposed for justification, it never suggests that such a disposition is possible apart from the grace of God.

[97] WA 1, 147, concl. sec.

[98] Cf. *Contra duas epist. pelag.,* 4, 6, 16.

[99] WA 18, 730, 26f.; 731, 6f.; 11ff.

[100] The Erlangen Edition of Luther's works has "serva" instead of "servit."

[101] WA 1, 147, concl. secunda, coroll. I: "Voluntas hominis sine gratia non est libera, sed servit, licet non invita."

he means by *serva voluntas* here is nothing more than the biblical (Johannine) and Augustinian concept of slavery to sin:

(a) As scriptural proof he cites the doctrine of Jn. 8: 34 [102] and 36, that sin makes us slaves and that only the Son of God can liberate us from this slavery.

(b) He insists—as he does in *De servo arbitrio*—that this slavery is a voluntary one: "But he serves voluntarily, not unwillingly."

(c) The citation from Augustine, *Contra duas epist. pelag.*, I, 3, 6, makes it clear that both before and after justification man has *liberum arbitrium;* but only the man whom the liberator has freed has *liberum arbitrium* to do what is good.

(d) Finally, Luther uses the same text from Augustine, *Contra Iul.*, 2, 23, that he had used in the *Lectures on Romans* in a perfectly Catholic context.[103]

4. When a man does what he is able to do he sins, since he can neither will nor think [good] by his own powers.[104]

As is evident from Luther's explanation of this thesis, he is speaking of the man who does what is in himself without grace (*exclusa gratia*). Recalling what we have seen previously concerning the analogous use of the terms "sin," "justice," etc. in Scripture and in Augustine, this thesis of Luther is not to be regarded as incompatible with Catholic teaching. The thesis has a long and respectable Catholic tradition behind it, a tradition which found magisterial approval in canon 22 of the Second Council of Orange.[105] That Luther does not intend to reject the possibility of ethical or natural goodness in the unjustified man is seen from his earlier remarks in *Conclusio prima, corollarium III*. Following Augustine, he holds that the infidels who keep the natural law will be punished less severely by God than those who definitely violate it.[106]

D. *Disputatio contra scholasticam theologiam* (SEPTEMBER 4, 1517):
THESES FOR FRANZ GÜNTHER [107]

These theses, prepared by Luther for Günther to defend in a public disputation at Wittenberg, represent a continuation of Luther's "war against the philosophical theology" [108] of the *moderni* and a "defense

---

[102] Luther mistakenly attributes this verse to Paul "Rom. 7."
[103] Cf. above p. 228.
[104] WA 1, 148, concl. sec., coroll. II: "Homo, quando facit quod in se est, peccat, cum nec velle cogitare ex seipso possit."
[105] DS 392.
[106] WA 1, 146f.
[107] WA 1, 224-228. Grane, pp. 369-385 offers a valuable analysis of these theses. Especially useful are his references to the texts of Gabriel Biel which Luther attacks.
[108] Grane, p. 376.

of classical theology, namely, Augustine's." [109] Grane's study has made it overwhelmingly clear that it was precisely Biel's theology against which Luther was reacting most strongly.[110] With Vorster we hold it to be equally certain "that the opponents against whom Luther is fighting on the question of *liberum arbitrium,* for the most part, no longer stood on the soil of the Thomistic doctrinal tradition; furthermore, the concept of freedom which Luther opposes had long since exceeded the Thomistic interpretation of the free will's relation to God." [111]

This disputation contains almost a complete outline of Luther's new theology. However, we shall confine ourselves simply to the points which have direct bearing on our theme:

1. Luther insists on the total inability of the unjustified man to will or do anything but evil.[112] The will of the unjustified man "necessarily elicits an evil and deformed act without God's grace." [113] Thus there can be no disposition for grace by man's own unaided efforts.[114]

Here we have not a denial of natural goodness, but a complete disinterest in speculations about it. This stems from Luther's correct insight that merely ethical goodness, or the righteousness of men, is totally irrelevant for salvation. Thus Luther designates as an invention (*terminus fictus*) the thesis that man can naturally love God above all things.[115] Luther's meaning becomes clearer when we look at thesis 77: "Every work of the law without God's grace appears good externally, but inwardly it is a sin." [116] Is this not precisely what Paul means when he contrasts justice before men to justice before God? [117] Is it not what Augustine means when he says that a work can be good *ex officio*

---

[109] P. 375.

[110] Already in the last century, Luthardt, p. 65, said of Biel's Semipelagian theology: "Seine Theologie ist es, zu welcher Luther sich in den entschiedensten bewussten Gegensatz stellt." Vignaux, *Luther commentateur des Sentences*, p. 45, says that Luther chose Biel "comme principal adversaire" in this *Disputatio*. In defense of Biel, Grane, p. 377, remarks: "Sicher ist, dass z.B. Biel seine eigenen Motive nicht wieder erkennen würde." Luther reacted, says Grane, in a manner "die Biels theologische Intentionen eigentlich schlecht entspricht. Luthers 'Missverständnisse' sind unvermeidlich, weil er alles auf Grund seiner Auffassung über Aufgabe und Methode der Theologie versteht." We believe, on the contrary, that Luther understood Gabriel Biel's Neo-Semipelagian tendencies correctly and that his reaction against them was completely justified.

[111] P. 314.

[112] WA 1, 224; Thesis 4: "Veritas itaque est quod homo arbor mala factus non potest nisi malum velle et facere."

[113] *Ibid.:* Thesis 7: "Sed necessario elicit actum difformem et malum sine gratia dei."

[114] *Ibid.:* Theses 26, 29f.

[115] WA 1, 225: Thesis 18; cf. WA 56, 274.

[116] WA 1, 227.

[117] Rom. 4: 2.

but not *ex fine?* While we may find some ambiguous statements in Luther on this point, it is good to remember that similar ambiguities can also be found in Augustine.[118] The Luther scholar, therefore, must not apply a stricter standard of interpretation to Luther than he does to Augustine. It must further be kept in mind that Luther here, as in the *Disputatio* of 1516,[119] is speaking of the power of fallen man without the grace of God.

2. As in the *Lectures on Romans* Luther does not deny that the distinction between *necessitas consequentiae* and *consequentis* is invalid. He simply reasserts his view that nothing is gained by it: "nihil quoque efficitur." [120]

As in previous works Luther gives no indication that he grasps the real meaning of this distinction. The distinction, in some form or another, has been made not only by the Scholastics, but by all Christian thinkers as far back as Boethius and Augustine. They saw the need of such a distinction of two kinds of necessity in order to maintain *both* the infallibility of God's foreknowledge and predestination *and* man's *liberum arbitrium*. If one does not make such a distinction or if he thinks the distinction achieves nothing then he will probably either deny God's infallible foreknowledge or man's free will. But, as Augustine said, as Christians and philosophers we profess both: foreknowledge as a part of our faith; free choice as a condition of responsible living.[121] Thus he, and the main stream of the Catholic tradition after him, found it necessary to distinguish a necessity resulting from God's infallible foreknowledge—which did not exclude man's freedom—and a necessity which is incompatible with free will.

3. An important departure from the Augustinian-Thomistic exegetical tradition is evident in Luther's assertion that if anyone says of such texts as Zach. 1: 3; Jas. 4: 8; Lk. 11: 9 and Jer. 29: 13 that "one refers to nature, the other to grace" ("unum naturae, alterum gratiae sit"), then he says the same thing as the Pelagians.[122] This is not correct. Nor is it correct to say with Vogelsang that Luther here thinks in the closest harmony with Augustine.[123] Vogelsang calls upon Augustine's *De gratia et libero arbitrio*, 5, 10 to support his view.[124] But it is precisely in *De gratia et libero arbitrio* that Augustine teaches that the

---

118 Cf. the excursus: The Different Meanings of "Sin," . . . in Augustine.
119 Cf. footnote 96 above.
120 WA 1, 225: Thesis 32.
121 *De civ. Dei,* 5, 10.
122 WA 1, 225: Thesis 28. We shall find this assertion repeatedly in DSA.
123 See vol. 5, *Luthers Werke* (Berlin, 1955), p. 322, footnote.
124 *Ibid.*

biblical imperatives are a divine proof of the existence of free will.[125] And when Augustine criticizes the Pelagians in Chapter 5, 10 of this work, it is not because they deduce free will from such texts as Zach. 1: 3, but because they think this and similar texts mean that grace is not a gift but something merited. Biel, like the Semipelagians, understood Zach 1: 3 to mean that man can begin the journey to salvation by doing what he is capable of doing, apart from grace.[126] Luther is therefore perfectly justified in rejecting the view of the Pelagians and of Biel, but he goes too far when he rejects the idea that the biblical texts in question imply that man has *liberum arbitrium*. Augustine and Thomas Aquinas are just as much opposed to the heretical exegesis of the Pelagians as is Luther. They do not oppose it, however, by denying man's free will.

E. *Disputatio Heidelbergae Habita* (APRIL 26, 1518)

Coming to the *Heidelberg Disputation* we pass over Luther's 95 *Theses on Indulgences* (October 31, 1517), simply recalling the words of Luther cited from *De servo arbitrio* in our Introduction to the effect that the matter of indulgences was a trifle [127] in comparison to the question of the free will.

Of the forty theses which Luther drew up for this disputation, a dozen are concerned with arguments against Aristotelian philosophy.[128] Of those remaining, the one which concerns us most directly is Thesis 13, a thesis which was later to be condemned in the bull of Leo X, "Exsurge Domine" (June 15, 1520): [129] "Free will after the fall, exists in name only and as long as it does what it is able to do, it commits a mortal sin." [130]

To understand Luther's meaning here, it is necessary to look at the explanation which he offers in his proof of the thesis:

The first part is clear, for the will is captive and subject to sin. Not that it is nothing, but that it is not free except to do evil. According to Jn. 8 [:34, 36], "Everyone who commits sin is a slave to sin . . . So if the Son makes you free, you will be free indeed." Hence St. Augustine says in his book, *The Spirit and the Letter*, "Free will without grace has the power to do nothing but sin"; and in the second book of *Against Julian*,

---

125 Cf. chapter 4, pp. 94f.
126 Cf. chapter 7, pp. 206f.
127 WA 18, 786, 28f.: "nugis potius quam caussis."
128 WA 1, 355: Theses 29-40.
129 DS 1486.
130 WA 1, 354: Thesis 13: "Liberum arbitrium post peccatum res est de solo titulo, et dum facit quod in se est, peccat mortaliter"; tr. H. Grimm, AE 31, p. 40.

"You call the will free, but in fact it is an enslaved will," and in many other places.
The second part is clear from what has been said above and from the verse in Hos. 13 [:9], "Israel, you are bringing misfortune upon yourself, for your salvation is alone with me," and from similar passages.[131]

Is this a denial of the existence of natural freedom in the unjustified man, the man who is a *servus peccati?* By no means. Luther says that the free will of the slave to sin is *not nothing.* It is, however, only free to do evil. Such statements can easily be reconciled with the Catholic tradition of Augustine and the Second Council of Orange. When Luther says that the *liberum arbitrium* in the unjustified man is only a name—"res de titulo solo"—we are to understand this as he intended it, namely, in terms of Jn. 8: 36, where we are taught that the sinner is not *truly* free and that the political liberty enjoyed by sinners is not *true* freedom— freedom in the most important sense of the word—as long as they are not yet liberated from their sins. Luther's teaching here is without question solidly biblical. On the other hand, it is also quite clear that he would not have encountered nearly so much opposition had he in his thesis stuck to the Johannine terminology instead of using the ambiguous phrase, *res de solo titulo,* which could easily have been interpreted to mean that Luther was denying the existence of *liberum arbitrium* outright. Why could he not simply have said: Freedom of the will after the fall is not *true* freedom? The meaning is identical in both cases. Whereas Luther's thesis employs a radical, new terminology that invites misunderstanding, the latter thesis is much more biblical.

Concerning the second part of the thesis, Luther seems to be doing nothing more than reaffirming the teaching of Augustine,[132] which was later accepted by Orange II [133]: "No one has anything of his own except his lies and his sins." Luther indeed makes this teaching more radical when he says "he sins mortally." But when we recall the diversity of meanings attached to the word "sin" in Scripture, in Augustine and in much of the Catholic tradition,[134] and when we keep in mind the Neo-Semipelagian understanding of *facere quod in se est . . . ,* against which Luther is reacting, then Luther's thesis does not seem to be so revolutionary.[135]

---

131 WA 1, 359f.; AE 31, pp. 48f.
132 *In Ioann. tract.,* 5, 1: PL 45, 1887.
133 DS 392.
134 Cf. Thomas, *In Rom.,* cap. 3, lect. 2, n. 277: "nullus est iustus in se ex seipso, sed ex se quilibet est peccator. . . ."
135 A valuable contribution to ecumenical theology would be a study of the development and nature of Luther's concept and theology of sin in the light of

Luther offers a different type of proof for the thesis in the preparatory notes for the *Heidelberg Disputation*.[136] Here he seeks to prove that: "outside of grace, the will of man is not free with reference to actions which are either contrary or contradictory to each other; the will is necessarily in bondage and captive even if it is free from all compulsion." [137] In order to demonstrate this thesis, says Luther, two things must first be noted: first the acts of a contrary will are willing and being unwilling (*velle et nolle*), while the acts of a contradictory will are either willing and not willing (*velle et non velle*) or being unwilling and not unwilling (*nolle et non nolle*); second, the issue here concerns the liberty of the will in relation to merit and demerit, not in relation to lower things where the will seems to be free both for contrary as well as contradictory acts.[138]

Having made these qualifications, Luther then says that the will of man, apart from grace, is not free "in contradictoriis"; otherwise the will would be freely able "to avoid every future sin." [139] If the will is free in such a way, it could avoid being drawn into sin. But this is false, since, as the "common saying" affirms, "apart from grace the will cannot remain free from mortal sin for a long time." [140] Nor does the will of man apart from grace have any freedom of contrariety, argues Luther, because, as Gen. 8: 21 teaches, the will is "always prone to evil." If it is always prone to evil, then it cannot be prone to good, the contrary of evil. Luther quickly asserts that this proneness is not a coercion, for "it is impossible that willing be coerced and not free; therefore, it is necessarily free and necessarily wills freely." [141] Therefore, concludes Lu-

---

Scripture, Augustine, Thomas, the late Scholastics and Trent. R. Hermann, *Luthers These "Gerecht und Sünder Zugleich"* (Gütersloh, 1930) is a helpful starting point for such an investigation. See the thorough analysis of Hermann's book by R. Kösters, *Luthers These "Gerecht und Sünder Zugleich" in der Interpretation Rudolf Hermanns* (Paderborn, 1967).

[136] WA 1, 365f.

[137] WA 1, 365: "Voluntas hominis extra gratiam non est libera actuum, seu contrariorum seu contradictorium, sed necessario serva et captiva, licet libera ab omni coactione;" tr. H. Grimm, AE 31, p. 58.

[138] *Ibid.*: "Nam respectu aliorum suorum inferiorum non nego, quod sit, imo videatur sibi libera tum ad contraria tum ad contradictoria."

[139] WA 1, 366.

[140] *Ibid.*: "voluntas extra gratiam non potest diu stare sine peccato mortali." Cf. Thomas Aquinas, I-II, q. 109, a. 8c.

[141] WA 1, 366: "impossibile est, quod velle sit coactivum et non liberum: ergo necessario est liberum et necessario libere vult." This is similar to what Augustine says in *De civ. Dei*, 5, 10: the will, when it wills, necessarily wills freely. Is not Luther here possibly admitting—and using—the distinction between absolute necessity and conditional necessity? In DSA he no longer conceives of *any* necessity that is compatible with free will.

ther: ". . . the will outside grace or in falling is unable not to fall and not to will evil by its own power. It is able, by the grace of God, not to fall or to stop falling." [142] This conclusion is in full agreement not only with Augustine, but also with Thomas Aquinas.

The thirteenth of Luther's Heidelberg theses may thus seem at first glance to be radical; his *meaning,* as we have just seen from the two different proofs and explanations he offers for it, is certainly not. The thesis may be ambiguous or misleading, but it is definitely not heretical. Yet it was precisely this thesis on free will that was condemned in the bull "Exsurge Domine" of 1520.

III. LUTHER AND ECK ON FREE WILL IN 1519

Before we look at this papal document and Luther's reaction to it, something should be said about the *Leipzig Disputation* which lasted from June 27 to July 14, 1519.[143] The adversaries were John Eck (1486-1543) on the one side and the Wittenbergers, Luther and Karlstadt (Andreas Bodenstein, 1480-1541), on the other. The main issues debated at Leipzig were the primacy and power of the Roman pontiff and the relation of grace to free will and to good actions. Although Luther touched upon both issues in his sermon on the Feast of Saints Peter and Paul, June 29, 1519,[144] the question of free will and grace was formally debated only by Eck and Karlstadt.[145]

In his sermon, Luther asserts, on the basis of Mt. 16: 17, Jn. 8: 32ff. and 36 and Rom. 3: 10ff and 23f., that the free will of man "can do nothing whatever by itself. Nor is it in the power of his free will to acknowledge or do good, but solely in the grace of God which makes him free. . . . Apart from grace he does not do God's will but his own, which is never good. The will was indeed free in Adam. But now it has been corrupted and made captive in sins through Adam's fall; yet it has kept the name of free will because it once was free and is to become free again through grace." [146] What Luther says here is both biblical and

---

[142] WA 1, 366: ". . . voluntas extra gratiam vel in cadendo constituta non potest non cadere et velle malum suis viribus, potest autem per gratiam Dei non cadere aut cessare a cadendo. . . ;" tr. Grimm, AE 31, p. 59.

[143] WA 2, 254-383.

[144] WA 2, 244-249.

[145] On the basic differences between Karlstadt and Luther see E. Kähler, *Karlstadt und Augustin. Der Kommentar des Andreas Bodenstein von Karlstadt zu Augustins Schrift De Spiritu et Littera* (Halle, 1952). Kähler maintains that this work was at least partly intended by Karlstadt to be a refutation of Luther by means of Augustine. Cf. Kähler, p. 4.

[146] WA 2, 247: ". . . gar nichts vermag aus ym selbs: und nit in seiner wilkuere frey steht guts zuerkennen adder thun: sundern allein in der gnaden Gottis die yn

Augustinian in substance, with one exception. When Luther says that man's will is called free only because it was once free and because, through grace, it can again become free, he restricts the name "free" in a manner which is foreign not only to the Scholastics, but also to Augustine and to the teaching of the early councils of the Church.[146a]

Whatever Luther intends to say here concerning natural freedom— and this is impossible to determine from the immediate context—there is no question that his terminology is poor and misleading, for he does not adequately distinguish two realities that had long been recognized as distinct in the Catholic tradition: acquired freedom and natural freedom, that is, the freedom from sin that we receive solely through the grace of Christ, and the natural freedom of the will. Man always possesses the latter freedom (*liberum arbitrium*) even though it has been so "weakened and harmed" by original sin that without grace, it can no longer do anything truly good in the sight of God.[147] Luther thus abandons the view he upheld in the *Lectures on Romans* and in the *Heidelberg Disputation* that the *liberum arbitrium* of the sinner at least

---

frey macht." Further: "an gnad thut er nit gottis willen sundern seiner eygnen willen: der nimmer gut ist. Er ist wol frey gewesen in Adam. Aber nw durch seynen fall verterbet und in sunden gefangen: doch den namen des freyen willens behalten darum das er frey gewest: und durch gnad widder frey werden soll." —It is ordinarily hazardous to use Luther's sermons to indicate developments in his thought. We make use of this sermon, however, first of all because of the theological context in which it was preached at Leipzig and secondly, because we find him making basically the same point in a later theological work, his reply to the bull, *Exsurge Domine*. Cf. below, footnote 229.

[146a] The assertion that man can be said to have free will because he once had it and can have it again is also found in Luther's work of the same year, *Contra malignum I. Eccii iudicium . . . defensio,* WA 2, 647, 10-13, as well as in the *Grund und Ursach* of 1521: WA 7, 448, 31-34; 449, 30ff. Luther seems to think that the Fathers of the Church also hold this view of *liberum arbitrium*. WA 2, 647, 28-31: "Quando ergo sancti patres liberum arbitrium defendunt, capacitatem libertatis eius praedicant, quod scilicet verti potest ad bonum per gratiam dei et fieri revera liberum, ad quod creatum est." This statement of the patristic teaching is to a considerable extent true. But it is not true to say that the Fathers taught that man has *liberum arbitrium* simply because he was once free in paradise. They all admit that he lost the *libertas* of paradise, but they are no less in agreement that he retained, however weakened, the power of choice which they called *liberum arbitrium*.

[147] Vg. DS 396: ". . . ita inclinatum et attenuatum fuerit liberum arbitrium . . . ut nullus postea . . . operari propter Deum quod bonum est, possit, nisi eum gratia misericordiae divinae praevenerit." It is true that Augustine gives the impression in certain passages, e.g. *Enchir.,* 30, 9, that man has no *liberum arbitrium* whatever as a result of sin. The difference between Luther and Augustine, however, is that when Augustine became aware that some were misunderstanding his position on *liberum arbitrium* he wrote *De gratia et libero arbitrio* precisely to express his conviction that man *always* possesses *liberum arbitrium*. Cf. the excursus: The Meaning of "servum arbitrium" in Augustine.

exists, even though, unaided by grace, it is free only to sin. It is especially relevant for our understanding of the Erasmian position on free will to note that Luther is rejecting the conception of *liberum arbitrium* as the power of a man to will good or evil. Thus, in the *Contra malignum I. Eccii iudicium . . . defensio* (1519), written shortly after the debate, he says that this is what everyone, at least the uneducated person, understands by *liberum arbitrium*.[148] It is sufficient here to recall that neither Augustine nor Thomas Aquinas understood *liberum arbitrium* in this way!

In contrast to some of the contemporary Catholic apologists who upheld a non-Augustinian, sometimes humanistic doctrine of free will against Luther,[149] John Eck offers a doctrine of grace and free will which is similar, though not identical, to the doctrine of Augustine and Thomas Aquinas. Already in his *Chrysopassus* of 1514 Eck had maintained: (1) the sovereign causality of God in all created actions,[150] (2) that good is to be attributed to God first of all, while evil has man as its principal cause,[151] (3) that even the *initium salutis* comes from God [152] and (4) that man's merits before God are in no way a matter of strict justice but are completely dependent on God's ordinance.[153]

---

[148] WA 2, 647, 5-8: "Nam omnis homo, saltem rudis, audiens liberum arbitrium, intelligit ipsum aeque posse in bonum et in malum, prorsus non cogitans, quod solum possit in malum: inde procedet in fiducia sui, praesumens, posse se ad deum ex suis viribus converti."

[149] Cf. P. Mandonnet, "Frères Prêcheurs," DTC, 6, 912ff. Jörgensen, p. 80 and Zickendraht, pp. 183ff. regard John Fisher's doctrine of grace and free will in his *Assertiones Lutheranae Confutatio* (Paris, 1523), as at least ambiguous, if not actually Semipelagian, especially concerning the axiom, "facienti quod in se est, etc." Jedin, however, *Des Johannes Cochlaeus Streitschrift De libero arbitrio hominis 1525* (Breslau, 1927), pp. 35f., shows convincingly that Fisher held that the preparation for grace is only possible with the help of special grace. Jedin, p. 26 also defends the orthodoxy of Conrad Wimpina (Koch, ca. 1460-1531) on this point. Whereas Luthardt, *Die Lehre vom freien Willen*, p. 71, claims that Wimpina, *Anacephaleosis* (1528) attacked the fatalistic tendencies of Wyclif and Luther by defending Semipelagianism, Jedin, *Des Joh. Cochlaeus Streitschrift*, p. 26 defends Wimpina's teaching as being fundamentally Thomistic.

[150] *Chrysop.*, II, 60: "Deus est ita causa efficiens hominum, quod ipso non agente nihil aliud agit; et cuiuscumque effectus etiam naturalis Deus est potior causa quam creatura."

[151] *Ibid.*, III, 71.

[152] *Ibid.*, III, 95: ". . . initium salutis nostrae deo inspirante habemus. . . ." III, 63b: "Initium salutis nostrae deo miserante habemus. . . ." In *ibid.*, IV, 7, Eck gives two principles which differentiate his teaching from the Pelagians: "Nam primo ponimus peccatum originale quod negavit Pelagius, Secundo quia initium salutis nostrae cum Augustino ponimus deo inspirante et movente quod ille negavit." Cf. above chapter 7, footnote 106.

[153] *Ibid.*, III, 95: "Fatemur ingenue non esse iusticiam et natura rei inter illos actus nostros et praemium veluti iam centies diximus." ". . . nulla sunt merita ex

That Eck has not developed a harmonious, fully Augustinian-Thomistic doctrine of grace, free will and merit is seen from the fact that in the *Chrysopassus* he holds to a doctrine of predestination based on foreseen merits (*praedestinatio propter merita praevisa*).[154]

At the Leipzig Disputation Eck gave a Thomistic, distinctly non-Bielian explanation of *facere quod in se est:* "Man can do good by doing what he is able to do, always presupposing, however, the help of grace. . . ."[155] Eck also admits that God causes the *whole* meritorious act. He does not say, however, that God is the *total* cause.[156] According-ing to Eck the free will has its own activity in performing a good act, but it is an activity which is dependent on God's grace: "I think that free will has its own special activity in the good work, but an activity which comes from God and grace." [157] This text makes it clear, as Jedin says, that Eck wanted only to exclude the idea that grace was the only oper-ative factor in a good act.[158]

In his *Enchiridion locorum communium* of 1525 Eck gives a fully Augustinian statement on free will:

We hold that free will can do nothing good by itself. . . . The grace of God enables it to do something. Therefore no man thinks anything good by himself but only by the special grace of God. This grace is under-

---

natura rei, sed solum ex acceptatione et ordinatione dei. . . ." Eck then cites one of the characteristic theses of Augustine: "Deus non remunerat in nobis merita nostra, sed dona sua."

[154] *Ibid.*, III, 82f. Cf. J. Greving, *Johann Eck als junger Gelehrter* (Münster, 1906), pp. 127f. Greving, pp. 94-104 has shown that Eck was always a syncretist, but his early preference for the *moderni* developed into an appreciation for the older theologians of the High Scholasticism. It may be true that Biel had a profound influence on Eck, as Oberman, *The Harvest*, p. 19; cf. p. 427, maintains. But in the light of the texts which we have just presented it seems safe to say that this influence did not extend to Eck's doctrine of justification.

[155] "Liquet posse hominem facere bonum faciendo quod in se est; semper tamen auxilium gratiae non excludendo . . . Et hoc est facere quod in se est." Citation from Luthardt, pp. 110f.

[156] "Deum effective producere totum opus meritorium, sed non totaliter." Cita-tion from O. Seitz, *Der authentische Text der Leipziger Disputation* (Berlin, 1902), p. 26. Karlstadt regarded this distinction as an innovation. Cf. Seitz, p. 53. In his *Resolutiones Lutherianae super propositionibus suis Lipsiae disputatis,* drawn up after the disputation of 1519, Luther seems to reject Eck's distinction completely when he says: The free will is purely passive "in omni actu suo." The good act comes from God "totus et totaliter." Cf. WA 2, 421. The reason Luther offers for saying that our good acts are totally from God, namely, because the entire activity of man's will depends upon the divine activity, is something that neither Eck nor any Thomist would dispute. This gives us reason to think that we are dealing here more with an apparent opposition than a real one.

[157] Jedin, *Des Cochlaeus Streitschrift*, p. 28, footnote 35.

[158] *Ibid.*, p. 28.

stood not only as the grace which is charity and which makes one pleasing to God, but also of the prior, gratuitous movement by which God inspires, nudges and calls man to good.[159]

It is most interesting, but not surprising, therefore, to find that Luther, *Contra malignum I. Eccii iudicium . . . defensio* insists that Eck really agrees with his doctrine of *servum arbitrium* and that any difference is merely verbal. Eck conceded to Karlstadt, argues Luther, that the free will before grace only has power to sin. Where, then, is the liberty of the will, he asks? [160] This argument shows once again that Luther blurs the distinction between natural freedom (*liberum arbitrium*) and acquired freedom (Christian freedom), a distinction which he himself once recognized. This lack of clarity results in a substantial modification of the traditionally received theological terminology concerning *liberum arbitrium*. Thus Luther, unlike Augustine, Thomas Aquinas and the entire Catholic dogmatic tradition, is no longer willing to say, as he did in his own *Lectures on Romans* only three years previously: man "is indeed always free naturally." [161]

Despite his novel and misleading *terminology* Luther's *intention* is nevertheless perfectly clear. He may ask: "Where is sinful man's free will?" But in asking this question he is not really questioning the *existence* of *liberum arbitrium* in fallen man, but its power and its value as far as salvation and Christian freedom are concerned. That *this* is Luther's fundamental intention and not a doctrine of determinism or necessitarianism is made clear from the fact that he repeats again and again in his writings of 1519 and 1520 the thesis: "Free will prior to grace is capable only of sinning." [162] This is not a heretical thesis. It is a thesis of Augustine, the "doctor of grace," a thesis which has been accepted by the official teaching authority of the Roman Catholic Church.[163]

---

159 "Deinde fatemur liberum arbitrium ex se solo non posse in bonum sed nihil esse, sed gratia Dei facit ut aliquid possit, ideo nullus homo ex se cogitat aliquid boni sed ex gratia Dei speciali. Tertio dicunt hoc non solum intelligi de gratia quae est charitas et gratum facit Deo, sed etiam de motione gratuita praevia, qua Deus inspirat, pulsat et vocat hominem ad bonum." Citation from Jedin, p. 29.

160 WA 2, 647, 1-5: "Scito ergo, lector, et certus esto, Eccium nihil prorsus in hac re dissentire mihi, nisi ad meram vocem et speciem. Quod ut noscas adverte. Eccius Lipsiae concessit, liberum arbitrium ante gratiam non valere nisi ad peccandum: ergo non valet ad bonum sed tantum ad malum. Ubi ergo libertas eius?" Cf. WA 2, 702, 32f.

161 WA 56, 385: ". . . liberum quidem semper est naturaliter."

162 "Liberum arbitrium ante gratiam non valet nisi ad peccandum." Cf. *Contra malignum I. Eccii. . . :* WA 2, 647, 3ff. The thesis is found approximately ten times in the letter to Eck of November 7, 1519: WA 2, 700-708; WABR 1, 439-458.

163 Cf. Augustine, *In Ioann. tract.,* 5, 1 and DS 392.

IV. THE BULL *EXSURGE DOMINE* (JUNE 15, 1520) AND LUTHER'S REPLY: *ASSERTIO OMNIUM ARTICULORUM* . . . (DECEMBER, 1520)

A. *Exsurge Domine* [164] was the first official pronouncement of the Roman Church on Luther's doctrine. The bull was the culmination of the Church's investigation of Luther, which began in June of 1518. The termination of this investigation may be considered to be January 3, 1521, the date of the publication of the bull *Decet Romanum Pontificem,* in which Pope Leo X excommunicated Luther and his followers.

Exsurge Domine censured 41 propositions of the Reformer in the following terms: "All and each of the above mentioned articles or errors . . . we condemn, disapprove and completely reject as respectively heretical, or scandalous, or false, or offensive to pious ears, or seductive of simple minds, and as opposed to Catholic truth." [165]

With the exception of proposition 25, all of the censured articles can be found word for word in one or another of Luther's writings.[166] Proposition 36 is the one which directly concerns our study. As we have noted, it is from the *Heidelberg Disputation* of 1518: "Free will after sin is an empty word; and when a man does what is in him, he sins mortally." [167] We have already expressed our view that, taken in context and considering Luther's own explanation of what he meant by it, the Heidelberg proposition can be defended with little difficulty in the light of the doctrine of Orange II, and in terms of Augustine's theology. Can such a view be sustained in the light of the condemnation of proposition 36 in *Exsurge Domine?* We believe it can. *Exsurge Domine* made use of an "in globo" condemnation,[168] that is, all of the propositions were condemned *either* as heretical, *or* as scandalous, *or* false, *or* as offensive to pious ears, *or* as seductive of simple minds, etc. But there is no indication as to *which* of these censures applies to *which* proposition.

---

[164] Cf. Jedin, I, pp. 170-177; H. Roos, "Exsurge Domine," LThK, 3, 1319. Propositions 1-20 and 37-40 had already been censured by the theological faculty of the University of Louvain on November 7, 1519.

[165] DS 1491: "Praefatos omnes et singulos articulos seu errores tanquam, ut praemittitur, respective haereticos, aut scandalosos, aut falsos, aut piarum aurium offensivos, vel simplicium mentium seductivos, et veritati catholicae obviantes, damnamus, reprobamus, atque omnino reicimus;" tr. R. Deferrari, *The Sources of Catholic Dogma* (St. Louis-London, 1957), p. 243.

[166] Cf. H. Roos, "Die Quellen der Bulle 'Exsurge Domine,'" in: *Theologie in Geschichte und Gegenwart, Festschrift M. Schmaus,* ed. by J. Auer and H. Volk (München, 1957), III, pp. 909-926.

[167] DS 1486: "Liberum arbitrium post peccatum est res de solo titulo; et dum facit, quod in se est, peccat mortaliter."

[168] Cf. the formulation in footnote 165.

The *"respective"* in the formula of condemnation simply tells us that each proposition merits one or more of the censures.[169] It is therefore impossible from *Exsurge Domine* alone to determine whether proposition 36 is condemned as heretical or merely as "offensive to pious ears." [170]

"In globo" censures were first employed by the teaching office of the Church in the condemnation of the Fraticelli in 1318.[171] Censures of this type received their highest endorsement when they were used at the Council of Constance in 1415.[172] Since the rejection of Quesnel's teaching by Pope Clement XI in 1713, however, the Church has virtually abandoned *in globo* censures.[173] The most obvious reason for their abandonment seems to be the ambiguity which is intrinsically attached to them. When such censures are used it is most difficult, if not impossible to say with certainty which censures apply to which error—or to which assault on pious ears.[174] Thus a situation results which seems partially to illustrate Rahner's view, that it is possible for a dogmatic statement of the Church to be qualified in itself as true and yet at the same time be rash, presumptuous, dangerous, equivocal, seductive, forward, etc.[175]

Further to be considered is the fact that a censure such as "offensive to pious ears" does not necessarily relate to the doctrine itself but to the inadequate *expression* of the doctrine.[176] When the teaching office of the Church censures such a thesis as proposition 36 of *Exsurge Domine,* it may simply be doing so because the wording is misleading or inadequate, especially when the thesis is taken out of context.[177] The Church unquestionably has the duty and therefore the right to supervise the language in which her preachers and teachers proclaim and explain the Word of God. The necessity for "a communal *linguistic* ruling on ter-

---

[169] X. Le Bachelet, "Baius," DTC, 2, 66.

[170] On the history and meaning of these various qualifications see H. Quilliet, "Censures Doctrinales," DTC, 2, 2101-2113; J. Cahill, *The Development of the Theological Censures after the Council of Trent (1563-1709)* (Fribourg, 1955); A. Kolping, "Qualifikationen, theol.," LThK, 8, 914-919.

[171] Cf. DS 910-916.

[172] Cf. DS 1225 and 1251.

[173] DS 2357. Cf. Cahill, p. xviii.

[174] Luther himself pointed out the inadequacy of such a censure in his *Adversus execrabilem Antichristi bullam* (1520).

[175] "What is a Dogmatic Statement?", *Theol. Inv.,* V, pp. 45f.

[176] Cf. Quilliet, DTC, 2, 2108; Kolping, LThK, 8, 918. It was at Eck's insistence—against the more moderate and sensible judgment of Cardinal Cajetan—that the *in globo* condemnation was used. Eck later admitted that the condemnations in the bull were unclear and that they should have been supported by scriptural arguments. Cf. Jedin, I, pp. 174f.; H. Boehmer, *Martin Luther: Road to Reformation,* 3rd ed. (New York, 1960), p. 352.

[177] Pope Pius V admitted that some of the censured propositions of Baius could be given a correct interpretation; DS 1980.

minology," as Rahner has suggested,[178] stems primarily from the fact that the Church's dogmatic statements have an ecclesial character, which implies that they "ought to be brief, understandable by all and accommodated to the consciousness of faith of a wider audience." [179]

Briefly stated, it would be incorrect to assume that proposition 36 of *Exsurge Domine* was censured as heretical or even as false. It was much more probably censured because, taken out of context and apart from Luther's own explanation of the thesis, the thesis seemed to convey the idea that Luther was rejecting the natural freedom of choice which man possesses before and after the fall. Without calling into question the right and duty of the Church's teaching authority to be vigilant in doctrinal matters, one can indeed raise the question whether the magisterium in the matter before us spoke relevantly and with real understanding of the nature of the problem.

So far, although we have noted a certain inadequacy in Luther's statements about necessity and contingency in the *Lectures on Romans* and a tendency to confuse natural freedom and acquired freedom, we have not encountered in him any outright rejection of man's natural freedom. We do find a denial that fallen man can choose what is good without grace, but there is no denial that he can choose. Luther has simply but radically used Johannine and Augustinian language to emphasize how unauthentic and inconsequential this natural freedom of the sinner is in comparison to the freedom unto which Christ liberates us.

B. *Assertio omnium articulorum M. Lutheri per bullam Leonis X novissimam damnatorum* (December, 1520) [180] and *Grund und Ursach aller Artikel D. Martin Luthers, so durch römische Bulle unrechtlich verdammt sind* (March 1, 1521) [181]

If we have thus far been able to acquit Luther of any *real* break with the authentic Catholic tradition on free will, we are able to do so only with the greatest difficulty when we examine his reply to *Exsurge Domine*. He received the bull on October 11, 1520. On November 29, 1520 he wrote to Spalatin that he had already begun a Latin and a German reply to the bull.[182] Between May and November of 1520 Luther had worked tirelessly to publish such important Reformation writings as the *Sermon on Good Works, On the Babylonian Captivity of*

---

[178] *Theol. Inv.*, V, p. 54. Cf. P. Fransen, *Divine Grace and Man*, 2nd ed. (New York, 1965), pp. 30f.

[179] *Theol. Inv.*, V, p. 54.

[180] WA 7, 94-151.

[181] WA 7, 308-457.

[182] WABR 2, 220, 5ff.

the Church, On Christian Freedom,[183] Address to the Christian Nobles of the German Nation and Against the Bull of the Antichrist. Of Luther's great writings of this year, Lortz says that they "represent . . . both in content as well as form his historically most significant utterances as a reformer." [184] The last-named work was a brief, undetailed answer to Exsurge Domine. In the Latin version of it, Adversus execrabilem Antichristi bullam,[185] Luther expresses his disbelief that the bull came from the pope. He preferred to think it was the work of his arch-enemy, Eck. In any case, says Luther, whoever wrote the bull is the anti-Christ! Luther pointed out the ambiguous nature of the in globo censure and insisted, quite reasonably, that his opponents should clearly attach a specific note of censure to each proposition they wish to condemn.[186]

The Latin and the German versions of Luther's formal, detailed reply to Exsurge Domine differ significantly. The Latin version of Luther's defense of proposition 36 is not only twice as long as the German,[187] but is also much more radical.[188] The radicality of the Assertio consists above all in the fact that Luther leaves himself clearly open to the charge of necessitarianism or theological determinism. In his previous writings Luther's concept of the unfree will was basically nothing more than the biblical doctrine of man's slavery to sin, to injustice and to Satan. This slavery, as we have seen in Chapter 2, like any other kind of slavery, is in no way incompatible with man's natural freedom or freedom of choice, although it certainly limits the area of what can be effectively willed: freedom from sin on the one hand, freedom from corporal imprisonment or captivity on the other. Nor does the biblical concept of slavery to sin imply in any way a doctrine of universal necessity.

---

[183] Lortz, I, p. 233, says of this work: "Es gibt unter Luthers Schriften wohl auch keine, die den Katholiken wehmütiger stimmt. Denn hier zeigt sich am deutlichsten, was die ganz ungewöhnliche christliche Kraft Luthers für die Reform der Kirche in der Kirche hätte erreichen können." As we indicated earlier, despite its name, this work makes no contribution to Luther's doctrine of unfree will that cannot be found in the other works we have examined. This "frömmste aller Schriften des Reformators" (Lortz, I, p. 232) is an essay on the meaning of Christian freedom from works and a description of the loving, free Christian service of God and neighbor. It is not a treatise on man's free will.

[184] Ibid., p. 225.

[185] WA 6, 597-612.

[186] Cf. R. Bainton, Here I Stand, 8th ed. (New York, 1961), pp. 125f.

[187] The Assertio fills about seven pages of the WA, while the Grund und Ursach takes up less than three.

[188] Grisar and Jedin, Des Cochlaeus Streitschrift, pp. 12ff., agree that the Assertio is even more radical than DSA.

In the *Assertio omnium articulorum,* however, Luther does not limit himself simply to the biblical arguments which are already familiar to us.[189] He uses another argument which is found neither in Scripture nor in Augustine—nor anywhere in the Catholic tradition. It is the argument that the will is not free because all things happen by absolute necessity:

. . . it is necessary to revoke this article. For I have wrongly said that free will before grace exists in name only. I should have said frankly: "free will is a fiction, a name without a correspondent in reality." Because no one indeed has power freely to think of good or evil, but (as the thesis of Wyclif condemned at Constance correctly teaches) all things happen by absolute necessity. This is what the poet meant when he said: "all things are determined by a fixed law." And Christ says in Mt. 10: "The leaf of a tree does not fall to the ground without the will of your Father . . ." and in Is. 41 he insults them when he says: "Do good or evil if you can." [190]

Such an argument gives an entirely new ring and meaning to Luther's doctrine of *servum arbitrium.* First of all, if *all* things happen by absolute necessity, then the assertion which Luther makes in earlier and in later writings—that man has *liberum arbitrium* "in inferioribus"—is meaningless.[191] Secondly, the fact that Luther cites a fatalistic pagan poet [192] to support his thesis of absolute necessity is an *a priori* indication that this concept of *servum arbitrium* is neither strictly biblical nor

---

[189] These arguments prove clearly that fallen man without grace can do nothing but sin, taking sin here to mean any action which is not truly pleasing *coram Deo.* The question of "natural goodness" is simply by-passed. This biblical concept of *servum arbitrium,* as we have seen in previous chapters, is by no means peculiar to Luther. It is shared by Augustine, by Thomas Aquinas, by the overwhelming majority of Catholic theologians prior to Luther and also by the official teaching authority of the Church, especially in the teachings of Second Orange and in the other councils which condemned Pelagian errors.

[190] WA 7, 146, 3-12: "Unde et hunc articulum necesse est revocare. Male enim dixi, quod liberum arbitrium ante gratiam sit res de solo titulo, sed simpliciter debui dicere 'liberum arbitrium est figmentum in rebus seu titulus sine re'. Quia nulli est in manu sua quippiam cogitare mali aut boni, sed omnia (ut Viglephi articulus constantiae damnatus recte docet) de necessitate absoluta eveniunt. Quod et Poeta voluit, quando dixit 'certa stant omnia lege', Et Christus Matth. x 'Folium arboris non cadit in terram sine voluntate patris vestri omnes numerati sunt'. Et Esa. xli eis insultat dicens 'Bene quoque aut male si potestis facite'."

[191] Cf. WA 56, 385; 1, 365; 18, 638, 4-11; 662, 6f.; 672, 7-11; 752, 7; 781, 8ff.; 24, 584, 14ff.; 40/1, 293.

[192] WA 7, 146, footnote 1 attributes this quotation to Manilius. This is not correct. The identical citation is found in DSA: WA 18, 618, 1 and there Luther attributes it to Vergil (*Aen.* 2, 324).

Christian.[193] The two biblical texts Luther adds to his citation from Vergil have no probative value whatever for the thesis: "all things happen by absolute necessity." We have already commented on Luther's use of a saying similar to Mt. 10: 29.[194] Concerning Is. 41: 23, it suffices to say that it would be difficult to find an exegete before or after Luther who uses this text to support a doctrine of universal absolute necessity.

In the next paragraph of the *Assertio* we find Luther saying that, from our earthly perspective, things appear arbitrary and fortuitous, but from God's viewpoint all things are necessary, because they happen not as we, but as he wills.[195] Once again, because he fails to distinguish two kinds of necessity as Augustine and Thomas do, Luther arrives at a conclusion which is at least ambiguous. If Luther takes "necessaria" to mean an absolute necessity that excludes man's free will—and from what we have just seen this does not seem to be an unfair interpretation—then he dissociates himself from the doctrine of providence taught by Thomas and Augustine and finds himself in the company of the fatalists, whose doctrine both Thomas and Augustine rejected.[196]

EXCURSUS: *Was Luther a Determinist?*

In view of the text from the *Assertio* which we have just examined (WA 7, 146, 3-12; 146, 30—147, 2) and other texts from *De servo arbitrio* (WA, 18, 615, 12—618, 18; 635, 17-22; 709, 21f.) a number of authors, both Catholic and Protestant, have not hesitated to call Luther a determinist or a fatalist. Various designations are used to describe this aspect of Luther's thought. We shall cite only Protestant

---

[193] Luther seems to be unaware, both here and in DSA: WA 18, 617, 23-618, 18, that Augustine and most of the early Fathers defended *liberum arbitrium* against the fatalists.

[194] Cf. pp. 232f.

[195] WA 7, 146, 30ff.

[196] Cf. footnote 65 above. Augustine recognizes different types of fatalists. One group holds that fate is what is bound to happen, even despite the will of God or of men. Luther is certainly not a fatalist in this sense. Another group speaks of fate, but they mean by this the will and power of God. These persons have a correct insight, says Augustine, but their terminology is bad: they should not use the misleading word "fate." "Si propterea quisquam res humanas fato tribuit, quia ipsam Dei voluntatem vel potestatem fati nomine appellat, sententiam teneat, linguam corrigat": *De civ. Dei*, V, cap. 1, Thomas, I-II, q. 116, a. 1c. In this group, however, continues Augustine, there are those—the Stoics—who correctly say that God allows nothing to remain unordered. But they err in thinking that *liberum arbitrium* is taken away by God's certain knowledge of this order, just as Cicero errs when he supposes that man's *liberum arbitrium* is incompatible with God's foreknowledge. Cf. *De civ Dei*, V, cc. 5, 8, 9f.

authors: "absolute determinism": F. Kattenbusch, *Luther's Lehre vom unfreien Willen,* pp. 25f. and 48f.; closely following this terminology is Fr. W. Schmidt, *Einleitung und Erläuterung zu: Vom unfreien Willen,* (München, 1923), p. 393; J. Huizinga, *Erasmus and the Age of Reformation* (New York, 1957), p. 163; "déterminisme totale": J. Boisset, *Erasme et Luther: Libre ou serf-arbitre?* (Paris, 1962), p. 116; "determinism": Zickendraht, *op. cit.,* p. 7; "ethical-religious determinism": E. Hirsch, *Luther-Studien,* I/II (Gütersloh, 1954), pp. 134f.; "religious determinism, but not psychological or philosophical determinism": W. von Loewenich, *Luther und der Neuprotestantismus* (Witten/Ruhr, 1963). In an earlier study, "Gott und Mensch in humanistischer und reformatorischer Schau. Eine Einführung in Luthers Schrift De servo arbitrio," in *Humanitas-Christianitas* (Gütersloh, 1948), pp. 86f., von Loewenich hesitated to call Luther's doctrine of *servum arbitrium* deterministic, primarily because this was not Luther's central concern. He admits, however, that Luther's affirmation of universal necessity and of *liberum arbitrium in inferioribus* are "statements which are not readily harmonized;" "predestinarian determinism": M. Richter, *Die Stellung des Erasmus zu Luther und zur Reformation in den Jahren 1516-1524,* diss. (Leipzig. 1900), p. 68; W. Pannenberg, "Der Einfluss der Anfechtungserfahrung auf den Prädestinationsbegriff Luthers," in: *KuD* 3 (1957), p. 29; "fatalism": H. Zahrnt, *Luther deutet Geschichte* (München, 1952), p. 207, footnote 66. H. J. Iwand calls Luther a determinist insofar as he teaches the strict determination of all events, but not in the sense of blind fate. (Cf. Pesch, "Freiheitsbegriff," *Catholica* 17 [1963], p. 233, footnote 116).

The following authors reject the claim that Luther is a determinist. They all have one thing in common: they base their judgment solely on the texts where Luther recognizes *liberum arbitrium in inferioribus* (cf. above footnote 192), but ignore the texts which led the above-named authors to conclude that Luther is a determinist. They take Luther's doctrine of *servum arbitrium* to be rooted *solely* in the biblical doctrine of sin. Conspicuously absent in these authors is a consideration of WA 7, 146, 6-12 and WA 18, 615, 12-17: K. Barth, *Kirchliche Dogmatik,* IV/2, pp. 558f.; H. Bornkamm, "Erasmus and Luther," in: *Das Jahrhundert der Reformation* (Göttingen, 1961), p. 50; Fr. Gogarten, "Sittlichkeit und Glaube in Luthers Schrift 'De servo arbitrio,' " in: *Zeitschr. f. Theol. u. Kirche* 47/2 (1950), 243ff., 248; A. Peters, *Glaube und Werk* (Berlin-Hamburg, 1962), p. 259, footnote 6; G. Ebeling, "Luther: II. Theologie," RGG, 4, 516. In his more recent study, *Luther: Einführung in sein Denken* (Tübingen, 1964), pp. 246ff., Ebeling acknowledges that there are texts in Luther which teach absolute necessity; he refrains from calling this determinism, however, because of the narrow way in which he defines determinism. Other Luther researchers who simply overlook the problem presented by the "necessitarian" texts include, according to Pesch, "Freiheitsbegriff," in: *Catholica* 17 (1963) p. 233, footnote 116: R. Hermann, E. Seeberg, P. Althaus and E. Schott.

Another group of authors who deny that Luther is a determinist or fatalist have this in common: their concept of determinism is too narrow. They seem to think that they have proven their case by refusing to attribute to Luther a doctrine of *philosophical, psychological* or *metaphysical determinism,* but forget that there can also be a *theological* or religious determinism and fatalism which is based on God's foreknowledge and predestination. Cf. G. Fonsegrive, "Déterminisme," *DTC,* 4, 641-647; J. Bouché, "Fatalisme," *DTC,* 5, 2095-2098; K. H. Miskotte, "Determinismus," *RGG,* 2, 97-100; A. Willwoll, "Determinismus," *LThK,* 3, 258f. Authors in this group include G. Ebeling, *Luther,* p. 256; H. Bornkamm, *Erasmus und Luther,* p. 50; W. Elert, *Morphologie des Luthertums,* Bd. I (München, 1958²), pp. 22 and 384f. Another common characteristic of this group is its insistence that Luther's doctrine of *servum arbitrium* is strictly biblical and theological, in no way connected with philosophy. For example, Iwand, MA, p. 312, says: "Luther's doctrine is derived from Scripture and from it alone." And Ebeling, *Luther,* p. 257, believes that Luther's statements on the absolute necessity of all happenings are not to be understood as theoretical statements, "but only as a confession, that is, in faith as praise of God ..." Cf. R. H. Fischer, "A Reasonable Luther." in: *Reformation Studies* (Richmond, Va., 1962), p. 36. These views overlook the fact that Luther was convinced that the absolute necessity of all events to the exclusion of *liberum arbitrium* was a truth forced upon the natural reason not only of confessing Christians, but also of pagans. Cf. WA 7, 146, 8f.; 18, 617, 23ff.; 718; 15-19. As E. Erikstein, *Luthers Praedestinationslehre ...* (Oslo, 1957), p. 159, has shown from abundant citations, Luther "adduces a concept of necessity ... by drawing upon every available means from logic, the concept of God, the poets, popular philosophy and scholasticism."

Still another group of authors is willing to call Luther a determinist in a watered-down sense that would also make Thomas Aquinas and Augustine determinists. Thus according to Pannenberg, *op. cit., KuD* 3 (1957), p. 114, a theologian is either a synergist (Pelagius, Ockham) or a determinist (Augustine, Thomas Aquinas, Luther). This unusual opinion is based on Pannenberg's equally unusual definition of determinism: "The causal interpretation of God's all-powerful activity in salvation ... is to be designated as theological determinism." Pannenberg seems to be dependent on Seeberg, III, pp. 402 and 405 and Loofs, p. 438, both of whom consider Thomas Aquinas to be a determinist. According to Loofs, *ibid.,* it seems that any doctrine which holds that God in some way moves the will is deterministic. But surely it is a misuse of words to designate as a determinist a theologian who very clearly upholds free will in man. Pannenberg has surprisingly little to say about the problem of free will both in the essay just mentioned and in his article, "Prädestination IV, Dogmatisch," *RGG,* 5, 487ff. Another adulterated definition of determinism is that proposed by E. Schwiebert, *op. cit.,* p. 693: "the panorama of human life unfolding according to a divine pattern." According to this definition not only would Luther, the teacher of absolute necessity, be a determinist, but also such defenders of free will as Augustine and Thomas Aquinas.

As a result of his peculiar definition of determinism, Vorster, *op. cit.,* pp. 360f. and 366, has no difficulty in denying that Luther is a determinist. Vorster, p. 313, correctly notes that, for Luther, man has no power of decision or rejection in relation to God. Yet Vorster is not willing to call this even a "religious determinism," "for determinism means that man's will is delivered over by God to an indwelling power and to an inevitability which destroys its spontaneity," p. 366. According to Vorster, it is not the destruction of human freedom, but of the will's spontaneity which constitutes determinism. Granting this peculiar definition, Vorster is, of course, correct: Luther is no determinist.

It is easy to see, after reviewing the literature, that the answer to the question: Was Luther a determinist? depends not only on a consideration of *all* the relevant texts, but also to a great extent on our understanding of what a determinist is. Because there is little agreement on the definition of determinism, the question we have posed will have as many different answers as there are definitions. There are even some Thomists who hold that Thomas Aquinas taught a certain kind of determinism: a non-necessitating pre-determination. Cf. Garrigou-Lagrange, *God: His Existence and His Nature,* Vol. II, 6th ed. (St. Louis 1955), pp. 530ff. In our opinion it is more meaningful and less ambiguous to ask: Did Luther teach a doctrine of absolute necessitarianism, that is, a necessitarianism which excludes free will? Here as elsewhere, however, we are interested not only in what Luther said, but also in what he meant.

There can be no doubt that Luther *said* that all things happen out of absolute necessity. We wish, however, to offer several considerations which point to the genuine possibility that Luther, even though he used the language of a theological determinism or necessitarianism, did not really understand the meaning and the implications of the *necessitas absoluta* which he affirmed in the *Assertio,* and that it would therefore, be incorrect to call him a determinist in the strict sense, that is, in his intention as well as in his verbal formulation: (1) the fact that his thinking on contingency and necessity lacked clarity, as we have already seen in our examination of the *Lectures on Romans* and as we shall see again in *DSA;* (2) the fact that he does not see what difference it makes to say that things happen by *necessitas consequentiae* (conditioned necessity) or by *necessitas consequentis* (absolute necessity); (3) the fact that in the *Grund und Ursach*—the German version of the *Assertio* —Luther does not use the argument from universal necessity, and that in *DSA:* WA 18, 699, 15, he omits the word "absoluta" when restating the proposition of Wyclif condemned by the Council of Constance, thus proposing a thesis: "everything happens by necessity," to which Augustine, Boethius and Thomas Aquinas could subscribe, so long as *necessitas* is not taken in an absolute sense; (4) the fact that Luther tells us that by "mera necessitas" he *means* nothing else than that man can neither will nor do anything good without special grace (WA 18, 667, 16; 670, 26 and 28); (5) the fact that Luther continually upholds the existence of man's *liberum arbitrium* "in inferioribus." If Luther understood *necessitas absoluta* in the Scholastic sense, this "exception" would be a manifest contradiction, since he says *"all things* happen by absolute necessity." One should not presume that a thinker of Luther's caliber is guilty of such an obvious contradiction. Therefore we should interpret benignly and in a less than strict sense his assertion: "All things happen by absolute necessity."

Thus to the question: Did Luther teach a doctrine of absolute necessitarianism? we should answer: according to the accepted sense of the words he uses, yes; according to his intention, no. We are happy to find ourselves in agreement here with the following Protestant theologians, all of whom admit that Luther uses deterministic language, but who maintain that determinism was certainly not Luther's intention, interest or concern: Luthardt, *op. cit.,* pp. 133f.; McGiffert, *Protestant Thought before Kant* (New York, 1962), p. 29; von Loewenich, "Gott und Mensch in humanistischer und reformatorischer Schau," pp. 86ff.; H. Bandt, *op. cit.,* pp. 120f.; Miskotte, RGG, 2, 97; Erikstein, *op. cit.,* p. 165. Bandt, *Luthers Lehre vom verborgenen Gott,* p. 120 recognizes that Luther, both in *DSA* and in the *Assertio,* certainly used "the phrase 'the necessity' of all events in a very misleading way." If we cannot without qualification agree with Bandt, p. 121, that Luther was no spokesman for determinism, we are in full agreement with him when he says Luther "at least did not intend" to teach determinism.

In the *Assertio* Luther does not hesitate to accept one of the obvious practical conclusions of his necessitarian premise, namely, that if man has no power of free choice, then God works even the evil works done by sinful men:

. . . it is not even in man's power to do or to think evil. In Eph. 1 Paul says truly: "God works all things in all." [197] . . . God also works the evil deeds in the ungodly, as Prov. 16 says: "The Lord has made everything for his own purpose, even the wicked for the evil day." [198] And Rom. 1: "God has given them up to a reprobate sense, so that they do what is not fitting." [199] And Rom. 9: "Whom he will he hardens and he has mercy on whom he will." Just as he says of Pharaoh, Ex. 9: "For this purpose I have raised you up that I may show in you my power." [200] Therefore God is frightful in his judgments and in his works.[201]

It need hardly be pointed out that the biblical texts cited by Luther admit of other interpretations than the radical one he has given, especially when we look at them in their context. Scripture does teach us of the all-embracing power of God, but it never says explicitly that God causes or works the evil deeds of sinners. The Church's tradition of

---

[197] ". . . non est homo in manu sua, etiam mala operans et cogitans. Et vere Paulus Eph. i. dixit: 'Deus operatur omnia in omnibus'." WA 7, 145, 25ff. Cf. I Cor. 12: 6; Eph. 1: 11 and Phil. 2: 13.

[198] Prov. 16: 4.

[199] Rom. 1: 28.

[200] Rom. 9: 17f.; Ex. 9: 16.

[201] WA 7, 144, 34–145, 4.

scriptural interpretation before Luther always admitted that God permits sin, that he can leave sinners in their misery, that even sin can be used by God for good purposes and that God sometimes punishes men by hardening their hearts through the withdrawal of his grace, which is always given freely. But awareness of the numerous biblical texts telling us of God's unique holiness, sinlessness and detestation of evil, coupled with reflection on the very nature of sin, prevented the Catholic tradition of biblical interpretation from saying that God causes or works sin in the sinner.

As with other radical assertions of Luther, however, we must pose the ecumenical question: What did Luther *mean* when he said, "God also works evil deeds in the ungodly?" Neither here nor in a corresponding place in *DSA* [202] is it perfectly clear what Luther means. He does not treat the question *ex professo,* as Thomas Aquinas does, for example.[203] Is it not possible that Luther intends the same thing that Thomas and other Scholastics intended when they held that God is the cause of the sinful acts of sinners, but not of the sin itself? Even the formulations of Luther and Thomas are strikingly similar: "God also works evil deeds in the ungodly" (Luther); "the action of sin is from God (Thomas, *De Malo,* q. 3, a. 2) and "God is the cause of the act of sin" (Thomas, I-II, q. 79, a. 2).[204] It is possible that Luther meant something else. The point we wish to make, however, is that it would be unfair to say Luther clearly did mean something else, something Manichaean, for he has never been asked what he really meant! Perhaps Luther meant to say that "God produces the evil as well as the good works, not only permissively, but also properly and by himself"—a thesis which was condemned by Trent.[205] Perhaps he would have rejected such a thesis. There is no way to determine this for certain. At least we know of no work, however, in which he qualifies his thesis by saying that God produces evil works not only permissively, but also properly and by himself.

If one's knowledge of Luther is restricted solely to Grisar's well-known work, he believes that Luther taught a doctrine of the absolute passivity of man's will which is incompatible with Catholic doctrine. Grisar quotes Luther as saying: "We suffer each and every thing. Toward God free will ceases." [206] Aside from the fact that one cannot

---

[202] WA 18, 709, 28-36.

[203] Cf. *De Malo,* q. 3, aa. 1 and 2; I-II, q. 79, aa. 1-3; *In Rom.,* cap. 1, lect. 7, nn. 137-140.

[204] Even Trent (DS 1556) seems to be willing to accept as Catholic the thesis: Deus mala opera permissive operatur.

[205] Sess. VI, can. 6: DS 1556.

[206] *Luther,* I, p. 518, esp. footnote 1.

overlook the general context of Luther's statements on the passivity of the will,[207] it is an even more basic rule of interpretation to consider the immediate context in this case, the full sentences from which the above-cited partial sentences were taken. Referring to the petition of the Lord's prayer, "Thy will be done . . .", Luther writes: "We live, we do and we suffer each and every thing not as we, but as he wills. The free will which manifests itself toward us and in relation to temporal things ceases in relation to God." [208] Is one expressing an unorthodox doctrine of passivity when he says that man lives, acts and suffers all things according as God wills? And when Luther says: Free will ceases in relation to God, but not in relation to earthly things, we encounter nothing that we have not seen before. He is simply restating his conviction that fallen man is not free to move toward God in any way, not even to prepare himself to return to God.

This reminds us again that we cannot lose sight of Luther's concern if we are to interpret the *Assertio* fairly and in its total context. Luther's concern here was surely not to propagate a doctrine of absolute necessitarianism. His unquestionable concern was to refute and to destroy the exaggerated Neo-Semipelagian view of free will that found its expression in the Ockham-Biel interpretation of the Scholastic axiom: *facienti quod in se est, etc.* From the beginning to the end of the *Assertio* Luther attacks the Bielian doctrine "that free will is able to prepare itself to enter into grace." [209] From beginning to end he attacks the Neo-Semipelagian doctrine which places "the necessary grace of God in the power of man." [210] His basic concern is clearly discernable when he asks: "And how is it possible that, without the Spirit, he is able by the power of his nature to have a desire for the Spirit or to prepare himself for the Spirit by doing what he is able to do?" [211]

Any Catholic theologian could and should have asked this same question of Gabriel Biel. The fact that Luther was not joined by more Catholics in his rightful protest against this threat to the biblical, Augustinian and Thomistic doctrine of the grace of Christ can be explained to *some* extent by the mysterious disappearance of the proceedings and teachings of the Second Council of Orange. But even apart from Orange

---

207 See our remarks above, esp. in footnote 91, on Luther's statements in the *Lectures on Romans* concerning the passivity of the will.

208 WA 7, 146, 32ff.

209 WA 7, 143, 2f. WA 7, 147, 38–148, 13 is a brilliant exposition of the fallacy of Neo-Semipelagianism.

210 WA 7, 148, 8f.: ". . . gratiam Dei necessariam in potestatem hominis ponit."

211 WA 7, 147, 17ff.: "Et quommodo possibile est, ut sine spiritu ex natura sua possit pro spiritu concupiscere seu ad spiritum se praeparare faciendo quod in se est."

II, the New Testament was available and Augustine was available from which one could have seen the error in this new form of Semipelagianism. Why more theologians prior to Luther did not arise to refute the Neo-Semipelagianism is a question that cannot be answered here. And this is not the most important question for us, for Luther did not separate from the Church of the Catholic *theologians,* but from the Church of the *papacy.* It was not the theologians whom he called the Antichrist, but the pope. He came to this conclusion not through careful ecclesiological and historical arguments, which were always a secondary basis for his judgment that the pope was the Antichrist. He reached this conclusion primarily because of two convictions, both of which appear in the *Assertio:* (1) that the pope himself teaches Biel's error,[212] and (2) that such an erroneous doctrine has *prevailed* in the Church to the detriment of many people, especially the unlearned.[213] The first charge is not true: no pope has taught, at least in his capacity as pope, that fallen man can prepare himself for justification simply by the power of free will without the prevenient grace of God. On the other hand, there is a great deal of truth to Luther's second contention, which carries with it an implicit indictment that the pope, Christ's vicar and appointed shepherd over the whole flock, was not faithful to his pastoral office, that he was not vigilant in his duty to uphold sound doctrine throughout the Church. We have already expressed our view in the last chapter that negligence in the exercise of the papal and episcopal teaching office was the greatest of the many evils in the late medieval Church and that it was the most important single motive which prompted Martin Luther to begin his reformation of the doctrine, not the morals, of the Church. We wish to re-affirm this view now, and to specify that the particular doctrine which Luther found *most* in need of reform was not the doctrine of indulgences or of the papacy, but the doctrine concerning free will. In the *Assertio,* as in *DSA,* he stresses the primacy and centrality of this question:

In the other articles on the papacy, councils, indulgences and other unnecessary trumpery the levity and foolishness of the pope and his associates ought to be tolerated, but in this article, which is the most

---

212 WA 7, 143, 1ff.: "Tu dicis, quod liberum arbitrium possit se parare, ut intret ad gratiam. Contra Christus dicit. . . ." WA 7, 148, 8-11: "Videris mihi peior esse Pelagio, dum gratiam dei necessariam in potestatem hominis ponis, quam ille penitus negavit necessariam. Minus, inquam, videtur impium gratiam in totum negare quam eam nostro studio et opere parari ac velut in manu nostra reponere."

213 WA 7, 148, 11ff.: "Et tamen praevaluit haec operatio erroris, quia speciosa et placens naturae liberoque arbitrio ut difficile sit eam confutare, praesertim apud rudes et crassos animos."

important of all and the greatest of our concerns, one must grieve and weep that these wretches so rave.[214]

When we grant at least the partial validity of Luther's implicit indictment of the pope's neglect of his teaching office, we are not saying that the pope had allowed the entire Church to fall into error on the doctrine of grace. We have given reasons in Chapter 7 why we do not think this was the case. But we do say that at least in the part of the Church that Luther knew, there was a serious misunderstanding of the Gospel, not simply among certain theologians, but among wide sectors of the common people whom Luther undoubtedly had encountered.[215] Academic theology, then as now, is seldom without its practical influence on the faithful, for good or ill. The point of academic theology which had this destructive effect on the popular understanding of the absolute necessity of grace. We have given reasons in Chapter 7 why we do not think this truly good before God, was, of course, the doctrine of free will contained in the Bielian understanding of the axiom "facienti quod in se est. . . ." It was *this* concept of free will—not Augustine's or Thomas'—which Luther rejected in order to uphold the grace of God.

Luther believed that the *Grund und Ursach,* which appeared on March 1, 1521, was a better version of his reply to the papal bull than the *Assertio.*[216] From an ecumenical standpoint, one can agree that it is better since it is less divisive and less radical in its formulations. Above all, there is no hint of absolute necessitarianism. As in the *Assertio,* Luther stresses again the central importance of his thesis concerning free will. Even though some of the 41 censured propositions were concerned with the papacy, with purgatory, with indulgences and with the sacraments, Luther designates the one pertaining to free will as the main issue:

In other matters the frivolity and the blindness of the pope could be tolerated, but when it comes to this chief article of the faith it is a pity that they are so senseless. Here they completely ruin everything that God has given us through Christ.[217]

When we look at Luther's defense of the censured proposition 36, we find no argument from the absolute necessity of all events or any sugges-

---

[214] WA 7, 148, 14ff.: "In caeteris autem articulis, de Papatu, Conciliis, indulgentiis aliisque non necessariis nugis, ferenda est levitas et stultitia Papae et suorum, sed in hoc articulo, qui omnium optimus et rerum nostrarum summa est, dolendum ac flendum est, miseros sic insanire."

[215] Cf. Lortz, I, pp. 99-111; 124 and 173ff.

[216] WABR 2, 251, 7f.: "Vernacula melior est, quam sit latina."

[217] WA 7, 449; tr. C. Jacobs, rev. by G. Forell, AE, 32, p. 93.

tion that God is the ultimate source even of man's sins, as we encountered in the *Assertio*. We find instead a completely biblical argument which does *not* prove that the sinner lacks natural freedom or *liberum arbitrium*, but simply that the sinner without grace and faith can do nothing but sin.[218] This proposition, as we have already seen, can readily be incorporated into the Catholic doctrinal tradition.

The importance of theological language and formulation becomes manifest in this work. Luther is greatly concerned about what we *call* "free" and that to which we give the *name* "freedom". He is not so interested in denying man's power to choose—*liberum arbitrium*—as he is in denying that this should be *called* freedom.[219] Thus, Luther argues: If man's free will apart from God's grace can only sin, "where is then the freedom" to do anything but sin? [220] "Is it freedom to be unable to do anything but evil?" [221] "Is that freedom to be a prisoner of the devil's will?" [222]

From the standpoint of the Catholic tradition, the answer to these questions is quite simple: in one sense the sinner is free and in another sense he is not! The sinner is *not* free to do anything relevant to salvation apart from God's grace. He is free, however, in the sense that he always possesses natural freedom or *liberum arbitrium*. When the Catholic tradition constantly upholds the latter thesis, this in no way implies that man is free to do anything for salvation without grace. It was only in a non-authentic "episode" [223] of Church history, an episode which Luther knew at first hand, that certain theologians asserted that the

---

[218] As biblical evidence Luther uses: Rom. 14: 23; II Tim. 2: 25f., Jn. 8: 33ff.; Gen. 6: 3,15; 8: 21; Gal. 5: 17.

[219] As we have seen from his earlier works, this is a pastoral concern. For example, in the *Resolutiones Lutherianae super propositionibus suis Lipsiae disputatis* (1519): WA 2, 424, 15-22, Luther says to Eck: "Si dices 'Est tamen aliquo rerum sensu, liberum arbitrium esse dominum non excludendo gratiam,' respondeo: 'Sive sit sensus sive non, Theologum decet loqui ad usum Theologiae et sacrae scripturae. . . .' Fateor, liberum arbitrium posse dici dominum, Principem, Episcopum, Regem et alia quaecunque, sed haec periculo gratiae dei et scripturae intelligendae dicuntur, quae servitutis vocabulo nos signat et qui aliter liberum arbitrium intelligit, non intelligit." Luther is thus willing to admit the reality of that which is commonly called *liberum arbitrium*, but he believes that this is a departure from biblical language and that it endangers the doctrine of grace, for Scripture, apart from Christian freedom, speaks only of slavery or servitude. If anyone understands *liberum arbitrium* apart from this servitude then he has not understood it correctly. Cf. WA 2, 647, 5-8; 7, 145, 35f.

[220] WA 7, 445, 36.

[221] WA 7, 445, 38: "Ist das frey das nirgen zu taug den zum Bosen?"

[222] WA 7, 447: "Ist das freiheit nach des teufels willen gefangen sein. . . ." Luther then appeals to his favorite text from Augustine, where Augustine calls man's will *servum* rather than *liberum arbitrium*: *Contra Iul. pelag.*, 2, 8, 23.

[223] That is Loofs' expression.

sinner could do something of value before God by his own free will without grace. It is hard to over-estimate the passionate intensity with which Luther rejected this concept of free will. With a remarkably sound and profound biblical intuition he, like Augustine, saw that "This error of free will is a special doctrine of the Antichrist." [224] Happily, in the *Grund und Ursach,* Luther indicates that he does not consider that the "error of free will" consists in the mere affirmation that man has natural *liberum arbitrium.* He writes: "It is a profound, blind error to teach that the naturally free will can turn itself to the Spirit apart from grace. . . ." [225] This is not the denial of the existence of "the naturally free will," then, but the denial of the exaggeration of its powers in relation to salvation!

Nevertheless, it is clear that Luther wants a reformation of theological language in view of the fact that the term "free will" is not biblical and since it has led many into serious error. "The papists," he insists, "have distorted all words and have created a new language" by claiming that the will is free even though it can only sin.[226] Therefore, he says, "I wish that the term 'free will' had never been invented. It is not in Scripture and should more aptly be called 'self will'." [227] If one wishes to use the term free will, adds Luther, he should apply it to the regenerate man, for "the man who is without sin is certainly free. But those who remain in sin are unfree and prisoners of the devil." [228] Using a far-fetched example, Luther will also allow the sinner to be called "frey willige" since this man wishes to become free through grace, just as a beggar might be called a rich man because he can become rich. Any other designation of a sinner as "free," contends Luther, would easily mislead simple people.[229]

How are we to evaluate Luther's suggested revision of accepted theological language? First of all we must note that Luther, properly conscious of the importance of theological language, is correct in saying that the term *liberum arbitrium* is not found in Scripture. He seems to admit that the reality is there when he attacks the exaggeration—not the existence—of the power of the "naturlich frey will." But in the light of the affirmation of *liberum arbitrium* by so many Church Fathers, councils and theologians, is it correct to say that, by using the term, "free

---

[224] WA 7, 451: "Dieser yrthum von freyen willen ist eyn eygen Artickel des Endchrist."

[225] WA 7, 447.

[226] WA 7, 447, 7f.

[227] WA 7, 449, 24f.

[228] WA 7, 449, 26-30: ". . . der mensch der on sunde ist der self ist gewislich frey. . . . Die aber ynn den sunden liegen sein unfrey und des Teuffels gefangen."

[229] WA 7, 449, 31ff.

will," the "papists . . . have created a new language?" The mere fact that
the term *liberum arbitrium* is not a biblical term cannot be regarded as
the decisive motive behind Luther's attack on *liberum arbitrium*. As is
well known, Luther had no difficulty in accepting other non-biblical terms
such as "person," "Trinity," etc. His main reason for opposing the term
liberum arbitrium is based, as we have already suggested, on his *pastoral*
concern that people, especially simple persons, are misled by this term
into thinking that man's conversion depends primarily not on the grace
and mercy of God but on the good use a man makes of his free will.[230]

Has not Luther put his finger on a problem that is widespread even
today: the Pelagian tendency present in many Christians which inclines
them to think that the effectiveness of God's grace depends ultimately on
our free acceptance of it or that our response to the Gospel is mainly a
matter of free resolutions? Forgotten in this popular understanding of
grace is the fact that our very free acceptance of grace and our good
resolutions themselves are the work of grace! How often do preachers,
under the guise that they "do not want to frighten the people" by teaching them of the mystery of predestination and of the absolute necessity
of grace for every salutary act simply succeed in having before them
a congregation of superficially unfrightened—but often scrupulous—
Semipelagians and legalists who are confident that God does—or has
done—his part and that it is up to them to do the rest? One need only
ask the average Catholic, or modern Protestant, a few questions concerning grace and predestination to discover that many of them—including those who have been catechized and preached to for years—
have very little awareness of the absolute sovereignty of God's grace,
and therefore of the mystery of God himself. How easy it is to find
even educated Catholics who are not aware that there is not only a
Calvinistic, but also a Lutheran and a Catholic doctrine of predestination. When the Catholic theologian F. Norris, asserted: "We are all
Pelagians at heart," [231] he was merely echoing in 1964 what Luther
wrote in 1519: that Pelagianism is the error of every century, "very
often suppressed, but never stamped out." [232]

Luther's conviction that a popular Pelagianism "prevailed," coupled
with the doctrinal error (Neo-Semipelagianism) that he himself learned
from the works of Gabriel Biel and other late Scholastic theologians led
him to the conclusion that the best way to combat this heresy was

---

[230] Cf. footnote 219 above.
[231] "The 'De Ecclesia' Tract in the Seminary," in: *Apostolic Renewal in the
Seminary* (New York, 1965), p. 196.
[232] WA 5, 485: "saepius oppressus quidem, se nunquam extinctus."

through a radical revision of accepted theological language: by elimi-
nating completely the term *liberum arbitrium*—a word that Satan invented to lure men away from God [233]—and by replacing it with the
term *servum arbitrium,* or at least "our own will" (*eygen wille*), Luther
hoped to restore the primacy of the grace of Christ and to teach the
helplessness of man's "eygen wille" without grace. In this way men
could be led back to the "way of God."

It is a matter of historical record that the Church did not accept
Luther's proposal. It can very plausibly be argued that the official teaching authority of the Church did not even understand his pastoral-
cathechetical intention. The *magisterium* simply was concerned with the
fact that Luther had called the *liberum arbitrium* of the sinner an
"empty word." Without taking Luther's explanation of his thesis into
account, the Church authorities censured it, as we have seen, in a most
ambiguous way.

Even supposing, however, that the Church authorities did understand
the pastoral-theological concern behind Luther's radical thesis, can we
assume that Luther's proposal would have been accepted? We do not
believe so. Our view is not based simply on the fact that the term *liberum
arbitrium* had played such an integral and legitimate role in Catholic
theology since the pre-Augustinian Fathers. We are taking into account
also the fact that, by abandoning the terms "free will" or power of free
decision in favor of some other term, it is more than possible that the
carefully balanced dialectic of grace and free will upheld against the
Stoic fatalists and Manichaeans on the one hand, and against every kind
of Pelagianism on the other would be endangered.

In his legitimate concern for defending the absolute necessity of God's
grace for even the beginning of salvation, Luther seems to have ignored
the possibility of other errors, that of fatalism, necessitarianism or
quietism. We have already seen how Luther himself did not avoid suggestions of fatalism and determinism in his attack on the exaggeration of
the powers of free will. The Church had struggled all too mightily in an
earlier age on behalf of the unity and holiness of God and man's responsibility for sin. These were the truly theological motives, not any
false humanistic desires to extol the powers of man, which led the
Church to affirm officially man's free will. Therefore even in the face
of serious misunderstanding of the role of man's *liberum arbitrium,*
both in a particular school of theology as well as in practical piety, the

---

[233] WA 7, 145, 33-36: "Unde non est dubium, Satana magistro in Ecclesiam
venisse hoc nomen 'liberum arbitrium' ad seducendos homines a via dei in vias
suas proprias."

Church could not have been sympathetic to a proposal that would correct one error by opening the door to others. The authoritative teachers of the Church could have little interest in a new theological formulation designed to uphold the doctrine of the absolute necessity of God's grace for every action that is truly good *coram Deo* if, in doing so, the doctrine of God's unity or holiness could be called into question.

It must be remembered also, that to be fully consistent in his program of a reform of theological language, Luther would have to abolish from the Christian vocabulary *all* use of the word freedom except Christian freedom. But not even the Bible does this! The Jews did not misunderstand Jesus' words about freedom [234] because they were infatuated with the concept of *liberum arbitrium* but because of their pride in their *political* freedom.[235] Jesus did not tell them to abolish this concept of freedom from their vocabulary. He told them instead of *another kind* of freedom corresponding to another kind of slavery. This was the all-important freedom. Only through it is a man *truly* free. In this way Jesus gave us a "new language"—not by abolishing other concepts of freedom—but by revealing to us a new kind of freedom.

The Catholic-Evangelical preacher [236] should therefore try to correct the Pelagian tendency present in all of us not by denying that man has free will or by saying that political freedom is not worthy to be called freedom. He should rather proclaim constantly that *genuine* freedom belongs only to the sons of God. Even though natural freedom and political freedom are good gifts of God for which we should be continually grateful, we should strive for and pray for the greatest gift of freedom, the freedom by which the Son of God makes us free. While never calling into question the role of man's free decision in faith and in Christian living, the Christian preacher will fulfill Luther's genuinely Catholic concern by proclaiming more clearly and emphatically the great New Testament doctrine that, apart from the grace of Christ, our free will cannot make even the slightest beginning toward faith, and that,

---

[234] Jn. 8: 33.

[235] It was at least an exaggeration for the Jews to say they have never been slaves to anyone. They were once enslaved in Egypt and in Babylon and even at the time in which they spoke they were under Roman political domination.

[236] The Roman Catholic theologian today suffers from none of the ambiguities in the doctrine of the necessity of grace which marked late Scholastic theology. Unlike the late Scholastics he is guided by the teachings of Second Orange as well as by Trent. A persistent problem today, however, is that when seminarians are confronted with the classical debate between Molinism and the Bañez-Thomists on the relation of grace and free will, many seminarians declare that they "follow Thomism, but Molinism is easier to preach." But what they preach is often some form of Semipelagianism!

as far as Christian living is concerned, it is God who works in us both the willing and the performance of our actions.[237]

In 1519 Luther was still a Catholic reformer. In 1520 he was the first of the Protestant reformers. Luther's transformation from a reformer-within-the-Roman Catholic Church [238] to a reformer-outside-the-Roman Catholic Church [239] was largely occasioned by the condemnation of much of his teaching in *Exsurge Domine*. The tragedy of this transformation from Catholic to Protestant reformer lies to a great extent in the fact that there was no true dialogue or meeting of minds between the Church and Luther prior to his separation from the Church. There was mostly simply a mutual rejection of formulas, with little understanding of the intention and concern of the other.

From the standpoint of the Church's *magisterium* or teaching office, the propositions condemned in *Exsurge Domine* were censured, as we have already noted, most ambiguously. It would not be difficult, on the one hand, to *conceive of* a sense in which each of the propositions is *either* heretical, *or* scandalous, *or* offensive to pious ears. But on the other hand the commission which drew up the bull threatening excommunication made no real effort to come to grips with the meaning of Luther's propositions *as he explained them*. The legitimate Catholic sense which Luther intended proposition 36 to have received no acknowledgment whatever in the bull.[240] If the commission were not concerned with Luther's meaning, but only with what he wrote, with his

---

[237] It is significant that Phil. 2: 13, to which we have just referred, such an important text for teaching the sovereignty of God even over man's free will, is a text that is never read publicly in the liturgy of the Church! The same is true of many other texts which are so often cited by Augustine, Luther—and Catholic works of *theology*—as the biblical loci for the doctrines of predestination, grace, faith, Christian freedom, and law and works. For example, the following passages are *never* read publicly in the Mass on Sundays or on feast days: Rom. 1: 7; 4: 25; 8: 28-34; 9; Gal. 3: 1-15; I Cor. 4: 7 (Augustine's chief argument against the Pelagian concept of merit); Eph. 2: 8f.; Jn. 6: 66; 8: 31-36 (!). John 15: 5 is read only on the feast of a martyr in Paschaltide. Hopefully at least some of these texts will be included in the more extensive selection of biblical readings currently being worked out for the Service of the Word by the post-conciliar liturgical commission.

[238] As K. Adam, *The Roots of the Reformation* (New York, 1951), p. 28, has said, had Luther brought his "magnificent qualities to the removal of the abuses of the time, . . . had he remained a faithful member of his Church," he would have been a saint comparable to Thomas Aquinas and Francis of Assisi.

[239] In terms of the *Constitution on the Church* and of the *Decree on Ecumenism* of the Second Vatican Council, it is incorrect to speak of Luther simply as being "outside the Church." He was separated from the Roman Catholic Church, but nevertheless retained a "certain, though imperfect, communion with" that Church: *Decree on Ecumenism*, n. 3, par. 1.

[240] This sense is perfectly evident in both the original setting of the proposition,

theological language, then this too should have been made clear.[241] Karl Rahner has made us aware of the fact that "ecclesiastical declarations of doctrine . . . also contain implicitly a determined terminology about which one cannot pose the question of truth but at the most the question of aptness. Of course, those who teach and define are not always conscious of this; indeed most of the time they are not conscious of it. . . ."[242]

After offering several historical illustrations of his point Rahner adds: "The interesting thing about this is . . . the fact that nowhere in these declarations of the Church's *magisterium* is the question seen explicitly as one of terminology but that the matter is taught with the impression and presupposition that one is speaking about the reality itself."[243]

It would seem to be one of the chief ecumenical duties of the Church's *magisterium* to be conscious of the distinction between talking about an issue and the issue itself [244] or, as Pope John XXIII expressed it in his opening address at the recent Council, between the *truth* contained in a doctrine and the formulation of that truth.[245] In contrast to the spirit in which *Exsurge Domine* was composed, there is much evidence that the Second Vatican Council was sensitive to this distinction. It has, in fact, officially been accepted by the council in the *Decree on Ecumenism*.[246]

As far as Luther's reaction to *Exsurge Domine* is concerned, we also find a lack of the ecumenical spirit: the will to unity of the Church rooted in charity and in an interest to understand the concerns of his opponents. He had encountered a Neo-Semipelagian concept of free will in Gabriel Biel's theology which severely diminished the importance of the grace of Christ. Unfortunately, when the papal bull censured his assertion that the free will is an "empty word," Luther concluded that

---

the *Heidelberg Disputation*, as well as in the defense of it in the *Grund und Ursach*.

[241] Cardinal Ottaviani, as we have noted in the Introduction, footnote 46, has made it clear that this is how he understands the censure of books by the Holy Office (now the Congregation of the Doctrine of the Faith).

[242] *Theol. Inv.* V, p. 55.

[243] *Ibid.*, p. 57.

[244] *Ibid.*, p. 59.

[245] *Concilium Oecumenicum Vat. II*, AAS 54 (1962) 792: "Est enim aliud ipsum depositum fidei, seu veritatis, quae veneranda doctrina nostra continentur, aliud modus, quo eaedem enuntiantur, eodem tamen sensu eademque sententia."

[246] *Decretum de Oecumenismo*, cap. II, 6: ". . . in doctrinae enuntiandae modo —qui ab ipso deposito fidei sedulo distingui debet. . . ;" citation from *Catholica* 19 (1965), 28. It is important to note the admission made in the decree that there can be deficiencies in the mode of expressing a doctrine: ". . . si quae . . . etiam in doctrinae enuntiandae modo . . . minus accurate servata fuerint, opportuno tempore recte debiteque instaurentur": *ibid.*

this was a defense of Biel's false concept of the power of free will. Like those who had condemned his proposition, he too committed the ecumenical sin: [247] he rejected their view without asking: "What did you mean by that?"

The censuring of Luther's thirty-sixth proposition was certainly no endorsement of the Ockham-Biel Neo-Semipelagianism. No pope or council ever approved an understanding of free will that would make it responsible for the beginning of salvation. But Luther thought that the pope had done precisely this. That is why he thought the pope was the Antichrist. And this was his greatest mistake. Even as late as 1535 Luther showed a tragic misunderstanding of the authentic Catholic doctrine when he said that he would not only carry the pope on his shoulder but would also kiss his feet, if the pope would teach that we are justified solely by the grace of Christ.[248] Even at such a late date Luther did not realize that this is what the pope does teach!

In saying this we certainly do not wish to cast all the blame for the misunderstanding on Luther. Why did the Roman Catholic Church have to wait until the year after Luther's death to reaffirm clearly the Pauline-Augustinian-Orange II doctrine of man's bondage to sin?

When we said that the pope *does* teach that we are justified solely by the grace of Christ, we do not mean that he continually teaches this truth clearly and effectively or that he was teaching it clearly during Luther's lifetime. That the papal teaching office should be exercised in such a way is most desirable, but not even the Roman Catholic Church's teaching about papal infallibility implies that the bishop of Rome will exercise his teaching office as unfailingly, as alertly and as devotedly as the Good Shepherd exercised his ministry.

The doctrine of papal infallibility simply means that the bishop of Rome, in view of the promise of Christ to send the Holy Spirit of Truth to the whole Church, cannot err when he is teaching the Gospel to the whole Church in his role as delegated shepherd of the whole Church.[249] In the ordinary exercise of his ministry, according to Roman Catholic doctrine, it is quite possible as long as the Church is on her pilgrim journey, for the bishop of Rome to be insensitive to problems of the times, to be negligent in preaching relevantly and to be lacking in vigilance and theological discernment.

---

[247] Surely the lack of pastoral understanding which characterizes the condemnation of Luther in *Exsurge Domine,* as well as Luther's equally harsh designation of the pope as the Antichrist, should be listed among the "sins against unity" for which Catholics and Lutherans should humbly seek "pardon from God and the separated brethren": *Decree on Ecumenism,* ch. II, n. 7.

[248] WA 40/1, 181, 11ff.

[249] Cf. Jn. 21: 15-18.

Even when the pope or a council teaches infallibly, it is still possible, according to Catholic theology, for this teaching to be ineffective due to misunderstanding of the problem or the situation. It is still possible for a true teaching to be irrelevant, to be lacking in clarity, to be too late to meet the need, or, because of its wording, to invite misunderstanding.[250]

It is possible for theologians, preachers, laity, bishops and popes as private teachers—to teach something in the Church that is not the teaching of the Church. A pope—because of negligence, insensitivity to the situation or lack of knowledge—can likewise fail to teach something that is the teaching of the Church. In this sense one could argue that the popes in Luther's time did not effectively teach the Catholic doctrine that the very beginning of salvation is due solely to the inspiring action of the Holy Spirit and grace within us.

The popes of Luther's day certainly did not censure the late Scholastic theologians such as Biel who had—most probably unwittingly—departed from the teaching of the Catholic doctrine of the Second Council of Orange. In this sense again it could be said that the popes of Luther's time did not teach that we are saved solely by the grace of Christ.

Without prejudice to a correctly understood and necessary doctrine of infallibility, then, it is quite proper to see even this doctrine as leaving great room for fallibility in the Church and in the papacy. History can provide us with innumerable examples of the fallibility of the infallible Church of Christ.

It is only in the light of the foregoing restrictions that we say that the pope—and the Catholic Church—do teach that we are saved solely by the grace of Christ. When we say that the pope does teach this evangelical truth, we mean simply that this is the official, authoritative, defined teaching of the Church of which the bishop of Rome is the leading visible pastor. It is this authentic teaching—not the distortions of it that have existed and exist still among both Catholics and Protestants—that should form a common bond between Catholic and Evangelical Christians. The tragedy of the 16th century was that distortions of this Evangelical-Catholic truth on both sides led to a division of those who called themselves Evangelicals on the one hand and Catholics on the other.

---

[250] Cf. K. Rahner, "What is a Dogmatic Statement?," *Theol. Inv. V*, pp. 45ff.

PART TWO

ERASMUS: DE LIBERO ARBITRIO

9

The Erasmian Doctrine of Free Will as Set Forth in *De libero arbitrio* (1524) and Clarified in *Hyperaspistes Liber* I (1526) and *Liber* II (1527)

I. BACKGROUND OF *DE LIBERO ARBITRIO*

Luther's *Assertio* encountered swift opposition from Catholic apologists.[1] We are concerned here with only one of these replies, *De libero arbitrio diatribe sive Collatio,* written in 1524 by Erasmus of Rotterdam.[2] This was the book which directly provoked Luther's major work, *De servo arbitrio.*

The early positive attitude of Erasmus toward Luther[3] began to

---

[1] These replies included the *Determinatio theologiae facultatis Parisiensis super doctrina Lutheriana hactenus per eam visa,* of April 15, 1521; the book by Bishop John Fisher of Rochester, England: *Confutatio assertionis Lutheranae* (1523). J. von Walter accepts the argument of Zickendraht pp. 43ff., that DLA is dependent on the work by Fisher: "Die neueste Beurteilung des Erasmus," in: *Jahresbericht der Schlesischen Gesellschaft f. vaterländische Kultur;* 89 (1911/12), 17. For other Catholic reactions to the *Assertio* see *Erasmus-Luther: Discourse on Free Will,* tr. and ed. E. F. Winter (New York, 1961), p. 5, footnote 4.

[2] We shall use as our text the edition of Johannes v. Walter, *Quellenschriften zur Geschichte des Protestantismus,* Heft 8 (Leipzig, 1910) = Walter. Cf. *Desiderii Erasmi de libero arbitrio diatribe sive collatio 1524,* in *Opera Omnia,* ed. LeClerc, Vol. IX (Leyden, 1706), 1215-1247.

[3] The early relations between Luther and Erasmus as well as the background of the controversy are traced by Max Richter, *Die Stellung des Erasmus zu Luther und zur Reformation in den Jahren 1516-1524,* diss. (Leipzig, 1900); (a short summary of this work can be found in DTC, 9, 1287ff.); Freitag, "Einleitung zu de servo arbitrio," in: WA 18, 552-559; Ch. Andler, *Étude critique sur les relations d'Érasme et de Luther* (Paris, 1909); Zickendraht, pp. 1-25; J. MacKinnon, *Luther and the Reformation,* vol. III (London, 1929), pp. 224-273; K. A. Meissinger, *Erasmus von Rotterdam,* 2nd ed. (Berlin, 1948), pp. 238-71; H. Bornkamm, "Erasmus und Luther," in: *Das Jahrhundert der Reformation* (Göttingen,

change gradually, first to a posture of silent caution, then to one of outright opposition as Luther's criticisms began to be directed not simply against Scholastic theology and abuses in the Church, but against the teachings and authority of the Church itself. It was Luther who first of all saw that there were fundamental differences between himself and the most influential scholar in Europe. As early as 1516 Luther was convinced that Erasmus did not understand what Paul meant by the justice of the law.[4] In 1517, in a letter to Johann Lang, Luther made it known that his respect for Erasmus was decreasing daily.[5] In this same letter Luther also indicates what is to be the basic difference behind the future controversy: "The judgment of the man who attributes something to free will is different from that of the man who knows of nothing but grace." [6]

G. Krodel sees the Leipzig Disputation of 1519 as the decisive point in Erasmus' change of heart toward Luther.[7] By the middle of 1522 Erasmus had made known his intention to write against Luther.[8] It is well known that when Erasmus hesitated to carry out his plan, Pope Hadrian VI, King Henry VIII of England and other Catholic leaders urged him on.[9] This is hardly proof, however, "that Erasmus attacked Luther entirely against his will" and "without any freedom whatever." [10] Whereas the attacks on the *Assertio* by such opponents of Luther as Johannes Cochlaeus and Henry VIII centered mainly on the theses concerning the sacraments which were censured in *Exsurge Domine*, Erasmus concentrated on proposition 36.[11] In a letter to

---

1961), pp. 36-55; also in: *Luther-Jahrbuch* (1958), pp. 1-11; J. Boisset, *Érasme et Luther* (Paris, 1962), pp. 5-27.

[4] WABR 1, 70. Luther's interpretation of *iustitia legis* here is the same as that of Thomas Aquinas: cf. I-II, q. 100, a. 12; q. 106; *In Rom.*, cap. 3, lect. 4, n. 317.

[5] WABR 1, 90.

[6] *Ibid*: "Sed aliud est iudicium eius, qui arbitrio hominis non nihil tribuit, aliud eius, qui praeter gratiam nihil novit."

[7] "Luther, Erasmus and Henry VIII," in: *Archiv fur Reformationsgesch.*, 53 (1962), 75.

[8] Cf. Zickendraht, p. 11. Krodel, p. 77 has found evidence that Erasmus first thought of writing against Luther in August of 1521. He refers to the letter of Erasmus in P. S. Allen, *Opus Epistolarum*, vol. 4, 1228, 50ff.

[9] See A. Renaudet, *Études Érasmiennes (1521-1529)* (Paris, 1939), pp. 193ff.; 202-206. Even before 1522 Erasmus had been urged to declare himself publicly against Luther by Pope Leo X and others. Cf. Freitag, WA 18, 529-579; Zickendraht, 1-25.

[10] Freitag, pp. 577ff.

[11] As early as the Diet of Worms (1521) the papal nuncio and former teacher of Erasmus, Jerome Aleander, listed the thesis of the unfree will as one of Luther's main errors. Other Catholic controversialists who attacked Luther's thesis 36 include: Ambrose Catharinus, O.P. (1521); Jacobus Hochstratten, O.P. (1522); Kasper Schatzgeyer, O.F.M. (1522); Lambertus Campester, O.P. (1523); Joh.

Zwingli of August 31, 1523, Erasmus listed the doctrine of *servum arbitrium* as one of Luther's three fundamental errors.[12] Without offering any evidence for his view, G. Ebeling [13] asserts that Erasmus surely acted unwittingly when he put his finger on the central point of Luther's theology.[14]

II. ERASMUS' CONCEPT OF FREEDOM IN *DE LIBERO ARBITRIO*: A REFLECTION OF THE THEOLOGICAL UNCLARITY OF THE LATE MIDDLE AGES

The book which A. von Harnack has judged to be "the crown" of Erasmus' works [15] was written within a week or ten days.[16] It was completed on May 13, 1524.[17] The Greek word "diatribe" in the title of the work means simply a discussion or conversation, basically the same meaning as the Latin word "collatio." It has nothing in common with the modern English use of the word, which conveys the idea of bitter criticism or invective.[18] On the contrary, *De libero arbitrio* was written with such characteristic Erasmian moderation, elegance and gentleness—though not without occasional irony—that some scholars have understood this reserve as a lack of Erasmus' personal involvement in the question.

EXCURSUS: *Was Erasmus a Skeptic, Uncommitted to the Christian Faith?*

It is evident from Erasmus' writings as well as from the knowledge we have of his personal life that he did not share Luther's personal inquietude, anguish and spiritual crises. It would be grossly unfair, however, to conclude from this difference of religious temperament that Erasmus lacked deep Christian conviction. Those who question Eras-

---

Dietenberger, O.P. (1524); Joh. Eck (*passim*) and Joh. Cochlaeus (1525). Cf. Jedin, *Des Joh. Cochlaeus Streitschrift*, pp. 20-36. Jedin, p. 37 calls DLA "the most famous of the Catholic polemical works against Luther on the question of the freedom of the will."

[12] Cf. P. Smith, p. 340.

[13] "Luther," RGG, 4, 515.

[14] Cf. G. L. Plitt, "Luthers Streit mit Erasmus über den freien Willen. . . .," in: *Studien der evangel.-protest. Geistlichen des Grosshergthums Baden* 2 (1876), 206; Walter, pp. VII f.; DTC, 9, 1289.

[15] *Dogmengeschichte*, 4th ed., vol. III, p. 841; citation from P. Smith, pp. 426ff.; cf. Freitag, WA 18, 593; Richter, p. 60.

[16] The preparation for writing had surely taken a long time. Cf. Walter, p. XI.

[17] Zickendraht, p. 23.

[18] P. Smith, p. 346; Walter, p. 1, footnote 2; Schumacher, *Vom freien Willen* (Göttingen, 1956²), p. 9, footnote 2.

mus' sincerity or personal commitment to Christ and his teaching almost always try to support this judgment by pointing to the passage in *De libero arbitrio* where Erasmus points out a basic difference between himself and Luther. In contrast to the "triumphalist tone of Luther in the Assertio" (Walter, p. 3, footnote 3), Erasmus says that he does not like to make assertions. He writes: "So great is my dislike of assertions that I prefer the views of the skeptics wherever the inviolable authority of Scripture and the decisions of the Church permit . . ." (tr. E. Winter, *Erasmus-Luther: Discourse on Free Will* [New York, 1961], p. 6. Cf. Walter, I a 4: p. 3, 15-18).

In *De servo arbitrio* Luther attacked this "skepticism" of Erasmus at great length (WA 18, 603, 1-605, 30; Cf. WABR 7, Nr. 2093). Many later authors have accepted Luther's view that Erasmus is a skeptic. M. Richter, for example, *Die Stellung des Erasmus,* p. 60, thinks that Erasmus had "no real concern for faith; he was too much of a skeptic for that. . . ." Other authors who share this view, to some extent at least, include G. L. Plitt, p. 207; Zickendraht, pp. 28ff. (however note his caution on p. 63); Huizinga, *Erasmus and the Age of Reformation,* p. 116; J. Jundt in his foreword to *Luther: Traité du Serf-arbitre,* tr. D. de Rougemont (Paris, 1937), p. 13; Lortz, I, p. 127; *idem.,* "Erasmus Kirchengeschichtlich," in: *Aus Theologie und Philosophie:* Festschr. f. F. Tillmann (Düsseldorf, 1950), pp. 293ff., 301; H. Bornkamm, "Luther und Erasmus," pp. 47f.; E. Schwiebert, p. 691; Packer and Johnston, p. 43; Boisset, pp. 34, 77f.; Vorster, p. 248f., 254, Siirala, p. 112.

These authors seem to have based their judgment about Erasmus' skepticism not simply on Erasmus' words, but on Luther's interpretation of Erasmus' words. Erasmus never said that he would be inclined to follow the attitude of the Skeptics in all questions, but only on those disputed points where no conclusive answer can be had either from Scripture or from the magisterial decisions of the Church. Thus, although Erasmus is aware of many disputed questions concerning the nature of free will, there can be, in his mind, no dispute concerning the existence of free will. This distinction Luther did not see. His misunderstanding of Erasmus is perhaps justifiable on the grounds that Erasmus expressed himself ambiguously in *De libero arbitrio.* But it is inexcusable that the later Luther—and later scholars to the present day—should continue to misunderstand Erasmus after Erasmus had clarified his meaning in his reply to *De servo arbitrio,* the *Hyperaspistes = Hyp.* (Liber I, 1526; Liber II, 1527. Our citations are from the Leyden edition of the *Opera Omnia,* Vol. X, 1254-1536).

In Hyp. I, 1258-1262, Erasmus claims that Luther has seriously misrepresented his statement about the "sententia Scepticorum": "You distort my words into calumny. Do I hold that nothing at all is to be asserted? I expressly said that we cannot be skeptical concerning the teaching of Scripture or that which the authority of the Church hands on to us. I do not waver from any article of the faith, as anyone can see from my writings. Concerning truths of the faith, I neither desire nor have a skeptical attitude. In fact I would not hesitate to face death for them." This sentence is never mentioned by those who point out that Erasmus once said that he would not have the strength to be a martyr like Thomas More.

Authors who accuse Erasmus of having a skeptical attitude also overlook his understanding of skepticism. In *Hyp.* I, 1258 D he takes this term to mean simply the attitude of lengthy deliberation before deciding some disputed issue. In this sense even the Church has been skeptical, says Erasmus: "I speak of debated issues in which the Church was once skeptical and considered them for a long time before defining them. [As examples he cites the doctrine of the Church concerning the procession of the Holy Spirit, the doctrine of purgatory, the approval of the expressions "homoousion," "transubstantiatio," etc.] It is of such questions that I speak. If the Church has not defined anything and I am asked what I think, I answer that it isn't clear to me. . . . After the Church has defined something, I follow this decision and cease to be a skeptic" (*Hyp.* I, 1258 E). He does not have an aversion to the Scripture, but to quarrels about disputed questions (1258 F). He is not against assertions but against a hasty settlement of questions: "A temeritate definiendi abhorret animus, non ab asserendo" (1259 A).

Further, he does not condemn absolutely those who seek to inquire into an unclear question in a moderate disputation, but those who argue violently and divisively (1259 B). Finally, Erasmus replies to Luther's charge (WA 18, 609, 15f.) that he regards the question of free will as useless. In a very forceful passage, overlooked by Lortz, Schwiebert, *et al.,* who think that Erasmus considered the whole controversy as a more or less non-committal disputation, Erasmus writes: "I regard the question, 'Is there free will?' so far from being useless that I think it is heretical to doubt it. This is a truth which has been handed down by orthodox Christians with a great consensus, a truth which the Church has clearly defined, a truth no longer to be disputed, but to be believed" (*Hyp.* I, 1259 D).

There are many scholars who have neither accepted Luther's unfair claim that Erasmus is a skeptic nor ignored Erasmus' own explanation in *Hyp.* of the meaning of his words in *De libero arbitrio.* Even Zickendraht, 63 admits that Erasmus is *not* skeptical about "central questions of faith" and says that Luther therefore seems to have done him an injustice. Walter, XXIII, footnote 1 is nevertheless correct when he writes: "Zickendraht emphasizes the skeptical utterance of Erasmus too strongly. . . . One may not call into doubt the steadfastness of Erasmus' belief in free will." Walter says elsewhere, "Die neuste Beurteilung des Erasmus," p. 18: "It is completely false to make Erasmus a skeptic. He believed thoroughly in the existence of free will. . . . The only person who can call Erasmus a skeptic is the person who ignores Erasmus' other religious writings." Similar defenses of Erasmus have been made by P. Smith, p. 356; Meissinger. *Erasmus,* p. 396; J. P. Whitney, *Reformation Essays* (London, 1939), p. 81f.; K. H. Oelrich, *Der späte Erasmus und die Reformation* (Münster, 1961), pp. 127f.; R. Padberg, *Erasmus als Katechet* (Freiburg, 1956), pp. 5 and 128. One of the merits of Padberg's study is that he shows how much the Erasmus image of later generations has been influenced by Luther's opinion of him. Cf. Padberg, pp. 5-9. The image of Erasmus which was painted by Luther is at least as unreliable as the image of Luther fashioned by Cochlaeus, which, as Herte has shown, had such an important influence on the later Catholic attitude toward Luther.

A. THE INTRODUCTION TO *De libero arbitrio*

One of the most striking things about the introductory part of *De libero arbitrio* [19] is that Erasmus shows little appreciation of the true meaning of Luther's thesis of the unfree will, namely, that the will of fallen man apart from grace is totally incapable of doing anything for salvation, totally unfree to do anything that is good *coram Deo*. Instead of coming to grips with this biblical concept of man's slavery to sin, Erasmus concentrates his attention on the secondary, non-biblical supporting argument which Luther used in the *Assertio*—but not in the *Grund und Ursach*—the argument from the absolute necessity of all events. Repeatedly Erasmus attacks the view that all things happen "by mere necessity." [20] In the eyes of Erasmus, Luther's thesis of *servum arbitrium* is simply one more example of determinism or necessitarianism, to be ranked alongside the deterministic doctrine of Manichaeus and the necessitarian doctrine supposedly held by Wyclif.[21]

The intention of Erasmus is clear: to uphold the justice and the mercy of God by affirming free human responsibility.[22] Jedin states Erasmus' thought as follows:

The just God rewards and punishes accordingly to merits. This presupposes a varying cooperation by man's will. Otherwise one could not explain why God rewards the one and punishes the other. The merciful God cannot punish where only necessity holds sway and where there is no freedom. Even though a rewarding without merits is worthy

---

[19] Walter, pp. XVIII f. divides DLA into four parts: I: introduction; II: biblical texts which speak in favor of free will; III: explanation of the biblical texts which seem to speak against free will; IV: formulation of the view of Erasmus and evaluation of the views of his opponents. Both DLA and DSA are summarized by MacKinnon, III, pp. 242-273.

[20] Walter, II a 12, p. 31, 8-13; II a 14, p. 32, 20f.; II a 18, p. 38, 19-22; II b 1, p. 39, 3. 7. 10. 24 and *passim;* cf *Hyp.*, II, 1487 A.

[21] Walter, I b 2, p. 13, 6-9.

[22] Oelrich, pp. 129f. emphasizes the pastoral aspect of Erasmus' concern. Erasmus showed that he was quite open to an important concern of Luther: "to destroy false self-confidence and to ascribe everything to God." Cf. Jedin, *Des Cochlaeus Streitschrift,* pp. 38f.; Walter, IV 2, pp. 77, 22-78, 17. Boisset, p. 30 erroneously depicts Erasmus as a merely intellectual reformer. Further, he sets up a false opposition when he says, that for Erasmus the Reformation "was to be a new theology, for Luther, a new piety": p. 31.

of God, it is unthinkable that God should punish a sinner who did not deserve punishment.[23]

Jedin rightly asks, however,

. . . granting that the justice and mercy of God are upheld by the affirmation of the free will, isn't another aspect of the divine nature threatened by it namely, God's omnipotence and universal causality? [24]

We ask further: Has Erasmus in his defense of free will overlooked the absolute necessity of grace for every salutary act? In his assertion of *liberum arbitrium* has he not forgotten the biblical doctrine of fallen man's servitude to sin? If one were to consider only Erasmus' definition of free will, he would have to answer these questions affirmatively!

B. ERASMUS' DEFINITION OF *liberum arbitrium*

At the end of Part I (Walter's edition) of DLA Erasmus gives this definition of liberum arbitrium: "By liberum arbitrium . . . we mean the power of the human will by which man can apply himself toward or turn himself away from the things which lead to eternal salvation." [25] "In this controversy over free will," writes Iwand, "the issue centers precisely around this definition!" [26] What are we to think of Erasmus' definition? In the light of the *status quaestionis* which we have presented at great length and in relation to the basic intention of Luther's thesis of unfree will, it must be said that Erasmus' definition is seriously defective.[27]

---

[23] Jedin, *Des Cochlaeus Streitschrift*, pp. 37ff.; cf. Walter, I a 8, pp. 6, 10-7, 22; II b 3, p. 42, 13-20.

[24] Jedin, *Des Cochlaeus*, pp. 37f.

[25] Walter, I b 10, p. 19, 7-10; *Op. Omnia*, IX, 1220 F-1221 A: "Vim humanae voluntatis, qua se possit homo applicare ad ea, quae perducunt ad aeternam salutem, aut ab iisdem avertere."

[26] "Die Freiheit des Christen und die Unfreiheit des Willens," in: *Solange es heute heisst, Festschr. f. R. Hermann* (Berlin, 1957), p. 138.

[27] E. de Moreau, "La crise religieuse du XVIe siècle, Livre I. Luther et Lutheranisme," in: Fliche-Martin, *Histoire de l'Eglise* . . . (Paris, 1950), p. 93 cites this definition as proof that "l'humaniste rationalise trop et néglige la grâce." The definition is surely one of the "extraordinary blunders" which, according to P. Hughes, *The Reformation in England* (London, 1948), I, p. 123, characterize DLA. In *Hyp.*, I, 1320 A-1328 E, Erasmus explains his definition, shows how Luther interpreted it in the worst possible way and points out that his definition does not *exclude* grace. This is all true, and to this extent we cannot call Erasmus a Pelagian. However, the fact that his definition does not *include* grace explicitly is what makes it a bad, seriously incomplete definition. E. W. Kohls, *Die Theologie des Erasmus*, vol. II (Basel, 1966), p. 79, footnote 176 overlooks this important point.

In the first place, Erasmus makes no distinction here between natural and acquired freedom. If he is using *liberum arbitrium* in the sense of man's natural, inborn freedom, there is no indication whether he is speaking of man's free will before or after the fall. Only a few lines later, but without any logical connection with his definition, Erasmus describes the incorrupt will of Adam and of the angels as "free in the sense that, if they wish, they could turn themselves from what is good toward what is evil." [28] How does this description of the will in man's original condition differ from the description of the will in Erasmus' definition, which, one would suppose, refers to the will of man in his present, *fallen* situation? If Erasmus is defining the free will of sinful man, as is most likely the case, he gives no hint whatever that such a man is enslaved to sin,[29] until he is liberated by grace. He gives no indication that the sinner by his own power of free will cannot choose the path which leads to eternal life unless his will receives this power through grace. Yet this was always the basic meaning of Luther's thesis of the unfree will.

Both before Erasmus wrote DLA and in DSA itself Luther repeatedly says that the thesis of the unfree will is a question of what fallen man can do without grace. The definition of Erasmus therefore simply does not come to grips with Luther's thesis. The entire work, *De libero arbitrio,* is really not a genuine confrontation with Luther's position. It is simply an attempt to refute a secondary aspect of this position, Luther's necessitarianism. Even in this attempt Erasmus was not successful, for, as we shall soon notice, in attacking the necessitarian aspects of Luther's thesis, he himself takes a position that is difficult to distinguish from Semipelagianism!

One might also ask concerning Erasmus' definition: Does not this definition recall the concept of free will which Augustine held in his own book, *De libero arbitrio*—a concept which he later discarded? [30] Instead of making it clear that man's will accepts grace only because of a previous grace enabling the will to do so,[31] does not the definition imply that the efficacy of God's grace depends on man's will? Does it not imply that the "beginning of salvation," in the sense of Augustine and of

---

[28] Walter, II a 2, p. 20, 10ff.

[29] Erasmus does not in fact deny original sin and its consequences, as we shall soon note. Cf. below footnote 37. The point is, however, that he does not integrate this doctrine into his definition of free will. It is surely not necessary to mention either original sin or grace in a definition of man's natural freedom. But if one defines free will in terms of *salus aeterna* as Erasmus has done, *then* it is necessary!

[30] See above chapter 4, pp. 72ff.

[31] D 177; 180; 199.

Orange II,[32] is not a gift of grace but something of which we are naturally capable?

Finally, it would be difficult to find a previous author, who, like Erasmus, defines man's *natural* freedom in terms of a *supernatural* goal —eternal salvation—without mentioning grace! Compare the definition of Erasmus with that of Peter Lombard, for example: free will in the wayfarer "is the faculty of reason and will by which good is chosen with the help of grace, or evil in the absence of grace." [33] Even Biel does not define free will in terms of salvation, but only in terms of *natural* goodness or evil: "There is free will between alternatives because the will can be moved spontaneously to those things which reason (*ratio*) judges to be good or evil." [34]

We have serious reservations concerning Erasmus' definition of free will. We wish, however, to treat him no less fairly than we have treated Luther. We should therefore try to see what Erasmus *means* by his definition. Fortunately there is more to *De libero arbitrio* than the definition. Having barely begun his Old Testament argument on behalf of free will, Erasmus digresses into a theological consideration of the effects of sin and of the relation of freedom to grace.[35] He grants that man's intellect has been darkened but not destroyed by sin [36] and that the will, by means of which we choose or avoid, has been corrupted to the extent that it cannot be healed by its own natural powers. It has lost its freedom and is compelled to serve the sin to which it once willingly

---

[32] Cf. D 178.

[33] *Lib. Sent.*, II, d. 24, cap. 3. Citation from Grane, p. 135, footnote 68. MacKinnon, III, p. 245 asserts without evidence that Erasmus' definition follows that of Peter Lombard. Luther, on the contrary, recognized that Lombard's definition was not only different from, but also superior to Erasmus'. WA 18, 665, 6ff. Erasmus' definition is very similar to the one found in Thomas Aquinas, *De Ver.*, q. 24, a. 1, arg. 6 *except* that Erasmus leaves out the words "gratia assistente!"

[34] In *Sent.*, II, d. 25, q. un. F.; translation based on Latin text in Grane, p. 136.

[35] Walter, II a 2-12; pp. 20, 7-31, 13; *Op. Omnia*, IX, 1221-1224. There is no need for us to investigate Erasmus' scriptural argument. This has already been done quite well by Zickendraht, pp. 32-46. Even though he questions the exegesis in DLA in several places (above all, Erasmus' interpretation of Jn. 1: 12), Zickendraht concludes that Erasmus' scriptural argument in general is a faithful rendering of the texts he cites. Erasmus is at his exegetical best where he, like Augustine and Thomas and others, shows that there are two types of biblical texts, those teaching the necessity of grace and those pointing to the freedom of the will: (Walter, III a 17, pp. 58, 19-60, 23; *Op. Omnia* IX, 1234 D; 1235 B). It would be unjust to say that Erasmus did not understand Pauline theology. His commentary on a very central text of this theology, Rom. 9: 20, is just as incisive as that of Augustine, Thomas or Luther: "Ita si deus deserit hominem in peccatis, sic natus est, nulla est iniuria: si vocat ad iustitiam, gratuita est misericordia." In *Ep. Pauli ad Rom. Paraph., Op. Om.* VII, p. 595.

[36] Walter, II a 3, p. 21, 12ff.; ". . . per peccatum obscurata est, non extincta." *Op. Om.*, IX, 1221 D.

consented. But once the sin has been forgiven by the grace of God, the will is again made free.[37] In the light of these clarifications one may raise the question: If Erasmus were interested only in proving the *existence* of free will, why couldn't he have defined *liberum arbitrium* as he does here, simply as the power by which we choose or avoid something? Why didn't he say in the definition, as he does here, that man's will after the fall is *not free* to improve itself and that it must serve sin unless grace liberates it?

In DSA [38] Luther correctly points out the inadequacy of Erasmus' definition in the light of the earlier statement he had made in DLA that apart from the mercy of God, neither the will nor the effort of man is effective.[39] Similarly, when Erasmus in many later places[40] admits that the will without grace is not free for truly good acts, but that with grace it can do all things, Luther, with full justification,[41] repeatedly exposes the contradiction. The controversy, says Luther, according to Erasmus' own statement of purpose, was supposed to be about the power of free will, not about the power of grace! [42] Any reader of the *Diatribe* will be able to agree with Luther when he says to Erasmus: "the free will which you define is one thing; that which you defend is another." [43]

Although Luther has correctly pointed out a serious inconsistency in DLA, he is unfair to Erasmus in that he does not give sufficient recognition to Erasmus' statements on the need for grace. Thus, he frequently calls Erasmus a Pelagian.[44] In the *Hyperaspistes* Erasmus firmly denies

---

37 Walter, II a 3, p. 21, 14-18: ". . . voluntas, qua eligimus aut refugimus, hactenus depravata fuit, ut suis naturalibus praesidiis non posset sese revocare ad meliorem frugem, sed amissa libertate cogebatur servire peccato, cui se volens semel addixerat. Sed per dei gratiam condonato peccato hactenus facta est libera. . . ." *Op. Om.,* IX, 1221 D. Boisset is unfair in claiming that Erasmus believes that man journeys to God the same today as he did before the fall. In contrast to this, says Boisset, Luther teaches that God must come to man because the fall broke the bond that enabled man to journey to God. The text just cited is sufficient to show the groundlessness of Boisset's assertion.

38 WA 18, 664, 32-36.

39 Cf. Walter, I a 8, p. 6, 10-17.

40 Walter, III b 2, p. 62, 5-8. This passage, however, gives us further reason for hesitation. Erasmus speaks not of the "proclivitas ad malum in *omnibus* hominibus," but "in *plerisque* hominibus." Cf. III b 3, p. 62, 22ff.; III c 13, p. 76, 27-31; IV 8, p. 82, 20-27; IV 16, p. 90, 11f.; and, above all, IV 8, p. 83, 7-11.

41 We disagree with Meissinger, *Erasmus,* p. 319, who thinks that Luther is unfair to Erasmus here.

42 Cf. Luther's reply to DLA (Walter, III c 13, p. 76, 27-31) in DSA, WA 18, 754, 21-755, 18; also WA 18, 693, 16f.; 753, 22f.

43 WA 18, 668, 3f.

44 WA 18, 664, 14-24. Luther said that Erasmus was even worse than the Pelagians, but he never went as far as Schwiebert, p. 694, who says that Erasmus teaches that "man needs partially to redeem himself."

this accusation.[45] A number of Protestant scholars agree that Luther's accusation was exaggerated and unfair.[46] As Walter has shown, one finds the fullest statement of Erasmus' own position only at the end of DLA—in Part IV. Luther did not take these later elaborations seriously. He was content merely to show that such later statements contradicted the definition. Almost exclusively on the basis of the definition Luther judged Erasmus to be a moralist, an exponent of "works-piety." This is another example of the lack of ecumenical spirit that characterized the decisive period of the Reformation. An opponent was read not in order to understand him, but to refute him!

J. von Walter has very plausibly suggested that the still widespread view of Erasmus as a mere moralist can be traced back to Luther's one-sided judgment of him: "One may ask, how is it that one continually tries to find in Erasmus the mere moralist? I believe that Luther bears the responsibility for this. It is very interesting to note that in DSA Luther does not reply to DLA from beginning to end. This is especially unfortunate in view of the fact that Luther did not notice that the main part of the *Diatribe* is its conclusion. Here Erasmus explains what he actually thinks about the problem of free will and grace. Luther clearly overlooked the plan of DLA. At least Erasmus continually complained about this in the *Hyperaspistes*. As a result Luther emphasized repeatedly in DSA that Erasmus upheld on the one hand the full freedom of the will—thus making him a moralist, but maintained on the other hand the need for grace—thus reflecting Pauline thought. Luther regarded the moralizing aspect as the genuine position of Erasmus. Erasmus continued to be portrayed in this light in later research. This view seemed plausible especially in view of Erasmus' energetic invective against the Scholastics which gave the impression that he had nothing whatever in common with Scholasticism. This is not true. On the contrary it was precisely from the Scholastics that Erasmus received his views concerning Church authority and grace. To regard the king of the humanists as a precursor of deism or to imagine that he even shows anti-supernaturalistic tendencies is completely unjustified. Whoever does this is guilty of 'modernizing' Erasmus." [47]

---

[45] *Hyp.*, I, 1324 C.

[46] Cf. F. Kattenbusch, *Luthers Lehre vom unfreien Willen*, p. 28; Freitag, WA 18, 664, footnote 1; O. Scheel, "Erläuterungen zu vom unfreien Willen," (Berlin, 1905), p. 537, footnote 82; F. W. Schmidt, *Erläuterungen zu Luthers "Vom unfreien Willen"* (München, 1923), p. 424; Mackinnon, III, p. 271. One may still ask, however, if Erasmus had an adequate understanding of Pelagianism. We do not think so. See below footnote 59.

[47] Walter, "Die neueste Beurteilung des Erasmus," pp. 16f. (Further observations on the relationship between Erasmus and Scholasticism are found in Walter,

C. ERASMUS BETWEEN NEO-SEMIPELAGIANISM AND AUGUSTINE

Joseph Lortz has listed the widespread unclarity in late medieval theology as one of the basic conditions without which the Reformation would have been unthinkable.[48] This thesis has recently been confirmed by Jedin: "The magisterial condemnation of current errors concerning the faith was unquestionably urgent. For twenty-five years the highest teaching authority of the Church had not spoken. It is true that universities had censured erroneous propositions of Luther, Zwingli and their followers and that theologians had attempted to refute them. Nevertheless the question was frequently raised: 'Which are binding articles of faith and which are simply theological opinions?'" [49]

We find in the *De libero arbitrio* of Erasmus a tragic example of this unclarity *precisely* concerning the question that was for Luther the very heart [50] of his Reformation: What can the sinner do for salvation without the help of grace? As we have seen in the state of the question, the interpretation of the New Testament given by Augustine, confirmed by the II Synod of Orange and reaffirmed by Thomas Aquinas and other Scholastics is that the sinner can do absolutely nothing for salvation without grace. Even the preparation of the sinner for justification is

---

pp. XXVIII-XXXI). Walter's judgment has been confirmed by the study of A. Flitner, *Erasmus im Urteil seiner Nachwelt* (Tübingen, 1952), pp. 10f. Cf. the reply of L. Bouyer, *Erasmus and the Humanist Experiment* (London, 1959), pp. 122-152 to A. Renaudet's view that Erasmus was a "modernist before the event." See also G. Ritter, "Die Geschichtliche Bedeutung des deutschen Humanismus," in: *Historische Zeitschr.*, 127 (1923), 442-445; J. P. Dolan, Introduction to *Erasmus: Handbook of the Militant Christian* (Notre Dame, Ind., 1962), pp. 17ff. Vorster, pp. 242f. sees Erasmus as the root of even worse evils than moralism, modernism or deism. Without considering any of the numerous statements of Erasmus on the need for grace, Vorster claims that he teaches a doctrine of "uneingeschränkter Entscheidungsfähigkeit, [die] ein gerader Weg zu modernen Atheismus [führt!]" Vorster, p. 16, feels that it is unnecessary to bring Erasmus and Luther into dialogue since this would mean confronting a "mouse with an elephant." Is Vorster referring here to Erasmus' own sarcastic reference to himself as a "musca" (not a "mus" or a "musculus") in comparison to the "elephanto," Luther? Cf. Walter, I a 2, p. 2, 6.

[48] *Die Reformation*, I, pp. 137f.; 205-210. Cf. Seeberg, III, p. 761. Oberman, *The Harvest*, p. 186, footnote 2 has questioned this thesis. It seems, however, that Oberman is defending the clarity—"the unity and consistency"—of the theological system of such *individual* theologians as Gabriel Biel. Lortz, on the other hand, is referring to the *general* unclarity within the contemporary Catholic theology concerning such questions as: What is Catholic doctrine? Which opinions are incompatible with Catholic doctrine? The question of the preparation for justification is a good illustration of the theological unclarity on the eve of the Reformation.

[49] *Der Abschluss der Trienterkonzils 1562/63*, (Münster, 1963), pp. 6f.; cf. pp. 77f.

[50] WA 18, 786, 27.

itself the work of grace. We have likewise seen how, in the absence of any knowledge of the canons of Orange II and in the absence of a knowledge—or an acceptance—of the teaching of Augustine on the necessity of grace for the very preparation of a truly good will, certain late Scholastics developed a new form of the doctrine of the Semi-pelagians which had been condemned by Orange II. These theologians were not formally heretical since they were unaware that their teaching had been long ago condemned by the Church. Far more culpable were the shepherds of the Church who had allowed the true doctrine to become so obscure that the once-condemned error could reappear.

Erasmus of Rotterdam was merely reflecting the theological unclarity of his time when he listed the Neo-Semipelagian view as one that could be held by Catholics, even though he knew that it was not the "probable opinion." What he calls the "sententia probabilis" is actually the *official teaching* of the Church which had been defined by the Second Council of Orange and which had been declared to be a "truth of faith" by Thomas Aquinas.[51] This teaching was later to be reaffirmed by the Council of Trent. Here is how Erasmus describes the "probable opinion": ". . . those who flee the greatest distance from Pelagius attribute much to grace and almost nothing to free will although they do not take it away completely. They deny that man can will good without special grace and they deny that he can begin, make progress or become perfect without the principal and perpetual aid of divine grace." [52]

Erasmus erroneously attributes the following Neo-Semipelagian view of Ockham and Biel to Duns Scotus: [53] ". . . having not yet received the

---

[51] I-II, q. 114, a. 5, ad 1.

[52] "Qui longissime fugiunt a Pelagio, plurimum tribuunt gratiae, libero arbitrio pene nihil nec tamen in totum tollunt: negant hominem posse velle bonum sine gratia peculiari, negant posse incipere, negant posse progredi, negant posse perficere sine principali perpetuoque gratiae divinae praesidio," Walter, II a 12, p. 30, 22-27; cf. *ibid.*, II a 10, pp. 27, 15-28, 7. Erasmus attributes this view to Augustine, Thomas (*Hyp.* I, 1328 E; 1382 D) and Bernard (*Hyp.* II, 1522 B).

[53] Walter, p. 27, footnote 1 dismisses without comment the study of Minges, *Die Gnadenlehre des Duns Scotus* and asserts, as if Minges' book did not exist: "Erasmus stellt die Lehre des Duns Scotus und seiner Schule richtig dar." For this judgment Walter depends mainly on Seeberg and Loofs. He, like Schumacher, p. 32, footnote 1, accepts as certain, for example, the claim of Seeberg that Augustine's writing about free will "nich mehr als ein Spiel mit Worten ist." On p. 20, footnote 2 we find an example of Walter's faulty knowledge of the Scholastics. After indicating that Thomas Aquinas is in basic agreement with Augustine on the necessity for grace, Walter says: "Erst Duns Scotus lehrte, dass der Mensch vor dem Falle aus blossen Naturkräfte Gott uber alles lieben könne. . . ." Cf. *ibid.*, p. XXVIII and *idem*, "Die neueste Beurteilung. . . ," p. 16. Walter doesn't realize that Thomas Aquinas teaches exactly the same as Scotus on this point. Walter likewise doesn't give sufficient attention to the fact that many Scholastics conceived of both a natural and a supernatural love of God

grace which forgives sin, man can, by his natural powers, perform works which, as they say, are morally good, by which justifying grace is merited not *de condigno* but *de congruo*. . . ." [54] In *Hyperaspistes* Erasmus describes the "Scotist" view more fully: ". . . he thinks that by morally good works, [performed] by the common power of nature, man can merit *de congruo* the efficacious grace of God: because the goodness of God would not allow anyone to perish who in some way would become capable of divine grace." [55] We need hardly mention that this position is almost identical to Biel's Neo-Semipelagian view. As far as Erasmus knows, the Church has not rejected this position. He himself neither defends it nor attacks it.[56] What saves Erasmus from formal error is not only his unawareness that the Church *had* condemned this error, but also his fundamental attitude of obedience to the teaching office of the Church. At the end of *Hyperaspistes* we find evidence of his orthodox attitude: ". . . whatever has been discussed by us I submit to the Catholic Church, prepared to correct anything that has departed from the truth." [57]

Another interesting clarification that we find in the *Hyperaspistes* is Erasmus' admission that the definition of free will which he gave in *De libero arbitrio* can be applied *either* to the (orthodox) Augustinian-Thomistic view or to the allegedly Scotist opinion, which is actually the Neo-Semipelagian view![58] It is thus perfectly clear that Erasmus, although he personally inclines to the "sententia probabilis" of Augus-

above all things. The last-mentioned kind of love of God by merely natural powers is unquestionably excluded both by Scotus and by Thomas.

[54] Walter, II a 9, pp. 26, 15-27, 2: ". . . homo nondum accepta gratia, quae peccatum abolet, naturae viribus exercere posset opera moraliter, ut vocant, bona, quibus non de condigno, sed de congruo promereantur gratiam gratum facientem. . . ."

[55] *Hyp.* I, 1327 D and E: ". . . putat per opera moraliter bona, per influxam naturae communem, hominem posse Dei gratiam efficacem promereri de congruo: quod Dei benignitas non patiatur quemquam interire, qui modo sed quod aliquo pacto fiat capax divinae gratiae." Cf. *ibid.*, 1323 D.

[56] *Hyp.* I, 1327 E: "Hanc opinionem quoniam Ecclesia, quod quidem sciam, nondum reiecit, ego nec defendo nec explodo." *Ibid.*, 1330 D: "Quam sententiam non arbitror ab Ecclesia damnatam, . . ." 1364 D; 1378 C and D. In *Hyp.* II, 1467 F, he says of the "Scotistic" view: "quam opinionem nunquam rejeci." In a letter to Thomas More (March 30, 1527: Allen, VII, *Epist.* 1804) Erasmus says of the same opinion "mihi non displicerit opinio . . . nisi refrageretur Paulus. . . ." Citation from Oelrich, p. 125. In our opinion Oelrich reads too much into the "mihi non displicerit." It has the same meaning as the expression we have just cited from *Hyp.* II, which was written at about the same time.

[57] *Hyp.* II, 1536 E and F.

[58] *Hyp.* I, 1323 D: "Utrique sententiae locum reliquit mea definitio, quod neutrum omnino refellam, licet in eam propensior, quae plus tribuit gratiae." Cf. Walter, p. XXX; Jedin, *Des Cochlaeus Streitschrift*, p. 40.

tine and Thomas, sees nothing un-Catholic about the Bielian, Neo-Semipelagian position. In Book II of *Hyperaspistes* we find a number of revealing passages which indicate Erasmus' failure to grasp the seriousness of the Church's early struggle against Semipelagianism.[59] For example, developing the concept of "natural or common" grace that he had mentioned in *De libero arbitrio*,[60] Erasmus distinguishes a "human faith" which is "a kind of knowledge preparing for the light of faith" from a "faith justifying by grace." Then he explains: ". . . as there are degrees of justice, so there are degrees of gifts until you reach that which is merely natural. But even this is grace, since God is the author of nature. Thus Augustine is needlessly afraid of saying that the beginning of grace arises from man." [61] Erasmus seems completely unaware that Pelagius had said exactly the same thing to Augustine: free will is a gift of God; therefore no other gift is necessary! In this sense Pelagius could also say as Erasmus does: "we ascribe all to God's goodness." [62]

On the final pages of the *Hyperaspistes,* Erasmus again shows his inability to comprehend Augustine's insistence that the beginning of faith comes from God and that it does not lie in the power of man's free will to begin the journey to salvation. Augustine, says Erasmus, has a "scruple . . . lest the beginning of faith seem to arise from free will." [63]

---

[59] Erasmus did not even grasp the extent of the Pelagian error. He thought it was simply the view that man, once his free will had been set free and sanctified by grace, required no new grace! This watered-down version of Pelagianism resembles that which Ockham and Biel describe, but bears little similarity to the Pelagianism which Augustine combatted. Luther was fully justified in charging: Erasmus would make "Pelagium pene Evangelicum": WA 18, 666, 30-667, 1. Other indications of Erasmus' poor understanding of Pelagianism are found in the fact that he more than once confused Pelagian works with those of orthodox authors. He ascribed several books to Jerome, for example, which were really written by Pelagians. Cf. J. Forget, "Jêrome," DTC, 8, 924. He likewise published in 1528 the *De gratia Dei et humanae mentis libero arbitrio* of Faustus of Riez, a Semipelagian bishop of the fifth century, Cf. above chapter 5. Furthermore, Erasmus expressed regret that he did not know of this work before he wrote DLA. He could then have used its arguments against Luther! Cf. Renaudet, p. 39; H. Humbertclaude, *Érasme et Luther* (Fribourg, 1909), pp. 222-241; RGG, 2, 889.

[60] Walter II a 11, pp. 28, 21-29, 12. This *gratia*, says Erasmus, is the same as the "influxus naturalis."

[61] *Hyp.* II, 1413 E: ". . . ut sunt iustitiae gradus, ita sunt et donorum, donec pervenias ad id quod mere naturale, atque hoc ipsum habet suam gratiam, cum auctor naturae sit Deus, ut frustra metuat Augustinus, ne initium gratiae dicatur ab homine proficisci."

[62] Walter, I a 8, p. 6, 16: "totum ascribamus divinae benignitati." Cf. above chapter 4, pp. 82f.

[63] *Hyp.* II, 1526 D: "ne gratia initium videatur a libero arbitrio proficisci." Erasmus made no secret of the fact that he preferred Origen and St. John Chrysostom to Augustine. Cf. Humbertclaude, pp. 11-15. Feret, "Érasme," in: *Catholicisme*, 4, 373 has called attention to the parallels between the scriptural

Then, speaking of the assent which the sinner gives to grace, Erasmus seems to offer as his own opinion the following: "we assent—and that is something we certainly can do by our natural powers: I am not speaking of the assent which justifies, but which in some way prepares us." [64] He then tries to reassure his readers with an affirmation that any good Pelagian could make: God's grace is not endangered "since whatever good that remains in us, as well as everything which we can do and which we are, is a gift of God." [65] Again: ". . . one need not fear having grace seeming to originate from the powers of nature, since this very natural good itself, as we have stressed, is a free gift of God." [66]

Erasmus is unable to see much difference between Semipelagianism and the Catholic doctrine defended by Augustine and defined by II Orange. Thus, he says, a great deal of the controversy between Julian of Eclanum and Augustine "involved a verbal rather than a real difference." [67] Similarly, of the opinion of the Neo-Semipelagian Scholastics, he says: "they do not depart greatly from the view of Augustine; they differ more in words rather than in fact." [68] The probable opinion of Augustine is held by those "who tend to exaggerate the grace of God." Actually, he says, "there is only a slight difference between the two opinions," i.e., between the Augustinian and the Neo-Semipelagian views. [69]

We shall present one final testimony for the doctrinal uncertainty not only of Erasmus, but of much of the Church during the most decisive

---

argument for free will in Origen's *Peri Archōn* and in DLA. The fact that Erasmus had little esteem for the "doctor gratiae" is regarded by Humbertclaude as proof for the thesis: Erasmus is a mere "moralist." We have already indicated our reasons for disagreeing with this evaluation.

[64] *Hyp.* II, 1528 E: "assentimur, quod certe possumus naturae viribus: de assensu loquor, non qui iustificat, sed qui praeparat aliquo modo."

[65] *Ibid.*, and 1529 A: "quoniam hoc ipsum, quod in nobis relictum est boni, et totum hoc quod possumus aut sumus, Dei donum est."

[66] *Hyp.* II, 1532 A: "Rurus non est metuendum ne gratia videatur ex naturae viribus oriri, cum hoc ipsum, ut crebro diximus, naturae bonum sit gratuitum Dei donum . . ."

[67] *Hyp.* II, 1524 D: "nasci ex verbis videtur potius quam ex re ipsa."

[68] *Hyp.* II, 1532 D: "non ita multum dissidere ab opinione Augustini, nisi quod variant in vocabulis potius quam in re."

[69] *Hyp.* II, 1467 F: "minimum interest inter has duas opiniones." J. P. Dolan, p. 45, following P. Mesnard, *Essai sur le Libre Arbitre,* p. 60, overlooks this and the aforementioned texts when he concludes that Erasmus and Thomas Aquinas are in basic agreement on the question of meriting the first grace. They at least disagree in that Erasmus thinks this question is still a matter of opinion, while Thomas regards it as a "veritas fidei" that the *initium fidei* lies with God, not with our free will. A similar criticism could be made of P. Imbart de la Tour, *Les Origines de la Réforme,* vol. III (Paris, 1914), pp. 95f., who concentrates only on Erasmus' anti-Pelagian, pro-Augustinian statements.

period of the Reformation on the very question that was at the heart of Luther's Reformation concern. In a work written in 1528 in reply to attacks that had been made on him by some Spanish monks, Erasmus writes: "Some think that we have the power to will good but not to do it. Some, that we can neither will nor do good. Some hold that we can will good—but only imperfectly, and this is why the grace of God is necessary. Some deny even this to man and hold that man's good resolutions are not aided by God but are given by him. Some say we are free because we have the power to will, even though we are not able to will the good. This kind of liberty is also found in evil persons. Others hold that freedom involves the power either to do good or evil. The Scholastic theologians teach that man can merit grace *de congruo* by works which are morally good." [70]

In view of this disagreement Erasmus believes he is justified in suspending judgment: "until I hear the voice of the Church. I regard as articles of faith not any mere opinions of the Scholastics but those truths which are certainly attested to by clear scriptural proof or which are publicly accepted or taught by General Councils." [71] Very interesting is the fact that Erasmus is aware of the teachings of the "Africanae Regionis Concilium" in which Augustine played such an important role, but he does not feel bound by them since they are not taught by a universal synod.[72]

The uncertainty surrounding this decisive Reformation issue, an uncertainty to which Erasmus gives abundant testimony, was only to be overcome through the rediscovery of the canons of the Second Council of Orange during the fourth decade of the 16th century and through the reaffirmation of this ancient Catholic teaching by the Council of Trent. It is no exaggeration to say that until this clarification took place, Martin Luther was one of the few theologians in Germany who unhesitatingly defended the biblical and Catholic teaching on man's bondage to sin. He proclaimed that fallen man could do nothing whatever without grace to prepare himself for salvation. This he did at a time in which many, many Catholics—including Erasmus—had either lost this truth or were uncertain about it.

---

[70] *Apol. contra Monach. Hisp.*, in: *Op. Omnia*, IX, 1091. Cf. *Adv. Geront.*, in: *Op. Omnia*, IX, 988.

[71] *Adv. Geront.*, in: *Op. Omnia*, IX, 988.

[72] *Ibid.*, 989. Cf. Humbertclaude, p. 68.

PART THREE

LUTHER: DE SERVO ARBITRIO

10

Luther's Doctrine of Unfree Will according to His Main Work, *De servo arbitrio,* with Reference to His Later Teaching and to the Development of Lutheran Theology

I. BACKGROUND AND STRUCTURE OF
DE SERVO ARBITRIO (1525)

The *De libero arbitrio* of Erasmus appeared in print on September 1, 1524, probably at Basel. Within a month two other editions were published in Antwerp and Cologne.[1] Already on September 30 Melanchthon could write to Erasmus from Wittenberg that the book had been received. Even though Melanchthon closed the letter with the words, "Luther reverently greets you," he gave hints that a violent controversy might result over *De libero arbitrio*.[2] More than a year passed before Luther answered *DLA*. Even though Luther had, as early as November 17, 1524, declared his intention to answer Erasmus, he had too many prior commitments and urgent preoccupations to permit him to make an immediate reply. As Freitag has pointed out in his detailed account of the reception of *DLA,* Luther first had to write against Karlstadt and the "heavenly prophets," then work on the *Adnotationes ad Deuteronomium Mose* and, finally, he had to take a literary stand against the rebelling peasants before he could begin his reply to Erasmus.[3] One might also add another preoccupation: Luther's adjustment

---

[1] Walter, pp. xiii, xvi f.
[2] Allen, V, 1500.
[3] WA 18, 579-583; cf. Richter, pp. 61-64; P & J, pp. 38f.; Zickendraht, pp. 50-57; Rupp, pp. 269ff.

to married life which began on June 27, 1525. In *DSA,* however, Luther denies that any of these factors prevented him from writing an earlier answer to Erasmus. It was simply his "disgust, disinclination and distaste" with *DLA.*[4]

This unusual delay in replying to Erasmus' attack is no proof that Luther took more than a year to consider his answer. We can only be certain that Luther was totally involved in his refutation of *DLA* from September 25, 1525.[5] The delay does prove, however, that *DSA* was not written in polemical haste and that Luther had much time for reflection in preparation for the actual composition of *DSA.* We emphasize this point because one sometimes encounters a view which seeks to modify or excuse some of the "exaggerations" in *DSA* on the ground that it was written hastily and in the midst of controversy. Luther, in fact, expressly denies that his doctrine of the unfree will was developed "in the heat of battle." [6] Lütkens has correctly pointed out that Luther, in his refutation of Erasmus, united into a systematic whole all the elements of his position which had previously emerged only in a scattered fashion. We therefore cannot see in this book the product of excessive haste, but only the fruit of the most thoughtful reflection and interior composure." [7]

De servo arbitrio was completed between November 11 and 18, 1525. It appeared in print at Wittenberg in the "month of December" of the same year.[8] Seven other editions were published in 1526.[9] As soon as Luther had finished his Latin manuscript Justus Jonas began his translation into German, which appeared in January 1526 under the title: *Das der freie Wille nichts sey.*[10]

Next to Luther, Erasmus was the most influential intellectual figure in Northern Europe. Among his opponents Luther regarded Erasmus as by far the most formidable.[11] It is therefore not surprising that Luther gave special attention to *DLA*. It was, he said, the only work of his adversaries which he had read in entirety.[12]

De servo arbitrio was four times as long as Erasmus' book. It was written in a sharp, polemical tone which infuriated Erasmus [13] and prompted him to write the *Hyperaspistes*—longer than both *DLA* and

---

4 WA 18, 601, 29-32.
5 Freitag, pp. 581f.
6 WA 18, 756, 1-5.
7 *Luthers Prädestinationslehre,* p. 9.
8 Freitag, pp. 582f.
9 *Ibid.,* pp. 598f.
10 Iwand, MA, p. 265; cf. Freitag, p. 599.
11 Meissinger, *Erasmus,* p. 276.
12 WA 25, 27, 24; WATR 2, 318, 16; 4, 641, 12; 6, 234, 9.
13 Renaudet, p. 287 says of DSA: Luther "n'a jamais écrit en termes plus

DSA combined.[14] An effort by Luther to placate Erasmus in a letter shortly after the appearance of *DSA* was rejected by Erasmus in a bitter letter of April 11, 1526.[15]

Luther "took up the *Diatribe* almost sentence by sentence in order to refute it, instead of setting forth the few central issues in his own creative way. As a result, his book is to a great extent formless and monotonous."[16] *De servo arbitrio* begins with a long preface—one-fourth of the entire book—in which he answers Erasmus' introduction, attacks his "skepticism" and develops several important points of his own theology.[17] Coming to the main body of the book, Luther outlines the course of the controversy.[18] He first begins with a systematic refutation of Erasmus, starting with Erasmus' definition of free will and his concept of law and Gospel.[19] Secondly, he examines and refutes Erasmus' biblical argument [20] and, finally, he concludes with his own presentation of the biblical doctrine of *servum arbitrium*.[21]

De servo arbitrio is an extremely rich book, not only because it is the fullest statement of Luther's central reformation concern, "the real thing" (*res ipsa*) and "the essential issue" (*summa caussae*),[22] but also because of Luther's digressions on such important themes as law and Gospel, the clarity of Scripture,[23] responsibility for sin, the relation between faith and reason and his doctrine of *Deus absconditus* and *Deus praedicatus*.[24] The concept of God which Luther unfolds in *DSA* itself provides sufficient material for a monograph. However, in order to continue our investigation of the theme that we have traced from Scripture to the time of Luther, and in order not to get lost in these secondary themes—important and interesting as they are—we shall limit our investigation to the main theme of the book: the doctrine of the unfree will. We shall touch upon the above-mentioned themes insofar as they are essential for an understanding of the central theme. As M. Doerne has

---

hostiles contre personne." MacKinnon, III, p. 266, on the contrary, thinks that DSA is "moderate and measured in style"!

[14] Cf. Freitag, pp. 583ff.

[15] Allen, VI, 1688; Freitag, pp. 568f.

[16] Meissinger, *Erasmus*, p. 276; H. Bornkamm also calls DSA "formlos:" RGG, 4, 489.

[17] WA 18, 600, 661.

[18] WA 18, 661, 26ff.

[19] WA 18, 661-699.

[20] WA 18, 699-756.

[21] WA 18, 756-786.

[22] WA 18, 786, 27.

[23] Cf. R. Hermann, *Von der Klarheit der heiligen Schrift* (Berlin, 1958).

[24] The most thorough investigation of the problem of *Deus absconditus* has been done by H. Bandt, *Luthers Lehre vom verborgenen Gott* (Berlin, 1958).

said of *DSA:* "One must remember: it is not entitled 'On Predestination' or 'On the hidden God,' but 'On the unfree will'." [25]

Before proceeding to a detailed examination of *DSA,* we offer the following survey of literature especially relevant to *DSA:* For the older literature see Freitag, WA 18, 597. Especially valuable from the 19th century are J. Lütkens, *Luthers Praedestinationslehre im Zusammenhang mit seiner Lehre vom freien Willen,* diss. (Dorpat, 1858) and Ch. E. Luthardt, *Die Lehre vom freien willen und seinem Verhältnis zur Gnade in seiner geschichtlichen Entwicklung dargestellt,* (Leipzig, 1863).

H. Humbertclaude, *Erasme et Luther* (Fribourg, 1909). The critique of Erasmus by this Catholic theologian is especially good. His conviction that Erasmus is a Semipelagian prevents him from giving sufficient attention to Erasmus' statements on the need for grace. His interpretation of Luther is unfortunately too greatly influenced by Denifle. He fails to search for the real intention behind Luther's necessitarian statements and doesn't take into account the biblical doctrine of man's bondage to sin. This book has been greatly neglected in the German research.

K. Zickendraht, *Der Streit zwischen Luther und Erasmus . . .* (Leipzig, 1909). Unfortunately there is no confrontation with Humbertclaude, since both works appeared independently but almost simultaneously. Zickendraht's most serious shortcoming is that he passes over the difficult "necessitarian" passages and fails to discuss Luther's doctrine of *Deus absconditus.* Since 1909 there have been no studies of the controversy between Erasmus and Luther as extensive as those of Humbertclaude and Zickendraht.

F. Gogarten, "Nachwort" to his new edition of Justus Jonas' translation of *DSA* (München, 1924); reprinted in *Glaube und Wirklichkeit* (Jena, 1928), pp. 13-43 and in: *Theologische Bücherei,* vol. 17 (München, 1963), pp. 191-218. For a confrontation with Gogarten's bold interpretation of *DSA,* an interpretation clearly influenced by the dialectical theology of the 1920's, see K. Holl, "Gogartens Lutherauffassung. Eine Erwiderung," in: *Die christliche Welt,* 38 (1924), 307-314; reprinted in: Holl, *Gesammelte Aufsätze,* vol. III (Tübingen, 1928).

Other relevant studies include: M. Peisker, "Zum Problem von Luthers De servo arbitrio," in: *Theol. Studien u. Kritiken,* 98/99 (1926), 212-258; R. Hermann, "Willensfreiheit u. gute Werke im Sinne der Reformation," reprinted in: *Gesammelte Studien zur Theologie Luthers und der Reformation,* (Göttingen, 1960), pp. 44-76, and "Zu Luthers Lehre vom unfreien Willen," in: *Greifswalder Studien zu Lutherforschung. . . ,* 4(1931), pp. 17-38; E. Schott, "Luthers Lehre vom servum arbitrium in ihrer theologischen Bedeutung," *Zeitschr. f. system Theologie,* 7 (1929), 399-430.

H. J. Iwand has contributed several studies to the literature on *DSA:* "Die grundlegende Bedeutung der Lehre vom unfreien Willen für den Glauben," in: *Blätter aus dem evang. Prediger-Seminar Kloster Neu-*

---

[25] Doerne, "Gottes Ehre am gebundenen Willen," in: LuJ, 22 (1938), 46.

hof/Ostpr., 1 (1930), 5-19; reprinted in: *Um den rechten Glauben: Ges. Aufsätze* (München, 1959), pp. 13-30; "Studien zum Problem des Unfreien Willens," in: *Zeitschr. f. syst. Theol.,* 8 (1930), 216-250; reprinted in: *Um den rechten Glauben. . . . ,* pp. 31-61; "Die Freiheit des Christen und die Unfreiheit des Willens," in: *Solange es heute heisst: Festgabe für R. Hermann zum 70. Gerburstag* (Berlin, 1957), pp. 132-146; reprinted in: *Um . . . Glauben,* pp. 247-268; theological introduction and notes (the latter in collaboration with Bruno Jordahn) to the MA, pp. 253-315.; on pp. 266f. there is a brief survey of the relevant literature.

See also: H. Lammers, *Luthers Anschauung vom Willen* (Berlin, 1935), S. Normann, *Viljefrihet og forutsbestemmelse i den lutherske reformasjon* (Oslo, 1933). The same views are expressed in Normann's essay, "De servo arbitrio als Ausdruck lutherischen Christentums," in: *Zeitschr. f. system. Theologie,* 15 (1937), 303-338. M. Doerne, "Gottes Ehre am gebundenen Willen: Evangelische Grundlagen und theologische Spitzensätze in De servo arbitrio," in: *LuJ,* 22 (1938), 45-92; Gerald Smith, "Luther and Free Choice," in: *The Modern Schoolman,* 20 (1943), 78-88; W. von Loewenich, "Gott und Mensch in humanistischer und reformatorischer Schau: Eine Einführung in Luthers Schrift De servo arbitrio," in: *Humanitas-Christianitas,* (Gütersloh, 1948), pp. 65-101; von Loewenich discusses the *Deus absconditus* doctrine in: *Luthers Theologia Crucis,* 4th rev. ed. (München, 1954), pp. 21-54; and "Pharaos Verstockung. Zu Luthers Lehre von der Prädestination," in: *Viva Vox Evangelii: Festschr. f. H. Meiser* (München, 1951), pp. 196-214; reprinted in: *Von Augustin zu Luther* (Witten/Ruhr, 1959), pp. 161-179. L. Schauenberg, *Luthers Lehre vom verborgenen, alleinwirksamen Gott und von der Unfreiheit des Willens: Eine Darlegung der philosophischen Grundgedanken von De servo arbitrio unter Heranziehung gleicher Gedanken aus den anderen Schriften,* typewritten diss. (Göttingen, 1949). Y. Alanen, *Valinta ja vastuu,* (Helsinki, 1955); also, "Das Wahrheitsproblem in der Bibel und in der griechischen Philosophie," KuD 3 (1957), 23-239. L. Pinomaa, "Unfreier Wille und Prädestination bei Luther," in: *Theol. Zeitschr.,* 13 (1957) 339-349. Alanen and Pinomaa were the leading figures in the sharp debate which arose twenty years ago among Finnish Lutherans. The debate began with the appearance of the first Finnish translation of *DSA*. Pinomaa represents the view, held by most of the Finnish theologians who took sides in the debate, that the basic meaning of *DSA* is the proclamation of the sovereignty of divine grace and the "God-ness" of God. According to this view Luther's doctrine of predestination in *DSA* has nothing to do with philosophical determinism. The opposite view, held by Professor Alanen, and with him many pastors, holds that *DSA* contains an untenable determinism which is not only inconsistent with Scripture and with Luther's own teaching as a whole, but which is also incompatible with the responsible, personal decision that is essential to Christian faith. Cf. our Introduction, pp. 13f. (The author is indebted to Professor T. A. Kantonen of Wittenberg University, Springfield, Ohio, for a clarification of the issues involved in this controversy carried on in the Finnish language.) P. Althaus, *Die Theologie Martin Luthers* (Gütersloh, 1962), pp. 99-107; 238-248. J. Boisset, *Erasme et Luther: Libre ou serf-arbitre?* (Paris, 1962). This work contributes little to an understanding of either side of the controversy between Erasmus and Luther. The author presents a completely outdated view of Erasmus, and his interpretation of Luther is dominated too much by his desire to understand Luther in terms of the philosophy of M. Blondel. M. Seils, *Der Gedanke vom Zusammenwirken Gottes und des Menschen in Luthers Theologie* (Gütersloh, 1962). Seils completed this study in 1959. It is therefore important to note the qualification he makes in the foreword written in 1962: The three years "between writing and publication mean also for me personally a difference in outlook from that which I then wrote. Above all, I would like to have written the section dealing with the problem of the will more precisely": p. 8. O. J. Mehl, "Erasmus contra Luther," in *LuJ* 29 (1962), 52-64. O. Pesch, "Freiheitsbegriff und Freiheitslehre bei Thomas von Aquin und Luther," in: *Catholica* 17 (1963), 197-244. H. Vorster, *Das Freiheitsverständnis bei Thomas von Aquin und Martin Luther* (Göttingen, 1965). Independently of each other Vorster and Pesch have discovered "that Thomas' theology of freedom embodies a doctrine of the 'bondage of the will' which is basically not at all far removed from Luther's doctrine": Pesch, *ibid.*, p. 198, footnote 1.

II. LUTHER'S CONCERN IN *DE SERVO ARBITRIO*

Martin Luther was a Scholastic, but not just a Scholastic. He was also a Reformer of the Church and of the Church's theology. Even after 1520 he continued to use Scholastic terminology alongside the increasingly biblical and personal language of his theology of the cross. When reading Luther, therefore, we cannot read him as if he were *just* a Scholastic. On the other hand, it would be an error to think his theology was *totally* different from the tradition in which he was educated. It would be most inaccurate to suppose that he is writing *purely* as a biblical theologian, or *purely* in personalist or existentialist or non-objectivizing terms.

If we are to read Luther correctly we must remember that he sometimes uses Scholastic terms in their classical, Scholastic sense and sometimes in a new sense—which must be proved, not assumed, to be new in each specific case. Sometimes he develops certain biblical ideas such as that of the hidden God and gives them an importance which they did not have in the Scholastics. Sometimes when he is writing in his new, paradoxical style of Reformation theology, he uses phrases and makes assertions which are not found among the Scholastics and which seem to contradict accepted Catholic doctrine. For example, Luther writes to Melanchthon: "Sin courageously, but believe more courageously" and says often: "man is saved by faith alone without any works." Yet *in another context* he attacks the Antinomians for their moral laxity! [26] He preaches constantly that we are saved by faith alone without works and that even "good" works are sins. Yet he explains in other places that he was referring to works of the law, works which do not proceed from faith and love. With grace all of man's works can be good, says Luther.[27] He even goes so far as to say that works are "necessary" for salvation (!) even though they do not "effect" salvation.[28] As is well-known, Luther teaches that faith is *fiducia,* a total, trusting self-surrender to God. Yet, in the best Scholastic tradition, Luther says in another place—and this not in one of his early, "Scholastic" works—that faith is situated primarily in the intellect and has as its object the truth, while hope is seated in the will and has for its object God's goodness! [29] Again, Luther can reject the whole concept of *ex opere operato,* and yet in another place teach almost precisely what Catholic theology understands by this term! [30]

These examples of the coexistence of Reformation theology and Scholastic theology even in the mature writings of the Reformer remind us that a statement written by Luther does not necessarily have the same meaning that the same statement would have were it written by a Scholastic theologian. Roman Catholic theologians, especially those who have been trained in Scholastic theology with its considerable uniformity of terminology, must try to get the "feel" of the whole of Luther's thought —at least on a specific question—before making judgments about individual statements of Luther. We must note any new uses of words or special definitions that we find in his writings. We must observe which statements constantly recur in Luther's writings. We must note the structure of Luther's statements. Does a particular statement have the structure of a personal confession of a sinner, or that of an "objectivizing" Scholastic? [31] Above all, we must never simply judge Luther's formulations solely in terms of traditional Catholic formulations. As A. Brandenburg has said: we must always take into account "that Luther, even when he is teaching, is a preacher and a herald, that

---

[26] Cf. Lortz, I, pp. 293ff.

[27] WA 18, 754, 32ff.

[28] WA 39/1, 96, 6ff.; cf. P. Althaus, "Sola fide numquam sola," in: *Una Sancta,* 16 (1961), 227-235.

[29] WA 40/2, 25, 27-27, 23.

[30] In his *Large Catechism,* WA 30/1, 218, 24 Luther says: ". . . when the word accompanies the water, baptism is valid, even though faith be lacking. For my faith does not constitute baptism but receives it": tr. Tappert, p. 443.

[31] Cf. E. Schlink, *The Coming Christ. . . ,* pp. 16-84. O. Pesch, *Theologie der Rechtfertigung,* pp. 935-948, calls Luther's style of theology "existentiell," that of Thomas Aquinas "sapiential."

his words must be understood as organic words, that we must not press them with excessive logic. . . . One has to presume a certain "logical" imprecision in individual statements by Luther and must appeal to a number of statements to confirm what he really intends to say." [32]

Having made these preliminary observations on Luther-interpretation, we now turn to the question: What was Luther's concern when, in *DSA,* he taught "that free will is nothing?" [33] Was his concern, as Denifle has suggested, his desire to be bound no longer to self-discipline and mortification? [34] Was his concern, as Grisar and Humbertclaude have asserted, his wish to uphold a deterministic doctrine of absolute necessity? Or are we to understand Luther's doctrine of unfree will simply as a product of "the German temperament?" [35] Luther's concern in *DSA* was none of these. It was rather the same thoroughly Catholic concern which motivated his attack on free will in the *Lectures on Romans,* the Scholastic disputations and the *Grund und Ursach,* namely, the desire to uphold the absolute necessity of God's grace for every human act that has any relevance for salvation (*bonum coram Deo*) and to strike down every doctrine which places the beginning of salvation or the effectiveness of God's grace in the power of fallen man's free will.

In view of his assertion that the doctrine of the unfree will is the "turning point of things" (*cardo rerum*),[36] it is not surprising that his concern should involve a number of central Christian truths. Thus his utterly central Reformation concern—his "summa caussae"—can be expressed in a number of ways: 1. *DSA* is concerned with "a theological anthropology." [37] 2. At the same time, the thesis of unfree will is a testimony of the "omnipotence or God-ness of God." [38] "*DSA* is the book about the God-ness of God," the assertion of which belongs to the gospel of justification.[39] 3 (a). *DSA* is concerned with the grace of God. According to Luther's own words he is fighting in *DSA* "against free will on behalf of the grace of God." [40] 3 (b). More specifically, in

[32] *Gericht und Evangelium,* pp. 9f.; cf. Bandt, p. 20; Vorster, pp. 283f.
[33] This is the title of the translation by Jonas of 1526.
[34] Cf. Strohl, p. 5.
[35] Paquier, "Luther," DTC, 9, 1287.
[36] WA 18, 786, 30; 721, 25; 614, 3.
[37] Erikstein, p. 264, footnote 13.
[38] Vorster, pp. 285.
[39] Doerne, pp. 60f. According to Ebeling, *Luther,* pp. 298f. DSA could just as well be entitled "De deo."
[40] WA 18, 661, 28; 771, 17. Bandt, p. 117 calls this sentence Luther's "Schlüsselwort, von dem her wir seine Schrift . . . zu interpretieren haben." *Ibid.,* p. 111: "Das Grundanliegen dieses Buches ist ganz offensichtlich die zentrale reformatorische Botschaft von der freien, dem Menschen völlig ungeschuldeten und von ihm durch keinerlei Werke zu erwerbenden Gnade Gottes in Jesus Christus." Cf.

addition to asserting the marvelous reality and power of grace, it is "undoubtedly a basic concern of this book decisively to emphasize the complete *freedom of living grace* over against a widespread emasculation and domestication of the biblical concept of God in medieval teaching." [41]

4 (a). Should one choose to express negatively the concern described in 3 (b), one could say that it is Luther's constant concern to eliminate from theology and from pastoral practice every kind of Pelagianism. As we have seen, from the time of the *Lectures on Romans* anti-Pelagianism was one of Luther's deepest concerns.[42] Repeatedly in *DSA* he identifies Erasmus' defense of free will with Pelagianism. 4 (b). More specifically, Luther announces that he is concerned not with what the will can do *with* grace. He is interested much more in showing that man's will *without* grace can do nothing whatever that is good or just in the eyes of God.[43]

4 (c). In the *Assertio* and in the *Grund und Ursach* we noticed Luther's rejection of any idea of a preparation or disposition for, or a merit of justification—even *de congruo*—by fallen man's unaided free will. The same concern is evident in *DSA*.[44] 5. From still another perspective we can say: "the thesis of unfree will has no other meaning for Luther than the safeguarding of the totality of sin." [45] According to Scripture, man in the concrete is a "slave of sin and as such is bound, imprisoned and miserably lost." [46] He is so blind that he thinks he is free and happy.[47] He has fallen completely into the power of Satan.[48] Thus man is in no way capable of turning toward God or to the gifts of salvation by his own powers.[49] "Without a doubt," says Bandt, "this is the real theme of *DSA*, a theme to which Luther reverts unflaggingly in a number of his exegetical passages." [50]

6. Finally, we encounter the same pastoral concern in *DSA* that we

---

ibid., pp. 118 and 143. See also H. Zahrndt, p. 199 and M. Doerne, p. 52: "Luthers ganze . . . Lehre vom unfreien Willen will nur die Bewährung des Evangeliums von der freien Gnade in Jesus Christus sein."
[41] Bandt, p. 143.
[42] Cristiani, "Réforme," DTC, 13, 2027-2030, in his enumeration of the positive and negative influences on Luther, completely overlooks this central concern.
[43] Cf. WA 18, 753, 36-39; 767, 32—768, 4; Vorster, p. 310.
[44] WA 18, 759, 15-18; 26ff.; 762, 19ff.; 769, 24—771, 14. According to L. Pinomaa, "Unfreier Wille und Prädestination bei Luther in DSA," in: *Theol. Zeitschrift,* 13 (1957), 340, this book is ultimately concerned with the possibility of the *dispositio ad gratiam.*
[45] Doerne, p. 49.
[46] Bandt, pp. 111f.
[47] WA 18, 679, 23.
[48] WA 18, 659, 6; 679, 25; 707, 10; 750, 13.
[49] Cf. Erasmus' definition, Walter, 1 b 9, p. 19, 8ff. and WA 18, 665, 15.
[50] Bandt, p. 112.

have seen in Luther's earlier writings.[51] Here as earlier he urges that the very word "free will" be abolished because, as pastoral experience shows, people are "pitifully deceived and led astray." [52] What the people understand by this term, he says, is far removed from anything that theologians believe and discuss.[53] The people understand free will to be "a power of freely turning in any direction, yielding to none and subject to none." [54] The people do not realize that *liberum arbitrium* [55] actually refers only to a "tiny spark" of power and that "this is totally ineffective of itself, since it is the devil's prisoner and slave." [56] If the people understood this, says Luther, they would probably stone us as deceivers when we speak of free will.[57]

Has not Luther once again laid his finger upon a real problem frequently experienced by the preacher and catechist? All too often a Roman Catholic catechist or teacher is met with astonishment when he explains to the average Catholic that even man's free will acts, insofar as they exist, are totally dependent on God's creative and sustaining activity for their very existence. Almost always he is asked: Then how is our will really free? Luther's proposal to abandon the term free will because it misleads the Christian people should raise the following questions in the minds of all preachers: What is the actual concept of free will held by the average Christian? Isn't it more often than not a Semipelagian concept? How often does a preacher or catechist proclaim or teach that God is the sovereign creator and Lord not only of all *things,* but also of all *free acts?* Such an explanation will not lead to a clear understanding of the mysterious relationship between God's creative and sustaining activity, but it will at least lead the people to realize that there *is* a mystery here for Christians, but not for Pelagians!

In explaining the intimate relationship of God's creativity to our free acts something must, of course, be said about the problem and the mystery of evil. Again the preacher will not solve the problem or explain

---

51 Cf. chapter 8, pp. 266ff.

52 WA 18, 637, 4f.: ". . . praesertim cum nobis cognitum perspectumque sit misere falli ac seduci eo vocabulo populum."

53 *Ibid.,* 6f. This is an unusual concession inasmuch as Luther here seems to grant that the theologians have a correct understanding of the term. He says just the opposite not only in his earlier works, but even in this book. Cf. WA 18, 662, 7ff., where he not only says that the "populum," in distinction to the "Theologi," but that "omnes" have a false conception of *liberum arbitrium.*

54 Tr., P & J, p. 105; WA 18, 637, 9f. Cf. WA 18, 662, 7ff. Vorster, p. 370 erroneously thinks this is Luther's own definition.

55 Luther's use of the term here indicates that he does not deny the *existence* of *liberum arbitrium!* Cf. WA 18, 638, 4-111.

56 WA 18, 637, 10ff. Cf. P & J, p. 106.

57 WA 18, 637, 10-14.

the mystery, but he will at least state the mystery: that God is holy and is in no way responsible for sin, that we do evil and are evil because of the misuse of our freedom through a free rejection of the grace that is offered to all, and that evil has a completely different structure and relation to God than does good.

The inevitable question: Why does God permit some people to sin and to be lost?, can only be properly answered in terms of the widely ignored biblical doctrines of predestination and election. How seldom are the Christian people told that if they are saved it is only because God has *chosen* them to be saved? Paul the Apostle regularly addressed the Christians of his day as the saints called and elected by God. The rarity of such forms of address today corresponds to the extent to which the preaching of the doctrine of election is neglected. It is difficult to understand how the Christian preacher can neglect to speak of election and calling when God has revealed himself as a God who elects and calls according as he pleases. Does one really believe in the mysterious God of the Old and New Testaments unless he believes in a God of election and predestination? Often a preacher will say that he does not preach about these mysteries because he does not want to frighten his people. But this is an indication that the preacher has not taught them of the certitude and hope that are ours as a result of our hope in Jesus Christ! [57a]

In addition to what we have already said in chapter 8, p. 269, we offer the following comments on Luther's proposal for a revision of theological language. We agree with Luther that "our words should be proper, pure, sober . . ." (WA 18, 638, 2). We question however, whether the replacement of the Catholic thesis: man "is indeed always naturally free" (WA 56, 385), by the thesis that "free will is a vain word" (WA 18, 670, 35f.) will be any less misleading to people. The traditional Catholic thesis of *liberum arbitrium* must always be explained in its relation to grace and to God's continuous conserving action so that all Semipelagianism is excluded. This has not always been done, neither in Luther's time nor in our own.

On the other hand, does not Luther's proposal to abolish the term free will also mislead people? Does he not have the difficult task of explaining to the people that, even though they have no free will, they must still live a Christian life, and must still *choose, resolve,* or *decide* to follow the path of love instead of selfishness, the path of Christian discipline instead of antinomianism? If many Catholics explain free will

---

[57a] Cf. Rom. 9: 31; Phil. 4: 13, Col. 1: 27. See. S. Pfürtner, *Luther and Aquinas on Salvation* (New York, 1965).

in an un-Catholic, Semipelagian way, how many of Luther's early followers could correctly explain the necessity of good works and the keeping of the commandments for salvation?

It is important to note that later Lutherans, beginning with Melanchthon, did not follow Luther's proposal to abolish the term free will. The question at issue is really: Is the term free will at fault, or the Christian preacher or catechist who does not explain the absolute dependence of the free will on God's grace for every salutary act? Even Luther seems to grant that the latter is the case. He says that he would allow the people to use the term free will *if* it were correctly explained! [57b] Calvin likewise rejected the term *liberum arbitrium*—but not the reality—because he believed it was misleading. In his *Institutes,* II, 2, 5, he said he would not object to the term *if* someone were to use it without an erroneous signification!

We have already indicated our conviction that Luther's concerns in *DSA,* which we have enumerated above, are, with the exception of the sixth, which we have evaluated separately, fully Catholic concerns. These concerns are all mutually related and are all in full conformity with Scripture. These concerns have been shared not only by Augustine, Anselm, Peter Lombard and Thomas Aquinas, but also by earlier (Second Council of Orange) and later (Trent) authoritative teaching documents of the Church.

Unfortunately, *De servo arbitrio* cannot be so simply analyzed. It is necessary to point out that there is more in this book than the Catholic-Lutheran thesis that the unjustified man is unable, unfree to do anything for salvation by his own fallen power of free will. It is true, as Bandt has said, that "Luther's fundamental thesis of the unfree will first of all seeks to express the captivity of the sinful human will in relation to the grace of God, which remains free in the face of all human pretensions, demands and 'merits'." [58] However, it is also correct, as Bandt points out, that the thesis of the unfree will has another, much more general meaning. "Unfree will" signifies for Luther not only man's bondage to sin but also that, from the standpoint of God's will, everything we do "happens by necessity" (*omnia necessitate fieri—si Dei voluntatem spectes:* WA 18, 615, 31; 617, 19), since all of our activity which is not directed by God's Word and Spirit is subject to the general omnipotence of God (WA 18, 752, 12). [59]

The following is representative of a fairly wide attitude toward *DSA:* "Luther like the Bible, treats man from three viewpoints. Man is God's

---

[57b] Cf. WA 18, 638, 4-9.
[58] P. 118.
[59] *Ibid.*

image. Man is a sinner. Man becomes a new creature in Christ according to the image of Christ. It is the methodological peculiarity of this
book that Luther here consciously limits the anthropological theme to
the doctrine of man as sinner." [60] This is unquestionably Luther's intention in *DSA,* but he does not stick to it! Although it is his announced
purpose to treat of the *homo peccator* without grace and although he insists that he is not interested in what the fallen man can do with grace,
he nevertheless uses an argument for his thesis of *servum arbitrium* which
has *nothing whatever to do with the fact that man is a sinner.* This
argument for the unfree will is based on the fact that man is a *creature!*
This is the argument that free will is "completely thrown down and cast
under foot" by the very fact that "God foreknows nothing contingently,
but that He foresees, purposes, and does all things according to His own
immutable, eternal and infallible will. This bombshell knocks 'free will'
flat, and utterly shatters it." [61] Luther argues further that everything we
do, everything that happens, however they may appear to us to be done
mutably and contingently, in reality happen necessarily and immutably
"if you consider the will of God." [62] Here Luther is clearly not arguing
for the unfree will because of man's sinfulness, but because of his crea-
tureliness! Man has an unfree will because of God's necessitating, infallible foreknowledge of all things. According to this argument it is im-
material whether a man has been justified or not. In either case he would
have no free will because in either case God foresees all that he does.
Would not this argument also apply to the will of Christ, as well as to
Adam and to Satan before they sinned? Such reasoning is not simply a
more radical and more universal argument for the thesis of *servum
arbitrium.* It implies an altogether different concept of *servum arbitrium*
than the one based on the biblical doctrine of man's servitude to sin.[63]

In contrast to many Luther scholars who too readily bypass this part
of *DSA,* Doerne faces the problem: "One would like to hear more
clearly that this unfreedom which follows from the *generalis motus
omnipotentiae* is different from the unfreedom which Luther had in
mind from beginning to end, namely, the guilt-ridden fate of that human
existence which has decided against God. In contrast to this genuine
'cardo rerum' (WA 18, 786, 30) which the Reformer called into the
arena against Erasmus, the *necessitas* which the all-powerful God imposes on his creatures is something 'formal.' Unless we draw a sharp

---

[60] Doerne, p. 48.
[61] WA 18, 615, 13ff.
[62] *Ibid.,* 31ff.
[63] It was much more than inadequate terminology which led Luther away from
his genuine concern. Cf. RGG, 2, 97.

boundary line here, the entire meaning of the thesis of *servum arbitrium* might be transformed. Then it will no longer be a judgment concerning man's sinful will but only the ascertaining of his creaturely subjection." [64]

From still another point of view, one can agree with E. Schlink that Luther's doctrine of *servum arbitrium* was "not primarily a statement of theological reflection but the confession of the sinner." [65] Yet it is also true that Luther does present his thesis of unfree will as an expression of theological reflection on the nature of the divine will and foreknowledge.

We shall now examine more closely this two-fold concept of unfree will, emphasizing the explanations and elaborations of Luther which we have not yet seen in our investigation of his earlier writings.[66]

III. LUTHER'S NECESSITARIAN CONCEPT OF UNFREE WILL

In the previous chapter we saw that Erasmus, in his attack on proposition 36 of the *Assertio,* did not attack Luther's main concern—the affirmation of the Johannine-Pauline-Augustinian doctrine of man's bondage to sin—but his non-biblical argument based on the absolute necessity of all events. We have also tried to show that Luther, despite certain misleading formulations, was, at least in his intention, not a determinist. In *DSA,* however, instead of trying to clarify the meaning of what he had said about *necessitas absoluta,* Luther not only repeated his necessitarian thesis, but also reaffirmed it more vigorously and expounded it at greater length.

A. THE STRUCTURE OF LUTHER'S NECESSITARIAN ARGUMENT:
A STATEMENT OF THEOLOGICAL REFLECTION IN THE STRUCTURE
OF DESCRIPTION, AS WELL AS A CONFESSION OF DIVINE PROVIDENCE [67]

Luther's necessitarian argument against free will can be stated as follows: God foresees nothing contingently. He foresees, designs and does everything with an immutable, eternal and infallible will. Therefore free will is "entirely destroyed." [68] Luther also states it in the following

---

[64] Doerne, pp. 85f. Cf. Lütkens, p. 52. Other scholars who have pointed out the two-fold basis for *servum arbitrium* include H. Jedin, *Des Joh. Cochlaeus Streitschrift;* E. Erikstein, p. 168; E. de Moreau in: Fliche-Martin, vol. 16, pp. 93f.; and recently G. Ebeling, *Luther,* pp. 248ff. L. Pinomaa, p. 340 exemplifies the view which sees DSA only as an expression of man's helplessness as a result of sin, but which applies to the justified and the non-justified alike. See also Schwiebert, pp. 689f.

[65] *The Coming Christ. . . ,* p. 175.

[66] Cf. chapter 8.

[67] Cf. Schlink, *The Coming Christ. . . ,* pp. 174ff.

[68] WA 18, 615, 13ff.: ". . . Deus nihil praescit contingenter, sed quod omnia

way: God's will and knowledge is eternal and changeless. Therefore it follows irrefutably: everything that we do, everything that happens, even though it appears to us to happen changeably and contingently, in reality happens necessarily and immutably from the standpoint of God's will.[69]

Authors who insist that Luther's thesis of unfree will is derived "from Scripture and from it alone," [70] or who assert that Luther's thesis has nothing to do with philosophical or metaphysical thinking [71] will be hard-pressed to reconcile the foregoing argument with their generalizations. We do not say that this is a *purely* philosophical argument, for it is clear that Luther's major premise is biblical: that God foreknows all things. We should remember, however, that this is not a belief peculiar to the Bible. It was held in pagan antiquity even apart from biblical revelation. Luther acknowledges this fact when he points out to Erasmus that even pagan poets [72] have rejected the idea of free will because of their belief in the foreknowledge of the gods. The knowledge of divine predestination and foreknowledge, says Luther, has remained in the world no less strongly than the notion of the divinity itself.[73] Thus, although Luther's own argument for universal necessity against free will is based partly on revelation, he regards his thesis as a truth which can be attained even by the natural reason of non-believers!

We have emphasized that only part of Luther's necessitarian argument is based on revelation: the major premise. There is, however, an implicit minor premise in his argument which has nothing whatever to do with biblical revelation, namely, the proposition: whatever God foresees and foreknows must happen necessarily; otherwise God could be mistaken.[74] Without affirming this proposition Luther cannot reach his

---

incommutabili et aeterna infallibilique voluntate et praevidet et proponit et facit. Hoc fulmine sternitur et conteritur penitus liberum arbitrium. . . ."

[69] WA 18, 615, 29-33: "Si volens praescit, aeterna est et immobilis (quia natura) voluntas, si praesciens vult, aeterna est et immobilis (quia natura) scientia. Ex quo sequitur irrefragabiliter, omnia quae facimus, omnia quae fiunt, etsi nobis videntur mutabiliter et contingenter fieri, revera tamen fiunt necessario et immutabiliter, si Dei voluntatem spectes."

[70] Iwand, MA, p. 312; cf. p. 300.

[71] Cf. Pinomaa, "Unfreier Wille und Prädestination bei Luther," p. 349; Th. Sartory, "Das Mysterium der Kirche in reformatorischer Sicht," in: *Mysterium Kirche* (Salzburg, 1962), vol. II, pp. 904f. See above chapter 8, footnote 68.

[72] WA 18, 617, 24: "gentiles Poetae."

[73] WA 18, 618, 12-15.

[74] This proposition is found explicitly in WA 18, 710, 5. Lütkens, p. 71 represents a view accepted by many modern Luther scholars (Pannenberg, G. Nygren, *et al.*). When he criticizes J. Müller, *Lutheri de praedestinatione et libero arbitrio doctrina* (Göttingen, 1832), p. 274 for saying that Luther uses causal argumentation here. This seems to be a quarrel over words. Luther speaks constantly of God's

conclusion. Luther's minor premise is manifestly a philosophical, meta-physical thesis.[75] Thus, whereas a non-believer could reach the same conclusion as Luther on purely philosophical or rational grounds,[76] for Luther the conclusion was a *theological* conclusion, that is, a theological assertion which is derived from two premises, one of which is a revealed truth, the other a truth of natural reason.[77]

M. Schüler describes Luther's necessitarian argument as follows: "God's immutable all-embracing causality . . . compels the recognition of the absolute, metaphysical unfreedom of creatures. . . . No doubt or darkness remains: *everything* happens necessarily (WA 617)." [78] It is difficult to see how this argument against free will, which can be found not only in *DSA* but in Vergil and other fatalistic pagan thinkers, can be said to have the "structure of personal encounter" or of "a confession of sins." [79] It seems much more to be an "objectivizing assertion about the relation of man in his actions to God in his actions [80] "in the structure of description." [81] However—and this is of decisive importance for a correct interpretation of Luther's necessitarian argument—it must be recognized that Luther's statements concerning the necessity of all human activity are in no way motivated by a desire to defend a doctrine of cosmic necessity. Although these statements may be ambiguous in comparison with what the Scholastics had said concerning freedom and necessity, they are nevertheless to be understood first of all as expres-sions of Luther's firm Catholic belief in the biblical doctrine of divine providence. As such, they not only have the structure of description but

---

"operare," "agere" and "facere" in man. Are not these operations all a form of "causare?" Cf. chapter 4, pp. 78-81.

[75] On the non-biblical sources of Luther's concept of necessity, cf. Erikstein, p. 159. See also Doerne, p. 88.

[76] Cf. Zickendraht, p. 186; Pannenberg, "Der Einfluss der Anfechtungserfah-rung. . . ," p. 117, footnote 30; W. von Loewenich, "Luthers theologia crucis," p. 88.

[77] Cf. Schlink, "Der theologische Syllogismus als Problem der "Prädestinations-lehre," in: *Einsicht und Glaube, Festschr. f. G. Söhngen* (Freiburg-Basal-Wien, 1962), pp. 299 and 318. In this essay Schlink says many valuable things about predestination. We cannot agree with his conclusion, however, that in the doc-trine of predestination, "logisch richtige Folgerungen aus theologisch unbestreit-baren Prämissen zu irrigen Aussagen führen," p. 318. In each example he offers of such erroneous conclusions, we believe it can be shown that the conclusion is not "unavoidable."

[78] "Luthers Gottesbegriff nach seiner Schrift De servo abritrio," *Zeitschr. f. Kirchengesch,* 55 (1936), 553.

[79] Cf. Schlink, *The Coming Christ. . . ,* pp. 173ff.

[80] Pesch, "Ein katholisches Anliegen," 312f. Cf. above chapter 8, footnote 68. See also Alanen, "Das Wahrheitsproblem," p. 235.

[81] Schlink, p. 174f.

also the structure of a confession, not necessarily the confession of a sinner, but of one who believes in divine providence. The doctrine of providence and the related doctrine of predestination,[82] as Luther rightly believes, absolutely exclude any concept of *liberum arbitrium* as "a power . . . yielding to none and subject to none." [83] Unfortunately, Luther does not say clearly, as did Augustine, Boethius, Anselm, Thomas Aquinas, *et al.,* that man truly has *liberum arbitrium* and can truly make free decisions, which are infallibly foreseen by God and which are governed by his providence.

B. The Meaning of Luther's Necessitarian Argument for Servum Arbitrium: A Denial of Natural Freedom of the Will or an Affirmation of God's Providence?

When Luther says in *DSA* and in the *Assertio* that all things happen necessarily as a result of God's infallible foreknowledge and immutable will, his readers—especially those with some background in Scholastic theology—could easily conclude that he is denying the existence of the natural freedom of the will. Many Catholic theologians and Reformation scholars have interpreted Luther precisely in this way. The Scholastics affirmed that some things happen contingently and not necessarily. Luther says that even though the things we do seem to us to be done contingently, they really happen necessarily.[84] There seems to be, therefore, a clear contradiction between the Scholastic and Catholic affirmation of contingency and free will and Luther's denial of the same. We readily admit that, from the standpoint of Scholastic theology, Luther's argument is at least ambiguous.

For the following reasons,[85] however, we maintain that it is incorrect to interpret Luther's necessitarian argument for *servum arbitrium* as a denial of the existence of man's natural freedom.

1. First of all, Luther does not say in the conclusions of his argument: therefore, there is no free will. He says rather: therefore, "it is completely thrown down and trampled under foot" ("sternitur et conteritur penitus liberum arbitrium").[86] If Luther had intended to deny the existence of *liberum arbitrium* by this argument—something

---

[82] Cf. Iwand, p. 275.

[83] WA 18, 637, 7-10.

[84] WA 18, 615, 31f.: "omnia quae fiunt etsi nobis videntur mutabiliter et contingenter fieri, revera tamen fiunt necessario et immutabiliter, si Dei voluntatem spectes."

[85] The following reflections supplement that which was said in the excursus: Was Luther a Determinist?

[86] WA 18, 615, 15; cf. 722, 4.

we have not seen in any of his previous writings [87]—he could have said
so in such a clear phrase as: therefore there is no free will,[88] or with
such words as: "it is totally excluded, destroyed, annihilated, etc." He
could even have repeated his statement from the *Assertio:* therefore "all
things happen by absolute necessity." [89] Instead, Luther used a strong
figure of speech: "sternitur et conteritur penitus liberum abiritrium,"
which the MA has interpreted too extremely as: thus "the free will is cut
down and completely annihilated." The context of *DSA* and the figura-
tive language seem to us better preserved by the paraphrase: "thus the
free will is thrown to the ground and stepped upon in the dust." The
meaning of the necessitarian argument is therefore: because God infallibly foresees and ordains all things, any concept of the free will as a
proud, independent power existing apart from God's providential rule
is shattered; even the free will must be seen as humbly subject to
God's power. Like Augustine, Luther is opposing those who, in defending free will, commit the "sacrilege" of withdrawing free will from God's
providence.[90]

2. Our second reason for contending that Luther's necessitarian
argument is not a true denial of man's natural freedom is that Luther
does not conclude here—as he did in the *Assertio*—that all things happen "by absolute necessity." According to Boethius,[91] Thomas,[92] et al.
this and the "necessity of coercion" are the only kinds of necessity
which are incompatible with free will. Instead Luther says: "all things
. . . happen necessarily and immutably, if you consider the will of God."
Is he not saying here precisely what Boethius, Thomas and other Scholastics have said, namely, that on the condition or supposition that God
wills something to happen it will happen infallibly, most certainly or
necessarily, that is, by a necessity of infallibility (*ex necessitate infall-*

---

[87] This applies also to the *Assertio* when it is interpreted in the light of the
Grund und Ursach.

[88] Even in this case, however, the question would have to be asked: In what
sense is there no free will? In the Augustinian-Thomistic sense? In the Ciceronian?
In the Bielian? Luther does say elsewhere: "nullum esse liberum arbitrium" (WA
18, 635, 24) and "liberum arbitrium nihil est" (WA 18, 719, 31; 722, 13). It is
our view, however that in each of these places the meaning is: there is no *liberum
arbitrium* which is not subject to God's infallible foreknowledge and immutable
will and which escapes the *necessitas immutabilitatis* (*infallibilitatis*) which follow
from the infallibility and immutability of the *scientia* and *voluntas Dei.* This will
be seen clearly in point (2).

[89] In this case we would ask again, as we did earlier in our analysis of WA 7,
146, 6-12, chapter 8, p. 259: What does Luther mean by *necessitas absoluta?*

[90] In *De Civ. Dei*, I, 5, 9 Augustine says of Cicero: "Cum vult facere liberos
fecit sacrilegos." For Thomas' attitude on this question see chapter 6, p. 156.

[91] Cf. chapter 4, footnote 74.

[92] Cf. chapter 6, p. 151.

ibilitatis)? [93] We are convinced that this question is to be answered affirmatively even though Luther in *DSA* as well as in the *Lectures on Romans* and in the *Disputatio contra scholasticam theologiam* rejects the distinction between *necessitas consequentis* (*absoluta*) and *necessitas consequentiae* (*conditionata*). In both places Luther rejects the "two necessities" as irrelevant—and for the same reason. The fact that things do not happen *necessitate consequentis,* he says, simply means that the creature is not God! [94]

In *DSA,* as in the *Lectures on Romans,* Luther fails to see that the high Scholastics at least, following Boethius and Augustine, distinguished the two types of necessity not to prove that man is not God, but to show that God's infallible foreknowledge—a truth of faith—does not exclude man's free will, the basis of human responsibility. The Catholic tradition believes just as strongly as Luther that God's infallible knowledge cannot be deceived and that his immutable will most certainly is fulfilled. It even recognizes that things happen by necessity (*suppositionis; consequentiae*) as a result of God's foreknowledge and will. But this was never a necessity which excluded man's *liberum arbitrium,* without which there could be no moral order of sin, true virtue, reward and punishment.

Luther rejects the traditional distinction of the two kinds of necessity as a trick, a *ludibrium.*[95] But just as in the case of his rejection of the concept of *ex opere operato* in name and in an unauthentic sense, but not in reality, it seems that he does not reject the distinction of the two necessities in its true meaning. Does he not actually admit the distinction when he says: "all things which we do . . . , even if they seem to us to happen mutably and contingently, nevertheless happen necessarily and immutably, *if you consider the will of God?*" Is not the phrase we have italicized the *condition* upon which our acts are necessary? The necessity spoken of in Luther's necessitarian argument is a necessity which arises as a result of God's willing and knowing. This is the same as saying that it is a necessity which occurs on the supposition or condition that God has willed and known an event. Luther therefore says in fact— if not in word—the same thing as Thomas does concerning *necessitas*

---

[93] Thomas, I-II, q. 112, a. 3c.

[94] WA 18, 617, 14-17; cf. chapter 8, p. 234. On this point see Vorster, pp. 337-349. Vorster, like Zickendraht, pp. 114f., is not critical enough of Luther's "reductio ab absurdum." Furthermore, he understands the concept "necessitas absoluta" univocally (p. 341), and overlooks the fact (p. 342) that Thomas grants the possibility of a *necessitas consequentis* (*absoluta*) in creatures. However, this is never an absolute necessity of existence, but of essence. Cf. *De Ver.,* q. 23, a. 4, I, q. 14, a. 13, ad 3; q. 22, a. 4. See chapter 8, pp. 234f. and G. Smith, p. 80.

[95] WA 18, 617, 14.

consequentiae. Do we not find a parallel to Luther's "necessary . . . if you consider" in Thomas Aquinas, who says ". . . the things known by God must be necessary according to the way in which they are subject to the divine knowledge . . . but they are not absolutely [necessary], that is, according to the way they are considered in their own causes." [96] It would thus be possible for Thomas to say with Luther: If you consider God's knowledge (will, predestination), man's will acts *necessarily* because it is not outside the infallible and immutable order of God's providence, knowledge and predestination.[97]

The difference between Thomas and Luther is that Thomas clearly says that the *necessitas consequentiae* by which all things willed by God happen does not exclude free will and contingency. We believe, however, that Luther implicitly says the same thing by the very fact that the necessity of which he speaks in his necessitarian argument is a necessity which is *conditioned* by God's knowing and willing. This seems to imply that, considered in themselves and apart from God's foreknowledge, our actions are mutable and contingent.

Although Luther, speaking of our acts, uses the phrase: ". . . they seem to us to happen mutably and contingently," [98] we do not agree with Vorster that the contingency of the human activity recognized by Luther "is in reality an illusion." [99] This interpretation lays too much

---

96 I, a. 14, a. 13, ad 3. Cf. *Quodl.,* XI, q. 3, art. un., ad 1.

97 Cf. *De Ver.,* q. 2, a. 12, ad 3; q. 6, a. 3; *In Metaph., Lib.* VI, lect. 3, n. 1216: I, q. 14, a. 13; q. 19, aa. 7 and 8; q. 23, a. 6; *Quodl.,* XII, q. 3. Vorster, p. 87, footnote 70 correctly notes that, for Thomas, the *necessitas consequentiae* or *infallibilitatis* is universally present, "weil es—ausserhalb der absoluten Notwendigkeit Gottes—nichts gibt, was nicht irgendwie bedingt ware." He is also correct when he (p. 343) says that Luther and Thomas agree on the thesis that "omnia quae facimus" or "quae fiunt. . . , facimus vel fiunt necessario et immutabiliter, si Dei voluntatem spectes."

98 WA 18, 615, 32.

99 P. 264. On p. 343 Vorster proposes an idea which we judge to be an extreme "theology of appearance." He writes: "Luther ist sich . . . klar, dass die theologisch verbindliche Charakterisierung nur die vom Willen Gottes ausgehende sein kann. So wie sich Sein und Werden von Gott her und vor Gott darstellen, so sind sie auch wirklich und so sind sie theologisch zu beschreiben. Jeder Aspekt, auch der einer phänomenalen Analyse oder einer Freiheitsontologie, kann demgegenüber nur *Schein* sein." For this reason, says Vorster, Luther deliberately avoids the formulation "alles geschehe 'mutabiliter et contingenter, si voluntatem hominis spectes'," and says instead: "etsi nobis videntur mutabiliter et contingenter fieri." This conception seems to us to call into question the reality of creation and of created action insofar as Vorster does not clearly affirm that free acts *really* are free in themselves when they are considered from the point of view of their proper causes ("absolute, secundum quod in propriis causis considerantur:" Thomas, I, q. 14, a. 13, ad 3). It should also be noted that there is no such thing as an adequate ontology of freedom which does not consider created freedom in relation to the knowledge, will and providence of God. Thomas Aquinas has

stress on the "seem" (*videntur*). Actually Luther is so interested in emphasizing the universal necessity (*conditionata*) which results from God's foreknowledge and will that he does not stop to reflect sufficiently on the contingency [100] and mutability of the will in itself (*absoluta*). This is one of the differences—and weaknesses—of his doctrine on free will in comparison with that of Augustine and Thomas.

The fact that Luther is not interested in defending a doctrine of absolute necessity is clearly seen in his comment on Erasmus' argument that Judas betrayed Christ freely. Equally clear from Luther's remarks concerning the betrayal by Judas is the fact that Luther did not really grasp the distinction of the two kinds of necessity. In line with many earlier thinkers, Erasmus says: "not every necessity excludes free will. . . .[101] Applying this principle to the betrayal of Christ by Judas, Erasmus writes: ". . . if you consider God's infallible foreknowledge and immutable will, it would be necessary for Judas to betray the Lord, and yet Judas could have changed his will or certainly would not have to have given in to an evil will." [102]

Erasmus continues: those who discuss this question with Scholastic subtlety admit a *necessitas consequentiae* but reject a *necessitas con-*

---

developed precisely this kind of an ontology of freedom—or theology of freedom. Yet he never loses sight of the *reality* of human freedom. For him, it is never "nur Schein." The created act ("ens secundum quid") as well as the created being ("ens completum in se subsistens in suo esse": cf. Thomas, *De Ente et Essentia*, cap. 7; I, q. 44, a. 2c) have their own reality distinct, but not independent of the divine reality. To say that the reality of either the created act or of the created being is *in seipso* "nur Schein" is to come dangerously close to pantheism. It is one of the fundamental truths of theology that creatures are related to God as their creator and that they participate in God's being—yet this created participation in being is really distinct from God's being. Vorster seeks to escape the charge of pantheism by saying, *ibid.*: "Die Seinskontingenz des Geschaffen . . . ist nie blosser Schein wie die Aktkontingenz, sondern sie ergibt sich zwingend aus der Freiheit Gottes gegenüber und zur Schöpfung." This statement is logically sound only if one grants Vorster's implicit premise, which we do not, namely, that the human act is not a being (Seindes). It is surely not an "ens completem," but an "ens accidentale" or an "ens secundum quid" and, as such, its contingence cannot be called "blosser Schein" any more than can the contingence of being. The fact that it is "only" an *ens secundum quid* with an *esse accidentale* does not mean that it is withdrawn "ab universali causa entium" (Thomas, I, q. 44, a. 2). The human act must be regarded as a creature of God. As such, it can *really* be contingent if the creator so wills.

[100] On Luther's non-Scholastic concept of contingency, see chapter 8, p. 233 and point (3) below.

[101] Walter, III, a 9, p. 52, 7f.: "Non omnis necessitas excludit liberum voluntatem . . ."

[102] *Ibid.*, lines 13-17: ". . . si spectes dei praecientiam infallibilem et voluntatem immutabilem, necessario eventurum est, ut Iudas prodat dominum, et tamen Iudas poterat mutare voluntatem suam aut certe poterat non suscipere voluntatem impiam."

sequentis.[103] According to the Scholastics, says Erasmus correctly, it *necessarily follows* that Judas would betray the Lord *if* God willed this to happen by his eternal will, but it does not follow that he betrays the Lord *necessarily*, since this wicked deed arises from his own evil will.[104]

In his response to Erasmus, Luther makes it clear at the outset that he does not say that Judas necessarily betrayed Christ in the sense of necessity of force or violence.[105] He affirms, rather, a *necessitas immutabilitatis* or *infallibilitas ad tempus* [106] which in no way excludes the voluntariness of Judas' betrayal.[107] Thus, when Luther says that Judas necessarily betrayed Christ, he means: "after the time had been predetermined by God, it infallibly had to happen that Judas should willingly betray Christ." [108]

It is of supreme importance to recognize that neither Augustine nor Thomas nor any truly Catholic theologian—not even Erasmus—would deny that, under the supposition of God's eternal will, all events—including the betrayal of Christ by Judas—infallibly happen at the time decreed by God. They happen, as Thomas and Luther say, *ex necessitate infallibilitatis*. In further agreement with Luther, the Catholic theological tradition teaches that this necessity of infalliblity does not destroy the voluntary character of human actions. However, in contrast to

---

[103] *Ibid.*, lines 19ff.

[104] *Ibid.*, p. 53, lines 1-5: "Fatentur enim necessario consequi, quod Iudas proditurus fuerit dominum, si hoc ab aeterno voluntate efficaci voluit deus, at negant consequi, quod ideo necessario proditurus sit, cum ex sua prava voluntate susceperit impium negotium." Neither the translation of Schumacher, p. 52, nor that of Winter, p. 52, adequately convey the two-fold sense in which Erasmus here uses the term "necessario."

[105] WA 18, 720, 31-721, 4. For a list of the places in DSA where Luther distinguishes *necessitas immutabilitatis* from *necessitas coactionis* see Iwand, MA, p. 296.

[106] WA 18, 720, 32 and 36. In contrast to this understanding of *necessitas immutabilitatis,* cf. WA 18, 634, 30f. where Luther says that this type of necessity means: "quod voluntas sese mutare et vertere alio non possit." Here *nec. immutabilitatis* has nothing to do with God's foreknowledge and predestination, but is the result of sin and the absence of the Spirit. *Ibid.*, 634, 21ff. This is evidence not only of Luther's two-fold argumentation for *servum arbitrium,* but also of the great terminological difficulty presented by DSA. We encounter another semantic ambiguity when Luther tells his readers that by "mera necessitas" he means nothing more than that man cannot will good without special grace! Cf. WA 18, 670, 25—30; 670, 19ff.; 667, 15 ff. and 21ff.

[107] WA 18, 720, 32f.: "Scimus . . . quod Iudas volendo prodidit Christum. . . ." In WA 18, 635, 12ff. Luther insists that man's actions are voluntary, i.e., spontaneous and not forced. A forced will is not *voluntas,* but *noluntas.*

[108] WA 18, 721, 2ff.: ". . . disputamus . . . an tempore praedefinito a Deo infallibiliter fieri oportuerit, ut Iudas volendo proderet Christum."

Luther, this tradition unanimously affirms that human acts, even though they are immutably decreed and infallibly foreknown by God, happen *freely* because they proceed from a free will. This is something Luther is very reluctant to say.[109]

Luther insists that once the *necessitas consequentiae* is admitted by Erasmus and the Scholastics, the question is already settled: the free will is "defeated and prostrate." [110] Nothing that is said about contingency or necessity of the consequent, that is, on the act itself, makes any difference! [111] We regard this statement as being a confirmation of our earlier suspicion, based on Luther's remarks in the *Lectures on Romans* and in the *Disputatio contra scholasticam theologiam*, that Luther does not truly understand the distinction between *necessitas consequentiae* and *consequentis*.[112] The distinction is admittedly not an easy one to grasp, as the frequently inadequate explanations of it by translators and commentators indicate.[113] We would have been more assured that Luther understood the distinction had he at least taken into account the classical illustration of the distinction: when a man sits, he

---

[109] Seils, pp. 100-113, is representative of a number of Luther scholars who erroneously think that because Luther teaches that the will is unforced and that man acts voluntarily, man's cooperation with God is therefore a *free* cooperation. Like many others Seils identifies voluntary activity with free activity. Pp. 112f. Other authors who incorrectly translate Luther's "voluntarie" with "libere" or "freiwillig," or who think that because Luther rejects the notion of a coerced will or affirms man's cooperation with God, he therefore holds to free will include: K. Holl, *Ges. Aufs.*, I, p. 65; Schüler, pp. 554f.; Prenter, *Spiritus Creator*, pp. 236 and 331, footnote 253; Löfgren, p. 116; Erikstein, pp. 27f. and 269, footnote 44; E. Schott, *Willensfreiheit*, RGG, 6, 1724; McDonough, pp. 50f., footnote 6; Boisset, p. 129. W. von Loewenich, *Luther und der Neuprotestantismus* (Witten/Ruhr, 1963), p. 418, on the contrary, states Luther's position accurately when he says that Luther views man's acts as happening voluntarily but necessarily, although not *ex necessitate coactionis*. Compare Luther's affirmation of the spontaneity of man's voluntary acts with the distinction between spontaneity and freedom outlined by P. Tillich, *Systematic Theology*, I, 3rd ed. (London, 1960), p. 205.

[110] WA 18, 722, 4f.: "Si enim necessitatem consequentiae concesseris, victum ac prostratum est liberum arbitrium."

[111] WA 18, 722, 5f.: ". . . nec quicquam iuvat vel necessitas vel contingentia consequentis." Cf. WA 18, 719, 12-19 where Luther also dismisses the distinction as irrelevant and misleading.

[112] This is our answer to the question raised by G. Smith, "Luther and Free Choice," p. 80: ". . . could one say that because Luther thinks the distinction impertinent, therefore did he fail to see the distinction itself?" Seils, p. 98 also doubts whether Luther understands the distinction.

[113] O. Scheel, p. 405 and the MA, p. 156 (cf. Iwand, MA, p. 277) translate "contingentia" as "Zufall." Scheel, *ibid.*, renders "consequentis" as "das Unbedingte." The translation of P & J, p. 221 and the note of F. W. Schmidt to *Luthers Lehre vom unfreien Willen* (München, 1923), p. 393 are much more accurate.

sits necessarily as long as he is sitting (by *necessitas consequentiae* or *suppositionis*), for it is impossible for him to sit and not to sit at the same time (*sensus compositi*); however, he sits freely or contingently (and not by *necessitas consequentis*), for it is always possible for him to stand (*sensus divisi*). This illustration of the two types of necessity shows, contrary to Luther, that it makes a great deal of difference if one says that an event happens *necessitate consequentiae* but not *necessitate consequentis*.

Luther overlooks the different senses in which "can" and "necessity" can be understood when he says to Erasmus: "How could Judas change his will while God's infallible foreknowledge stands? Could he change God's foreknowledge and make it fallible?" [114] A theologian could reply in Thomistic terms: God infallibly foresees that Judas will freely choose to betray Christ. As a consequence of God's foreknowledge, Judas' free betrayal is said to be necessary by necessity of supposition, immutability, condition or consequence, but not by absolute or consequent necessity. Because Judas' betrayal is the result of his free choice, as proximate cause, it can be said that *in one sense* (*sensus divisi*) Judas could have responded to the grace by which God enables all men to resist temptation [115] and could have asked Christ for forgiveness instead of betraying him. This was a *real* alternative for Judas before his actual betrayal of Christ.[116] In another sense (*sensus compositi*), however, under the supposition that God foresees that Judas will freely betray Christ and under the supposition that Judas is actually betraying Christ freely, then it is impossible that he not betray him. Thus Judas necessarily betrays Christ by necessity of consequence and in the composite sense, but he does not betray Christ necessarily, by necessity of the thing consequent and in the divided sense, but freely. In both senses God infallibly foresees the event.[117] Again we see that it *does* make a difference if one says that an event happens by necessity of consequence but not by necessity of the thing consequent.

The following conclusions can be drawn from Luther's reflections on the Judas betrayal:

(a) Luther's main purpose here is to insist vigorously that all things

---

[114] WA 18, 721, 8f.: tr. P & J, p. 220.

[115] I Cor. 10: 13.

[116] Vorster, p. 348, ignores Thomas' distinction of the "sensus divisus" and "sensus compositus" when he says without qualification: the *necessitas consequentiae* resulting from God's eternal will "schneidet bei Thomas *und* Luther die Möglichkeit des Auch-Anders-Könnens ab."

[117] *De Ver.*, q. 2, a. 12c: "Deus infallibiliter videt omnia contingentia." Cf. I, q. 14, a. 13c and ad 3.

happen by what the Scholastic tradition calls necessity of consequence.[118] He thus wishes to make it absolutely clear that God infallibly foreknows all events.

(b) By affirming the necessity of consequence and rejecting as a "mere phantom" [119] the applicability of the concept of necessity of the thing consequent because the two necessities "are directly opposed and contradictory," [120] Luther shows a fundamental misunderstanding of the distinction. The misunderstanding is based on his failure to see that there can be another kind of necessity besides violent necessity (coercion) and necessity of consequence (of immutability, infallibility), namely, a necessity of the thing consequent or absolute necessity—not of being (*esse*), but of becoming (*fieri*)—which excludes contingent becoming and therefore free will.

(c) On the other hand, Luther says it makes no difference to him if we say man's actions are contingent, as long as we grant him that they happen by necessity of consequence, thus assuring that we recognize God's infallible foreknowledge.[121] Does this last conclusion not show that Luther is much more concerned with upholding the doctrine of God's providence than in denying that the will is contingent *in the Scholastic sense* of this term?

It must be admitted that Luther asks a question which cannot be fully answered by any Catholic theologian, for it strikes at the mysterious relationship between God's infallible foreknowledge and most efficacious will and man's free will: "How, I ask you, will these two positions agree: 'Judas can will not to betray,' and: 'Judas must necessarily will to betray?' " [122] Even though the Catholic theologian will explain that there is no *contradiction* here, since the necessity of contingency by which Judas acts is a necessity which does not exclude free will, he is still confronted with the *mystery* that God is able to move man's free

---

[118] WA 18, 722, 4f.; 12f. Bandt, p. 147 oversimplifies when he says that Luther unequivocally rejects the distinction between the two necessities. Vorster, pp. 338f. on the contrary, correctly sees that Luther's judgment is, on the one hand, critical and negative, but "on the other hand, affirmative insofar as he makes use of the distinction himself."

[119] WA 18, 722, 16.

[120] *Ibid.*, 23.

[121] *Ibid.*, 4-8. Cf. footnote 111 above. The same indirect concession is made by Luther in the *Lectures on Romans,* WA 56, 383: "Si enim scis, quod nec tale consequentiae omnino fiet, quid refert ulterius scire, an sit contingens vel non pro hoc loco?" (The translation of this sentence by Ellwein in the MA of the Lectures on Romans, p. 290 is completely misleading.) Elsewhere in DSA, WA 18, 616, 2-12, we find a complete rejection of contingency by Luther. However, see point (4) below.

[122] P & J, p. 222; WA 18, 722, 21ff.

will infallibly but freely. If God's power is likened to any created power of our experience then we have a contradiction and an impossibility—not a mystery. But if we consider God's creative power as it truly is—as transcendent and as "efficacissima," as a power so great that it can effect even the free choices of men—then we have placed the doctrine of free will in the only context in which it cannot be distorted by any form of Pelagianism or false autonomy, namely, within the mystery of God's providence and all-embracing causality. Only then have we acknowledged the fully Catholic concern behind Luther's doctrine of *servum arbitrium*.[123]

3. Continuing with our examination of Luther's necessitarian argument, when he says "that 'free will' is obviously a term applicable only to the divine majesty," [124] we must again not take this to be a denial of the free will of man that is affirmed by the Catholic tradition. It is simply a denial of a concept of an absolutely autonomous, all-powerful free will in creatures. Every Catholic would agree with Luther that only the divine majesty "can do and does (as the Psalmist sings), 'what ever he wills in heaven and earth' " (Ps. 135.6).[125] Every Catholic would deny with Luther that such a concept of *liberum arbitrium* can be "ascribed to men." [126]

4. The Catholic tradition, as expressed in the language of Scholastic theology, affirms that man is able to perform some acts freely or contingently. By this terminology the Scholastics meant that it was really possible for certain events not to have happened. These are the contingent events resulting from free choice. In contrast to other events which happen necessarily or inevitably, a contingent event need not have

---

123 G. Smith, offers many helpful clarifications for understanding Luther's doctrine of *servum arbitrium*. Above all, he correctly sees that man's free choice must be related to God as creature to creator. P. 88. However, aside from the fact that he does not sufficiently distinguish Luther's two-fold argument for *servum arbitrium*, Smith reaches a conclusion which is only partly justified when he says: ". . . just as Luther denies freedom in choice by as much as he denies that God can cause it, so, by as much as one asserts that God causes it, may one assert free choice." *Ibid.* The second part of his statement is true; the first part is not. Luther does *not* deny that God can cause free choice. He neither affirms it nor denies it. He never really addresses himself to the question that concerned so many of the Scholastics: Does God's immutable will and infallible knowledge impose absolute necessity on all events, or does God will that some events should happen contingently? As we shall see in point (4) the contingency which Luther rejects has nothing to do with the contingency or freedom of the will affirmed by Thomas and other Scholastics.

124 P & J, p. 105; WA 18, 636, 28f.

125 WA 18, 636, 29f.; P & J, p. 105.

126 *Ibid.*

happened; another event or action was really possible had the free agent responsible for the action chosen otherwise.

When Luther says that although things "seem to us to happen . . . contingently," [127] they really cannot be contingent as long as God's creative and conserving will remains active,[128] does he truly contradict the Scholastic-Catholic view that man does some things contingently? We believe not. The contingency which Luther rejects is simply not the same as the contingency which Scholastic theologians such as Thomas Aquinas attributed to certain actions of man.[129] Luther rejects a contingency which is outside the order of God's will. The Thomistic-Scholastic notion of contingency, on the other hand, is not only not understood as being outside the order of God's will; it is, on the contrary, the result of God's will![130]

As we have already noted in our examination of Luther's *Lectures on Romans* and his *Assertio,* Luther identifies contingency with what Augustine, Thomas and early thinkers called chance or fortune (*casus* or *fortuna*).[131] In *DSA* we find the same understanding of contingency: "A deed cannot be called contingent unless we do it 'contingently,' i.e., by chance (as it were) and without premeditation;[132] that is, when our will or hand fastens on something presented to us as if by chance, without our having previously thought or planned anything about it." [133]

In his *Hyperaspistes* Erasmus asks if Luther believes that a chance or fortuitous happening is the same as a contingent one. He indicates his

---

[127] WA 18, 615, 31f.

[128] WA 18, 616, 5ff.

[129] Cf. the excursus in chapter 6, Contingency and Necessity in Thomas Aquinas.

[130] ". . . propter efficaciam divinae voluntatis." I, q. 19, a. 8c.; cf. I, q. 116, a. 1.

[131] WA 56, 383, 17ff.: "nulla est contingentia apud Deum simpliciter, sed tantum coram nobis. Quia etiam folium arboris non cadit in terram sine voluntate patris." Cf. Thomas, I, q. 19, a. 8c.: "Vult autem quaedam fieri Deus necessario, et quaedam contingenter . . . Deus voluit eos contingenter evenire. . . ." Compare Luther in the *Assertio,* WA 7, 146, 27-31: "Fallet nos miseros homines rerum humanarum in constantia seu (ut vocant) contingentia: oculos enim suos stultos mergunt in res ipsas operaque rerum, nec aliquando elevant in conspectum dei, ut res supra nos in deo cognoscerent. Nobis enim ad inferna spectantibus res apparent arbitriae et fortuitae, sed ad superna spectantibus omnia sunt necessaria."

[132] "Imprudentibusque" is adequately translated as "hastig" by MA, p. 25. Even better is the rendering "without premeditation" by P & J, p. 81. The term is presumably meant to be synonymous to "nihil de eo aut cogitavimus aut voluimus antea." Vorster, p. 345 does not catch the sense at all.

[133] "Contingens opus dici non potest, nisi quod nobis contingenter et velut casu imprudentibusque fit, Quia nostra voluntas vel manus illud arripit velut casu oblatum, ut qui nihil de eo aut cogitavimus aut voluimus antea:" WA 18, 616, 10ff.; P & J, p. 81.

disagreement with such an identification by citing the traditional distinction: "Something happens by chance or fortune when it takes place apart from our expectation and action. But that which is contingent, which Aristotle calls *endechomenon,* embraces the possibility of being or not being. . . ." [134]

For Thomas, Erasmus and the Scholastics generally, contingent events—unlike chance and fortune—are *really* contingent even in the eyes of God and not just in our eyes. God *really* wills that some things happen contingently.[135] Things which *appear* to us to happen *per accidens,* that is, by chance or fortune, *really* are ordered by the divine intellect, says Thomas.[136] They are not chance events in his eyes and they are subject to his providence.[137] Thomas never says, however, that the things which God has willed to happen contingently are only contingent in our eyes. Contingent events are indeed subject to God's providence, as are chance events, but they do not thereby cease to be contingent! [138]

Luther likewise seems to be directly contradicting the Thomistic-Scholastic theology when he says: *"being done contingently* does not, in Latin, signify that the thing done is itself contingent, but that it is done by a contingent and mutable [139] will—such as is *not* to be found in God!" [140] Thomas, on the contrary, although he does not admit that God has a mutable will, says that God does have a contingent or free will "with respect to those things which he does not will of necessity," that is, with respect to things other than his own goodness. Thus, God wills the whole order of creation freely,[141] for it was not absolutely

---

[134] "Verum haud scio an Lutherus credat idem esse casu fortuitove fieri, quod contingenter fieri, casu fortuitove fit quod accidit praeter expectationem aut operam nostram. Contingens autem, hoc est, quod Aristoteles vocat endechomenon, complectitur possibilitatem ad esse et non esse. . . ." *Hyp.* II, 1416 E. In *Hyp.* I, 1275 B, Erasmus sharply criticized Luther's definition of contingency. His point is well taken when he says: "Contingenter igitur facimus non tantum quod casu et imprudentes facimus, verum illud quoque quod scientes ac volentes facimus, sed quod in nostro arbitrio erat non facere."

[135] Cf. the citation from Thomas in footnote 131 above.

[136] I, q. 116, a. 1.

[137] *Ibid.*

[138] Cf. Thomas, I, q. 19, a. 8; 22, a. 4. On this point Vorster, pp. 343-349 has seriously misunderstood Thomas. Vorster applies to the Thomistic notion of *contingentia* the principles which Thomas applies to *fortuna* and *casus.* He thus comes to the conclusion that, for Thomas, in view of the knowledge and will of God, contingency is an illusion just as luck and chance are illusions. This is Luther's concept of *contingentia,* not Thomas'. Cf. footnote 131 above.

[139] MA, p. 25, translates "mutabili voluntate" as *un*changeable will (unveränderlichen Willen)!

[140] Tr. P & J, p. 81; WA 18, 616, 7ff.

[141] Cf. I, q. 19, aa. 3 and 10.

necessary that he create anything. However, since God's will is "alto-gether immutable," [142] Thomas says we should say "God wills change" rather than "God has a changeable will." [143] Further, supposing that God freely wills to create, one can say that God wills to create neces-sarily *ex suppositione* "because of the immutability of the divine will." [144]

A Scholastic theologian would be inclined to ask Luther how he can save the freedom of the divine will if he denies that God has a contin-gent will. This objection, however, is based on a Scholastic definiton of contingency which Luther does not share. When Luther denies that God has a contingent will, it is because, as we have seen above, he under-stands contingent to mean that which happens by *chance* and without forethought. *In this case* we must agree with Luther that God's will is not contingent! Once again we have discovered a contradiction in formu-lation where there is no contradiction in meaning.[145]

Luther is not the only theologian to have such a concept of contin-gency. As we have already seen, Archbishop Thomas Bradwardine in the 14th century similarly affirmed the necessity of all events and denied that anything happens contingently.[146] Like Luther, however, the con-cept of contingency rejected by Bradwardine is one which is identified with the pagan concept of fortune or fate, that is, a concept which leaves room for events which happen apart from God's providence. Unlike Luther, Bradwardine explicitly leaves room for a concept of contingency understood as a real possibility to choose between alternatives, a "con-tingentiam ad utrumlibet." [147]

Apart from Bradwardine, and possibly Wyclif,[148] we also find an antecedent for Luther's attitude toward contingency in the writings of the Italian humanist, Laurentius Valla (1407-1457). The similarity lies not in the fact that Valla's concept of contingency is, in content, the same as Luther's and Bradwardine's, but in the fact that Valla rejects

---

[142] I, q. 19, a. 7.
[143] *Ibid.*, ad 3.
[144] *Ibid.*, ad 4.
[145] This is not the same as saying there is full agreement in meaning.
[146] Chapter 7, p. 195.
[147] *Ibid.* Because this phrase has so often been misunderstood by writers who contrast Luther's doctrine of *servum arbitrium* with the Catholic doctrine of "liberum arbitrium," it is necessary to point out that neither for Bradwardine nor for the Scholastics—with the exception of the Ockham-Biel school—does this type of "libertas arbitrii" mean that a sinner is free to choose to believe or not simply by the power of his natural freedom of choice. Only with *gratia praeveniens* can the sinner make the free surrender of faith by which he is liberated from sin.
[148] Cf. chapter 7, p. 195.

the *proposition* that man's actions are contingent just as firmly as does Luther. In *DLA* Erasmus said that Valla "seems to agree" with the denial of free will by Manichaeus and Wyclif.[149] That Erasmus does not think Valla really denied free will is evident from his later affirmation, that hardly anyone has answered better than Laurentius Valla the question of how our free will is compatible with God's foreknowledge.[150] In contrast to his sharply critical attitude toward Erasmus, Luther had much praise for Valla, both as a writer and as a Christian.[151] He read Valla's work with great interest[152] and had special praise for his *De libero arbitrio et providencia divina*.[153]

Most important to notice is that Luther praises a work in which the natural freedom of man's will—in the traditional Catholic sense—is *defended!* This is another indication that his thesis of *servum arbitrium* is not directed against the *liberum arbitrium* upheld by the authentic Catholic tradition.

What is it that leads Luther to praise Valla's defense of free will while rejecting Erasmus' *De libero arbitrio?* We believe it is the fact that, unlike Erasmus and the Scholastics, but in agreement with Luther and Bradwardine, Valla admits that man acts *voluntarily* but denies that he acts *contingently*. Unlike Bradwardine and Luther, Valla does not reject the term because it implies that man's actions happen outside the order of God's providence, but simply because he thinks the word is barbaric and superfluous.[154] The similarity between Luther and Valla ceases with his rejection of the concept of contingency. For by denying contingency he does not affirm necessity: "It is false to say that because something does not happen contingently it happens necessarily. I am writing neither necessarily nor contingently, but voluntarily and with reflection. And God makes man by his will and by grace, not necessarily or contingently."[155]

---

[149] Walter, I b 2, p. 13, lines 6-11.

[150] *Ibid.*, III a 5, p. 49, 15ff.

[151] Cf. WATR 1, 109, 1ff; 2, 107, 6f.

[152] WATR 5, 333, 6.

[153] WATR 1, 109, 3: "De libero arbitrio bene disputat." This work which was placed on the Index (cf. J. Mercier, "Valla, Laurent," DTC, 15, 2525), was first printed at Strasbourg in 1482. It can be found in Valla's *Opera Omnia* (Basel, 1543), 999-1010. A modern edition has been published by M. Anfossi (Florence, 1934). Cf. the monograph by E. Maier, *Die Willensfreiheit bei L. Valla*, diss. (Bonn, 1911). A summary of the work can be found in Zickendraht, pp. 180f.

[154] *L. Vallae Dialecticorum Disputationum*, Lib. II, cap. 19, in: *Opera Omnia*, p. 717: "Possible contingens, impossibile necessarium, verum, falsum. . . . Quae partitio videtur mihi redundare numero, et verbis magis locuples esse quam rebus." *Ibid.*, p. 718: The word "contingenter" "mihi videtur e rure sumptum potius quam ex urbe ideo scabrium quiddam prae se ferre. . . ."

[155] *Ibid.*: "Et quod non contingenter, id fiat necessario, quod falsum est, nam

Further, while Luther holds that man acts voluntarily because he is a man, but necessarily because his actions are foreseen by God, Valla attributes neither contingency nor necessity to man's actions, even though he affirms the divine foreknowledge just as strongly as does Luther.[156]

As if an anticipation of Luther's question to Erasmus: "How could Judas change his will while God's infallible foreknowledge stands?" [157] Valla says: ". . . I deny that if it is possible for something to happen in another way than has been foreknown, it follows that the foreknowledge can err. . . ." [158] Valla is certain both of man's free will and God's foreknowledge. But how they are to be reconciled, he says, cannot be known by reason—only by faith.[159]

(5) The final and perhaps the most important reason for our contention that Luther's necessitarian argument for *servum arbitrium* is—despite appearances—not really a denial of man's natural free will is the fact that Luther explicitly and repeatedly affirms that man has *liberum arbitrium* "in the realm of things below him," [160] or "in respect of what is below him" [161] or "in his own kingdom" where man "is led by his own will and not by the precepts of another" [162] and where God "has granted him a free use of things at his own will." [163] Thus Luther can say: "I know that free will can do some things by nature; it can eat, drink, beget, rule, etc." [164] The free will is also able to sin, as Luther has always admitted.[165] Man does not have *liberum arbitrium,* how-

---

ego nunc neque necessario, neque contingenter scribo, sed voluntate et gratia non necessitate et contingenter."

[156] *De gr. et lib. arb.,* in: *Opera Omnia,* p. 1002: "non video quare cum deus presciscit aliquid ab homine faciendum. ut id facias. nulla necessitas est. quia voluntate id facis, quod autem voluntarium hoc nequit esse necessarium." It should be noted that Valla conceives of no other necessity than that which Luther and the Scholastics call "necessitas coactionis": "Nam nihil aliud est necesse esse quam cogi et vi fieri necessitateque constringi": *Opera Omnia,* p. 718.

[157] Tr. P & J, p. 220; WA 18, 721, 8f.

[158] *De lib. arb.,* in *Op. Omnia,* 1004: ". . . nego si possibile est aliter evenire quam praescitum est, consequens esse praescientiam falli posse. . . ."

[159] Copleston, III/2, p. 23.

[160] WA 18, 672, 7-13: "in rebus sese inferioribus"; cf. 671, 33-38; 781, 8ff. Tr. P & J, p. 150.

[161] WA 18, 638, 5f.: "respectu inferioris."

[162] WA 18, 672, 18f.: "fertur suo arbitrio absque praeceptis alterius." Tr. P & J, p. 151.

[163] *Ibid.,* 12f.: "usum rerum illi liberum pro arbitrio concesserit." Tr. P & J, p. 150.

[164] WA 18, 752, 7f.: "Scimus liberum arbitrium natura aliquid facere, ut comedere, bibere, gignere, regere. . . ." Tr. P & J, p. 265. Vorster, p. 264 asserts without evidence that, according to Luther, "even the freedom concerning the things beneath us is in reality an illusion."

[165] WA 18, 752, 9ff.; cf. 773, 17f.

ever, "toward God" [166] or "in the kingdom of God," [167] where man "is
led by the precepts of another, and not by his own will" and where he
"is led by the will and counsel of God." [168]

If one were to interpret Luther's necessitarian argument as a rejection
of the natural freedom of the will which has been upheld by the Catholic
tradition, he would have to say that Luther, in the various places just
cited, flatly contradicts himself. For surely God "foresees and decrees"
what man shall do "in the realms of things below him" such as eating
and ruling. Surely God foresees that men and angels will sin. But if
God's infallible foreknowledge causes all things to happen by *absolute*
necessity *to the exclusion of free will,* then it would be impossible for
Luther to say that these events "in the kingdom of man" happen freely.
But Luther says precisely this! Erasmus rebuked Luther many times
because he simultaneously affirmed universal necessity as a result of
God's foreknowledge and yet admitted free will "in the realm of things
below him." [169] Humbertclaude [170] and other modern authors do not
hesitate to say that Luther is guilty of a contradiction when he makes an
"exception" to the rule of universal necessity.

It is never a sound principle of interpretation to suppose that a thinker
of Luther's calibre *truly* contradicts himself in such an obvious way. It is
much better to assume that there is only an apparent contradiction.
There are, in fact, strong reasons to support this assumption. On the
preceding pages and in the excursus: Was Luther a Determinist?, we
have already looked at evidence for the view that Luther teaches a
doctrine not of absolute, but of conditional necessity, a *necessitas con-*
sequentiae, which the Scholastics regarded as being compatible with free
will. We regard Luther's admission that man has *liberum arbitrium* "in
the realm of things below him" as the strongest evidence that his necessitarian argument is not to be understood as excluding man's natural
freedom. This argument is to be understood primarily as an affirmation
of the infallibility of God's foreknowledge and the universality of his
providence. It is not a rejection of *liberum arbitrium* in the Catholic
sense, but of a pagan concept of autonomous *liberum arbitrium* which
would somehow be independent of God's sovereign and universal rule of
his creatures. [171]

---

[166] WA 18, 781, 10-14; cf. 751, 23f.; 37f.
[167] WA 18, 662, 6f.
[168] WA 18, 672, 16-19; P & J, p. 151.
[169] Cf. *Hyp.* I, 1289 E and F.; *Hyp.* II, 1342 B and C; 1343 A; 1416 A.
[170] P. 112.
[171] Such a concept of *liberum arbitrium* was held by the Epicureans. Cf.
Copleston, I/2, pp. 149f. Luther accuses Erasmus several times of being an Epi-
curean: WA 18, 620, 3 and 38. Cf. WATR 1, 187, 4: Erasmus "denkt uber Gott

To summarize: we have shown that Luther's necessitarian argument *can* be interpreted in the sense of Thomas Aquinas, namely, that all things happen necessarily (*ex suppositone*) in view of God's immutable will, but not by an absolute necessity which would exclude free or contingent actions. We hold, further, that Luther's argument *must* be so interpreted if we are to avoid accusing Luther of that type of glaring contradiction which one rarely finds in thinkers of Luther's stature.

C. CRITICISM OF LUTHER'S NECESSITARIAN ARGUMENT

To be able to say that Luther's necessitarian argument, when carefully examined, does not *contradict* the Catholic teaching on the existence of natural freedom is of decisive importance. This is not the same as saying, however, that there is *full agreement* between Luther's doctrine and that of the Catholic tradition. From the standpoint of the biblical and the Catholic theological traditions, we believe that Luther's necessitarian argument for *servum arbitrium* is open to the following criticism:

1. Even though Luther does not really deny the existence of man's *liberum arbitrium* as a result of God's providence, his lack of consistent affirmation of natural *liberum arbitrium* together with his frequent use of overly simple, absolute expressions not only makes it very difficult to determine that he does not deny this truth of the Catholic tradition, but sometimes gives the strong impression that he rejects the existence of free will in creatures. His argument is therefore unclear and misleading. In terestingly, this is the same charge Luther made against the contemporary concept of free will, especially the concept of free will held by "the people." Luther set out to abolish this misleading concept of free will. And yet, with his necessitarian argument, he simply replaced one allegedly misleading concept with another.

2. Luther is so concerned with defending the truth that all things happen necessarily when seen from the standpoint of God's foreknowledge and will (*necessitas consequentiae*) that he does not think it significant that the Scholastics deny that all things happen by necessity of the thing consequent. He thus shows a poor understanding of this important distinction which has been used by Christian thinkers at least since the time of Augustine. Instead of seeing it as a distinction intended precisely to uphold man's free will *and* God's providence and foreknowledge, he takes it to be merely a way of showing that a creature is not God.

---

wie Epikur." This was also one of Luther's main objections to Aristotle. Cf. WATR 5, 155, 1; 324, 16. Luther correctly sees that Cicero, in contrast to Aristotle, has a much better concept of God's providence, but he seems unaware of Augustine's disagreement with Cicero precisely because Cicero denied God's foreknowledge in order to save man's free will.

3.[172] Although one can find in Luther's works all three of the types of freedom described in Chapter 1, in *DSA* and in other writings Luther frequently fails to keep in mind that there is more than one way in which man can be said to be free. This failure to make distinctions—which he is very capable of doing, as Erasmus pointed out [173]—further contributes to making his doctrine of *servum arbitrium* so easily misunderstood. Thus, once Luther has established that all things are subject to God's infallible foreknowledge and immutable will, he concludes that "free will is thereby knocked down and trodden under foot." [174] What he really means, and all he really proves, is that a free will conceived as autonomous and independent from God's providence is thereby "knocked down and trodden under foot." But this is not the free will of Augustine or Thomas Aquinas, for example, which is never conceived of apart from God's providence, foreknowledge and will.

Luther says it is a verbal monstrosity, a misuse of language,[175] to say that man has free will even though he has lost his freedom and is in bondage to sin.[176] "These things are contrary to common sense, and utterly overthrow our use of language." [177] Yet the fact remains, as we have seen in the state of the question, that *every* Christian thinker—including Augustine, Bradwardine and Wyclif (!), as well as the Luther of the *Lectures on Romans*—has explicitly distinguished more than one use of the word "freedom" and has affirmed the possibility that man can lose his freedom from sin and can become a slave of sin while retaining his *liberum arbitrium*. Similarly, even though the writers who helped form the Christian tradition prior to Luther admit with him that God's infallible foreknowledge and efficacious will impose some kind of necessity on man's actions, this is never understood as a necessity which

---

172 This criticism applies to Luther's proposal to reform the language of theology and to the conclusion which Luther frequently draws from his biblical argument: if man is a slave to sin, he therefore has no free will.

173 *Hyp.* I, 1319 A and B: "Distinguitur Lex ab Evangelio. . . , interna Scriptura claritas ab externa, Deus a Scriptura, Deus praedicatus a non praedicato, spiritus Evangelicus a spiritu erroris, opinio negativa, quae nihil probat, ab affirmativa, cuius est probatio. Ostenditur duplex ostensio spiritus: duplex canon, caritatis et fidei: duplex necessitas, operis et temporis, rursum coactionis et immutabilitatis: duplex omnipotentia Dei, naturae et operationis: duplex respectus ad superiora et inferiora: discernuntur indicativa verba ab imperativis et subiunctivis . . . Non haec recenseo quod omnes tuas distinctiones improbem, sed quod tibi sumas in sacris Litteris explicandis quod aliis non permittis, et aliorum distinctiones soleas exsibilare, cum tuas haberi velis pro oraculis. Nobis occludis omnem exitium, et tibi vis patere tot cuniculos."

174 WA 18, 615, 15.

175 WA 18, 671f.: ". . . monstra verborum"; "abusum loquendi."

176 *Ibid.*, 5f.

177 P & J, p. 149; cf. WA 18, 671, 7f.: ". . . pugnant haec communi sensui et tollunt prorsus usum loquendi."

excludes *liberum arbitrium*. As Wyclif put it, we are moved by God necessarily without, however, excluding free will: "salva libertate arbitrii." [178]

When Luther says to Erasmus: "You would not call a slave, who acts at the beck of his lord, free," [179] we again find a confusion of different types of freedom which illustrates perfectly the misleading character of Luther's argument against free will. Is it not Luther who "overthrows established usage" when he asserts that the slave of sin is, in no accepted sense of the word, free? Even the master or lord of the slave knows that the slave at least has free will even though he enjoys no domestic freedom.

The New Testament itself recognizes that even the slaves who are urged to obey their masters [180] can be free in the deepest sense of the word, namely, with the freedom by which Christ has made us free.[181] Paul teaches, in fact, that it is precisely the *slave* of justice, the one who "acts at the beck of his lord," [182] who is truly free in the Christian sense. And we learn from Jesus that the politically free man can in reality be a slave—of sin.[183] It is astonishing that in the entire *De servo arbitrio* Luther does not cite either John 8: 33-36 or Romans 6: 16-22, both of which are central loci for the New Testament teaching on freedom and slavery.

Luther's statements on freedom and slavery are, therefore, in certain places [184] actually more rigid and oversimplified and less radical and paradoxical not only in comparison with common sense usage, but also in comparison with the usage of Scripture itself. The biblical authors see no difficulty at all in saying that a man is free in one sense and a slave in another. In a similar way, the Christian theological tradition has not regarded it as dangerous to say that a man has free will, even though he is a slave to sin. This tradition, in conformity with the paradoxical New Testament categories of freedom and slavery, was able to coin the radical, but superbly descriptive phrase, captivated—or liberated—free will (*liberum arbitrium captivatum* or *liberatum*).[185] This phrase, which expresses both the reality of man's free will and his slavery to sin, is far superior to Luther's alternative: either *servum* or *liberum arbitrium*.

---

[178] Cf. chapter 7, footnote 68.
[179] WA 18, 662, 9f.; P & J, p. 137.
[180] Col. 3: 22.
[181] Gal. 5: 1.
[182] Cf. WA 18, 662, 9f. and Rom. 6: 16ff.
[183] Jn. 8: 33f.
[184] We emphasize this because Luther is elsewhere much more flexible and cautious, for example, when he concedes that man has free will "in regno hominis."
[185] Cf. Augustine and Peter Lombard above, p. 236, footnote 49.

Luther's either/or concept of the freedom and bonadge of the will becomes more Catholic—but also more inconsistent—when, after denouncing and rejecting the concept and the very term, *liberum arbitrium,* he says: *except* for the things "in the kingdom of man."

4. The most serious criticism that can be directed against Luther's necessitarian argument for *servum arbitrium* is that he is so carried away by his legitimate desire to refute a Neo-Semipelagian concept of autonomous free will and to affirm the unfreedom of the sinner to do anything truly good, that he in one place eliminates all free decision from man not only in man's justification by faith but also in the sins man commits! The three previous criticisms of Luther's necessitarian argument have dealt with the unclarity and inappropriateness, of Luther's statements concerning the freedom of man's will, but have not questioned the basic soundness or orthodoxy of his intention. This fourth criticism, however, is concerned with a serious doctrinal deficiency in Luther's teaching on the unfree will.

We have already expressed our view that, when it is properly understood, Luther's necessitarian argument is not incompatible with the Catholic doctrine of man's free will. Here, however, we meet a continuation, or rather an over-extension of the necessitarian argument, in which Luther arrives at a concept of man's will which is opposed not only to the Catholic, but also to the later Lutheran dogmatic tradition.

A century ago the Lutheran theologian, Luthardt, rightly observed that *De servo arbitrio* was supposed to prove the unfreedom of the sinful will to do good. "In reality, however," says Luthardt, "Luther at least tried to prove the unfreedom of the created will . . . to make a moral decision." [186] Luther's arguments in *DSA,* maintains Pannenberg, rob "the encounter with Christ of its decision-character." [187] "Contrary to what we often think," writes Iwand, "in Scholastic theology personal decision is included in the reception of grace." [188] And contrary to a popular misconception,[189] a personal, free decision of faith is explicitly excluded by Luther's over-extended concept of *servum arbitrium.*[190] Luther indeed teaches that man's will acts "spontaneously and volun-

---

[186] P. 133.

[187] "Der Einfluss der Anfechtungserfahrung auf den Prädestinationsbegriff Luthers," in: *KuD* 3 (1957), 129.

[188] "Die Freiheit des Christen und die Unfreiheit des Willens," in: *Solange es heute heisst,* p. 135.

[189] F. Gogarten, *Was ist Christentum?,* 2nd ed. (Göttingen, 1959), p. 86 exemplifies this misunderstanding. He is rightly criticized by H. Lammers, pp. 18, 81-84.

[190] When W. von Loewenich, *Humanitas-Christianitas,* p. 89 says: "Die Lehre vom servum arbitrium will also den Personalismus nicht aufheben," "personalism" must not be understood here as involving a free decision of faith. It can only mean that man personally wills and loves goodness after he has been transferred

tarily" [191] and not by any necessity of coercion, but by necessity of immutability.[192] He does teach that man *cooperates* with God,[193] even, as we have seen, in justification itself.[194] But in *DSA* it is clear that Luther rejects the notion of man's freedom of election (*libertas eligendi*), that he does not take "libenti voluntate" to mean "by free will," and that he does not say that man's cooperation in justification or renovation by faith is a *free* cooperation involving a decision of man's free will.[195]

A number of authors erroneously maintain that Luther teaches "a freedom of decision" in justification, a "decision of faith," etc.: F. Gogarten, "Nachwort" to his new edition of *De servo arbitrio* (München, 1924), reprinted in: *Theologische Bücherei*, vol. 17 (München, 1963), p. 201; E. Erikstein, *op. cit.*, p. 163; H. Bornkamm, "Luther und der deutche Geist: Sammlung gemeinverständlicher Vorträge und Schriften aus dem Gebiet der Theologie und Religionsgeschichte," Nr. 70 (Tübingen, 1934), p. 8; also: *Das bleibende Recht der Reformation* (Hamburg, 1963), p. 27; M. Doerne, *op. cit.*, pp. 55ff., 72f.; J. Boisset, *op. cit.*, p. 129; H. Grass, "Glaube: V. Dogmatisch," RGG, 2, 1608f. W. Pauck, *The Heritage of the Reformation* (Glencoe, Ill., 1950), p. 20 says that faith, according to Luther, is a "free surrender." He bases this judgment not on Luther's *ex professo* teaching in *DSA*, but on a few citations from sermons such as Sermon Nr. 40, July 25, 1552 (WA 10/III, 239, 19ff.), the same text cited by Gogarten for a similar purpose in his essay: "Sittlichkeit und Glaube in Luthers Schrift *De servo arbitrio*," in: *Zeitschr. f. Theol. und Kirche*, 47 (1950), 243f. As H. Bandt, *op. cit.*, p. 20 has rightly noted, however, one must not seek to discover Luther's thought in complex manners in his sermons "because Luther expresses his thoughts in the sermons in a broad, intuitive way which is thus often less theologically precise and therefore of little help to us in the genuinely controversial questions."

The over-extension of the necessitarian argument is found in WA 18, 634, 14-635, 22. One may actually call this a third argument for

---

or changed from sin to goodness without any free decision on his part. Cf. *idem, Luther und der Neuprotestantismus*, p. 418.

[191] WA 18, 634, 25: "sponte et libenti voluntate facit."

[192] *Ibid.*, 21ff.

[193] WA 18, 753, 20-23.

[194] WA 18, 676, 29ff. Cf. chapter 8, p. 238 and WA 18, 754, 3; 15.

[195] WA 18, 754, 11-17; 767, 23f.: "Non (ait) probatur liberum arbitrium per legem, Non cooperatur ad iustitiam." Cf. WA 6, 530 (*De capt. babyl. eccl. prael.*, 1520): Faith "est opus Dei, non hominis . . . Caetera nobiscum et per nobis, hoc unicum in nobis et sine nobis operatur." Here we are no longer able to give a favorable interpretation to Luther's doctrine of "mera passivitas" as we were when we investigated the concept in the *Lectures on Romans*. Cf. chapter 8, p. 238. One of the few authors to see clearly this aspect of Luther's teaching is H. J. Iwand, MA, p. 254. See also Seeberg, IV/1, p. 206.

Luther's thesis of *servum arbitrium,* in distinction to the necessitarian argument and the biblical argument based on man's bondage to sin.[196] What makes this argument essentially different from the necessitarian argument is the fact that Luther gives the concept of "mere necessity" or "necessity of immutability" a meaning which it did not have in the original necessitarian argument. Furthermore, in this argument Luther's Satanology plays a role which it did not have in the argument based on the universal necessity of all events as a result of God's foreknowledge and will. In WA 18, 615, 31ff. the necessity of immutability, as we have shown, was conceived of as the necessity of consequence which results from God's eternal and immutable will. Here, however, even though Luther continues to distinguish necessity of immutability from necessity of coercion,[197] he uses the concept of necessity as though it were simply an absolute necessity, that is, a necessity in man's will *not* in reference to the will of God—not "si Dei voluntatem spectes" [198]—but in view of the captivity of man to sin and to Satan "when the Spirit of God withdraws." [199]

If the spirit of God is absent, man cannot change his will from willing evil to willing good.[200] This assertion of Luther is in full conformity with the biblical and Catholic tradition, which insists that liberating grace is necessary for such a change of will. But when Luther says that the change of our wills from sin to justice depends solely on the overcoming and the defeat of Satan by someone stronger—Christ—and neglects entirely to mention that the personal, free decision of the sinner—made possible, to be sure, only by the healing and liberating grace of God—is essential to justification, then he is no longer on biblical or Catholic ground.[201]

It is true that, according to the New Testament, the sinner cannot free himself from Satan's power.[202] It is also true, however, that there is no liberation from the power of Satan without man's free decision. For the call to justification and to salvation is addressed to the sinner from

---

[196] M. Schüler, "Luthers Gottesbegriff nach seiner Schrift De servo arbitrio," in: *Zeitschr. f. Kirchengesch.* 55 (1936), 554 has correctly distinguished the three arguments. We shall treat this third argument in connection with the necessitarian argument simply because Luther does so.

[197] WA 18, 634, 21. Nevertheless Luther several times describes the movement of the will by God in terms of force: "cogimur:" WA 18, 670, 10; God "rapit omnia omnipotentiae suae motu," WA 18, 753, 29ff., Cf. 752, 12ff.

[198] WA 18, 615, 33.

[199] WA 18, 634, 23. Cf. footnote 106 above.

[200] WA 18, 634, 23-29.

[201] WA 18, 635, 14ff.: "Si autem fortior superveniat et illo victo nos rapiat in spolium suum, rursus per spiritum eius servi et captivi sumus. . . ."

[202] W. Foerster, TDNT, 2, 79, 9f.; cf. TDNT, 2, 79.

whom the response of free obedience to Christ and to justice is required. And according to the New Testament *hypakoē* is always a free act of man, an act of religious decision.[203]

Luther is right in saying that the just man cannot be forced to do evil against his will, but surely it is contrary both to Christian experience—to which he appeals—and to biblical teaching to say that the Christian man has "no 'free will' to turn elsewhere, or to desire anything else, as long as the Spirit and grace of God remain in a man." [204] Does this not imply that sin is more God's turning away from us than our turning away from God? [205] How can Luther's doctrine here be reconciled with the doctrine that the Christian man, liberated from sin, is still at war with sin which is a *real danger* to him as long as he lives on earth? [206] How can Luther explain the warnings of the New Testament against possible loss of salvation [207] and the fact that in the New Testament the Christian is called to do battle against sin [208] if the Christian man has "no free will to turn elsewhere?"

It must finally be asked if Luther's concept of the relation of God and Satan to man's will corresponds to that of Scripture. We have already seen that in WA 18, 634, 37—635, 17 Luther conceives of man as being completely dominated either by God or by Satan. To a certain extent this corresponds to the Pauline doctrine that we are either slaves to justice or to sin. What is overlooked by Luther is the biblical teaching that this captivity or slavery essentially involves our *obedience,* an attitude of man which always involves a free decision.[209] Luther further overlooks the fact that it is man—not God—who is responsible for allowing Satan to dominate him.[210]

EXCURSUS: *Luther's Image of the Human Will as the Beast of Burden of God or Satan*

We find a still greater discrepancy between what Luther and the Bible teach about Satan's relation to God and man when we consider the image which Luther uses to illustrate the argument he presents in WA

---

[203] Cf. chapter 2, pp. 46f.

[204] P & J, p. 103; WA 18, 635, 5ff.

[205] Cf. A. Vögtle, "Sünde: IV. Im NT," LThK, 9, 1174.

[206] W. Grundmann, "Hamartanō: F. Die Sünde im NT, 2. Paulus," ThW, 1, 317, 24-27; cf. TDNT, 1, 317. See also K. Stendahl, "Sünde u. Schuld: IV. Im NT," RGG, 6, 487; Vögtle, "Sünde: IV. Im NT," LThK, 9, 1175.

[207] Cf. W. Joest, *Gesetz u. Freiheit,* pp. 165-169.

[208] K. Stendahl, "Sünde . . . im NT," RGG, 6, 487.

[209] See above p. 48.

[210] See above pp. 39f., esp. footnote 43.

18, 634, 37—635, 17. Immediately following his argument Luther writes: "So man's will is like a beast standing between two riders. If God rides, it wills and goes where God wills: as the Psalm says, "I am become as a beast before thee, and I am ever with thee" (Ps. 73: 22-3). If Satan rides, it wills and goes where Satan wills. Nor may it choose to which rider it will run, or which it will seek; but the riders themselves fight to decide who shall have and hold it."

Literature on Luther's "image": K. Zickendraht, *op. cit.,* p. 195; H. Jedin, *Des Joh. Cochlaeus Streitschrift,* pp. 33f., footnote 2; R. Hermann, *Von der Klarheit der heiligen Schrift,* pp. 110-126; A. Adam, "Die Herkunft des Lutherwortes vom menschlichen Willen als Reittier Gottes," in *LuJ* (1962) 25-34; H. Vorster, *op. cit.,* pp. 415-418.

K. Meissinger has said of this image: "There is no place in Luther's *servum arbitrium* which has been more frequently cited than these sentences, always, however, with a slight shudder": *Erasmus,* p. 309.

Luther uses Ps. 72 (73), 22f. as the biblical basis of his illustration. Jedin, *Des Joh. Cochlaeus Streitschrift,* p. 33, footnote 2 believes that the original form of the comparison between a man and a beast of burden can be found in Augustine's *Enarratio in Ps. 32, II.* n.n. 22f. (PL 36, 272). Cf. the *Ennarationes in Ps. 33, 5,* and 148, 2 (PL 36, 310; 37, 1938). There the disobedient, unbelieving man is likened to an animal who has to be bridled and whipped. The blows are the sufferings sent from God. In this comparison neither Satan nor God is the rider of man. It is true that Satan "has power as the tempter to evil, but the unpleasant alternative: God or Satan as lord of the soul is excluded. . . ." Jedin, *ibid.*

A. Adam, p. 29, has shown that there are antecedents for the image as far back in the history of theology as Origen. In him we find God depicted as the director of the faithful and Satan as the rider of the unbelievers. Adam, p. 33, argues that the element of struggle between God and Satan in Luther's image has its origin in Manichaeism, where there was a strong tradition of a battle between the Son of Brightness and the Son of Evil. Adam, p. 33.

Augustine, too, on the basis of Mt. 12: 29, conceived of the struggle between God and Satan. Cf. Augustine, *Epistle* 217 (*Ad Vitalem;* ca. 427 A.D.). One need not conclude with Adam, however, that it was from Augustine that Luther drew the second part of his image, the part concerning the struggle between God and Satan. Thomas Aquinas likewise recognized the existence of such a struggle in his interpretation of Mt. 12: 29: *Super Matt. Lect.* XII, nn. 1016-1019. We are not suggesting that Luther was influenced here by Thomas. We are simply pointing out the probability that certain elements of Luther's image were widespread in the post-Augustinian period.

When John Calvin employs the image for a purpose similar to Luther's, he simply attributes it to Augustine without an exact citation: "en quelque lieu." Cf. *Institutes,* II, 4, 1. (Calvin does not say, as does Luther, that it is not "in arbitrio" of man "ad utrum sessorem currere aut eum quaerere." This fact, coupled with Calvin's statement that man *obeys* his rider—a concept which is missing in Luther's use of the image —makes it easier to find a place in Calvin's theology for free will in the sense of free decision and consent.) Although Augustine knows of a struggle between Christ and Satan and although he can conceive of God sending suffering to men for the purpose of making men live better, similar to the reason for which a beast of burden is whipped, the image as it is used by Luther and Calvin cannot be found in Augustine.

As Zickendraht, p. 195, has shown, the image of Calvin and Luther is found not in any writing of Augustine, but in the pseudo-Augustinian work: *Hypomnesticon contra pelagianos et caelestinianos vulgo libri Hypognosticon sex* (PL 45, 1621-1638; written after 435 A.D.). Cf. L. Smits, *Saint Augustin dan l'œuvre de Jean Calvin*, I (Louvain-Paris, 1957), p. 188ff.; II (Louvain-Paris, 1958), p. 263; Portalié, "Augustin (Saint)," *DTC*, 1, 2307f. In *Hypomn*. III, 11, 20 (PL 45, 1632) we read: "I think the free will is rightly compared to a beast of burden. Thus it has been said: I have been made like a beast of burden before you (Ps. LXXII, 23): but grace is like the rider. . . ."

Like Luther, but unlike Augustine, the image as used in the *Hypomnesticon* is based on Ps. 72 (73): 22f. The main difference between the image in the *Hypomnesticon* and in Luther, as Zickendraht, p. 195, has shown (Jedin and Vorster agree with him), is that in the *Hypomnesticon* the *liberum arbitrium* is the animal and grace is the rider. Satan is not a rider, only a "herdsman" of the evil will. Further, says Zickendraht, *ibid.*, "Grace is depicted as the rider not merely to illustrate its 'taming' and guiding function, but precisely to explain the manner in which grace cooperates with free will, something that is prohibited by Luther." The cooperation of the free will is clearly stated: "The work . . . is imputed to both."

Zickendraht, influenced by the extremely broad concept of Semipelagianism held by Loofs, regards the *Hypomnesticon* as a "crypto-Semipelagian" work. This opinion has been revived by A. Adam, *op. cit.*, p. 27, who is followed by Vorster, p. 415. The idea of a cooperation of grace and free will is, however, not a peculiarity of Semipelagianism. It is perfectly good Augustinianism. See the excursus in Chapter 4: Synergism and Semipelagianism. Indicative of the fact that the *Hypomnesticon* is not a Semipelagian work is Luther's judgment that this book is one of Augustine's best writings! Cf. WATR, 2, 515, 22.

The Scholastics also occasionally illustrated the relationship between the will and grace by comparing it to that between a horse and its rider. See: Thomas Aquinas, I-II, q. 110, a. 4, obj. 1 and ad 1; cf. I-II, q. 109, a. 8, ad 3; III, q. 18, a. 1, ad 2; cf. Seckler, *op. cit.*, pp. 79 and 189, footnote 74. For Albert the Great, see Auer, *Die Entwicklung*, II, p. 186. John Duns Scotus, *Ord*. I, d. 17, pars 1, qq 1f.; cf. Auer, II, pp. 198ff. William of Ockham, *Sent* IV, dub., ad F. In Scotus and Biel emphasis is placed on the power of the free will to follow grace or not to follow it. Such a power of the free will is clearly presupposed in the use of the image by Thomas Aquinas and the *Hypomnesticon*. Gabriel Biel, *Sacri canonis misse expositio. . .* , 59 L and 29 K; see Oberman, *The Harvest*, pp. 162ff. Oberman agrees with Auer that the image of the horse and rider undergoes a new interpretation by Scotus, Ockham and Biel. It is important to notice, however, that in Thomas Aquinas, Albertus Magnus, Duns Scotus, William of Ockham and Gabriel Biel, the horse is always compared to the *liberum arbitrium*. Other authors who use the horse-rider image include John de Bassolis, *Sent.* I, d. 17; cf. Dettloff, *Die Entwicklung der Akzeptations-und Verdienstlehre von Duns Scotus bis Luther*, p. 159; John Eck, *Chrysoppasus*, IV, 2; cf. Greving, *Eck als junger Gelehrter*, p. 164, footnote 3. Eck also used the image in the *Leipzig Disputation*—as a proof for the free will! Cf. Seitz, *Der authentische Text der Leipzig Disputation*, p. 28. At the Council of Trent the comparison between the free will and an animal was rejected, possibly as a reaction against Luther's use of the image. Cf. *Conc. Trid.*, V, 390, 408.

Luther broke with the traditional use of the image in that he: (1) likened the animal not to the free will but to the *voluntas;* (2) denied that man's will has any free choice as to who will "ride" and dominate it; (3) made God himself and not grace the rider of the good will; (4) made Satan the rider of the evil will. Already in a sermon preached in 1524 (Oct. 9: WA 15, 714) Luther held that the devil was the rider of the man who lives without the Spirit of God. Cf. WA 16, 96f.; 112-117; 140-147; 150 (*Sermons on Exodus* from 1524); WATR 1, 176, 5.

In points (1) and (2) we see something which is peculiar to Luther's concept of the will: Man indeed has a will, but this is never a free will that is capable of freely deciding to follow Satan or of freely following God even under the action of grace. Nor is there any indication by Luther that the will *freely* consents to its domination by God or Satan. There is only a will (*velle*) to do what God or Satan wills. The direction of this *velle*—for good or evil—is determined *solely* by forces outside of man. It is determined solely by the outcome of the struggle between God and Satan. Iwand, MA, pp. 280ff., is one of the few scholars who shows awareness of the uniqueness of Luther's doctrine of the non-free will: "We see here that Luther, with his assertion of unfreedom (*necessitas*) in no way denies the reality of the will. On the contrary, it is Luther's view that only in this way does one do justice to the nature of the will. . . . Luther's recognition of the inner essential connection of will and necessity is that which is unique and significant in his position seen in the light of the history of man's struggle correctly to understand the nature of will, freedom and law."

Even though Luther several times in *DSA* says that he is not discussing what the will can do with grace, he nevertheless seems to give an answer to this question in the text we are considering: WA 18, 634, 14—635, 22. His answer is that even under the action of God man's will is not free. The traditional problem of the relationship between God's grace or saving action and man's free will is completely bypassed.

Instead of the biblical categories of man's (free) obedience to sin or to justice and man's *obedient* servitude to God (justice) or to Satan (sin), which presuppose the possibility that man can disobey God or can, with God's help, turn from sin to God (not simply *be* turned) and which therefore necessitate admonitions both to those who obey sin and those who obey justice, instead of the patristic categories of God's efficacious, liberating grace and man's *liberum arbitrium* (*captivatum* or *liberatum*), we find in *DSA* only the categories of a struggle between

God and Satan to see who shall control and hold captive man's purely passive will, passive in the sense that it can make no free decisions whatever. Here we find no divine call to conversion, no admonition to steadfastness in justice or to avoidance of sin, no struggle of man with Satan, no personal dialogue which presupposes a free response such as we find in Scripture, but only a domination of man's will by God or Satan without any free, personal action of man. We find only a struggle between God and Satan, only an unalterable, necessary *velle* of good or evil depending on whether the will is "ridden" by God or Satan.

Luther correctly emphasizes the biblical doctrine that the sinner is Satan's captive and is not free to escape. But here and elsewhere (WA 18, 749, 34–750, 38; 782, 30–783, 2) he overlooks the biblical teaching that man's liberation from Satan's captivity involves man's decision of faith and obedience, never forgetting that this decision is itself absolutely dependent upon the liberating grace of Christ.

W. von Loewenich, *Luther und der Neuprotestantismus,* p. 418, says of Luther's image of the rider and the horse: "It seems flatly to put an end to man as a personal being." He adds however: "This was certainly not Luther's intention." Von Loewenich insists here as he does in *Humanitas Christianitas,* p. 88, that the image is an analogy "which ought not to be pressed." This is, of course, correct. However, one must not overlook the fact that Luther's illustration does not stand in isolation but in direct connection with the carefully developed argument in WA 634, 14–635, 17. Neither in the argument nor in the image used to illustrate the argument can we find any evidence for von Loewenich's assertion: "Even with an unfree will man remains thoroughly a person; he is not simply an instrument": *Luther und der Neuprotestantismus,* p. 418. Only by re-defining "person" to exclude the element of free decision can one agree with von Loewenich that the man who is unable to choose between or to decide for God or Satan remains "thoroughly a person." Von Loewenich would undoubtedly agree that an animal with his vitality, spontaneity and powerful appetite is not simply an instrument. This does not, however, make the animal a person. (For Thomas Aquinas "person" and "instrument" are not mutually exclusive categories. An instrument can be an "inanimate instrument," an instrument animated by a "sensible soul" or an "instrument animated by a rational soul": III, q. 18, a. 1, ad 2. Even Luther understands man as an instrument of God: WA 40/3, 210, 14; 211, 3; 215, 6. See P. Althaus, *The Theology of Martin Luther,* p. 107.)

The "modernizing" interpretation of Luther's illustration by H. Schuster, *Martin Luther Heute,* does violence to Luther's words. According to Schuster, p. 122, the illustration means: "If humanity does not *allow* itself to be ruled by the spirit of God, it acts as basely and as stupidly as if it were possessed by the devil."

R. Hermann, *Die Klarheit der heiligen Schrift,* pp. 110-126 offers many worthwhile considerations for a better understanding of Luther's illustration especially by comparing Luther's use of Ps. 72 (73): 22f. in *DSA* and his interpretation of the same verse in the *First Lectures on the Psalms.* According to Hermann, Luther's doctrine of *servum arbitrium* under the devil means nothing more than that "the justification of ourselves lies outside of our strength and capability," p. 126. We welcome Hermann's understanding of unfree will as being in complete accord with the doctrine of the Catholic tradition. We cannot agree with him however when he thinks that this is also Luther's understanding.

Important to notice in our criticism of Luther's image and the argument connected with it is that the issue is not whether Satan dominates man. Thomas Aquinas admits this in his interpretation of Mt. 12: 26. Nor is there any disagreement concerning the struggle that exists between God and Satan. Cf. Thomas Aquinas, *Super Matt.*, cap. 12, n. 1017: ". . . when someone is master of his house, he can only be ejected if a stronger man appear" and Luther, WA 18, 635, 14f.: "But if a stronger man appears and overcomes Satan we are once more captives. . . ." The question is: Does Satan dominate us because we *obey* him and freely consent to him, as Thomas maintains, or does he dominate us simply because he has been victorious over God in the struggle to determine who shall dominate us, as Luther implies? Thomas Aquinas knows that Satan is "strong": *Super Matt.*, cap. 12, n. 1018, but he adds: "He is made stronger by consent, for he who consents gives up powers over himself. . . ." *Ibid*. Luther, on the other hand, simply says that man *wills* to go where Satan or God wish to go. This willing is explicitly opposed to a *free* willing. Nowhere in *DSA* does Luther call man's willing a *free willing* or a *free* consensus.

In addition to our main objection, that Luther leaves no place for a decision of faith or even for a decision to sin by man, other questions can be raised concerning Luther's concept of man's domination by either of two unfreely accepted masters. According to Scripture the Christian—not only Christ—struggles against Satan. Thus we find admonitions to resist Satan such as Eph. 6: 11 and James 4: 7. How can Luther explain such a struggle and such warnings if man's will plays no part in deciding for or against Satan? How can Luther explain the original sin of Satan? According to *DSA* (WA 18, 711, 7f.) God simply finds Satan's will evil: "Thus not creating [but] finding the will of Satan evil. . . ." Elsewhere Luther says Satan's sin came from his turning away from God (WATR 5, 5194) and from his rebellion against God (cf. Löfgren, pp. 125-141, esp. 132). But he doesn't say that this was a *free* turning away. Did Satan originally have a free will concerning good and evil? If so, does not Luther have to revise his assertion that all things are necessitated as a result of God's foreknowledge? Was God the "rider" of Satan's will before Satan turned away from him? If so, how could Satan change the direction of his will? Was it God who changed the direction of his willing from good to evil?

5. The questions we have just raised lead us to another criticism of Luther's necessitarian argument for the unfree will. This concept of unfree will makes it impossible for Luther to give a satisfactory explanation of man's responsibility for sin.

We have seen that the pre-Augustinian Fathers of the Church defended free will strongly against the fatalists, Marcionites, etc. in order to make *man*, not God, the originator of sin, in order, therefore, to uphold the holiness and sinlessness of God. Their attention was not focused on the necessity of grace as was Augustine's. When Augustine complemented the thought of the early Fathers, the Catholic theological tradition on sin received its decisive and lasting determination: man alone is responsible for sin. Personal sin always involves a misuse of man's free will. Man can be guilty of no personal sin unless he freely wills it. Although man can commit sin by the power of free will alone, he cannot will what is truly good by the power of free will alone apart from the grace of God.

The traditional Catholic concept of sin and free will was shattered by Luther. In contrast to the conviction that there is no responsibility for sin without the cooperation of man's free will, Luther developed a concept of responsibility without freedom.

As we have seen, it is extremely difficult to answer the question whether Luther really denied man's free will. One must make many distinctions and qualifications—just as Luther did. Yet concerning the question, how is man responsible for sin?, Luther could have simply answered as the Fathers, Augustine and the Scholastics have done by saying: Man is responsible because he has free will and because he sins through his own free choice. Luther does not say this. Even though he said many times previously—and even in *DSA* (WA 18, 752, 10f.)— that man has *liberum arbitrium* for sin, when he treats the question *ex professo* in *DSA,* he refuses to admit that responsibility for sin presupposes a free will. Luther develops his thoughts on man's responsibility for sin in the context of his explanation of the hardening of Pharaoh's heart: WA 18, 705, 14–733, 21.

In WA 18, 709, 5ff. Luther takes up the question of how God is said to work evil in us.[211] He begins his answer by saying that even reason concedes that: "God works all in all." [212] Furthermore, continues Luther, neither Satan nor man, fallen and abandoned by God, can will any good. "Since God moves and works all in all, he moves and works of necessity even in Satan and the ungodly. But he works according to what they are and what he finds them to be. This means that since they are evil and perverted themselves, when they are impelled to action by divine omnipotence they do only that which is perverted and evil. . . ." [213] "Here you see that when God works in and by evil men, evil deeds result; yet God, though he does evil by means of evil men, cannot

---

[211] "Quaeritur fortassis quo modo Deus mala in nobis dicatur operari, ut indurare, tradere desideriis, seducere et similia." WA 18, 709, 34 shows that Luther includes "peccatum" under "malum."

[212] *Ibid.,* 11f.

[213] WA 18, 709, 21-24; tr. P & J, p. 204.

act evilly himself, for he is good and cannot do evil; but uses evil instruments, which cannot escape the impulse and movement of his power." [214] Three things are to be noticed here:

(a) Luther bypasses the question of how Satan and man fell. He simply takes their falling away from God as a starting point and says that God "finds" sin in his creatures. But as Vorster correctly notes, Luther's assertion "that God in his decree, does not create new evil but only stirs up as an 'inquietus actor' the evil which is already present in man, simply moves the problem further into the past. . . ." [215] The question now is: Did Adam and Satan possess free will before their fall? If they did, must not Luther revise his entire necessitarian argument, since it was an argument which proves *universal* necessity as a result of God's foreknowledge? We have already expressed our view that Luther's necessitarian argument—even as it stands—can be reconciled with a concept of free will understood as freedom from absolute necessity. Our criticism of the argument was directed mainly against its ambiguity and its failure to come to grips with the traditional distinction of the "two necessities." However, had Luther begun to develop his doctrine of *servum arbitrium* after he had clearly stated that Satan and Adam have a *liberum arbitrium* and that only because of this *liberum arbitrium* was it possible for them—in contrast to animals—to sin, he would never have gotten himself entangled in his non-biblical necessitarian argument based not on the fact of sin, but on the fact of God's foreknowledge. He would then most likely have confined himself to developing the biblical-Augustinian-Catholic concept of *servum arbitrium:* that man, having sinned by a decision of his own free will, is enslaved to sin and is unable to escape unless liberated by Christ. This was, as we have shown, Luther's own early concept of *servum arbitrium.* [216]

Having appealed to a necessitarian argument in *DSA,* Luther knows that he cannot appeal to free will to explain the origin of sin. He simply ignores this question of central theological importance. That man and Satan have fallen is accepted by Luther as an unquestionable biblical truth. But *how* they have fallen he does not say. He will not say clearly with all previous theological tradition that they have fallen by a misuse of their free will. In *DSA* Luther carefully and deliberately avoids ex-

---

214 WA 18, 709, 28-31: "Hic vides Deum, cum in malis et per malos operatur, mala quidem fieri, Deum tamen non posse male facere, licet mala per malos faciat, quia ipse bonus male facere non potest, malis tamen instrumentis utitur, quae . . . potentiae suae non possunt evadere." Tr. P & J, p. 204.

215 P. 362.

216 Earlier Luther had taught that man originally had *liberum arbitrium* but lost it as a result of his fall. Afterward the will was free only for sinning and for things of the natural order. Cf. chapter 8, p. 246, esp. footnote 146.

plaining sin in terms of man's free will.[217] In contrast to his earlier, Augustinian doctrine that "free will before grace avails only for sinning," [218] Luther now teaches that man has no free will even concerning sin: "Concerning God or the things which pertain to salvation or *damnation* he has no free will" [219] (emphasis added). By ignoring the problem of the origin of sin, as Pannenberg has pointed out. Luther ignores "the most important theological argument for free will." [220]

(b) Furthermore, to say simply that man has responsibility for his sin because he wills his sin and yet to deny that this is a *free* willing of the sin, to deny that man could have avoided sinning is to give "responsibility" a new definition.[221] Responsibility without freedom is as incomprehensible to civil justice as it is to the pre-Lutheran theological tradition. But it is precisely in terms of these two problems: the responsibility of man for his actions and the origin of evil in God's good creation that "every theological rejection of free will must justify itself." [222]

(c) Because of his failure to discuss the origin of sin and through his emphasis on the all-embracing activity of God, Luther seems to make God the actual originator of sin. In our examination of Luther's *Assertio,* we tried to give an acceptable interpretation of Luther's thesis: "Deus operatur et mala opera in impiis." [223] We were able to give such

---

[217] Cf. Iwand, MA, p. 296. In one place Luther speaks of God *permitting* Adam to sin: WA 18, 712, 29ff.: "Cur permisit Adam ruere. . . ." It must be remembered, however, says E. Seeberg, *Luthers Theologie,* p. 71, followed by J. Richter, "Luthers 'Deus absconditus'—Zuflucht oder Ausflucht," in *Zeitschr. f. Religions- und Geistesgeschichte,* 7 (1955), 298, that "to permit," when applied to Luther's always-active God, does not mean "to allow," but "to effect."

[218] Cf. chapter 8, footnote 160; see also pp. 243f.

[219] WA 18, 638, 9f. But cf. WA 18, 753.

[220] "Christlicher Glaube und menschliche Freiheit," in: *KuD* 4 (1958): "Wenn Gott die Schöpfung gut hervorgebracht hat und wenn es keinen bösen Gegengott gibt, der gleich ewig wie der Schöpfer und nicht von ihm geschaffen wäre, dann muss doch das Böse in einem der—guten!—Geschöpfe Gottes seinen ersten Ursprung haben. Und dann muss dieses Geschöpf von vornherein ausser seiner geschöpflichen Hinordnung auf Gottes Willen die Möglichkeit gehabt haben, dem Willen Gottes auch widerstreben, für ihn, aber auch gegen ihn entscheiden zu können."

[221] Althaus, *Die Theologie M. Luthers,* pp. 140f. is one of the many authors who seem to see nothing unusual about Luther's concept of responsibility without freedom. These theologians seem to think that it is sufficient to say that man is responsible because he is willing, but they do not take notice of the great break Luther has made with all prior theological and philosophical tradition by his disjunction of *voluntarium* and *liberum.* Cf. also Löfgren, pp. 49, 81, 102, 125; Bandt, p. 120; Vorster, pp. 361f. and 368. Theologians who are not satisfied with Luther's explanation of man's responsibility for sin include Meissinger, *Erasmus,* p. 329; J. Richter, p. 298; Pinomaa, *Sieg des Glaubens,* p. 51; Pannenberg (see below).

[222] Pannenberg, "Christlicher Glaube und menscliche Freiheit," p. 272.

[223] Cf. chapter 8, p. 261.

an interpretation because of our view that in the *Assertio* and *Grund und Ursach* Luther still retained the idea that man's *liberum arbitrium* was responsible for sin. In *DSA,* however, where we meet the same thesis, "God, though he does evil by means of evil men, cannot act evilly himself. . . ," [224] one cannot suggest as readily as we did previously that Luther's meaning could simply be that of Thomas Aquinas and the Scholastics when they taught that God is the origin of the sinful *act* but not of the sin itself. According to the Catholic tradition the origin of sin is attributed solely to the created free will. In *DSA* where Luther, forced into a corner because of his necessitarianism, deliberately avoids explaining sin in terms of free will, one cannot say, as Vorster does, that Luther's explanation of the origin of evil stands "in immediate relationship" to the doctrine of Thomas Aquinas.[225] Vorster attributes to Luther the view that "not God, but Satan, not the creator but the creature creates evil." [226] Vorster, however, does not face the problem of how a creature can "create" evil if the creature has no free will.

Because Luther refuses to say that man's responsibility for sin is based upon a misuse of free will, he is led to affirm the justice of God while at the same time affirming that God condemns those who are unfree and who therefore are not deserving of condemnation.[227] To call this absurd, as Erasmus does, says Luther, is to apply the Erasmian standards of reason and man's idea of what is right to God. According to Rom. 9: 19, says Luther, this is precisely what the reason of the unbeliever does.[228] In his answer to Erasmus' objection, Luther invokes Rom. 11: 33 and the incomprehensibility of God's justice which is based upon this text.[229] That God's wisdom and justice are incom-

---

224 WA 18, 709, 29f.; P & J, p. 204.
225 P. 368.
226 *Ibid.* See also Löfgren, p. 98.
227 WA 18, 729, 23f.: God damns those "qui vitare non potest meritum damnationis." Cf. 686, 10f.; 730, 26 and 31f.: Deus damnat immeritos.
228 WA 18, 729, 11ff.
229 WA 18, 784, 11-16. WA 18, 729, 7-731, 13 is to be read in connection with 784, 1-785, 38. In WA 18, 686, 10f. Luther warns that it is not lawful for us to seek the reason for God's imputation of guilt to a man even when the man is unable to avoid guilt. This admonition is made within the context of Luther's comments on the distinction between *Deus praedicatus* and *Deus absconditus.* Important as this distinction is in Luther's concept of God, we cannot directly discuss it here. H. Bandt, has written the most extensive study on this theme. Cf. A. Brandenburg, *Gericht und Evangelium,* pp. 28-33; 114-121. Recently P. Althaus, *Die Theologie M. Luthers,* pp. 238-248 has accepted M. Doerne's criticism of Luther's doctrine of *Deus absconditus* without taking into account Bandt's assessment of Doerne's position. Pannenberg's interpretation of the relation of the *Deus absconditus* to *Deus revelatus,* "Der Einfluss der Anfechtungserfahrung auf den Prädestinationsbegriff Luthers," p. 189 follows closely the view of Kattenbusch and of the early W. von Loewenich, without taking into account Doerne's important criticism of these views. Pannenberg seems unaware that von Loewenich actually changed his position as a result of Doerne's criticism (cf. the post-script

prehensible to human reason is a truth affirmed not only by Luther but by the entire previous theological tradition. All Christian theologians since the time of Augustine have seen in Rom. 11: 33ff. a confession that God's wisdom infinitely transcends man's and that man cannot comprehend the reason behind God's judgments. None of these theologians, however, said that God's judgments *contradict* man's judgments or that God can be just even though he condemns men who do not *deserve* condemnation. There is a difference between incomprehensible and unreasonable!

H. J. Iwand concedes that the question of the condemnation of the sinner is not so bitter as long as one works within the context of free will. One can then find the basis for man's condemnation in man himself. Luther refused to take this approach to the problem. For him man's condemnation "reverts back to God." [230] Martin Doerne has pointed out that Luther's teaching that God condemns even those who do not deserve condemnation has nothing to do with the paradoxical and mysterious character of Christian faith, but is, instead, a contradiction to reason and to the very nature of justice. Citing Luther's words: ". . . the highest degree of faith is to believe that he is merciful, though he saves so few and damns so many; to believe that he is just, though of his own will he makes us perforce proper subjects for damnation. . . ," [231] Doerne comments: Luther "has twisted the genuine paradox of faith into the false form of logical contradiction. . . . That God condemns those who are undeserving is not an expression of faith, but the rational hardening of the testimony of faith into a contradiction." [232] Other Protestant authors who have sharply criticized Luther on this point include: F. Kattenbusch,[233] O. Ritschl,[234] K. Meissinger.[235] Authors who see that Luther is content to allow Christian faith to involve contradictions include: E. Erikstein,[236] M. Schüler,[237] K. D. Schmidt,[238]

---

to the latter's *Theologia Crucis*, 4th ed. (München, 1954). Bandt, pp. 158f. criticizes Kattenbusch for the same reasons as does Doerne.

[230] Iwand, "Die Freiheit des Christen und die Unfreiheit des Willens," p. 142.

[231] WA 18, 633, 15ff.: "Hic est fidei summus gradus, credere illum esse . . . iustum, qui sua voluntate nos necessario damnabiles facit. . . . ;" tr. P & J, p. 101.

[232] Pp. 89f.

[233] *Luthers Lehre vom unfreien Willen*, pp. 11 and 37. But cf. Kattenbusch's later essay, "Deus absconditus," in: *Festgabe f. J. Kaftan* (Tübingen, 1920), p. 178, footnote 11. See also the criticism by M. Doerne, p. 77.

[234] *Dogmengeschichte des Protestantismus* (Leipzig-Göttingen, 1926), II, p. 87; III, p. 127.

[235] *Erasmus*, p. 332.

[236] P. 17.

[237] "Luthers Gottesbegriff nach seiner Schrift, De servo arbitrio," in: *Zeitschr. f. Kirchengeschichte*, 55 (1936), 582.

[238] "Lutherische und katholische Rechtfertigungslehre," in: *Theologie und Verkündigung*, H. 5 (Lüneburg, 1946), p. 15.

W. von Loewenich,[239] H. Bornkamm.[240] While Schüler, Schmidt and von Loewenich agree that Luther's "anti-rational logic of faith . . . is an expression of genuine Christian faith," [241] Bornkamm says that the contradictions in Luther's statements concerning responsibility without freedom "are really only . . . apparent" contradictions.[242]

H. Bandt grants that Luther has a fondness for paradoxical formulations,[243] but he refuses to concede to Doerne, O. Ritchl et al. that the element of the contradictory and the irrational is essential to Luther's thought.[244] When Luther says "absurdum est" to believe in many of the doctrines of Christianity,[245] this does not mean, says Bandt, that Luther believes these doctrines are logical contradictions. They are absurd only in the sense that everything which is paradoxical and truly miraculous runs contrary to reasonable expectations and postulates.[246] Bandt overlooks, however, the fact that "absurd" can also mean that which manifestly contradicts a truth of which reason is certain. It is in this sense that Luther says the Christian faith is absurd to human reason when it teaches "that God, who is just and good, should require of 'free will' impossibilities; and that though 'free will' cannot will good and serves sin of necessity, He should yet lay sin to its charge. . . ." [247]

Bandt agrees with Doerne's statement: "That God condemns those who are undeserving, this is not an expression of faith." [248] "However,

---

239 *Luther und der Neuprotestantismus*, pp. 422f.

240 "Luther und Erasmus," p. 52.

241 Schüler, p. 582.

242 "Luther und Erasmus," p. 52.

243 P. 58.

244 Pp. 170-173. Contrary to Bandt, W. von Loewenich, *Luther und der Neuprotestantismus*, pp. 422f., says: "Es ist nicht schwer, Luther im einzelnen Widersprüche und logische Aporien nachzuweisen. . . ." If one considers Luther's statements on man's responsibility for his sins theoretically, continues von Loewenich, then "liegt hier ein reiner Widerspruch vor." *Ibid.* "The fact that Luther ends in confusion," concludes von Loewenich, "is a good sign for his theology; it is not 'systematic,' but existential. The antinomy of God's grace and man's freedom" (sic!) is insoluble. *Ibid.*

245 WA 18, 707, 12-35.

246 P. 172.

247 WA 18, 707, 32-35: "Absurdum manet (ratione iudice), ut Deus ille iustus et bonus exigat a libero arbitrio impossibilia, et cum liberum arbitrium non possit velle bonum necessarioque serivat peccato, tamen imputet ei." Tr. P & J., p. 201. Gerrish, *Grace and Reason*, p. 20, footnote 1, cites a number of places where Luther teaches: *ratio adversatur fidem*. Although Gerrish grants that Luther "certainly considers some of his beliefs to be contrary to reason" (p. 136), he rightly warns us "not to do less justice to subtlety of Luther's thought than he deserves" (p. 137). No one offers better guidance in understanding the subtleties of Luther's position on faith and reason than Gerrish himself.

248 Doerne, p. 90; Bandt, p. 172.

the way in which Doerne understands this sentence," continues Bandt, "is not the way Luther intended it." "The actual guilt of those whom God condemns," maintains Bandt, "is never questioned by Luther." [249] It seems to us that Bandt loses sight of the difficulty into which Luther has forced himself in *DSA*.

The early Luther, in common with previous Christian tradition,[250] knows that God only damns those who are deserving of damnation.[251] Yet the Luther of *DSA*, forced by his necessitarian argument, his extreme concept of God's all-embracing causality and his Satanology to deny that man's responsibility for sin lies in an abuse of his free will, finds himself unable to say that God damns only those who deserve damnation. Not once, but many times, we find Luther saying: "God damns those who do not deserve or cannot avoid deserving damnation!" [252] Bandt is not completely correct when he says that, for Luther, the actual guilt of those whom God condemns is never questioned. What Luther never questions is that God is just even when he condemns the undeserving ("immeritos damnat"). Luther *asserts* this constantly. Bandt overlooks the fact, of which Luther is aware, that this assertion is opposed not only to man's reason, but even to reason aided by the light of grace! Luther asks the Christian to *believe* that God is just, even though the light of *grace*—as well as the light of *nature*—insists that it is God's fault—not man's—that man is damned! [253] Here we have a concept of faith and reason that has no foundation in Scripture.

Christian apologists have always tried to show that there is no real contradiction in the Christian dogmas "that God became man, was the Son of a virgin, was crucified, and now sits at the right hand of the

---

[249] *Ibid.*

[250] Cf. Augustine, *Contra Iul.*, 3, 18, 35: "Bonus est Deus, iustus est Deus; potest aliquos sine bonis meritis liberare, quia bonus est; non potest quemquam sine malis meritis damnare, quia iustus est." Luther argues that, if God can have mercy on men who do not deserve mercy, he can damn men who do not deserve damnation: WA 18, 730, 15 - 731, 13. Even though he is justifiably acting against Erasmus' view that God elects some men because of the faith he finds in them (*ob credulitatem:* Walter, III a 14, p. 56, 25f.; 57, 17f.; cf. *Hyp.*, II, 1439A; 1448B), Luther falls into an equally unacceptable position when he ignores the fundamental distinction between God's mercy or goodness and his justice.

[251] Cf. p. 423.

[252] WA 18, 633, 15ff.; 686, 10f.; 729, 23f.; 730, 26f., 31f.; 731, 2f.; 5f.; 12f.; 784, 2.

[253] WA 18, 785, 29-37: "In lumine gratiae est insolubile, quomodo Deus damnat eum, qui non potest ullis suis viribus aliud facere quam peccare et reus esse. Hic tam lumen naturae quam lumen gratiae dictant, culpam esse non miseri hominis sed inqui Dei . . . At lumen gloriae aliud dictat, et Deum, cuius modo est iudicium incomprehensibilis iustitiae, tunc ostendet esse iustissimae et manifestissimae iustitiae, tantum ut interim id credamus. . . ."

Father," etc.[254] They have agreed with Paul (I Cor. 1: 23) that the doctrine of the cross is "foolishness to the Gentiles and a scandal to the Jews," [255] but they would not concede to Luther that this doctrine—or any Christian doctrine—is, in the strict sense of the word, absurd or truly contradictory to human reason, especially when it is illuminated by grace.[256] On the other hand, no Christian apologist prior to Luther has ever tried to defend as non-contradictory the truly contradictory assertion that God is just even though he condemns men who, according to the standard of reason illumined by grace, do not deserve condemnation. Luther is able to assert God's justice in such a case because of his extreme voluntarist conviction that, "what God wills is not right because he ought, or was bound, so to will; on the contrary, what takes place must be right, because he so wills it." [257]

Here we have an indication of a separation of the divine will from the divine intellect that was unknown to Thomas Aquinas and Scotus, but which is similar to the voluntaristic concept of God held by Gabriel Biel.[258] This concept of God makes it possible to say that God is just regardless of what he does and that there is really nothing that could conceivably be unjust for him. Does not the concept of justice thereby lose all meaning? Why call God just at all if his justice includes that which human reason calls just as well as unjust? Roman Catholic theology always recognizes the essential difference between God's justice and ours, but if there is no analogy whatever between God's justice and ours, why give it the same name? Why not assume an agnostic posture and say God is totally different from us—therefore we can say nothing meaningful about him or his "justice"?

Although Bandt tries—in our opinion without success—to free Luther from the charge that his doctrine of responsibility without freedom

---

[254] WA 18, 707, 24-27. We speak of *authentic* apologists not only because there is an authentic Catholic teaching on the relation of faith to reason (cf. D 1797), but also because we wish to indicate our awareness that there has been a "succession of Christian irrationalists which goes back at least to Tertullian": Gerrish, *Grace and Reason,* p. 135. Gerrish, pp. 49-56 offers some helpful considerations on the relation of the anti-intellectualism of the Ockhamist branch of Nominalism to Luther's own attack on reason.

[255] Cf. Thomas Aquinas, In *I ad Cor.,* cap. 1, lect. 3, n. 47; Erasmus, *Hyp.,* II, 1400 D: "Nec tamen in his [articles of faith] est quicquam absurdi, etiamsi sunt multa paradoxa."

[256] WA 18, 707, 24-27; cf. footnote 249 above.

[257] WA 18, 712; tr. P & J, p. 209.

[258] *De Ver.,* q. 23, a. 6c: "Dicere autem quod ex simplici voluntate dependeat iustitia, est dicere quod divina voluntas non procedat secundum ordinem sapientiae, quod est blasphemum." Concerning Biel, cf. Bandt, p. 120; Dettloff, *Die Entwicklung der Akzeptations- und Verdienstlehre,* pp. 358 and 361.

leads him to an anti-rational concept of faith, he admits that Luther's attempt to explain the relation of God to evil is a "faltering" and "not especially convincing attempt." Bandt adds: One must admit that this is one of the manifest weaknesses of the book on the unfree will. . . ." [259]

Bandt raises another important point of criticism when he asks whether eternal damnation is actually taught by such passages as Ex. 9: 12, Mal. 1: 2f. and Rom. 9: 11ff., or whether Luther reads into these texts certain basic thoughts of the traditional doctrine of predestination. He further asks the question whether the biblical concept of the hardening of the heart is identical with an eternal decree of damnation. Bandt finally asks: "Are we then permitted to understand God's decree of eternal damnation under any other aspect than that of his reaction to the guilty resistance of men? Must it not really be conceded that Luther allows himself here to be driven to assertions for the sake of consistency, assertions which go beyond the limits of biblical truth and which actually undermine his own position?" [260]

The authentic Catholic tradition has always recognized that the affirmation of both God's providence and foreknowledge as well as man's free will involve a genuine mystery—but never a contradiction. Only with the aid of the "light of glory" can we "see" the relation of these two realities. After he has argued on *rational* as well as on biblical grounds that free will is incompatible with God's foreknowledge, Luther inconsistently refuses to allow rational arguments to be used against his view that God condemns men who do not deserve condemnation.

6. Our final point of criticism is directed not against Luther's necessitarian concept of *servum arbitrium,* but against the hermeneutic principle by which Luther seeks to overthrow one of the almost universally accepted arguments for the existence of a power of free decision in man: the argument, namely, that commands, laws, prohibitions, invitations, admonitions and promises to which a condition is attached all presuppose or imply that the person receiving these commands, etc., has free will. We have encountered this argument for free will in authors from the time of Augustine [261] through Thomas Aquinas.[262] It is used also by Erasmus when he argues for free will on the basis of Sir. 15: 14-18.[263] Like Augustine and others before him, Erasmus invokes a num-

---

[259] P. 123.

[260] Bandt, pp. 155-159. Freitag, WA 18, 595, also sees Luther's exegesis of Rom. 9ff. as an unconvincing over-interpretation. Similarly H. Strohl, p. 186.

[261] See pp. 94f. The argument is used not only by "ethical idealists," as Iwand, MA, p. 290 thinks.

[262] See p. 145.

[263] Walter, II a 1-8, p. 19, 11-26.

ber of texts which presuppose free will: Gen. 4: 6f., Dt. 30: 15-19 [264] and Zach. 1: 3.[265]

To Erasmus' argument based on Sir. 15: 14-18, Luther answers by introducing into the Sirach text a distinction between two kingdoms: "In the one, he is led by his own will and counsel, not by any precepts and commandments of God; that is, in the realm of things below him. . . . In the other kingdom, however, man is not left in the hand of his own counsel, but is directed and led by the will and counsel of God." In the kingdom of God, therefore, "he is led by the precepts of another, and not by his own will." [266] We shall allow K. A. Meissinger to express our opinion of what he calls this "sophistic" interpretation: "Out of respect for the truth one must say here: No, that is directly the opposite of the simple and clear meaning of the text." [267]

In the course of his argument against Erasmus, Luther lays down a principle which forces him to stand alone in the history of Christian biblical interpretation. According to Luther, commands, conditional promises, imperatives, etc. do *not* prove the existence of free will, for: a) it is a principle of logic that conditional or imperative statements assert nothing indicatively [268] and b) it is a principle of Pauline theology that the reason for the divine legislation is that "God is trying us, that by his law he may bring us to a knowledge of our impotence, if we are his friends . . . or else, he is really and deservedly taunting and mocking us, if we are his proud enemies." [269] This is Luther's distinctive doctrine of the pedagogical function of the law. The law teaches us not what we *can* do but only what we *ought* to do.[270] God commands us to do what is impossible in order to goad us and to show us how incapable we are of doing any of the things he commands.[271] On the basis of Rom. 3: 20 Luther concludes: "The entire design and power of the law is solely to give knowledge, and that of nothing but sin; not to display or confer any power." [272]

---

[264] Cf. p. 34.

[265] Cf. above p. 97. Walter, II a 14-18, p. 32, 11-38, 22.

[266] WA 18, 672, 16-20; P & J, pp. 150f.

[267] *Erasmus*, p. 320.

[268] WA 16, 672, 30-35; 677, 23ff.

[269] WA 18, 673, 40-674; 1; tr. P & J, p. 153.

[270] WA 18, 676, 1ff., 16; 678, 44ff.

[271] WA 18, 676, 39-677, 1; 679, 33-37.

[272] WA 18, 677, 10ff.: "Tota ratio et virtus legis est in sola cognitione eaque non nisi peccati praestanda, non autem in virtute aliqua ostendenda aut conferenda"; tr. P & J, p. 158. Luther's assertion "tota ratio . . . legis est in sola cognitione . . . peccati" must not obscure the fact that Luther is aware of the civil function of the law (*usus primus, civilis* or *politicus*). Here he emphasizes

If one should grant, says Luther, that the law or imperative or conditional statements are proof of free will, then it would follow that free will is able by itself, without grace, to keep the commandments. But this is precisely the argument of the Pelagians, who, on the basis of Sir. 15: 14-18 denied grace altogether and ascribed everything to free will.[273]

Concerning Luther's argument from the rules of formal logic and grammar, one can certainly agree with him that the fact that someone is commanded or exhorted does not itself prove the existence of free will in the person concerned. One can even agree with him, "that the nature of words and the use of the language, even among men, is not always such as to make it an act of mockery to say to the impotent, 'If thou art willing,' 'If thou shalt do,' 'If thou shalt hear,'." [274] Luther offers a number of valid examples showing that imperatives do not always presuppose freedom to do what is commanded, but are sometimes used to show that a person is powerless to fulfill the command. What Luther does *not* show, however, is that when God commands, invites, forbids, etc., man's free will is *never* presupposed.[275] Formal logic may prevent us from concluding to the existence of free will from the mere fact that one person promises something to another person if that person fulfills a condition.[276] However, common sense and the rules of personal communication prevent us from saying that such conditional sentences spoken to other persons *never* presuppose that the other person has the ability to fulfill the condition. Luther's proposal to apply a derivative rule of formal logic to *every* divine law or command is therefore clearly exaggerated and one-sided because it ignores the rules of personal dialogue.[277]

---

the second and most important function, the *usus elenchticus, paedagogicus* or *theologicus*. This is *usus praecipuus legis*. It is the *lex accusans* which serves the purpose of leading man to a knowledge of his sins and thus to Christ. Highly debated among Lutherans is the meaning of the so-called *tertius usus legis* a concept which, at least in its wording, is found neither in Luther nor in Lutheran Confessional Statements. Cf. the Formula of Concord, Ep. VI and SD VI. See W. Joest, *Gesetz und Freiheit. Das Problem des tertius usus legis bei Luther und die neutestamentliche Parainese*, 3rd ed. (Göttingen, 1961); E. Wolf, "Gesetz: V. Gesetz und Evangelium, dogmengeschichtlich," in: RGG, 2, 1519-1526; P. Bläser, "Gesetz und Evangelium," in: *Catholica* 14 (1960), 1-22.

[273] WA 18, 674, 29-675, 19; 678, 21-28, 35f.; 682, 30ff.; 683, 4ff.

[274] WA 18, 673; P & J, p. 152.

[275] Cf. Erasmus, *Hyp.*, II, 1346 E and F.

[276] WA 18, 672, 30-35.

[277] It is interesting that Luther would accept Sir. 15: 14ff. as a proof for free will had the author, instead of using a conditional sentence, said: Man is able to keep the commandments: WA 18, 672, 35ff. Elsewhere Luther does not accept the command of Moses: "Choose life. . . ." (Dt. 30: 19), as evidence for free will: WA 18, 676, 29-33; 678, 10f. One wonders if Luther would have accepted

Luther's rejection of the traditional argument for free will seems even more questionable when one considers that the function of the law which Luther emphasizes, namely, the pedagogical function, "has no significance whatever in the Pauline statements concerning the Old Testament law." [278] When Luther claims that, if Erasmus' argument is valid, then the Pelagian position is true, he shows a remarkable forgetfulness of the fact that the greatest of all opponents of Pelagianism— Augustine—used exactly the same argument! [279] Whereas the Pelagians affirmed free will alone—or that free will *is* grace—and whereas Luther affirms grace alone, Augustine and Erasmus, and the Catholic tradition with them, affirm both grace and free will.[280]

Luther asks: "What shall we say to those (the Pelagians, I mean) who, on the basis of this passage, [Sir. 15: 14-18] denied grace altogether, and ascribed everything to 'free will'?" He adds: "If the *Diatribe's* inference stands good, the Pelagians have clearly won the day." [281] We are fortunately in a position to know how Augustine would answer Luther's question. He draws from Sir. 15: 14-18 and from Zach. 1: 3 the same inference as Erasmus—and the Pelagians! —that man has *liberum arbitrium*. But he by no means concedes that the Pelagians have won the day. In contrast to the Pelagians, Augustine upholds—*on the basis of other biblical texts*—the biblical and Catholic truth that the free will alone, without grace, cannot will anything truly good and cannot truly fulfill any of the commandments.[282] We are thus left with a paradox. Luther's charge that Erasmus opens the door to Pelagianism by arguing from the fact of the law to the existence of free will should therefore apply equally to Augustine, the greatest of all anti-Pelagians!

Luther's position here seems less incongruous when we remember that he had some reason to think—on the basis of Erasmus' definition —that Erasmus was defending the Pelagian thesis that free will without

---

Ps. 118 (119): 173 as evidence for free will: ". . . I have chosen your precepts." This text is cited neither by Erasmus nor by Luther.

[278] Bläser, "Gesetz und Evangelium," 22. Cf. Joest, p. 165. Doerne, p. 50, footnote 19 calls Luther's understanding of the law in his exegesis of Sir. 15: 15ff. one of the "entscheidenden Prämissen (und Einseitigkeiten) unserer Schrift." For further criticism of the reduction of the theological significance of the law to the *usus elenchticus* see Luthardt, p. 426; Meissinger, p. 322; Joest, p. 195.

[279] Cf. footnote 257 above.

[280] In the preceding chapter we have indicated where Erasmus has departed from the Catholic tradition. We need here only recall that the Semipelagians also held to grace and free will.

[281] WA 18, 674, 38ff.; P & J, p. 155.

[282] Cf. above pp. 95ff. Erasmus, too, insists against the Pelagians that grace is necessary for a good use of free will: *Hyp.*, II, 1358 E: "Ego cum Augustino

grace could have relevance for salvation. When Erasmus used the argument from law to prove the existence of free will—exactly as Augustine had done—Luther saw this as an attempt to prove a Pelagian concept of free will. It is regrettable that Luther did not combat the Pelagianism of his day as Augustine had done: not by denying the natural free will—or by appearing to do so—but by affirming clearly both the existence of natural free will and the necessity of grace. It is very interesting to note that his manner of argument is not that of Augustine, but of Pelagius. Both Pelagius and Luther say: If man has need of the grace of God then the will is not free.[283] The conclusion Luther reaches—grace alone— is, of course, directly opposed to that of Pelagius: free will alone. But it is also opposed to Augustine's grace and free will.[284]

IV. LUTHER'S BIBLICAL AND CATHOLIC CONCEPT OF *SERVUM ARBITRIUM*

We have found much to criticize in Luther's necessitarian concept of *servum arbitrium*. Nearly all of our criticism has been directed against Luther's use of such non-biblical concepts as necessity and contingency. Other points of criticism were raised against Luther's exaggerated interpretation of the biblical doctrine concerning Satan, the hardening of Pharaoh's heart and the significance of the law. When we turn to Luther's strictly biblical concept of man's enslavement by sin, however, we recognize at once a doctrine of *servum arbitrium* that is fully in conformity with the Catholic tradition of Augustine, Anselm, Peter Lombard, Thomas Aquinas, *et al.*, as well as with the teaching of the Second Council of Orange and of the Council of Trent.

In the final section of *DSA* Luther presents in masterful fashion the Pauline and Johannine doctrine of man's bondage to sin.[285] In this

---

gratiam jungo cum ˙˙ ero arbitrio. . . ." As Lütkens has pointed out, p. 75, it was very unfair of Luther to argue "als habe Erasmus durch seine Behauptungen die Notwendigkeit der Offenbarung und der Gnade Gottes für den Menschen völlig geleugnet und Christum und den Geist Gottes für durchaus unnütz erklärt."
[283] RJ 348. Cf. WA 18, 636, 4-13.
[284] The difference between Luther and Augustine is not as great as it seems at first sight once we note that Luther uses "liberum" in two senses without seeming to be aware of it. Augustine too, can call "liberum arbitrium sine gratia Dei" a *servum arbitrium*. But he does not say, as Luther does, that it is "prorsus non liberum:" WA 18, 636, 4ff. With Augustine it is always clear from the context that the *servum arbitrium* is a "liberum arbitrium captivatum," that the *servum arbitrium* is in some way free. With Luther one must search carefully to learn that when he says "liberum arbitrium sine gratia Dei prorsus non liberum," he really does not take "prorsus" to mean "in no sense at all." Luther does recognize, as we have seen, that man's free will without grace *is* free in relation to natural goodness, etc.
[285] WA 18, 756-783.

exegetical section, where Luther is not refuting Erasmus' arguments, but is developing his own, we find little which a Catholic theologian could not accept.[286] We shall not examine this section in detail simply because we have already seen so much of the same material in our biblical chapter and in our investigations of Augustine and Thomas Aquinas—though never have we seen the doctrine unfolded with such concentration and power! The fact that we do not scrutinize this part of *DSA* is, we emphasize, no indication that we regard this section as unimportant. On the contrary, we hold it to be the most important part of Luther's book, the part in which his deepest concern finds expression: the assertion of the absolute necessity of the grace of Christ against all Pelagian [287] efforts of man to free himself or save himself from slavery to sin, death and Satan simply by the power of free will.

M. Doerne has described Luther's biblical concept of *servum arbitrium* in the following way: "Man as he is today stands before God in guilty bondage. He is absolutely unable to overcome by himself the mortal threat to his very being which arises from his sin and guilt." According to Doerne, this is: "The evangelical-theological foundation of *De servo arbitrio*" and "an ultimate statement of Reformation anthropology." [288] We do not hesitate to say that this is also a fundamental statement of Catholic anthropology!

The questionable elements which we have found in Luther's necessitarian concept of *servum arbitrium* are completely absent in his biblical concept. Several times in this section, in contrast to the previous parts of the book, Luther places himself clearly on Augustinian-Catholic ground when he says that it is man's *liberum arbitrium* that is enslaved and unable to do anything truly good or righteous.[289] Luther speaks once more as he did earlier in *DSA* (WA 18, 615, 14f.), not of the *nonexistence* of *liberum arbitrium,* but of its helpless, prostrate condition in relation to salvation.[290] Luther is even prepared to grant that *liberum*

---

[286] That Erasmus cannot be regarded as fully Catholic concerning the biblical doctrine of slavery to sin can be seen from his negative comments on Luther's biblical argument. Cf. *Hyp.,* II, 1487A—1516 C.

[287] The concept of merit which Luther rejects in his biblical argument (WA 18, 769, 24 - 771, 33) is the Neo-Semipelagian concept of Gabriel Biel and other late Scholastics which we examined in chapter 7. See also the excursus in chapter 6: The Axiom: God does not deny grace . . . Neo-Semipelagianism? T. McDonough, p. 159 has shown that the theology of merit of Thomas Aquinas "bears no resemblance to the erroneous doctrines of merit which the Reformer attacks and refutes in his Commentary on Galatians." The same can be said of Luther's attack on merit in DSA.

[288] Doerne, p. 86.

[289] WA 18, 757, 17; 758, 1, 14f., 24f.; 759, 6-10, 15-20; 760, 14ff.; 765, 39f.; 766, 4-7; 775, 16ff.; 777, 5.

arbitrium is capable of naturally good works. He adds immediately, however, that these have nothing to do with righteousness before God.[291] According to one of Luther's exegetical principles, every time Scripture speaks of Christ we have testimony militating against the free will.[292] It is perfectly clear from the context, however, that he means: militates against the *proud* free will, the free will which seeks to escape the bondage to sin by its own powers.

Here we find no assertion of universal necessity, no denial that man's will is contingent. In fact, in contrast to the places where Luther developed his necessitarian concept of *servum arbitrium,* there is here a constant affirmation that man has a *liberum arbitrium,* but that this *liberum arbitrium* is totally unable to please God, totally unable to will anything truly good or righteous, that is, before God. Thus Luther's biblical concept of *servum arbitrium* is very close to the concept of the captive free will (*liberum arbitrium captivatum*) of Augustine and Peter Lombard. It is unquestionably a Catholic concept that is in complete harmony with the concept of *liberum arbitrium captivatum* of the Council of Trent:

> . . . whereas all men had lost their innocence in the prevarication of Adam [Rom. 5: 12, I Cor. 5:22], "having become unclean" [Is. 64: 6], and (as the Apostle says), "by nature children of wrath" [Eph. 2: 3], as [the Synod] has set forth in the decree on original sin, to that extent were they the servants of sin [Rom. 5: 20], and under the power of the devil and of death, that not only the Gentiles by the force of nature, but not even the Jews by the very letter of the law of Moses were able to be liberated from that condition, although free will was not extinguished in them. . . ." [293]

V. THE DOCTRINE OF *SERVUM ARBITRIUM* IN THE LATER LUTHER: A RETRACTION?

We do not propose to present a completely original investigation of Luther's doctrine of the unfree will in all of his writings after *DSA*. We wish instead simply to draw upon some older, partly forgotten studies, in order to throw some light on a theory recently revived by W. Pannenberg that the later Luther abandoned some of the more extreme aspects of his doctrine which are found in *DSA*.[294]

---

[290] WA 18, 757, 3, 6f.; 767, 10; 773, 20f.

[291] WA 18, 767, 40-768, 1; 771, 37-772, 9; 781, 8-13.

[292] WA 18, 782, 21-24.

[293] D 793.

[294] Cf. Pannenberg, "Einfluss der Anfechtungserfahrung auf den Prädestinationsbegriff Luthers," in: *KuD* 3 (1957), 109-139. This theory was already presented in 1568 by Chr. Lasius. Cf. Döllinger, *Die Reformation,* III (Regensburg,

Pannenberg sees in *DSA* a dualistic tension between the hidden God and the revealed God, coupled with a deterministic concept of predestination that allows no place for a decision of faith. Late in his life, however, says Pannenberg, Luther "clearly recognized that this deterministic concept of predestination which robs our encounter with Christ of its decision-character, ultimately makes the Incarnation and the redemptive work of Christ completely superfluous." [295] In the *Lectures on Genesis,* maintains Pannenberg, "Luther has become wary of the proposition that everything happens out of necessity." [296] "Even though Luther makes use of the concept of the hidden God in the *Lectures on Genesis,* he no longer defends his proposition: 'all things are absolute and necessary'. . . ." [297]

Pannenberg does not say that Luther retracted his *DSA* doctrine concerning God hidden and revealed. He holds, rather, that Luther overcame the anguish caused by the doctrine of predestination by emphasizing the *unity* of the revealed God and the hidden God. "This is Luther's final and decisive word on the question of overcoming the vexation caused by belief in predestination. . . . The resolution of doubts concerning one's own election through faith in the unity of the eternal God with Jesus Christ unavoidably destroys the deterministic scheme in which Luther earlier had thought of predestination." [298]

Pannenberg likewise does not say that Luther retracted his necessitarianism: he was simply wary about it and did not defend it. Yet the clear implication of Pannenberg's essay, as can be seen from statements which we have already noted, is that Luther, at the end of his life, began teaching that faith involves decision, thus abandoning his deterministic view of predestination. This would indeed represent a decisive repudiation of some of the most questionable theses of *DSA.* As much as we would welcome a demonstration showing that Luther abandoned his necessitarian outlook in later years, we do not believe that Pannenberg has proved that the later Luther reversed his position.

First of all, Pannenberg points to no clear text in the later Luther where Luther teaches that man's encounter with Christ in faith involves a free decision. Secondly, Pannenberg takes no account of the numerous

---

1848), p. 457. He was followed by P. Haberkorn, J. Gerhard, A. Rudelbach *et al.* Cf. Humbertclaude, p. 278.

[295] P. 129.

[296] Pannenberg, p. 138. These lectures were held between June 3, 1535 and November 17, 1545. They appeared in four parts from 1544 to 1554. Cf. Aland, p. 110.

[297] *Ibid.,* footnote 114. Cf. WA 43, 463, 5.

[298] Pp. 127f.

texts in Luther's later writings which simply reaffirm the totally passive role of man in faith—to the exclusion of all free decision—that we have noted in *DSA*. Such texts have been enumerated not only by Grisar,[299] but also by Lutheran scholars such as Lütkens.[300] In the *Smalcaldic Articles* of 1537—composed at the same time he was holding his *Lectures on Genesis*—Luther still held it to be "nothing but error and stupidity" when "scholastic theologians" taught that after the fall of Adam "man has a free will, either to do good and refrain from evil or to refrain from good and do evil." [301] It was also in this year of the *Lectures on Genesis* that Luther wrote his letter to Wolfgang Capito in which he extolled *DSA* and the *Catechism* as his best work.[302]

Thirdly, Pannenberg's suggestion that there is "an essential, real difference" [303] between *DSA* and the *Lectures on Genesis* concerning the doctrine of predestination presupposes a development in Luther's understanding of the relationship between the hidden God and the revealed God which does not stand up when one analyzes the texts themselves. In 1926 O. Ritschl [304] thought that he saw in the *Lectures on Genesis* an "implicit" correction of the dualistic tension in the concept of God which was found in *DSA*. In contrast to this view, which is similar to that of Pannenberg, Bandt emphasizes that in the *Lectures on Genesis,* Luther indeed worked out more strongly and clearly than in *DSA* the unity of the hidden and the revealed God. He nevertheless regards it as incorrect to speak of an "implicit correction" of *DSA,* that is, of "an essential, real difference" between the earlier and the later Luther.[305]

Fourthly, scholars in the last century—unmentioned by Pannenberg —have examined the same texts from the *Lectures on Genesis* as did Pannenberg, and in far greater detail, but they reached exactly the opposite conclusion! Early in the 19th century J. Müller showed that Luther held a doctrine of unconditional predestination both before and after the controversy with Erasmus.[306] Müller's thesis was attacked by A. Rudelbach,[307] who used the same arguments as Pannenberg. After a

---

[299] I, pp. 567-571.
[300] P. 90.
[301] *Schm. Art.*, III, Teil, 1, 5: BKS, p. 434, 17ff.; Tappert, p. 302. Cf. footnote 321 below.
[302] Cf. p. 6, footnote 7 above.
[303] P. 129.
[304] *Dogmengeschichte des Protestantismus*, III, pp. 10ff.
[305] Bandt, pp. 158f. Cf. WATR, 4, Nr. 5070 (1540). See also Brandenburg, *Gericht und Evangelium*, pp. 117f.
[306] *Lutheri de praedestinatione et libero arbitrio* (Göttingen, 1832).
[307] *Reformation, Luthertum und Union* (n.p., 1839), pp. 277-289.

careful analysis of Luther's commentary on Genesis 26: 9, J. Lütkens [308] raised the question: "Do we find any kind of a contradiction
between the commentary on this Genesis text and the doctrine which
Luther upheld against Erasmus?" He answers: "In no way." [309] It is
only the point of view which is different. Speaking of the Genesis commentary Lütkens says:

Luther does not treat the doctrine dogmatically, but from the point of
view of the correct attitude which the individual person should take
toward the question of predestination. In this perspective the means of
grace come to the fore and faith is placed in an immediate relation to
Christ but this is by no means a retraction or a disavowal of his earlier
teaching. Much more important is the fact that Luther expressly recognizes the distinction of the hidden and revealed will of God just as
much as he did in the work against Erasmus—and he even cites this
earlier teaching. [310]

"Even at this late date," concludes Lütkens, "Luther maintains that
everything happens necessarily. He cautions only against an exclusive
emphasis on this aspect of the doctrine and against drawing consequences which destroy the foundations of Christianity." [311] Although he
differs on several points from Lütkens' opinion, C. E. Luthardt finds
himself in substantial agreement with Lütkens. [312] Like Bandt and
Pannenberg and many other scholars, Luthardt sees a shift of accent in
the *Lectures on Genesis,* a shift away from the hidden will of God to
God's revelation of salvation in Christ Jesus. [313] Unlike Pannenberg,
however, he refuses, with Lütkens, to admit that Luther *retracted* any of
the doctrine of *DSA* concerning absolute necessity or predestination. [314]

Modern scholars who share the view that Luther never retracted or
abandoned the position he took in *DSA* include: M. Richter, [315] R.
Seeberg, [316] H. Strohl, [317] E. Erikstein [318] and G. Rost. [318a]

---

[308] *Luthers Prädestinationslehre im Zusammenhang mit seiner Lehre vom
freien Willen,* diss. (Dorpat, 1858).

[309] P. 84.

[310] *Ibid.*

[311] P. 87.

[312] *Die Lehre vom freien Willen und seinem Verhältnis zur Gnade* (Leipzig,
1863).

[313] Pp. 122 and 135.

[314] Pp. 85 and 135. It must not be overlooked, however, that even the later
Luther continued to assert, as he did in DSA, that man has free will in natural
things. Cf. footnote 42 of our Introduction.

[315] P. 70.

[316] *Dogmengeschichte,* IV/1, pp. 189ff.

[317] P. 154.

[318] P. vi.

Finally, it is difficult to conceive that Luther would substantially modify, in the manner suggested by Pannenberg, the ideas contained in a work which was "the fruit of very thoughtful reflection and innermost composure," [319] a work which, as late as 1537, Luther named as one of his two best theological efforts. As Lütkens says: "A complete and radical transformation of Luther's doctrine of predestination has to appear to us from the outset to be improbable." [320]

VI. LUTHER'S DOCTRINE OF *SERVUM ARBITRIUM* AND THE LUTHERAN CONFESSIONS

Aside from the denial in the *Smalcaldic Articles* of the ability of free will even "to refrain from good and to do evil," [321] it is striking how few of the elements of Luther's doctrine of the unfree will which we have had to criticize are found in the Lutheran Confessional writings. There is, first of all, no necessitarian concept of unfree will. In fact, the determinism of the Stoics and Manichaeans, "who taught that whatever happens must so happen and could not happen otherwise" is condemned as "delirium." [322] "Following the pattern of the *Augsburg Confession*, 18," comments Vorster, "the article of free will has become a permanent part of Lutheran dogmatics." [323]

Secondly, in contrast to the unclarity of *DSA* with its frightening implication that God is in some way responsible for sin since he is the only non-necessitated center of free choice, the Confessions make it perfectly clear that the cause of sin is not God, but the perverted will of the devil and of man: "causa peccati est voluntas malorum." [324] "God

[318a] *Der Prädestinationsgedanke in der Theologie Martin Luthers* (Berlin, 1966), pp. 72-76.

[319] Lütkens, p. 10.

[320] *Ibid.*

[321] S. A., III, 1, 5: Tappert, p. 302. Cf. The Solid Declaration = S.D. II, 33. This is not surprising since the articles are the work of Luther himself. The Augsburg Confession = A.C., XVIII, on the other hand, clearly affirms that man is capable of sin "by his own choice." The introduction to Part III of the S.A. states that the subsequent articles may still be discussed with "learned and sensible men." It would, however, be incorrect to take this to mean that what is said concerning free will is a negotiable matter. On the contrary, Luther insists that the teachings of the Scholastics on the natural powers of fallen man are "nothing but error and stupidity" and "thoroughly pagan doctrines" that cannot be tolerated: S.A., III, 1, 3 and 11.

[322] The Epitome = Ep., II, 8; Tappert, pp. 470f. Cf. S.D., II, 74. This thesis was asserted several times by Luther. Luther never taught the other aspect of the condemned Stoic-Manichaean doctrine: "et hominem omnia coactum facere." In the absence of necessitarian thinking in the Lutheran Confessions, we may presume something which we could not presume in DSA, that "volens" and "voluntarie" mean the same as "libere."

[323] Vorster, p. 264.

[324] A.C., XIX. The teaching of the A.C. that the will of man "se avertit a

is not the cause of sin, nor is he the cause of the punishment, the damnation. The only cause of man's damnation is sin. . . ." [325] Further, whereas Luther in *DSA* was reluctant to say with the Catholic tradition that sin involves a misuse of free will, Lutheran commentators on the Confessions do not hesitate to interpret the word "*voluntas*" in the *Augsburg Confession,* art. XIX, as free will or free decision.[326]

In the *Formula of Concord* the condemnation of the unrighteous is not attributed to any absolute predestination or reprobation decree of God, but to the active rejection of the word of salvation by the unbeliever.[327] Although "our election to eternal life does not rest on our piety or virtue, but solely on the merit of Christ and the gracious will of the Father," [328] the basis for condemnation (*causa perditionis*) "is not that God did not want them to be saved." [329] On the contrary, "God does not want any man to be damned. . . ." [330] "The only cause of man's damnation is sin. . . ." [331] They alone are damned who have despised the Word and have "resisted the Holy Spirit. . . ." [332] "The reason for such contempt of the Word is not God's foreknowledge, but man's own perverse will." [333] Although the Catholic theologian must show critical reserve toward the doctrine of predestination contained in *DSA*, he immediately recognizes that the predestination doctrine of the *Formula of Concord* is in fundamental agreement with that of the Catholic tradition.[334]

Deo"—not "avertitur"—can only with difficulty be reconciled with Luther's assertion in the S.A., III, 1, 5.

[325] S.D., XI, 81.

[326] Cf. E. Kinder, *Die Erbsünde* (Stuttgart, 1959), pp. 66-72 and Schlink, *Lutheran Confessions,* p. 42, footnote 3. Compare Luther's abstruse and evasive explanation of man's responsibility for sin with the clear statement of Kinder: "Dass der Mensch von seiner Freiheit nicht denjenigen Gebrauch macht, wozu sie ihm einzig gegeben ist. . . , sondern sie zur Abkehr von Gott missbraucht, das ist in keiner Weise durch Gott zu erklären. . . ." Pp. 66f.

[327] Cf. E. Kähler, "Prädestination: III. Dogmengeschichtlich," RGG 5, 486.

[328] S. D., XI, 75; Tappert, p. 628.

[329] S.D., XI, 78; Tappert, p. 629.

[330] S.D., XI, 81; Tappert, p. 629.

[331] *Ibid.* In contradistinction to Luther's explanation in DSA, the hardening of Pharaoh is understood in S.D., XI, 85 as "a punishment for his preceding sin": Tappert, p. 630.

[332] S.D., XI, 78.

[333] S.D., XI, 41: "Huius contemptus verbi non est in causa vel praescientia vel praedestinatio Dei, sed perversa hominis voluntas. . . ."

[334] Despite the reference to DSA in S.D., II, 44, we cannot agree with Luthardt, p. 133 that the Formula of Concord sanctioned DSA. There is a general approbation of DSA, but, as Luthardt himself recognizes, there are ideas in DSA "welche mit dem Bekenntnis der lutherischen Kirche unvereinbar sind." Lau, pp. 107f. notes that Luther's doctrine of predestination has never been officially approved by the Lutheran Church. On the relationship of Article XI of the Formula of Con-

Finally, in the Confessions—especially in the *Formula of Concord*—one encounters an element which was totally lacking in *DSA*—the element of a personal involvement or decision of free will in man's rebirth in Christ. In none of the confessional statements is there any suggestion that man is so totally passive in justification that he makes no free decision in determining whether God or Satan will "ride" him.

Man's will is at times described as being "purely passive," but this is explained in such a way as to admit an active response by man.[335] Although the *Formula of Concord* refers to unregenerated man—as does the Scripture—as a hard stone, as an unhewn timber and as a wild animal,[336] it nevertheless hastens to point out the differences between man and such sub-human creatures: man, after the fall, still has reason and can freely (*libere*) act "in outward or external secular things." [337]

In one place the *Formula of Concord* states: "There is . . . no cooperation on the part of our will in man's conversion." [338] As it stands, this thesis recalls the worst elements of *DSA*. And yet, when we consider the whole context of the *Solid Declaration,* Article II, which is entitled "Free Will or Human Powers," it is perfectly clear that what is being opposed in Article II is not the cooperation of the free will *under the action of grace* in conversion. What is opposed is the Pelagian idea that the unregenerate free will ("non renatum") or that free will by its own natural powers ("proprius et naturalibus suis viribus") can do something for man's conversion, righteousness, peace, and salvation, and can cooperate and obey, believe, and give assent when the Holy Spirit offers the grace of God and salvation through the gospels.[339] The clear implication of Article II, 18 is that the free will, illuminated and ruled by the Holy Spirit ("spiritu Dei illuminatum et rectum") *can* cooperate in man's conversion, justice and salvation and *can* "believe and give assent when the Holy Spirit offers the grace of God." [340]

---

cord to the earlier Lutheran Confessions see E. Schlink, *Theology of the Lutheran Confessions* (Philadelphia, 1961), pp. 288-295 and Seeberg, IV/2, 549f.

[335] Cf. Ep., II, 18; S.D., II, 89.

[336] S.D., II, 19; Tappert, p. 524.

[337] *Ibid.* Cf. S.D., II, 59.

[338] S.D., II, 44: ". . . non est . . . ulla cooperatio voluntatis nostrae in hominis conversione. . . . ;" Tappert, p. 529. Cf. S.D., II, 45.

[339] S.D., II, 18, 86, 89.

[340] Cf. Ep., II, 18 and S.D., II, 83, where it is taught that man's will "apprehendat gratiam" once it has been renewed and transformed by the Holy Spirit. In S.D., II, 67 we learn that man makes an assent of faith: "eidem (verbum Dei) . . . assentire . . . possunt." Luther also recognized an assent of faith: WA 43, 240; 243; 458; 40/1, 228. In contrast to the F.C., however, Luther gives us no reason to think that this is a *free* assent. Sometimes the impression is given that the free cooperation of the will under grace begins only *after* conversion (Ep., II, 18; S.D., II, 83), not *in* conversion itself. S.D., II, 18, as we have seen

Such a doctrine is in full harmony with the teaching of the Council of Trent that man's free will, *activated by God*, cooperates by assenting to God in order to obtain the grace of justification.[341] The Lutheran confessional statements thus overcome one of the chief objections against *DSA*, namely, that it leaves no place for man's free decision in faith.

The doctrine of man's "unfreedom" which is contained in the Lutheran confessional writings, especially in the *Formula of Concord*, corresponds closely to the biblical-Catholic doctrine that the free will of fallen man is totally incapable of doing anything that is truly good *coram Deo* or of freeing itself from its sinful situation. It must *be* freed by the grace of Christ. Then it becomes, in a formula reminiscent of Augustine, a liberated will (*arbitrium liberatum*).[342] The Holy Spirit *begins* the work of conversion in us; we are able to cooperate with him because of the new powers and the gifts he gives us.[343]

Finally, the Roman Catholic Church rejects, along with the Lutheran authors of the *Formula of Concord*, the "falsa doctrina et errores" concerning free will, the errors namely, of the Pelagians,[344] the Synergists [345]—and even the error which is attributed by the *Formula* to the "Papists and Scholastics"—which is in reality the error of the Neo-Semipelagians, as the *Epitome* recognizes.[346]

VII. THE DOCTRINE OF THE UNFREE WILL AND MODERN PROTESTANTISM

Modern Protestant theology understands the doctrine of the unfree will almost without exception not in the sense of the necessitarian concept of *DSA*, but solely in the sense of the biblical-Catholic concept of man's slavery to sin, which Luther so strongly emphasized in his main

---

indicates the activity of the free will which is illumined by the Spirit. Similarly, in S.D., II, 89, where we are told that the will does nothing in man's conversion, we also read: "but lets God alone work in him." "Lets" is an important interpretation of "patitur." From the Catholic viewpoint this means that the will, moved by grace, is "active" in man's conversion because it *freely* allows grace to operate. The will could oppose God's activity (S.D., II, 82f.). It does not do this, but allows God to act. Thus we have a free decision of the will made possible by grace!

341 D 814: "a Deo motum et excitatum."

342 S.D., II, 67.

343 S.D., II, 65.

344 S.D., II, 75.

345 S.D., II, 77.

346 The critical edition of *Die Bekenntnisschriften*, 5th ed. (Göttingen, 1963), p. 903, footnote 2, followed by Tappert, p. 536, footnote 7 is mistaken when it cites Trent, Sess. VI, ch. 1 and 5, as a source of this error. Cf. Ep., II, 10; S.D.,

work. "As far as I see," says H. J. Iwand, "and allowing for a few exceptions, the doctrine of the unfree will has not been upheld by the Protestant Scholastic dogmatics. The doctrine soon degenerated into an avowal of the mere incapacity of man to become justified in the sight of God by his own power. But that was not its original meaning." [347] The same scholar maintains that "modern Protestantism, with its doctrine of the self-movement of the human will, stands closer to Thomism than to the Reformation." [348] Pinomaa points out that *DSA* "has never found a place in the system of the majority of Lutheran theologians and even today does not find a place. The opposition between the true Luther and the Luther who has been distorted by the Lutheran tradition is nowhere more apparent than in the question of the freedom of the will." [349]

Already in his lifetime Luther saw several of his closest followers, above all, Melanchthon, reject his necessitarian concept of unfree will.[350] Melanchthon's break with Luther on this decisive point gave rise after Luther's death to a fierce struggle within Lutheranism: the Synergistic controversy.[351] The attitude which one took toward *De servo arbitrio* became one of the standards by which one was judged to be a Gnesio-Lutheran or a Philippist.[352] Although the *Formula of Concord* condemned synergism by name [353] and excluded the doctrine that the free will—by its *natural* powers—could cooperate in and prepare itself for justification, one must not take this to mean an unquali-

---

II, 76. For a much better appreciation of Trent by a Lutheran see P. Brunner, "Die Rechtfertigungslehre des Konzils vom Trient," in: *Pro Veritate* (Münster-Kassel, 1963), pp. 63f and 83f.

[347] "Die Freiheit des Christen und die Unfreiheit des Willens," p. 136. The formulation of Iwand indicates that he views negatively a development which we regard as a return to the genuine biblical understanding of man's unfreedom.

[348] "Die Freiheit des Christen," p. 134.

[349] "Unfreier Wille und Prädestination bei Luther," in: *Theologische Zeitschrift*, 13 (1957), 339f.

[350] Cf. Seeberg, IV/2, pp. 442-445; Luthardt, pp. 160-164; Zickendraht, pp. 176f.; A. Evard, *Étude sur les variations du dogme de la prédestination et du libre arbitre dans la théologie du Melanchthon* (Laval, 1901). Melanchthon regarded Luther's necessitarianism as the undermining of all discipline and as blasphemy: *Corp. Reform.*, 9, 766.

[351] On this controversy see: Döllinger, III, pp. 437-493; Seeberg, IV/2, pp. 490-495; W. Joest, "Synergismus," RGG, 6, 561f.

[352] According to Döllinger, III, p. 457, the "zealous" Lutherans such as Flacius, Spangenberg, Heshusius, as well as Brenz and Heerbrand, were determined not to allow the authority of DSA as a dogmatic canon to be challenged. Döllinger says that the first effort to question the authority of DSA was made by Chr. Lasius in 1568. Lasius argued, in a manner similar to Pannenberg centuries later, that Luther himself later retracted the content of DSA.

[353] S.D., II, 77f.

fied endorsement of the views of Matthias Flacius (1520-1575), the chief representative of the conservative party defending *DSA*.[354]

Historically, the main stream of Lutheran theology, as distinct from Luther's theology, has avoided Luther's necessitarianism and has consistently affirmed, along with the Catholic tradition, that faith involves a free decision on the part of man.[355] Kattenbusch defends later Lutheranism's break from *DSA*. In the final sentence of his still valuable doctoral dissertation he writes: ". . . concerning the doctrine of *servum arbitrium* and predestination, the Church which named itself after Luther was perfectly correct in leaving the paths trodden by its first great leader and in seeking other forms." [356]

W. Joest represents the thinking of the vast majority of modern Lutheran theologians when he writes: In saying " 'no' to sygergism, it must not be forgotten: a) that not faith and salvation, but unbelief and the corruption of man are unquestionably grounded in man himself. . . ; b) that man is moved through and in the action of grace to his own assent to faith and also to his own act of faith. . . ." [357]

In contrast to *DSA,* modern Protestant theology affirms almost unanimously that man's free will is involved not only in the sins which he commits but also in the faith in Christ through which he is liberated from his sins. Pannenberg has remarked that ". . . in present day Evan-

---

[354] Cf. Joest, RGG, 6, 561. Seeberg, IV/2, p. 548 thinks that Melanchthonism "triumphed" in the teaching of the F.C. on predestination. As far as synergism is concerned, says Seeberg, the F.C. recognized the views of Flacius but rejected his theory; the psychological insights of Melanchthon and his followers were, however, given consideration. *Ibid.,* p. 540. This is a much more nuanced judgment than that of Döllinger, III, p. 484, who simply asserts that the F.C. rejected Melanchthon's synergism.

[355] Luthardt, pp. 149-388 has carefully traced the doctrine of free will in Protestant theology after Luther. Cf. also W. Matthias, "Über die Lehre von der Willensfreiheit in der altlutherischen Theologie," in: *Zeitschr. f. Kirchengesch.,* 74 (1963), 109-133.

[356] *Luthers Lehre vom unfreien Willen und von der Prädestination nach ihren Entstehungsgründen untersucht,* diss. (Göttingen, 1875), p. 95. In addition to our criticism of DSA, the reader is also referred to the following Protestant Luther scholars: Luthardt, p. 133; G. L. Plitt, "Luthers Streit mit Erasmus über den freien Willen," pp. 208f.; Zickendraht, p. 178; J. MacKinnon, *Luther and the Reformation,* vol. 4, p. 268; Th. Harnack, *Luthers Theologie* (München, 1927), Bd. I, pp. 42 and 135; Pannenberg, "Der Einfluss der Anfechtungserfahrung. . . ," pp. 137f.; W. von Loewenich, "Zur Gnadenlehre bei Augustin und bei Luther," in: *Von Augustin zu Luther,* p. 87. Paul Tillich is not a Luther scholar. His criticism of Luther's doctrine of the unfree will is nevertheless highly relevant: "Luther's assertion that man's will is in bondage to demonic structures is meaningful only if man, in his essential nature, is free. . . . Only a being that has the power of self-determination can have a *servum arbitrium,* a 'will in bondage', because a being without the power of self-determination has no 'arbitrium' ('capacity of decision') at all": *The Protestant Era* (Chicago, 1951), p. 129.

[357] RGG, 6, 562.

gelical theology there is on this question a seldom-reached broad consensus among theologians of the most varied directions." [358] Among the
theologians who affirm free will he lists: F. Gogarten, R. Bultmann, E.
Brunner, P. Althaus and K. Barth.[359] According to Pannenberg:

This fact can only be explained by the important theological reasons for
affirming free will, despite all the reservations one may have against it.
Two such reasons are to be mentioned above all: the interest in upholding the responsibility of man for his actions and the closely related
question of explaining the origin of evil in God's good creation. Every
rejection of the free will on theological grounds must do justice to both
of these problems.[360]

In addition to the theologians mentioned by Pannenberg, the following
Protestant theologians are among the many who hold that sin and man's
responsibility for sin presuppose a free decision of the will: E.
Schlink,[361] M. Doerne,[362] R. Hermann,[363] K. L. Schmidt,[364] and R.
Niebuhr.[365]

Highly indicative of the tenor of modern Protestant thought in the
question of free will is the following declaration of the Faith and Order
Conference at Edinburgh (1937):

We do not . . . hold that the action of the divine grace overrides human
freedom and responsibility. . . . [W]e men owe our whole salvation to

---

[358] "Christlicher Glaube und menschliche Freiheit," in: *KuD*, 4 (1958), 270ff.

[359] To this list can be added the following names: Schlink, "Der theologische
Syllogismus. . . ," p. 300; W. von Loewenich, *Der moderne Katholizismus*, 2nd
ed. (Witten, 1956), p. 27; W. Pauck, *The Heritage of the Reformation*, pp. 5 and
19; P. Brunner, "Die Freiheit des Menschen in Gottes Heilsgeschichte," in: *KuD*,
5 (1959), 238-257; H. Braun, "Glaube: III. Im NT," RGG, 2, 1596; H. Grass,
"Glaube: V. Dogmatisch," RGG, 2, 1608f.; W. A. Visser't Hooft; cf. E. C.
Bianchi, "Dr. W. A. Visser't Hooft," in: *America*, 109 (1963), 356. Each of these
theologians regards a free personal decision or a free obedience as an essential
element of faith in Christ. The role of the free will and of man's decision has in
fact been so stressed in certain circles of modern "activist" Protestantism that
P & J, p. 58 can say: "the present-day Evangelical Christian [has] semi-Pelagianism
in his blood." Cf. R. E. Chiles, "Methodist Apostasy: From Free Grace to Free
Will," in: *Religion in Life*, 3 (1958), 438-449; summarized in: *Theology Digest*,
7 (1959), 108-112.

[360] P. 272.

[361] "Der theologische Syllogismus. . . ," p. 307; *Lutheran Confessions*, pp.
108ff.; "Urstand: V. Dogmatisch," RGG, 6, 1213.

[362] Pp. 91f.

[363] "Willensfreiheit und gute Werke im Sinne der Reformation," in: *Gesammelte Studien zur Theologie Luthers und der Reformation* (Göttingen, 1960),
p. 60. Hermann erroneously thinks that Luther also affirms the activity of *free*
will in sin.

[364] TDNT, 1, 589.

[365] *An Interpretation of Christian Ethics*, 2nd ed. (New York, 1958), pp. 86f.

his gracious will. But, on the other hand, it is the will of God that his grace should be actively appropriated by man's own will and that for such decision man remains responsible.[366]

This statement, coupled with the overall tendency of modern Protestant theology, which we could illustrate by numerous examples, makes clear that the doctrine of the Council of Trent concerning free will need not be seen as a factor which separates the Catholic Church from the other Christian confessions. The development toward the clear affirmation of free will and decision-making within Lutheran theology and Protestant theology in general represents an abandonment of the un-Catholic tendencies in Luther's *DSA*. For this reason, and in view of the unique significance which Luther attached to *De servo arbitrio,* the following words of the Lutheran theologian, H. Mulert, should provoke deep reflection in everyone who is concerned with promoting "the restoration of unity among all Christians": [367]

[W]hich Protestant Christians, moreover, which Lutheran Churches, take seriously the content of Luther's main systematic work, "On the Enslaved Will"? But if we do not follow the Reformer in his central ideas, then it is natural for our Catholic brothers to ask whether the separation of the Church was necessary at all or whether it was even justifiable.[368]

One must not, however, think that with the rejection of the un-Catholic currents of *DSA,* modern Protestant theology has abandoned the main stream of the Reformer's thought. Martin Luther's abiding concern was an evangelical-biblical and, therefore, a Catholic concern. Thus, one is not surprised when such a representative Lutheran theologian as Edmund Schlink expresses Luther's biblical doctrine of the unfree will in a fully Catholic way: "The Protestant *servum arbitrium* . . . was . . . primarily . . . the confession of the sinner that he cannot break through the spell of guilt and forlornness by any act of his own." [369]

---

[366] *A Documentary History of the Faith and Order Movement,* ed. L. Vischer (St. Louis, 1963), pp. 43 and 41.

[367] The Decree on Ecumenism of Vatican Council II, Introduction, n. 1.

[368] *Christliche Welt,* n. 20 (1930); citation from Schütte, p. 68.

[369] *The Coming Christ. . . ,* p. 175.

Conclusions

1. In the Bible, the term "freedom" is limited to that which we have called circumstantial freedom and acquired freedom. Nevertheless, man's ability to make decisions and to choose (natural freedom—*liberum arbitrium*) is clearly implied.

2. Scripture offers testimony concerning the foreknowledge, predestination and providence of God, but it never implies that any kind of necessity is imposed upon man which excludes free choice.

3. In the New Testament the sinner is characterized as a slave of sin. Only through faith in Jesus Christ, a faith which involves obedience and, therefore, free surrender, can the sinner be liberated from his bondage.

4. Although the Bible never questions the holiness and the sinlessness of God, it does not treat the problem of the ultimate origin of sin. By this we mean that Scripture does not explicitly concern itself with the problem of the relationship between God's omnipotence and man's freedom.

5. The pre-Augustinian Fathers emphasized *liberum arbitrium*. This stress was not motivated by humanistic tendencies or by any undervaluation of the necessity of grace, but by the intention to make man alone—and not God—responsible for sin.

6. In his defense of the necessity of the grace of Christ for every salutary act—even for the beginning of salvation—against the (Semi-) Pelagians, Augustine never denied man's natural freedom. It is true that man lost the *libertas* from sin through the fall of Adam and therefore needs grace to free him once more. Liberating grace does not, however, exclude *liberum arbitrium*, as Augustine emphasizes in *De gratia et libero arbitrio*.

7. "Voluntary" (*voluntarie, volens*) was almost always identified with

367

"free" (*libere*) by Augustine and the theological tradition which followed him. Thomas Aquinas is one of the exceptions.

8. Augustine's concept of *servum arbitrium* represents a faithful interpretation of the biblical truth which we have formulated above in conclusion 3.

9. The basic elements of Augustine's doctrine of *servum arbitrium* were accepted by the Second Synod of Orange (529 A.D.) and, through the approbation of various popes and the Council of Trent, were elevated to the status of dogmas of the Church. Through circumstances still not yet explained, the canons of the Second Synod of Orange were unknown during the Middle Ages from the 10th until the 16th century.

10. The early Scholastics were, in general, faithful to the heritage of Augustine. This faithfulness was reflected also in their fundamental acceptance of Augustine's doctrine of grace and free will.

11. Thomas Aquinas, at the outset of his theological career, was not aware of the Augustinian doctrine of grace in its mature form. As soon as he became aware of it, however, he embraced it in its entirety, making only minor modifications.

12. Influential late-Scholastics of the Ockham-Biel school had little appreciation of Augustine's radical biblical doctrine of grace. Some of these theologians taught a doctrine of preparation for justification by man's purely natural powers of reason and free will apart from the illuminating and liberating grace of Christ, a doctrine which one can designate as Neo-Semipelagianism. In fairness to these theologians, it must be pointed out that they were unaware that their teaching in this respect had previously been condemned by Church synods. See conclusion 9.

13. It was in the Ockham-Biel school that Luther received his theological formation. The young Luther was, like Gabriel Biel, a theologian whose works he certainly read, a Neo-Semipelagian. Through his deep study of Scripture and of the works of Augustine, Luther came to recognize that his own position was heretical. He therefore began to combat the false theology which he had learned from his "Catholic" teachers.

14. Luther's first reaction against Neo-Semipelagianism was as energetic as it was justified. It is quite correct to designate his basic Reformation transformation as a movement from an un-Catholic outlook to a Catholic one. Despite some ambiguities, Luther's early attacks on free

will should be interpreted as a defense of the Augustinian doctrine of the powerlessness of free will without grace in matters of salvation.

15. In the *Assertio omnium articulorum* (1520) Luther, who began his campaign against free will on biblical grounds, began to rely also on a necessitarian argument.

16. In his rejection of Luther's doctrine of "mere necessity" in his works, *De libero arbitrio* and *Hyperaspistes,* Erasmus did not do justice to the traditional Catholic doctrine. Even though he recognized both free will and the necessity of grace, he was nevertheless unable to understand why Augustine opposed so vigorously the thesis that the beginning of salvation could be attributed to fallen man's free will. Moreover, he was not aware of the fact that he was not dealing simply with an opinion of Augustine, but with the authentic teaching of the Church. Cf. conclusion 9.

17. In his answer to Erasmus, *De servo arbitrio,* in which Luther enunciated what was for him "the essential issue," the Reformer employed two basic arguments: one necessitarian, the other biblical.

18. A careful analysis of the necessitarian argument, which is made more complicated by Luther's peculiar understanding of the distinction between necessity of consequence and necessity of the thing consequent, shows that Luther's assertion of the necessity of all events *need not* be understood deterministically, to the exclusion of *liberum arbitrium,* but ought to be understood as the expression of Luther's belief in God's providence. The necessitarian argument, however, leads Luther into a theological predicament, since it makes it impossible for him to explain in a convincing way that man alone—and not God—is the cause of sin. It furthermore leaves no place in his theology for a personal decision of faith.

19. In Luther's biblical argument one sees the realization and the expression of his central Reformation concern. In contrast to his necessitarian argument, this one is fully Catholic and fully Evangelical.

20. The biblical concept of man's slavery to sin, as found in Luther's main work, has been accepted by the Lutheran confessional writings as well as by most contemporary Protestant theologians, to the exclusion of the necessitarian argument. Between *this* concept of *servum arbitrium* and the doctrine of the Roman Catholic Church there is no difference which is capable of justifying the separation of the Churches.

Select Bibliography

I. Sources and Translations

Alexander of Hales. *Summa Theologica.* 2 vols. Quaracchi, 1924-48.

Alfons de Castro. *Adversus omnes haereses libri XIV.* Coloniae, 1549.

Anselm of Canterbury. *De veritate.* In: PL 158.

────── *De libertate arbitrii.* In: PL 158.

────── *De concordia praescientiae et praedestinationis nec non gratiae Dei cum libero arbitrio.* In: PL 158.

Aristotle. *Metaphysics.* Loeb Classical Library, Nr. 271, 4th ed. London-Cambridge, Mass., 1956.

Augustine. *Obras de San Augustin.* Edicion en latin y castellano. 18 vols. Biblioteca de autores Christianos. Madrid, 1949ff.

Die Bekenntnisschriften der Evangelisch-Lutherischen Kirche, 4th ed. Göttingen, 1959.

Bernard of Clairvaux. *De gratia et libero arbitrio.* In: *Sancti Bernardi Opera.* Vol. III, *Tractatus et Opuscula,* ed. Cistercienses: J. Leclercq et al. Rome, 1963.

Biel, Gabriel. *Lectura super canone misse in alma universitate Tuwingensi ordinarie lecta.* Rutlingensis, 1488.

────── *Epithoma expositionis Canonis Misse.* Tübingen, 1499.

────── *Gabrielis Biel Canonis Misse Expositio,* ed. H. Oberman and W. Courtenay. 4 vols. Wiesbaden, 1963-1967.

Boethius. *De consolatione philosophiae.* In: PL 63.

Bonaventure. *Opera Omnia.* 10 vols. Quaracchi, 1882-1902.

The Book of Concord. The Confessions of the Evangelical Lutheran Church, tr. and ed. T. Tappert. St. Louis, 1959.

Bradwardine, Thomas. *De causa Dei contra Pelagium et de virtute causarum, libri tres.* London, 1618; reprinted Frankfurt, 1964.

Concilii Tridentini Actorum Tomus 5. Pars altera: Acta post sessionem tertiam usque ad Concilium Bononiam translatum, ed. S. Ehses. Freiburg, 1911.

Duns Scotus, John. *Opera Omnia.* Vatican City, 1950ff.

Eck, John. *Chrysopassus praedestinationis.* n. p., 1514.

Erasmus, Desiderius. *Desiderii Erasmi Roterodami Opera Omnia,* ed. J. Clericus. Lugduni Batavorum, 1703-1706.

Erasmus, Desiderius. *Opus Epistolarum,* ed. P. S. and H. M. Allen. Oxford, 1906-1947.

──── *De libero arbitrio diatribe sive collatio,* ed. J. von Walter. *Quellenschriften zur Geschichte des Protestantismus.* No. 8. Leipzig, 1910; 2nd ed., 1935.

──── *Vom freien Willen,* verdeutscht von O. Schumacher, 2nd ed. Göttingen, 1956.

──── *Erasme de Rotterdam: Essai sur le Libre Arbitre,* tr. P. Mesnard. Paris-Alger, 1945.

──── *Erasmus-Luther: Discourse on Free Will,* tr. and ed. E. F. Winter. New York, 1961.

──── *Erasmus von Rotterdam: Auswahl und Einleitung* by Fr. Heer. Frankfurt-Hamburg, 1962.

Determinatio theologicae facultatis Parisiensis super doctrina Lutheriana hactenus per eam visa. Wittembergae, 1521.

Lombard, Peter. *Libri IV Sententiarum.* Quaracchi, 1916.

Luther, Martin. *D. Martin Luthers Werke.* Kritische Gesamtausgabe. Weimar, 1883ff.

──── *Luthers Werke in Auswahl,* ed. O. Clemen, et al. 8 vols. Bonn-Berlin, 1912-56.

──── *Luther's Works: American Edition,* ed. J. Pelikan and H. Lehmann. St. Louis-Philadelphia, 1955ff.

──── *Dokumente zu Luthers Entwicklung (bis 1519),* ed. O. Scheel, 2nd ed. Tübingen, 1929.

──── *Vom unfreien Willen,* übersetzt v. O. Scheel. In: Ergänzungsband 2 der *Berliner Laienausgabe.* Leipzig, 1905.

──── *Vom unfreien Willen,* Neue Überarbeitung der Übersetzung von Justus Jonas nach dem lateinischen Original mit Einleitung und Erläuterungen v. Fr. W. Schmidt. In: M. Luther, *Ausgewählte Werke,* vol. 5, ed. H. Borcherdt. München, 1923.

──── *Vom unfreien Willen.* Nach der Übersetzung v. Justus Jonas herausgegeben und mit einem Nachwort versehen von Fr. Gogarten. München, 1924.

──── *Vom unfreien Willen.* Verdeutscht v. O. Schumacher. Göttingen, 1937.

──── *Dass der freie Wille nichts sei, Antwort D. Martin Luthers an Erasmus von Rotterdam.* Vol. 1 der Ergänzungsreihe von M. Luther, *Augsewählte Werke,* hrsg. v. H. H. Borcherdt u. Georg Merz, neu übersetzt v. B. Jordahn mit einer Einführung v. H. J. Iwand. München, 1954; reprint, 1962.

──── *Vom unfreien Willen* (Teilübersetzung). In: *Luther Deutsch: Die Werke Martin Luthers in neuer Auswahl fur die Gegenwart.* Vol. 3, hrsg. v. K. Aland. Stuttgart-Göttingen, 1961.

──── *Traité du serf arbitre,* tr. D. de Rougemont. Paris, 1936.

──── *On the Bondage of the Will,* tr. J. I. Packer and O. R. Johnston. London, 1957.

Luther, Martin. *Lectures on Romans,* tr. and ed. W. Pauck. In: *Library of Christian Classics.* Vol. XV. Philadelphia, 1961.

Suarez, Francisco de. *Opera Omnia.* Paris, 1856ff.

Thomas Aquinas. *Summa contra Gentiles,* ed. Leonina manualis. Roma, 1934.

———— *Summa Theologiae.* Taurini-Romae, 1948.

———— *Quaestiones Disputatae.* 2 vols., 9th ed. Taurini-Romae, 1953.

———— *Quaestiones Quodlibetales.* 9th ed. Taurini, 1956.

———— *Super Evangelium S. Matthaei Lectura.* 5th ed. Taurini-Romae, 1951.

———— *Super Evangelium S. Ioannis Lectura.* 5th ed. Taurini-Romae, 1952.

————*Super Epistolas S. Pauli Lectura.* 2 vols., 8th ed. Taurini-Romae, 1953.

———— *Die menschliche Willensfreiheit.* Texte zur thomistischen Freiheitslehre ausgewählt und mit einer Einleitung versehen v. G. Siewerth. Düsseldorf, 1954.

Valla, Laurentius. *Opera Omnia.* Basel, 1543.

———— *Laurentii Vallensis Oratoris Clarissimi de libero arbitrio et providencia divina.* Strasbourg, n.d. (probably 1482).

II. Secondary Sources

Adam, A. "Der Herkunft des Lutherwortes vom menschlichen Willen als Reittier Gottes," in: LuJ (1962), 25-34.

Adler, M. J., director. *The Idea of Freedom: A dialectical examination of the conceptions of freedom,* for The Institute for Philosophical Research. 2 vols. New York, 1958-1961.

Aland, K. *Hilfsbuch zum Lutherstudium.* 2nd ed. Gütersloh, 1957.

Alanen, Y. "Das Wahrheitsproblem in der Bibel und in der griechischen Philosophie," KuD 3 (1957), 230-239.

Albrecht, A. "Neuere katholische Versuche zur Würdigung der theologischen Anliegen Luthers," *Una Sancta,* 18 (1963), 174-183.

d'Alès, A. "Providence," *Dictionnaire Apologetique,* 4, 433-474.

Althaus, P. *The Theology of Martin Luther,* tr. R. Schultz. Philadelphia, 1966.

———— *Die Theologie Martin Luthers,* Gütersloh, 1962.

Altmann, P. *Erwählungstheologie und Universalismus im Alten Testament.* Beihefte zur Zeitschr. f. die Alttestamentliche Wissenschaft, hrsg. v. Georg Fohrer, Nr. 92. Berlin, 1964.

Amand, D. *Fatalisme et liberté dans l'antiquité grecque.* Louvain, 1945.

Amann, E. "Occam: I. Vie; II. Oeuvres," DTC, 11, 864-876.

———— "Semi-pélagiens," DTC, 14, 1796-1850.

Antoniotti, L.-M. "Prédestination, Grâce et Libérté," *Rev. Thomiste,* XLVI (1966), 437-456.

Auer, J. *Die Entwicklung der Gnadenlehre in der Hochscholastik.* 2 vols. Freiburg, 1942 and 1951.

——— "Gnade: III. Geschichte der Gnadenlehre," LThK, 4, 984-991.

——— "Prädestination: I. Geschichtlich," LThK, 8, 662-665.

Bachelet, F. Le. "Baius," DTC, 2, esp. 64-111.

Bainton, R. H. *The Reformation of the Sixteenth Century,* 5th ed. Boston, 1960.

——— *Here I Stand: A Life of Martin Luther,* 8th ed. New York, 1961.

——— *Studies on the Reformation,* London, 1964.

Bandt, H. *Luthers Lehre vom verborgenen Gott.* Eine Untersuchung zu dem offenbarungsgeschichtlichen Ansatz seiner Theologie. In: *Theologische Arbeiten,* hrsg. v. H. Urner, Bd. VIII. Berlin, 1958.

——— "Verborgenheit Gottes," RGG, 6, 1256-1260.

Bardy, G. "Jean Chrysostome," DTC, 8, 660-690.

——— *La conversion au christianisme.* In: *Theologie.* No. 15. Paris, 1949.

Barth, H. *Die Freiheit der Entscheidung im Denken Augustins.* Basel, 1935; new ed. 1965.

Barth, K. *Church Dogmatics,* tr. G. Bromiley. IV/2. Edinburgh, 1958.

Bauer, K. "Die Heidelberger Disputation Luthers," *Zeitschr. f. Kirchengesch.,* XXI (1901), 233-268.

Baumgartner, Ch. *La Grâce du Christ.* Tournai, 1963.

Bellucci, D. "Faith and Justification in the Early Works of Luther," *Unitas,* XVII, n. 2 (1965), 113-133.

Bertram, G. "Synergos," ThW 7, 869-875.

Bläser, P. "Gesetz und Evangelium," *Catholica,* XIV (1960), 1-23.

——— "Gesetzesgerechtigkeit," LThK, 4, 829f.

Boehmer, H. *Luther im Lichte der neueren Forschung,* 4th ed. Leipzig-Berlin, 1917.

——— *Martin Luther: Road to Reformation,* tr. J. W. Doberstein and T. Tappert, 3rd ed. New York, 1960.

Boisset, J. *Erasme et Luther: libre ou serf-arbitre?* Paris, 1962.

Bonhoeffer, Thomas. *Die Gotteslehre des Thomas von Aquin als Sprachproblem.* Tübingen, 1961.

Bornkamm, G. *Das urchristliche Verständnis von der Freiheit.* Neckauer Hefte, Nr. 8. Heidelberg, 1961.

——— "Die christliche Freiheit." In: *Das Ende des Gesetzes.* Vol. I. München, 1961, pp. 133-138.

Bornkamm, H. "Der verborgene und der offenbare Gott." In: *Theologie und Verkündigung.* No. 2. Lüneburg, 1946.

——— "Probleme der Lutherbiographie." In: *Lutherforschung Heute.* Referate und Berichte des 1. Internationalen Lutherforschungskongresses, Aarhus, 18-23 August, 1956, hrsg. v. V. Vajta. Berlin, 1958.

Bornkamm, H. "Luther und Erasmus." In: *Das Jahrhundert der Reformation*. Göttingen, 1961, pp. 36-55.

————— "Faith and Reason in the thought of Erasmus and Luther." In: *Religion and Culture: Essays in Honor of Paul Tillich,* ed. W. Leibrecht. New York, 1959.

————— *The Heart of Reformation Faith,* tr. J. Doberstein. New York, 1965.

Bouché, J. "Fatalisme," DTC, 5, 2095-2098.

Bouillard, H. *Conversion et grâce chez S. Thomas d'Aquin.* Paris, 1944.

Bourke, V. *Will in Western Thought: An Historico-Critical Study.* New York, 1964.

Bouyer, L. *The Spirit and Forms of Protestantism,* tr. A. V. Littledale. Westminster, Md., 1961.

————— *Erasmus and the Humanist Experiment,* tr. F. X. Murphy. Westminster, Md., 1959.

Brandenburg, A. "Hinweise zur Methodik der Arbeit an der Luthertheologie." In: *Begegnung der Christen. Festschr. f. O. Karrer,* hrsg. v. M. Roesle und O. Cullmann. Frankfurt-Stuttgart, 1959, pp. 496-500.

————— "Protestantismus in katholischer Sicht," *Evangelisches Kirchenlexicon.* Vol. III. Göttingen, 1960, 360-372.

————— *Gericht und Evangelium: Zur Worttheologie in Luthers Erster Psalmenvorlesung.* Konfessionskundliche u. Kontroverstheologische Studien, hrsg. v. J.-A. Möhler Institut. Vol. 4. Paderborn, 1960.

————— "Thomas und Luther im Gespräch," *Catholica* XVI (1962), 77ff.

Brown, R. McA. *The Spirit of Protestantism.* New York, 1961.

Brunner, P. *Luther und die Welt des 20 Jahrhunderts.* Göttingen, 1961.

————— Die Rechtfertigungslehre des Konzils von Trient." In: *Pro Veritate, Festgabe f. Erzb. L. Jaeger und Bischof W. Stählin,* hrsg. v. E. Schlink und Bischof H. Volk. Münster-Kassel, 1963, pp. 59-96.

Bultmann, R. *Primitive Christianity in its Contemporary Setting,* tr. R. Fuller, 4th printing. New York: Meridian, 1956.

————— *Theology of the New Testament,* tr. K. Grobel. 2 vols. New York, 1951-55.

————— *History and Eschatology.* New York: Harper Torch Book, 1962.

Burrows, M. *An Outline of Biblical Theology.* Philadelphia, 1946.

Callus, D. *The Condemnation of St. Thomas at Oxford.* Aquinas Paper No. 5, 2nd ed. London, 1955.

Chéné, J. "Que signifiaient 'initium fidei' et 'affectus credulitatis' pour les semipélagiens?," *Recherches de science religieuse,* 35 (1948), 566-588.

————— *La Théologie de Saint Augustin: Grâce et Prédestination.* Lyon, 1961.

Clark, Francis. *Eucharistic Sacrifice and the Reformation.* London-Westminster, Md., 1960.

———— "A New Appraisal of Late-Medieval Theology," In: *Gregorianum,* XLVI (1965), 733-765.

Clark, Mary T. *Augustine, Philosopher of Freedom: A Study in Comparative Philosophy.* New York-Tournai-Paris-Rome, 1958.

Cristiani, L. "Réforme," In: *Dict. apologetique,* 4, 582-622.

———— "Réforme," DTC, 13, 2020-2097.

Daniel-Rops, H. *The Protestant Reformation,* tr. A. Butler, Vol. I. New York, 1963.

Denifle, H. *Luther und Luthertum in der ersten Entwicklung. Quellenmässig dargestellt.* Mainz, 1904-06.

Dettloff, W. *Die Lehre von der Acceptatio Divina bei Johannes Duns Scotus mit besonderer Berücksichtigung der Rechtfertigungslehre.* Werl, 1954.

———— *Die Entwicklung der Akzeptations- und Verdienstlehre von Duns Scotus bis Luther.* Münster, 1964.

Dillenberger, J. and Welch, C. *Protestant Christianity.* New York, 1958.

Dinkler, E. "Prädestination bei Paulus. Exegetische Bemerkungen zum Römerbrief." In: *Festschrift für G. Dehn.* Neukirchen, 1957, pp. 81-102.

Dion, H. -M. "La Prédestination chez Saint Paul," *Recherches de Science Religieuse,* LII (1965), 5-43.

Dodd, C. H. *The Epistle of Paul to the Romans.* 2nd ed. London-Glasgow, 1960.

Doerne, M. "Gottes Ehre am gebundenen Willen. Evangelische Grundlagen und theologische Spitzensätze in De servo arbitrio." In: *Luther-Jahrbuch,* 1938, pp. 45-92.

Dolan, J. P. Introductory Essay to *Erasmus: Handbook of the Militant Christian.* Notre Dame, 1962, pp. 7-58.

———— *History of the Reformation: A Conciliatory Assessment of Opposite Views.* New York-Tournai-Paris-Rome, 1965.

Dupont, J. *Gnosis: La connaissance religieuse dans les Épîtres de Saint Paul.* Louvain-Paris, 1949.

Ebeling, G. "Luther II. Theologie," RGG, 4, 495-516.

———— *Luther: Einführung in sein Denken.* Tübingen, 1964.

Eichrodt, W. "Vorsehungsglaube und Theodizee im Alten Testament." In: *Festschrift O. Procksch zum 60. Geburtstag.* Leipzig, 1934, pp. 45-70.

———— *Theology of the Old Testament,* tr. J. Baker. Vol. II. Philadelphia, 1967.

Elert, W. *Morphologie des Luthertums.* 2 vols., corrected reprint of 1st ed. München, 1958; tr. W. Hansen, *The Structure of Lutheranism.* St. Louis, 1962.

Erikstein, E. *Luthers Praedestinationslehre geschichtlich dargestellt bis einschliesslich "De servo arbitrio."* Doctoral dissertation, Göttingen University Faculty of Theology. Typed. Oslo, 1957.

Fairweather, W. "Freewill and Foreordination: Development of Doctrine in the Apocryphal Period." In: *A Dictionary of the Bible,* ed. J. Hastings, 6th impression. Extra volume. Edinburgh, 1927, pp. 272-308.

Farrelly, M. J. *Predestination, Grace and Free Will.* Westminster, Md., 1964.

Feckes, C. *Die Rechtfertigungslehre des Gabriel Biel und ihre Stellung innerhalb der nominalistischen Schule.* Münsterische Beiträge zur Theologie. H. 7. Münster, 1925.

———— "Die Stellung der nominalistischen Schule zur aktuellen Gnade." In: *Römische Quartalschrift* XXXII (1924), 157-165.

Féret, H.-M. "Érasme," *Catholicisme. Hier-Aujourd'hui-Demain.* Paris, 1948ff. Vol. 4, pp. 269-375.

Ferguson, J. *Pelagius.* Cambridge, 1956.

Fischer, R. H. "A reasonable Luther." In: *Reformation Studies. Essays in Honor of Roland H. Bainton,* ed. F. H. Littell. Richmond, 1962.

Flick, M. "Semipelagianismus," LThK, 9, 650ff.

Flitner, A. *Erasmus im Urteil seiner Nachwelt: Das literarische Erasmusbild von Beatus Rhenanus bis zu Jean Leclerc.* Tübingen, 1952.

Foerster, W. "Diabolos: D. The NT view of Satan," TDNT 2, 79ff.

Forget, J. "Jérome (Saint)," DTC, 8, 894-983.

Fortman, E. D., ed. *The Theology of Man and Grace: Commentary.* Milwaukee, 1966.

Fransen, P. "Orange," LThK, 11, 1188ff.

———— "The Authority of the Councils." In: *Problems of Authority,* ed. J. M. Todd. Baltimore-London, 1962, pp. 43-78.

———— *Divine Grace and Man,* tr. G. Dupont. Revised ed. New York, 1965.

———— "How Should We Teach the Treatise on Grace?" In: *Apostolic Renewal in the Seminary in the Light of Vatican Council II,* ed. J. Keller and R. Armstrong. New York, 1965, pp. 139-163.

Freitag, A. "Einleitung zu Luthers De servo arbitrio." In: WA 18 (1908), pp. 551-597.

Fritz, G. "Orange (Deuxième Concile d')," DTC, 11, 1087-1103.

Fuchs, E. "Freiheit: I. Im NT," RGG 2, 1100-1104.

Garrigou-Lagrange, R. *De Deo Uno.* Paris, 1938.

———— *God: His Existence and His Nature,* tr. B. Rose. 6th ed. Vol. II. St. Louis, 1955.

———— *Predestination,* tr. B. Rose. 5th ed. St. Louis-London, 1953.

Gasquet, F. A. *The Eve of the Reformation.* London, 1913.

Gelin, A. *The Key Concepts of the Old Testament,* tr. G. Lamb. New York, 1963.

Gerest, R.-C. "Du Serf-Arbitre à la Liberté du Chretien: Les cheminements de Martin Luther." *In Lumière et Vie,* XII (1963), 75-120.

Gerrish, B. A. *Grace and Reason: A Study in the Theology of Luther.* Oxford, 1962.

Gilson, É. *Introduction à l'étude de Saint Augustin.* Paris, 1943.

Gnilka, J. *Die Verstockung Israels: Isaias 6, 9-10 in der Theologie der Synoptiker.* Studien zum Alten und Neuen Testament. H. III. München, 1961.

———— "Verstocktheit . . . in der Schrift," LThK, 10, 740f.

Godet, P. "Érasme," DTC 5, 388-397.

Gössmann, E. *Metaphysik und Heilsgeschichte: Eine theologische Untersuchung der Summa Halensis (Alexander von Hales).* Mitteilungen des Grabmann Instituts der Univ. München, hrsg. v. M. Schmaus. München, 1964.

Gogarten, F. "Nachwort" to his *Neuausgabe von Justus Jonas' Übersetzung von De servo arbitrio.* München, 1924. Reprinted in *Theologische Bücherei.* Bd. 17, Teil II. München, 1963, pp. 191-218.

———— "Sittlichkeit und Glaube in Luthers Schrift 'De servo arbitrio.'" In: *Zeitschrift für Theologie und Kirche,* XLVII/2 (1950), 227-264.

Grabmann, M. "Das Weiterleben und Weiterwirken des moraltheologischen Schrifttums des hl. Thomas von Aquin im Mittelalter." In: *Aus Theologie und Philosophie: Festchr, f. F. Tillmann.* Düsseldorf, 1950, pp. 64-83.

———— *Die Geschichte der katholischen Theologie seit dem Ausgang der Väterzeit,* 2nd ed. Darmstadt, 1961.

Grane, L. *Contra Gabrielem. Luthers Auseinandersetzung mit Gabriel Biel in der Disputatio Contra Scholasticam Theologiam 1517,* übers v. E. Pump, *Acta Theologica Danica.* Vol. IV. Gyldendal, 1962.

Greving, J. *Johann Eck als junger Gelehrter: Eine literar-und dogmengeschichtliche Untersuchung über seinen Chrysopassus Praedestinationis aus dem Jahr 1514.* Reformationsgeschichtliche Studien und Texte. H. 1. Münster,1906.

Grisar, H. *Luther.* 3. Bde. Freiburg, 1911/12.

Grislis, E. "Martin Luther's View of the Hidden God," *McCormick Quarterly,* XXI (1967), pp. 81-94.

Grundmann. W. "Agathos," TDNT 1, 10-17. "Harmartanō, F. Sin in the NT." TDNT 1, 302-320. "Anagkazō," TDNT 1, 344-347. "Kakos," TDNT 3, 469-481.

Haikola, L. *Studien zu Luther und zum Luthertum.* Uppsala-Wiesbaden, 1958.

Hamel, A. *Der junge Luther und Augustin.* 2 Bde. Gütersloh, 1934/5.

Hedde, R. and Amann, E. "Pélagianisme," DTC, 12, 675-715.

Heim, K. *Das Wesen der Gnade und ihr Verhältnis zu den natürlichen Funktionen des Menschen bei Alexander Halesius.* Leipzig, 1907.

Heynck, V. "Der Anteil des Konzilstheologen Andreas de Vega O.F.M.

an dem ersten amtlichen Entwurf des trienter Rechtfertigungsde-
kretes," *Franziskanische Studien,* XXXIII (1951), 49-81.

Heinisch, P. *Theology of the Old Testament,* tr. W. Heidt. Collegeville,
1955.

Hennig, G. *Cajetan und Luther.* Ein historischer Beitrag zur Begegnung
von Thomismus und Reformation. Stuttgart, 1966.

Hermann, R. "Zu Luthers Lehre vom unfreien Willen," *Greifswalder
Studien zur Lutherforschung und neuzeitlichen Geisteschichte.* H. 4.
Berlin, 1931, pp. 17-38.

——— "'Willensfreiheit und gute Werke im Sinne der Reformation."
In: *Gesammelte Studien zur Theologie Luthers und der Reformation.*
Göttingen, 1960, pp. 44-76.

——— *Luthers These "Gerecht und Sünder Zugleich."* 2nd ed. Darmstadt, 1960.

——— *Von der Klarheit der heiligen Schrift: Untersuchungen und
Erörterungen über Luthers Lehre von der Schrift in De servo arbitrio.* Berlin, 1958.

Hesse, F. *Das Verstockungsproblem im Alten Testament. Eine Fröm-
migkeitsgeschichtliche Untersuchung.* Beihefte zur Zeitschrift für die
alttestamentliche Wissenschaft. H. 74. Berlin, 1955.

Hirsch, E. *Lutherstudien.* 2 Bde. Gütersloh, 1954.

Holl, K. *Gesammelte Aufsätze zur Kirchengeschichte.* Bd. I: Luther.
7th ed. Tübingen, 1948.

——— "Gogartens Lutherauffassung. Eine Erwiderung," *Die christliche
Welt,* XXXVIII (1924), 307-314. Reprinted in: *Gesammelte Aufsätze.* Bd III: Der Westen. Tübingen, 1928, pp. 244ff.

Huenermann, F. *Wesen und Notwendigkeit der aktuellen Gnade nach
dem Konzil von Trent.* Forschungen zur christlichen Literatur-und
Dogmengeschichte, hrsg. v. A. Ehrhard and J. P. Kirsch. T. XV, fasc.
4. Paderborn, 1926.

Huizinga, J. *Erasmus and the Age of Reformation,* tr. F. Hopman. New
York, 1957.

Humbertclaude, H. *Érasme et Luther: Leur Polémique sur le Libre Arbitre. Paris,* 1909.

Imbart de la Tour, P., *Les Origines de la Réforme.* Vol. III. Paris, 1914.

Iserloh, E. *Gnade und Eucharistie in der philosophischen Theologie des
Wilhelm von Ockham.* Wiesbaden, 1956.

Iwand, H. J. *Rechtfertigungslehre und Christusglaube: Eine Untersuchung zur Systematik der Rechtfertigungslehre Luthers in ihren Anfän-
gen.* Leipzig, 1930. Reprinted photo-mechanically. Darmstadt, 1961.

——— "Die Freiheit des Christen und die Unfreiheit des Willens." In:
Solange es heute heisst, Festgabe f. R. Hermann. Berlin, 1957, pp.
132-146. Reprinted in: *Um den rechten Glauben: Gesammelte Aufsätze.* Theologische Bücherei, 9. München, 1959, pp. 247-268.

——— "Theologische Einführung und Anmerkungen (in Verbindung
mit B. Jordahn) zu Luthers Schrift Dass der frei Wille nichts sei."

Ergänzungsband I zur Münchener Lutherausgabe. München, 1954, pp. 253-315.

Jedin, H. *Des Johannes Cochlaeus Streitschrift De libero arbitrio hominis 1525.* Breslauer Studien zur historischen Theologie, 9. Breslau. 1927.

—— *Girolamo Seripando.* Bd. I. Würzburg, 1937.

—— *A History of the Council of Trent,* tr. E. Graf. 2 vols. St. Louis, 1957-61.

—— "Die Deutschen am Trienter Konzil 1551/52," *Hist. Zeitschr.,* CLXXXVIII (1959), 1-16.

—— "The Council of Trent and Reunion: Historical Notes," *The Heythrop Journal,* III (1962), 3-14.

—— *Der Abschluss des Trienter Konzils 1562/63. Ein Rückblick nach vier Jahrunderten.* Katholisches Leben und Kämpfen im Zeitalter der Glaubensspaltung. Vereinsschriften der Gesellschaft zur Herausgabe des Corpus Catholicorum. Nr. 21. Münster, 1963.

—— "Wo sah die vortridentinische Kirche die Lehrdifferenzen mit Luther?" *Catholica* XXI (1967), pp. 85-100.

Jörgensen, A. Th. "Was verstand man in der Reformationszeit unter Pelagianismus?," *Theol. Studien und Kritiken,* LXXXIII (1910), 63-82.

Joest, W. *Gesetz und Freiheit: Das Problem des tertius usus legis bei Luther und die neutestamentliche Parainese.* 3rd ed. Göttingen, 1961.

—— "Synergismus," RGG, 6, 561f.

Johnston, O. R. (see Packer).

Jonas, H. *Augustinus und das paulinische Freiheitsproblem: Ein philosophischer Beitrag zur Genesis der christlich-abendländischen Freiheitsidee.* Forschungen zur Religion u. Literatur des Alten und Neuen Testamentes, hrsg. R. Bultmann u. H. Gunkel. N.F., H. 27. Göttingen, 1930. New ed. Göttingen, 1965.

Jongh, H. de. "La faculté de théologie de l'université de Louvain au XV⁰ siècle et au commencement du XVI⁰ siècle," *Rev. d'Histoire Eccl.,* XI (1910), 263-318.

—— *L'ancienne faculté de théologie de Louvain au première siècle de son existence (1432-1540).* Louvain, 1911.

Jundt, A. Foreword to the French tr. of *De servo arbitrio: Traité du Serf Arbitre,* tr. D. de Rougemont. Paris, 1936.

Jungmann, J. *The Mass of the Roman Rite,* 2 vols., tr. F. Brunner. New York, 1951-55.

Kähler, E. *Karlstadt und Augustin: Der Kommentar des Andreas Bodenstein von Karlstadt zu Augustins Schrift De Spiritu et Littera.* Einführung u. Text. Halle (Saale), 1952.

Kattenbusch, F. *Luthers Lehre vom unfreien Willen und von der Prädestination nach ihren Entstehungsgründen Untersucht.* Göttingen, 1875.

Kattenbusch, F. "Deus absconditus bei Luther." In: *Festgabe f. J. Kaftan.* Tübingen, 1920, pp. 170-214.

Kelly, J. N. D. *Early Christian Doctrines.* 2nd ed. New York, 1960.

Kinder, E. *Die Erbsünde.* Stuttgart, 1959.

Kittel, G. "Hypakoē," TDNT 1, 224f.

Köberle, J. *Sünde und Gnade im religiösen Leben des Volkes Israel bis auf Christum.* München, 1905.

Kohls, E. W. *Die Theologie des Erasmus,* 2 vols. Basel, 1966.

Krodel, G. "Luther, Erasmus and Henry VIII," *Archiv f. Reformationsgesch.,* LIII (1962), 60-78.

Köstlin, J. "Luthers Sätze vom freien Willen in der Heidelberger Disputation vom Jahre 1518." In: *Zeitschrift für Kirchengesch.,* XXI (1901), 517-523.

Kramm, H. H. *The Theology of Martin Luther.* London, 1947.

Küng, H. *Justification. The Doctrine of Karl Barth and a Catholic Reflection,* tr. T. Collins, E. Tolk, D. Granskou. New York, 1964.

Kuss, O. *Der Römerbrief: Übersetzt und Erklärt.* 2 Lieferungen. Regensburg, 1957-59.

Laemmer, H. *Die vortridentinische katholische Theologie des Reformationszeitalters.* Berlin, 1858.

Lammers, H. *Luthers Anschauung vom Willen.* Berlin, 1935.

Landgraf, A. M. *Dogmengeschichte der Frühscholastik.* Bd. I/1, Regensburg, 1952.

Lau, F. *Luther,* tr. R. H. Fischer. London, 1963.

Leff, G. *Bradwardine and the Pelagians.* Cambridge, England, 1957.

Lindhagen, C. *The Servant Motif in the Old Testament: A Preliminary Study to the "Ebed-Yahweh Problem" in Deutero-Isaiah.* Uppsala, 1950.

Link, W. *Das Ringen Luthers um die Freiheit der Theologie von der Philosophie.* 2nd ed. München, 1955.

Löfgren, D. *Die Theologie der Schöpfung bei Luther.* Forschungen zur Kirchen- und Dogmengeschichte. Bd 10. Göttingen, 1960.

Løgstrup, K. E. "Wille, Wahl und Freiheit." In: *Zeit und Geschichte: Dankesgabe an R. Bultmann zum 80 Geburstag,* hrsg. v. E. Dinkler. Tübingen, 1964, pp. 517-530.

Loewenich, W. v. "Gott und Mensch in humanistischer und reformatorischer Schau. Eine Einführung in Luthers Schrift De servo arbitrio." In: *Humanitas-Christianitas.* Gütersloh, 1948, pp. 65-101.

———— "Pharaos Verstockung. Zu Luthers Lehre von der Prädestination." In: *Viva Vox Evangelii: Festschr. für H. Meiser.* München, 1951, pp. 196ff. Reprinted in; *Von Augustin zu Luther.* Beiträge zur Kirchengeschichte. Witten (Ruhr), 1959, pp. 161-179.

———— *Luthers Theologia Crucis.* 4th ed. München, 1954.

———— "Zur Gnadenlehre bei Augustin und bei Luther." In: *Von Augustin zu Luther.* Witten (Ruhr), 1959, pp. 75-87.

———— *Luther und der Neuprotestantismus.* Witten, 1963.

Lohse, B. "Die Bedeutung Augustins für den jungen Luther," KuD, XI (1965), 116-135.

Loofs, F. "Der articulus stantis et cadentis ecclesiae," *Theologische Studien und Kritiken,* XC (1917), 323-400.

———— *Leitfaden zum Studium der Dogmengeschichte.* 1 and 2. Teil, 6. durchgesehene Aufl., hrsg. v. K. Aland. Tübingen, 1959.

Lortz, J. *Die Reformation in Deutschland,* 2 vols. 4th ed. Freiburg, 1962.

———— "Erasmus—kirchengeschichtlich." In: *Aus Theologie und Philosophie: Festschrift für F. Tillmann.* Düsseldorf, 1950, pp. 271-326.

Lucas, H. *The Renaissance and the Reformation,* 2nd ed. New York, 1960.

Lütkens, J. *Luthers Prädestinationslehre im Zusammenhange mit seiner Lehre vom freien Willen.* Diss. Dorpat, 1858.

Luthardt, C. E. *Die Lehre vom freien Willen und seinem Verhältnis zur Gnade in ihrer geschichtlichen Entwicklung dargestellt.* Leipzig, 1863.

Lyonnet, S. *Les Épitres de Saint Paul aux Galates et aux Romains.* 2nd ed. Paris, 1959.

———— "Saint Paul: Liberty and Law." In: *The Bridge.* A Yearbook of Judaeo-Christian Studies. New York, 1961. Summarized in: *Theology Digest,* 11 (1963), 12-18.

Mackinnon, James. *Luther and the Reformation.* 4 vols. London-New York, 1925-30.

Maurer, W. *Von der Freiheit eines Christenmenschen: Zwei Untersuchungen zu Luthers Reformationsschriften 1520/1521.* Göttingen, 1949.

McDonough, T. M. *The Law and the Gospel in Luther: A Study of Martin Luther's Confessional Writings.* Oxford, 1963.

McGiffert, A. C. *Protestant Thought Before Kant.* London, 1911; New York, 1962.

McSorley, H. J. "Luther und Thomas von Aquin über die Prädestination." In: *Oekumenica: Festschrift für E. Schlink zum 60. Geburtstag,* hrsg. v. R. Herrfahrdt und A. Gerwinat. Heidelberg, 1963, pp. 17-20.

———— "Was Gabriel Biel a Semipelagian?" in: *Wahrheit und Verkündigung.* Michael Schmaus zum 70. Geburtstag, ed. L. Scheffczyk, W. Dettloff, R. Heinzmann. München-Paderborn-Wien, 1967. Vol. II, pp. 1109-1120.

———— "Luther, Trent, Vatican I and II," *McCormick Quarterly,* XXI (1967), pp. 95-104.

Meersch, J. van der. "Grâce," DTC, 6, 1554-1689.

Mehl, O. J. "Erasmus contra Luther," *Luther-Jahrbuch,* XXIX (1962), 52-64.

Meissinger, K. A. *Erasmus von Rotterdam.* 2nd ed., Berlin, 1948.

———— *Der katholische Luther.* München, 1952.

———— *Luther: Die deutsche Tragödie 1521.* München, 1953.

Meyenfeldt, F. H. von. *Het Hart (Leb, Lebab) In Het Oude Testament*. Leiden, 1950.

Minges, P. *Die Gnadenlehre des Duns Scotus auf ihren angeblichen Pelagianismus und Semipelagianismus geprüft*. Münster, 1906.

——— J. *Duns Scoti doctrina philosophica et theologica*. 2 vols. Quaracchi, 1930.

Moreau, É. de. *Histoire de l'Église en Belgique (1378-1559)*. Vol. 4. Bruxelles, 1949.

——— "La crise religieuse du XVIᵉ siècle. Livre Premier: Luther et Lutheranisme." In: *Histoire de l'Église depuis les origines jusqu'à nos jours*, ed. A. Fliche and V. Martin. Vol. 16. Paris, 1950, pp. 11-163.

Most, G. *De gratia et praedestinatione*. Rome, 1963.

Mousnier, R. "Saint Bernard and Martin Luther," *American Benedictine Review*, XIV (1963), 448-462.

Müller, J. *Lutheri de praedestinatione et libero arbitrio doctrina*. Göttingen, 1832.

Müller, O. *Die Rechtfertigungslehre nominalistischen Reformationsgegner: Bartholmäus Arnoldi von Usingen, O.E.S.A. und Kaspar Schatzgeyer, O.F.M. über Erbsünde, erste Rechtfertigung und Taufe*. Breslauer Studien. Bd. 8. Breslau, 1940.

Niederwimmer, K. *Der Begriff der Freiheit im Neuen Testament*. Berlin, 1966.

Nygren, A. *Augustin und Luther: Zwei Studien über den Sinn der augustinischen Theologie*. Aufsätze u. Vorträge zur Theologie u. Religionswissenschaft. H. 3. Berlin, 1958.

Nygren, G. *Das Prädestinationsproblem in der Theologie Augustins*. Forschungen zur Kirchen und Dogmengeschichte. Bd. 5. Göttingen, 1956.

Obendiek, H. *Der Teufel bei Martin Luther*. Berlin, 1931.

Oberman, H. A. *Archbishop Thomas Bradwardine: A Fourteenth Century Augustinian*. Utrecht, 1958

——— "Reformation, Preaching, and Ex opere operato." In: *Christianity Divided: Protestant and Roman Catholic Theological Issues*, ed. D. J. Callahan, H. A. Oberman, and D. J. O'Hanlon. London-New York, 1961, pp. 223-239.

——— " 'Facienti quod in se est Deus non denegat gratiam,' Robert Holcot, O.P., and the Beginnings of Luther's Theology," *Harvard Theological Review*, LV (1962), 317-342.

——— *The Harvest of Medieval Theology: Gabriel Biel and Late Medieval Nominalism*. Cambridge, Mass., 1963.

——— "Das tridentinische Rechtfertigungsdekret im Lichte spätmittelalterlicher Theologie," *Zeitschr. f. Theol. u. Kirche*, LXI (1964), 251-282. Tr. "The Tridentine Doctrine on Justification in the Light of Late Medieval Theology," *Journal for Theology and the Church*, 3 (1967), 28-54.

——— "Duns Scotus, Nominalism, and the Council of Trent." In:

John Duns Scotus: 1265-1965, ed. J. K. Ryan and B. M. Bonansea. Washington, 1965, pp. 311-344.

——— *Forerunners of the Reformation: The Shape of Late Medieval Thought.* Illustrated by Key Documents. New York-Chicago-San Francisco, 1966.

Oeing-Hanhoff, L. "Zur thomistischen Freiheitslehre," *Scholastik,* XXXI (1956), 161-181.

Oelrich, K. H. *Der späte Erasmus und die Reformation.* Reformations-philosophische Studien und Texte. H. 86. Münster, 1961.

Packer, J. I. and Johnston, O. R. "Historical and Theological Introduction" to *The Bondage of the Will.* London, 1957, pp. 13-57.

Padberg, R. *Erasmus als Katechet.* Untersuchungen zur Theologie der Seelsorge. Bd. 9. Freiburg, 1956.

——— "Glaubenstheologie und Glaubensverkündigung bei Erasmus von Rotterdam: Dargestellt auf der Grundlage der Paraphrase zum Römerbrief." In: *Verkündigung und Glaube, Festgabe f. Franz X. Arnold,* hrsg. v. T. Filthaut and J. Jungmann. Freiburg, 1958, pp. 58-75.

Pannenberg, W. "Der Einfluss der Anfechtungserfahrung auf den Prädestinationsbegriff Luthers," KuD, III (1957), 109-139.

——— "Christlicher Glaube und menschliche Freiheit," KuD, IV (1968), 251-280.

——— "Prädestination: IV. Dogmatisch," RGG, 5, 487ff.

Paquier, J. "Luther," DTC, 9, 1146-1335.

Pauck, W. *The Heritage of the Reformation.* Glencoe, Illinois, 1950. Revised and enlarged edition, 1961.

Peisker, M. "Zum Problem von Luthers De servo arbitrio," *Theol. Studien u. Kritiken,* 98/99 (1926), 212-258.

Pelikan, J. *The Riddle of Roman Catholicism.* New York-Nashville, 1959.

Pesch, O. H. "Ein katholisches Anliegen an evangelische Darstellungen der Theologie Luthers," *Catholica,* XVI (1962), 304-316.

——— "Philosophie und Theologie der Freiheit bei Thomas von Aquin in quaest. disp. 6 de malo," *Münchener Theologische Zeitschr.,* XIII (1962), 1-25.

——— "Freiheitsbegriff und Freiheitslehre bei Thomas von Aquin und Luther," *Catholica,* XVII (1963), 197-244.

——— "Zum 'Gespräch zwischen Luther und Thomas'," *Catholica,* XVIII (1964), 27-47.

——— "Thomas von Aquin im Lichte evangelischer Fragen," *Catholica,* XX (1966), 54-78.

——— "Zur Frage nach Luthers reformatorischer Wende," *Catholica,* XX (1966), 216-246; 264-280.

——— *Die Theologie der Rechtfertigung bei Martin Luther und Thomas von Aquin.* Band 4, Walbergerger Studien der Albertus-Magnus-Akademie. Mainz, 1967.

Peters, A. *Glaube und Werk: Luthers Rechtfertigungslehre im Lichte der heiligen Schrift.* Arbeiten zur Geschichte und Theologie des Luthertums. Bd. 8. Berlin-Hamburg, 1962.

Pfürtner, S. *Luther and Aquinas on Salvation,* tr. E. Quinn. New York, 1965.

Piepkorn, A. C. "Grace," *Encyclopedia of the Lutheran Church,* ed. J. Bodensieck. Vol. II, 947-958. Minneapolis, 1965.

Pinomaa, L. "Unfreier Wille und Prädestination bei Luther," *Theol. Zeitschrift,* XIII (1957), 339-349.

———— *Sieg des Glaubens: Grundlinien der Theologie Luthers,* bearbeitet und hrsg. v. H. Beintker. Göttingen, 1964. Tr. *Faith Victorious.* Philadelphia, 1963.

Plagnieux, J. "Le Chrétien en face de la loi d'après de De spiritu et littera de Saint Augustin." In: *Theologie in Geschichte und Gegenwart, Michael Schmaus zum 60. Geburtstag,* hrsg. v. J. Auer und H. Volk. München, 1957, pp. 725-754.

Plinval, G. de. *Pélage, se écrits sa vie et sa doctrine.* Lausanne, 1943.

Plitt, G. L. "Luthers Streit mit Erasmus über den freien Willen in den Jahren 1524-1525," *Studien der evangelisch-protestantischen Geistlichen des Grossherzogthums Baden,* II (1876), 205-214.

Portalié, E. "Augustin (Saint)," DTC, 1, 2268-2472. Tr. by R. Bastian, *A Guide to the Thought of St. Augustine.* Chicago, 1960.

———— "Augustinisme (Développement historique de 1')," DTC, 1, 2501-2561.

Prenter, R. *Spiritus Creator,* tr. J. Jensen. Philadelphia, 1953.

Quell, G. "Hamartanō: Sin in the OT," TDNT 1, 267-286.

———— "Eklegomai: B. Die Erwählung im AT," ThW 4, 147-173.

Rad, Gerhard von. *Old Testament Theology.* tr. D. Stalker. 2 vols. New York, 1962-65.

Rahner, K. "Augustin und der Semipelagianismus," *Zeitschr. f. kath. Theol.,* LXVI (1938), 171-196.

———— "Freiheit: III. Kirchl. Lehramt; IV. F. in der Tradition; V. Systematisch," LThK, 4, 331-336.

———— "Prädestination: III. Systematisch," LThK, 8, 668ff.

———— "Was ist eine dogmatische Aussage?" in *Catholica,* XV (1961), 161-184. Reprinted in: Rahner, *Schriften zur Theologie.* Bd. V. Einsiedeln-Zürich-Köln, 1962, pp. 54-81. Tr. K. Kruger. *Theological Investigations.* Vol. V. Baltimore-London, 1966, pp. 42-66.

———— "Würde und Freiheit des Menschen." In: *Schriften,* II, pp. 247-277. Tr. "The Dignity and Freedom of Man." In: *Theol. Inv.,* II, pp. 235-265.

———— *Theological Dictionary,* in collaboration with H. Vorgrimler, Tr. R. Strachan. New York, 1965.

Reijnen, H. *Erasmus en Luther.* Hilversum, 1937.

Renaudet, A. *Études Érasmiennes (1521-1529).* Paris, 1939.

Renaudet, A. *Érasme, sa pensée religieuse et son action d'après sa correspondence (1518-1521)*. Paris, 1926.

Rengstorf, H. "doulos, etc.," TDNT 2, 261-280.

Richter, J. "Luthers 'Deus absconditus'—Zuflucht oder Ausflucht?" *Zeitschr. f. Religions-und Geistesgesch.*, VII (1955), 289-303.

Richter, M. *Die Stellung des Erasmus zu Luther und zur Reformation in den Jahren 1516-1524*. Diss. Leipzig, 1900.

Ritter, G. *Studien zur Spätscholastik I: Marsilius von Inghen und die okkamistische Schule in Deutschland*. Sitzungsberichte der Heidelberger Akademie der Wissenschaften, phil.-hist. Kl., 4. Abhdlg. Heidelberg, 1921.

———— *Studien zur Spätscholastik II: Via antiqua und via moderna auf den deutschen Universitäten des XV. Jahrhunderts*. Photomechanical reproduction of the edition: Heidelberg, 1922. Darmstadt, 1963.

———— *Luther: His Life and Work*, tr. J. Riches. London, 1963.

Rivière, J. "Justification," DTC, 8, 2078-2277.

———— "Mérite," DTC, 10, 574-785.

Rondet, H. *Gratia Christi*. Paris, 1948.

Rupp, G. *The Righteousness of God*. London, 1953.

———— *Protestant Catholicity*. London, 1960.

Rzadkiewicz, A. L. *The Philosophical Bases of Human Liberty According to St. Thomas Aquinas*. Washington, 1949.

Saint-Blancat. L. "La théologie de Luther et un nouveau plagiat de Pierre d'Ailly," *Positions Luthériennes,* IV (1956), 61-77.

Scheel, O. *Martin Luther: Vom Katholizismus zur Reformation*. 2 Bde. 4th ed. Tübingen, 1921.

Schelkle, K. H. *Paulus, Lehrer der Väter: Die altkirchliche Auslegung von Römer 1-11*. 2nd ed. Düsseldorf, 1959.

Schillebeeckx, E. "The Tridentine Decree on Justification: A New View," *Concilium,* vol. 5 (1965), pp. 176-179.

Schlier, H. "Haireomai, etc.," TDNT 1, 180-184.

———— "Eleutheros, etc.," TDNT 2, 487-502.

———— "The Law of Perfect Freedom," in: *Man Before God*. New York, 1966, pp. 52-67.

Schlinder, A. "Gnade und Freiheit. Zum Vergleich zwischen der griechischen und lateinischen Kirchenväter," *Zeitsch. f. Theol. u. Kirche,* 62 (1965), pp. 178-195.

Schlink, E. *Theology of the Lutheran Confessions,* tr. P. Koehneke and H. Bouman, Philadelphia, 1961.

———— *The Coming Christ and the Coming Church*. Philadelphia, 1968.

———— "Der theologische Syllogismus als Problem der Prädestinationslehre." In: *Einsicht und Glaube: Festschr. f. G. Söhngen*. Freiburg-Basel-Wien, 1962, pp. 299-320.

Schmaus, M. *Katholische Dogmatik,* Bd. I, 6th revised ed. München,

1960; Bd. II/1: 6th revised ed. München, 1960; Bd. III/2: 5th revised ed. München, 1956.

Schmidt, F. W. "Einleitung und Erläuterungen zu Martin Luthers Vom unfreien Willen." In: *Martin Luther: Ausgewählte Werke*, hrsg. v. H. H. Borcherdt. Bd. 5. München, 1923.

———— "Eine kurze Bemerkung zu Gogartens Ausgabe von Luthers de servo arbitrio," *Die christliche Welt*, XXXVIII (1924), 941ff.

Schmidt, K. D. *Lutherische und katholische Rechtfertigungslehre*. Theologie und Verkündigung. H. 5. Lüneburg, 1946.

Schmidt, K. L. "Proorizō," ThW 5, 457.

Schott, E. "Willensfreiheit," RGG, 6, 1719-1725.

Schottenloher, O. "Erasmus," RGG, 2, 534-537.

Schrenk, G. "Eklegomai: C. . . in der LXX und im jüdisch-hellenistischen Schrifttum," ThW, 4, 173-181.

———— "Eudokeō, etc.," TDNT 2, 738-742.

———— "Thelō, etc.," TDNT 3, 44-62.

Schüler, M. *Prädestination, Sünde und Freiheit bei Gregor von Rimini*. Stuttgart, 1934.

Schüler, M. "Luthers Gottesbegriff nach seiner Schrift De servo arbitrio," *Zeitschr. f. Kirchengesch.*, LV (1936), 532-593.

Schuster, H. *Martin Luther Heute: Zeitbedingtes und Bleibendes*. Stuttgart, 1958.

Schwarz, R. *Fides, Spes und Caritas beim jungen Luther unter besonderer Berücksichtigung der mittelalterlichen Tradition*. Arbeiten zur Kirchengeschichte. H. 34. Berlin, 1962.

Schwiebert, E. G. *Luther and His Times*. St. Louis, 1950.

Seckler, M. *Instinkt und Glaubenswille nach Thomas von Aquin*. Mainz, 1961.

Seeberg, R. *Lehrbuch der Dogmengeschichte*. Bde. I, II and IV/2 = photo-mechanical reproduction of 3rd ed.; 5th ed. Basel-Stuttgart, 1960. Bde. III and IV/1 = reproduction of 4th ed.; 6th ed. Basel-Stuttgart, 1960.

Seebohm, F. *The Oxford Reformers: John Colet, Erasmus and Thomas More*. 2nd ed. revised and enlarged. London, 1869.

Seils, M. *Der Gedanke vom Zusammenwirken Gottes und des Menschen in Luthers Theologie*. Beiträge zur Förderung christlicher Theologie. Bd. 50. Gütersloh, 1962.

Smith, G. "Luther and Free Choice," *The Modern Schoolman*, XX (1943), 78-88.

Smith, P. *Erasmus: A Study of His Life, Ideals and Place in History*. New printing. New York, 1962.

Sodeur, A. "Luthers Schrift de servo arbitrio im Lichte der modernen Philosophie," *Protestantische Monatshefte*, X (1906), 319-325.

Söhngen, G. *Gesetz und Evangelium: Ihre analoge Einheit*. München, 1957.

Souter, A. *Pelagius's Expositions of Thirteen Epistles of St. Paul*. Vol. I:

Introduction. Cambridge, 1922; Vol. II: Text and Apparatus Criticus. Cambridge, 1926.

Spicq, C. *Dieu et L'Homme selon le Nouveau Testament.* Lectio Divina, 29. Paris, 1961.

Stakemeier, E. *Glaube und Rechtfertigung.* Freiburg, 1937.

────── *Der Kampf um Augustin: Augustinus und die Augustiner auf dem Tridentinum.* Paderborn, 1937.

────── *Über Schicksal und Vorsehung.* Luzern, 1949.

Stendahl, K. "Sünde und Schuld: IV. Im NT," RGG, 6, 484-489.

Stegmüller, F. "Zur Gnadenlehre des spanischen Konzilstheologen Domingo de Soto." In: *Das Weltkonzil von Trient,* hrsg. v. G. Schreiber. Bd. I. Freiburg, 1951, pp. 169-230.

Stephan, H. *Luther in den Wandlungen seiner Kirche.* 2nd rev. ed. Berlin, 1951.

Strohl, H. *Luther Jusqu'en 1520.* 2nd rev. ed. Paris, 1962.

Tavard, G. *Protestantism.* Faith and Fact Books: 137. London, 1959.

Todd, J. M. *Luther: A Biographical Study.* Westminster, Md., 1964.

Tresmontant, C. *Essai sur la Pensée Hebraïque.* Lectio Divina, 12. 2nd ed. Paris, 1956.

Vajta, V., ed. *Lutherforschung Heute.* Referate und Berichte des. 1. Internationalen Lutherforschungskongresses, Aarhus, 18-23 August, 1956. Berlin, 1958.

Vawter, B. "Scriptural Meaning of 'Sin'," *Theol. Digest,* X (1962), 223-226.

Vignaux, P. "Occam," DTC, 11, 876-889.

────── "Nominalisme," DTC, 11, 717-784.

────── *Justification et prédestination au XIVe siecle: Duns Scot, Guillaume d'Ockham, Pierre Auriole, Grégoire de Rimini.* Paris, 1934.

────── *Nominalisme au XIVe Siècle.* Montreal-Paris, 1948.

────── "Luther: lecteur de Gabriel Biel (Disputatio contra scholasticam theologiam, 5-19; III Sent., d. xxvii, q. u. a. 3, dub. 2)," *Église et théologie,* XXII (1959), 33-52.

────── *Philosophy in the Middle Ages: An Introduction,* tr. E. Hall, New York, 1959.

Vigoroux, F. "Liberté," *Dictionnaire de la Bible,* 4, 237f.

Vogel, H. "Praedestinatio Gemina." In: *Theologische Aufsätze: K. Barth zum 50. Geburtstag.* München, 1936, pp. 222ff.

Vorster, H. *Das Freiheitsverständnis bei Thomas von Aquin und Martin Luther.* Kirche und Konfession. Bd. 8. Göttingen, 1964.

Vriezen, Th. C. *An Outline of Old Testament Theology.* Newton, Mass., 1961.

────── "Sünde und Schuld: II. Im AT," RGG, 6, 478-482.

Walter, J. von. "Die neueste Beurteilung des Erasmus," *Jahres-Bericht der Schlesischen Gesellsch. f. vaterländ. Kultur,* LXXXIX (1911/12), 1-18.

Walter, J. von. "Die Ja- und Neintheologie des Erasmus." In: *Moderne Irrtümer im Spiegel der Geschichte*. Leipzig, 1912.

Wang Tch'ang-Tche, J. *Saint Augustin et les vertus des Païens*. Paris, 1938.

Watson, P. S. *Let God be God: An Interpretation of the Theology of Martin Luther*. 4th ed. London, 1960.

Weijenborg, R. "La charité dans la première théologie de Luther (1509-1515)," *Revue d'histoire ecclésiastique*, XLV (1950), 617-669.

Werner, K. *Die Scholastik des späteren Mittelalters*. 4 Bde. Wien, 1881-1887.

Wolf, E. *Peregrinatio: Studien zur reformatorischen Theologie und zum Kirchenproblem*. 2nd rev. ed. München, 1962.

Zahrnt, H. *Luther deutet Geschichte*. München, 1952.

Zickendraht, K. *Der Streit zwischen Erasmus und Luther über die Willensfreiheit*. Leipzig, 1909.

Zumkeller, A. "Hugolin von Orvieto über Prädestination, Rechtfertigung und Verdienst," *Augustiniana*, IV (1954), 109-156; V (1955), 5-51.

Index of Names

Abelard, P., 125
Adam, A., 102, 336f.
Adam, Karl, 270
Adler, Mortimer, 19, 25-29, 129, 147
Ahlbrecht, A., 12
Ailly, Peter d', 185, 197
Alanen, Y., 14, 301, 312
Aleander, J., 278
Albert the Great, 197, 337
Ales, A. d', 59, 112
Alexander of Hales (*Summa Halensis*), 137, 168, 197, 202f., 205, 208-213, 223
Altaner, B., 108
Althaus, P., 227, 257, 301, 303, 339, 343f., 365
Altmann, P., 32
Amand, D., 59
Amann, É., 65, 73, 104, 112ff., 116, 118, 120f., 187, 193
Ambrose, St., 74, 88
Andler, C., 277
Anfossi, M., 326
Anselm of Canterbury, 26, 129-134, 136, 148, 211, 221, 308, 313, 353
Aristotle, 17, 26, 27, 31, 36, 130, 141-144, 212f., 230, 233, 243, 324, 329
Athanasius, St., 32
Aubert, Roger, 118f.
Auer, A., 59
Auer, Johannes, 59, 79, 104, 116, 122, 133, 135, 137f., 163, 169f., 172, 192, 200, 204, 213, 337
Augustine, cc. 4 & 5 *passim;* 4, 15, 16, 26, 31, 32, 54, 130, 132-136, 141ff., 146ff., 154, 156-159, 161, 164-168, 171ff., 178f., 181, 186f., 190f., 196ff., 200f., 203, 205ff.,
211ff., 217, 219f., 225, 227-230, 233, 235-251, 255f., 258f., 261, 262-266, 270, 272, 284f., 288-293, 308, 313ff., 317f., 329ff., 336f., 341, 345, 349, 352-355, 367ff.; (Pseudo-Augustine), 102
Aureolus, Petrus, 197
Ayer, A. J., 26f.

Bachelet, X. Le, 252
Bainton, Roland, 8, 254
Bainvel, J., 129
Baius, 16, 68, 91, 120, 164
Bandt, Helmut, 14, 223, 230, 260, 299, 304f., 321, 333, 343f., 346-349, 357f.
Barth, Heinrich, 103, 108
Barth, Karl, 16, 50, 257, 365
Barth, T., 213
Bartmann, B., 108
Bassolis, John de, 338
Bardy, G., 59
Bäumker, F., 129
Baumgärtel, F., 32
Bavel, T. van, 63
Bea, Cardinal A., 15
Beck, H., 59
Behm, J., 32
Bellarmine, Robert, 139
Bellucci, Dino, 227
Benignus, Brother, 145, 154
Berdyaev, Nicholas, 10
Bergson, Henri, 26
Bernard of Clairvaux, 133f., 136, 160, 211, 219, 224f., 289
Bertram, G., 103
Beyer, H., 45
Bieder, W., 32
Biel, Gabriel, 17, 20, 137, 148, 170, 175f., 178, ch. 7 *passim*, 217-227,